JN099391

英文
詳説日本史
JAPANESE HISTORY for High School

佐藤 信　五味文彦　高埜利彦 編
Sato Makoto　Gomi Fumihiko
Takano Toshihiko

近藤成一
亀井ダイチ利永子
亀井ダイチ アンドリュー 翻訳
Kondo Shigekazu
Rieko Kamei-Dyche
Andrew T. Kamei-Dyche

まえがき

『詳説日本史』が英語になりました。

『詳説日本史（日 B309)』は日本の高校で使用された教科書です。教科書のようにバランスのとれた形で、日本の通史を英語で刊行したものは、たぶん今まであまりなかったと思います。かつて『詳説日本史』で学ばれた方も、そうでない方も、今度は英語で読んでみませんか。

この本は、もちろん英語を母語とする方にも読んでいただきたいのですが、日本語を母語とするけれども英語での発信に興味のある方に使っていただくことを想定しています。ふだん日本語を使っておられる方なら、この本に書かれていることは、たとえ詳しいことは知らなくても、なんとなく聞いたことがあると思います。この本では、歴史用語については、日本語の原語を小さな赤字で併記してあります。そういうところを手がかりにしていけば、辞書を使わなくても、本書を読み通すことが可能になるでしょう。

英語を母語としない方が英語の本を読むとき、いずれは辞書の助けを借りるにしても、まずは辞書を使わずに多読・速読してみることが大切です。そういう時、内容についてある程度見当のついている本を英語で読むということがすごく有効です。この本をそのように使っていただいてもいいと思います。

この本は高校で使用された教科書をベースにしておりますので、要点を押さえてバランスのとれた詳細な通史を英語で読んでいただくことができます。日本史の研究を英語で発信しておられる亀井ダイチ利永子さんとアンドリューさんご夫妻のご尽力により、それが可能になりました。私は翻訳監修という立場で本書の制作に関わらせていただきました。

日本語で書かれた文章を英語に直しましたので、英語として不自然な表現も残っています。はじめから英語で書く文章なら異なる表現になるようなところでも、『詳説日本史』の表現を残したところがあります。どの程度英語の表現に合わせて、どの程度元の表現を残すかについて、亀井ダイチご夫妻は苦労して検討してくださいました。翻訳が大変なことから本書の刊行までずいぶん時間がかかってしまいましたが、困難を乗り越えて刊行までこぎつけたことについて、亀井ダイチご夫妻をはじめとして、本書の刊行に携わられたすべての方に感謝したいと思います。

『詳説日本史』を英語で読むことで、日本の歴史を新たな視点から見直していただければ幸いです。

近藤成一

Preface from the Translators

Our intention in undertaking this translation was to create an English edition that would, to the greatest extent possible, accurately and smoothly reflect the original Japanese text. Because the English text occupies more space than the Japanese, unfortunately some tables needed to be removed; copyright issues also led to some images being replaced or removed. In spite of the obstacles involved, great effort was expended to produce the best possible English version of the work.

We generally employed the historical terminology used among scholars of Japan writing in English, rather than popular expressions or the terms used by the English mass media, which are often outdated or inaccurate. Exceptions include some cases where particular terms were likely to be confusing for Japanese readers, such as the names of political parties. Note that while the mass media may render Japanese names using English name order, historians overwhelmingly render Japanese names using Japanese name order. Translation notes have been provided to help explain the rationale behind some significant editorial choices and help the reader to understand the issues involved in translating a history textbook. Key terms include Japanese text to help readers situate them in context or look up more about them elsewhere.

Japanese readers may be surprised at the extent to which Japanese terms are used by scholars writing in English, since there has increasingly been a trend to retain Japanese words that lack close English equivalents. Readers may also notice that standard English conventions regarding Japanese terminology can be inconsistent: castle names substitute "castle" for "-jō" (thus, 姫路城 becomes Himeji Castle) whereas temple names may add "temple" but always retain "-ji" (thus, 浅草寺 becomes Sensōji Temple or Sensōji, but not Sensō Temple). Occasionally events and international agreements have significantly different names in English than in Japanese: 西南戦争, for instance, is usually called the Satsuma Rebellion, and while in Japanese the treaties 日米和親条約 and 日露和親条約 have similar names, their official English titles – the Japan-US Treaty of Peace and Amity, and the Treaty of Commerce and Navigation between Japan and Russia, respectively – notably differ.

In some cases in this book we translated a term in more than one way, either to avoid repetition (as English eschews being overly repetitive), or because the Japanese term was quite inclusive, preventing a one-size-fits-all translation. Moreover, words evolve over time, so with a term like "bushi" (武士) that meant different things in different eras the translation may change depending on the context.

It is our sincere hope that this volume retains the comprehensive coverage of the Japanese text while being accessible to a wide variety of readers, and that studying it by itself or together with the Japanese version will be a thought-provoking and rewarding experience.

Rieko Kamei-Dyche & Andrew T. Kamei-Dyche

***Prefatory Notes**

1. Through 1872, when Japan decided to adopt the Gregorian calendar, there was a difference of about a month between the Japanese Calendar and the Western one. In this text, all dates prior to that time follow Japanese reckoning instead of being converted to the Western calendar. Months in Japanese reckoning are given numerically (e.g. third month) to avoid confusion, since they do not correspond to the Western calendar months.
日本がグレゴリオ暦の採用を決定した1872（明治５）年までは、日本暦と西暦とは１カ月前後の違いがあります。本文では、それ以前の日付は西暦に換算せず、日本暦に準じています。日本暦の月は西暦の月に対応していないため、混乱を避けるために、数字で表しています。（例：３番目の月）

2. Japanese names are rendered in Japanese order (family name first).
日本人の名前は、日本語順（姓名の順）で示しています。

3. Macrons are consistently used to indicate long vowels in Japanese, even in cases where they are commonly dropped in English (thus Tōkyō rather than Tokyo).
長音記号は、英語では一般的に省略されることがあっても、日本語での長母音を示すために統一的に使用しています。（例：Tokyo ではなく Tōkyō）

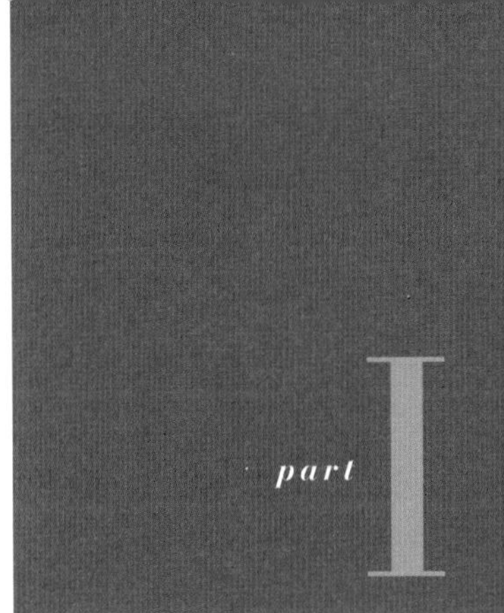

The Primeval & Ancient Eras

Chapter

1

The Dawn of Japanese Culture

1 The Beginnings of Culture

The Japanese Archipelago and the Japanese People

The earliest humans appeared on earth around 7 million years ago in the late Miocene 中新世 epoch of the Neogene 新第三紀 period in the geological time scale. Human evolution continued throughout the late Neogene and Quarternary 第四紀 periods. The Quarternary period is divided into two epochs, the **Pleistocene** 更新世 and the **Holocene** 完新世, with the transition between the two occurring more than ten thousand years ago. The Pleistocene, also called the **Ice Age** 氷河時代, was characterized by the alternation of cold glacial stages and relatively warm interglacial stages. During the former, the sea level dropped dramatically compared to the level today.

At least twice during this epoch, a land bridge is thought to have connected the Japanese archipelago and the northeastern part of the Asian continent, enabling large mammals such as *Stegodon orientalis* and *Palaeoloxodon naumanni* to cross over. It is possible that humans, hunting these animals, also arrived in the Japanese archipelago from the Asian mainland through the same route, although there is not yet clear

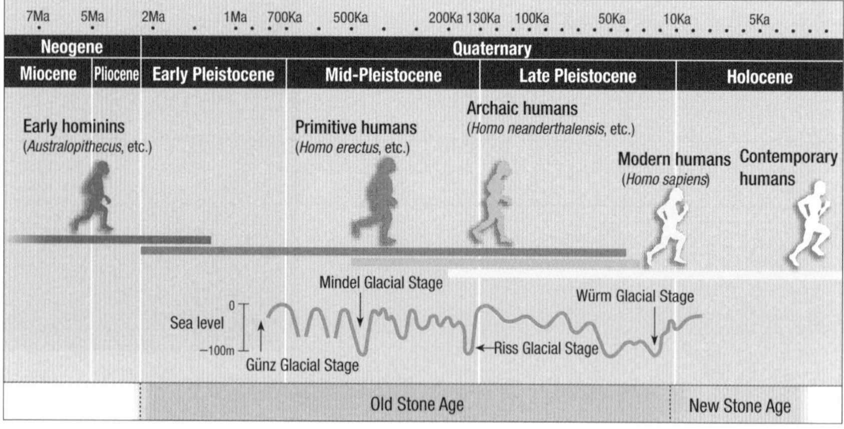

HUMAN EVOLUTION AND GEOLOGICAL TIMETABLE
Modern humans (*homo sapiens*) appeared around the middle of the Pleistocene, about 200 thousand years ago.

evidence for this hypothesis. With the end of the last glacial stage of the Pleistocene, the sea level rose once again during the Holocene epoch, and thus the Japanese archipelago, roughly as we know it today, was formed more than ten thousand years ago.

Based on the study of fossil hominids, it is widely accepted that humans emerged in the order of early hominins (*Australopithecus*, etc.)[1], primitive humans (*Homo erectus*, etc.), archaic humans (*Homo neanderthalensis*, etc.), and modern humans (*Homo sapiens*). So far, all of the hominid fossil finds from Pleistocene Japan, such as the Hamakita (浜北人) people in Shizuoka (静岡県) Prefecture, and the Minatogawa (港川人) people and Yamashitachō (山下町洞人) Cave people in Okinawa (沖縄県) Prefecture, belong to the category of modern humans[2]. The Minatogawa people are believed to have originated in the southern hemisphere. The first indigenous Japanese were possibly the Jōmon (縄文人) people, the offspring of people who originally inhabited the southern region of the Asian continent. However, the culture of the late old stone age and early Jōmon people also had strong elements of northern culture. Consequently, it is impossible to state their origin with certainty until more discoveries are made. Later, these early Japanese mixed with new arrivals from northern Asia from the Yayoi (弥生時代) period[3], which is said to explain the mixed ancestry of the modern

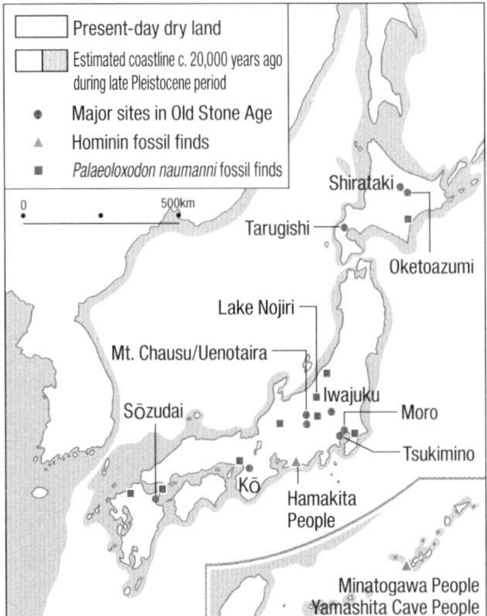

JAPANESE ARCHIPELAGO TOWARD THE END OF THE PLEISTOCENE

As can be seen, Tsushima 〈対馬〉 and the Korean peninsula, and Honshū 〈本州〉 and Hokkaidō 〈北海道〉, were both separated by the last glacial stage toward the end of the Pleistocene.

[1] In no other region outside of Africa have *Australopithecina* fossils been discovered, suggesting an African origin for humanity.

[2] It was theorized that the Akashi people 〈明石人〉 remains excavated in Akashi, Hyōgo Prefecture 〈兵庫県〉, in 1931 were those of a primitive human, but recent research has confirmed that the remains were of a modern human and may have even dated from the Holocene epoch.

[3] Present-day Asians (Asian ethnicities) can be divided into southeast Asians, who are descendants of people who migrated from Africa to southeast Asia tens of thousands of years ago, and northeastern Asians, who inherited characteristics from people who had lived in north Asia and adapted to its very cold climate 20 to 30 thousand years ago.

Japanese[4]. Today's ethnic Ainu (アイヌ) people in Hokkaidō and the people living in Japan's southern islands, including Okinawa, are said, however, to still retain dominantly Jōmon features.

Life in the Paleolithic Era

The time period before humans discovered the use of metal tools is called the Stone Age (石器時代)[5], and mainly corresponds to the Pleistocene. In the Paleolithic period (Old Stone Age) (旧石器時代), simple tools like **chipped stone tools** (打製石器) were dominant. Then, in parallel with the transition to the Holocene, more sophisticated polished stone tools appeared in the Neolithic period (New Stone Age) (新石器時代). Previously, it was believed that no sites from the Paleolithic period existed in the Japanese archipelago. However, in 1949 chipped stone tools buried in the Kantō loam layer (関東ローム層) formed during the Pleistocene were excavated at the **Iwajuku site** (岩宿遺跡) in Gunma Prefecture[6]. Afterwards, other stone tools from the Pleistocene were discovered at sites across the archipelago, thus confirming the existence of Paleolithic culture in Japan[7].

The people in this period subsisted on **hunting** (狩猟) and **gathering** (採取) of wild plant foods. They hunted large mammals, such as *Paraeoloxodon naumanm*, *Megaloceros giganteus* and *Alces alces*, with a stone spear which consisted of a stone tool such as a **knife-shaped implement** (ナイフ形石器) or a **projectile point** (尖頭器) attached to a wooden stick. To search for plant foods and game, they continuously moved within certain areas near rivers or streams. They lived in simple tent-like shelters, or temporarily in caves.

They likely lived in small groups of around ten people. When several such groups came together, they could form a sort of tribe able to obtain materials for stone tools from distant locations and distribute them among themselves.

---

[4] Grammatically, the Japanese language, along with Korean and Mongolian, is grouped under the Altaic language family of northern Eurasia. However, it has lexical elements of possible southern origin, and thus its precise history is still debated.

[5] Archeology, an academic discipline that studies human history through ruins and artifacts, divides past human culture into the stone, bronze and iron ages, based on the material of tools used. In the case of the Japanese archipelago, the Jōmon period coincided with the stone age, but from at least the middle phase of the Yayoi period that followed iron tools were already used along with bronze ones, equivalent to the iron age. Therefore, a strict bronze culture appears to be absent from Japan's archeological past.

[6] Aizawa Tadahiro 〈相沢忠洋〉, an independent archaeologist, discovered stone tools from the Kantō loam layer at this site in 1946, and an academic excavation followed in 1949.

[7] Many sites from the Paleolithic period discovered in Japan date back as far as the Upper Paleolithic period around 36 thousand years ago. Efforts to discover earlier sites from the Middle (approximately 36 to 130 thousand years ago) and/or the Lower (approximately 130 thousand years ago) Paleolithic period are underway in multiple regions.

Toward the end of the Paleolithic period, a small stone tool called a **microlith**[8] 細石器 appeared. The microlithic culture developed extensively in the region from northeast China through Siberia, and was transmitted to the Japanese archipelago from the north.

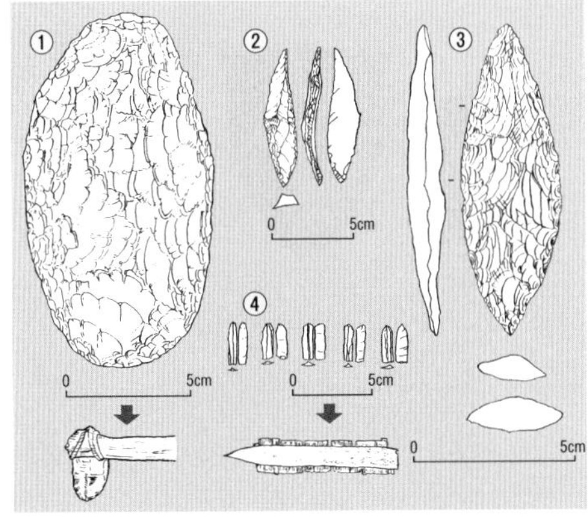

PALEOLITHIC STONE TOOLS AND THEIR USAGE
① Chipped stone axe (Suzuki site〈鈴木遺跡〉, Tōkyō), ② knife-shaped stone tool (Sunagawa site〈砂川遺跡〉, Saitama Prefecture〈埼玉県〉), ③ projectile point (Tsukimino site〈月見野遺跡〉, Kanagawa Prefecture〈神奈川県〉), ④ microlith (Oketoazumi site〈置戸安住遺跡〉, Hokkaidō).

The Emergence of Jōmon Culture

During the Holocene approximately ten thousand years ago, the earth's climate became warmer, and the natural environment became closer to what we have today. The vegetation changed, with the older subarctic coniferous forests giving way to deciduous broadleaf trees like Japanese beech and Japanese oak in eastern Japan, while evergreen broadleaf trees such as *Castanopsis* flourished in western Japan. Large mammals died out, replaced by smaller and more agile animals like Japanese deer and boar.

People's lifestyle also changed significantly in response to the transformation of the natural environment, resulting in what we call **Jōmon culture** 縄文文化. The Jōmon period spanned from about 13 thousand years ago to approximately 2,500 years ago when the Yayoi period, distinguished by paddy-field rice farming, began. Distinguishing characteristics of Jōmon culture include the use of bows and arrows to hunt thriving small and mid-sized animals, earthenware used mainly for cooking plant foods, and the creation of **polished stone tools** 磨製石器[9].

The earthen vessels from this period are called **Jōmon earthenware** 縄文土器, because many of them bear jōmon (cord patterns) impressed by a rope (twisted thread) used to smooth out the surface. These earthen vessels were low-fired and often thick and dark brown in color. The Jōmon period is generally classified into six sub-periods

---

[8] A microlith is a stone tool made by fitting several smaller stone tools (microblades〈細石刃〉) of 3-4 cm in length into grooves on the side edges of a wooden or bone shaft. The archaeological sites from this period include the well-known Shirataki site〈白滝遺跡〉 in Hokkaidō.

[9] The wide distribution of polished stone tools clearly indicates that the Jōmon culture corresponds to the Neolithic cultures in Eurasia. However, whereas the Western Asian or Chinese Neolithic societies shifted to food production from agriculture and/or livestock breeding, the Jōmon culture in Japan fundamentally remained a hunter-gatherer culture.

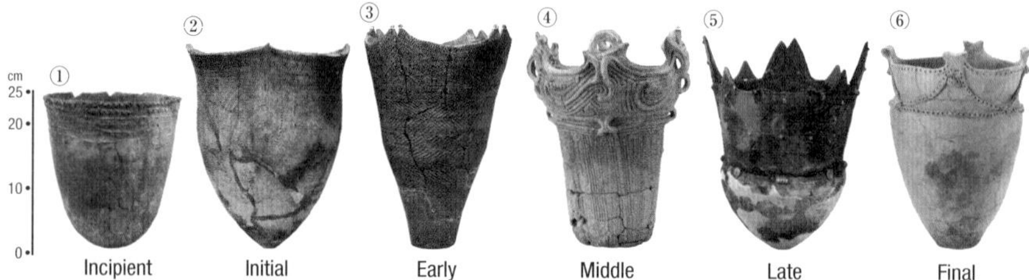

TRANSITION IN JŌMON EARTHENWARE
Most Jōmon earthenware are deep dishes, but other types, such as shallow bowls and vessels on stands or with spouts have also been discovered.

based on the developmental stages of the pottery: incipient, initial, early, middle, late and final. Among these, the incipient Jōmon pottery[10] is currently considered to be one of the oldest types of earthenware in the world. Similar ancient earthenware has been discovered on the Asian continent, but it is evident that the people living in the Japanese islands at the time also successfully adapted to the environmental change from the Pleistocene to the Holocene and produced a new culture at an early stage.

Lifestyle and Beliefs of the Jōmon People

People in the Jōmon 縄文時代 period adapted to the dynamically transformed natural environment. In particular, as the climate became warmer, they increasingly relied on plant foods, including gathered nuts such as chestnuts, walnuts, Japanese horse chestnuts and acorns as well as Japanese yams. Moreover, they also started from the early Jōmon period the management and expansion of chestnut forests, the protection and growing of yams, and the cultivation of beans, perilla, gourds, and more[11]. It has been argued that the Jōmon people were possibly starting farming of rice, wheat, millet and Japanese millet, although not to the extent of full-fledged agriculture. Many artifacts from this period such as chipped stone hoes for digging, and stone dishes and grinders for the grinding of nuts, have been unearthed.

For hunting, people used bows and arrows and often made use of pitfall traps. Game mostly consisted of Japanese deer and wild boar. The rise of the sea level, which

---

[10] Incipient Jōmon earthenware was either circular-shaped with a round bottom, or square-shaped with a flat bottom. These are thought to reflect the shapes of leather bags and woven baskets that the first producers patterned their vessels on. Decorative styles included mumon〈無文〉 (undecorated or plain), ryūkisenmon〈隆起線文〉 (raised lines) and tsumegatamon〈爪形文〉 (nail-shape). The cord-marked pattern became common during and after the early Jōmon phase.

[11] Japanese horse chestnuts and acorns must be soaked in water or boiled in an earthen vessel in order to remove their harsh taste and make them edible. This technique seems to have already been known in the early Jōmon phase.

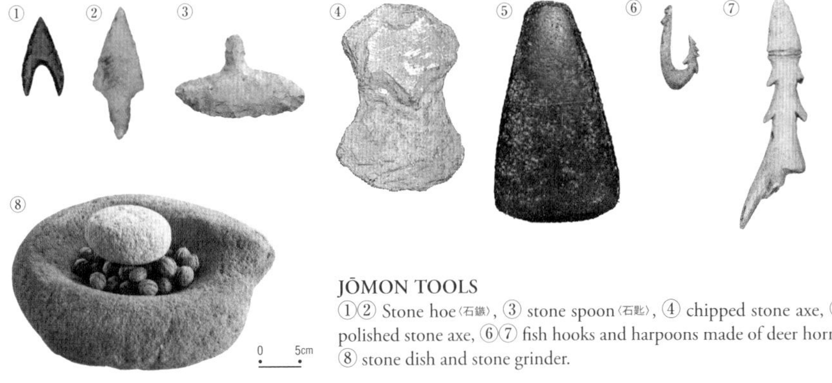

JŌMON TOOLS
①② Stone hoe〈石鏃〉, ③ stone spoon〈石匙〉, ④ chipped stone axe, ⑤ polished stone axe, ⑥⑦ fish hooks and harpoons made of deer horns, ⑧ stone dish and stone grinder.

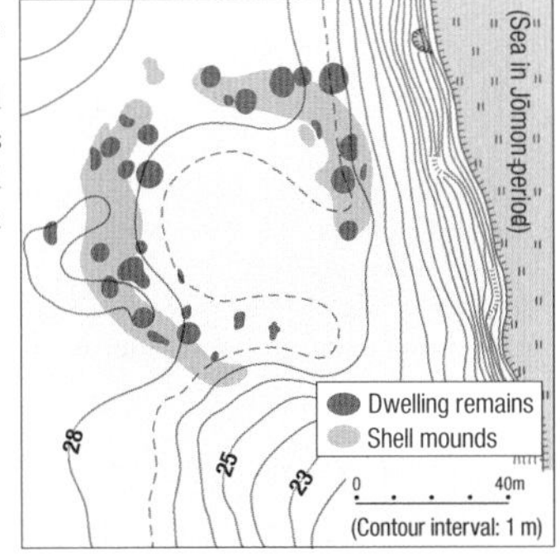

SHELL MOUNDS (KAINOHANA SHELL MOUNDS〈貝の花貝塚〉, CHIBA PREFECTURE)
Remains of about 33 dwellings were discovered under horseshoe-shaped shell mounds spread over a terrace. The central space where nothing was found was probably used for gatherings or festivities. Such a structural arrangement suggests that community life was regulated by certain sets of rules.

made the Japanese islands rich in deep inlets of various sizes, also led to the development of fishing. This is evidenced by numerous **shell mounds**〈貝塚〉[12] from the Jōmon period across Japan. People widely engaged in net-fishing with **bone tools**〈骨角器〉 such as fish hooks, harpoons and fishing spears, along with stone sinkers and earthen sinkers. Extant evidence, such as remains of dugout canoes that have been discovered in various locations and the Jōmon sites on Izu Ōshima〈伊豆大島〉 Island and, further south, Hachijōjima〈八丈島〉 Island, suggests that the Jōmon people were capable of open-seas navigation.

As the ways of obtaining food diversified, people's lifestyle became more stable

---

[12] Shell mounds are heaps of rubbish, piled in layers, that people had disposed of, such as seashells left after their contents had been eaten. They contain human-made artifacts such as earthen vessels, stone tools and bone tools, as well as the bones of humans, animals and fish that were preserved by calcium derived from seashells. These mounds are thus important sources that can offer insight into the lives of people and the natural environment at the time. Modern Japanese archaeology was spearheaded by the excavation of the **Ōmori shell mounds**〈大森貝塚〉 in Tōkyō by Edward Sylvester Morse〈モース〉, the American naturalist, in 1877.

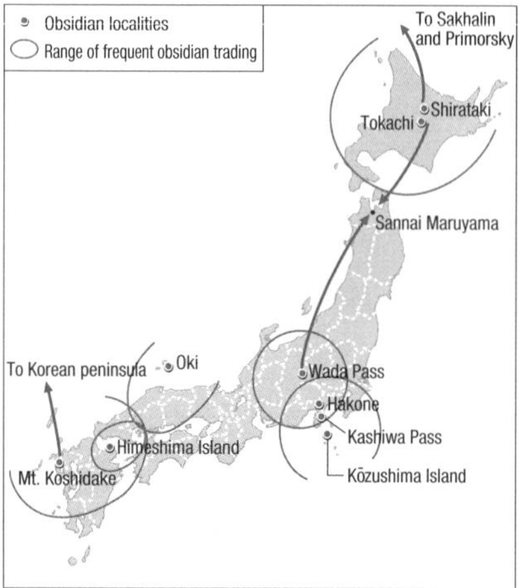

MAJOR OBSIDIAN LOCALITY DISTRIBUTION IN THE JAPANESE ARCHIPELAGO

Obsidian was commonly used for making stone tools. Confirmed localities include Shirataki, Hokkaido, and Wada Pass〈和田峠〉, Nagano Prefecture. The wide distribution of stone tool finds offers information about exchanges and trade among localities and consuming regions.

and sedentary. People started to live in a **pit-house** 竪穴住居, a dwelling made of a dugout in the ground covered by a roof. A pit-house had a hearth in the center, and was likely inhabited by a small family who cooked, ate and slept together. Settlements of several families were often built on a sunny hilltop near a waterside so as to secure drinking water. Often, a few pit-houses surrounded an open space, sometimes with a series of food storage pits and grave pits. Sometimes, as was the case with **Sannai Maruyama site** 三内丸山遺跡 in Aomori Prefecture 青森県, a large-scale village could also include large pit-houses possibly meant for communal living. In light of these facts, the basic unit of Jōmon society is thought to have been a group of 20 to 30 people, making 4 to 6 pit-house households.

Such groups established marriage ties with their neighbors as well, thereby enabling the exchange of various types of information. It is known that the Jōmon people also practiced trade with groups from a considerable distance, as shown by the distribution of **jade** ひすい (jadeite) and raw materials for stone tools such as **obsidian** 黒曜石. People worked together to secure their communal life; men focused on hunting and crafting stone tools, and women on gathering nuts and making earthenware pottery. Even in cases where groups had leaders, it is thought that they lacked status differentiation or

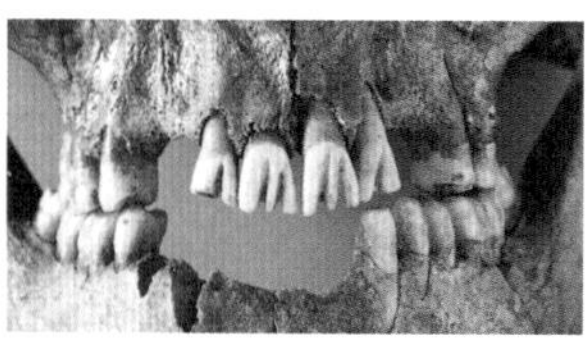

DOGŪ, SEKIBŌ AND TOOTH EXTRACTION

Left: shakōki〈遮光器〉 (light-blocking device) dogū excavated from Ebisuda site〈恵比須田遺跡〉 in Miyagi Prefecture〈宮城県〉 (Height 36.1 cm). Center: sekibō excavated from Misawa 1 site〈美沢1遺跡〉, Hokkaidō (Length 42.2 cm). Tooth extraction was a custom of extracting healthy adult teeth. Above: 4 lower incisor teeth and 2 upper canine teeth were extracted, with 4 upper incisor teeth chipped in a fork-like shape.

any concept of rich and poor.

The Jōmon people appear to have believed that spiritual forces resided in all natural objects and natural phenomena. This form of belief is called **animism** (アニミズム). They tried to ward off disaster and prayed for good harvests through magical practice. Excavated artifacts suggesting such animistic practice include **dogū** (土偶) (clay figures) that represented the female body and **sekibō** (石棒) (stone poles), polished stones that served as phallic symbols. The **tooth extraction** (抜歯) that became common from the middle of the Jōmon period could have been part of initiation rites into adulthood, which could indicate customs designed to maintain strict discipline within a group. Many of the dead were interred in a fetal position in what is called **flexed burial** (屈葬), probably out of fear that the spirits of the dead could harm the living.

BURIAL METHOD IN JŌMON PERIOD (TSUKUMO SHELL MOUNDS〈津雲貝塚〉, OKAYAMA PREFECTURE)
A common burial method in Jōmon times was flexed burial in which the body was tightly bent when interred. The corpse shown here had the knees and waist closely bent, arms held in front of the chest, and had a decorative belt around the waist.

2 The Establishment of Agricultural Society

Yayoi Culture

The Jōmon culture continued for more than ten thousand years in the Japanese archipelago. During that time, around 6,500 to 5,500 BCE, in China the cultivation of millet (awa (アワ) and kibi (キビ)) emerged in the middle stream region of the Yellow River (黄河) in the north, while rice farming started around the lower stream region of the Yangzi River (長江) in the south. In this way, agricultural societies became predominant in China. Then, from around

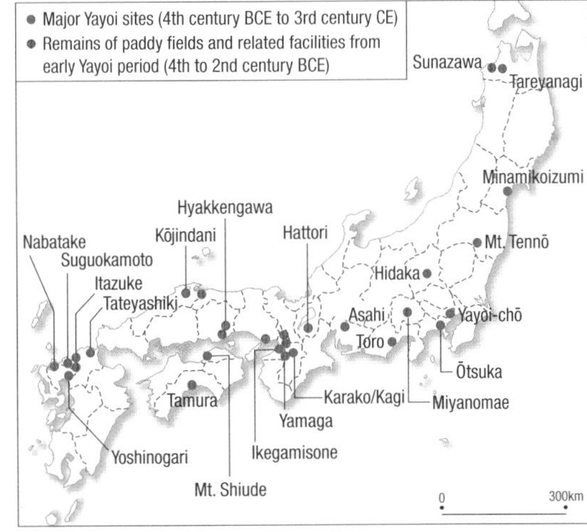

MAJOR YAYOI SITES

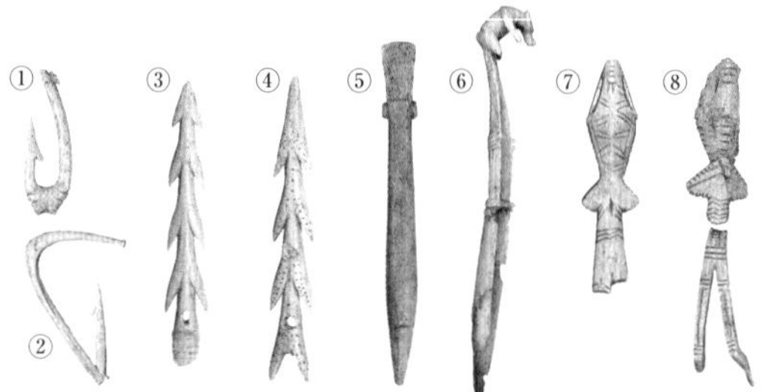

BONE TOOLS FROM RESIDUAL JŌMON CULTURE
(USU-MOSHIRI SITE〈有珠モシリ遺跡〉, HOKKAIDŌ)
①② Fish hooks, ③④ harpoon heads with barbs, ⑤ spear, ⑥ spoon with bear relief, ⑦⑧ spoons with whale relief. These are thought to have been crafted specifically as funerary goods.

the 6th century BCE, iron tools developed and agricultural production further expanded throughout the Spring and Autumn period〈春秋時代〉 (770-403) and the Warring States period〈戦国時代〉 (403-221). The development of agricultural culture exerted a strong influence on surrounding regions, and eventually found its way to the Japanese islands through the Korean peninsula.

Toward the end of the Jōmon period about 2,500 years ago, paddy field rice growing began in the northern part of Kyūshū〈九州〉 near the Korean peninsula[13]. After a brief period of trial adaptation, the **Yayoi culture**〈弥生文化〉 centering on **paddy field rice farming**〈水稲農耕〉 emerged in western Japan, and in due course spread to eastern Japan as well. In this way, most of the Japanese islands except for Hokkaidō and the southwestern islands advanced to the food production phase from hunting-gathering subsistence[14]. This period of time from about the 4th to mid-3rd century BCE is called the **Yayoi period**〈弥生時代〉[15].

The Yayoi culture was a new type of culture, founded on paddy field rice farming and accompanied by the development of new tools and techniques. These included **metal tools**〈金属器〉 made of bronze (an alloy of copper and tin) and, from the middle of this period, iron, as well as polished stone tools introduced from the Korean peninsula, such as stone knives〈石包丁〉 for harvesting rice and stone axes used to cut down and process

[13] Remains of wet rice fields from the late Jōmon period have been discovered across western Japan including the Nabatake site〈菜畑遺跡〉 in Saga Prefecture〈佐賀県〉 and the Itazuke site〈板付遺跡〉 in Fukuoka Prefecture〈福岡県〉, indicating that wet rice farming had already begun in this period. Some scholars argue that the stage at which wet rice cultivation had begun in some parts of Japan while Jōmon pottery was still being utilized should be defined as the incipient Yayoi period.

[14] Whereas the Jōmon culture was widely distributed throughout the area equivalent to the present-day Japanese archipelago, the Yayoi culture did not extend to Hokkaidō and the southwestern islands. Instead, a hunter-gatherer culture called "**residual Jōmon culture**〈続縄文文化〉" in Hokkaidō, and "**shell mound culture**〈貝塚文化〉" in the southwestern islands, continued. In Hokkaidō from the 7th century onward there existed the Satsumon culture〈擦文文化〉, named for its Satsumon (brush-marked) pottery, and the Okhotsk culture〈オホーツク文化〉 that featured Okhotsk pottery, both of which were based on hunting and gathering.

[15] The Yayoi period is classified into early, middle, and late phases based on the sequence of pottery development.

wood, and weaving techniques. As for earthenware, there was a shift to a new style of red-burnished pottery called **Yayoi earthenware** 弥生土器[16], major examples of which included cooking jars 甕, storage pots 壺, serving bowls 鉢 and pedestal bowls 高杯.

EARLY YAYOI EARTHENWARE (① ITAZUKE SITE, FUKUOKA PREFECTURE, ②③④ IMAGAWA SITE 〈今川遺跡〉, FUKUOKA PREFECTURE)
From left: large and small jar-shaped earthen vessels, pot-shaped earthen vessel, pedestal earthen vessel.

These new techniques of paddy field rice farming[17] and metal tool production were introduced from China and the Korean peninsula. Some Yayoi skeletons excavated in northern Kyūshū and the Chūgoku 中国 and Kinki 近畿 regions of Honshū are taller than Jōmon skeletons, and have characteristically flat and narrow faces. At the same time, the Yayoi culture also clearly inherited elements of Jōmon tradition such as basic techniques of pottery making, chipped stone tools and pit-house dwellings. Based on these facts, it is likely that the Yayoi culture was a product of collective creation by the indigenous Jōmon people and new arrivals who came to the Japanese archipelago not necessarily in great number but who brought new technologies from the Korean peninsula where agricultural society with metal tool technology had already taken root.

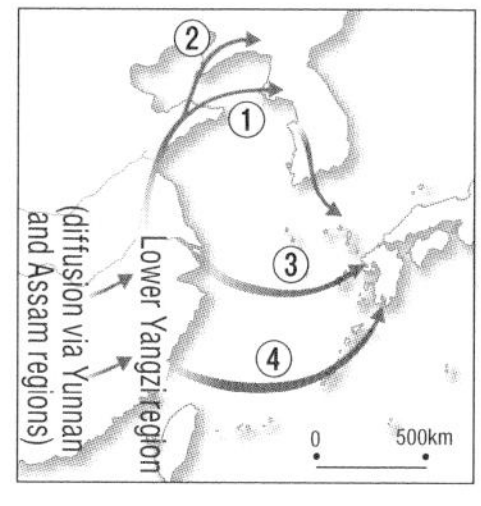

RICE DIFFUSION ROUTES

Life in the Yayoi Period

Food production brought about major changes in lifestyle. Many paddy fields in this period were small-sized, with sides several meters long, but had a well-developed

[16] Yayoi pottery is named after the location where earthen vessels of this style were discovered at the Mukōgaoka shell mounds 〈向ヶ岡貝塚〉 in Hongō-Yayoi-chō 〈本郷弥生町〉 (present-day Yayoi 2-chōme in Bunkyō-ku 〈文京区〉), Tōkyō, in 1884.

[17] The introduction of the techniques of wet rice cultivation in the Yayoi period from the southern part of the Korean peninsula has been confirmed by the discovery of corresponding remains there and in the Japanese archipelago. Rice originated in the Yunnan region 〈雲南〉 of China and the Assam region of India, and is thought to have arrived in Japan by way of the lower stream region of the Yangzi River, the Shandong peninsula 〈山東半島〉, and then the west coast region of the Korean peninsula. There are alternative theories of how rice diffusion reached Japan, such as through the Shandong and Liaodong peninsulas 〈遼東半島〉 and then the Korean peninsula, or through direct introduction from the lower Yangzi region. It was even argued at one time that rice was introduced via the southwestern islands.

REMAINS OF EARLY YAYOI PADDY FIELDS
Tamura site〈田村遺跡〉 in Nankoku City〈南国市〉, Kōchi Prefecture〈高知県〉, spread over natural levee at about 7-8 m elevation on right bank of Monobe River〈物部川〉 estuary. This photograph shows matrix-like arrangements of ridges over paddy fields, indicating that paddy fields used to be compartmentalized in smaller plots compared to present size.

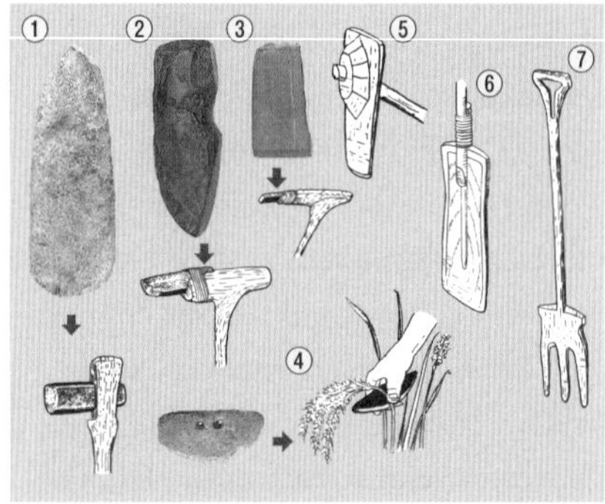

YAYOI FARMING TOOLS
① Polished clam-shaped thick stone axe (for logging), ② column-like single-edged stone axe, ③ flat single-edged stone axe, (②③both for woodworking), ④ stone knife, ⑤ hoe, ⑥⑦ spades. Examples of usage shown for ①-④.

system equipped with channels for irrigation and drainage. Furthermore, it is known that rice planting had already been introduced.

For cultivation, wooden spades and hoes were used, and rice spikes were harvested with stone knives. Grain thrashing to remove husks was performed with a wooden mortar (木臼) and a vertical pounding pole (竪杵), and the husked grains were stored in **stilt warehouses** (高床倉庫) and/or storage pits. Initially, people used polished stone tools to make wooden farming utensils, but later on they began to use iron tools such as axes, planes (鉇) and knives. In the later Yayoi period, many stone tools were no longer in use, and iron tools became more common. With farming tools with iron heads becoming more widespread, **dry paddy field** (乾田) farming developed in the mid-to-late Yayoi period in addition to the **wet paddy field** (湿田) cultivation that had already been practiced[18]. In some regions, cultivation of upland rice and various coarse grains was explored. Hunting and fishing were also actively practiced along with agriculture, and the domestication of pigs began.

The common Yayoi dwelling was a pit-house as in the Jōmon culture, but stilt warehouses on dug-standing pillars and stilt dwellings also increased in settlements. Settlements grew in size and number of dwellings, and some large-scale settlements appeared in various regions, no small number of which were **moated settlements** (環濠集落) with deep moats or mounds.

[18] Wet paddy fields have a high groundwater level and require a drainage system. Their yields are comparatively low. On the other hand, dry paddy fields have a low groundwater level and require an irrigation system. The alternation of drainage and irrigation enriches the soil and results in higher productivity.

The deceased were buried in a common burial ground near the settlement. There were many cases of **extended burial** (伸展葬), with the type of tomb being a hole in the ground, a wooden coffin or a stone coffin made by putting together stone plates. In the northern part of Kyūshū, we find the remains of **dolmens** (支石墓) consisting of several large flat stones, as well as large jar coffins especially made for burial purposes. In eastern Japan, early Yayoi tombs in which the bones of the dead were stored in earthen vessels have also been discovered.

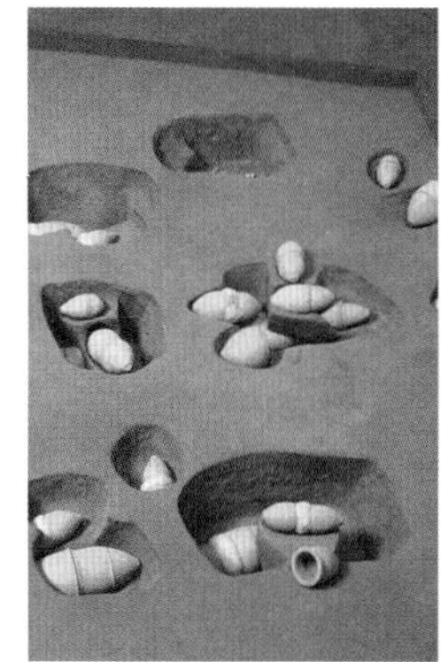

JAR COFFIN (NAGAOKA SITE〈永岡遺跡〉, FUKUOKA PREFECTURE, RESTORED MODEL) **AND HUMAN BONES**
Left: restored model of jar coffin. Right: inside jar coffin and interred bones of deceased. In the Yayoi period, earthenware vessels were commonly used for children, but special jar coffins were used for adults in northern Kyūshū.

Another characteristic of Yayoi burial practice was the wide distribution of **burial mounds** (墳丘). **Square burial mounds with ditches** (方形周溝墓) have been discovered in many locations, with larger ones emerging later in the period. Prominent examples of this type of mound are the **Tatetsuki Tumulus** (楯築墳丘墓) discovered in Okayama Prefecture (岡山県) that features two rectangular extended premises on both sides of a circular mound more than 40 meters in diameter, and the **Trapezoidal Tumuli with Four Extended Corners** (四隅突出型墳丘墓) in the San'in region (山陰地方) in western Japan. Some of the **jar coffins** (甕棺墓) found in northern Kyūshū from the mid-Yayoi period were found to contain funerary goods including more than 30 Chinese mirrors and bronze weapons. These large-scale mounds and tombs with many burial goods suggest the existence of stratified societies and the emergence of powerful leaders in multiple regions.

In settlements, people performed rituals to pray for, or offer thanks for, good harvests, with ceremonial bronze implements[19], such as **bronze bell-shaped vessels** (銅鐸), **bronze swords** (銅剣), **bronze pikes** (銅矛) and **bronze dagger-axes** (銅戈). Bronze bell-shaped vessel finds are widely distributed in the Kinki region, whereas flat bronze swords are found in the central region of the Seto Inland Sea (瀬戸内) area, and bronze pikes and dagger-axes are common in northern Kyūshū. This suggests that there emerged several regions

[19] Bronze bell-shaped vessels have their origin in bronze bells that emerged on the Korean peninsula. Bronze swords, pikes and dagger-axes were derived from practical bronze weapons from the peninsula. These were adapted for ritual purposes in the Japanese archipelago and gradually grew in size. During the Yayoi period, many bronze ritual implements were crafted, although iron tools were also made except during the early phase. Therefore, from the perspective of archaeological periodization most of the Yayoi period can be defined as an iron age.

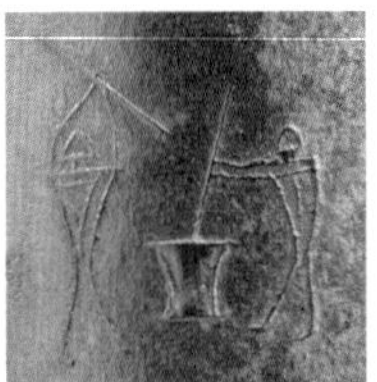

SCENES IN RELIEF ON A BRONZE BELL
Left: grain thrashing using wooden mortar and vertical pounding pole (Sakuragaoka site〈桜ケ丘遺跡〉). Right: stilt warehouse (allegedly excavated in Kagawa Prefecture).

BRONZE PIKES AND BRONZE BELL-SHAPED VESSELS DISCOVERED AT KŌJINDANI SITE〈荒神谷遺跡〉
At Kōjindani site, Hikawa-chō〈斐川町〉, in Izumo City〈出雲市〉, Shimane Prefecture, 6 bronze bell-shaped vessels and 16 bronze pikes were stored together in one hole. Just nearby, as many as 358 bronze swords were also buried. Moreover, at neighboring Kamo Iwakura site〈加茂岩倉遺跡〉 in Unnan City〈雲南市〉, Shimane Prefecture, 39 bronze bell-shaped vessels were found to have been similarly buried in one place.

that used common ceremonial tools. These ritual items, shaped like bells or oversized weapons, were seldom buried in individual tombs, but rather used for rituals that involved the whole settlement. It has been argued that these ritual implements were usually stored buried in the ground, and were only taken out on the occasion of rituals.

The Emergence of Small Polities

The Yayoi period saw the emergence of moated settlements as well as stone and metal weapons unknown to the Jōmon culture. The emergence of farming cultures around the world led to armed settlements with defensive facilities that suggest warfare started to take place over accumulated surplus products and crops.

The Japanese archipelago also entered this period of warfare, with dominant communities absorbing neighboring settlements to form political groupings called **kuni** (クニ). The deceased found in jar coffins with a volume of funerary goods from the mid-Yayoi period and/or those interred in graves with large mounds were likely kings of such small polities.

Chinese historical texts also record the state of small polities in the Japanese archipelago. According to the "**Treatise on Geography**" (『漢書』地理志) in the 1st-century ***Book of Han***, the people of "Wa" (倭)[20] were divided into more than a hundred such polities that

[20] In China at the time, people on the Japanese archipelago were called "Wa people〈倭人〉," and their polities "Wa-koku〈倭国〉." However, from the late 7th to early 8th centuries people on the archipelago began to use the term "Nihon〈日本〉," and this term came to be used in Chinese historical texts for the first time during the Tang Dynasty〈唐〉.

YOSHINOGARI SITE〈吉野ヶ里遺跡〉**(RESTORED)**
The site has a double circular moat, and the area inside the outer moat is as large as 40 ha. Also, remains of structures with wooden posts that could have been watchtowers have been discovered in the inner moat's protruding areas.

GOLDEN SEAL
A farmer dug up this golden seal by chance on Shikanoshima Island in present-day Fukuoka Prefecture in 1784. The seal bears an inscription customarily read as "King of Na in Wa of Han〈「漢委奴国王」〉." This type of seal was used to seal a confidential communication. (Each side 2.3 cm, weight 109 g)

regularly sent envoys to **Lelang Commandery**〈楽浪郡〉[21].

Moreover, the "**Treatise on Eastern Barbarians**"〈『後漢書』東夷伝〉 in the ***Book of the Later Han*** records that in 57 CE an envoy from the king of the country of Na〈奴国〉 of Wa came to Luoyang〈洛陽〉, the capital of the Later Han Dynasty[i], and received a seal from Emperor Guangwu〈光武帝〉. It also states that in 107 CE a king called Suishō〈帥升〉 and some others made a tribute of 160 slaves〈生口〉 to Emperor An〈安帝〉[22]. Na was a small polity that existed near present-day Fukuoka City. The **golden seal**〈金印〉 discovered on Shikanoshima〈志賀島〉 Island in the same area is thought to be the one bestowed upon the king of Na by Emperor Guangwu.

The kings of these small polities had the advantage of being able to obtain advanced goods from China and the Korean peninsula, and are thought to have sent envoys to China in order to consolidate their authority over their neighboring polities within the Japanese islands.

The Yamatai Federation

On the Chinese continent, the Later Han Dynasty was overthrown in 220, and the age of the Three Kingdoms of Wei〈魏〉, Wu〈呉〉 and Shu〈蜀〉 began. The "Records of Wei," part of the *Records of the Three Kingdoms*〈『三国志』〉, a historical text covering this period, contains a

---

[21] The Lelang Commandery was one of four commanderies on the Korean peninsula established in 108 BCE by Emperor Wu〈武帝〉 of the Former Han Dynasty〈前漢〉. It is supposed to have been located near present-day Pyongyang〈平壌〉, and was renowned for its refined Chinese-style culture.

[22] Regarding the latter text, a slightly different rendering of Suishō's realm is also recorded. This prompted an argument over whether he was a king of Wa or merely that of a smaller polity within Wa. However, even if he had been regarded as the king of Wa, it is believed that this just referred to a federation of small polities in northern Kyūshū.

section called "**Account of the Wa People** 「魏志」倭人伝[23]." According to this text, a major conflict broke out in Wa around the end of the 2nd century, and the unrest continued for some time. Therefore, various small polities elected the female ruler of Yamatai 邪馬台国, Himiko 卑弥呼, as their common queen, which resolved the conflict and brought about a federation of 29 small polities led by Yamatai. Himiko sent an envoy to the Emperor of Wei in 239, and received the title "King of Wa, Friendly to Wei," 「親魏倭王」 a golden seal, and many bronze mirrors. As a shaman, she was regarded as being able to skillfully communicate with the spirits, and ruled with spiritual authority.

Yamatai had status distinctions such as that between taijin 大人 (people of high status) and geko 下戸 (commoners), and to some extent had a kind of governing structure, and a taxation and penal system, as well as markets. Later in life, Himiko waged a war with a polity called Kunakoku 狗奴国, but died in 247 or immediately thereafter. She was succeeded by a male ruler but unrest persisted. Then, a woman related to Himiko, named **Iyo** 壱与（台与） (or Toyo) assumed the throne, and finally brought an end to the turmoil. In 266, a queen of Wa (possibly Iyo) sent an envoy to Luoyang, now the capital of the Jin 晋 Dynasty that succeeded Wei. This is the last time that Wa is mentioned in the Chinese historical record. For the following 150 years or so, Wa disappears from the Chinese written sources.

There are two major theories regarding the location of Yamatai. One holds that it was Yamato 大和 in the Kinki region, while the other argues that it was in northern Kyūshū. The **Kinki theory** 近畿説 asserts that a broad political federation extending from the central Kinki region to northern Kyūshū already existed in the early 3rd century. This theory holds that Yamatai provided the basis for the later Yamato polity ヤマト政権. On the other hand, the **Kyūshū theory** 九州説 maintains that the Yamatai federation was centered on northern Kyūshū and had relatively limited reach. According to this theory, either the Yamato polity was established separately in the eastern region and later absorbed the Yamatai federation in Kyūshū, or Yamatai extended its control eastward to finally result in the founding of the Yamato polity[24].

[23] *The Records of the Three Kingdoms* was compiled in the 3rd century by Chen Shou〈陳寿〉 of the Jin Dynasty.

[24] Remains of a large-scale, systematically arranged structure from around the early 3rd century were discovered at the **Makimuku site**〈纒向遺跡〉 in Sakurai City〈桜井市〉, Nara Prefecture〈奈良県〉 in 2009. It has attracted considerable attention for its possible connection to Yamatai.

3 Kofun and the Yamato Polity

The Emergence of Kofun and the Yamato Polity

Large burial mounds had already been built in various areas in the late Yayoi period, but from the mid-to-late 3rd century much larger-scale tombs called kofun 古墳, most notably **keyhole-shaped kofun** 前方後円墳, began to be built mainly in western Japan. Many of these early kofun[25] were either keyhole-shaped or trapezoid-and-square-shaped 前方後方墳, and shared common set characteristics such as a **pit-style stone chamber** 竪穴式石室 that housed a long wood coffin and many ritual **funerary goods** 副葬品, such as large numbers of bronze mirrors.

Since kofun were constructed based on common customs shared by chieftains of various regions, it is thought that a cross-regional political federation had already been established prior to the emergence of the kofun themselves. The largest-scale kofun from this early period are found in Nara Prefecture (Yamato), where major clans based in the central Kinki region had formed a political federation. This political federation centering on the Yamato region is called the **Yamato polity** ヤマト政権. The kofun had spread as far as central Tōhoku 東北地方 (the northeast) by the mid-4th century at the latest, indicating that an extensive area of eastern Japan had been integrated into the Yamato polity by then[26].

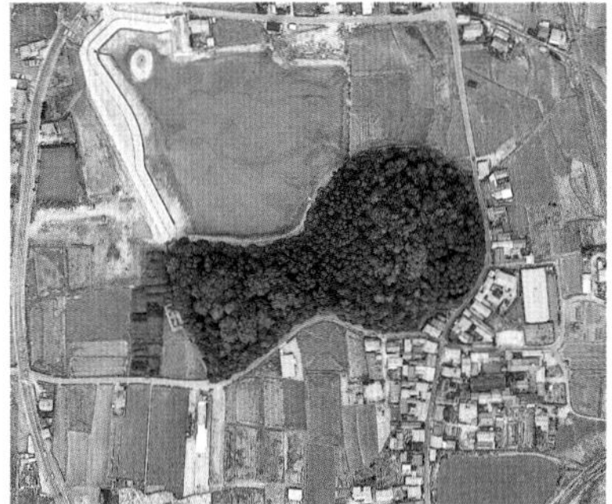

HASHIHAKA KOFUN
Located in Sakurai City, Nara Prefecture, this is the largest keyhole-shaped kofun from the incipient Kofun period.

---

[25] The first half of the early Kofun period is called the incipient period. The largest kofun from this period is Hashihaka Kofun〈箸墓古墳〉 in Nara Prefecture. It is a keyhole-shaped kofun with a mound of 280 m in length, and is far larger than other contemporary kofun such as Urama Chausuyama Kofun〈浦間茶臼山古墳〉 in Okayama Prefecture (keyhole-shaped kofun, length 140 m) and Ishizukayama Kofun〈石塚山古墳〉 (keyhole-shaped kofun, length about 120 m) in Fukuoka Prefecture. Keyhole-shaped kofun were common in western Japan while trapezoid-and-square-shaped kofun were dominant in eastern Japan during this period.

[26] The period in which kofun were constructed is called the Kofun period and spans the mid-3rd to 7th centuries. The Kofun period is classified into an early stage (mid-3rd to latter 4th century), a middle stage when the kofun were largest (latter 4th to end of 5th century), and a late stage (6th to 7th centuries). The final part of the late stage in the 7th century when keyhole-shaped kofun were no longer built is also called the final stage. The final stage of the Kofun period corresponds to the Asuka period〈飛鳥時代〉 from the perspective of political history.

Kofun in the Early and Middle Stages

Kofun can take various forms, such as keyhole-shaped, trapezoid-and-square-shaped, round, or square. The most common types of kofun are round and square types, but all of the large kofun are of the keyhole-shaped variety and were employed by major chieftains in various regions[27]. **Haniwa** 埴輪 (clay figurines) were arranged on top of the kofun mounds, while fukiishi 葺石 (roofing stones) were used for covering slopes, and no small number of kofun were surrounded by moats. In the early stage, haniwa often took the form of cylinders, houses, and tools such as shields, quivers, or parasols[28].

HANIWA PLACED ON A KOFUN (WATANUKI KANNON'YAMA KOFUN〈綿貫観音山古墳〉, RESTORED MODEL)
A cylindrical haniwa is seen on the mound, and human-shaped haniwa are in front of the stone chamber.

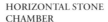

PIT-STYLE STONE CHAMBER
Yukinoyama Kofun〈雪野山古墳〉 stone chamber, Shiga Prefecture. A ceiling stone has been removed.

HORIZONTAL STONE CHAMBER
Bakuya Kofun〈牧野古墳〉 stone chamber, Nara Prefecture. A house-shaped stone coffin made of tuff is housed inside this burial chamber.

---

[27] All kofun from the 1st to 46th when arranged by length of the mound are of the keyhole-shaped variety. Some round and square kofun from the late Yayoi period had a causeway over the ditch surrounding them. This causeway is thought to have developed into the protruding area of the keyhole-shaped kofun or the trapezoid-and-square-shaped kofun (in the latter case, the trapezoid part).

[28] The cylindrical haniwa originated in a particular type of cradle for a special pot that was placed on the tombs of powerful provincial leaders in the Kibi〈吉備〉 region (present-day Okayama and eastern Hiroshima〈広島県〉 prefectures) during the late Yayoi period. In contrast with cylindrical haniwa, haniwa resembling houses or tools from the second half of the early stage as well as human- and animal-shaped haniwa from the mid-middle stage are called figural haniwa.

Burial chambers in the early and middle stages consisted of a **pit-style stone chamber** (竪穴式石室) which accommodated a wood or stone coffin, or a **pit-style tomb with a clay-covered coffin** (粘土槨). In the late stage, a **horizontal stone chamber** (横穴式石室)[29] became more common. The funerary goods from the early stage include, together with iron weapons and farming tools, many objects with ritualistic and religious significance, notably a considerable amount of bronze mirrors, especially **triangular-rimmed mirrors** (三角縁神獣鏡) with gods and sacred animals[30], and bracelet-like stone objects. This suggests that the deceased entombed in kofun at this time, who were chieftains of various regions, possessed shamanistic characteristics. On the other hand, the increase in iron weapons and armor among funerary goods during the middle stage indicates an increasingly military aspect of the deceased.

IRON ARMOR
Right: a protector or armor for the upper body called tankō〈短甲〉. Left: a helmet.

TRIANGULAR-RIMMED MIRROR WITH GODS AND SACRED ANIMALS
The rim's cross-sectional surface is triangular. This mirror was discovered at Kurozuka Kofun〈黒塚古墳〉 in Nara Prefecture.

The largest kofun is the **Daisenryō Kofun** (大仙陵古墳) (Tomb of Nintoku Tennō (仁徳天皇)[ii]), constructed in Ōsaka (大阪) during the middle stage. It is a keyhole-shaped kofun with a mound of length 486 m, encircled by two or three moats. If we include the area around the main mound where a series of smaller subordinate kofun (baichō (陪冢)) are located, the entire precinct is up to 80 ha in size[31]. Enormous kofun like the Daisenryō Kofun, along with others like the second-largest one, the Kondagobyōyama Kofun (誉田御廟山古墳) (Tomb of Ōjin Tennō (応神天皇陵)) in Ōsaka, are thought to be the tombs of **ōkimi/daiō** (大王) (great kings)[iii] of the Yamato polity in the 5th century.

---

[29] A horizontal stone chamber consists of a burial chamber and a corridor leading to the outside of the mound. It differs from a pit-type burial in that it allows additional burials. The horizontal stone chamber emerged in northern Kyūshū around the beginning of the middle stage through influence from the Korean peninsula, and became a common burial practice by the late stage.

[30] One hypothesis maintains that they were crafted in Wei, one of the Three Kingdoms, with which Yamatai had a diplomatic relationship, while another theory argues that they were made by Chinese craftsmen settled in the Japanese archipelago.

[31] If it is supposed that 2,000 workers were deployed each day, it is estimated that a total of 6,800,000 workers and a duration of 15 years and 8 months would have been required to construct it.

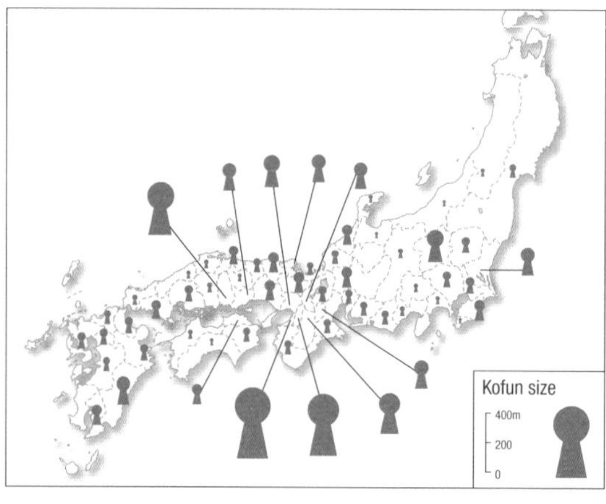

LARGE KEYHOLE-SHAPED KOFUN FROM MID-KOFUN PERIOD
This map shows the size of large kofun by province during the middle stage of the Kofun period (5th century). It reveals the relative standing of each province within the political confederacy centering on the Kinki region.

BIRD'S-EYE VIEW OF DAISENRYŌ KOFUN
(NINTOKU TENNŌ-RYŌ KOFUN 〈仁徳天皇陵古墳〉)
This large kofun occupies the central place within the Mozu Kofun Cluster 〈百舌鳥古墳群〉 scattered across a region east of Sakai City〈堺市〉 in Ōsaka.

Enormous middle-stage keyhole-shaped kofun have been discovered not only in the central Kinki region but also in Gunma Prefecture (Kamitsukeno 上毛野), the northern part of Kyōto 京都 (Tango 丹後), Okayama Prefecture (Kibi), Miyazaki Prefecture 宮崎県 (Hyūga 日向), and elsewhere. In particular, Tsukuriyama Kofun 造山古墳 has a mound 360 m in length and is the fourth largest kofun in the Japanese archipelago. This shows that regional elites in these areas held significant standing within the political federation called the Yamato polity.

Relations with Other States in East Asia

In China, the Three Kingdoms period was followed by the establishment of the Jin Dynasty. However, in the early 4th century the Jin fled south due to the intrusion by non-Han ethnic peoples (Wu Hu 五胡, "five barbarians") such as the Xiongnu 匈奴 from the north. Thus, China was divided into north and south, and the Southern and Northern Dynasties period 南北朝時代 began. This caused a weakening of China's influence on its neighboring peoples, which in turn encouraged the emergence of new states in East Asia one after another.

A new state of **Goguryeo** 高句麗 (?-668) emerged in northeastern China and then expanded its territory into the northern part of the Korean peninsula, and finally took control of the Lelang Commandery in 313. Meanwhile, three confederacies of statelets called **Mahan** 馬韓, **Byeonhan** 弁韓, and **Jinhan** 辰韓 that had been established in the southern part of the Korean peninsula gave way to new states like **Baekje** 百済 (mid 4th c. -660) that emerged out of Mahan, and **Silla** 新羅 (mid 4th c. -935) out of Jinhan, in the 4th century.

GWANGGAETO STELE
This stele was erected by Jangsu〈長寿王〉 to commemorate his father's achievements, and was placed near the tomb of Gwanggaeto. (Height, about 6.4 m)

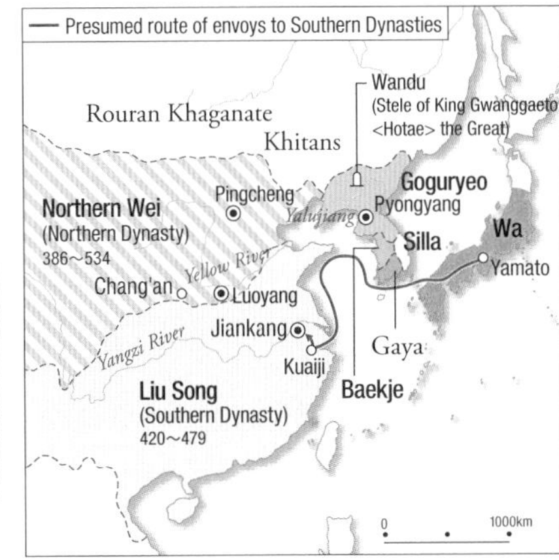

EAST ASIA, 4TH TO 5TH CENTURIES

Wa (the Yamato polity), which had been engaging in a long-standing friendly relationship with the Gaya Confederacy 加耶（加羅）諸国[32] in the former Byeonhan region in order to secure iron resources in the southern part of the Korean peninsula, allied with Gaya and Baekje in a war against Goguryeo when the latter tried to seek southward expansion in the late 4th century. The inscription on the **Gwanggaeto Stele of Goguryeo** 好太王碑[33] refers to the warfare between that state and Wa. The people of Wa, who had not previously known mounted warfare, learned those techniques through fighting with Goguryeo cavalry troops[34]. This is evidenced by harnesses found in kofun on the Japanese archipelago from the 5th century. The Wa people also adapted various technologies from Baekje and Gaya. Furthermore, many migrants (**toraijin** 渡来人) crossed the sea and

---

[32] While Baekje emerged out of the Mahan Confederacy, and Silla out of the Jinhan Confederacy, a confederacy of statelets persisted in the Byeonhan region in the southern part of the Korean peninsula from the 4th until the 6th century. These statelets were called Gaya. *Nihonshoki* 〈『日本書紀』〉 refers to Gaya by the name Mimana〈任那〉.

[33] This stele stands in present-day Ji'an in Jilin Province〈吉林省〉 in China, where the capital of Goguryeo was located. Its inscription chronicles the achievements by King Gwanggaeto (Gwanggaeto the Conqueror), and is a valuable historical resource that provides information about the contemporary political situation on the Korean peninsula. It includes a reference to Wa, as follows: "Baekje and Silla were former subjects of Goguryeo and had been paying tribute to us, whereas Wa came over from the other side of the sea in 390 and defeated Baekje and ....Silla, and thus made them their own subjects." Various interpretations of this reference to Wa have been suggested and debated.

[34] There used to be a theory that insisted on a cultural discontinuity that divided the early stage of the Kofun period and the middle stage, and maintained that the military tone of the middle-stage kofun derived from a conquest of the Japanese islands by Eurasian nomads (Horserider theory).

brought various technologies and cultures to Japan.

Moreover, Wa rulers had been sending envoys to the imperial court of the Southern Dynasties (420-589) of China for about a hundred years from the early 5th century in order to secure their diplomatic and military positions with respect to the southern part of the Korean peninsula. **"An Account of the State of Wa" in the *Book of Song*** (『宋書』倭国伝) mentions **five kings of Wa** (倭の五王)[35] named San (讃), Chin (珍), Sei (済), Kō (興), and Bu (武), successively paying tribute to Chinese emperors.

The Reception of Continental Culture

Frequent contact with the Korean peninsula and China brought new technologies to the Japanese archipelago. Advanced iron tools, Sue ware (須恵器) ceramics, weaving, metal crafts, and civil engineering were some of these technologies, introduced especially through migrants from the peninsula[36].

The Yamato polity organized migrants into several groups by their expertise, such as Korean metalwork (韓鍛冶部), pottery (陶作部), brocade weaving (錦織部), and saddle-making (鞍作部), and settled them in various locations. The use of **kanji** (漢字) also began. The phonetic use of kanji allowed Japanese personal names and place names to be expressed in writing, as can be seen in the inscription on the double-edged iron sword excavated at the Inariyama Kofun (稲荷山古墳) in Saitama Prefecture. It was also a group of migrants called fuhito-be (史部) who kept records of various events and financial matters, and prepared diplomatic letters by using kanji.

In the 6th century, **Confucianism** (儒教) was introduced by scholars of Chinese classics who arrived from Baekje. The Wa elites also absorbed other

DOUBLE-EDGED IRON SWORD EXCAVATED FROM INARIYAMA KOFUN

[35] Of the five kings of Wa mentioned in "An Account of the State of Wa" in the *Book of Song*, it is almost consensus that Sei and his sons, Kō and Bu, correspond to the sovereigns Ingyō〈允恭〉, Ankō〈安興〉, and Yūryaku〈雄略〉 in *Nihonshoki* and *Kojiki*〈『古事記』〉 (two texts referred to as "Kiki〈記紀〉" collectively). As for San, arguments are ongoing over whether he corresponds to Ōjin, Nintoku or Richū, while Chin could be either Nintoku or Hanzei〈反正〉.

[36] The Kiki contain stories about Wani〈王仁〉, Achino-omi〈阿知使主〉 and Yuzukino-kimi〈弓月君〉, the ancestors of Kawachinofumi-uji〈西文氏〉, Yamatonoaya-uji〈東漢氏〉, and Hata-uji〈秦氏〉, respectively, who came to the Japanese archipelago and assisted the Yamato polity with writing and other skills.

forms of knowledge, such as medicine, divination, and calendar systems. **Buddhism** 仏教 was also introduced through the Korean peninsula[37]. *Teiki* 「帝紀」 (lore centering on the genealogy of the great kings) and *Kyūji* 「旧辞」 (lore about the court), which provided a basis for the early-8th-century historical texts *Kojiki* and *Nihonshoki*, are believed to have been compiled around this time.

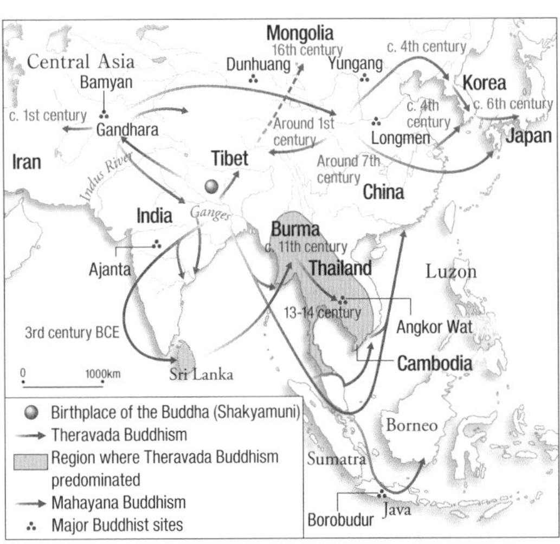

DIFFUSION OF BUDDHISM

Changes in Kofun Culture

In the late Kofun period in the 6th century, there was a major shift in Kofun themselves. The conventional pit-style of burial chamber was replaced by a **horizontal stone chamber** 横穴式石室 like those commonly found on the Korean peninsula, and simultaneously the burial of voluminous earthenware became prevalent as part of a new funerary rite. Sepulchers that were dug into hillsides or mountain slopes also appeared in various regions. **Haniwa** 埴輪 figures in the form of humans or animals were increasingly used. A group of such haniwa placed on the mound as well as around the kofun was probably intended to reproduce the funeral ceremony or preserve how

HANIWA
Above: a gabled-house haniwa (height 53.2 cm). Left: a sitting priestess (height 69.5 cm).

---

[37] The Buddhism disseminated to Japan belonged to the Mahayana tradition introduced via the northern route through Central Asia, China and the Korean peninsula. It is said that King Seong〈聖明王〉(Seiō or Meiō) of Baekje introduced Buddhist statues and teachings during the reign of Kinmei Tennō〈欽明天皇〉. There are two major theories about the date of the introduction of Buddhism, one supporting 538 based on *Jōgū Shōtoku Hōō Teisetsu*〈「上宮聖徳法王帝説」〉(Biography of Shōtoku Taishi〈聖徳太子〉) and *Gangōji Engi*〈「元興寺縁起」〉(Legends of Gangōji Temple〈元興寺〉), and the other supporting 552 based on *Nihonshoki*. Currently, the former is more widely accepted. However, it is suspected that Buddhism had already been professed by then among some of the migrants from the continent.

CLUSTERED KOFUN
Niizawasenzuka clustered kofun〈新沢千塚古墳〉in Nara Prefecture. The site consists of approximately 370 kofun of various sizes and shapes, scattered across the hilly district. The majority of the kofun are round kofun of about 10-20 m in diameter.

WALL PAINTING IN TAKEHARA KOFUN〈竹原古墳〉STONE CHAMBER
Figures like ships and a pack-horse man are depicted along with a mystic animal that appears to be the Azure Dragon, one of the Chinese Four Symbols, on the inner wall of the horizontal stone chamber of Takehara Kofun in Miyawaka City〈宮若市〉, Fukuoka Prefecture. Some scholars maintain that such ships and horses symbolize vehicles to the next life.

the deceased used to preside over the ceremony.

Distinct regional flavor became part of kofun culture. In northern Kyūshū, stone haniwa in the form of humans or horses were placed on the kofun, while **decorated kofun** 装飾古墳, in which the kofun or horizontal chambers were ornamented with petroglyphs or color paintings, appeared across Kyūshū as well as in Ibaraki 茨城県 Prefecture and Fukushima 福島県 Prefecture.

On the other hand, there were also changes in kofun from the latter half of the 5th century to the 6th century. While large keyhole-shaped kofun continued to be built in the central Kinki region, in the Kibi region, where previously large keyhole-shaped tombs were also common, this was no longer the case. This demonstrates that the nature of the Yamato polity had undergone a significant shift from a confederacy of major chieftains of various regions to a more centralized arrangement in which regional leaders were subordinated to the central elites in the Kinki region centered on the great king.

In parallel with these changes in the Yamato polity, the number of small kofun jumped dramatically, and collections of small kofun called **clustered kofun** 群集墳 came to be widely constructed even in mountainous areas and on small islands. This proves that the wealthy farming classes, who previously could never have imagined having their own kofun, started to build them for themselves. It is likely that the Yamato polity sought to put the emerging wealthy farming classes under its direct control by embedding them into the Yamato status structure that had previously been composed only of the ruling elites.

RESIDENCE OF A PROVINCIAL ELITE FAMILY IN THE KOFUN PERIOD
In those days, elite families lived in residences separated from the settlements of the common people. Mitsudera I site〈三ツ寺Ⅰ遺跡〉 in Takasaki City〈高崎市〉, Gunma Prefecture, is the site of one of the largest residences inhabited by provincial elites during the 5th to 6th centuries. The square lot with sides of about 90 m in length is surrounded by a moat of 30-40 m in width, and the inner side of the moat is slated with river cobbles to a height of 3 m.

SETTLEMENT DATING FROM THE KOFUN PERIOD (KUROIMINE SITE〈黒井峯遺跡〉, GUNMA PREFECTURE, RESTORED MODEL)
Remains of a mid-6th-century settlement were discovered under the pumice layer resulting from the eruption of Mt. Haruna's Futatsu Peak〈榛名山二ツ岳〉. This settlement was composed of several units of household residences made of pit-houses with a few ground-level dwellings, a stilt warehouse and so forth.

Life in the Kofun period

The Kofun period was a time when there came to be a clear distinction in lifestyle between the elite rulers (chieftains) and the populace who were ruled. The elites lived apart from the general populace in residences with moats and fences, where they also engaged in political matters. These residences appear to have been equipped with warehouses to store surplus products and crops.

HAJI WARE (ABOVE) **AND SUE WARE** (RIGHT)
Early-Kofun period Haji pot and late-Kofun period Sue legged pot.

The populace lived in settlements without moats, with several units (yashikichi 屋敷地) each of which consisted of a number of pit-houses, ground-level houses and stilt warehouses. In the 5th century, due to influence from the Korean peninsula pit-houses came to be commonly equipped with built-in hearths.

From the early through early middle Kofun period, red-burnished **Haji ware** 土師器, an evolved version of Yayoi pottery, was still being produced and used. In the 5th century, the harder and grayish **Sue ware** 須恵器 was introduced from the Korean peninsula, and began to be used alongside Haji ware. As for clothing, the most common style was separate upper and lower garments, consisting of a shirt-like upper garment with horse-riding-style trousers (hakama 袴) for men or a skirt (mo 裳) for women, as depicted in haniwa figures.

The most important rituals for people in the Kofun period were those related to

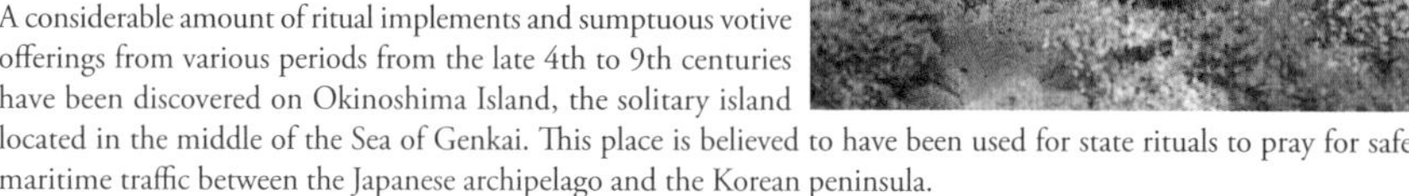

OKINOSHIMA ISLAND IN FUKUOKA PREFECTURE (ABOVE) AND MEGALITH CLUSTER AROUND THE RITUAL SITE ON THE ISLAND (RESTORED MODEL)
A considerable amount of ritual implements and sumptuous votive offerings from various periods from the late 4th to 9th centuries have been discovered on Okinoshima Island, the solitary island located in the middle of the Sea of Genkai. This place is believed to have been used for state rituals to pray for safe maritime traffic between the Japanese archipelago and the Korean peninsula.

farming, especially the **Toshigoi no Matsuri** (祈年の祭) (rite for a good harvest) in spring and the **Niiname no Matsuri** (新嘗の祭) (great harvest rite) in autumn. In place of the bronze ritual implements that had been used during the Yayoi period, bronze mirrors and iron weapons and farming tools, which have been discovered as funerary goods in kofun, became important ritual items. In the 5th century, stone replicas of these articles were produced in great number for ritualistic purposes.

The people believed that spirits resided in remarkable natural objects such as bell-shaped stately mountains, tall trees, great rocks, solitary islands in distant seas, and stream pools. These sacred places became the object of worship, and no small number are linked to Shintō (神社) shrines that exist today. The custom of worshipping the ancestors of one's clan is also believed to have started during this period[38].

Various ritual practices were also performed, such as misogi (禊) and harae (祓), purification methods intended to ward off misfortune; **futomani** (太占), a method of divination by baking deer bones; and **kukatachi** (盟神探湯), a method to judge one's guilt at a trial by forcing the accused to put their hand into boiling water to see if injury occurred or not.

The End of the Kofun Period

From the end of the 6th to the early 7th century, the keyhole-shaped kofun, which had been built by major regional chieftains, ceased to be constructed. The reason for the simultaneous timing of this development in multiple regions is likely that the

[38] Remains of ritual sites and religious artifacts from the Kofun period have been found around Ōmiwa Shrine〈大神神社〉 in Nara Prefecture, which deifies Mt. Miwa〈三輪山〉 and has only a front shrine with no inner shrine where an object of worship is usually placed, and Okitsu Shrine〈沖津宮〉 of the Munakata Taisha〈宗像大社〉 in Fukuoka Prefecture, which worships Okinoshima Island〈沖ノ島〉, the solitary island in the middle of the Sea of Genkai〈玄界灘〉. These shrines are still maintained today and imply the continuity of Shintō nature worship rituals since the Kofun period.

Yamato polity had imposed a strict regulation on the construction of keyhole-shaped kofun. During this period, the Sui Dynasty unified southern and northern China and was showing signs of eastward expansion toward the Korean peninsula. Reacting to these developments in the East Asian sphere, Wa also sought to achieve a centralized state structure centered on the great king. This was probably the backdrop behind the decision to break away from the old confederacy type of political organization represented by the keyhole-shaped kofun.

Even though the keyhole-shaped kofun ceased to be constructed, kofun still continued to be built for about another 100 years. Archeologists call this period the final stage of the Kofun period, and its kofun final-stage kofun. The ruling elites who used to build keyhole-shaped kofun now started to construct large round or square kofun, but in provinces it was only the influential elites appointed as local chieftains who were accorded a large round or square kofun. The largest of these final-stage kofun are the Ryūkakuji Iwaya Kofun 龍角寺岩屋古墳 (square kofun, each side 80 m) in Chiba prefecture and Mibu Kurumazuka Kofun 壬生車塚古墳 (round kofun, diameter 80 m) in Tochigi 栃木県 Prefecture. These kofun are thought to have been built by influential elites in eastern Japan appointed as local chieftains.

Moreover, in the mid-7th century, the tomb of the great king in the Kinki region became an **octagonal kofun** 八角墳. This was most likely because while the great kings used to build keyhole-shaped kofun like other chieftains, just larger in size, now they sought to build an octagonal type that was permitted only to them in order to demonstrate their superiority over the other chieftains. Ruling elites continued to build kofun until around the end of the 7th century, but after that it seems that only the great kings, members of their clan, and a smattering of other ruling elites who supported the rule of the great kings built traditional kofun with mounds. The end of the keyhole-shaped kofun, as well as the emergence of octagonal kofun and the cessation of kofun construction by ruling elites, can be seen as part of a major shift in the political system from a simple unified state to a more organized and elaborate state structure known as the Ritsuryō 律令国家 state.

The Yamato Polity and Its Political System

From the latter 5th to the 6th century, the Yamato polity with the great king at its center gradually consolidated a ruling structure that put under its control the regional elite class from the Kantō area through to central Kyūshū. "An Account of the State of Wa" in the *Book of Song* records that five kings of Wa in succession paid tribute to Chinese emperors and were recognized as kings of Wa. Moreover, "A Diplomatic Letter addressed to the Chinese Emperor from Bu, King of Wa," dated

478, describes the expansion of the realm of Wa and the subjugation of regional chieftains in eastern, western and northern Japan. This dovetails with the development of large keyhole-shaped kofun centering on the Kinki region. Further, both the double-edged iron sword discovered at Inariyama Kofun in Saitama Prefecture and the single-edged iron sword unearthed at Etafunayama 江田船山古墳 Kofun in Kumamoto 熊本県 Prefecture have inscriptions mentioning Great King 「獲加多支鹵大王」 Wakatakeru, along with the names of respective local chieftains who assisted his rule. This great king was King Bu of Wa, also known as Yūryaku Tennō.

LARGE SWORD DISCOVERED AT OKADAYAMA I KOFUN IN SHIMANE PREFECTURE

It lacks an upper half. It has an inscription that reads "Nukatabe no omi."

From the 5th to 6th centuries, the Yamato polity implemented a ruling structure called the **uji-kabane system** 氏姓制度. In this system, the ruling elites were organized into **uji** 氏 (clans) based on blood relations or other political relationships, which then shared responsibilities in the Yamato polity. The great king in turn gave them **kabane** 姓 (hereditary titles)[39].

The kabane included **omi** 臣 (regional elites claiming royal descent) and **muraji** 連 (prominent regional elites). Elites chosen from each category, called ōomi 大臣 (supreme omi) and ōmuraji 大連 (supreme muraji) respectively, carried out the central governance. Beneath those, officials called **tomo no miyatsuko** 伴造 took charge of responsibilities such as military affairs, finance, religious services, foreign affairs, and documentation, assisted by a lesser category of officials named tomo 伴, who were grouped according to different responsibilities, and the subordinates of tomo, be 部. The migrants were also organized into tomo and be according to the knowledge and technology they brought with them, and were assisted by subordinates called shinabe 品部 (tomobe). The residences of the powerful princes and influential families engaged in governance, and the palace where the great king resided, were concentrated in the southern part of the Nara basin. Each of these elite families was served by minor clans from the central region, provincial elite families, and tomo. Powerful families had their own private

---

[39] Examples of kabane (hereditary titles) include: "omi" for Kazuraki〈葛城〉, Heguri〈平群〉 and Soga〈蘇我〉, whose names were taken from place names in the Kinki region, "muraji" for Ōtomo〈大伴〉 and Mononobe〈物部〉, whose names signified their profession, "kimi〈君〉" for powerful regional families, and "atai〈直〉" for regional ruling families. One of the oldest examples of kabane is "Nukatabe no omi〈額田部臣〉" inscribed on the large sword discovered at Okadayama I Kofun〈岡田山1号墳〉 in Shimane Prefecture.

land (**tadokoro** 田荘) and servants (**kakibe** 部曲), which provided them with financial resources. Uji and the households that constituted them also had slaves called yatsuko ヤツコ（奴婢） (nuhi).

Some provincial elites resisted the expansion of the great king's power. In particular, at the start of the 6th century, an official named Iwai 磐井 in charge of the administration of the Tsukushi 筑紫国 (Chikushi) Province launched a major rebellion with support from Silla. It took two years for the great king's forces to suppress the **Iwai Rebellion** 磐井の乱, whereupon northern Kyūshū was put under royal control as **miyake** 屯倉. The Yamato polity gradually subordinated the occasionally rebellious provincial elites under its control, and in various areas they established miyake and created a service group of subordinates called **nashiro** 名代 and **koshiro** 子代. During the 6th century, regional elites were appointed as **kuni no miyatsuko** 国造 (local chieftains). While the Yamato polity guaranteed their local rule, they were required to serve the polity by providing various services. These included sending their children to the great king's court to serve as toneri 舎人 or uneme 采女 (personal attendants), offering local specialties as tribute, supervising the people working under miyake and nashiro and koshiro, and participating in military service.

Translators' Notes

[i] The Later Han Dynasty, also called the "Eastern Han," should not be confused with the other Later Han (947-951) of the Five Dynasties and Ten Kingdoms era. In English, Chinese historical eras are named after the ruling dynasties (so for example, "Ming Dynasty" refers to the Chinese state during 1368-1644, and the empire that state controlled, as well as to the era itself). Note that this does not correspond to how Chinese states actually called themselves (the Ming Dynasty was officially the "Great Ming" (大明), for instance).

[ii] The characters for "tennō" (天皇) literally mean "heavenly sovereign," but the term is difficult to translate because of the special character of the royal institution in Japanese history and how it has evolved over time. 19th-century politics led to the term frequently being rendered as "emperor," a practice that has continued to be followed by the contemporary mass media and government, but this is not really appropriate for "tennō," especially in the context of premodern history. "Emperor" denotes a supreme and absolute ruler with military power over a large area, and derives from the Latin "imperator," a title for ancient Roman military commanders. None of this suits the Japanese tennō, who possessed spiritual authority, not military power, and was never an absolute ruler. "King," corresponding to 王, does not work either (one reason the court adopted "tennō" in the first place was to distinguish the Japanese ruler from local kings who had come before), and while "sovereign" works in general contexts it is not always appropriate, especially in contemporary Japan where the tennō is a symbol of the nation rather than a sovereign. It was therefore decided to retain the term as "tennō" in most contexts in this textbook. As a proper title, it is capitalized when applied to specific individuals (e.g. Saimei Tennō).

[iii] Normally, "ōkimi" (or "daiō") is rendered as "great king," irrespective of gender. Unlike Japanese and Chinese, English usually employs gendered terms for rulers (king, queen) but often makes no distinction between a queen on the throne and a queen who is merely the consort of a king (see the note for "queen consort"). To avoid confusion, "great king" is therefore used in this textbook for all ōkimi, including both male and female rulers.

Chapter

2

The Formation of the Ritsuryō State

1 The Yamato Court of the Asuka Period

Changes in East Asia and the Development of the Yamato Polity

In the 6th century, the Korean peninsula saw the kingdoms of Baekje 百済 and Silla 新羅, under pressure from Goguryeo 高句麗, expand their territories southwards to incorporate the small states of the confederacy of Gaya 加耶[1]. The confederacy gradually disintegrated and by 562 had come under the full control of Baekie and Silla. This was followed by the decline of the influence of the Yamato ヤマト政権 polity on the Korean peninsula, which had been based on its ties with Gaya. At the beginning of the 6th century, the Ōtomo 大伴氏 family, who were the leading figures in the government, lost power due to their policies concerning the Korean peninsula[2]. In the middle of the century, a conflict developed between the Mononobe 物部氏 family and the rising Soga 蘇我氏 family[3]. Through collaboration with migrants from the continent, the Soga family took control of the court finances[4] and actively set about putting the administrative

KOREAN PENINSULA IN THE 6TH CENTURY

---

[1] Gaya, situated in the south of the Korean peninsula, was a state ruled by the city-state of Geumgwan Gaya (Gimhae)〈金官国（金海）〉 for the first half of its history, and by that of Daegaya (Goryeong)〈大加耶国（高霊）〉 in the latter half. Although this state had diplomatic relations with countries such as Baekje, Silla, and Wa〈倭〉, Gaya itself is said to have had strong characteristics of a confederacy consisting of small states.

[2] At the beginning of the 6th century, Ōtomo no Kanamura〈大伴金村〉 lost his position when he was accused of misgovernment by allowing Baekje to conquer the western areas of Gaya.

[3] A conflict occurred between the Soga family〈蘇我氏〉, which favored introducing advanced culture and Buddhism, and the Mononobe and Nakatomi families〈中臣氏〉, which opposed this due to their support for indigenous tradition and beliefs. In 587 the Soga family defeated the Mononobe family and established a powerful position.

[4] The Soga family was in charge of the Mitsu no Kura〈三蔵〉 (Three Treasuries), namely the Imikura〈斎蔵〉 (Ritual Articles Treasury), the Uchitsukura〈内蔵〉 (Royal Family Treasury), and the Ōkura〈大蔵〉 (State Treasury). They are also believed to have been involved in the management of miyake〈屯倉〉 (royal properties).

system in order and promoting the acceptance of Buddhism.

In 589, East Asia entered an era of great change as the **Sui Dynasty**（隋） (581-618) of China unified the Northern and Southern Dynasties（南北朝）, and commenced its expansion towards surrounding neighbors including Goguryeo. In Japan, in 587 the Ōomi（大臣） **Soga no Umako**（蘇我馬子） (?-626) defeated the Ōmuraji（大連） **Mononobe no Moriya**（物部守屋） (?-587) and in 592, he seized power by assassinating Sushun Tennō（崇峻天皇） (r. 587-592). This led to Suiko Tennō（推古天皇） (r. 592-628), who was the consort of the late Bidatsu Tennō（敏達天皇）, ascending the throne. Amidst international tensions, Soga no Umako and Suiko's nephew **Prince Umayato**（厩戸王（聖徳太子）） (Shōtoku Taishi, 574-622) worked together to build a state system of government. In 603 the **Twelve Level Cap and Rank System**（冠位十二階） was put into place, and in 604 the **Seventeen-article Constitution**（憲法十七条） was promulgated. The Twelve Level Cap and Rank System was created in order to reorganize the court system, previously based on clans, into one where ranks were granted based not on ancestry but on individual talent and achievements. The Seventeen-article Constitution was intended to instill in the clans an awareness of what it entailed to be government officials. It also put a great emphasis on Buddhism as the new political philosophy. In this way the organization of central and local administration[5] proceeded under the court's direction. The diplomatic relationship with China was also resumed in this period through the dispatch of an envoy to Sui (**kenzuishi**（遣隋使）). Following the first envoy, who as recorded in the *Book of Sui*（『隋書』） was dispatched in 600, Ono no Imoko（小野妹子） was sent as kenzuishi in 607. The message carried by the second envoy, unlike those written in the era of the Five Kings of Wa（倭の五王）, did not situate Wa as a subject of the Chinese emperor, which Emperor Yang of Sui（煬帝） (r. 604-618) considered insolent.

In 618, the Sui Dynasty collapsed and was followed by the **Tang Dynasty**（唐） (618-907), and witnessing the rise of this powerful empire, Wa began sending envoys again. These envoys (kentōshi（遣唐使）), beginning with Inukami no Mitasuki（犬上御田鍬） in 630, adopted the latest changes in East Asia in order to establish a centralized political structure. Scholars and monks who accompanied the envoys, such as Takamuko no Genri（高向玄理） (?-654), Minabuchi no Shōan（南淵請安） (?-?), and Min（旻） (?-653), returned to Japan after a long period of studying, and brought back with them new knowledge of Chinese systems, thought, and culture, which came to strongly influence politics from the middle of the 7th century onwards.

---

[5] According to the *Book of Sui*, a Chinese historical account, in the 7th century Wa had local leaders called "kuni〈クニ〉," which were similar to regional officials in China, and "inagi〈イナギ〉," which in turn were similar to township heads. It is believed that ten inagi were under one kuni.

The Court and Culture of the Asuka Period

From the end of the 6th century, many palaces of the ōkimi (大王) (great king) were constructed at Asuka (飛鳥), located in the southern part of the Nara Basin (奈良盆地). While powerful members of the royal family and major elite families had their own residences separate from the palaces, the centralization of these palaces and the building of facilities related to the court nearby led the Asuka area to gradually turn into a large city, eventually becoming a royal capital city (**kyūto** 宮都).

VIEW OF THE WESTERN PRECINCT OF HŌRYŪJI TEMPLE
There was a fire at the Main Hall in 1949, which damaged a great part of the wall paintings. The Inner Gate, Main Hall, Five-storied Pagoda, and Cloister of this temple feature elements of Asuka style, and are believed to be some of the most ancient wooden structures in the world. An entasis bulge can be seen in the middle of the wooden pillars of the Main Hall and Cloister.

The culture from the first half of the 7th century was characterized by a prominent role for Buddhism, which was propagated by the royal family and the Soga family. This **Asuka culture** (飛鳥文化) was heavily influenced by the cultures of Baekje, Goguryeo[6] and the Northern and Southern Dynasties of China through the activities of migrants. Furthermore, it shares some similarities with cultures in West Asia, India and Greece. There were many temples built, including Asukadera (Hōkōji) (飛鳥寺（法興寺）)[7] by the Soga family, Kudaraōdera (百済大寺), attributed to Jomei Tennō (舒明天皇) (r. 629-641), and Shitennōji (四天王寺) and Hōryūji (Ikarugadera) (法隆寺（斑鳩寺）)[8] attributed to

---

[6] It is believed that a monk from Baekje, Gwalleuk〈観勒〉, brought the knowledge of the calendar, and a monk from Goguryeo, Damjing〈曇徴〉, introduced methods for coloring, papermaking, and ink.

[7] The construction of Asukadera, founded by Soga no Umako, was completed in 596. This was the first temple to bear true elements of Garan architecture with a pagoda and a main hall. Engineers from Baekje took part in the construction. Unlike the traditional method where posts embedded in the ground were used for building, it was built by placing wooden pillars atop foundation stones and laying tiles on the roof. When Asukadera was excavated, artifacts that were of the same type as those found in kofun were discovered from the foundation stone of the pagoda's central pillar. This proves that Buddhism in Japan was adopted by syncretizing the religion with ancient Japanese beliefs and practices.

[8] In *Nihonshoki*〈『日本書紀』〉, there is a reference to Hōryūji burning down in 670. There had been a controversy among historians since the Meiji period over whether the temple was a reconstruction or not, as it had been described as having an ancient style of architecture. The current Main Hall and Five-storied Pagoda are believed to have been reconstructed according to the excavation reports from the site of Wakakusa-Garan〈若草伽藍〉, one of the original buildings of Hōryūji.

THE STATUE OF HANKASHIYUI OF CHŪGŪJI TEMPLE
A wooden statue made from a camphor tree from the latter half of the 7th century. It takes a contemplative pose with one leg on the knee and a hand touching its cheek. The face wears a benevolent expression. Influence from the art style of one of the Southern Dynasties (Liang〈梁〉) can be seen in this piece. (Height 87.9 cm)

GILT-BRONZE SHAKYAMUNI TRIAD OF HŌRYŪJI TEMPLE
Gilt-bronze statues attributed to Kuratsukuri no Tori, enshrined in the middle of the Shumi platform〈須弥壇〉. The influence of the Northern Wei style can be seen in their stern and solemn expression. (Height 86.4 cm [central figure], 90.7 cm [left flanking figure], 92.4 cm [right flanking figure])

KUDARA KANNON OF HŌRYŪJI TEMPLE
A wooden statue made from a camphor tree. The name "Kudara Kannon" was given in the modern era. The statue is tall and has sloping shoulders. The jug of water held in the hands gives a noble impression. (Height 210.9 cm)

TAMAMUSHI MINIATURE SHRINE〈玉虫厨子〉OF HŌRYŪJI TEMPLE
A miniature shrine made of black lacquered Japanese cypress. Wings of jeweled beetles are displayed under the metallic fretwork on its fittings. Drawings based on Buddhist fables can be seen on the sides of its miniature palace and the Shumi platform. (Height 233 cm)

Prince Umayato. Such temples came to replace kofun (古墳) as indicators of a family's authority. Garan (temple) architecture (伽藍建築), a continental style that applied new technology using foundation stones and roof tiles, was introduced. As for Buddhist sculpture, one style adopted the clear-cut and stern expression of sculptures from the Northern Wei (北魏) style of the Northern and Southern Dynasties, as can be seen in pieces like the gilt-bronze statues of the Shakyamuni Triad of Hōryūji Temple (法隆寺金堂釈迦三尊像) attributed to Kuratsukuri no Tori (鞍作鳥). Another style was wooden sculptures with a gentle expression, such as the Hankashiyui (半跏思惟像) of Chūgūji (中宮寺) Temple and the Kudara Kannon (百済観音像) of Hōryūji Temple.

2 The Road to the Ritsuryō State

The Taika Reforms

In the mid-7th century, the Tang Dynasty, with a strong and advanced political structure, commenced a military campaign against Goguryeo. Amidst this international tension, neighboring countries felt pressured to establish centralized governments and consolidate their territory. In the case of Wa, Soga no Iruka 蘇我入鹿 (?-645) attempted to consolidate his own power by killing Prince Yamashiro 山背大兄王 (?-643), the son of Prince Umayato. However, this was not successful, because Prince Naka no Ōe 中大兄皇子 (626-671), with the help of Soga no Kurayamada no Ishikawa Maro 蘇我倉山田石川麻呂 (?-649) and Nakatomi no Kamatari 中臣鎌足 (614-669), established a centralized government with members of the royal family as its core. In 645, he brought about the deaths of Soga no Emishi 蘇我蝦夷 (?-645) and Iruka (**Isshi Incident** 乙巳の変). Kōgyoku Tennō 皇極天皇 (r. 642-645) abdicated in favor of Prince Karu 軽皇子, who ascended the throne as Kōtoku Tennō 孝徳天皇 (r. 645-654). A new government was established with Prince Naka no Ōe as crown prince, Abe no Uchi no Maro 阿倍内麻呂 as minister of the left, Soga no Kurayamada no Ishikawa Maro as minister of the right, Nakatomi no Kamatari as inner palace minister, and the envoys Takamuko no Genri and Min as senior scholars. The palace was moved from Asuka to Naniwa 難波宮 where political reforms proceeded.

In the new year of 646, the **Reform Edict** 改新の詔 was promulgated, setting forth the policy of abolishing the private land and servant systems, and transitioning to a system of state ownership of land and people[9]. This policy aimed to determine the population and amount of cultivated land in the realm, and to develop a standardized tax system. Local administrative institutions called kōri 評[10] were established across the country, and the bureaucratic system of the central government was also reorganized. The great Naniwa Palace was also constructed. This centralization occurred in the context of the expanding authority of the kingship and Prince Naka no Ōe[11]. These reforms in

[9] The lines in *Nihonshoki* that mention the edict appear to have been embellished to match the Taihō Code〈大宝令〉 and its successors. Therefore, it is necessary to exercise careful consideration when examining what the actual plans for reform were at this point in time.

[10] References to kōri in various parts of Japan can be found on mokkan〈木簡〉 (documents on wood) and kinseki-bun〈金石文〉 (documents on metal or stone) from the 7th century, such as the Fujiwara-kyū Mokkan〈藤原宮木簡〉. The establishment of kōri based on requests made by regional clans is also recorded in documents such as *Hitachi no Kuni Fudoki*〈『常陸国風土記』〉.

[11] Under Prince Naka no Ōe's initiative, Prince Furuhito no Ōe〈古人大兄王〉, a candidate for the throne from the Soga family, Soga no Kurayamada no Ishikawa Maro, and later Prince Arima〈有間皇子〉, a son of Kōtoku, were eliminated, and the centralization of power proceeded apace.

the era of Kōtoku Tennō are known as the **Taika Reforms** 大化改新.

The Road to the Ritsuryō State

On the Korean peninsula, the Tang Dynasty allied with Silla, and defeated Baekje in 660 and Goguryeo in 668. Under the reign of Saimei Tennō 斉明天皇 (r. 655-661, Kōgyoku who re-ascended the throne after the death of Kōtoku), Wa sent a military expedition to support Baekje restoration forces which had continued to resist Tang and Silla. However, in 663, they were defeated by the allied forces of Tang and Silla in the **Battle of Baekgang** 白村江の戦い. The aftermath of this event led to Silla establishing control over the Korean peninsula, and finally uniting it in 676. After the defeat, defensive policies were undertaken in Wa, and by 664 sakimori 防人 (guards who protected border regions) and tobuhi 烽 (signal beacons) were stationed on Tsushima 対馬, Iki 壱岐 Island, and in Tsukushi 筑紫 Province. Fortifications such as Mizuki 水城 Fort, Ōno 大野城 Fort, and Kii 基肄城 Fort were also build to protect strategically important locations in the Kyūshū region under the supervision of exiled Baekje nobles. Ancient Korean-style fortresses were built from Tsushima up to Yamato 大和. As for domestic policies, in 664 clan heads (uji 氏上 no kami) were appointed in order to organize the clans through measures such as verifying the system of private people belonging to clans. In 667, Prince Naka no Ōe moved the capital to Ōtsu Palace 大津宮 in the Ōmi 近江 region, where he ascended the throne as **Tenji Tennō** 天智天皇 (r. 668-671) the following year. In 670, he instituted the **Kōgo Nenjaku** 庚午年籍, which was the first family registry system in Japan[12].

In 672, a year after Tenji died, a dispute over succession (**Jinshin War** 壬申の乱) broke out between Prince Ōtomo 大友皇子 (648-672), Tenji's son who was leading the Ōmi court, and Prince Ōama 大海人皇子 (631?-686), the younger brother of Tenji. Prince Ōama moved to Mino 美濃 in the eastern provinces where he was successful in mobilizing the local clans in his favor, and thus defeated Prince Ōtomo. The next year he took the throne as **Tenmu Tennō** 天武天皇 (r. 673-686) at the Asuka Kiyomihara Palace 飛鳥浄御原宮. This dispute led to the collapse of the powerful central clans who sided with the Ōmi Court, resulting in Tenmu gaining a tremendous amount of power and enabling the formation of a centralized government orientated around himself[13].

In 675, Tenmu abolished the system of private people belonging to clans, and instituted a bureaucratic system by declaring the ranks of officials and the system

---

[12] Some historians believe that Tenji was also responsible for the Ōmi Code〈近江令〉, the first collection of laws in Japan, but there are doubts as to whether or not this code was ever completed.

[13] It is believed that the use of the title "tennō〈天皇〉" (heavenly sovereign) instead of "ōkimi" (great king) began around this time. The deity of Ise〈伊勢〉, to whom Tenmu prayed for victory in the war, also became a deity worshipped in state rituals from this era (Ise Grand Shrine〈伊勢神宮〉).

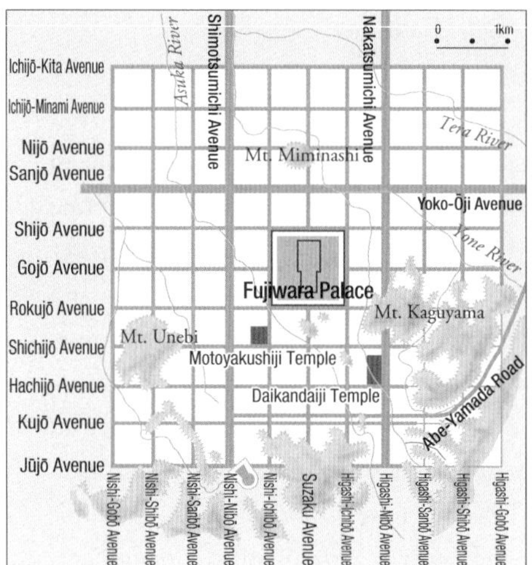

RESTORED GRID PATTERN DIAGRAM OF FUJIWARA-KYŌ
The size of Fujiwara-kyō was approximately 5.3 km square, with the Fujiwara Palace in the center. Many powerful members of the royal family and elite families were required to live here.

of their promotion. In 684, he implemented the **Yakusa no Kabane** 八色の姓 **(eight-rank system)** to form a new hierarchy of clans with the sovereign at the center. He also sought to improve the government's political structure by minting coins (**Fuhonsen** 富本銭), initiating the compilation of the Ritsuryō 律令 (penal and administrative codes) and official history, as well as by constructing a new capital (Fujiwara-kyō) based on a Chinese model (tojōsei 都城制). However, Tenmu died prior to the completion of these initiatives.

Tenmu's queen consort (kōgō 皇后)[i], Jitō 持統天皇 (r. 690-697), ascended the throne after him and continued his policies. In 689 a legal code known as the **Asuka Kiyomihara Code** 飛鳥浄御原令 was put into effect, and in the following year a new family registry system (Kōin Nenjaku 庚寅年籍) was established to further collect information about the population. In 694, Jitō Tennō moved the capital from Asuka to **Fujiwara-kyō** 藤原京[14], the first full-scale capital.

Hakuhō Culture

The culture of the era from the latter half of the 7th century to the beginning of the 8th is called the **Hakuhō culture** 白鳳文化. Emerging in the early days of the Ritsuryō state under the reigns of Tenmu and Jitō, it is often described as lively in character. It was based on Buddhism and influenced by the culture of the early Tang Dynasty, which arrived first by way of Silla in the 7th century, and later via the envoys in the 8th century.

Buddhism in this era expanded rapidly under state promotion, such as the founding of temples like Daikandaiji 大官大寺 and Yakushiji 薬師寺 under Tenmu. Local clans also competed

[14] Unlike other palaces which were used as the capital under the reign of a single sovereign, Fujiwara-kyō remained the capital for the reigns of three. The capital city was built around the palace in a grid pattern (jōbōsei〈条坊制〉) adopted from China, and powerful members of the royal family and central elites were required to reside there. There were also buildings for important government affairs and rituals, built in a Chinese style with roof tiles and foundation stones, such as the Daigokuden〈大極殿〉(Throne Hall) and Chōdōin〈朝堂院〉(Audience Hall). In this way, Fujiwara-kyō became a capital that symbolized the new centralized state.

with each other to build such institutions. Buddhist sculptures such as the bronze Buddha head of Kōfukuji 興福寺 Temple conveyed a peaceful expression. As for paintings, influence from India and regions west of China can be seen in the wall paintings in the Main Hall of Hōryūji Temple, whereas the influence of China and the Korean peninsula can be seen in the paintings on the walls of the Takamatsuzuka Kofun 高松塚古墳.

Elites began to adopt Chinese learning and compose classical Chinese poetry, while on the other hand the conventions for writing waka 和歌 (Japanese poems) also came to be established. Moreover, as the centralization of the state system got underway, the period witnessed the diffusion of Chinese characters and Confucian thought, not only among officials in the center but also among local elites.

EAST PAGODA OF YAKUSHIJI TEMPLE
Built around 730, this structure is believed to represent the design styles of the Hakuhō period. The three-storied pagoda has a mokoshi〈裳階〉(decorative pent roof) on each floor. (Height 34.1 m)

YAKUSHI TRIAD IN MAIN HALL OF YAKUSHIJI TEMPLE〈薬師寺金堂薬師三尊像〉
This gilt-bronze statue is the main image of Yakushiji. The carving has a soft but realistic expression full of dignity. Theories suggest that this statue was made during the Yōrō era〈養老年間〉(717-723), when the Main Hall of Yakushiji was built. (Height 254.8 cm [central figure], 311.8 cm [left flanking figure], 309.4 cm [right flanking figure])

BRONZE BUDDHA HEAD OF KŌFUKUJI TEMPLE
This was originally the head of the central statue of Yamadadera Temple's〈山田寺〉Yakushi Triad. It was sculpted in 685 to console the soul of Soga no Kurayamada no Ishikawa Maro. (Height 98.3 cm)

WALL PAINTINGS OF THE TAKAMATSUZUKA KOFUN (WESTERN WALL)
A wall painting on the inner walls of a stone burial chamber, painted in color over plaster. Aside from groups of men and women, the Chinese Four Symbols and constellations were also depicted. The influence from wall paintings of the Tang Dynasty and Goguryeo can also be seen in these works.

The Taihō Code and Bureaucracy

In 701, the **Taihō Code** 大宝律令 was completed by Royal Prince Osakabe 刑部親王 (?-705)[ii] and Fujiwara no Fuhito 藤原不比等 (659-720), which finalized the Ritsuryō system of governing the state[15]. "Ritsu" 律 refers to what would today be a penal code, and "ryō" 令 signifies regulations pertaining to administrative and bureaucratic duties as well as the taxation and labor of the populace.

The central administrative system contained two councils: the **Jingikan** 神祇官 (**Council of Shrine Affairs**), which was in charge of rituals for the deities, and the **Daijōkan** 太政官 (**Council of State**), which managed governmental affairs. Under the Daijōkan, responsibilities were divided among the **Hasshō** 八省 (**Eight Ministries**). The administration was handled by the **kugyō** 公卿 (**senior nobles**), including the daijōdaijin 太政大臣 (supreme minister), sadaijin 左大臣 (minister of the left), udaijin 右大臣 (minister of the right), and dainagon 大納言 (senior counselors). These positions were filled with appointees chosen from the powerful clans.

As for local administration, the country was divided into the **Kinai** 畿内 (capital region) and **shichidō** 七道 (**seven circuits**), with smaller divisions consisting of **koku** 国 (**province**), **gun** 郡 (**district**), and **ri** 里 (**township**, which would later be renamed gō 郷). Kokushi 国司 (provincial governors), gunji 郡司 (district chieftains), and richō 里長 (township heads), were appointed to administer these respective regions. Provincial governors were nobles[iii] sent from the capital to govern a province from an administrative headquarters called kokufu 国府 (or kokuga 国衙). District chieftains, on the other hand, were appointed from among traditional local elites who had formerly held the post of local chieftains (kuni 国造

[15] Ritsu and ryō were compiled for the first time in Japan under the Taihō Code, and it was during the same period that the country name "Nihon"〈「日本」〉 started to be used officially. Although the Ritsuryō system in Japan was modeled after the system of the Tang Dynasty, certain adjustments were implemented to meet the specific needs of the state. In 718, the **Yōrō Code**〈養老律令〉 was completed by Fujiwara no Fuhito and some other officials. However, this code, which was implemented in 757, was not substantially different from the Taihō Code.

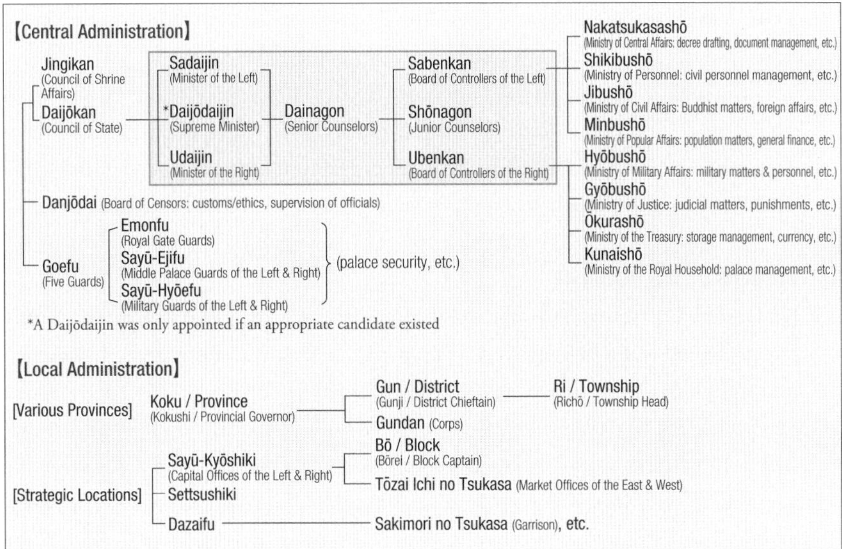

TABLE OF THE RITSURYŌ BUREAUCRATIC SYSTEM

no miyatsuko). They governed their gun from a district office known as a gūke 郡家 (or gunga 郡衙). There were also other administrations established, such as the Sakyōshiki 左京職 (Left Capital Office) and Ukyōshiki 右京職 (Right Capital Office) in the capital city, the **Settsushiki** 摂津職 in Naniwa, and the **Dazaifu** 大宰府 which managed Saikaidō 西海道 (Kyūshū), and was located in the northern part of the island which was a region with both diplomatic and military value. These administrations employed many officials, who were required to be able to write documents in Chinese characters and possess an understanding of Confucianism.

Under the Taihō Code, officials received numeric ranks, and their posts were determined according to their rank through the Kan'isōtōsei 官位相当制 (rank and post congruence system). Officials were paid, depending upon their rank and post, in fuko 封戸 (residence units), denchi 田地 (farming fields), and roku 禄 (goods)[16], but they were also exempted from taxes such as chō 調 and yō 庸 (taxes paid in kind and delivered), and zōyō 雑徭 (additional labor tax)[17]. Nobles above the fifth rank enjoyed further privileges, and their children (and grandchildren if above the third rank) were granted ranks according

[16] The salaries of officials were paid in several ways: fuko, a system where the fūshu〈封主〉(owner of the fuko) would receive tax collected from a ko〈戸〉as salary in forms called ifu〈位封〉and shikifu〈職封〉; farming lands, in forms called iden〈位田〉and shikiden〈職田〉; and kiroku〈季禄〉, a salary paid in kind twice a year.

[17] As long as the crime was not serious, nobles and officials had the prerogative to be discharged from punishment by accepting dismissal from their post or paying compensation.

to the father's (or grandfather's) rank. This system was called the **On'i no Sei**〈蔭位の制〉 **(grace rank system)**, and it served to sustain the aristocratic class[18].

The judicial system had five punishments: chi〈笞〉 (whipping), jō〈杖〉 (caning), zu〈徒〉 (forced labor), ru〈流〉 (exile), and shi〈死〉 (death). In the provinces, chi was the most severe punishment the gunji were given jurisdiction to use. Crimes against the state or sovereign and parricide were tried as especially serious in order to protect the political and social order[19].

Burdens on the Populace

Under the Ritsuryō state, members of the populace were registered in a **koseki**〈戸籍〉 **(family registry)** and **keichō**〈計帳〉 **(tax registry)**. Each person belonged to a certain ko〈戸〉 (residential unit)[20], with a representative called a koshu〈戸主〉 (residential unit head). Fifty ko comprised a ri〈里〉. Each ko as a unit was assigned a number of **kubunden**〈口分田〉 **(distributed fields)**[21] that were subject to taxation. The koseki was updated every six years, and based upon the registration, every male or female of six years of age or older was entitled to a kubunden of a fixed size. Private ownership of houses and surrounding lands was legal, but the buying and selling of the kubunden was not permitted. Kubunden granted to people who had died were returned to the state the next time the koseki was updated, under the **Handen Shūju Law**〈班田収授法〉 **(field allotment system)**[22].

The populace was subject to various levies, such as so, chō, yō and zōyō. **So**〈租〉 was a tax consisting of approximately three percent of the rice harvested from fields like the kubunden, and which was generally stored in the provinces. **Chō**〈調〉 and **yō**〈庸〉 were taxes

---

[18] Aside from the grace rank system, high-ranking officials could also be promoted in a shorter period of time compared to their lower-ranking counterparts, who were gradually promoted following working evaluations over a number of years.

[19] Serious crimes, such as treason against the sovereign and parricide, were called Hachigyaku〈八虐〉 (eight unpardonable crimes), from which no one, including people of high rank, could be excused.

[20] Ko were organized groups that consisted of more than one family. A typical ko would be made up of approximately 25 people. For a certain time in the first half of the 8th century, they were called gōko〈郷戸〉 and a smaller sub-ko called bōko〈房戸〉, consisting of a small family of around ten people, was created under them. In the same period, the name "ri" in the koku/gun/ri division was changed to "gō," and the gōri system〈郷里制〉, where several ri would be organized under one gō, was implemented.

[21] Ryōmin〈良民〉 men were assigned two tan〈段〉 (1 tan = 360 bu〈歩〉 = 11.9 ares) and women were assigned two thirds of that. Privately-held nuhi〈奴婢〉 (slaves) were assigned a third of the amount given to ryōmin, depending upon their sex. The actual size of the distributed fields differed according to the geographic specifics of the area.

[22] The Handen Shūju Law was intended to abolish the system of clans ruling the land and people in order for the state to be able to control the population directly, but the implementation of this law required the cooperation of local elites such as the district chieftains.

paid by silk, cloth, yarn and local products to the central government, imposed mainly on adult men who had to deliver these goods as **unkyaku** 運脚 (carriers) to the capital. **Zōyō** 雑徭 was a corvée where people were obliged to work on projects under the authority of the provincial governors, such as water-related construction, or carry out routine tasks for the kokufu for up to sixty days a year. There was also a system called **suiko** 出挙 (or kusuiko 公出挙)[23] where the government made loans (often of rice seed) in spring, which were repaid at a high rate of interest when the harvesting season came in autumn.

Military service in the Ritsuryō state saw one out of every three to four adult males drafted. These men were then trained by the **gundan** 軍団 (corps) in the provinces. Some would become eji 衛士 or **sakimori** 防人[24]. Eji were troops who guarded the palace, while sakimori were troops who protected the shorelines of Kyūshū. In principle, troops were required to provide their own weapons and food. This duty was a heavy burden for the populace because it required them to pay while also giving up a productive source of labor.

A social hierarchy divided the population into two classes, **ryōmin** 良民 (upper class) and **senmin** 賤民 (lower class). There were five sub-groups (**goshiki no sen** 五色の賤) within the senmin: ryōko 陵戸 (tomb guards), kanko 官戸 (official servants), and kunuhi 公奴婢（官奴婢） (kannuhi; official slaves) were publicly-owned people; ke'nin 家人 (clan servants) and shinuhi 私奴婢 (private slaves) were people owned privately. Although the senmin only comprised a few percent of the whole population, some of the major temples and clans owned many hundreds of such servants or slaves.

[23] Suiko was originally implemented by clans in order for farmers to be able to sustain their standard of living. Under the Ritsuryō system, it was transformed into a state tax (kusuiko), and the rice earned as interest became an important source of revenue for the provinces.

[24] Troops from eastern provinces were assigned to become sakimori and served under the Dazaifu for three years. The *Man'yōshū*〈『万葉集』〉 contains many waka composed by sakimori who moved far from their homes to Kyūshū.

3 The Heijō-kyō Era

Envoys to Tang China

The Tang Dynasty, which in 618 had replaced the Sui Dynasty and unified China, formed a great empire controlling vast territory, and therefore exerted a strong influence on surrounding regions. Exchange with West Asia thrived, and Chang'an (Xian) 長安（西安）, the capital, flourished as a cosmopolitan metropolis.

Countries in East Asia also interacted with Tang China, including Japan, which sent **kentōshi** 遣唐使 envoys every twenty years from the 8th century[25]. Starting from the ambassador, a Japanese envoy mission included students and trainee monks, sometimes amounting to four vessels with approximately 500 people aboard. However, the poor shipbuilding and navigational techniques of the age, combined with the rise in political tensions, caused envoys to change their sailing course from the shorelines of Silla to crossing the East China Sea, resulting in many missions suffering from shipwrecks. The kentōshi brought back the advanced political systems and international culture of the Tang Dynasty, which had a major impact on Japan. In particular, **Kibi no Makibi** 吉備真備 (693?-775) and **Genbō** 玄昉 (?-746), who after returning from China were given important posts by Shōmu Tennō 聖武天皇, also had great political influence[26].

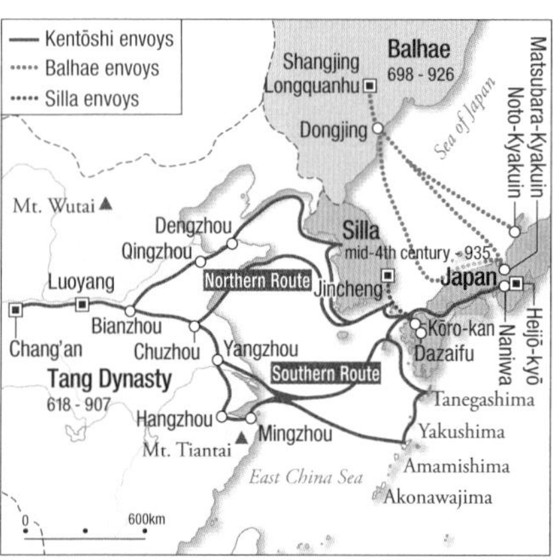

EAST ASIA AND THE JAPAN-CHINA ROUTE IN THE MID-8TH CENTURY

Japanese envoys first took the northern route, but after relations with Silla worsened in the 8th century, they started to take the riskier southern route.

Although there were also many envoys sent back and forth to Silla, which had unified the Korean peninsula, tensions arose from time to time when Japan addressed the kingdom, which had

---

[25] Until the system was abolished in 894 due to a proposition by Sugawara no Michizane〈菅原道真〉, envoys travelled to China more than 10 times.

[26] Abe no Nakamaro〈阿倍仲麻呂〉, who was a student accompanying the envoys, remained in Tang China due to a shipwreck which occurred upon his return journey to Japan. He was later made a high official by Emperor Xuanzong〈玄宗〉, interacted with poets like Wang Wei〈王維〉 and Li Bai〈李白〉, and finally died there.

become much stronger, as a subordinate state[27]. By the end of the 8th century, envoys to Silla were few in number, but in contrast to diplomatic relations the exchange among private merchants became more frequent. On the other hand, the exchange of envoys increased between Japan and **Balhae**(渤海) (698-926), a state founded mostly by the Mohe(靺鞨族) people living in far northeast China and refugees from the former kingdom of Goguryeo. In 727, Balhae sent an envoy to Japan wishing to have diplomatic exchange due to its hostile relations with the Tang Dynasty and Silla. Tensions between Japan and Silla were also high, resulting in Japan and Balhae establishing a friendly relationship[28].

Heijō-kyō: The Nara Capital

In 710, Genmei Tennō(元明天皇) (r. 707-715) moved the capital from Fujiwara-kyō to **Heijō-kyō**(平城京), in the northern part of the Nara Basin. Thus began the era known as the **Nara period**(奈良時代), which lasted until the capital was moved to Nagaoka-kyō(長岡京), and then Heian-kyō(平安京), in Yamashiro(山背国) Province.

Heijō-kyō was modelled after **Chang'an**(長安), the capital of Tang China, and shared the same characteristics of **jōbōsei**(条坊制), a method in which land was divided into straight streets orientated east-west and north-south in a grid pattern. The capital city was separated into two halves by Suzaku Avenue(朱雀大路), a north-south street running down the middle. There was an eastern side (sakyō(左京), or left cap-

DIAGRAM OF HEIJŌ-KYŌ

The 74 m wide Suzaku Avenue divided the capital into western and eastern halves. The city did not have walls (rajō〈羅城〉) surrounding it. After the capital was moved to Nagaoka-kyō, the site of Heijō-kyō was turned into paddy fields, except for areas with large temples. Remains of the capital survive to the present.

---

[27] When the Tang Dynasty fell into confusion through the rebellion of An Lushan〈安禄山〉 and Shi Siming〈史思明〉(An Lushan Rebellion〈安史の乱〉, 755-763), Fujiwara no Nakamaro〈藤原仲麻呂〉 planned a military campaign against Silla in unison with Balhae, advancing its troops towards Tang and Silla, but this did not come to fruition.

[28] Wadōkaichin have been discovered in fortress remains in Balhae, and artifacts of Balhae origin have been unearthed on the Sea of Japan coast, revealing that there had been interaction between the two states.

RESIDENCE OF PRINCE NAGAYA (RESTORED MODEL)
Prince Nagaya's residence covered 4 chō〈町〉(approx. 250 m^2) in the third ward of the western capital, and consisted of spaces for rituals, living, and household management.

ital), and a western side (ukyō 右京, or right capital), with the Heijō 平城宮 Palace located in the central north area. Located in the palace precinct were the Dairi 内裏 (sovereign's private quarters), the Daigokuden and Chōdōin where political affairs and rituals took place, and the governmental offices of the Nikan 二官 (Two Councils) and Hasshō (Eight Ministries). Inside the capital city lived nobles, officials, and commoners, and great temples with fine Garan-style architecture were built, starting with Daianji 大安寺, Yakushiji, Gangōji 元興寺, Kōfukuji, and later on Tōdaiji 東大寺 and Saidaiji 西大寺. The population of Heijō-kyō is believed to have been around 100,000.

Excavation of preserved sites of the Heijō Palace have uncovered remains of the palace itself, government offices, and gardens, as well as artifacts such as mokkan that reveal details of ancient court life and the financial structure that supported it.

Excavation of the Heijō-kyō ruins has uncovered residential sites and the way people belonging to each class lived, from the mansions of noblemen such as Prince Nagaya 長屋王 to the houses of lower-ranking bureaucrats. Through this research it has become clear that districts of the 5th Ward and further north, which were closer to the Heijō Palace, held a series of grand mansions built by aristocrats, while districts such as the 8th and 9th Wards, which were more distant from the palace, held the smaller housing of lower officials.

In both the eastern and western sides, there were state-run markets called **Ichi** 市, supervised by the Ichi-no-Tsukasa 市司 (market official). At the Ichi, goods were brought from the provinces and cloth and yarn paid to bureaucrats as salary was exchanged. In 708, the era name was changed to Wadō 和銅 because bronze had been presented to the government from Musashi Province 武蔵国. Further, following on from the Fuhonsen under Tenmu's reign in the 7th century, coins similar to those of Tang China called **Wadōkaichin** 和同開珎 were minted[29]. This coinage was used as currency for the construc-

[29] After Wadōkaichin in the beginning of the Nara period, the minting of bronze coins by the government was carried out twelve times until the Kengen Taihō〈乾元大宝〉were produced in the mid-10th century. These were called the "Honchō (Kōchō) Jyūnisen〈「本朝（皇朝）十二銭」〉" (Twelve Coins of the Royal Court), but the number of instances of coin minting became thirteen upon the discovery of the Fuhonsen.

tion of the capital, such as payments to the workers involved. Although the government sought to circulate the Wadōkaichin by issuing a law called the **Chikusenjoi-rei** 蓄銭叙位令, bartering of goods such as rice and cloth remained common outside of the areas surrounding the capital and the Kinai region.

FUHONSEN (LEFT, DIAMETER 2.4 CM) **AND WADŌKAICHIN** (RIGHT, DIAMETER 2.4 CM)
Both the Fuhonsen (bronze coin) and the Wadōkaichin (silver/bronze coin) were modeled after coins minted by the Tang Dynasty, and have been discovered in the Kinki region〈近畿地方〉 and other provinces.

Provincial Administration and "Remote Areas"

To serve as a transportation system connecting the central region to the provinces, routes called kandō (or ekiro) 官道（駅路） were organized spreading out mainly from the Kinai area surrounding the capital to the various provincial kokufu. Collectively these comprised seven routes (or "circuits"), such as the Tōkaidō 東海道. A station system was created where stations called **umaya** 駅家 were placed 16 km apart from each other, and used by government officials for administrative purposes. There were also roads called denro 伝路 that branched off from the ekiro, connecting to the gūke which structured the transportation network in the area[30].

Kokufu 国府（国衙） (or kokuga, provincial headquarters) was the office from which the provincial governor, who was dispatched from the capital, would govern the province. It was equipped with various facilities such as the kokuchō 国庁（政庁） (or seichō) where government affairs and rituals took place, the administrative buildings where various practical matters were handled, the governor's residence, and warehouses, thereby making it the political and economic center of the area. Later on, a kokubunji 国分寺 (provincial temple) would also be built close to the kokufu, making the latter the cultural heart of the province as well. The **gūke** 郡家（郡衙） (or gunga), from which a district chieftain governed their district, was similar to the kokufu and had facilities

SHIMOTSUKE KOKUCHŌ (RESTORED MODEL)
The kokuchō (seichō) was an official institution for administrative affairs and rituals, and functioned as the center of the kokufu. At the kokuchō of Shimotsuke Province〈下野国〉 (Tochigi City〈栃木市〉), there was an open space surrounded by the seiden〈正殿〉 (central palatial house), which was also the zenden〈前殿〉 (front palatial house), and the east and west wakiden〈脇殿〉 (side palatial houses), inside a square area accessed via the southern gate.

---

[30] In the areas of Tōkai, Tōsan〈東山〉, Hokuriku〈北陸〉, San'in〈山陰〉, San'yō〈山陽〉, Nankai〈南海〉, and Saikai, where the ekiro of the seven circuits are presumed to have existed, remains of ancient roads built by the government have been discovered. They run in straight lines on flatlands with ditches on the sides, and are standardized into certain widths (12 m, 9 m, 6 m).

GŪKE OF TSUZUKI DISTRICT〈都築〉 **IN MUSASHI PROVINCE** (RESTORED MODEL)
A series of large stilt structures, believed to be gūnchō, are arranged in a "U" shape, with facilities such as log-cabin-style warehouses with raised floors (shōsō〈正倉〉) lined up neatly.

such as the gunchō 郡庁, administrative buildings, the chieftain's residence, and warehouses. Moreover, the chieftain would also have their ujidera 氏寺 (clan temple) built nearby, making the gūke the center of the district. It is thought that the practical governance of areas was carried out by the district chieftains, who were appointed for life from the traditional local elites, unlike the provincial governors who had terms of office. Textual evidence such as mokkan and bokusho-doki 墨書土器 (pottery with ink-writing) have also been excavated from remains of gūke, revealing how Chinese-character culture had spread even in the provinces under the document-based precepts of the Ritsuryō system.

The government made efforts to expand agricultural lands by introducing iron tools for farming and advanced irrigation methods, while also supervising the mining of mineral resources such as bronze in Nagato Province 長門国 and gold in Mutsu Province 陸奥国. Moreover, they sent specialists in silk farming and high-quality weaving to provincial areas in order to foster production, resulting in local goods which could be used to pay taxes.

Having realized a political structure based on Ritsuryō, the central government, having gained sufficient power, turned to expanding its territory. As a provision against a people the government referred to as the **Emishi** 蝦夷, who lived in the Tōhoku region 東北地方, two forts, called Nutari-no-Saku 渟足柵 and Iwafune-no-Saku 磐舟柵, were constructed on the coast of the Sea of Japan in the mid-7th century when Japan faced external pressure due to Tang China's campaign against Goguryeo. Under the reign of Saimei Tennō, Abe no Hirafu 阿倍比羅夫 (dates unknown) was dispatched and established ties with the Emishi in the regions further north such as Akita 秋田. However, the territories controlled by the government in this period remained settlements situated near the coast of the Sea of Japan. In the 8th century, a military campaign approach also came to be pursued against the Emishi[31]. In 712, Dewa Province 出羽国 was established on the coast of the

---

[31] The government's policies against the Emishi had two aspects, consisting of giving special treatment to obedient groups, while suppressing those who resisted. Furthermore, the government adopted a policy of "using barbarians against barbarians."

Sea of Japan, followed by the construction of Akita Fort 秋田城, while on the Pacific coast, following on from the fortifications made in the latter half of the 7th century, **Taga Fort** 多賀城 (later the kokufu of Mutsu Province) was built. These two forts became the bases for the administration of Dewa and Mutsu and for the campaigns against the Emishi.

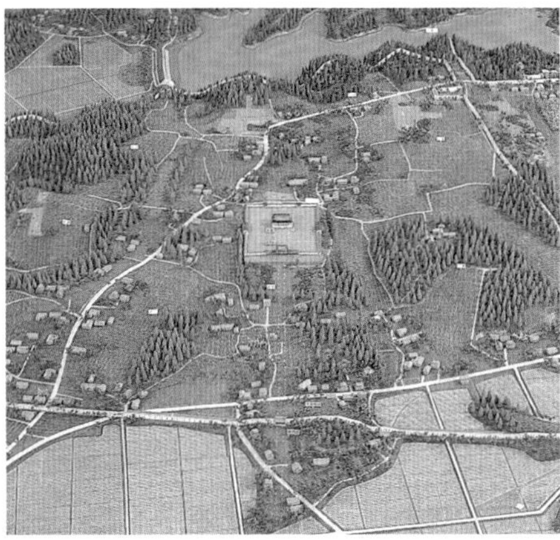

RUINS OF TAGA FORT (RESTORED MODEL)
Taga Fort had a seichō, where administrative affairs and rituals were conducted, towards the center of the fort surrounded by walls made of mud and wooden planks. There were also office structures for practical matters, warehouses, and barracks for soldiers. Mokkan and lacquer documents (urushigami monjo〈漆紙文書〉) used for document-based administration have been discovered at this site.

Meanwhile, in the areas of southern Kyūshū controlled by a people called **Hayato** 隼人, in the beginning of the 8th century Satsuma Province 薩摩国 and then Ōsumi Province 大隅国 were established after resistance was suppressed. Various southwestern islands, such as Tanegashima 種子島 and Yakushima 屋久島 which became administrative divisions, came to be in a tributary relationship in which they provided local products like bishop wood to the government.

The Emergence of the Fujiwara Family and Political Turmoil

In the beginning of the 8th century, when power was relatively balanced between royal family members and prominent nobles, the Ritsuryō system was established mainly by **Fujiwara no Fuhito** 藤原不比等. However, as the Fujiwara family 藤原氏 became politically influential, this balance collapsed with the downfall of traditionally powerful families such as the Ōtomo and the Saeki 佐伯氏. Fujiwara no Fuhito built close relations with the royal family by having his daughter, Miyako 宮子, marry Monmu Tennō 文武天皇 (r. 697-707), and then having the crown prince born between them (who later ascended the throne as **Shōmu Tennō** 聖武天皇, r. 724-749) marry another daughter of his, **Kōmyōshi** 光明子 (701-760).

After the death of Fuhito, a member of the royal family, **Prince Nagaya** 長屋王 (?-729)[32], took power by becoming minister of the right. With the Fujiwara family facing the loss of their position as maternal relatives to the sovereign, in 729 the four sons of

[32] Son of Prince Takechi〈高市皇子〉(son of Tenmu Tennō) who was active in the Jinshin War, and husband of Royal Princess Kibi〈吉備内親王〉, sister of Monmu Tennō. Fuhito also had one of his daughters marry Prince Nagaya. The residence of this prince is known to have been an influential cultural salon from the descriptions seen in the *Kaifūsō*〈『懐風藻』〉 and *Man'yōshū*, and the remains of a large mansion situated inside Heijō-kyō have been excavated.

Fuhito – Muchimaro 武智麻呂 (680-737), Fusasaki 房前 (681-737), Umakai 宇合 (694-737), and Maro 麻呂 (695-737) – engineered a plot and forced Prince Nagaya, who had become the minister of the left, to commit suicide (Prince Nagaya Incident 長屋王の変). They then installed Kōmyōshi as queen consort[33]. However, in 737 the four brothers died one after another in a smallpox epidemic, leading to a temporary decline in the power of the Fujiwara family. In the meantime, **Tachibana no Moroe** 橘諸兄 (684-757), a man of royal descent, seized power while Kibi no Makibi and Genbō, who had returned from Tang China, became active with the backing of Shōmu Tennō.

In 740, Fujiwara no Hirotsugu 藤原広嗣 (?-740) led a major rebellion in Kyūshū, demanding the removal of Kibi no Makibi and Genbō from the government, but this ended in failure (Fujiwara no Hirotsugu Rebellion 藤原広嗣の乱)[iv]. In the years following this incident, Shōmu moved the capital many times, to Kuni 恭仁京, Naniwa, Shigaraki 紫香楽宮, and elsewhere.

This political situation, coupled with famine and epidemics, led to great social anxiety. Under these circumstances, Shōmu, a devout believer in Buddhism, attempted to restore order by adopting the Buddhist ideology of a state under spiritual protection. In 741, he issued the **Kokubunji Konryū no Mikotonori** 国分寺建立の詔 (Edict for Establishing Provincial Temples), and had kokubunji (provincial temples) and kokubun-niji 国分尼寺 (provincial nunneries) built in the provinces[34]. Further, in 743 the tennō announced the **Daibutsu Zōryū no Mikotonori** 大仏造立の詔 (Edict for Building a Great Statue of the Buddha) at Shigaraki in the Ōmi Province. In 745, upon returning to Heijō-kyō, the project of building a Great Buddha was continued in Nara. In 752, a grand eye-opening ceremony for the completed Great Buddha was celebrated under the reign of Kōken 孝謙天皇 Tennō (r. 749-758), Shōmu's daughter[35].

In Kōken's time, **Fujiwara no Nakamaro** 藤原仲麻呂 (706-764) strengthened his political position by making ties with Dowager Queen Consort Kōmyō. Naramaro 橘奈良麻呂 (721-757), the son of Tachibana no Moroe, attempted to remove Nakamaro, but was defeated (Tachibana no Naramaro Rebellion 橘奈良麻呂の変). Nakamaro was granted a new name, Emi no Oshikatsu 恵美押勝, upon supporting Junnin Tennō's 淳仁天皇 (r. 758-764) rise to the throne. Later he was also given special financial prerogatives, monopolized power, and finally became

---

[33] Under the Ritsuryō system, only a member of the royal family could become queen consort. A queen consort could temporarily govern the state after the death of the sovereign, at times assume the throne as a tennō herself, and be able to have a say in the royal succession.

[34] Because the project was of enormous scale, construction progress in provincial areas was slow, prompting the government to later ask local elites for help.

[35] This grand ceremony was attended by Retired Sovereign Shōmu, Dowager Queen Consort Kōmyō, Kōken Tennō, all the military and civil officials, Indian and Chinese monks, and ten thousand Japanese monks.

taishi 大師 (daijōdaijin).

Emi no Oshikatsu became isolated in the court upon the death of Kōmyō, who had been his most influential supporter. In 764, in fear of crisis he started a rebellion against Retired Sovereign Kōken[v], who had been favoring a monk named **Dōkyō** 道鏡 (?-772) since he had cured her illness, prompting a conflict with Junnin Tennō. However, this coup d'état failed because the Kōken side struck before him (Emi no Oshikatsu Rebellion 恵美押勝の乱). Junnin was dethroned and exiled to Awaji 淡路 Island, and Kōken re-ascended the throne as Shōtoku Tennō 称徳天皇 (r. 764-770).

With the support of Shōtoku, Dōkyō was granted the title of daijōdaijin zenji 禅師 (supreme minister and mediation master). Later he became hō-ō 法王 (literally "dharma king") and having gained power, ruled the state based on the teachings of Buddhism[36]. In 769, Shōtoku, heeding an oracle from Usa Shrine 宇佐神宮, attempted to give the throne to Dōkyō, but this plan was stopped by Wake no Kiyomaro 和気清麻呂 (733-799) and others[37]. After Shōtoku's death, the monk, no longer having influential backing, was banished[38]. The enthronement of the next tennō proceeded under the influence of Fujiwara no Momokawa 藤原百川 (732-779), a member of the Shikike 式家 (the branch of the Fujiwara family descended from Fujiwara no Umakai) from the Fujiwara family. As a result, a grandson of Tenji Tennō, **Kōnin Tennō** 光仁天皇 (r. 770-781), ascended the throne, thus ending the long lineage of Tenmu Tennō's line. In Kōnin's time, there was an attempt to rebuild the Ritsuryō system and the state finances, which had fallen into turmoil in the years under Dōkyō's Buddhism-based rule.

The Populace and Land Policies

In the 8th century when the Ritsuryō system developed, there were advancements in agriculture, and the use of iron tools became more common. The lifestyle of people also changed. **Stilt houses** 掘立柱住居 on flatlands gradually spread from western Japan and replaced the pit-houses. The structure of families was also different from today. Marriage started with a system called **tsumadoi-kon** 妻問婚 in which the man would first visit the woman's house. The couple would stay at either of their parents' houses for a period of time,

---

[36] Many temples and Buddhist-related objects were made in this period, which can be seen from the construction of Saidaiji and making of the Hyakumantō〈百万塔〉(one million pagodas).

[37] The oracle of Hachiman〈八幡〉, the deity of Usa Shrine in Kyūshū, urged that Dōkyō be made tennō, but Wake no Kiyomaro, who was sent as a messenger to bring back this message, gave a conflicting report and prevented the monk from ascending the throne. It is believed that behind Kiyomaro's actions were nobles who supported him, like Fujiwara no Momokawa, and who were opposed to Dōkyō.

[38] Dōkyō was exiled to Shimotsuke Province to be the director of Yakushiji Temple, and died there.

MURAKAMI SITE〈村上遺跡〉 **(RESTORED MODEL)**
A restoration of the remains of a village from around the 8th century (Yachiyo City〈八千代市〉, Chiba Prefecture〈千葉県〉) that was built on the hills of the eastern provinces. Houses of the eastern provinces at the time were generally pit-style buildings, and a typical village would consist of several pit houses, one or two stilt-style facilities such as a warehouse, and a well. Some villages have also been found that had a simple Buddhist structure.

and eventually came to have a home for themselves. The husband and wife would keep their own surnames even after marriage, and each had his or her private property. Although the Ritsuryō system emphasized paternal inheritance following China's patriarchal family system, it is believed that within most families women had a strong influence over deciding the division of labor and raising children.

Aside from cultivating the distributed kubunden, farmers[vi] also cultivated fields owned by the state (jōden〈乗田〉) or by temples and nobles. In principle, these lands were borrowed for one year, and one fifth of the crops were to be paid as land interest (chinso〈賃租〉) to the government or owner. Life could be difficult for farmers as they also had military service and other duties like corvée, such as zōyō, and transporting goods as unkyaku. In addition, famine could occur frequently due to erratic weather and pests. Although the provincial governors and district chieftains promoted agriculture, the lives of farmers remained unstable[39].

In order to address a shortage of kubunden fields caused by population growth, and to increase tax revenue, in 722 the government set out a million chō〈百万町歩開墾計画〉 (1 chō = 2.45 acres) development plan[40], and in 723, the **Sanze Isshin Law**〈三世一身法〉 was implemented. This law approved the ownership of newly-cultivated lands with new irrigation facilities for up to three generations, while newly-cultivated lands with old irrigation facilities were only allowed to be owned for one generation, therefore aiming to expand arable lands through the efforts of the people. In 743, the government issued the **Konden Einen Shizai Law**〈墾田永年私財法〉 which guaranteed permanent private ownership of the cultivated

---

[39] It could be said that the "Hinkyū Mondōka〈貧窮問答歌〉" (dialogue on poverty), a poem about the hardships of farmers composed by Yamanoe no Okura〈山上憶良〉 that appears in the *Man'yōshū*, was motivated by sympathy for their situation.

[40] The government attempted to increase fertile fields by supplying farmers with food and tools, and having them cultivate land for ten days, but little was accomplished.

fields[41]. This law was an active policy by the government to strengthen its control over land by increasing the amount of state-owned fields, but it also resulted in motivating nobles, temples, and local elites to expand their own private lands as well[42]. In particular, great temples such as Tōdaiji would monopolize vast fields, and with the help of the governors and district chieftains, would use nearby farmers or wanderers to build irrigation facilities and carry out large cultivation projects. This type of cultivation is called **early shōen** 初期荘園 (estates)[43].

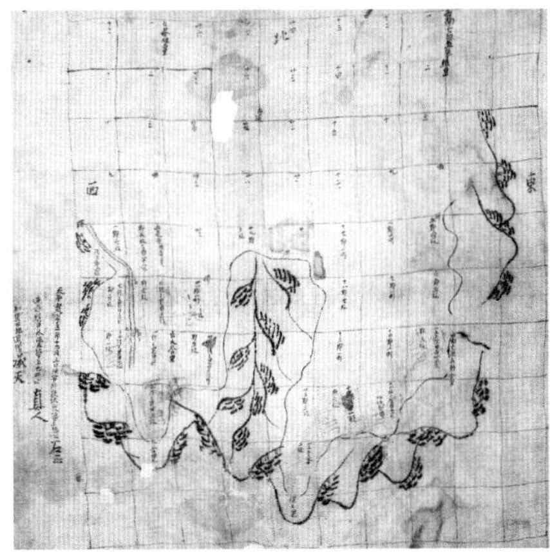

DIAGRAM OF NEWLY-OPENED FIELDS ON KUSO'OKI ESTATE HELD BY TŌDAIJI TEMPLE
A diagram created in 759 of newly-opened fields on Kuso'oki Estate〈糞置荘〉, held by Tōdaiji, in Asuwa District〈足羽郡〉, Echizen Province〈越前国〉 (Fukui City〈福井市〉). The mountains and paddy fields show a square-shaped division, and share the same characteristics that can be seen in the landform today.

The changes in agriculture led to the emergence of wealthy farmers and poor farmers. Among those suffering from poverty, some would commit **furō** 浮浪, meaning they abandoned their kubunden and left the land registered on their koseki to wander in other provinces. There was also an increasing number of cases of **tōbō** 逃亡, where people would run away from duties such as palace construction projects in the capital, and seek protection under local elites. On the other hand, even among wealthy farmers there were some who became wanderers for their own benefit, or who sought to evade taxation by becoming unapproved Buddhist monks (shidosō 私度僧) or the attendants of nobles. By the end of the 8th century, the state finance and military system started to become affected greatly due to a drop in quality of chō and yō goods, a large amount of taxes in arrears, and by the weakening of soldiers.

---

[41] The size of newly-cultivated fields was restricted by class, varying between 500 chō for princes of the highest royal rank or noblemen of the first rank to 10 chō for those of the lowest rank and commoners below that. Furthermore, these new arable lands were classified as yusoden〈輸租田〉, which made them subject to taxation.

[42] Later, in 765, cultivating new lands was temporarily banned except for temples, but after the exile of Dōkyō, in 772 the cultivation of fields and permanent private ownership of newly-cultivated lands was approved again.

[43] An early shōen was managed from an office at its center, and was dependent upon the provincial governor and district chieftain's control over the area. It had no people specifically belonging to it (shōmin〈荘民〉), and the system declined as the chieftain's authority weakened.

4 Tenpyō Culture

Tenpyō Culture and the Continent

In the Nara period, wealth was concentrated in the capital due to the establishment of a centralized polity. A sophisticated aristocratic culture developed revolving around Heijō-kyō. The culture of this period is called **Tenpyō culture** 天平文化, taking its name from the era of Shōmu Tennō's reign. It had a cosmopolitan character, strongly influenced by the culture of Tang China that was brought back by the kentōshi and valued by nobles of the era.

The Compilation of State History, and the *Man'yōshū*

Reflecting on the rise of a state consciousness awakened by the establishment of the Ritsuryō state, the government decided to compile a state history as China had done in order to demonstrate the origins of its rule and the process through which the state had formed and developed.

The state history compilation project begun in Tenmu Tennō's time was completed in the Nara period, in the form of ***Kojiki*** 『古事記』 (Records of Ancient Matters) and ***Nihonshoki*** 『日本書紀』 (Chronicles of Japan). *Kojiki*, completed in 712, was compiled by Ō no Yasumaro 太安万侶（安麻呂） (?-723). The contents were based on the recollections of Hieda no Are 稗田阿礼 (654?-?), who had been made to read *Teiki* 「帝紀」 and *Kyūji* 「旧辞」 (historical texts passed down within the court) by Tenmū Tennō. It was a narrative that covered from the time of myths and folklore until the reign of Suiko[44], and was written in a form of Japanese that used Chinese characters for both phonetic value and meaning. *Nihonshoki*, which was completed in 720, was compiled mainly by Royal Prince Toneri 舎人親王 (676-735), and written in chronological order using classical Chinese following the format of Chinese historical accounts. It covered history from the age of the gods until the era of Jitō Tennō, and included myths, folklore, *Teiki* and *Kyūji*, with an emphasis upon the sovereigns[45].

---

[44] The myths begin with a tale of the deities of creation and the birth of the country, and continue to the descent of the grandson of Amaterasu from the heavens〈天孫降臨〉, the eastern campaign of Jinmu Tennō〈神武天皇〉, and the conquest of the provinces by Prince Yamato Takeru〈日本武尊〉. These myths were written from the standpoint of the Ritsuryō state, and are not believed to be historically accurate.

[45] Some sections were written based on Chinese classical literature and laws that existed when the compilation was edited, so credibility needs to be considered. Nevertheless, it is an important

In 713, in line with the historical accounts, each province was ordered to record its local goods, folklore, and the name origins of mountains, rivers, and fields, in a type of chorography called **Fudoki** 風土記 (provincial gazetteer)[46].

Nobles and bureaucrats were required to have knowledge of Chinese poetry and prose. In 751, the oldest extant collection of Chinese poems written by Japanese poets, the ***Kaifūsō*** 『懐風藻』 (Fond Recollections of Poetry), was compiled. It consisted of poems written in classical Chinese since the latter half of the 7th century by such poets as Prince Ōtomo, Prince Ōtsu 大津皇子 (663-686), and Prince Nagaya. From the middle of the 8th century, literati known for Chinese poetry and prose included Ōmi no Mifune 淡海三船 (722-785) and Isonokami no Yakatsugu 石上宅嗣 (729-781)[47]. Traditional Japanese waka poems were also written in this period by many people ranging from the sovereign to commoners. The ***Man'yōshū*** 『万葉集』 (Ten Thousand Leaves) was an anthology that contained approximately 4,500 waka written up until 759, including those composed not only by poets and nobles of the court, but also by sakimori and commoners of the eastern provinces, among others. Many of these poems express sentiments in a clear style, and are profoundly moving[48].

As for educational institutions, to train bureaucrats a **Daigaku** 大学 (royal academy) was established in the capital, and **Kokugaku** 国学 (provincial academies) were established in the provinces. Admission to the Daigaku was prioritized for youth whose fathers were nobles or officials serving the court, while in the case of the Kokugaku, the sons of district chieftains were given priority. Students needed to complete their course at

---

source of ancient Japanese history. The compilation of history by the court that began with *Nihonshoki* continued through the Heian period〈平安時代〉, with *Shoku Nihongi*〈『続日本紀』〉, *Nihon Kōki*〈『日本後紀』〉, *Shoku Nihon Kōki*〈『続日本後紀』〉, *Nihon Montoku Tennō Jitsuroku*〈『日本文徳天皇実録』〉, and *Nihon Sandai Jitsuroku*〈『日本三代実録』〉. These six official histories, written in Chinese characters, are collectively known as the "**Rikkokushi**〈『六国史』〉" (Six State Histories).

[46] Five provincial gazetteers – those of Hitachi〈常陸国〉, Izumo〈出雲国〉, Harima〈播磨国〉, Bungo〈豊後国〉, and Hizen〈肥前国〉 –currently remain. The only record still in a nearly complete state is *Izumo no Kuni Fudoki*〈『出雲国風土記』〉.

[47] Isonokami no Yakatsugu renovated his residence into a temple. It contained a facility similar to a library that stored many books, not limited to Buddhist scriptures. This facility was named Untei〈芸亭〉, and was open to people wishing to study.

[48] With regards to well-known poets, the first generation (until the reign of Tenji Tennō) includes Prince Arima and Princess Nukata〈額田王〉; the second generation (until the transition to Heijō-kyō) includes Kakinomoto no Hitomaro〈柿本人麻呂〉; the third generation (until the beginning of the Tenpyō era, 729-749) includes Yamanoe no Okura, Yamabe no Akahito〈山部赤人〉, and Ōtomo no Tabito〈大伴旅人〉; and the fourth generation (until the reign of Junnin Tennō) includes Ōtomo no Yakamochi〈大伴家持〉 and Ōtomo no Sakanoue no Iratsume〈大伴坂上郎女〉. It is said that the editor of the *Man'yōshū* was Ōtomo no Yakamochi, but the truth remains unknown.

the Daigaku and pass an examination before becoming a bureaucrat[49].

The Development of State Buddhism

During the Nara period, Buddhism spread under the patronage of the state. The concept of **chingo kokka**鎮護国家 (spiritual realm protection), which held that Buddhism had the power to bring stability to the country, was a particularly prominent characteristic of Buddhism in this era.

In the great monasteries of Nara, many Buddhist theories from India and China were studied, and the **Nanto Rokushū**南都六宗 (Six Southern Schools of Nara Buddhism)[vii] were formed, comprising the Sanron三論宗, Jōjitsu成実宗, Hossō法相宗, Kusha倶舎宗, Kegon華厳宗, and Ritsu律宗 sects. Gien義淵 (?-728) of the Hossō Sect taught many pupils such as Genbō and **Gyōki**行基 (668-749). Rōben良弁 (689-773) of the Kegon Sect studied the Avatamsaka Sutra under the guidance of monks from Tang China and Silla, and took part in the establishment of Tōdaiji Temple. Dōji道慈 (?-744), who went to study in China and taught the Sanron Sect upon his return, was also involved in projects such as the founding of Daianji Temple.

Monks of this period were recognized as not just religious specialists, but leading intellectuals who had the most advanced knowledge of civilization. Therefore, there were also cases of monks such as Genbō, who was promoted by Shōmu Tennō and exerted great influence over politics. The efforts of figures like **Ganjin**鑑真 (Jianzhen, 688?-763), who after many failed attempts was finally able to reach Japan and lecture on Buddhist precepts, also contributed to the development of Japanese Buddhism[50].

However, Buddhism was also subject to heavy restrictions by the government. Generally, monks were prohibited from carrying out activities outside of their temples.

---

[49] The subjects taught at the Daigaku were the Myōgyōdō〈明経道〉, which taught Confucian texts such as the Five Classics〈五経〉 (*Book of Changes*, *Book of Documents*, *Book of Songs*, *Spring and Autumn Annals*, and *Book of Rites*), the Myōbōdō〈明法道〉, which taught jurisprudence such as the Ritsuryō system, and other matters such as pronunciation, calligraphy, and mathematics. Later in the 9th century, a new subject called the Kidendō〈紀伝道〉 was organized, which taught classical Chinese and history. Apart from the above, studies such as Yin and Yang〈陰陽〉 theory, calendar studies, astronomy, and medicine were also taught by various bureaucratic units.

[50] To officially become a monk at the time one was required to take part in tokudo〈得度〉 (ascetic practices), and accept Buddhist precepts through an inititation (jukai〈受戒〉). When Ganjin arrived in Japan he introduced the true precepts of Buddhism when initiated into the monastic community. Ganjin later founded Tōshōdaiji Temple, and remained there for the rest of his life. Shōmu, Kōmyō and Kōken were initiated in Buddhism by Ganjin himself. To hold these initiation ceremonies, a kaidan〈戒壇〉 (ordination platform) was built inside Tōdaiji Temple. Subsequently in 761, two more kaidan were built for those in distant lands, one at Tsukushi Kanzeonji Temple〈筑紫観世音寺〉 in Kyūshū, and the other at Shimotsuke Yakushiji Temple in the eastern provinces. The three sites were together named the "Three Kaidan of the Royal Court."

In spite of these circumstances, there were some monks, such as Gyōki, who enjoyed wide public support because along with propagating religion they contributed to society by building irrigation facilities and settlements for relieving the poor[51].

Under the influence of the Buddhist concept of spiritual realm protection, large-scale projects such as the construction of provincial temples or the Great Buddha were commenced under Shōmu Tennō. However, the vast temple estates and magnificent garan-style architecture of monasteries, supported under government policies to protect Buddhism, imposed a heavy burden on state finances. In the process of adapting to Japanese society, Buddhism was seen as a tool for **genzeriyaku** 現世利益 (worldly gains). It was also integrated with old beliefs of ancestor veneration, with the production of Buddhist statues or the copying of sutras being undertaken to console ancestral spirits. Furthermore, a new religious concept, **shinbutsu-shūgō** 神仏習合 (syncretism of kami 神 and Buddhas), evolved which explained that kami and Buddhas were in their essence fundamentally the same[52]. There were also monks who rejected the politicization of Buddhism and left their temples, engaging in ascetic practices in the mountains. They later became the core group of new Buddhist sects in the Heian period.

Art of the Tenpyō Period

Supported by the development of Buddhism, and the wealthy lifestyles of the court, nobles, and temples, many great works of art were created in the Nara period.

In terms of architecture, there were structures of grandeur built using foundation stones and roof tiles in temple compounds and palaces. The Denpō 伝法堂 Hall (Hall for Enshrinement of the Dharma) of Hōryūji (originally an aristocratic residence), the Lecture Hall of Tōshōdaiji 唐招提寺 (originally a palatial structure of Heijō Palace), the Hokke 法華堂 Hall (Lotus Hall) of Tōdaiji, the Main Hall of Tōshōdaiji, and the Treasury of Shōsōin 正倉院 are all representative buildings, characterized by symmetry and grandeur.

With regards to sculpture, there were many Buddhist statues, with a harmonious style and various expressions. In addition to the gilt-bronze and wooden statues from earlier times, the techniques of making **sozō** 塑像 (clay statues) and **kanshitsuzō** 乾漆像 (dry-lac-

[51] Gyōki was later granted the title of Daisōjō〈大僧正〉(highest rank in the Buddhist clergy), and helped to build the Great Buddha. His association with public works was motivated by the Buddhist notion that happiness and virtue are created by dedicating oneself to good deeds. Kōmyō's establishment of the Hiden'in〈悲田院〉where orphans and ill people were accommodated, and the Seyakuin〈施薬院〉, which functioned as a hospital inside Heijō-kyō, were also related to this Buddhist belief.

[52] This phenomenon was in part influenced by China, where an ideology similar to shinbutsu-shūgō had already come into existence through the fusion of Buddhism and traditional Chinese beliefs.

TREASURY OF SHŌSŌIN
One of the warehouses of Tōdaiji Temple. From the right, it is divided into the north, center, and south sections. It stored the belongings of Shōmu and various documents. The structure has a raised floor, and is built in an azekura-zukuri〈校倉造〉(log-cabin) style where triangular timbers are jointed upon each other. This treasury was classified as a chokufū〈勅封〉(sealed under royal order) warehouse that required the sovereign's permission to be opened.

quered statues) were developed. The former was a method where clay was applied on wood, while the latter was made by having a prototype, which was subsequently removed, covered with layers of lacquered hemp cloth. In the Hokke Hall of Tōdaiji Temple, Buddhist statues of the Tenpyō culture have been preserved in clusters, the most notable being the dry-lacquered statue of Fukūkenjaku Kannon 不空羂索観音像 (Amoghapasa, a form of Avalokiteśvara, Bodhisattva of Mercy), and other clay statues such as Nikkō Bosatsu 日光菩薩 (Suryaprabha, Bodhisattva of Sunlight), Gakkō Bosatsu 月光菩薩 (Candraprabha, Bodhisattva of Moonlight), and Shukongōshin 執金剛神像 (Vajra-Wielding Deity). In Kōfukuji Temple the dry-lacquered statues of Shaka Jūdaideshi 釈迦十大弟子像 (Ten Great Disciples of Shakyamuni) and Hachibushū 八部衆 (Devas of the Eight Classes), including the statue of Ashura 阿修羅像 are also well known.

Although paintings are few in number, there are exemplary works such as the *Jukabijinzu* 樹下美人図 (Beauties Under Trees) depicted on the *Chōmōryūjo Byōbu* 鳥毛立女屏風 (Folding Screen of Women with Bird Feathers) preserved at the **Shōsoin** 正倉院, and the *Kichijōtenzō* 吉祥天像 (Image of the Deity Kichijōten) preserved at Yakushiji Temple, which share the voluptuous look and splendid style typical of Tang influence. Paintings in scrolls of the *Illustrated Sutra of Cause and Effect in the Past and Present* 過去現在絵因果経, which depicts the life of the Buddha Shakyamuni, are believed to be the origins of what are later known as emakimono 絵巻物 (illustrated scrolls).

As for crafts, the collection preserved in the treasury of the Shōsōin is well known. Mainly consisting of objects favored by Shōmu Tennō and donated to Tōdaiji Temple after his death by Kōmyō, these items include clothing, furnishings, musical instruments, and equipment for war. Within this collection, some of the works are outstandingly well preserved, such as the *Radenshitan no Gogen Biwa* 螺鈿紫檀五絃琵琶 (five-stringed red sandalwood lute with mother-of-pearl inlay), the *Shikkohei* 漆胡瓶 (lacquered ewer), and the *Hakururi no Wan* 白瑠璃碗 (white lapis lazuli bowl). These crafts are also proof that Japan had interacted with not only Tang China but with West and South Asia as well, and

FUKŪKENJAKU KANNON OF HOKKE HALL, TŌDAIJI TEMPLE
The main image located in Hokke Hall. Dry-lacquered statue. It depicts a form of Kannon who saves many people using a rope. The design portrays a mystical figure full of dignity. The high quality of craftsmanship in this statue can be seen from the aureole and the crown decorated with beads and glass. (Height 362 cm, right side: Nikkō Bosatsu 207.2 cm, left side: Gakkō Bosatsu 204.8 cm)

KICHIJŌTENZŌ OF YAKUSHIJI TEMPLE
Kichijōten is a goddess of happiness and virtue. The original painting is drawn on hemp cloth. This is a copy made in 1891.

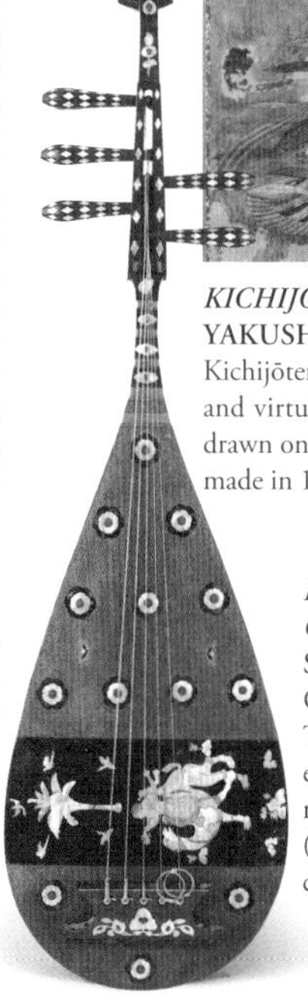

RADENSHITAN NO GOGEN BIWA OF SHŌSŌIN (TREASURY OF SHŌSŌIN)
This instrument depicts an ethnic man of the western regions riding a camel. (Surface area: height 108.1 cm, width 30.9 cm)

represent the high level of cultural sophistication and cosmopolitanism in the court life of the era. Moreover, the Hyakumantō (one million pagodas) and the *Hyakumantō Dharani* (dharani prayers in one million pagodas)[53] stored inside them, which were made under the orders of Shōtoku Tennō after the rebellion of Emi no Oshikatsu, are also indicators of the high crafting technology of this period.

[53] Although there is a debate over whether the *Hyakumantō Dharani* were printed using woodblocks or copperplates, they are said to be the earliest extant printing that can be dated.

5 The Formation of the Heian Courtly State

The Move to Heian and the Wars Against the Emishi

Under Kōnin Tennō, policies were carried out to rebuild the polity through simplifying the administration and finances, and alleviating the burdens on the public. In 781, just before his death, the throne was acceded to **Kanmu Tennō** 桓武天皇 (r. 781-806), a prince born between Kōnin and Takano no Niigasa 高野新笠 (?-789), a descendant of a family with migrant origins.

Kanmu continued the policies set down by his father. Seeking to exclude the negative influence of Buddhist politics and strengthen the authority of the sovereign, in 784 he moved the capital from Heijō-kyō to **Nagaoka-kyō** 長岡京 in Yamashiro Province. However, after the move, Fujiwara no Tanetsugu 藤原種継 (737-785), Kanmu's confidant who had supervised the construction of the new capital, was assassinated. This incident resulted in Royal Prince Sawara 早良親王 (750-785, Kanmu's younger brother)[54], the crown prince suspected of being the mastermind, and the traditional local elites such as the Ōtomo and Saeki families, being purged. In 794 the capital was moved again, to **Heian-kyō** 平安京, and the Chinese character for writing the "shiro" of "Yamashiro" was changed from "ridge" 背 to "castle." 城 The approximately 400 years from this transition to the founding of a bakufu 幕府 (warrior government)[viii] in Kamakura 鎌倉 by Minamoto no Yoritomo 源頼朝 is called the **Heian period.** 平安時代

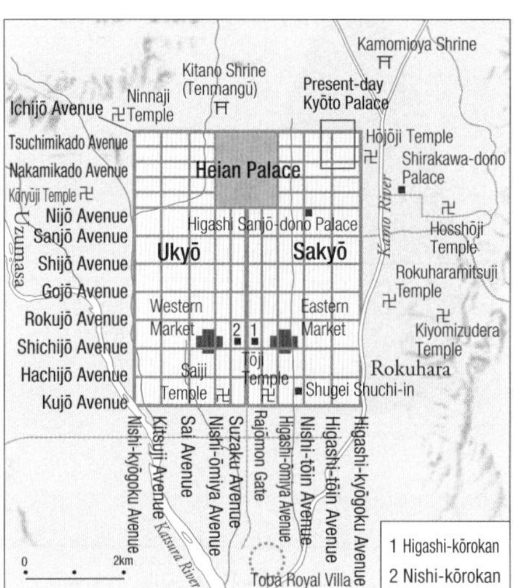

DIAGRAM OF HEIAN-KYŌ
It covered approximately 4.5 km from east to west, and approximately 5.2 km from north to south. The structure of the capital was similar to Heijō-kyō. The population in the western side declined from early on, while the eastern side became more heavily populated.

In the Tōhoku region, fortifications were being built from the Nara period. On the Mutsu Province side,

[54] Royal Prince Sawara starved himself to death. Subsequently, the mother and queen consort of Kanmu Tennō died, and the vengeful spirit of the prince was blamed for the misfortunes. In addition, the fact that the construction of Nagaoka-kyō was taking far too long also played a role in the move to Heian-kyō.

forts were positioned along the Kitakami River 北上川, extending power northwards from Taga Fort. The government also expanded its influence northwards on the Dewa Province side, starting from Akita Fort, along the coastline of the Sea of Japan. Forts, which contained within their walls government buildings and warehouses located around a central seichō, also served as administrative centers. Cultivation of lands surrounding the forts was carried out by farmers (sakuko 柵戸) of the Kantō region who migrated there[55]. In this way, control over Emishi territory proceeded through using forts as bases. In 780,

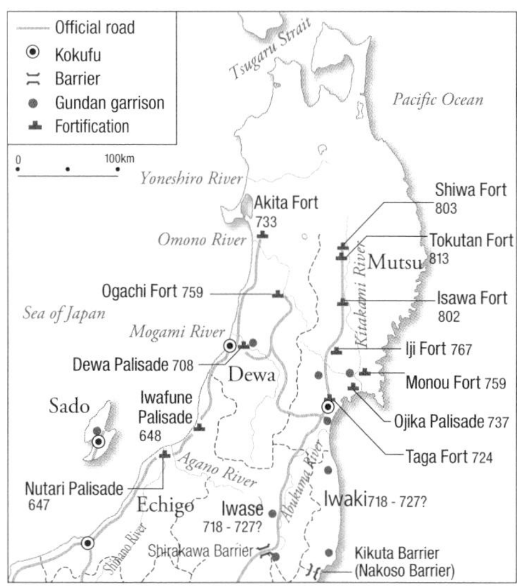

FORTS IN THE TŌHOKU REGION

The forts in the Tōhoku region were built consecutively along the Kitakami River or the Sea of Japan as they moved northwards. Solidifying administrative control over the new territories was realized based on these fortifications.

however, during the reign of Kōnin Tenno, a revolt lead by **Korehari no Azamaro** 伊治呰麻呂 (dates unknown), a member of an Emishi clan that had previously submitted to royal authority, occurred. This revolt expanded into a large-scale rebellion resulting in Taga Fort being temporarily captured and burnt. Following this event, wars continued in the Tōhoku region for over thirty years.

In 789, under Kanmu Tennō's reign the government appointed Ki no Kosami 紀古佐美 (?-797) as Seitō Taishi 征東大使 ("General of Eastern Conquest"), and sent a large force in an attempt to suppress the Emishi in the Isawa region 胆沢地方, located in the middle reaches of the Kitakami River. However, the government troops suffered a total defeat at the hands of the chief of the group, Aterui 阿弖流為 (?-802). Subsequently, **Sakanoue no Tamuramaro** 坂上田村麻呂 (758-811), who had become Seii Taishōgun 征夷大将軍 ("Great General for Subduing Barbarians"), built **Isawa Fort** 胆沢城 in the Isawa region in 802, and moved the Chinjufu 鎮守府 (pacification headquarters) from Taga Fort to this new fort after forcing Aterui to surrender. The following year, he founded Shiwa Fort 志波城 by the upper reaches of the Kitakami River, and used it as a frontline base for governing the Tōhoku region[56]. Similarly, on the

---

[55] Emishi groups who chose to submit were relocated to regions west of Kantō as Fushū〈俘囚〉(assimilated Emishi).

[56] In the time of Saga, Funya no Watamaro〈文室綿麻呂〉was sent to the Tōhoku region as a general and founded the final fort, Tokutan Fort〈徳丹城〉.

Sea of Japan side the reach of the Ritsuryō state extended up to the basin of the Yoneshiro River 米代川.

The wars in Tōhoku and the construction of Heian-kyō became a heavy burden for the state's finances and the public. In 805, Kanmu Tennō held a debate on the matter called the Tokusei 徳政相論 (benevolent government) Dispute, and announced the discontinuation of the two enterprises[57].

Political Reforms in the Early Heian Period

During his long reign, Kanmu Tennō successfully established the sovereign's authority, and actively proceeded with political reforms.

He made particular efforts to amend provincial politics that had become the cause of the state's financial decline. The supernumerary governors and district chieftains, who had increased over the years, were abolished, and a new post called the **Kageyushi** 勘解由使 (Office to Oversee Provincial Governors' Performance)[58], which strictly supervised the transfer of provincial governorships, was established.

In 792, after seeing a decline in the quality of soldiers recruited from the public, the old military system and soldiers, except for in Tōhoku and Kyūshū, were abolished. They were replaced by a new military system called **Kondei** 健児[59]: a small, elite force consisting of the sons of district chieftains and strong farmers who applied for the post. However, these reforms never achieved the expected results.

The reforms of Kanmu Tennō were carried on by his successors, Heizei Tennō 平城天皇 (r. 806-809) and Saga Tennō 嵯峨天皇 (r. 809-823). Shortly after his enthronement, in 810 Saga came into conflict with his brother, Retired Sovereign Heizei, who sought to return the capital to Heijō-kyō, creating a chaotic political situation called "Nisho Chōtei" 「二所朝廷」 (Two Courts). Saga quickly organized troops, allowing him to seize victory. In the

---

[57] Fujiwara no Otsugu 〈藤原緒嗣〉 opened the debate by criticizing the two enterprises, arguing that the military affairs and capital construction had caused suffering for the people, against which Sugano no Mamichi 〈菅野真道〉 argued back, insisting upon their continuation. Kanmu Tennō sided with Otsugu and announced the end of the war against the Emishi and the construction of Heian-kyō.

[58] New administrative posts that were not defined under the Ritsuryō system were called **ryōge no kan** 〈令外官〉 (extralegal posts). The kageyushi was one of these, and was responsible for inspecting the giving and receiving of geyujō 〈解由状〉, a document which was given from a new provincial governor to his predecessor when there were no acknowledged problems during the latter's term regarding the collection of tax and management of state-owned properties.

[59] Depending upon the size of the province and military needs, a quota between 20 to 200 soldiers was regulated accordingly in each province and appointed to protect the kokufu or maintain public order on a duty rotation of 60 days.

aftermath, Heizei became a monk, his lover Fujiwara no Kusuko 藤原薬子 (?-810) committed suicide, and Kusuko's brother, Fujiwara no Nakanari 藤原仲成 (764-810), was executed by archery (Retired Sovereign Heizei Incident 平城太上天皇の変, or Kusuko Incident 薬子の変). At the time, a new post called **Kurōdo no Tō** 蔵人頭 had been created to function as the chief secretary of the sovereign for the purpose of delivering royal orders quickly to the Daijōkan offices. Fujiwara no Fuyutsugu 藤原冬嗣 (775-826) was the first man to be appointed. The secretariat was called Kurōdo-dokoro 蔵人所, and the officials belonging to this section called kurōdo 蔵人 were later to be given important roles in the court as aides of the sovereign. Saga Tennō also founded the **Kebiishi** 検非違使, which was a police force that operated inside Heian-kyō. This organization would subsequently be given the right to administer justice, eventually taking on an important role in governing the capital.

Revisions of laws were also conducted under Saga Tennō. In order to supplement the Ritsuryō regulations with laws introduced in accordance with changes in society since the introduction of the Ritsuryō system, the *Kōnin Kyakushiki* 弘仁格式 was compiled. It consisted of **kyaku** 格, or supplementary laws, and **shiki** 式, which were detailed regulations for the actual enforcement of these laws. The *Kōnin Kyakushiki* was compiled for the convenience of conducting political affairs in coordination with the practical realities of administrative departments. Following this, the *Jōgan Kyakushiki* 貞観格式 and the *Engi Kyakushiki* 延喜格式 were compiled. All three compilations together are called the **Sandai Kyakushiki** 三代格式[60].

Changes in Local Regions and Courtier Society

From the latter half of the 8th century through to the 9th, the gap between rich and poor farmers significantly widened. Both wealthy and impoverished farmers used various means, such as furō and tōbō, to evade the burdens imposed on them. On the koseki registries, the number of false records (**giseki** 偽籍) in which more women were recorded instead of men – to avoid the burdens of military service, corvée, and tax imposed on the latter – increased. As a result, inconsistencies occurred between the Ritsuryō system and the actual social situation. This issue, and the complicated

[60] Among the documents, the *Ruijū Sandai Kyaku*〈『類聚三代格』〉, which was a collection of three generations of kyaku, and the *Engi Shiki*〈『延喜式』〉 still remain. Besides the kyaku and shiki, kōtai shiki〈交替式〉 (transfer shiki) for three generations (Enryaku〈延暦〉, Jōkan, and Engi) were also created, outlining regulations for the transfer of provincial governorships. In 833, the ***Ryō no Gige***〈『令義解』〉 (Commentary on the Administrative Code) which officially unified the interpretation of the administrative code, was compiled by Kiyohara no Natsuno〈清原夏野〉. In the latter half of the 9th century, the *Ryō no Shūge*〈『令集解』〉(Collective Commentaries on the Administrative Code) which was a compilation of annotations on the code, was compiled by Koremune no Naomoto〈惟宗直本〉.

procedures of the system, made conducting the distribution of fields and collection of taxes (Handen Shūju) difficult.

In an effort to enforce Handen Shūju, Kanmu Tennō revised the law so that each piece of land was to be distributed for a period of twelve years (ikki 一紀) instead of every six years when the koseki was updated. Some burdens were lifted in order to keep people as subjects in the system, such as the interest rate on official rice loans, which was dropped from 50 to 30 percent, and the period of the corvée being reduced from 60 to 30 days. However, these measures were not effective, and by the 9th century there was an increasing number of regions that had not distributed fields for 30 or 50 years.

Unable to sustain state finances because of the amount of unpaid chō and yō, the government took various measures to secure financial resources. These included not only cracking down on provincial governors and district chieftains for wrongdoings and neglecting taxes, but also establishing **kueiden** 公営田 (state-managed fields) under the Dazaifu administration in 823, and, in the Kinai region in 879, **kanden** 官田 (court-managed fields, also known as gangyō-kanden 元慶官田), both of which attempted to gain income by directly managing fields using rich farmers to raise revenue. However, each government bureau would later own their own sources of revenue called shoshiden 諸司田 (bureau-managed fields), and officials similarly gained ownership of newly-cultivated lands and thereby made themselves less dependent on state finances. The sovereign too gained their own arable fields called **chokushiden** 勅旨田 (royal grant fields), and royal family members were also granted lands by the tennō. A small number of royal family members and nobles who had close relationships with the sovereign, called Ingū Ōshinke 院宮王臣家 (royal and noble houses), owned many private lands, and put pressure on state finances while enjoying great influence[61].

Tang-Style Culture and Heian Buddhism

The culture that thrived from the move to Heian-kyō until the end of the 9th century is called **Kōnin-Jyōgan culture** 弘仁・貞観文化, after the era names of the sovereigns Saga and Seiwa 清和天皇. This culture developed around the aristocracy in Heian-kyō. **Monjō-Keikoku thought** 文章経国思想, which aimed to bring prosperity to the realm through the literary arts, became pervasive and fostered the development of classical Chinese learning in the court[62]. For Buddhism, newly-introduced sects named Tendai 天台宗 and Shingon 真言宗 became widespread,

[61] Low-ranking officials were eager to become housemen (kenin) of the Ingū Ōshinke. Influential local farmers who were opposed to the governor would also enter the sphere of the Ingū Ōshinke seeking protection.

[62] The *Ryōunshū*〈「凌雲集」〉(814), *Bunka Shūreishū*〈「文華秀麗集」〉(818), and *Keikokushū*〈「経国集」〉(827) were three compilations of classical Chinese poetry and prose prepared at royal command.

leading to the popularity of **esoteric Buddhism** 密教 (**mikkyō**).

Saga Tennō highly valued Tang Chinese culture. He gave palatial buildings Tang-style names and reorganized court rituals by adopting Chinese rites. He also adopted a policy of recruiting for politics intellectual courtiers gifted in literature or learning, and had them participate in governing the state.

Within the aristocracy there was a strong emphasis on the composition of classical Chinese poetry and prose as education, which led to the spread of Chinese literature. Courtiers mastered Chinese characters and used classical Chinese as though they were writing in their own language. This became part of the foundation for the emergence of Kokufū 国風文化 culture in later years. Noted intellectuals of the era included Saga Tennō himself, Kūkai 空海 (774-835), Ono 小野篁 no Takamura (802-852), and Sugawara no Michizane (845-903). Kūkai was a gifted writer and was known for *Bunkyō Hifuron* 「文鏡秘府論」, a collection of his work that examined writing classical Chinese poetry, and his poetry collection *Shōryōshū* 「性霊集」 (also known as *Henjō Hokki Shōryōshū* 「遍照発揮性霊集」). Sugawara no Michizane was also well known for his Chinese poems in *Kanke Bunsō* 「菅家文章」.

Study at the Daigaku was also highly valued. The Myōgyōdō, which taught Confucianism, and the Kidendō (or Monjōdō 文章道), which taught Chinese history and literature, were especially popular courses. Thus, **Daigaku Bessō** 大学別曹[63], a sort of dormitory, came to be built for the children of aristocrats. Moreover, the Shugei Shuchi-in 綜芸種智院, a comprehensive school founded by Kūkai, was very well known for opening its doors to commoners as well.

Due to the negative effects caused by the deep involvement of Buddhism in politics in the latter half of the Nara period, the great temples located in Nara did not accompany the government when the moves to Nagaoka-kyō and Heian-kyō were conducted by Kanmu Tennō. Instead, Kanmu and Saga supported the new sects of Buddhism developed by Saichō and Kūkai.

Saichō 最澄 (767-822) was from Ōmi Province, and trained to become a monk at the provincial temple of Ōmi and on Mt. Hiei 比叡山. In 804, he travelled to Tang China accompanying the envoys, where he learned the teachings of the **Tiantai Sect** 天台宗, and founded the Tendai Sect upon his return. Saichō also aimed to create a new original kaidan called the Daijō-kaidan 大乗戒壇 (Mahayana ordiation platform) in contrast to the traditional initiation ceremonies practiced at the kaidan of Tōdaiji Temple. This plan was met

---

[63] A Daigaku Bessō was a facility that functioned like a dormitory affiliated with the academy. Students would receive their stipends and study at the Daigaku using books. Famous dormitories include the Kōbun-in〈弘文院〉of the Wake family〈和気氏〉, the Kangaku-in〈勧学院〉of the Fujiwara family, the Shōgaku-in〈奨学院〉utilized by the Ariwara family〈在原氏〉and royal family members, and the Gakukan-in〈学館院〉of the Tachibana family〈橘氏〉.

with strong opposition from the Southern Schools of Nara Buddhism, against which Saichō defended himself by writing the *Kenkairon* 『顕戒論』 (Clarification of the Precepts). After his death, the new kaidan was officially approved, and the temple founded by Saichō, **Enryakuji Temple** 延暦寺 on Mt. Hiei, which began as a thatched hut, was later to become a center of Buddhist studies, as well as a monastery to pray for the safety and protection of Heian-kyō. Many monks were trained in this Buddhist complex including the Pure Land 浄土教 Buddhist master Genshin 源信, and the founders of Kamakura New Buddhism.

Kūkai 空海 hailed from Sanuki Province 讃岐国 and moved to the capital to study at the Daigaku. He become a Buddhist devotee after writing the *Sangō Shiiki* 『三教指帰』 (Indications of the Goals of the Three Teachings), which argued that Buddhism was a superior philosophy to Confucianism and Daoism. In 804, he travelled to China and studied esoteric Buddhism in Chang'an. Kūkai returned to Japan two years later and founded the **Shingon Sect** 真言宗[64] after building **Kongōbuji Temple** 金剛峰寺 on Mt. Kōya 高野山 in Kii Province 紀伊国. Similarly, Kyō-ō Gokokuji (Tōji) 教王護国寺（東寺） Temple in the capital, which was granted to Kūkai by Saga Tennō, also became a center of esoteric Buddhism.

After the death of Saichō, his disciples **Ennin** 円仁 (794-864) and **Enchin** 円珍 (814-891), who had also travelled to China, began to fully adopt esoteric teachings into the Tendai Sect[65]. Although both the Tendai and Shingon sects prayed for the peace of the realm and society, they were also supported by members of the royal family and nobles who sought to gain worldly benefits such as avoiding misfortune through **kajikitō** 加持祈禱 (rituals for empowerment) and pursuing happiness.

From around the 8th century, there was a trend towards kami-Buddhist syncretism, which can be seen in the building of jingūji 神宮寺 (temple annex affiliated with a shrine) in shrine complexes, enshrining Buddhist guardian deities as chinju 鎮守 (guardian kami) inside monastery grounds, and performing sutra recitations for the kami. These practices became more widespread as the Heian period dawned. The Tendai and

[64] "Shingon" means the true words of Dainichi Nyorai〈大日如来〉, and was referred to as mikkyō (literally "secret teachings") for its secrecy and depth. In contrast to kengyō〈顕教〉 (apparent teachings), which aimed at enlightenment through studying the teachings of the Buddha through sutras and performing ascetic practices, mikkyō aimed at enlightenment by teaching and mastering secretive mystic powers.

[65] The mikkyō of the Shingon Sect is called Tōmitsu〈東密〉 (Mikkyō of the East), whereas the mikkyō of the Tendai Sect is known as Taimitsu〈台密〉 (Mikkyō of Tendai). Ennin wrote a diary of his difficulties studying mikkyō in China from his departure in 838 until his return in 847, under the title *Nittō Guhō Junreikōki*〈『入唐求法巡礼行記』〉 (Record of a Pilgrimage to China in Search of the Law). From the end of the 10th century, the schools of Ennin and Enchin were in conflict, with the former faction called the Sanmon (Mountain) Branch〈山門派〉 after Enryakuji, and the latter called the Jimon (Temple) Branch〈寺門派〉 after Onjōji (Miidera)〈園城寺（三井寺）〉.

Shingon sects also became the roots of another religion called **Shugendō** 修験道, for, unlike Nara Buddhism, the new sects had built temples on mountains and performed ascetic practices in mountainous areas which syncretized with ancient mountain worship. Shugendō was a practical religion which believed that through ascetic training in the mountains one could be a yamabushi 山伏 (mountain ascetic) endowed with mystical powers. Practitioners worshipped mountains such as Mt. Ōmine 大峰山 in the Yoshino 吉野 district of Nara Prefecture, and Mt. Haku 白山 in the Hokuriku region.

Esoteric Buddhist Art

As both the Tendai and Shingon sects started to prosper, the mystical style of **esoteric Buddhist art** 密教芸術 developed in new ways. Architecturally, the placement of halls and pagodas of new temples in the mountains were arranged in unconventional compositions. The Main Hall of Murōji 室生寺 Temple is a representative structure of this period.

Many statues related to esoteric Buddhism such as the Nyoirin Kannon 如意輪観音 (Cintāmanicakra, a form of Avalokiteśvara in a half-lotus position) and Fudō Myō-ō 不動明王 (Wisdom King Acala) were made. A great number of these Buddhist statues were made by a technique called **ichiboku-zukuri** 一木造 (made from one block of wood), and convey a mystical impression. There were also many sculptures of kami made under the influence of kami-Buddhist syncretism, of which those in Yakushiji Temple of Sōgyō-Hachiman 僧形八幡神像 (Hachiman in the Guise of a Buddhist Monk) and Queen Consort Jingū 神功皇后像 are well known.

STATUE OF SITTING SHAKYAMUNI〈釈迦如来坐像〉OF MURŌJI TEMPLE

A life-size sitting statue made of Japanese torreya by the ichiboku-zukuri technique, preserved in the Miroku Hall〈弥勒堂〉of Murōji. The sculpture portrays a plump figure with a warm expression, while the clothing is sharply expressed. (Height 106.3 cm)

MAIN HALL OF MURŌJI TEMPLE

The size of the façade was formerly 5 ken〈間〉(approx. 9.1 m) high, and the sides 4 ken (approx. 7.3 m) across. The roof was covered by thin wooden shingles. The characteristics of this building can be ascertained from the simplistic structure which can be seen in the way the pillars are set up. Parts of the front were added in the Edo period〈江戸時代〉. This site is one of the few that preserves the structure of a temple founded in a mountainous area in the beginning of the Heian period.

RYŌKAI MANDALA (TAIZŌKAI)
A mandala that illustrates the universe of esoteric Buddhism in a pattern with Dainichi Nyorai located in the center. The painting conveys the Diamond Realm and the Womb Realm as a pair. (Vertical length 81 cm, width 65.9 cm)

STATUE OF NYOIRIN KANNON OF KANSHINJI TEMPLE
The main image of Kanshinji〈観心寺〉. It is a sitting statue that uses both wood and the dry-lacquer technique. The statue is believed to be the most representative image of Nyoirin Kannon, which had connections with esoteric Buddhism. (Height 109.4 cm)

Mystical Buddhist paintings such as the image of Fudō Myō-ō at Onjōji Temple, called the "Yellow Fudō (黄不動)," were also produced. Techniques to make **mandalas** (曼荼羅), images that express the esoteric Buddhist universe, were also developed in this period, as can be seen in paintings such as the Ryōkai Mandalas (両界曼荼羅) of Jingoji (神護寺) Temple and Kyō-ō Gokokuji Temple. A mandala is a drawing that illustrates the Kongōkai (金剛界) (Diamond Realm), representing the wisdom of Dainichi Nyorai (Vairocana, a Buddha highly regarded in esoteric Buddhism), and similarly the Taizōkai (胎蔵界) (Womb Realm), representing compassion, in a systematic pattern. A well-known painter belonging to this age was Kudara no Kawanari (百済河成) (782-853).

Tang-style calligraphy became popular and noted calligraphers started to emerge including Saga Tennō, Kūkai, and Tachibana no Hayanari (橘逸勢) (?-842), who would later be collectively known as the "**Sanpitsu** (三筆)" (Three Brushes).

Translators' Notes

[i] A sovereign's partners are usually referred to as consorts (后). The primary partner of a male sovereign is popularly called a queen, empress, etc., but it is important to distinguish between a woman whose partner occupies the throne (a queen consort) and a woman who occupies the throne herself (a queen regnant). The mother of a tennō and/or the partner of a deceased tennō may become known as a dowager queen or dowager queen consort, and as the latter more closely approximates the Japanese 皇太后 that is what this textbook employs.

[ii] The English terms "prince" and "princess" are quite inclusive, and are sometimes even used in reference to non-royals, but 親王 is a title that emphasizes the holder is a legitimate or high-ranking prince/princess, usually a sibling or child of a tennō. Appending "royal" emphasizes this distinctive characteristic.

[iii] The term "貴族," primarily used in this textbook to refer to a social class in ancient and classical Japan, is usually rendered in English as "nobles" or "nobility," which does not necessarily connotate an association with a court, while "公卿" or "公家," referring to the people and families associated with the royal court, is best rendered in English as "courtiers" (a person who belongs to or serves a court). However, they are often used synonymously in Japanese history, and accordingly in English it sometimes sounds more natural to render them the other way around. Moreover, each term is occasionally translated as "aristocrats," particularly in the adjective form when referring to the society or culture of the ruling class (e.g. aristocratic culture).

[iv] "Ran" (乱) is an inclusive term for an event that in English could encompass "disturbance," "revolt," "rebellion" or "war." Sometimes scholars favor just one of these terms, but this is not ideal since a short uprising may be called a "disturbance" in English but a long civil war certainly not. Therefore, rather than consistently translating "ran" in one way, this textbook uses a term appropriate for the specific event in question.

[v] "太上天皇," "上皇" and "～院," all terms used for a tennō who abdicated, are usually rendered by scholars today in English as "retired sovereign." Because many former tennō became monks/nuns, older English scholarship tended to refer to them as "cloistered," and therefore insei was often translated as "cloistered rule." However, because not every abdicated tennō became a monk/nun, and because their authority had little to do with religion, "retired sovereign" is a more accurate term, and is the one used consistently in this textbook. As a proper title, it is capitalized when applied to specific individuals (e.g. Retired Sovereign Hanazono).

[vi] "農民" is often translated as either "farmer" or "peasant." The latter, due to its association primarily with feudalism and the medieval era (especially in Europe) is appropriate in some contexts, but not in others, especially when used before or after the feudal era. This textbook therefore uses "farmer" consistently. Also see the note for "百姓" in Chapter 6, Section 4.

[vii] Organized forms of Buddhism (～宗) are usually translated as either "sect" or "school," but since subdivisions of those groups are also called "school," and sometimes "sect," this can be confusing. This textbook therefore translates the major forms as "sects" and the subdivisions as "schools," but the term Nanto Rokushū is an exception as it is customarily rendered "Six Southern Schools."

[viii] "Bakufu" (幕府) has no direct equivalent in English; it means literally "tent government," but refers to a government led by warriors (i.e., those in the "baku," a commander's tent on the battlefield). For decades, English writers have used the neologism "shogunate," but while this is still common in the mass media and among some specialists of modern Japan, it does not accurately reflect what a bakufu was (the key point is military rule, not rulership by a shōgun, most of whom lacked real power). Therefore, some premodern scholars use "warrior government" or "military government," but increasingly simply using "bakufu" has become the norm among scholars in English, and this textbook has followed suit.

Chapter

3

Aristocratic Rule and Native Japanese Culture

1 Regental Politics

The Rise of the Northern Fujiwara Family

Until the middle of the 9th century, Kanmu Tennō 桓武天皇 and Saga Tennō 嵯峨天皇 held the aristocracy in check, and asserted strong leadership in governance. However, the **Fujiwara family** 藤原氏, and in particular the **Hokke** 北家 or northern branch, gradually cut into the center of power by deepening its ties with the royal famiy.

Fujiwara no Fuyutsugu 藤原冬嗣 of the Hokke, who was deeply trusted by Saga Tennō and was appointed Kurōdo no Tō 蔵人頭, built marital relations with the royal family. His son, **Fujiwara no Yoshifusa** 藤原良房 (804-872), consolidated the supremacy of the Hokke among the Fujiwara branches through the Jōwa Incident 承和の変 in 842, while holding the rival families, represented by figures like Tomo (Ōtomo) no Kowamine 伴（大伴）健岑 (dates unknown) and Tachibana no Hayanari 橘逸勢, in check.

Yoshifusa successfully enthroned his 9-year-old grandson as Seiwa Tennō 清和天皇 (r. 858-876) in 858, and eventually became the **sesshō** 摂政 (regent)[i] as maternal grandfather of the sovereign. In the Ōtenmon Incident 応天門の変 of 866[1], he managed to oust the Tomo 伴氏 and Ki 紀氏 families. **Fujiwara no Mototsune** 藤原基経 (836-891), who succeeded Yoshifusa, was instrumental in the abdication of Yōzei Tennō 陽成天皇 (r. 876-884), and enthroned Kōkō Tennō 光孝天皇 (r. 884-887). To repay Mototsune, Kōkō Tennō appointed him to the new post of **kanpaku** 関白 (regent for an adult sovereign). Further, Mototsune opposed the royal edict which Uda Tennō 宇多天皇 (r. 887-897) issued at the time of his enthronement, and forced him to withdraw it in 888 (Akō Incident 阿衡の紛議). This resulted in even more consolidation of the political power vested in the office of kanpaku[2]. In this way, the northern branch

[1] A senior counselor, Tomo no Yoshio ‹伴善男›, set fire to the Ōtenmon Gate and laid the blame on Minister of the Left Minamoto no Makoto ‹源信›, but was exiled after his deed was brought to light.

[2] The royal edict issued by Uda Tennō stated that Mototsune would be appointed as an "akō," an equivalent of kanpaku referred to in the Chinese classics. However, Mototsune refused to

of the Fujiwara family rapidly expanded its influence within the central government.

After Mototsune's death, Uda Tennō dispensed with sesshō and kanpaku because his **gaiseki** 外戚 (maternal relatives) were not from the Fujiwara family, and instead promoted the scholar **Sugawara no Michizane** 菅原道真. However, during the reign of **Daigo Tennō** 醍醐天皇 (r. 897-930) that followed, Fujiwara no Tokihira 藤原時平 (871-909) exiled Michizane by means of a plot[3].

During the first half of the 10th century under Daigo Tennō's rule, there was an attempt to revive the Ritsuryō 律令体制 system through such means as calling for the distribution of cultivated fields and the decree to regulate the estate system (Engi no Shōen Seiri-rei 延喜の荘園整理令). Other developments included the compilation of *Nihon Sandai Jitsuroku* 『日本三代実録』 (History of Three Reigns of Japan), the last of the Rikkokushi 六国史 (Six State Histories), legal codes such as *Engi Kyaku* 『延喜格』 and *Engi Shiki* 『延喜式』, and a royal anthology of waka 和歌, *Kokin Wakashū* 『古今和歌集』 (Collection of Poems Ancient and Modern). Daigo's son, Murakami Tennō 村上天皇 (r. 946-967), issued a type of copper coin called Kengen Taihō 乾元大宝, which was the last of the twelve royal coins (Honchō [Kōchō] Jūnisen 「本朝（皇朝）十二銭」). The *Engi Shiki* went into effect shortly after his death. Since both Daigo and Murakami ruled without appointing sesshō or kanpaku, their reigns were later praised as **Engi Tenryaku no Chi** 「延喜・天暦の治」 (reigns of the Engi and Tenryaku eras). However, in between these reigns Fujiwara no Tadahira 藤原忠平 (880-949) served as sesshō and kanpaku, taking control of the Daijōkan 太政官. In 969, after the passing of Murakami Tennō, Minamoto no Takaakira 源高明 (914-982), one of Daigo's sons who had been serving as the minister of the left, was ousted in the **Anna Incident** 安和の変, firmly establishing the power of the northern branch of the Fujiwara family. Henceforth, the post of either sesshō or kanpaku was almost always maintained, and usually occupied by the offspring of Fujiwara no Tadahira.

Regental Politics

The sesshō acted in the tennō's stead when the sovereign was too young to govern,

---

carry out any duties, insisting that akō in the classics was merely a post without actual responsibilities. As a result, the sovereign had to retract the edict and assign anew the role of kanpaku to Mototsune. The kanpaku was involved in every communication, written or otherwise, between the sovereign and the Daijōkan, hence the name of the position ("kanpaku" means "to be involved and report").

[3] In 901, Michizane, the minister of the right at the time, was relegated to the position of Dazai no Gon no Sochi〈大宰権帥〉(provisional governor of the Dazaifu〈大宰府〉), and he died there. After his death, Michizane came to be feared as a vengeful spirit. In order to pacify his spirit, the Kitano Tenmangū Shrine〈北野天満宮〉in Kyōto, and the Dazaifu Tenmangū Shrine in Dazaifu where he was interred, were built. Later on, Sugawara no Michizane came to be widely worshipped as Tenjin〈天神〉, a patron deity of scholarship.

while the kanpaku assisted an adult tennō as his chief advisor. The political system of the second half of the 10th through 11th centuries is called **Sekkan Seiji** 摂関政治 (regental politics), as during this time sesshō and kanpaku were consecutively appointed and usually occupied the highest position in the government. The Fujiwara branch families that produced these sesshō and kanpaku were called the **Sekkanke** 摂関家 (regental families). The sesshō or kanpaku, holding the highest position within the greater Fujiwara family, also held the post of uji no chōja 「氏長者」 (clan head)[4] of the Fujiwara, and held immense power, controlling the allocation of titles and positions.

There were continuous struggles over the posts of sesshō and kanpaku within the Sekkanke, but such conflicts died down at the end of the 10th century when **Fujiwara no Michinaga** 藤原道長 (966-1027) came to power[5]. Michinaga wed his four daughters to sovereigns and crown princes, and held power in the court for about 30 years. Three consecutive generations of sovereigns – Go-Ichijō 後一条天皇 (r. 1016-1036), Go-Suzaku 後朱雀天皇 (r. 1036-1045), and Go-Reizei 後冷泉天皇 (r. 1045-1068) – had Michinaga as their maternal grandfather. **Fujiwara no Yorimichi** 藤原頼通 (992-1074), who succeeded his father Michinaga, served as sesshō and kanpaku for about 50 years during the reigns of the same three sovereigns. Thus, during these years the power of the Fujiwara Sekkanke had been stabilized.

In courtier society at the time, it was common for a married couple to either live together with the wife's parents or live by themselves in a new household. Much importance was placed on ties with the maternal side; the husband was patronized by his wife's father, and children were raised by maternal relatives. As the closest maternal relatives of the sovereign, sesshō and kanpaku could wield immense power by taking advantage of the vast, traditional authority of the tennō.

State administration under the regental system consisted of the tennō ruling the country by directing both central and provincial officials in uniform fashion through the Daijōkan. Major administrative matters were deliberated by the leading courtiers of the Daijōkan, and in most cases policies were issued and transmitted in the form of official documents such as Daijōkanpu 太政官符 (Daijōkan directive) or Senji 宣旨 (royal decree)

---

[4] The uji chōja of the Fujiwara family was responsible for the management of various family-related institutions, such as their clan temple, Kōfukuji Temple〈興福寺〉, their clan shrine, Kasugasha Shrine〈春日社〉, and their Daigaku Bessō〈大学別曹〉, called Kangakuin〈勧学院〉. The uji chōja was also entitled to recommend a family member on the occasion of a conferment of a court rank or an appointment to a post.

[5] Prominent examples include the struggle between brothers Fujiwara no Kanemichi〈藤原兼通〉 and Kaneie〈兼家〉, and that between uncle and nephew Fujiwara no Michinaga and Fujiwara no Korechika〈藤原伊周〉. The internal strife within the Fujiwara Sekkanke subsided for a while at the end of the 10th century after Korechika was demoted and Michinaga was promoted to the minister of the left.

with approval from the sovereign (or regent). Issues of high priority, such as finance and foreign affairs, were discussed in a meeting called Jin no Sadame 陣定, which was held in the residential palace guardrooms. The opinion of the senior courtiers was solicited, and the sovereign could then refer to this when making decisions.

Since sesshō and kanpaku controlled appointment of positions, middle- and lower-ranking nobles came to be subordinated to the upper echelon led by the Sekkanke. Eventually, the order and limits of promotion became almost entirely determined by lineage and maternal relationships. In this context, some middle- and lower-ranking nobles sought the favor of the senior nobles, such as the Sekkanke, in order to be recruited as keishi 家司 (household officials) to manage household affairs for them, while pursuing lucrative posts such as that of provincial governor.

Changes in Foreign Affairs

Envoys from Silla 新羅 had stopped coming to Japan at the end of the 8th century, but in the first half of the 9th merchants from there began to come to Japan to trade. By the second half of the 9th century, merchants from Tang 唐 China were coming more frequently, prompting the court to establish mechanisms to ensure smooth trade with them while promoting imports of books and crafts such as ceramics. Against this backdrop, when Sugawara no Michizane was appointed envoy to Tang 遣唐使 in 894 he argued that it was not necessary to take the tremendous risk of overseas travel to maintain official relations with Tang, a state that he considered to already be in decline. As a result, based on Michizane's proposal, the dispatch of envoys was cancelled.

In 907, the Tang Dynasty, which had been the political and cultural center of East Asia, fell. It was succeeded by a number of states that rose and fell in what came to be called the Five Dynasties and Ten Kingdoms 五代十国 era (907-979). Among those states was Wuyue 呉越国 (907-978), the capital of which was Hangzhou 杭州 on the eastern coast of China. Merchants from Wuyue came to Japan and introduced the culture of their region. Eventually, China was reunified under the **Song Dynasty** 宋（北宋） (Northern Song, 960-1127), but Japan decided not to pursue offi-

EAST ASIA IN THE 10TH AND 11TH CENTURIES

cial diplomatic relations with the dynasty both to avoid entanglement in East Asian upheavals and because of the Sinocentric structure of international relations (tributary system 朝貢関係).

However, Song merchants frequently came to Hakata 博多 in Kyūshū 九州, bringing books, medicines, and craftwork like chinaware, while gold, mercury, pearls, sulfur and so on were exported from Japan[6]. Although travel overseas was banned for Japanese under law, Buddhist monks seeking to make a pilgrimage to Mt. Tiantai 天台山 or Mt. Wutai 五台山 were occasionally permitted to do so. Thus, some Buddhist monks visited the Asian continent aboard Song merchant vessels, and introduced many things from Song back home. Examples include Chōnen 奝然 (938-1016), who travelled to China at the end of the 10th century, and Jōjin 成尋 (1011-1081), who went in the mid-11th[7].

In the northeastern regions of China, Balhae 渤海, with which Japan had enjoyed a friendly relationship since the Nara period 奈良時代, was overthrown by the **Khitans** 契丹 (Liao 遼 Dynasty, 916-1125) in the first half of the 10th century[8]. On the Korean peninsula, **Goryeo** 高麗 (918-1392) was established in the beginning of the 10th century, and eventually absorbed Silla and unified the Korean peninsula. Japan, on the other hand, did not seek diplomatic relations with either Liao or Goryeo, although merchants and other people continued to come and go between Japan and Goryeo.

2 Native Japanese Culture

Developments in Japanese Literature

From the second half of the 9th century to the 10th, a new culture emerged out of the cultures that had been imported from the Asian continent until then. This new culture, centered on courtier society, incorporated native Japanese tastes and sentiments, and was moreover shaped by the climate and natural world of Japan to produce an elegant

---

[6] Since gold was a specialty product indigenous to the Ōshū region〈奥州〉, Ōshū started to gain attention. In *Shinsarugakuki*〈「新猿楽記」〉(An Account of the New Monkey Music), a work of fiction from the 11th century, the main character, a merchant boss, is described as engaged in the import and export of various articles both Japanese and Chinese, traveling across Japan from Fushū〈俘囚〉in the east (Ōshū) to Kikai Island〈貴賀の島〉(southern Kyūshū) in the west.

[7] The statue of Shakyamuni〈釈迦如来像〉that Chōnen brought back was enshrined in Seiryōji Temple〈清凉寺〉in Saga〈嵯峨〉, Kyōto, and received great devotion. The Buddhist scriptures which Chōnen also brought back were dedicated to the Sekkanke.

[8] A group of the Jurchen people〈女真人〉known as Toi〈刀伊〉inhabited the northeastern coastal region (present-day Primorsky Krai), and were under the control of the Khitans. Later they established the Jin Dynasty〈金〉.

and sophisticated style of art and literature. Because the culture of the 10th and 11th centuries accentuated and reflected native sensibilities, it is called **Kokufū Bunka** 国風文化 (native Japanese culture)[ii].

The birth of native culture is symbolized by the development of **kana characters** かな文字. These include **hiragana** 平がな characters, which were simplified cursive forms of Man'yōgana 万葉がな (Chinese characters used to represent sounds in Japanese), and **katakana** 片かな, which evolved from the appropriation and simplification of fragments of Chinese characters. Both forms were already in use in the 9th century for phonogramic writing, but became more widely used at the start of the 11th century. This enabled the written expression of people's feelings and sentiments in the Japanese language in a lively manner, which in turn resulted in the emergence of many literary works.

The composition of waka flourished. In 905, the first royal anthology of waka, the ***Kokin Wakashū*** 『古今和歌集』, was compiled by Ki no Tsurayuki 紀貫之 (?-945) and others[9]. The subtleties and refined artifice of the waka in this collection came to be called "Kokin style," and established the norm for waka poetry for the following generations.

Nobles wrote documents solely in Chinese characters in official settings, but their writing greatly departed from Chinese conventions and instead took on Japanese styles[10].

Kana characters, on the other hand, were not used in official settings, except for waka. However, they came to be commonly used in everyday life, and gave birth to a number of notable literary works. Representative works of the kana monogatari かな物語 (prose narratives) are *Taketori Monogatari* 『竹取物語』 (The Tale of the Bamboo Cutter) based on legends, *Ise Monogatari* 『伊勢物語』 (The Tales of Ise) which belongs to the genre of uta (poem) monogatari 歌物語, and ***Genji Monogatari*** 『源氏物語』 (The Tale of Genji) written by Murasaki Shikibu 紫式部 (dates unknown), lady-in-waiting to Queen Consort Shōshi 彰子 (988-1074, a daughter of Fujiwara no Michinaga). *The Tale of Genji* is a masterpiece of prose fiction that chronicles the life of court nobles, and is counted as one of the highest achievements of Japanese literature along with ***Makura no Sōshi*** 『枕草子』 (The Pillow Book), a collection of essays on the actual experience of courtly life by Sei Shōnagon 清少納言 (dates unknown), lady-in-waiting to Queen Consort Teishi 定子 (976-1000, a daughter of Fujiwara no Michitaka 藤原道隆). *Eiga Monogatari* 『栄華物語』 (The Tale of Flowering Fortunes), a historical narrative that celebrates

---

[9] From the *Kokin Wakashū* through the *Shin Kokin Wakashū*〈『新古今和歌集』〉 in the early Kamakura period〈鎌倉時代〉, a total of eight anthologies of waka were compiled at royal command. Collectively, they are called the *Hachidai-shū*〈八代集〉.

[10] Partly because of the increase in ceremonies and events at the court since the 10th century, nobles kept journals written in Chinese characters to record details of events. The handwritten original of Fujiwara no Michinaga's diary, ***Midō Kanpakuki***〈『御堂関白記』〉, is still extant.

the glory of Michinaga's successful career, was also written in kana by a woman. It is accepted that the first diary in kana was *Tosa Nikki* 「土佐日記」 (The Tosa Diary), written by Ki no Tsurayuki, a male courtier, but many other kana diaries were written by women serving in the court and exemplify a detailed and tender consideration of their subjects.

The flourishing kana literature of this period owed much to the talented women whom the courtiers selected to attend to their daughters serving in the inner palace.

Pure Land Buddhism

The Buddhist sects predominant during the regental era were Tendai 天台宗 and Shingon 真言宗. These sects were patronized by nobles who regarded prayer offerings as a means of obtaining worldly benefits. Meanwhile, syncretism of Buddhism and indigenous kami 神 belief gave rise to the **theory of Honji Suijaku** 本地垂迹説[11], which held that kami were manifestations of Buddhist deities. Another notable development was goryō shinkō 御霊信仰, a widespread belief through which people sought to escape disasters like plague or famine by worshipping onryō (vengeful spirits) or ekishin 疫神 (pestilence deities), and to this end **goryōe** 御霊会 (spirit pacification rituals) were frequently held[12].

Along with the spread of various beliefs that purported to bring worldly benefits, **Pure Land teachings** 浄土教 (Jōdo-kyō) also became popular as a way to escape from the anxieties of the world. These teachings profess that that worship of the Buddha Amida (Amitabha) can lead one to be reborn in the Pure Land upon death, attaining enlightenment and liberation from pain and suffering. The monk **Kūya** 空也 (903-972) preached this in the markets of the capital around the mid-10th century, followed by **Genshin** 源信 (Eshin Sōzu 恵心僧都, 942-1017) who exhorted nenbutsu 念仏 (chanting of the name of Amida) as a means to such rebirth in the *Ōjōyōshū* 「往生要集」 (Essentials of Rebirth in the Pure Land). This resulted in Pure Land teachings gradually gaining believers not only in the aristocracy but also among the commoners.

Belief in the Pure Land was reinforced by **Mappō thought** 末法思想[13]. Rampant crime

---

[11] The concept maintained that a kami was a temporary manifestation of a Buddhist deity. Later, each kami came to be associated with a particular Buddhist deity; for example, the original identity of the sun goddess, Amaterasu Ōmikami〈天照大神〉, was said to be Dainichi Nyorai〈大日如来〉, and so on.

[12] Goryōe began around the mid-9th century as a prayer offering to pacify the souls of those defeated in political conflicts, such as Royal Prince Sawara〈早良親王〉, but it eventually grew into a ritual for protection from plague. Festivals at Kitano Tenmangū and Gionsha (Yasaka Jinja) shrines〈祇園社（八坂神社）〉originally developed from goryō shinkō.

[13] Mappō thought held that after the death of Shakyamuni〈釈迦〉, the world went through three stages: the age of true dharma (shōbō〈正法〉), the age of imitated dharma (zōbō〈像法〉), and the age of the end of dharma (mappō), the last of which was believed to begin in 1052.

and brawls, in addition to the anxiety caused by natural disasters, were thought to match the image of Mappō, the Buddhist era of decline, and drove people to yearn for salvation in the Pure Land. In this context, many collections of legends of people who were believed to have been reborn in the Pure Land proliferated, first and foremost being *Nihon Ōjō Gokurakuki* 『日本往生極楽記』 (Records of Japanese Reborn in Paradise), authored by Yoshishige no Yasutane 慶滋保胤 (?-1002). Also common was the practice in various locations of copying Buddhist scriptures, such as the Lotus Sutra 法華経, and burying them in cylindrical containers under **kyōzuka** 経塚 (sutra mounds) to preserve their wisdom for the next generation[14].

Native Japanese Art

Native Japanese styles were also evident in arts and crafts. Aristocratic residences came to be built in a new Japanese style called **shinden-zukuri** 寝殿造, using plain wood with cypress bark thatching. The design used open spaces, and tatami 畳 mats or round straw cushions for sitting. Partitions such as fusuma 襖 (sliding doors) and screens 屏風 were often painted with Chinese landscapes or motifs from the classics (kara-e 唐絵, or Chinese painting), or with Japanese seasonal motifs painted with gentle brushstrokes and sophisticated coloring (**Yamato-e** 大和絵, or Japanese painting)[15].

Interior furnishings were also often crafted with techniques developed in Japan such as **maki-e** 蒔絵[16] and **raden** 螺鈿[17]. These crafts combined splendid decoration with a refined impression, and were much-prized as exports. As for calligraphy, the Chinese-style calligraphy that had been prevalent in the past gave way to Japanese-style calligraphy (**wayō** 和様) characterized by elegant brushstrokes. Three masters (**Sanseki** 三跡（蹟）) of wayō calligraphy were Ono no Michikaze 小野道風 (894-966), Fujiwara no Sukemasa 藤原佐理 (944-998), and Fujiwara no Yukinari 藤原行成 (972-1027). Beautiful

KATAWA-GURUMA RADEN MAKI-E TEBAKO 〈片輪車螺鈿蒔絵手箱〉(COSMETICS BOX IN MAKI-E LACQUER AND MOTHER-OF PEARL INLAY)
Features a design of a cow cart with its wheels half-submerged in water.

[14] One of the well-known examples is Kinpusen Kyōzuka〈金峯山経塚〉 in Yoshino〈吉野〉, which contained a copy of the Lotus Sutra in a gilt-bronze cylindrical container buried by Fujiwara no Michinaga in 1007.

[15] Kose no Kanaoka〈巨勢金岡〉 was one of the representative early Yamato-e artists.

[16] In the maki-e technique, a pattern is drawn with lacquer, and then gold, silver and/or other metal powders are applied to complete the decoration.

[17] Radenwork is produced by having sliced and polished pieces of mother-of-pearl, cut into various forms, inlayed in a lacquer surface. The material was taken from shells like those of green turban snails, harvested around southern islands such as Amami Ōshima〈奄美大島〉 and Kikaijima〈喜界島〉.

THE BYŌDŌIN HŌŌDŌ
In 1052, Fujiwara no Yorimichi remodeled his villa in Uji〈宇治〉 into Byōdōin Temple. The Amida hall, named Hōōdō (Phoenix Hall), was completed in 1053. Its design – a central hall with mokoshi〈裳階〉 (decorative roof below the true roof) with two-storied smaller structures on either side – is said to resemble a phoenix spreading its wings.

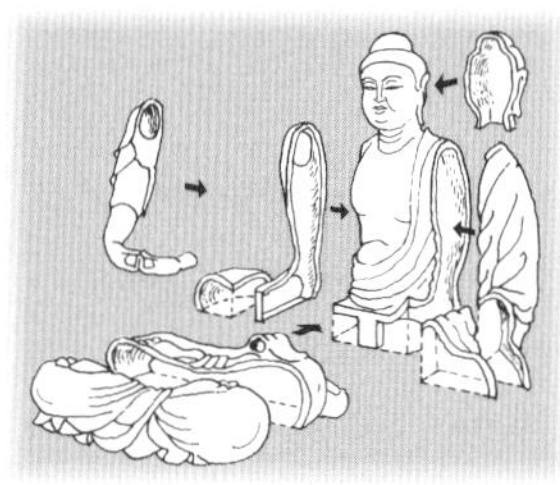

YOSEGI-ZUKURI

books and Yamato-e adorned with their calligraphy were valued as furnishing goods and gifts.

The popularization of Pure Land teachings inspired the creation of many works of art and architecture. **Hōjōji** 法成寺, a Buddhist temple constructed under Fujiwara no Michinaga's sponsorship and famed for its splendor, was a grand structure centered on the Amida Hall 阿弥陀堂. The **Byōdōin Hōōdō** 平等院鳳凰堂 (Phoenix Hall of Byōdōin Temple), constructed by Michinaga's son, Fujiwara no Yorimichi, is representative of Amida halls of the time. The main image of Amida there was created by the sculptor **Jōchō** 定朝 (?-1057). Jōchō perfected the technique called **yosegi-zukuri** 寄木造[18] in place of the more conventional ichiboku-zukuri 一木造, and responded to the increased demand for Buddhist statues in the context of Mappō thought. **Raigō-zu** 来迎図, drawings that depicted a Buddha appearing to lead the dying to the Pure Land were also popular and produced in great number.

Aristocratic Life

Formal wear for a male aristocrat was an outfit called **sokutai** 束帯, or its simplified form **ikan** 衣冠, while women wore **nyōbō shōzoku** 女房装束 (jūnihitoe 十二単) including a karaginu 唐衣 (wide-sleeved jacket) and mo 裳 (apron-like train). These fashions were partly patterned after Chinese outfits but dynamically arranged and adapted for Japanese taste and use[19]. The main material for clothing was silk, and patterns and color combinations reflected delicate and refined Japanese tastes.

---

[18] The ichiboku-zukuri technique uses one whole chunk of a tree to carve a Buddhist statue, whereas in the yosegi-zukuri, sculptors share in the carving of several different parts of a statue and then assemble them. The latter technique enabled the more efficient production of statues.

[19] Everyday wear for male courtiers consisted of nōshi〈直衣〉 or kariginu〈狩衣〉, which were simplified types of formal wear, while women wore kouchigi〈小袿〉 and hakama〈袴〉.

SHŌJU RAIGŌ-ZU〈聖衆来迎図〉(A RAIGŌ "WELCOMING APPROACH" IMAGE OF THE DESCENT OF THE BUDDHA AMIDA WITH CELESTIAL ENTOURAGE [PART])
Depicts the Buddha Amida descending from the Pure Land with 32 Buddhas and bodhisattvas to welcome the dying who have achieved enlightenment. (Length 129 cm, width 158 cm)

The diet was relatively simple, and meals were usually prepared twice a day. Oil was not used, and due to Buddhist influence neither was animal meat.

At an age between 10 to 15 years old, children underwent a coming-of-age ceremony, called **genpuku**元服 for boys and **mogi**裳着 for girls. Afterwards, they were treated as adults, and boys could start their careers as officials in the court. Most nobles lived in the eastern side of the capital, with the most prominent families, like the Sekkanke, living in grand mansions. They seldom left the capital except to visit temples and shrines in the surrounding areas, such as Hasedera長谷寺 in Yamato.

From about the mid-9th century, **annual events** (nenjū gyōji年中行事)[20] either originating in China or evolving from old Japanese customs became further developed and refined, and took root in courtly life.

Nobles were concerned about fate and fortune; they participated in prayer offer-

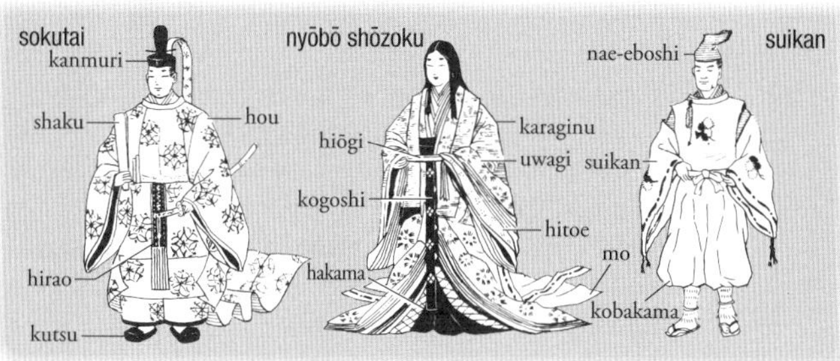

SOKUTAI, NYŌBŌ SHŌZOKU, SUIKAN
The sokutai's color differed according to rank. Women's formal wear in the court was nyōbō shōzoku, the beauty of which was emphasized through a layer of inner robes of different colors. Suikan〈水干〉 and hitatare〈直垂〉 were mostly worn by commoners and warriors.

[20] Annual events included Shintō〈神道〉 rituals such as Ōharae〈大祓〉 (Great Purification Rite) and Kamo no Matsuri〈賀茂祭〉 (Kamo Festival), Buddhist rituals like Kanbutsu〈灌仏〉 (Buddha's birthday), entertainment events like the star festival and sumai〈相撲〉 contests, and even administrative ceremonies such as joi〈叙位〉 (rank promotion ceremony) and jimoku〈除目〉 (post assignment ceremony).

ings to avoid calamities, sought to invite good luck, and lived their everyday lives within various restrictions determined by divination[21]. Having invested tremendous effort to these ends, they experienced deep disappointment when their wish for worldly achievements like wealth or promotion were not fulfilled. This partly explains why they sought solace in Pure Land teachings and salvation in the afterlife.

3 Provincial Administration and Warriors

Zuryō and Fumyō

Limitations of the Ritsuyō system began to be apparent around the beginning of the 10th century. In a decree issued in 902, the government sought to reorganize administrative laws by issuing a decree that prohibited illegal possession of land (**Engi no Shōen Seiri-rei**〈延喜の荘園整理令〉), implemented distribution of land, and so on. However, the koseki〈戸籍〉 (family registry) and keichō〈計帳〉 (tax registry) systems, as well as Handen Shūju〈班田収授〉, became difficult to manage. As a result, the collection of taxes like so〈租〉, chō〈調〉 and yō〈庸〉 was jeopardized, and the central and local government finances could no longer be maintained[22].

Facing such crises, from the late 9th century to the early 10th century the government established a system to oversee the transfer of provincial governorships. In this new system, significant power and responsibility was given to the highest position among the officials dispatched to the provinces (usually the governor). This position

---

[21] The aristocrats' outlook was largely influenced by Onmyōdō〈陰陽道〉 (the way of Yin〈陰〉 and Yang〈陽〉) which derived from Chinese Yin-Yang five-phase theory〈陰陽五行説〉, where everything including astronomical phenomena and the calendar system were interpreted in relation to good or bad luck. Their everyday activities were constrained by whether the day was deemed lucky or unlucky. When something unusual happened, they would have the event's meaning divined. To observe taboos, they would confine themselves inside their residence and refrain from performing certain kinds of activities (**monoimi**〈物忌〉), or if one's destination was in an unlucky direction, then first he/she would go in a different direction, stay overnight there, and then leave for the unlucky direction anew (**katatagae**〈方違〉).

[22] According to the koseki in Awa Province〈阿波国〉 from 902, a breakdown of 5 households comprising 435 individuals consisted of 59 males and 376 females. It is evident that the female headcount was intentionally increased so as to maximize the allocated land without incurring the obligation to pay taxes in labor and kind. Obviously, it was not practical to carry out the allocation of land based on such spurious family registration. In fact, after 902 there are no historical documents indicating that allocations were ordered. The *Ikenfūji Jūnikajō*〈「意見封事十二箇条」〉 (Statement of Opinion on Twelve Matters), which Miyoshi no Kiyoyuki〈三善清行〉 submitted to Daigo Tennō〈醍醐天皇〉 in 914, describes the extent of the government's financial misery and confusion in the provinces.

came to be called **zuryō** 受領 (custodial provincial governor, but literally meaning "receipt"), because the successor took over the assets of the province from their predecessor.

The zuryō assigned cultivation of farmland to influential farmers (**tato** 田堵)[23], and imposed taxation in the form of kanmotsu 官物 (comprehensive tax assets; originating from taxes like so, chō, and yō, and kusuiko public loans) and rinjizōyaku 臨時雑役 (extraordinary tax levies paid in labor) derived from the old zōyō 雑徭 corvée. The taxable farmland was divided into tax collection units called **myō** 名, with each myō being named for its **fumyō** 負名, the person obliged to collect and forward its taxes. The fundamental principle of the Ritsuryō system centered on taxation based on adult males listed on the family registry thus disintegrated, and in its place a system of taxation based on land with collection from fumyō by zuryō was established.

Previously, it had been the district chieftains who were responsible for duties such as collecting and transporting taxes and documentation, but now the zuryō exercised strong leadership over not only chieftains but also his own subordinates to achieve collection of taxes, thereby securing his own income as well as supporting state finances[24]. On the other hand, those provincial governors who were not zuryō came to be excluded from taking actual responsibilities, and instead it became common for them to receive income without relocating to their assigned province (a practice called **yōnin** 遙任, meaning absentee appointment).

Some zuryō were greedy and tried to reap great profits[25], which occasionally led to their being sued for tyranny by district chieftains and influential farmers. An example of one such suit, against Fujiwara no Motonaga 藤原元命 (dates unknown), is the **Owari no Kuni Gunji Hyakushōra Ge** 「尾張国郡司百姓等解」 (Petition by District Chieftains and Farmers of Owari Province) of 988.

At the time, the purchase of positions was common. Such practices included **jōgō** 成功, in which nobles provided funds out of their personal assets to finance courtly

---

[23] Some tato extended their influence by cooperating with provincial governors and engaging in large-scale farming, in some cases becoming wealthy enough to be called daimyō tato〈大名田堵〉(great landowner).

[24] The offices where zuryō worked (kokuga〈国衙〉) and their residences (tachi〈館〉) increased in importance, whereas the role played by the district office, which had been directly managing local administration, dwindled in contrast.

[25] The avarice of zuryō is illustrated by an episode in the *Konjaku Monogatari-shū*〈『今昔物語集』〉(Collection of Tales from Times Past), an anthology of folk and didactic short narratives. The story goes that Fujiwara no Nobutada〈藤原陳忠〉, governor of Shinano Province〈信濃守〉, fell down a ravine, but he climbed up with a basket-full of oyster mushrooms that were growing along the slope, saying "One should never return empty-handed; a zuryō must grab even the dirt where he falls."

rituals or the construction of temples or shrines in exchange for an office, and **chōnin** 重任, in which reappointment to a lucrative position was assured in the same manner. In this way, the post of zuryō became a sort of concession and was often appointed by means of jōgō or chōnin.

Eventually, in the second half of the 11th century, zuryō too often chose not to relocate to their assigned provinces except on the occasion of succession, and instead sent down a **mokudai** 目代 (deputy provincial governor) to the rusudokoro 留守所[26]. The mokudai would then supervise the **zaichō kanjin** 在庁官人 (resident local officials), the appointment of which was a hereditary prerogative of the elites in that province.

The Development of Estates

In the late 10th century, some people among the influential farmers and the offspring of provincial governors who had settled down in provinces were exempted from taxes such as the labor duty, and in turn developed land. These people came to be called **kaihatsu ryōshu** 開発領主 (land-opening proprietors)[iii] in the 11th century.

Some kaihatsu ryōshu donated their land to powerholders in the capital in order to avoid interference from the provincial headquarters. The land was then turned into an estate (shōen 荘園) belonging to the powerholder, with the former kaihatsu ryōshu now a **shōkan** 荘官, or estate manager (formally called geshi 下司, whereas azukaridokoro 預所 referred to a custodian sent by the powerholder). The powerholder who had received the land was called a **ryōke** 領家, and if they in turn donated the estate to a higher-ranking noble or powerful royal, this superior proprietor was called a **honke** 本家[27]. Estates developed in this way are known as **kishinchikei shōen** 寄進地系荘園 (donated shōen).

Over time, against a backdrop of the wealth of nobles or powerful temples and shrines, the number of estates exempt from taxation (**fuyu** 不輸) by the government increased. Later on, there were even estates permitted tax exemptions by a zuryō for the duration of their term of office[28]. Eventually, as the development of shōen progressed, conflicts between the proprietors and the provincial headquarters concerning the scope and objects of tax exemption intensified. There were many cases where estate man-

---

[26] When a governor was absent, their provincial headquarters was called a rusudokoro.

[27] Whichever of the ryōke or honke exercised actual control was called the honjo〈本所〉. In the Kinai region〈畿内〉 and its surrounding areas, powerful temples and shrines owned many small estates that they had collected from farmers.

[28] Estates that were exempted from taxes (by a written document issued by the government, such as a directive issued by the Daijōkan or the Ministry of Popular Affairs) were called **kanshōfu-shō**〈官省符荘〉, and estates exempted from taxes by the permission of the provincial governor were called **kokumen-shō**〈国免荘〉.

agers were able to block on-site inspection (**fu’nyū** 不入) by regional inspectors (such as kendenshi 検田使[29]) by taking advantage of the clout of their proprietors. As a result, in the second half of the 11th century, the tax revenue that zuryō transferred to the central government decreased. With the destabilization of their income (such as fuko 封戸) stipulated by the Ritsuryō system, the royal family, Sekkanke, and major temples and shrines actively sought donations of estates in order to compensate.

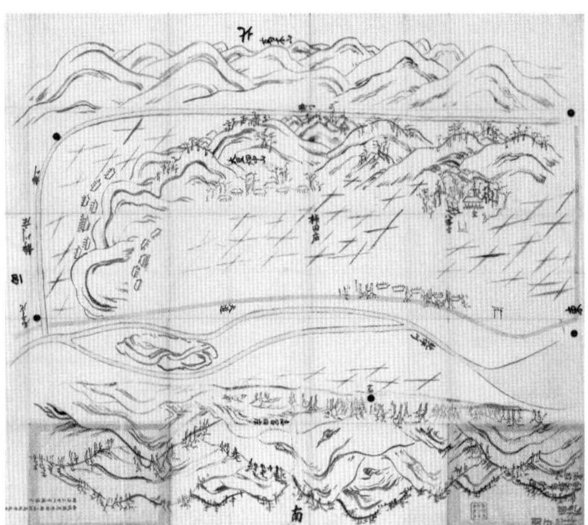

ILLUSTRATION OF AN ESTATE
This depicts Kaseda Estate〈桛田荘〉 in Kii Province〈紀伊国〉, which belonged to Jingoji Temple〈神護寺〉. It is a valuable historical source for studying village life on an estate. A Hachiman shrine〈八幡宮〉 was located at the northeast end of the estate, and dwellings of villagers faced the main street running along the Kinokawa River〈紀伊川（紀ノ川）〉 or the foot of the mountain. The boundary of the estate's territory is indicated by the four corners and the southern spot on the river. This estate was developed at the beginning of the 9th century, and donated to Jingoji Temple around the end of the 12th century.

Local Insurrections and the Rise of Warriors

Local politics experienced drastic structural change from the late 9th to 10th centuries, during which the offspring of governors in the provinces and local elites began to arm themselves in order to maintain or increase their power, resulting in armed conflicts in various regions. To quell such conflicts, the government appointed mid- or lower-ranking nobles as ōryōshi 押領使 (envoys appointed to pacify a region) or tsuibushi 追捕使[30] (envoys appointed to pursue and capture a criminal). Some of these people chose to remain in the assigned provinces as resident local officials, a number of which became influential **bushi** 武士[iv] (**tsuwamono** 兵, or warriors)[31].

These warriors, as leaders of their followers such as ienoko 家子 (relatives) and rōtō 郎党（郎等） (armed retainers), engaged in military clashes with each other, and at times even rebelled against the governors.

---

[29] A kendenshi was an official responsible for investigating crop conditions in a province to assess the amount of taxes and labor duty.

[30] Both ōryōshi and tsuibushi were dispatched to capture bandits and subdue insurgency in provinces. They were originally temporary positions, but later became permanently stationed in their assigned posts.

[31] The term “bushi” initially referred to a military officer serving the court in the capacity of military arts.

Gradually, these warriors came to form confederacies, and especially in remote areas large **bushidan** 武士団 (warrior bands) started to emerge, mainly centered on the offspring of governors who had remained in provinces after their terms of office. In particular, in eastern Japan (in the present-day Kantō 関東地方 region), which bred quality horses, bushidan that excelled in mobility grew rapidly.

Taira no Masakado 平将門 (?-940), a member of the **Kanmu Heishi** 桓武平氏 (descendants of Kanmu Tennō; also called the Taira 平 or the Heike 平家) that had earlier settled in eastern Japan, was based in the Shimousa 下総国 region. Over the course of repeated conflicts with his relatives he ended up confronting the provincial governor as well, eventually rising in revolt in 939 (**Taira no Masakado Insurrection** 平将門の乱). Masakado captured the provincial headquarters of Hitachi 常陸国, Shimotsuke 下野国, and Kōzuke 上野国 Provinces, and occupied most of eastern Japan, proclaiming himself a new sovereign. However, ultimately he was defeated by other bushi from the region, especially Taira no Sadamori 平貞盛 (dates unknown) and Fujiwara no Hidesato 藤原秀郷 (dates unknown).

Almost simultaneously, the former governor of Iyo 伊予国 Province, **Fujiwara no Sumitomo** 藤原純友 (?-941), also revolted with pirates in the Seto Inland Sea 瀬戸内海 (**Fujiwara no Sumitomo Insurrection** 藤原純友の乱), and captured the provincial headquarters of Iyo as well as the Dazaifu. However, he too was defeated, by Minamoto no Tsunemoto 源経基 (?-961), the founder of the **Seiwa Genji** 清和源氏 (descendants of Seiwa Tennō; also called the Minamoto 源). Thus, these insurrections in eastern and western Japan (together called the Tengyō Insurrections 天慶の乱) were put down, but they exposed the decreased military capability of

STRUCTURE OF A WARRIOR FAMILY

A warrior household was formed around a shujin〈主人〉(master), who was followed by ienoko, each of whom employed rōtō and genin〈下人〉/shojū〈所従〉(rōtō subordinates) as followers.

A WARRIOR GUARDING A GATE (*KOKAWADERA ENGI EMAKI*〈『粉河寺縁起絵巻』〉[ILLUSTRATED SCROLL OF THE LEGEND OF KOKAWADERA TEMPLE], PART)

This image shows the residence of a local elite in Kawachi Province〈河内国〉, and a warrior standing guard at the gate with a bow and arrows.

the court, and resulted in a further strengthening of provincial bushi organization.

The court and nobility, recognizing the power of the warriors, took them into their service as **samurai**. They were assigned duties such as serving as bodyguards for nobles and policing the capital, or guarding the palace like the **Takiguchi no Musha** that had been established in the late 9th century. In particular, Minamoto no Mitsunaka (912?-997) from the Seiwa Genji, who had settled in Settsu Province, and his sons Yorimitsu (948-1021) and Yorinobu (968-1048), were patronized by the Sekkanke as a reward for their service, which enhanced their prestige and influence. In the provinces, it became common for warriors to be organized under the governors as tachizamurai or kunizamurai[32], or appointed as ōryōshi or tsuibushi, and share the responsibility for maintaining security.

The Rise of the Minamoto

At the turn of the 11th century, in order to expand and protect their private landholdings, the kaihatsu ryōshu extended their influence through becoming zaichō kanjin or retainers of nobles settling in the provinces, and then local bushidan[33]. Eventually, they began to look up to the Seiwa Genji or Kanmu Heishi, who were of noble descent, as **tōryō** (leaders). Consequently, both of these families organized various local warrior bands, and grew into powerful **buke** (warrior families).

In 1028, Taira no Tadatsune (967-1031) led an uprising (**Taira no Tadatsune Insurrection**) that spread from Kazusa to the entire Bōsō peninsula, before it was subdued by Minamoto no Yorinobu. This feat enabled the Genji to establish themselves in eastern Japan.

In the northern region of Mutsu Province, the Abe family, who were local elites, wielded considerable influence and were clashing with the provincial governor. Yorinobu's son, Minamoto no Yoriyoshi (988-1075), set out for Mutsu as the newly-appointed governor, and with his son Yoshiie (1039-1106) led the warriors of eastern Japan against the Abe forces. With the aid of the Kiyohara family, local elites from Dewa Province, they vanquished the Abe forces (**Former Nine Years' War**, 1051-1062). Later, when an internal conflict arose within the Kiyohara family,

---

[32] Tachizamurai were those warriors directly subordinate to the zuryō, and consisted of ienoko and rōtō, whereas kunizamurai were local warriors organized to serve as the military forces of a provincial headquarters.

[33] When the Toi (Jurchen) pirates invaded northern Kyūshū in 1019, the warriors in Kyūshū, under the leadership of Fujiwara no Takaie〈藤原隆家〉, the Dazai no Gon no Sochi (provisional governor of the Dazaifu), drove them away. This indicates that by then bushidan had already come to be formed in contemporary Kyūshū as well.

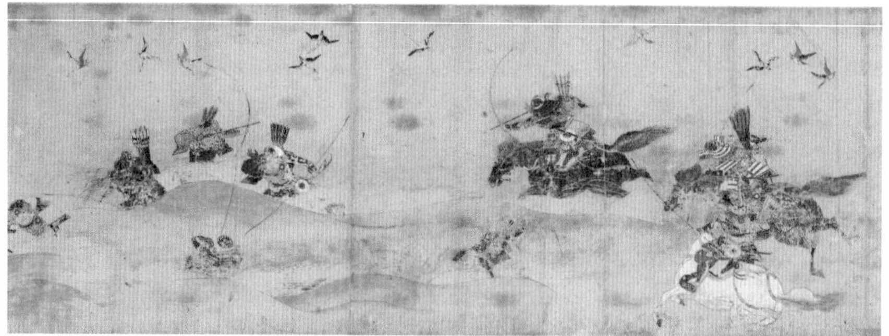

LATER THREE YEARS' WAR (*GOSANNEN KASSEN EMAKI*〈「後三年合戦絵巻」〉 [ILLUSTRATED SCROLL OF THE LATER THREE YEARS' WAR], PART)
This image depicts Yoshiie's forces attacking the enemy in an ambush upon noticing a disturbance in the formation of flying geese at the Kanezawa Fort〈金沢柵〉 (in present-day Akita Prefecture).

which had become a major powerholder in the Mutsu and Dewa Provinces, Yoshiie, now the governor of Mutsu, intervened and suppressed the conflict by supporting Fujiwara (Kiyohara) no Kiyohira 藤原（清原）清衡 (1056-1128) to contain the infighting (**Later Three Years' War** 後三年合戦, 1083-87). After this, the offspring of Kiyohira (the Ōshu Fujiwara family 奥州藤原氏), based in Hiraizumi 平泉 in Mutsu Province, maintained their power to rule the Ōu 奥羽 region, while the Minamoto family took advantage of these wars to strengthen their ties with warrior bands in eastern Japan and solidify their position as leaders of the warrior families.

Translators' Notes

[i] The post of "sesshō" (摂政) was developed first to mean a person who assisted a tennō, acting in their stead if they were too young or sick to rule, and "kanpaku" (関白) later to mean the same role but for an adult ruler. In English, however, both are usually rendered "regent" without any clear distinction. To avoid confusion, rather than conflating the terms under one English heading, in this text "sesshō" and "kanpaku" were retained.

[ii] Writers may frequently translate "国風" as "national," but the latter is a distinctly modern concept that sounds strange and unsuitable for discussing the ancient past. "Native culture" is more suitable but could be misconstrued, whereas "native Japanese culture" avoids this problem and makes the meaning clear for English speakers.

[iii] This term referred to people who cleared new land for development and were rewarded with the right to own it, making "land-opening proprietor" an appropriate translation.

[iv] "Bushi" (武士) began as an inclusive term for warriors but at the end of the Sengoku era began to refer to a distinct social class. Because the meaning and usage of the term changed over time, this text prefers "warrior" for the premodern era, and "bushi" for the late Momoyama and Edo periods (when bushi became not only a social class but also primarily government bureaucrats rather than fighters). "Samurai," which in the mid-classical era referred to warriors recruited to serve as guards for people or places, tends to be used today either as a synonym for "bushi" and/or as an umbrella term for Japanese warriors, but historically these usages are not accurate.

part II

The Medieval Era

Chapter

4

The Establishment of Medieval Society

1 The Emergence of Insei and the Taira Family

Reform of the Estate System

When the daughter of regent Fujiwara no Yorimichi 藤原頼通 failed to produce an heir, a sovereign without any maternal relationship to a sesshō 摂政 or kanpaku 関白 ascended the throne. This was **Go-Sanjō** 後三条天皇 (r. 1068-72), a tennō whose strong individuality led him to appoint erudite scholars such as Ōe no Masafusa 大江匡房 (1041-1111) and actively engage in political reforms[1].

In particular, the tennō was concerned that the increase in estates was putting pressure on public land (**kōryō** 公領/**kokugaryō** 国衙領, meaning land under a provincial governor's control), and issued the **Enkyū no Shōen Seiri-rei** 延久の荘園整理令 (Enkyū-era decree to regulate the estate system) in 1069[2]. The **Kiroku Shōen Kenkeijo** 記録荘園券契所 (or Kirokusho 記録所; office for the investigation of estate documents) was established, and screened evidence documents (kenkei 券契) submitted by estate proprietors and reports from provincial governors. Any estates that did not meet the standards, such as those with recent registration dates or which lacked sufficient paperwork, were banned. The Sekkanke 摂関家 were not exempt from this policy, which produced substantial results[3].

Due to this estate reform, the estates held by nobles, or by temples and shrines, became clearly separated from those held by provincial governors as public land.

---

[1] When Go-Sanjō Tennō issued the Shōen Seiri-rei he also set a standard size for masu〈枡〉(a measure of volume). This size of masu was called **senjimasu**〈宣旨枡〉(official masu) and was used until the Taikō Kenchi〈太閤検地〉(cadastral survey by Toyotomi Hideyoshi〈豊臣秀吉〉). However, various types of masu were used on estates.

[2] The first Shōen Seiri-rei was issued in 902 by Daigo Tennō〈醍醐天皇〉. Similar edicts were issued several times, such as the one in 1045 that cancelled newly-issued estates. However, the implementation of these decrees depended on the provincial governors, which prevented the system from being fully implemented.

[3] Among the estates owned by Iwashimizu Hachimangū Shrine〈石清水八幡宮〉, only 21 out of 34 were approved, with the remaining 13 being banned.

This prompted nobles and religious institutions to reorganize the estates they held. Meanwhile, to respond to local elites and land-opening proprietors who were gaining power over public land, governors reorganized the territory in their provinces into new units such as **gun** 郡 (district), **gō** 郷 (township), and **ho** 保 (hamlet). They then appointed the elites and proprietors to oversee these and collect taxes, as gunji 郡司, gōji 郷司, and hōji 保司, respectively. Moreover, provincial headquarters were outfitted with new administrative organs, such as tadokoro 田所 (land management offices) and saisho 税所 (tax offices), managed by resident local officials under the supervision of governor's deputies.

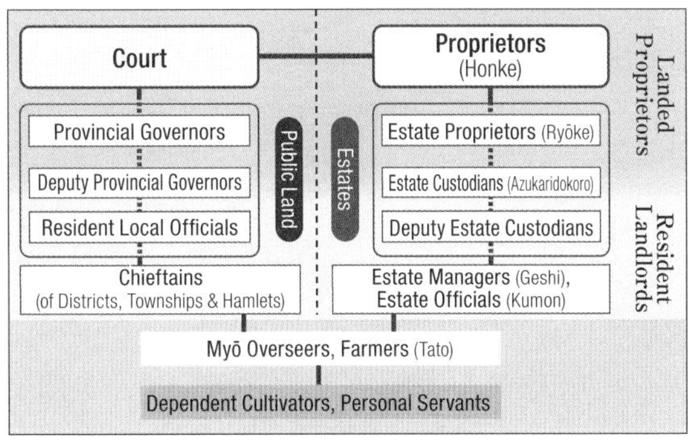

THE STRUCTURE OF SHŌEN KORYŌSEI

Since the local officials and district chieftains managed public land as if it were their own estates, or donated it to estate proprietors, the older provincial organization system (province, district and locality) based on the hierarchical Ritsuryō 律令制度 system transformed into a new system, **Shōen Kōryōsei** 荘園公領制 (public land and private estate system), in which public land and private estates of various types co-existed in a more horizontal fashion.

Under this newly-structured estate and public land system, most of the cultivated land became myō 名 (unit for tax assessment and collection), and was allocated to influential farmers such as tato 田堵. These farmers, however, gradually expanded their rights as contractors of myō, and came to be called myōshu 名主 (myō overseers). These myōshu had part of their land cultivated by their subordinates like genin 下人 (dependent cultivators), and part of it cultivated by farmers called sakunin 作人 (tenant cultivators). Moreover, the myōshu paid **nengu** 年貢 **(annual rent), kuji** 公事 **(tax owed to government)**, and **buyaku** 夫役 **(labor service)**[4] to the proprietors, and played a pivotal role among the farmers.

The Beginnings of Insei

Shirakawa Tennō 白河天皇 (r. 1072-86) followed in the footsteps of his father Go-Sanjō and

[4] In addition to the annual land tax paid mainly with rice and silk, myōshu were also responsible for paying taxes with craft products or local specialties such as yarn, charcoal, and vegetables, as well as service rendered in labor. This evolved from the kanmotsu〈官物〉 and rinjizōyaku〈臨時雑役〉 imposed on the tato contracted by the provincial governors to manage the myō.

HOSSHŌJI TEMPLE (RESTORED MODEL)
Hosshōji Temple symbolized the power of the retired sovereign, and was rebuilt every time it burnt down. However, it was not restored after it burnt down in the Nanbokuchō era〈南北朝時代〉.

conducted direct royal rule, but in 1086 he abdicated the throne, which then passed to young Horikawa Tennō 堀河天皇 (r. 1086-1107). Shirakawa then, as the jōkō 上皇 or **in** 院 (retired sovereign)[5], established the In no Chō 院庁 (office of the retired sovereign), and while protecting the sovereign held onto real political power through **Insei** 院政 (government by a retired sovereign).

Retired Sovereign Shirakawa (in 1086-1129) won over the provincial governors, who supported his enforcement of estate reform. He held control over personnel affairs, and strengthened his position by organizing the **Hokumen no Bushi** 北面の武士 (retired sovereign's guards) at his palace, and having among his intimates warriors from both the Minamoto (Genji 源氏) and Taira (Heike 平家) families. Eventually, after the death of Horikawa, Shirakawa launched a full-scale Insei system. Under this framework, edicts issued by the In no Chō called **In no Chō Kudashibumi** 院庁下文 and orders from the retired sovereign called **inzen** 院宣 gradually came to affect overall government of the state.

Initially, Insei began as a way to keep royal succession limited to the monarch's direct descendants. However, it came to exert political power in an autocratic manner irrespective of legal code or social custom. The system endured for more than a century, spanning the reigns of Shirakawa, Toba 鳥羽上皇 (in 1129-56) and Go-Shirakawa 後白河上皇 (in 1158-79, 81-92). Consequently, the Sekkanke strove to make ties with the retired sovereigns in order to regain some degree of power.

The retired sovereigns showed deep respect for Buddhism and took the tonsure, becoming known as **hō-ō** 法皇 (dharma sovereigns). They constructed large temples such as the **Rokushōji** 六勝寺 (six royal temples)[6], built pagodas and statues, and conducted grand Buddhist ceremonies. They occasionally went on the Kumano 熊野詣 and Kōya 高野詣 pilgrimage

---

[5] The term "in" originally referred to the residence of the retired sovereign, and later began to refer to the retired sovereign himself. Nyoin〈女院〉 referred to the consort or daughter of a tennō who received almost the same treatment as a retired sovereign.

[6] Rokushōji referred to six temples with the character "shō〈「勝」〉" (victory) in their names, built by the royal family during the Insei era, such as Hosshōji Temple〈法勝寺〉 built by Shirakawa Tennō and Sonshōji Temple〈尊勝寺〉 built by Horikawa Tennō.

routes in the Kii 紀伊 mountain range. They also built detached palaces on the outskirts of Kyōto in places like Shirakawa 白河 and Toba 鳥羽. In order to fund these palaces, the purchase of ranks and posts through practices such as jōgō 成功 became widespread, leading to the degeneration of administrative organization.

Society during the Insei Era

A retired sovereign was surrounded by a group called **In no Kinshin** 院近臣 (retired sovereign's intimates)[7], consisting of people such as wealthy zuryō and family members of his consorts and nursemaids, whom he provided with estates or profitable provinces. Especially during the time of Retired Sovereign Toba, estates were not only concentrated in the hands of these people, but also increasingly donated to powerful nobles and major temples as well[8]. Estates with fuyu 不輸 and fu'nyū 不入 became common, and the reach of fu'nyū was moreover increased to the extent of keeping out police authorities, resulting in estates becoming more independent.

Around this time, the system of public land also changed. **Chigyōkoku** 知行国 (proprietary provinces held by nobles or religious institutions)[9] and **inbunkoku** 院分国 (provinces that provided income to the retired sovereign himself) spread, resulting in public land becoming more like private holdings of the retired sovereign, or provincial proprietors and governors, that formed the economic base to support Insei.

Major temples also owned many estates, organized lower-ranking monks into **sōhei** 僧兵 (armed monks), and fought against the provincial governors. Through **gōso** 強訴 (forced petition or protest by a religious institution), they carried sacred trees or por-

---

[7] The intimates who served the retired sovereign as inshi〈院司〉(retired sovereign's officials) in the In no Chō initially did not have high positions in the court system. The majority had experience serving as provincial governors in various provinces.

[8] Retired sovereigns gave large amounts of estates to their close female relatives, whom they accorded (as nyoin) the same privileges as retired sovereigns. They also donated many estates to temples. For example, an estate cluster that Retired Sovereign Toba passed to his daughter Hachijōin (Hachijōin cluster〈八条院領〉) consisted of almost 100 estates at the end of the Heian period, and an estate cluster that Retired Sovereign Go-Shirakawa donated to Chōkōdō Temple (Chōkōdō cluster〈長講堂領〉) came to number almost 90 estates by the start of the Kamakura period. By the end of the Kamakura period, these estate clusters were inherited by, respectively, the Daikakuji (junior) and Jimyōin (senior) lines of the royal family, and became their economic foundations.

[9] This system gave high-ranking nobles the right to rule a province as a chigyōkokushu〈知行国主〉and collect profits from that province. The chigyōkokushu appointed their own sons or close relatives as provincial governors, and dispatched mokudai to the provinces to control them. This system was created in order to secure income for those nobles because their stipends had come to exist in name alone.

ARMED MONKS (PART OF A COPY OF *TENGU ZŌSHI EMAKI*〈『天狗草紙』〉)
Most of the armed monks were originally warriors from the local regions. This illustrated scroll depicts armed monks of Kōfukuji Temple, their heads covered with surplices, equipped with armor and long swords.

table shrines to the court and tried to force it to answer their demands[10]. Fearful of the authority of the deities, the court was unable to resist this pressure from the temples, and used warriors as guards and to suppress protests, which increasingly brought warriors into the center of the political sphere.

In the provinces, warriors in each area established their own **tachi** (館) (residence) and strengthened the ties with their own kin and the region. In the Ōu (奥羽) region in particular, when Fujiwara no Kiyohira (藤原清衡) took control of Okurokugun (奥六郡) (present-day Iwate (岩手県) Prefecture) he expanded his control over the whole area by establishing **Hiraizumi** (平泉) in Mutsu Province (陸奥国) as his base. The **Ōshū Fujiwara family** (奥州藤原氏) flourished for over a hundred years through the generations of Kiyohira, Motohira (基衡) (?-1157?), and Hidehira (秀衡) (1122?-87), during which, through the wealth generated from local specialties including gold and horses, they introduced the culture of Kyōto, while nurturing their own culture through trade with the northern regions[11].

During the Insei era, private ownership of land developed, and retired sovereigns, major religious institutions, and warriors all began to form their own authority. In this way, broadly power came to be decentralized, and the tendency to shape society through the direct use of one's own power became predominant. This heralded the dawn of medieval society.

---

[10] The armed monks of Kōfukuji Temple〈興福寺〉were called Nara Hōshi〈奈良法師〉, and made protests by entering Kyōto with a sacred sakaki tree〈榊〉from Kasuga Shrine〈春日神社〉. On the other hand, those from Enryakuji Temple〈延暦寺〉were called Yama Hōshi〈山法師〉, and protested by carrying in the portable shrine from Hiyoshi Shrine〈日吉神社〉. Kōfukuji and Enryakuji were called Nanto and Hokurei〈南都・北嶺〉, respectively. These actions by major temples that had preached protection of the realm exemplified how society in Insei times was characterized by the use of force over law.

[11] After the two wars in Ōshu in the 11th century, the Ōshu Fujiwara family established their base there, and used it as a means to bring northern products to the capital. Backed up by the power of gold, the family flourished around Hiraizumi and established splendid temples like Chūsonji〈中尊寺〉and Mōtsūji〈毛越寺〉. Recent excavations in Hiraizumi have revealed the cultural influence of both Kyōto and the northern regions. It has become evident that widespread cultural exchange had occurred, including across the Sea of Japan, and with Hokkaidō, as well as even further north.

The Hōgen and Heiji Disturbances

As the Genji extended their reach in eastern Japan as leaders of warrior families, the number of warrior bands there that sought protection for their land by donating it to Minamoto no Yoshiie 源義家 increased, prompting the court to quickly prohibit the practice. After Yoshiie, the power of the Genji declined somewhat due to conflicts within the family. Meanwhile, the **Ise Heishi** 伊勢平氏, a branch of the Kanmu Heishi 桓武平氏 named for being based in Ise 伊勢国 and Iga 伊賀国 provinces, came to power through forming ties with the retired sovereign.

Most notable among these was Taira 平正盛 no Masamori (dates unknown), who attacked Minamoto no Yoshichika 源義親 (?-1108), the son of Yoshiie who had been rebelling in Izumo 出雲. Tadamori 忠盛 (1096-1153), Masamori's son, subjugated pirates in the Seto Inland Sea 瀬戸内海 and thereby gained the confidence of Retired Sovereign Toba, becoming a tenjōbito 殿上人 (person with special permission to enter royal presence) and becoming valued as a warrior as well as a royal intimate. **Taira no Kiyomori** 平清盛 (1118-81), Tadamori's son, then further expanded the influence of the family.

In 1156, not long after Toba's death, Sutoku 崇徳上皇 (1119-64), who had struggled with Toba over the succession, united with the minister of the left, Fujiwara no Yorinaga 藤原頼長 (1120-56), who had been fighting with his brother, the regent Tadamichi 藤原忠通 (1097-1164), over regental succession. Together, they gathered warriors like Minamoto no Tameyoshi 源為義 (1096-1156) and Taira no Tadamasa 平忠正 (?-1156). On the other hand, **Go-Shirakawa** 後白河天皇 (r. 1155-58), who had succeeded Toba, mobilized warriors such as Taira no Kiyomori and Minamoto no Yoshitomo 源義朝 (1123-60, a son of Tameyoshi), based on the advice from his intimate **Fujiwara no Michinori** 藤原通憲 (1106-59, also called Shinzei 信西) and Tadamichi. They attacked Sutoku's forces and defeated them, resulting in the exile of Sutoku to Sanuki 讃岐, and the execution of Tameyoshi and many other warriors (**Hōgen Disturbance** 保元の乱).

Subsequently, due to the discord among the intimates of Go-Shirakawa, who began his rule as a retired sovereign in 1159, Fujiwara no Nobuyori 藤原信頼 (1133-59), one of the intimates who despised

Tennō Side	Go-Shirakawa (Younger brother)	Kanpaku Tadamichi (Elder brother)	Kiyomori (Nephew)	Yoshitomo (Child)
	Royal Family	Fujiwara Family	Taira Family	Minamoto Family
Retired Sovereign Side	Sutoku (Elder brother)	Minister of the Left Yorinaga (Younger brother)	Tadamasa (Uncle)	Tameyoshi (Father)

CHART OF RELATIONSHIPS IN HŌGEN DISTURBANCE

Michinori (Shinzei) ↓ [Committed suicide]	Kiyomori	Shigemori	Yorimori
Fujiwara Intimates of Retired Sovereign	Taira Family		
	Minamoto Family		
Nobuyori ↓ [Beheaded]	Yoshitomo ↓ [Murdered]	Yoshihira ↓ [Beheaded]	Yoritomo ↓ [Exiled to Izu]

CHART OF RELATIONSHIPS IN HEIJI DISTURBANCE

Michinori (who was close to Kiyomori), took up arms along with Yoshitomo and pushed Michinori to commit suicide. However, Nobuyori and Yoshitomo were destroyed by Kiyomori's superior forces, and Yoshitomo's child Yoritomo 源頼朝 was exiled to Izu 伊豆 (**Heiji Disturbance** 平治の乱).

Although the number of warriors involved in these two disturbances was rather small, it had become clear that even conflicts within courtier society could be resolved by military force, and thus Kiyomori's position and power as a warrior leader soared.

The Taira Polity

Following the Heiji Disturbance, Kiyomori gained promotion by supporting Go-Shirakawa with his military might, and by rendering services such as constructing Rengeōin 蓮華王院 Temple. This resulted in him assuming the position of supreme minister in 1167. The Taira 平氏 family, including of course Kiyomori's son Shigemori 平重盛 (1138-79), all gained high positions, and no one could compete with their influence.

Behind the onset of the Taira family's golden age was the growth of **bushidan** 武士団 (warrior bands) in each area. Kiyomori appointed some of his family members as **jitō** 地頭 (land overseers) responsible for managing local estates and public lands. He succeeded in turning warriors in western Japan, from the Kinai 畿内 through the Seto Inland Sea to Kyūshū, into his kenin 家人[12].

The economic base of the Taira family consisted of their proprietary provinces, of which at their height they controlled about half of the total amount across the country, their estates, which numbered as many as 500 at their peak, and **trade between Japan and Song China** 日宋貿易, in which the Taira family had invested great effort since Tadamori's time. From the second half of the 11th century, merchant ship traffic between Japan and Goryeo 高麗 or Song China increased. Trade thrived in the 12th century when the Song Dynasty became the **Southern Song** 南宋 (1127-1276) after defeats by the **Jin Dynasty** 金 (1115-1234) of the Jurchens 女真人 from the north. In response to this situation, Kiyomori promoted trade by having **Ōwada no Tomari** 大輪田泊 (present-day Kōbe City 神戸市) in Settsu 摂津 repaired to secure the Seto Inland Sea route, and then bringing Song merchants into the Kinai region[13]. This pro-active foreign policy by Kiyomori resulted in many rare

---

[12] In warrior society, followers were generally referred to as "kenin," but under the Kamakura Bakufu〈幕府〉 they were called gokenin〈御家人〉 (i.e., kenin with the honorific prefix "go〈「御」〉") out of respect for the shōgun〈将軍〉, reflecting the status of warriors.

[13] In the trade between Japan and Song China, Japan exported mainly gold, mercury, sulfur, wood, rice, swords, lacquerware, and fans, while from the continent it imported primarily Song coins, pottery, perfumes, medicines, and books. Among these imports, some, such as perfumes and medicines, were originally from Southeast Asia.

treasures, Song coins, and books being brought to Japan by Song ships, which had a significant influence on Japan both culturally and economically, while the trade profits became an important economic base for the Taira polity.

On the other hand, Kiyomori made his daughter Tokuko 徳子 (1155-1213, Kenreimon-in 建礼門院) the queen consort of Takakura Tennō 高倉天皇 (r. 1168-80), and put their child on the throne as Antoku Tennō 安徳天皇 (r. 1180-85), who he could then dominate as a **gaiseki** 外戚 (**maternal relative**). In this regard the Taira polity strongly resembled regental politics, and despite being run by warriors it had strong aristocratic characteristics. Because the Taira family expanded their control by occupying all the important posts, they were despised by established families who had been deprived of power.

In particular, the conflict between the Taira and Go-Shirakawa's intimates became intensified, leading to an incident in 1177 in which Fujiwara no Narichika 藤原成親 (1138-77) and the monk Shunkan 俊寛 (dates unknown) attempted to overthrow the Taira family at Shishigatani 鹿ケ谷 on the outskirts of Kyōto (**Shishigatani plot** 鹿ケ谷の陰謀). This ended in failure, and in 1179 Kiyomori confined Go-Shirakawa to the Toba Palace 鳥羽殿, took coercive measures such as punishing many nobles below the regent, seizing their posts, and taking control of the state mechanisms, leaving him in charge of the political realm.

The concentration of Kiyomori's power appeared to have reached its peak. However, this monopolization of political authority also prompted the consolidation of the retired sovereign, nobles, religious institutions, and the Minamoto family as an opposition force, which resulted in rapidly bringing about the fall of the Taira family.

The Culture of the Insei Era

The courtier culture at the start of the Insei era took on fresh and rich forms as it began to incorporate the culture of local areas shaped by warriors and commoners.

Retired Sovereign Go-Shirakawa himself studied **imayō** 今様, the popular songs of the commoners, and compiled a collection, ***Ryōjinhishō*** 『梁塵秘抄』 (Songs to Make the Dust Dance), reflecting the deep relationship between nobles and commoner culture at the time. Aside from imayō, other forms of popular vocal or musical practice included saibara 催馬楽, which developed from ancient folk songs, and rōei 朗詠, which were recited Japanese or Chinese poems. Performing arts such as **dengaku** 田楽 ("field music," a type of ritual theatre) and **sarugaku** 猿楽 ("monkey music," a type of comic theatre) were also popular among both commoners and nobles, and were performed at goryōe 御霊会 such as the Gion 祇園祭 Matsuri, as well as in ceremonies in the great temples.

Further, there was the ***Konjaku Monogatarishū*** 『今昔物語集』 (Tales of Times Now Past), a collection of some 1,000 tales from India, China, and Japan, which clearly depicted the lifestyles and activities of warriors and commoners. Starting with the *Shōmonki* 『将門記』,

MŌTSUJI TEMPLE GARDEN REMAINS (LEFT) **AND RESTORED MODEL** (RIGHT)
Established during the time of Motohira, the second head of the Ōshu Fujiwara family, and completed during the time of Hidehira, the third head. The buildings burned down in the medieval era but the remains of the Pure Land Garden were maintained in good condition.

THE GREAT HALL OF FUKIJI TEMPLE
The oldest Amida hall architecture in Kyūshū located on the Kunisaki peninsula〈国東半島〉 in Ōita Prefecture〈大分県〉, demonstrating a typical example of the spread of Pure Land Buddhism to local regions. The inside of the hall displays a "welcoming approach" image and a seated statue of Amida〈阿弥陀如来〉 in the Jōchō style〈定朝様〉.

which portrayed Taira no Masakado's insurrection 将門の乱, early gunki monogatari 軍記物語 (military tales) also came to be written, such as *Mutsuwaki* 『陸奥話記』, which portrayed the Former Nine Years' War 前九年合戦. Such works reveal the extent to which nobles of the time were interested in the happenings in local areas as well as warriors and commoners.

On top of the fictional tales from the previous era, impressive historical tales such as *Ōkagami* 『大鏡』 (The Great Mirror) and *Imakagami* 『今鏡』 (The New Mirror) were written in Japanese styles, and demonstrate how nobles in a time of transition were looking back on past history.

Nobles, warriors and commoners were linked together by religious preachers, called **hijiri** 聖 or **shōnin** 上人, who helped spread the philosophy of Pure Land Buddhism 浄土教 throughout the country. Masterpieces of architecture related to Pure Land Buddhism, such as Amida halls 阿弥陀堂, and created by local elites still remain in various places in Japan. These include the **Golden Hall of Chūsonji Temple** 中尊寺金色堂 in Hiraizumi built by the Ōshū Fujiwara family, the Shiramizu Amida Hall 白水阿弥陀堂 in Mutsu, and the Great Hall of Fukiji 富貴寺大堂 Temple in Bungo 豊後, Kyūshu. Moreover, the Itsukushima Shrine 厳島神社 in Aki 安芸, where the Taira family worshipped, retains the splendid *Heike Nōkyō* 『平家納経』 (sutras dedicated by the Taira)

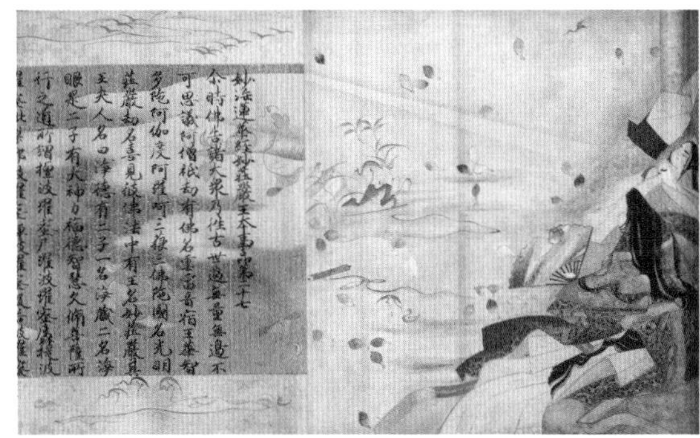

ITSUKUSHIMA SHRINE *HEIKE NŌKYŌ* (COPY)
Taira no Kiyomori made the deity of Itsukushima Shrine the patron deity of the Taira family. He dedicated copies of Buddhist sutras, such as the Lotus Sutra, in prayer for the prosperity of the family.

SHIGISAN ENGI EMAKI
(THE FLYING GRANARY, PART)
Dated from the 12th century, it depicts stories of a monk called Myōren〈命蓮〉whose rice bowl flew away and carried the rice storehouse of a chōja〈長者〉(powerful local elite) all the way to Mt. Shigi. It dynamically portrays the lives and customs of commoners.

SENMEN KOSHAKYŌ
The customs of those days were depicted in Yamato-e style on a fan along with the text of a sutra. The drawing depicts a Jūrasetsunyo〈十羅刹女〉(woman guardian of the Lotus Sutra) on the right protecting a man reciting the sutra.

indicating the prosperity and aristocratic character of the family.

During this period, illustrated scrolls expressing the progress of time through pictures and narrative developed through the techniques of Yamato-e 大和絵. *Genji Monogatari Emaki* 『源氏物語絵巻』 (Illustrated Scroll of the *Tale of Genji*) was made at noble request, while some illustrated scrolls depicted life in Kyōto under Insei, such as *Ban Dainagon Emaki* 『伴大納言絵巻』 (Illustrated Scroll of Senior Counselor Tomo), which portrayed the Ōtenmon Incident 応天門の変, and *Nenjūgyōji Emaki* 『年中行事絵巻』 (Illustrated Scroll of Annual Events) which covered the annual events of the court. *Shigisan Engi Emaki* 『信貴山縁起絵巻』 (Illustrated Scroll of the Legends of Mt. Shigi 信貴山) skillfully portrayed the way of life of hijiri, along with landscapes and people, while *Chōjū Giga* (Caricatures of Animals and Humans) vividly depicted personified animals. Looking at these illustrated scrolls or the pictures on the bottom of *Senmen Koshakyō* 『扇面古写経』 (ancient sutra manuscripts on a fan) can illuminate the lives and society of commoners in the local areas.

2 The Establishment of the Kamakura Bakufu

The Genpei War

In 1180, Taira no Kiyomori confined Retired Sovereign Go-Shirakawa and put his own grandson, Antoku, on the throne, which triggered dissent towards the autocratic rule of the Taira from local warrior bands as well as the nobles and major temples in the capital region.

Observing this situation, Prince Mochihito 以仁王 (1151-80), a son of Go-Shirakawa, together with Minamoto no Yorimasa 源頼政 (1104-80) who was based in the Kinai region, raised an army to defeat the Taira. The prince's edict 令旨 calling for troops was relayed to warriors in various provinces.

In response to this development, the armed monks of temples like Onjōji 園城寺 (Miidera) and Kōfukuji rose up, followed by warrior bands in multiple areas, beginning with **Minamoto no Yoritomo** 源頼朝 (1147-99), who had been exiled to Izu, and Minamoto no Yoshinaka 源義仲 (1154-84), who was in Kisodani 木曽谷, Shinano 信濃国. The civil war soon spread across the whole country, and continued for over five years (**Jishō-Juei War** 治承・寿永の乱).

The Taira family initially moved the capital to **Fukuhara-kyō** 福原京 (present-day Kōbe). Fukuhara had the fine harbor of Ōwada no Tomari nearby and served as the Taira base for controlling the Seto Inland Sea, but the nobles and major temples opposed the transfer, and the capital was moved back to Kyōto after only half a year. The Taira sought to address these developments by consolidating their power in the Kinai region. However, the family's foundation was weakened by several unfortunate events, including Kiyomori's sudden death and a famine that struck the Kinai and western provinces. In 1183, they were defeated by Yoshinaka in the Hokuriku 北陸 region, prompting them to escape to the western provinces with Antoku Tennō. Minamoto no Yoritomo, who made ties with the retired sovereign, dispatched his brothers Noriyori 源範頼 (dates unknown) and Yoshitsune 源義経 (1159-89) to defeat Yoshinaka. He then fought against the Taira family in the Battle of Ichi no Tani 一の谷の合戦, in Settsu Province, and the Battle of Yashima 屋島の合戦, in Sanuki, before finally defeating them in 1185 at the Battle of Dan no Ura 壇の浦の戦い in Nagato 長門国.

The local warrior bands had played a major role in this series of battles, seeking to establish a new political system that would strengthen and expand their control over territory in opposition to provincial governors or estate proprietors.

The Kamakura Bakufu

Within the forces that opposed the Taira family, the warrior bands of the eastern provinces rallied around Yoritomo, who was a leader of warrior families as well as the direct heir of the Minamoto family, and grew into a powerful force. As he raised his forces, Yoritomo, endeavoring to implement vassalage relations on a wide scale, established a base in **Kamakura** 鎌倉 (in Sagami 相模), and, through taking control of estates and public land, guaranteed the rights of retainers to manage their territories.

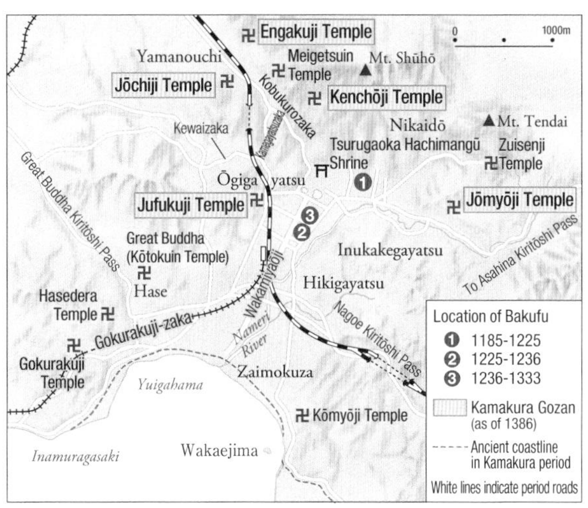

OVERVIEW OF KAMAKURA
Since the time of Minamoto no Yoriyoshi〈源頼義〉, Kamakura was a Minamoto stronghold, surrounded by small hills on three sides, and overlooking the sea to the south. The bakufu was established here by Yoritomo.

In 1183, when the Taira fled the capital, Yoritomo negotiated with Go-Shirakawa in Kyōto and gained his approval for territorial rights in both the Tōkaidō 東海道 and Tōsandō 東山道 regions of the eastern provinces[14] (royal decree of the tenth month of 1183 寿永二年十月宣旨).

In 1185, after the defeat of the Taira family, Go-Shirakawa, fearful of Yoritomo becoming too powerful, ordered Yoshitsune to subdue him. Yoritomo sent his forces to Kyōto to pressure Go-Shirakawa, gaining thereby the right to: 1) appoint **shugo** 守護 (military governors) for provinces[15]; 2) appoint jitō for estates and public lands, and collect five shō 升 (approximately 9 kg) of rice provisions from each tan 段 of land; and 3) control the resident local officials with actual power in the headquarters of various provinces. In this way, Yoritomo's regime expanded its control from the east into the west as well, and established the **Kamakura Bakufu** 鎌倉幕府 as a warrior government.

Afterwards, Yoritomo destroyed the Ōshū Fujiwara family for sheltering the fugitive Yoshitsune[16]. Then, in 1190, he realized his ambition to proceed to the

---

[14] The extent of the eastern provinces over which the bakufu could exert significant control eventually came to be considered the 15 provinces eastward of Tōtoumi〈遠江〉 and Shinano.

[15] Shugo were originally known as sōtsuibushi〈惣追捕使〉 (provincial constables) or kuni jitō〈国地頭〉 (jitō appointed to each province), but were later standardized as shugo.

[16] After the death of Fujiwara no Hidehira, his son Yasuhira〈藤原泰衡〉 gave into Yoritomo's request and killed Yoshitsune. However, in 1189, Yoritomo proceeded with his army to Ōshu to subjugate Yasuhira for sheltering Yoshitsune, and was able to put the provinces of Mutsu and Dewa〈出羽〉 under his control.

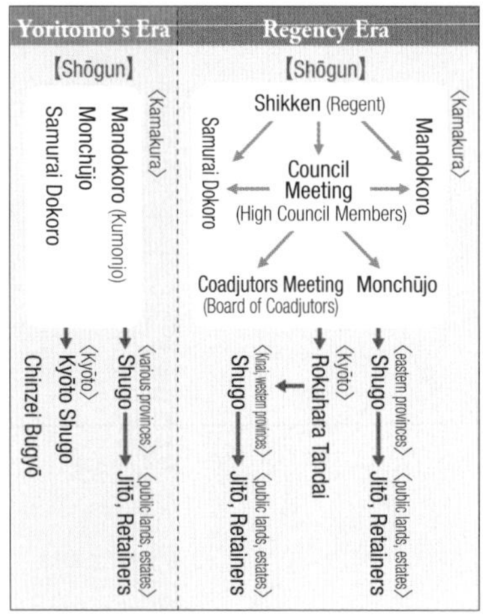

ORGANIZATIONAL STRUCTURE OF KAMAKURA BAKUFU

capital and assume the position of Ukonoe Taishō 右近衛大将 (senior captain of the inner palace guards of the right), and after the death of Go-Shirakawa in 1192, he was appointed **Seii Taishōgun** 征夷大将軍[17]. The period from the establishment of the Kamakura Bakufu to its collapse is called the **Kamakura period** 鎌倉時代.

The governing structure of the bakufu was simple and practical. The central administration was set up in Kamakura, and consisted of the **Samurai Dokoro** 侍所 (Board of Retainers), which managed retainers, the **Mandokoro** 政所 (Board of Administration, originally called Kumonjo 公文所), which handled government affairs and finance, and the **Monchūjo** 問注所 (Board of Inquiry), which was responsible for judicial matters. Low-ranking nobles were invited from Kyōto to support Shōgun Yoritomo as his main close advisors[18].

Shugo and jitō were installed in the local regions. In principle, one shugo was appointed per province, mainly from among the powerful retainers from eastern provinces. They were responsible for matters such as **daibon sankajō** 大犯三カ条 (three regulations for great crimes)[19], organizing retainers within the province, maintaining social order and carrying out police duties during peacetime, and leading the province's warriors

[17] The term "bakufu" was originally a Chinese word referring to the curtain tent put up on the front lines during a military campaign in which a general made decisions. In Japan, the term was used as a Chinese-style means of referring to the Ukonoe Taishō or the Seii Taishōgun, but evolved to mean the government established by a warrior leader. As for Seii Taishōgun, this originally referred to a temporary commander appointed to subdue the Emishi〈蝦夷〉. However, after the appointment of Yoritomo, the meaning changed to mean the post of government official who led the warriors.

[18] Wada Yoshimori〈和田義盛〉, a retainer from the eastern provinces, was appointed chief of the Samurai Dokoro, while the Mandokoro was headed by Ōe no Hiromoto〈大江広元〉, and the Monchūjo by Miyoshi no Yasunobu〈三善康信〉, who were both of noble background.

[19] Daibon sankajō represented the most important duties of a shugo in peacetime, namely recruiting retainers as Kyōto Ōbanyaku (guards for the palaces of the sovereign and retired sovereign in the capital), and apprehending rebels and murderers. The Kyōto shugo was considered important from the perspective of the bakufu's relationship with the court, and later evolved into the Rokuhara Tandai〈六波羅探題〉 responsible for managing retainers in the western provinces. In Kyūshū, meanwhile, the Chinzei Bugyō〈鎮西奉行〉 (Commissioner for Kyūshū) was appointed to manage the retainers in this region and take on the power of the Dazaifu〈大宰府〉 to carry out administration.

during times of war. They also governed the resident local officials, and, particularly in the eastern provinces, took over the administrative matters that used to be handled by the provincial headquarters, playing the role of regional administrators.

Jitō were appointed from among retainers, and were responsible for collecting and delivering taxes, managing land, and maintaining peace and order[20]. Most of the estate managers, including former geshi (下司), became jitō newly appointed by Yoritomo. The rights of retainers were widely guaranteed, but jitō were appointed mainly in territories where lands had been confiscated from rebels, particularly the Taira family.

The Bakufu and the Court

The vassalage relations between **shōgun** (将軍) and **retainers** (gokenin) (御家人) formed the foundation of the bakufu regime. As the lord, Yoritomo appointed retainers as jitō, guaranteeing their control over land they had inherited (**honryōando**) (本領安堵), and/or granting them new territories (**shin'on kyūyo**) (新恩給与). This was called **go'on** (御恩) (rewards), to which retainers reciprocated by providing **hōkō** (奉公) (service) as followers. Their duties included providing military service in times of war, and serving in peacetime as Kyōto Ōbanyaku (京都大番役) in the capital or as guards (鎌倉番役) protecting the shōgunal residence in Kamakura.

In this way, the warrior bands, which had been expanding their power in various regions as land-opening proprietors since the Insei era, and especially those in the eastern provinces comprised of retainers under the bakufu, were appointed as jitō and had their control over territory guaranteed by the shōgun[21]. The eastern provinces were substantially under the control of the bakufu, which held the administrative and judicial authority. In other regions, the responsibilities of the provincial headquarters, carried out under the provincial governors, were absorbed by the bakufu through the shugo[22].

The system of vassalage, in which, through the provision of land, lord and vas-

---

[20] Jitō were to some extent appointed under the Taira polity as well, but their salary depended on the customs in each area and was not fixed. Thus, by Yoritomo making their responsibilities clear, he also deprived provincial governors or estate proprietors of the ability to appoint or dismiss officials, and instead put this right in the hands of the bakufu.

[21] Most of the retainers from the western provinces were not appointed as jitō. Instead, they registered as retainers through the shugo, and served guard duty in the capital, while receiving protection from the bakufu.

[22] **Ōtabumi**〈大田文〉 were land survey documents that recorded the area of fields in a piece of land within a province, as well as the names of the proprietor and jitō. They were originally prepared by a provincial headquarters. The fact that the bakufu ordered resident local officials in various provinces to draw up ōtabumi showed that the bakufu had come to control those provincial headquarters.

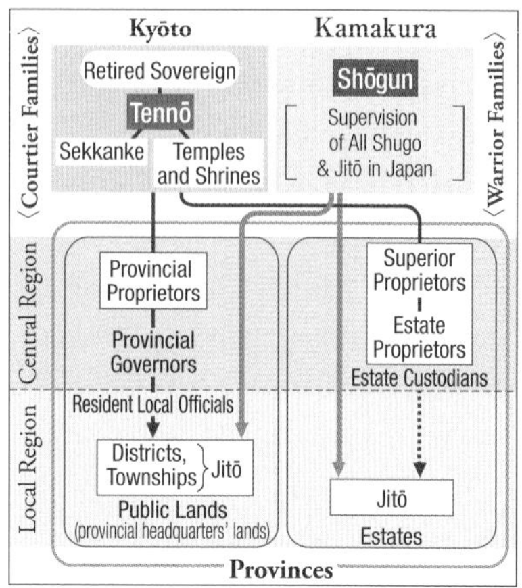

ORGANIZATIONAL STRUCTURE OF DUAL POLITY CONTROL BY COURT AND BAKUFU

sals were connected by rewards and service, has been called **feudalism** 封建制度. The Kamakura Bakufu was the first polity established based on this system, and, through the installation of shugo and jitō, this Japanese form of feudalism was for the first time established as a state system[23].

However, in this period the power of the estate proprietors – mainly consisting of the royal court, nobles, and major religious institutions – continued to exert great influence, resulting in a two-dimensional character (dual polity) of control in both the political and economic spheres. The court appointed provincial governors to manage general administration across the whole country, while nobles and religious institutions took most of the profits from their lands as zuryō or estate proprietors. Under these various powerholders were many warriors who did not serve the bakufu.

Shōgun Yoritomo himself also owned many chigyōkoku 知行国 (Kantō Chigyōkoku 関東知行国), as well as many estates (Kantō Goryō 関東御領), including lands confiscated from the Taira family, which became the economic base of the bakufu[24].

The relationship between the court and the bakufu was also regulated by royal decrees or laws issued by the court called shinsei 新制 (new royal laws)[25]. Both the court and the bakufu shared similarities as rulers. The bakufu maintained peace and order across the country through shugo and jitō, and punished jitō who failed to deliver land taxes. In this way, on the one hand the bakufu helped to maintain the rule of the court and the estate and public land system.

However, on the other hand, the bakufu tried to assert control over not only the eastern provinces, but other regions as well, leading to many disputes between

[23] Feudalism refers to a legal system within the ruling class whereby the relationship of go'on and hōkō between lord and vassal is established through the granting of lands.

[24] The Kantō Chigyōkoku (or Kantō Gobunkoku〈関東御分国〉) granted to Yoritomo by the court numbered 9 provinces at their peak, while the Kantō Goryō lands he held, which had been confiscated from the Taira, numbered more than 500.

[25] After the 10th century, laws and legislation issued by the royal court since the compilation of the Ritsuryō codes came to be called shinsei. The estate reform decrees were one example of shinsei. Shinsei continued to be issued during the Kamakura period as courtier law, and gradually the bakufu came to follow this pattern and issue laws called shinsei as well.

shugo or jitō on one side and provincial governors or estate proprietors on the other. Gradually, the estate managers in each area were replaced by jitō, and the bakufu's control increased, which deepened the conflict.

3 Warrior Society

The Rise of the Hōjō Family

The Kamakura Bakufu was initially led by the charismatic leader Minamoto no Yoritomo as a form of autocracy. However, after his death, when his young sons **Yoriie** 源頼家 (1182-1204) and **Sanetomo** 源実朝 (1192-1219) took the reins, there was an increasing demand for retainers to be positioned at the forefront of the political scene[26]. Seeking to seize the initiative, powerful retainers continued to fight amongst themselves. While many retainers were eliminated, the **Hōjō family** 北条氏, originally a family of resident local officials in Izu Province, came to power.

In 1203, **Hōjō Tokimasa** 北条時政 (1138-1215), who was the father of Yoritomo's wife, Masako 北条政子 (1157-1225), removed then-shōgun Yoriie from power[27], and installed the latter's younger brother, Sanetomo, as shōgun in order to seize real power over the bakufu. The position Tokimasa took was called **shikken** 執権 (shōgunal regent), a title that his son, **Yoshitoki** 北条義時 (1163-1224), then inherited. Yoshitoki also defeated Wada Yoshimori (1147-1213), the chief (bettō 別当) of the Samurai Dokoro (Wada Rebellion 和田合戦), and became chief of both the Samurai Dokoro and the Mandokoro, thereby firmly establishing his position. Thereafter, the position of shikken was inherited by the Hōjō family for generations.

The Jōkyū War

The royal court in Kyōto, witnessing the founding and rise to power of the bakufu, had been in the process of political reorganization. At the center of this process was **Retired Sovereign Go-Toba** 後鳥羽上皇 (in 1198-1221). He reinforced the Insei system through such measures as taking control of the vast royal estates scattered around the country, and establishing a new group of retired sovereign's guards (Saimen no Bushi 西面の武士) to

[26] After the death of Yoritomo, bakufu administration was run by a council consisting of 13 members, including his close associates of noble origin such as Ōe no Hiromoto and Miyoshi no Yasunobu, and powerful retainers such as Hōjō Tokimasa, Kajiwara Kagetoki〈梶原景時〉, Miura Yoshizumi〈三浦義澄〉, Hiki Yoshikazu〈比企能員〉, and Wada Yoshimori.

[27] At that time, Tokimasa had Hiki Yoshikazu, who was Yoriie's guardian, killed. Yoriie was confined in Shuzenji Temple〈修禅寺〉 in Izu, where he was assassinated a year later in 1204.

strengthen the court's military capabilities. In doing so, he sought to restore the authority of the court vis-à-vis the bakufu.

In the midst of this, Shōgun Sanetomo, who had been attempting to cooperate with Go-Toba, was assassinated by Yoriie's son Kugyō 公暁 (1200-19) in 1219. This resulted in the court-bakufu relationship becoming unstable[28]. In 1221, Go-Toba raised an army to subjugate Hōjō Yoshitoki, by winning over warriors in the Kinai and the western provinces, armed monks from the major temples, and also some warriors in the eastern provinces who were opposed to the expanding power of the Hōjō family.

However, contrary to the hopes of the retired sovereign's side, the vast majority of the warriors from east Japan rallied in response to a call from Hōjō Masako (Yoritomo's wife), and fought against the court. The bakufu dispatched a force to Kyōto, led by Yasutoki 北条泰時 (1183-1242) and Tokifusa 北条時房 (1175-1240), who were Yoshitoki's son and younger brother respectively. The result, a month later, was a resounding victory for the bakufu side. All three retired sovereigns of the time were exiled[29]. This chain of events is called the **Jōkyū War** 承久の乱.

After this war, the bakufu began to be involved in royal succession, and created the **Rokuhara Tandai** 六波羅探題 (bakufu deputies for Kyōto). The Rokuhara Tandai were responsible for keeping an eye on the court, guarding the capital and its environs, and supervising western Japan. The bakufu also confiscated around 3,000 estates from nobles and warriors who had supported Go-Toba, and appointed as jitō retainers who had shown distinguished performance during the war[30].

These policies made it possible for the bakufu to extend its power over the estates and public lands in the Kinai region and western Japan. In the court, the practice of **Insei** 院政 continued under the supervision of the bakufu, but the character of the dual polity system of court and bakufu had drastically changed. The bakufu had gained the

---

[28] After the death of Sanetomo, Hōjō Yoshitoki attempted to have a royal become the shōgun, but this ended in failure due to the refusal of the retired sovereign. Consequently, the bakufu invited Fujiwara no Yoritsune〈藤原頼経〉, a baby from the Sekkanke as well as a distant relative of Yoritomo, to take the position. The two shōguns (Yoritsune and his successor) who came from the Sekkanke are known as the Fujiwara (or Sekke〈摂家〉) shōguns.

[29] The bakufu dethroned Chūkyō Tennō〈仲恭天皇〉, and sent the retired sovereigns into exile: Go-Toba to the Oki Islands〈隠岐〉, Tsuchimikado〈土御門上皇〉 to Tosa〈土佐〉 (and later Awa〈阿波〉), and Juntoku〈順徳上皇〉 to Sado Island〈佐渡〉.

[30] When the bakufu assigned new jitō after the war, they set a new standard (shinpo rippō〈新補率法〉) for those confiscated lands where the salary for the jitō was insufficient, to guarantee the salary for these **shinpo jitō**〈新補地頭〉. The standard was to provide a jitō with 1) 1 chō〈町〉 (1.18 ha) of land per 11 chō of fields, 2) 5 shō (9 kg) of rice (kachōmai〈加徴米〉) per 1 tan (0.12 ha) of fields, and 3) half of the income from mountains and rivers.

dominant position, and begun to intervene in both royal succession and court politics.

Hōjō Regency Politics

After the Jōkyū War, the bakufu experienced a period of development under the leadership of Hōjō Yasutoki, the third shikken. Following Masako's death, Yasutoki established the post of **rensho** 連署 (cosigner) to assist the shikken, and installed powerful members of the Hōjō family in this position. Moreover, he selected 11 people from among the influential retainers or those who possessed political acumen, and installed them as **Hyōjōshū** 評定衆 (High Council members)[31]. Together with the shikken and rensho, these individuals would manage administrative affairs and judicial trials, conducting politics under a council system.

In 1232, Yasutoki promulgated the 51-article **Goseibai Shikimoku** 御成敗式目 (also called Jōei Shikimoku 貞永式目), and widely disseminated it among retainers. This law code determined the duties and jurisdiction of shugo and jitō based on precedents since the time of Yoritomo, as well as the customs and ethics of warrior society known as dōri 道理. It clarified the criteria for judging disputes between different retainers, or between retainers and estate proprietors, and was the first properly codified instance of warrior law.

Along with this law code, which pertained to areas under bakufu administration, there was also courtier law, which had developed from the Ritsuryō codes and applied to areas under court control, and estate proprietor law, which were still in effect. However, as the bakufu's power developed, the influence of warrior law, with its emphasis on fair judgement, grew, and eventually came to affect territories subject to courtier law or estate proprietor law as well[32].

By implementing the council system, enacting the law code, and actively adopting Kyōto culture, Yasutoki's policies entrenched regency politics. These policies were inherited by his grandson, **Hōjō Tokiyori** 北条時頼 (1227-63). In 1247, after consolidating the position of the Hōjō family by destroying the family of Miura Yasumura 三浦泰村 (?-1247) (Hōji Conflict 宝治合戦), Tokiyori demanded that the court reform its political and structural mechanisms. Under the reign of Retired Sovereign Go-Saga 後嵯峨上皇 (in 1246-72), a

---

[31] As they were important positions, Hyōjōshū were initially chosen from among influential retainers, but later most of them came to be taken by Hōjō family members. Although there was no fixed number of members, it was usually 14 or 15.

[32] Individual laws enacted thereafter as needed were called shikimoku tsuika〈式目追加〉(additional laws). In this manner, the laws issued by the Muromachi Bakufu〈室町幕府〉were called "Kenmu irai tsuika〈建武以来追加〉," meaning "laws enacted since the Kenmu era." This demonstrates that the Goseibai Shikimoku was still effective as a fundamental law code even under the rule of the Muromachi Bakufu.

high council was established for the Insei system (**In no Hyōjōshū** 院評定衆), and the bakufu came to wield strong influence within the court. Moreover, Tokiyori established the **Hikitsuke** 引付 (Board of Coadjutors) underneath the High Council (Hyōjō), and appointed people to it (**Hikitsukeshū** 引付衆). These members specifically handled lawsuits from retainers pertaining to land, in order to make the process quicker and fairer[33].

Eventually, the shōguns, which for some time (after Sanetomo) had been coming from the Fujiwara family, were succeeded by royal (princely) shōguns. This began when the bakufu invited Royal Prince Munetaka 宗尊親王 (1242-74), a son of Retired Sovereign Go-Saga, to become the first royal shōgun. In total there were four royal shōguns, but they were nominal figures and lacked real power. The bakufu eagerly adopted continental culture, constructed Kenchōji 建長寺 Temple (a full-scale Zen 禅宗 Buddhist temple), and turned Kamakura into a warrior capital. The upshot of all this was the further strengthening of regency politics under Tokiyori, and at the same time, a heightening of the autocratic tendencies of the Hōjō family.

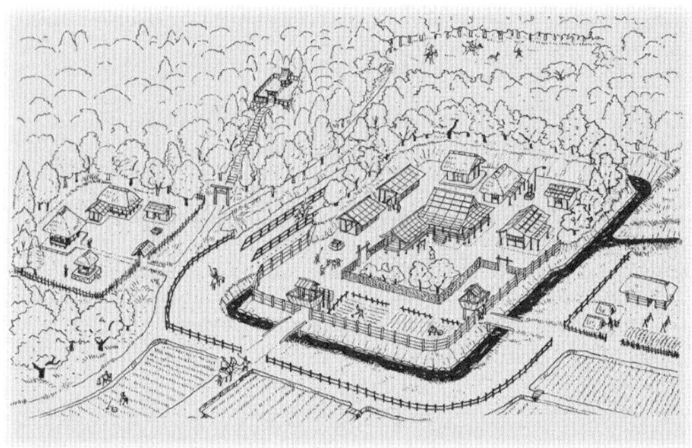

RESIDENCE OF A LAND-OPENING PROPRIETOR
This image is a reconstruction based on yakata depicted in illustrated scrolls, such as *Ippen Shōnin Eden*〈『一遍上人絵伝』〉(Illustrated Biography of the Preacher Ippen), as well as archaeological excavations. These residences were surrounded by a moat, and nearby were directly-managed lands. On the left side there is a family temple.

Warrior Life

Warriors up until this time had developed from land-opening proprietors, living on inherited lands and expanding their territory. They built their residences (**yakata** 館, or tachi)[34] in areas of relatively high elevation close to rivers, and surrounded them with moats or trenches and walls. Around these residences, they established lands under their direct control[35]

---

[33] The Hikitsuke originally consisted of three sections called ban〈番〉, each of which was headed by a chief chosen from the Hyōjōshū. Under the chief were several Hikitsukeshū who prepared drafts for judicial decisions, which were then approved by the Hyōjō.

[34] These served as a type of fortification, equipped with training facilities and defensive structures, while also being a center for agricultural management. The building structures were quite simple, with pillars inserted in the earth, and an annex where armed retainers resided.

[35] These lands were known by such terms as tsukuda〈佃〉, kadota〈門田〉, shōsaku〈正作〉, and yōsaku〈用作〉.

that were exempt from annual government taxes and duties, and which they had their servants or local farmers cultivate. Warriors endeavored to clear new farmland, and as land managers such as jitō they collected taxes from farmers and delivered them to the provincial headquarters or estate proprietors, receiving in return kachōmai (supplementary tax) as a fixed income.

KASAGAKE (*OBUSUMA SABURŌ EMAKI*〈『男衾三郎絵巻』〉 [ILLUSTRATED SCROLL OF OBUSUMA SABURŌ], PART)
A type of mounted archery competition in which wooden boards were used as targets. The name "kasagake" comes from the straw hats (kasa〈笠〉) that were originally used as targets.

In principle, warriors applied the **bunkatsu sōzoku** 分割相続 **(divided succession)** system[36] to share land among their sons and daughters. However, warriors regarded the main line (sōke 宗家, or honke 本家) of their family as their leaders, and developed their activities under blood tie relationships. These resulted in clans called ichimon 一門 (or ikka 一家), consisting of a main line and branch families (bunke 分家). The main line leader was called **sōryō** 惣領 (or **katoku** 家督), and other members were called shoshi 庶子. In wartime, an ichimon fought together under the leadership of its sōryō. During peacetime, sōryō were responsible for organizing festivals to honor their ancestors, or rituals dedicated to the family's patron deities.

The above system, called the **sōryō system** 惣領制, served as the foundation for the political and military structure of the Kamakura Bakufu. The sōryō were charged with managing most of the duties of their ichimon, including not only delivering taxes to proprietors or provincial headquarters, but also military service for the bakufu, and they divided up these responsibilities among their shoshi. Shoshi were also retainers, however, and through the sōryō were connected to the bakufu.

Warriors often led a simple life. They placed importance on developing martial arts to protect their status, and would regularly practice yabusame 流鏑馬 (mounted archery), kasagake 笠懸 (long-distance mounted archery), inuoumono 犬追物 (practicing archery against dogs), and makigari 巻狩 (group hunting)[37]. The ethics that emerged from daily warrior life came to be called "buke no narai," 「武家のならい」 "tsuwamono no michi," 「兵の道」 or "kyūba no michi," 「弓馬の道」

---

[36] In the family system of this era, the status of women was relatively high. Women inherited property like men, and there were cases where women became retainers or jitō. In this era, virilocal marriage became common.

[37] Many narratives that show the simple lifestyle of warriors have survived. For example, Yoritomo admonished his vassal, Fujiwara Toshikane〈藤原俊兼〉 (a deputy governor), for wearing luxurious clothes by cutting Toshikane's sleeves with his sword, and Hōjō Tokiyori, when enjoying sake〈酒〉 with Osaragi Nobutoki〈大仏宣時〉, licked miso〈味噌〉 for a snack.

and were characterized by an emphasis on bravery, loyalty to one's master, respecting the honor of one's family and clan, and a keen sense of shame. These would much later become the origin of Bushidō 武士道.

Warrior Land Management

Seeking to expand their sphere of influence, warriors often caused disputes with neighboring warriors or land proprietors over tax collection and territorial boundaries.

After the Jōkyū War in particular, disputes over management rights escalated as many warriors from eastern Japan were appointed as jitō in the Kinai and western regions as well, and gained new lands there. It was for this reason that the bakufu sought to establish fair judicial procedures.

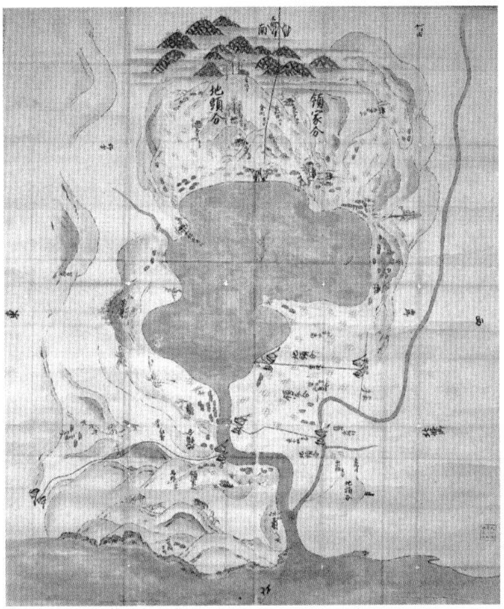

DIAGRAM OF SHITAJI CHŪBUN IN TŌGŌ NO SHŌ〈東郷荘〉, IN HŌKI PROVINCE〈伯耆国〉
A diagram based on a shitaji chūbun made between a proprietor and a jitō in the mid-13th century. The paddy fields, mountains and forests, as well as pastures were divided into two sides, for the proprietor and the jitō. On both sides of the dividing line are the signatures of the shikken and rensho, showing that the division was approved.

Facing the expansion of jitō power, proprietors of estates and public lands also complained to the bakufu in an attempt to suppress trends such as jitō refusal to pay tax. However, it gradually became impossible to deter the jitō because they had strong foundations in their territories. To settle a dispute, the proprietors had no choice but to make a contract with the jitō, called **jitō ukesho** 地頭請所, to entrust operation of the land to the jitō in exchange for a certain amount of tax. Alternatively, they would give a substantial amount of land to the jitō and make an agreement based on mutual management (**shitaji chūbun** 下地中分).

Since the bakufu encouraged concerned parties to settle disputes on their own through a compromise agreement (wayo 和与), the right to control land gradually shifted to the jitō.

4 The Mongol Invasions and the Decline of the Bakufu

The Mongol Invasions

Even under the Kamakura Bakufu, there were no official diplomatic relations between Japan and Song China. However, on the other hand, private trade and movement of

EAST ASIA IN THE 13TH CENTURY

merchants and monks continued to frequently occur following the active foreign exchange of the Taira polity. In this way, the Japanese archipelago came to be included in the East Asian trade sphere centered on Song China.

At the beginning of the 13th century, Chinggis (Genghis) Khan (チンギス＝ハン) (1167?-1227) emerged in the Mongolian steppe, unified Mongolian tribes, and conquered from Central Asia to southern Russia. After that, his successors carried out campaigns to Europe, and destroyed the Jin Dynasty in the east, establishing a great empire that spanned the Eurasian continent from east to west. A grandson of Genghis Khan, **Khubilai Khan** (フビライ＝ハン) (r. 1260-94), relocated the capital to Dadu (Beijing) (大都（北京）) to govern China, and chose the name **Yuan Dynasty** (元) (1271-1368) for his realm. After subjugating Goryeo (高麗), he strongly demanded many times that Japan pay tribute to the Yuan.

However, Shōgunal Regent **Hōjō Tokimune** (北条時宗) (1251-84), successor to Tokiyori, rejected these demands. In response, in 1274 the Yuan Dynasty dispatched approximately 30,000 troops, including forces from Goryeo, to the islands of Tsushima (対馬) and Iki (壱岐). The troops landed in Hakata Bay (博多湾), located in northern Kyūshū. The bakufu called up retainers who held land in Kyūshū to intercept the Yuan forces, but the Japanese had difficulty fighting against the invaders, who used mass attack strategies and sophisticated weapons, whereas the Japanese favored individual fighting. Nevertheless, the Yuan forces also incurred serious damage, and had internal divisions, prompting them to retreat. This invasion is called the **Bun'ei Invasion** (文永の役) (named for the era in which it occurred).

Afterwards, the bakufu, to prepare for further invasion attempts, strengthened the **Ikoku Keigo Banyaku** (異国警固番役) (forces for defense against foreign enemies), comprised of retainers recruited to guard key areas in northern Kyūshū including Hakata Bay. The bakufu also constructed stone (石築地) defensive walls along Hakata Bay[38]. The Yuan Dynasty, having destroyed the Southern Song, dispatched a force of as many as 140,000 troops

[38] Ikoku Keigo Banyaku, which imposed military service on retainers in parts of Kyūshū, dated from before the Bun'ei Invasion. After the invasion, the system became more thoroughly organized. The construction of defensive walls was assigned not only to retainers, but also to landholders in the region.

PICTURE OF A BATTLE AGAINST THE YUAN ARMY (*MŌKO SHŪRAI EMAKI*〈『蒙古襲来絵巻』〉 [ILLUSTRATED SCROLL OF THE MONGOL INVASIONS], PART)
One scene from a land battle during the Bun'ei Invasion. The mounted Japanese warrior is Takezaki Suenaga〈竹崎季長〉 of Higo Province〈肥後〉, who was 29 years old at the time. The Japanese forces struggled against the gunpowder bomb weapons called "tetsuhau."

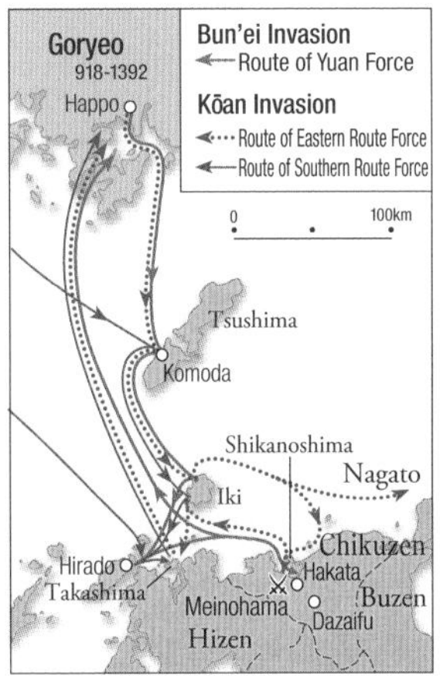

ROUTES AND LOCATIONS DURING THE MONGOL INVASIONS

RUINS OF A STONE DEFENSIVE WALL

to northern Kyūshū to invade Japan for the second time in 1281. However, they were blocked, and while struggling to land in Hakata Bay a typhoon struck their forces and caused serious damage, resulting in another retreat. This second invasion is called the **Kōan Invasion**〈弘安の役〉, and the two invasions together are known as the **Mongol Invasions**〈蒙古襲来〉 (genkō〈元寇〉).

The failure of both invasions was partly due to resistance among people from Goryeo and the Southern Song who had been invaded by the Yuan[39], but it was

[39] Goryeo in particular, which had capitulated only after 30 years of resistance, continued to resist the Mongols in many ways, such as the Sambyeolcho War〈三別抄の乱〉. While Khubilai Khan utilized Goryeo to negotiate with and attack Japan, the continuous resistance of Goryeo became an obstacle to invade Japan. Moreover, the people of the former Southern Song and Dai Viet〈大越〉 (Vietnam) started movements protesting the Yuan, which resulted in the Yuan Dynasty abandoning its plan for a third invasion of Japan.

mostly because the warriors in Kyūshū had fought very well under the leadership of the bakufu.

Politics after the Mongol Invasions

As the Yuan Dynasty did not abandon its plans to invade Japan despite having failed twice, the bakufu continued to be on the alert and mobilize retainers in Kyūshū as Ikoku Keigo Banyaku. Moreover, in addition to retainers, the bakufu obtained from the court the right to mobilize warriors on estates and public lands across the whole country. In other words, the bakufu took advantage of the Mongol invasions as an opportunity to expand its power in western Japan. For Hakata in particular, the bakufu sent members of the Hōjō family to serve as **Chinzei Tandai** 鎮西探題, and had them take control of the administration, judicial decisions, and leadership of the retainers in Kyūshū.

As the ruling power of the bakufu became enhanced across the country, the Hōjō family gained even more power. The power of the **tokusō** 得宗[40], who inherited the headship of the family, came to be especially strong. Accordingly, conflict between Hōjō deputies (miuchibito 御内人), who served the tokusō, and the original retainers became increasingly intense. In 1285, in the time of Hōjō Sadatoki 北条貞時 (1271-1311, a son of Tokimune), Taira no Yoritsuna 平頼綱 (?-1293), who was among these deputies a central figure (uchikanrei 内管領), defeated Adachi Yasumori 安達泰盛 (1231-85), one of the powerful retainers (**Shimotsuki Incident** 霜月騒動). A few years later Sadatoki responded by having Yoritsuna killed, and seized complete control of the bakufu.

Under the tremendous authority of the tokusō, the Hōjō and their deputies dominated bakufu politics. More than half of the shugo in the country were members of the Hōjō, as were most of the jitō. This political structure led by the tokusō is known as the **tokusō autocracy** 得宗専制政治.

The Situation in the Ryūkyū Islands and among the Ainu People

While the activities of the Mongols were shaking East Asia, in the Ryūkyū 琉球 Islands, to the south of the Japanese archipelago, the rulers (**aji** 按司) of the tribes expanded their power based on gusuku グスク fortresses. These tribes were gradually consolidated into three kingdoms, Hokuzan 北山 (Sanhoku 山北), Chūzan 中山, and Nanzan 南山 (Sannan 山南). In the Ryūkyū Islands, an agricultural lifestyle evolved from "shell mound culture 貝塚文化" around the 12th century, and gusuku came to be constructed. Initially, gusuku consisted of settlements and sanctuaries, but later, with the growing power of the aji, gusuku became castles

[40] "Tokusō" means the chief of the main line of a family. The word was said to have come from another name for Yoshitoki.

with solid stone walls.

Meanwhile, on Ezogashima 蝦夷ヶ島 (Hokkaidō) in the far north of Japan, in ancient times the Satsumon culture 擦文文化 and Okhotsk culture オホーツク文化 that developed from the "residual Jōmon culture" 「続縄文文化」 had become widespread[41]. Following these, **Ainu** アイヌ culture emerged in the 13th century. From Tosaminato 十三湊, a base in Tsugaru 津軽, the Ainu people conducted trade with the Andō 安藤（安東）氏 family, who were under the control of the tokusō. Some of the Ainu who inhabited Sakhalin (Karafuto) fought against the Mongols, showing that the Mongol influence stretched right across the Japanese archipelago.

Changes in Society

New developments in agriculture had begun to be seen around the time of the Mongol invasions. In the Kinai area and around western Japan, **nimōsaku** 二毛作, in which wheat was grown as a winter crop, came to be common. Grasses and trees from the countryside were utilized as fertilizer, and the use of iron farming tools as well as **cattle and horses** 牛馬 became more widespread[42]. Egoma 荏胡麻 (perilla, used for making kerosene) was grown, and

MARKET IN FUKUOKA, BIZEN PROVINCE (*IPPEN SHŌNIN EDEN*, PART)
The scene depicts warriors attempting to attack Ippen (the monk on the left side), who had been preaching in the market of Fukuoka〈福岡の市〉, Bizen Province〈備前〉 in 1278. On market day, many goods were showcased in temporary huts built along both sides of the road. We can see that the sale of goods was being actively conducted.

---

[41] "Residual Jōmon culture" refers to the culture lacking rice cultivation that followed the Jōmon culture. Satsumon culture had pottery with unique patterns, and spread from the northern part of Tōhoku to Hokkaidō and Sakhalin. It co-existed with the Okhotsk culture, which spread through the coast of the Okhotsk sea.

[42] In this era, daitōmai〈大唐米〉, which was a high-yield rice, was also imported. For fertilizer, **kari-shiki**〈刈敷〉 (cut grass that was laid in fields) and **sōmokubai**〈草木灰〉 (ashes made from grass and trees) were utilized.

people weaved silk and linen cloth. Craftsmen such as blacksmiths 鍛冶, imoji 鋳物師 (iron casters), and dyers 紺屋 lived in farming communities where they made products and walked to various places to sell them.

KASHIAGE (*SANNŌ REIGENKI EMAKI*《『山王霊験記絵巻』》 [ILLUSTRATED SCROLL OF MIRACLES OF THE SANNŌ SHRINE] PART)
The scene depicts a woman from the first half of the 13th century who was traveling from Kyōto to Kamakura to make a lawsuit. Being short on money, she borrowed some from a kashiage. On the edge of the veranda, we can see a long chain of coins.

Teikiichi 定期市 (regular markets) for buying and selling products were held in central areas of estates and public lands, at important points on transportation routes, or in front of temples and shrines. Moreover, **sansaiichi** 三斎市 (regular markets occurring three times per month) were not uncommon. In rural markets, local specialties and rice were bought and sold, and **gyōshōnin** 行商人 **(travelling merchants)** who brought clothes and crafts from the central areas started to appear.

In urban centers like Kyōto, Nara, and Kamakura, craftsmen and merchants who dealt with luxurious products gathered. Aside from the teikiichi, regular **misedana** 見世棚 (retail shops) appeared. Merchants and craftsmen in Kyoto and Nara were already affiliated with large religious institutions or the royal family from the late Heian period, and were granted the privilege to make and sell products. Later on, these people came to organize **za** 座 (professional guilds). Among za members, those affiliated with large temples or shrines were called jinin 神人, while those affiliated with the royal family were called kugonin 供御人.

Trade between distant places also became more common. Inns were located at important points on the land transportation network. In the ports in various regions, **toi** 問 (toimaru 問丸) – people who worked as middlemen, managed commission sales, and transported products – developed. As a means of trade, the use of currency became more frequent instead of paying in kind with products such as rice. On some estates, people started to pay their taxes in cash. The currency used for this purpose was **Sōsen** 宋銭 (Song coins), which were coins imported from China. For conducting distant trade, **kawase** 為替, which were bills of exchange, were used instead of transporting money. A financial institution called **kashiage** 借上 (high-interest lenders) also appeared.

Farmers actively responded to oppression and unlawful acts by jitō and estate proprietors. There were many cases of farmers uniting and filing lawsuits, or fleeing *en masse*. Farmers also contracted to have their taxes set at fixed rates.

The Decline of the Bakufu

The bakufu faced many difficulties due to the remarkable development of production and a distribution economy, as well as the enormous changes in society. The Mongol invasions cost great sacrifices on the part of retainers, but the bakufu could not sufficiently reward them, resulting in the loss of retainers' trust. In addition, many retainers had their territories divided into small portions through repeated divided succession, and on top of this, they faced the development of a monetary economy, leaving them poor. These changes also precipitated a decline in the status of women. The amount of assets given to women decreased, and the amount of inheritance that needed to be returned to the sōryō after their deaths increased.

As one of the measures to alleviate the struggles of poor retainers, in 1297 the bakufu issued the **Einin no Tokusei-rei** 永仁の徳政令 (Einin Ordinance, which cancelled debts). It prohibited the pawning or trading of retainers' lands, and restored to them for free territory that had already been pawned or sold. The bakufu also refused to accept money-related lawsuits involving retainers. However, the effect of these measures was just temporary.

While many small and medium-sized retainer households declined, there were also warriors who took advantage of the changes in the economic situation and expanded their power. Especially in the Kinai and surrounding regions, there were jitō who were against proprietors or newly-emerged warriors who were not retainers, and used force of arms to deny them the delivery of taxes. These warriors who opposed proprietors were called **akutō** 悪党 (evil bands), and this phenomenon came to spread in various regions.

Although the autocratic character of the tokusō was reinforced in order to resolve these issues, this merely resulted in even more dissatisfaction among retainers. In this way, the bakufu regime came to face a deep crisis.

5 Kamakura Culture

Kamakura Culture

The Kamakura period was a time in which on the one hand courtiers passed on traditional culture, while on the other hand a new culture, supported by warriors and commoners, developed. These new cultural practices then came to be passed down among families and groups of nobles and warriors.

One of the factors shaping the development of the new culture was the warriors from rural areas, whose rustic and down-to-earth dispositions influenced art and literature. Another factor came in the form of Southern Song and Yuan culture, which was brought not only by monks and merchants who had already been coming and going between Japan and the continent, but also by monks who escaped to Japan from China after the Mongol attacks on the Southern Song.

Kamakura Buddhism

As for the Buddhist tradition, the Kamakura period witnessed a general shift from practices that centered on Buddhist prayer rites (kitō 祈禱) and scholastic learning to a stronger emphasis on inner cultivation and a concern with a wider range of people, including commoners.

Hōnen 法然 (1133-1212) was the first person whose teachings represented this shift. Having studied Tendai 天台 doctrine, he developed a deep faith in the vows of the Buddha Amida 阿弥陀仏, and around the time of the Genpei War 源平争乱 he preached the teaching of **senju nenbutsu** 専修念仏, the exclusive practice of the recitation of the Buddha Amida's name. Hōnen emphasized that through the practice of **nenbutsu** 念仏, the simple recitation of "Namu Amida-butsu" 南無阿弥陀仏 (Glory to the Buddha Amida), all people would be reborn in the Pure Land of Bliss (Gokuraku Jōdo 極楽浄土). Eventually he came to be revered as the founder of the **Jōdo Sect** 浄土宗. His teachings received wide support from courtiers, such as Kujō Kanezane 九条兼実 (1149-1207) of the Sekkanke, as well as from many warriors and commoners. However, he was also intensely crticized by the Buddhist establishment, leading to his exile to Tosa Province and the persection of his disciples.

Shinran 親鸞 (1173-1262) was one of Hōnen's disciples, and was exiled to Echigo 越後国 Province. However, he eventually made his way to Hitachi 常陸国 Province in eastern Japan where he further developed Hōnen's teachings. Shinran advocated the doctrine of **akunin shōki** 悪人正機, which taught that it was people who had incurred great sin who were the most appropriate recipients of the Buddha Amida's saving grace. This teaching spread among the farmers and the provincial warriors, eventually leading to the establishment of the **Jōdo Shinshū Sect** 浄土真宗 (True Pure Land Sect, also called Ikkōshū 一向宗).

From the same strand of Pure Land teachings, a figure who appeared some years later was **Ippen** 一遍 (1239-89). He did not make distinctions among people, regardless of their karma or faith, and instead taught a form of nenbutsu that promised salvation for all. He freely distributed nenbutsu fuda 念仏札 (paper slips with the name of the Buddha Amida), and proselytized his teachings to commoners in various regions through the practice of **odori nenbutsu** 踊念仏 (dancing nenbutsu). His teaching came to be known as the **Jishū Sect** 時宗 (Time Sect) and was widely accepted by warriors and commoners in

SCENE OF DANCING NENBUTSU (*IPPEN SHŌNIN EDEN*, PART)
Ippen was called an "itinerant priest" as he travelled to various regions to spread his teachings. The people who followed Ippen were called the Jishū〈時衆〉(time assembly). In this scene, Ippen is with his disciples at a marketplace in Kyōto as he strikes a gong and dances while stomping around.

local regions.

Around the same time, **Nichiren** 日蓮 (1222-82) advocated a new method of salvation through exclusive faith in the Lotus Sutra 法華経. Although he began his training studying the teachings of the Tendai Sect, he eventually selected the Lotus Sutra as the most representative teaching of the Buddha Shakyamuni 釈迦 and taught that the practice of **daimoku** 題目, or the recitation of "Namu Myōhō Renge-kyō" 南無妙法蓮華経 (Glory to the Wonderous Teachings of the Lotus Sutra), was the correct path to salvation. Nichiren centered his prosetylization activities in the Kamakura region. By harshly criticizing other Buddhist sects, and for spreading a prophesy of the coming of a national crisis, he came under persecution from the Kamakura Bakufu. However, the teachings of the **Nichiren Sect** 日蓮宗 (also known as the Lotus Sect 法華宗) continued to spread widely among the warriors, merchants and craftsmen of the Kantō region.

The Buddhist sects that held the most significant influence among the warriors, mainly in the Kantō region, were the Zen 禅宗 sects. These emphasized the practice of zazen 坐禅 (sitting meditation) as a means of self-discipline, and taught that through it one could attain a state of enlightenment equivalent to that of the Buddha Shakyamuni. These teachings were first transmitted to Japan in the late 12th century by the Tendai priest **Eisai** 栄西 (1141-1215), who had travelled to Song China. Eisai was also skilled in performing prayer rites of the esoteric Buddhist tradition and received the support of courtiers and powerful members of the bakufu. He came to be revered as the founder of the **Rinzai Sect** 臨済宗. The bakufu placed great value on the Rinzai Sect. After Eisai's death, the bakufu financed the establishment of major Buddhist institutions, such as Kenchōji 建長寺 and Engakuji 円覚寺, in Kamakura, and invited a series of Chinese monks – such as Rankei Dōryū 蘭渓道隆 (Lanxi Daolong, 1213-78) and Mugaku Sogen 無学祖元 (Wuxue Zuyuan, 1226-86), who had come from the Southern Song – to head them. The bakufu's enthusiasm for Zen was partly because the latter's emphasis on strict training dovetailed with the warrior ethos of the time, and partly because the bakufu wanted to absorb new cultural trends from overseas; consequently, it sought to establish Zen as the leading trend among Buddhist institutions.

Among the Zen sects, **Dōgen** 道元 (1200-53) emphasized the exclusive practice of zazen and spread the teachings of the **Sōtō Sect** 曹洞宗. Dōgen, who studied under one of

Eisai's disciples, travelled to the Southern Song to advance his understanding of Zen teachings. Upon his return, he began actively promoting zazen, and established Eiheiji 永平寺 Temple in Echizen 越前国 Province. Through the proselyatization efforts of his disciples in the Hokuriku region that actively incorporated older forms of Buddhist teachings and practices, the Sōtō Sect spread far and wide[43].

These new forms of Buddhist teaching popularized in the Kamakura period shared several characteristics: they were critical of the corruption seen in the older Buddhist institutions, particularly those of Tendai and Shingon; they advocated a single practice (nenbutsu, daimoku, zen) as the sole method to attain salvation; they made their teachings available to a wider range of people, including warriors and commoners; and they came to be institutionalized as new sects that were passed on to later generations.

In response to these new Buddhist movements, the older Buddhist establishment also showed signs of development. In the early Kamakura period, **Jōkei** 貞慶 (1155-1213, also known as Gedatsu 解脱) of the Hossō 法相宗 Sect and **Myōe** 明恵 (1173-1232, also known as Kōben 高弁) of the Kegon 華厳宗 Sect placed effort into the revival of the Southern Schools 南都仏教 of Nara Buddhism by emphasizing the importance of Buddhist precepts. A little later, **Eizon** 叡尊 (1201-90, Shien 思円) and **Ninshō** 忍性 (1217-1303, Ryōkan 良観) of the Ritsu 律宗 Sect emphasized the Buddhist precepts as well, but were also engaged in social welfare by providing relief and care for the poor and sick[44]. They also garnered support from the Kamakura Bakufu, and influenced many people.

At the same time, Shugendō 修験道 practices connected to mountain asceticism from ancient times were also practiced under the established Buddhist sects. Furthermore, as shinbutsu-shūgō 神仏習合 thought spread, in the latter Kamakura period **Watarai Ieyuki** 度会家行 (dates unknown)[45], a Shintō priest of the Outer Shrine 伊勢外宮 of Ise Shrine, developed a unique Shintō theory influenced by the teachings of Kamakura Buddhism. This came to be known as **Ise Shintō** 伊勢神道（度会神道） (Watarai Shintō).

---

[43] The names "Rinzai" and "Sōtō" derive from the founders of the respective lineages in China. While the essential practice of the Rinzai Sect was **kōan mondō**〈公案問答〉, a form of meditation in which a student was given questions to contemplate as a means of attaining enlightenment, the Sōtō Sect advocated **shikantaza**〈只管打坐〉, a form of meditation in which a student emptied their mind to gain a state of true awareness.

[44] Ninshō established a relief center for the sick, the Kitayama Jūhakkendo〈北山十八間戸〉 in Nara, where he offered medical treatment and performed acts of charity.

[45] Watarai Ieyuki composed *Ruijū Jingi Hongen*〈『類聚神祇本源』〉 (Records on the Origins of Kami), in which he took issue with the notion of Honji Suijaku〈本地垂迹説〉 that held that kami were manifestations of Buddhas. He argued instead for Shinpon Butsujaku〈神本仏迹説〉, the notion that Buddhist deities were manifestations of Japanese kami.

The Origins of Medieval Japanese Literature

There were also new developments within the realm of literature. Saigyō 西行 (1118-90), who hailed from a warrior family, took the tonsure, and wrote refined waka 和歌 poetry as he traveled around various provinces during the tumultuous late Heian period, leaving behind a collection entitled *Sankashū* 『山家集』 (Collection of a Mountain Hut). Kamo no Chōmei 鴨長明 (1155?-1216), another noted poet, wrote *Hōjōki* 『方丈記』 (An Account of a Ten-Foot-Square Hut) in which he portrayed the ephemeral nature of all humanity and society. Right before the Jyōkyū War, Jien 慈円 (1155-1225)[46] composed ***Gukanshō*** 『愚管抄』 (Jotting of a Fool), in which he sought to identify fudamental principles underlying history and then interpret history based on those. All of these literary works of the time, moreover, convey the Buddhist notion of wishing to be reborn in the Pure Land.

The ***Shin Kokin Wakashū*** 『新古今和歌集』 (New Collection of Ancient and Modern Poems), a poetry anthology compiled at the command of Retired Sovereign Go-Toba, proved highly influential. The poetic style demonstrated by its compilers, such as Fujiwara no Sadaie 藤原定家 (1162-1241) and Fujiwara no Ietaka 藤原家隆 (1158-1237), revealed both a mastery of the Heian poetic tradition and the use of technical expressions, enabling them to produce new interpretations of conceptual beauty. These poetic styles were welcomed by the courtiers around Go-Toba, and many splendid poems were composed during this time, prompting some courtiers such as Sadaie to establish waka as a distinct family specialization.

As seen in the case of Go-Toba, the composition of poetry was deeply connected to politics, encouraging Shōgun Sanetomo to also take up poetry. He composed a number of poems in the classic style of the *Man'yōshū* 万葉集 and compiled the *Kinkai Wakashū* 『金槐和歌集』 collection. Indeed, it was not uncommon in this period for warriors to be involved in the composition of poetry.

The most representative literary genre of the period, however, was gunki monogatari, which were war tales based on battles and depicting the lively actions of real warriors. In particular, ***Heike Monogatari*** 『平家物語』 (The Tale of the Heike), which retells the rise and fall of the Taira family, is the masterpiece of the genre. It was recited with musical accompaniment in a performance called **heikyoku** 平曲 ("songs of the Heike") by **biwa hōshi** 琵琶法師 (literally "lute monks," traveling lute performers akin to bards), and came to be enjoyed widely, even by those who were illiterate.

---

[46] Jien was the younger brother of Kujō Kanezane, a regent who also had close ties to Yoritomo at the time when the Kamakura Bakufu was established. Jien also served as the head abbot of the Tendai Sect, and composed the *Gukanshō* in the years leading up to the Jōkyū War, partly in order to dissuade Retired Sovereign Go-Toba from seeking to vanquish the Kamakura Bakufu.

In terms of setsuwa 説話 (anecdotal literature), many works such as *Kokon Chomonjū* 『古今著聞集』 (A Collection of Tales Heard, Past and Present) were produced following the Jōkyū War. The most notable example was ***Tsurezuregusa*** 『徒然草』 (Essays in Idleness), written by the monk Kenkō 兼好法師 (1283?-1352?). It was a masterpiece that not only revealed the informed and acute observations of the author, but also reflected the distinctive culture of the Kamakura period.

A BIWA HŌSHI (*BOKI EKOTOBA* 〈『慕帰絵詞』〉, PART)

Within the realm of scholarship, the study of **yūsoku kojitsu** 有職故実, the ritual practices and precedents set by the royal court, and the study of the classics were actively pursued by courtiers out of respect for a bygone era. On the other hand, warriors in Kamakura, who had also begun to produce their own council system and codes of law under regency politics, became more interested in culture and scholarly pursuits in general, leading them to compile their own historical chronicle, ***Azuma Kagami*** 『吾妻鏡』 (Mirror of the East) that narrated the history of the Kamakura Bakufu. Kanezawa Sanetoki 金沢実時 (1224-76) of the Hojō family, and his descendents, established a private library known today as **Kanezawa Bunko** 金沢文庫 in the Kanezawa area of Mutsura 六浦, which had flourished as an outer harbor for Kamakura. They amassed a large collection of Japanese and Chinese texts, and in so doing established a center for learning.

Near the end of the Kamakura period, the Neo-Confucian teaching of Zhu Xi 朱熹 (1130-1200) of Song China was transmitted to Japan as **Sōgaku** 宋学 ("Song Learning") or Shushigaku 朱子学 (literally "Zhu Xi learning," but referring to the Cheng-Zhu School). Its theories of social hierarchy, known as **Taigi Meibunron** 大義名分論, were highly influential and later provided the theoretical justification for Go-Daigo Tennō's 後醍醐天皇 anti-bakufu movement.

New Directions in Art

New developments also occurred in various forms of art. In many cases, the catalyst was the restoration of various temples in Nara that had been destroyed during the Genpei War. The Buddhist priest **Chōgen** 重源 (1121-1206) travelled widely to solicit donations, and with the help of Chin Nakei 陳和卿 (Chen Heqing, dates unknown) from China invested great effort in reconstructing Tōdaiji 東大寺 Temple. The architectural style adopted at the time was called **Daibutsuyō** 大仏様 ("Great Buddha style"), which was reminiscent of continental splendor. The Nandaimon 南大門 Gate of Tōdaiji is representative of this style.

TŌDAIJI NANDAIMON GATE (LEFT) **AND ENGAKUJI SHARIDEN HALL** (RIGHT)
While the architectural style of the late Heian period leaned toward expressing beauty through decorations and handicraft, the characteristic of the Daibutsu style was to place emphasis on the beauty of the entire architectural structure as a whole, which through its unrestrained methods expressed a sense of boldness and strength. The Nandaimon Gate is representative of this style (height 26 m). On the other hand, using detailed wooden materials to express small-scaled, but orderly, beauty was the characteristic of the Zenshū style. The Shariden Hall that stands tall with its steep inclined roofs is a sharp contrast to the gentle slope and horizontal expressions of the Japanese-style architectural structures. The present building dates from the Muromachi period, and was likely moved here from another location. (Height 10 m)

This was followed by the new architectural style of **Zenshūyō** 禅宗様 ("Zen style," also called karayō 唐様 or "Chinese style") that was transmitted to Japan. This style was characterized by the combination of detailed parts to express a systematic beauty, and was used to build structures in Zen temples such as the Shariden 舎利殿 Hall of Engakuji. On the other hand, another popular new style called **secchūyō** 折衷様 ("eclectic style") combined continental characteristics with the soft aesthetics of Japanese styles dating back to the Heian period.

Along with efforts to restore the temples of Nara, Buddhist sculptors made Buddhist and portrait sculptures. Prominent sculptors included the father-son duo **Unkei** 運慶 (?-1223) and Tankei 湛慶 (1173-1256), and **Kaikei** 快慶 (dates unknown). Their work carried on the sculptural traditions of the Nara period, but was also characterized by a powerful realism that reflected the spirit of a new age, while depicting human emotion through rich expressions. In the mid-Kamakura period, the Great Buddha of Kamakura was constructed using new technologies that were introduced from the continent. This was made possible through the support of the bakufu, and the efforts of monks who travelled to solicit donations for temple construction and repair.

In the world of painting, the production of illustrated scrolls reached its peak during this period. These included not only illustrations of tales, called monogatari-e 物語絵, but also works that depicted battle scenes of warriors in action (such as *Mōko Shūrai Emaki* 『蒙古襲来絵巻』, Illustrated Scroll of the Mongol Invasions). There were also illustrated scrolls made to spread Buddhist teaching among a wide audience, including some covering the origin tales of temples and shrines (such as *Kasuga Gongen Genki* 『春日権現験記』, Chronicles of the Miracles of the Kasuga Deity) and some portraying legends of eminent priests (such as *Ippen Shōnin Eden*, Illustrated Biography of the Preacher Ippen).

As for **nise-e** (似絵), which were realistic portraits of individuals, this period saw the appearance of the masters Fujiwara no Takanobu (藤原隆信) (1142-1205) and his son Nobuzane (藤原信実) (1176?-1265?). The rise of nise-e alongside advancements in portrait sculpture indicates that there was a growing interest in the notion of individuality during this period. The practice of venerating portraits of Zen masters, known as **chinzō** (頂相)[47], also came to be transmitted from China in the mid-Kamakura period.

In terms of calligraphy, the elegant style of the Hosshōji School (法性寺流) was supplemented by the arrival of Song and Yuan calligraphic styles. Royal Prince Novice Son'en (尊円入道親王) (1298-1356), a son of Fushimi Tennō (伏見天皇) (r. 1287-98) established the **Shōren-in School** (青蓮院流) of calligraphy by incorporating Song styles into the Japanese styles dating back to the Heian period. As for handicrafts, as the influence of the warriors grew so too did the production of weapons and armor. The era gave rise to some of the most renowned swordsmiths, including Nagamitsu (長光) (dates unknown) of Bizen, Tōshirō Yoshimitsu (藤四郎吉光) (dates unknown) of Kyōto, and Masamune (正宗) (dates unknown) of Kamakura.

Moreover, under the significant influence of Song and Yuan styles, the production of ceramics in various regions showed great development, as can be seen in such styles as **Seto-yaki** (瀬戸焼)[48] and Tokoname-yaki (常滑焼) in Owari Province (尾張国) and Bizen-yaki (備前焼) in Bizen Province. These ceramics circulated widely across the Japanese archipelago. They have been discovered in not only the major centers of Kyōto and Kamakura, but also in excavations of harbors and inns at the sites of various towns such as Onomichi (尾道) in Bingo (備後) Province. These towns witnessed the rise of wealthy individuals referred to as utoku-nin (有徳人).

STATUE OF KONGŌRIKISHI〈金剛力士像〉 (OPEN-MOUTH FORM) **AT TŌDAIJI NANDAIMON GATE**
This is one of the wooden Niō guardian statues〈仁王像〉, with a height of roughly 8.5 meters, placed on the left and right sides of the Nandaimon Gate at Tōdaiji Temple. There is an agyō〈阿形〉 (open-mouth form), and an ungyō〈吽形〉 (closed-mouth form). These statues, constructed in a short period of time by Unkei, Kaikei, and others, show a vibrant and surging strength indicative of the power of the rising warriors. (Height 8.39 m)

---

[47] Along with chinzō sculptures, this style of artistic expression reached its peak in the following Muromachi period.

[48] It is said that Katō Kagemasa〈加藤景正〉, who travelled to Song China with Dōgen, transmitted Chinese manufacturing techniques of glazing to Japan and started the ceramics tradition in Seto. Although today it is generally understood that there is no historical basis for this account, there is no doubt that many Seto ceramics reveal strong influence from Song and Yuan techniques.

Chapter

5

The Evolution of Warrior Society

1 The Establishment of the Muromachi Bakufu

The Fall of the Kamakura Bakufu

Following the death of Retired Sovereign Go-Saga 後嵯峨法皇, the royal family was split into the **Jimyōin line** 持明院統, which was descended from Retired Sovereign Go-Fukakusa 後深草上皇 (in 1287-90), and the **Daikakuji line** 大覚寺統, which was descended from Kameyama Tennō 亀山天皇 (r.1259-74). Fighting over the right to ascend the throne, to rule as a retired sovereign, and to inherit the royal estates, both lines sought support from the bakufu 幕府 to gain an advantage over their rival. As a result, the bakufu frequently had to mediate between the two lines, which eventually led to an agreement that the throne would alternate between them (**ryōtō tetsuritsu** 両統迭立, alternate succession system).

Go-Daigo Tennō 後醍醐天皇 (r. 1318-39) of the Daikakuji line, who ascended the throne in this way, soon commenced direct rule and began asserting the power of the tennō in order to stabilize the status of the throne. Meanwhile, in the Kamakura Bakufu, Nagasaki Takasuke 長崎高資 (?-1333), the uchikanrei 内管領 serving under Shōgunal Regent Hōjō Takatoki 北条高時 (1303-33), wielded great power, generating strong resentment from retainers against the tokusō autocracy 得宗専制政治. Observing this situation, Go-Daigo, already displeased with the bakufu for its endorsement of the alternate succession system, began plotting to overthrow it. However, in 1324 his plot was revealed to the bakufu and so ended in failure (Shōchū Incident 正中の変). Go-Daigo next sought to raise an army in 1331, only to fail again (Genkō Incident 元弘の変). This resulted in Kōgon Tennō 光厳天皇 (r. 1331-33) of the Jimyōin line ascending to the throne with bakufu backing, while Go-Daigo was exiled to the Oki 隠岐 Islands the following year.

However, Go-Daigo's son, Royal Prince Moriyoshi 護良親王 (1308-35), and others including Kusunoki Masashige 楠木正成 (?-1336), mobilized anti-bakufu forces such as akutō 悪党 to rise up against the bakufu forces. After Go-Daigo managed to escape from Oki, more and more forces responded to his call and joined the fight against the bakufu. Eventually, Ashikaga Takauji 足利高氏（尊氏） (1305-58), a powerful retainer who was dispatched to the Kinai 畿内 region as the commander of the bakufu forces, also rebelled against the bakufu, defeating the Rokuhara Tandai 六波羅探題. Nitta Yoshisada 新田義貞 (?-1338), who raised an army in the

Kantō 関東 region, soon attacked Kamakura as well, defeating Hōjō Takatoki and his followers. Thus, in 1333 the Kamakura Bakufu was destroyed.

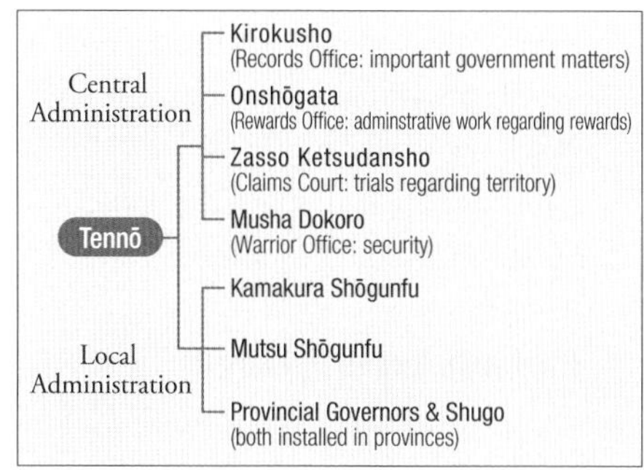

ORGANIZATIONAL STRUCTURE OF KENMU GOVERNMENT

The Kenmu Restoration

Go-Daigo immediately returned to Kyōto, where he dethroned Kōgon and began to rule. As the era name was changed to Kenmu 建武 in 1334, the tennō's new regime is called the **Kenmu Restoration** 建武の新政[1][i]. Go-Daigo sought to centralize authority in the position of the tennō, and to this end he rejected the bakufu, Insei 院政, and regency government systems. He issued a decree stating that all land ownership was to be determined by a royal **rinji** 綸旨 (tennō's edict)[2]. However, in reality it was not possible for matters to be settled solely by the tennō's authority. As a result, institutions like the **Kirokusho** 記録所 (**Records Office**) and **Zasso Ketsudansho** 雑訴決断所 (**Claims Court**), the latter of which replaced the bakufu's Hikitsuke 引付, were established in the capital, while provincial governors and shugo 守護 were positioned together in various provinces. He also set up regional government offices (shōgunfu 将軍府) in Mutsu 陸奥 (for the Tōhoku 東北 region) and Kamakura (for the Kantō region), and dispatched his sons there as governors. These offices could essentially be regarded as small-scale bakufu, considering how heavily they relied on the warriors who had served the former Kamakura Bakufu.

The new tennō-centered policies disregarded the customs that had been practiced in warrior society up until then[3], prompting dissatisfaction and resistance among many warriors. The makeshift political structures and complex internal rivalries brought about political stagnation and social disruption, which resulted in a rapid

---

[1] The name "Kenmu" comes from the era name used by the Chinese Emperor Guangwu〈光武帝〉 when he restored the Han Dynasty (Later Han Dynasty〈後漢〉). In order to demonstrate his authority, Go-Daigo also planned to construct a great palace precinct (daidairi〈大内裏〉) and issue copper coins and paper money to fund its construction.

[2] Go-Daigo admired the direct rule of Daigo〈醍醐天皇〉 and Murakami Tennō〈村上天皇〉, which was regarded as the height of royal rule. He himself chose his posthumous name, Go-Daigo, after Daigo Tennō whom he idealized.

[3] There were occasions that resulted in neglecting Article 8 of the *Goseibai Shikimoku*〈御成敗式目〉 which was considered an immutable law in warrior society. Article 8 stated that, "Land ownership cannot be transferred from the current owner when said owner has effectively ruled the land for over twenty years consecutively."

loss of public trust. Sensing the turn of the tide, Ashikaga Takauji, who had been secretly preparing to reestablish a bakufu, took advantage of the Nakasendai Rebellion 中先代の乱, which was started in 1335 when Hōjō Tokiyuki 北条時行 (?-1353), a son of Takatoki, occupied Kamakura. Takauji seized the opportunity to go to Kamakura and from there revolt against the Kenmu regime.

The Nanbokuchō Upheavals

In 1336, having seized control of Kyōto, Ashikaga Takauji put Kōmyō Tennō 光明天皇 (r. 1336-48) of the Jimyōin line on the throne and promulgated the **Kenmu Shikimoku** 建武式目 (Kenmu Code) which made public his immediate governmental policy in order to establish a bakufu[4]. Meanwhile, Go-Daigo, having escaped from Kyōto and taken refuge in the mountains of Yoshino 吉野, claimed to be the legitimate occupant of the throne. This was the beginning of a conflict between the **Southern Court** 南朝 (Daikakuji line) in Yoshino and the **Northern Court** 北朝 (Jimyōin line) in Kyōto, which spanned the country and lasted for sixty years, a time that came to be called the **Nanbokuchō** 南北朝の動乱 **(Era of Northern and Southern Courts) upheavals**.

Initially, the Southern Court was at a disadvantage, given that Kusunoki Masashige and Nitta Yoshisada had died in battle. However, it continued to fight, rallying behind **Kitabatake Chikafusa** 北畠親房 (1293-1354) and others, and building bases in regions such as Tōhoku, Kantō, and Kyūshū 九州. On the Northern Court side, in 1338 Takauji was appointed Seii Taishōgun 征夷大将軍, and he took up governance with his younger brother Ashikaga Tadayoshi 足利直義 (1306-52), dividing responsibilities between them. However, over time a conflict intensified between the supporters of Tadayoshi, who respected the legal order upheld since the establishment of the Kamakura Bakufu, and an emerging force centered around Takauji's shitsuji 執事 (deputy), Kō no Moronao 高師直 (?-1351), which desired to expand their territory by arms. Fueled further by a dispute over shōgunal succession, eventually in 1350 the two factions plunged into an armed confrontation (**Kannō Disturbance** 観応の擾乱). The conflicts continued even after Ashikaga Tadayoshi died in defeat, with three factions – Takauji's supporters (the bakufu), former Tadayoshi supporters, and the forces of the Southern Court – constantly changing political alliances among themselves for nearly a decade.

Against this backdrop of prolonged, widespread conflict was the collapse of the sōryō 惣領制 system, which had already begun to decline by the late Kamakura period. In

---

[4] It consists of a first section that stipulates the seat of the bakufu, and a second section with 17 articles that state the basic policies of the government at the time, in the form of responding to the inquiries of Ashikaga Takauji.

warrior society around this time, a head family and its branch families had become independent of one another, and **single succession** 単独相続 became common, where the heir of each family inherited all of the territory while the non-heirs were made subordinate to the heir. These changes caused division and conflict within warrior bands across various regions, leading to the expansion of the Nanbokuchō upheavals as one faction sided with the Northern Court while its opponents sided with the Southern Court. Under such circumstances, regional warrior bands that were mainly based on blood relations started to transform into ones that placed more emphasis on **regional bonds** 地縁的結合.

Shugo Daimyō and Kokujin Ikki

As local warriors began to gain more power during the ongoing upheavals, the shugo who led these warriors in their respective provinces began to take on a significant military role.

To mobilize local warriors, the bakufu greatly expanded the power of the shugo[5]. **Hanzei-rei** 半済令 (half-tax decrees), in particular, granted the shugo the authority to collect half the income from the annual land tax on estates and public lands within their province to fund military expenditures[6]. This was to have major consequences. The shugo used these rights to seize control of the estates and public lands within their provinces, and then parcel them out to warriors who they placed under their control. It became increasingly common for estate proprietors to entrust the shugo to undertake the collection of land tax from estates and public lands on their behalf, a practice known as **shugo-uke** 守護請 [7]. Shugo were conventionally appointed by the bakufu. However, some of them came to absorb the functions of the provincial headquarters, and established their authority over the territory of the entire province. Once the Nanbokuchō upheavals

---

[5] In addition to the official daibon sankajō〈大犯三カ条〉duties required of the shugo during the Kamakura period, they were also given new powers. For example, in a land dispute when one party, insisting on ownership of the land, harvested crops without permission (karita rōzeki〈刈田狼藉〉), the shugo had the ability to use force to stop this. They also had the ability to compulsorily enforce the bakufu's judicial decisions (shisetsu jungyō〈使節遵行〉).

[6] The half-tax decree first issued in 1352 had been applied for only a year and was limited to the three provinces of Ōmi〈近江〉, Mino〈美濃〉, and Owari〈尾張〉, where there was intense conflict. However, it later spread throughout the provinces and became a permanent policy that not only meant collecting half the annual land tax but also led to the division of land in halves.

[7] From the latter half of the Kamakura period it became common for estates and public lands to have local deputies (daikan〈代官〉) appointed who were entrusted to collect and deliver a set portion of the annual land tax (daikan-uke〈代官請〉). Jitō-uke〈地頭請〉 and shugo-uke were variants of this contract system, but there were also cases where Zen monks〈禅僧〉, merchants, or moneylenders were appointed as local deputies.

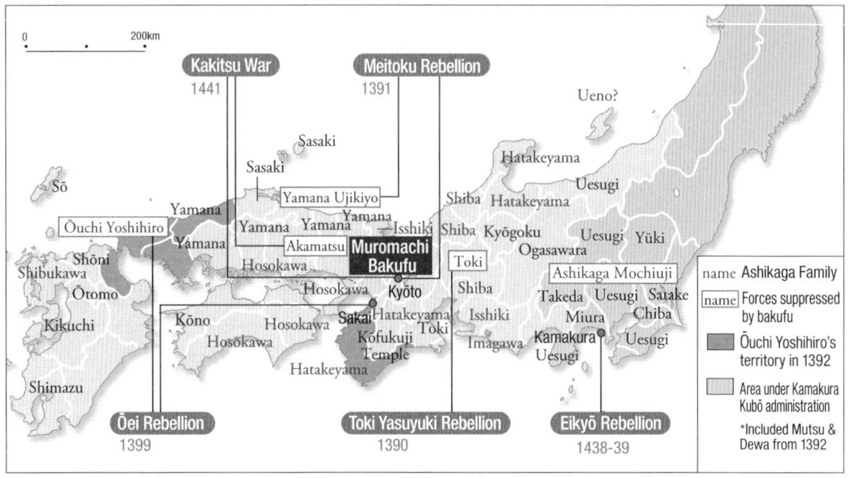

DISTRIBUTION OF SHUGO DAIMYŌ (MOSTLY AROUND EARLY 15TH CENTURY) **AND CONFLICTS** Only major conflicts before the Ōnin War〈応仁の乱〉are shown.

settled down, this control over provinces gradually began to become hereditary. The shugo during this period are sometimes referred to as **shugo daimyō**〈守護大名〉[ii] to differentiate them from the shugo during the times of the Kamakura bakufu.

However, some local warriors at the time who were lords such as jitō〈地頭〉, called **kokujin**〈国人〉, still had a strong independent streak, and the shugo consequently faced many difficulties in trying to vassalize them. In regions where the shugo had less authority, these kokujin often made a compact and formed a local league to settle disputes among themselves or to take control of farmers who had begun to become powerful. These local leagues are called **kokujin ikki**〈国人一揆〉[8]. These local warriors established an autonomous local authority by banding together, often fighting back against the control imposed upon them by the shugo.

The Muromachi Bakufu

With the Nanbokuchō upheavals having gradually settled down by the time Takauji's

[8] When medieval people worked together to achieve a goal, they would offer a pledge to Shintō or Buddhist deities to the effect of being of one mind (ichimi dōshin〈一味同心〉). A league united in such a way was called ikki[iii], and in addition to kokujin ikki there were various other ikki such as tsuchi ikki〈土一揆〉(farmers' league). With kokujin ikki, not a few had a contract made for all the alliance members to keep (ikki keijō〈一揆契状〉), stipulating such things as equality among all and decision-making by majority rule. To sign these contracts, people sometimes used a style called karakasa renpan〈傘連判〉(round robin document with the signatures signed in a circle) to show the equality of all participants.

grandson **Ashikaga Yoshimitsu** 足利義満 (1358-1408) became the third shōgun[9], the bakufu finally entered a stable period. Yoshimitsu negotiated with the Southern Court and brought about the **unification of the Northern and Southern Courts** 南北朝の合体 in 1392[10], successfully putting an end to the civil wars. He also placed under the bakufu's jurisdiction rights that had until then been held by the court, including the administration rights for Kyōto, which was the center of the country's commerce and industry as well as its political core[11], and the right to collect a special tax on land (tan-sen 段銭). By doing so, he was able to establish the bakufu as a countrywide, unified polity. In 1378, Yoshimitsu built a magnificent residence (Muromachi-dono 室町殿, or Hana no Gosho 花の御所) on Muromachi Avenue in Kyōto. As he conducted politics from this residence, his government came to be called the **Muromachi Bakufu** 室町幕府.

To take control of those shugo who had become powerful during the upheavals, Yoshimitsu attacked and destroyed the dominant shugo, such as the Toki 土岐氏, Yamana 山名氏, and Ōuchi 大内氏, in an effort to curtail their influence [12]. Yoshimitsu continued to exercise actual control over the bakufu as well as the royal court even after he stepped down as shōgun and became the supreme minister, and after he took the tonsure, eventually moving to a villa he built in Kitayama 北山 (Kitayama-dono 北山殿) in Kyōto[13].

The bakufu administrative structure was more or less established during this

---

[9] In Kyūshū, the turbulence continued for a long time because the Southern Court forces were able to maintain their power under the Kikuchi family〈菊池氏〉. The Kikuchi supported Go-Daigo's son, Royol Prince Kaneyoshi〈懐良親王〉, who was appointed Seisei Taishōgun〈征西大将軍〉. However, the Southern forces were gradually subdued by the Kyūshū Tandai〈九州探題〉, Imagawa Ryōshun (Sadayo)〈今川了俊（貞世）〉, dispatched by Yoshimitsu.

[10] Once Go-Kameyama Tennō〈後亀山天皇〉 of the Southern Court was persuaded by Yoshimitsu to enter the capital, Go-Komatsu Tennō〈後小松天皇〉 of the Northern Court became the only occupant of the throne.

[11] The rights pertaining to Kyōto transferred from the court to the bakufu included the policing and civil trial rights, and the right to levy commercial taxes on warehouse pawnbrokers and sake dealers.

[12] In 1390, Yoshimitsu defeated the Toki family that held the posts of shugo for the provinces of Mino, Owari, and Ise〈伊勢〉 (Toki Yasuyuki Rebellion〈土岐康行の乱〉). In 1391, he intervened in an internal conflict of the Yamana family, which held the shugo posts for 11 provinces in western Japan and were called Rokubun no Ichishū〈六分の一衆〉 (rulers of one-sixth of the sixty-some provinces that made up Japan at the time). Yoshimitsu defeated Yamana Ujikiyo〈山名氏清〉 and others (Meitoku Rebellion〈明徳の乱〉). In 1399, Ōuchi Yoshihiro〈大内義弘〉, another powerful shugo, was also suppressed by Yoshimitsu (Ōei Rebellion〈応永の乱〉). All of the above rebellions were provoked by Yoshimitsu.

[13] Yoshimitsu's wife became an honorary mother (junbo〈准母〉) of the tennō. The royal court also tried to grant the title of daijō hō-ō to Yoshimitsu posthumously as the honorary father of the tennō, but the fourth shōgun, Yoshimochi〈足利義持〉, declined this offer.

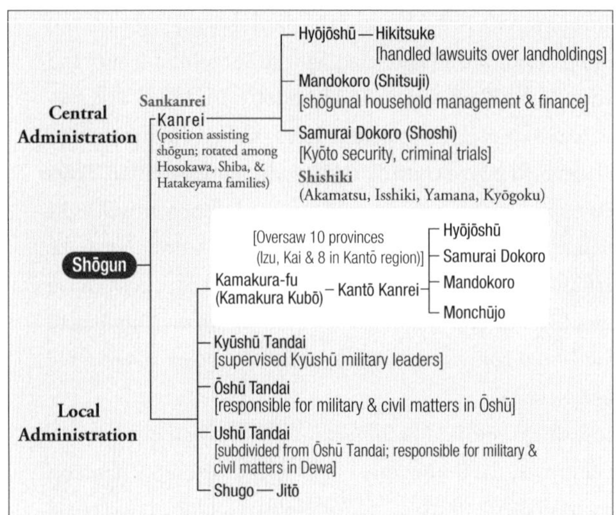

ORGANIZATIONAL STRUCTURE OF MUROMACHI BAKUFU

period. The **kanrei** 管領 (**deputy shōgun**) was the main post that assisted the shōgun. He would manage the primary administrative institutions such as the Samurai Dokoro 侍所 and Mandokoro 政所, and convey the shōgun's orders to the shugo in various provinces. This position was alternately appointed from among three branch families of the Ashikaga, namely the Hosokawa 細川氏, Shiba 斯波氏, and Hatakeyama 畠山氏 families (collectively termed **sankanrei** 三管領). It was also customary to appoint the Samurai Dokoro head (shoshi 所司), responsible for guarding Kyōto and its environs and for handling criminal trials, from among the Akamatsu 赤松氏, Isshiki 一色氏, Yamana 山名氏, and Kyōgoku 京極氏 families (collectively termed **shishiki** 四職). These powerful shugo resided in the capital, where they managed the bakufu administration and made decisions on major governmental matters. It was also common practice for the shugo to live in Kyōto to serve the bakufu while they entrusted managing their territories to **shugodai** 守護代 (**deputy shugo**).

The bakufu endeavored to build a military force to support the authority of the shōgun by organizing a force under its control called the **hōkōshū** 奉公衆 (**shōgunal guards**), composed of hereditary vassals of the Ashikaga family, families of the shugo, and influential local warriors. The hōkōshū usually worked guarding the shōgun in Kyōto. They were also entrusted with managing the **goryōsho** 御料所, which were the direct holdings of the shōgun in various provinces, and as a result, they served to keep the moves of the shugo in check.

The bakufu's finances consisted of income from the goryōsho, contributions from the shugo, and taxes imposed on jitō and retainers. Furthermore, the bakufu also imposed taxes called **dosō-yaku** 土倉役 on warehouse pawnbrokers, who engaged in high-rate moneylending in Kyōto, and **sakaya-yaku** 酒屋役 on breweries. These were in addition to tolls and customs at ports that were collected at strategically-placed checkpoints. The government also taxed the monks of the Kyōto Gozan 京都五山 temples (five great Zen 禅寺 temples) that widely engaged in financial activities under the protection of the bakufu. Additionally, the profits made through trade 日明貿易 between Japan and the Ming Dynasty and, later on, the buichi-sen 分一銭 (debt handling fee) became other sources of bakufu income. For state events such as the construction of a residential palace, taxes such as **tan-sen** 段銭 or **munebetsu-sen** 棟別銭 (**special levies on buildings**) were imposed across the country through the shugo.

Bakufu authorities for local administration included the **Kamakura-fu** 鎌倉府 (Kantō-fu 関東府) and the Kyūshū Tandai. Ashikaga Takauji had placed special importance on the Kantō region as a base of the Kamakura Bakufu, and tasked his son Ashikaga Moto'uji 足利基氏 (1340-67) with opening the Kamakura-fu to rule the eastern provinces as **Kamakura Kubō** 鎌倉公方 (Kantō Kubō 関東公方)[14]. Thereafter, this title was passed onto Moto'uji's descendants, while the post of **Kantō Kanrei** 関東管領 (**deputy for Kantō**) that assisted the Kamakura Kubō became a hereditary position for the Uesugi 上杉氏 family. Since the Kamakura-fu had more or less the same structure as the bakufu and held great authority, eventually frequent conflicts developed between it and the bakufu in Kyōto.

Trade with East Asia

While the Muromachi Bakufu was establishing its power from the late 14th century to the 15th century, the situation in East Asia had been undergoing a major shift.

Around the time of the Nanbokuchō upheavals, groups of pirates – mainly formed of residents of Tsushima 対馬, Iki 壱岐, and the Matsura 松浦 region in Hizen 肥前 – were raiding the coasts of the Korean peninsula and the Chinese continent. These fearsome people were called **wakō** 倭寇 (Japanese pirates). These pirates abducted people in the coastal regions of the Korean peninsula and looted food supplies such as rice and soy beans. Goryeo 高麗, being plagued by wakō activities, sent messengers to Japan, demanding that they be stopped. However, these demands went nowhere due to the internal upheavals Japan was experiencing at the time.

In China, Zhu Yuanzhang 朱元璋 (Emperor Hongwu 洪武帝, 1328-98) overthrew the Yuan 元 Dynasty in 1368 and established the ethnic Han Chinese **Ming Dynasty** 明 (1368-1644). The new dynasty sought diplomatic relations with neighboring countries in order to

[14] The Kamakura-fu ruled over the eight provinces of Kantō as well as the provinces of Izu 〈伊豆〉 and Kai 〈甲斐〉; later, it also gained control over the provinces of Mutsu and Dewa 〈出羽〉. Additionally, the shugo under the jurisdiction of the Kamakura-fu resided in Kamakura to serve it.

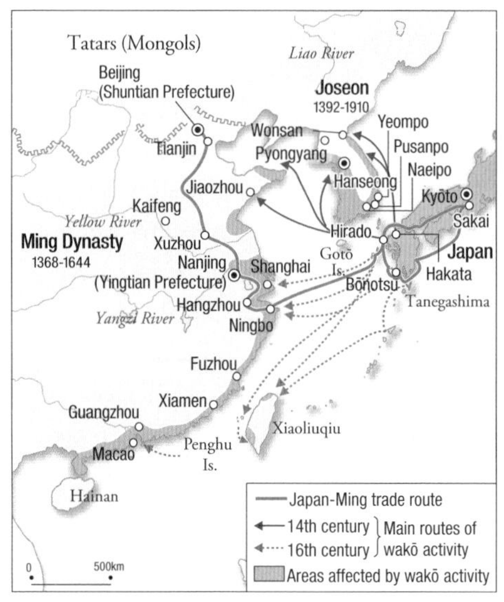

EAST ASIA AROUND THE 15TH CENTURY

reestablish a traditional international order with China at its center. No formal diplomatic relations had been established between Japan and China even after the Mongol Invasions (蒙古襲来), with only private merchant ships coming and going between the countries[15]. However, **Ashikaga Yoshimitsu** (足利義満), learning about the Ming Dynasty's request, dispatched an envoy to China in 1401 and opened diplomatic relations[16].

The **trade between Japan and Ming China** (日明貿易), conducted within an international order revolving around China, had to take the form of a king bringing tribute to the Ming emperor and receiving gifts in return (**tributary trade** (朝貢貿易))[17]. In addition, ships dispatched to Ming China were obliged to bring a certificate of proof called a **kangō** (勘合) (**tally**) issued by the Ming. As such, the trade between Japan and Ming China is also referred to as the **kangō bōeki** (勘合貿易) (**tally trade**).

The trade with Ming China was temporarily suspended due to the fourth shōgun

[15] Following the advice of Musō Soseki〈夢窓疎石〉, Ashikaga Takauji and his brother Tadayoshi 〈足利直義〉 decided to build Tenryūji Temple〈天龍寺〉 to pray for the soul of the late Go-Daigo Tennō. In order to procure funds to cover the cost of its construction, they dispatched a ship to Yuan China in 1342. This followed the precedent set by the Kamakura Bakufu, which in 1325 dispatched a ship to Yuan China for the purpose of funding repairs to Kenchōji Temple 〈建長寺〉. A sunken ship discovered off the coast of Sinan〈新安〉 in South Korea in 1976 is assumed to have been a trading vessel wrecked on its way to Japan from Yuan China in the first half of the 14th century.

[16] On the first ship dispatched to Ming China, Yoshimitsu sent as his chief envoy the monk Soa〈祖阿〉, a close advisor of his, along with Koitsumi〈肥富〉, a merchant from Hakata, as the deputy envoy.

[17] To establish diplomatic relations, Yoshimitsu sent an envoy to Ming China carrying an official message. He received a reply from the Ming emperor addressed to the "King of Japan, Gen [Minamoto] Dōgi〈源道義〉" (Dōgi was Yoshimitsu's Buddhist name) along with the Ming calendar. As a countermeasure against the wakō, the Ming Dynasty had a policy forbidding anyone but kings to conduct foreign trade (Sea Ban Policy〈海禁政策〉). This meant it was essential to receive the title of "king" from the Ming emperor to start trading with the Ming. Thereafter, the shōgun's official documents sent to Ming emperors were signed, "Your Subject, Minamoto, King of Japan." Furthermore, adopting the Ming calendar was a symbolic gesture to be a vassal of Ming.

PICTURE OF WAKŌ (*WAKŌ ZUKAN*〈『倭寇図巻』〉 [ILLUSTRATED SCROLL OF WAKŌ], PART)
This scroll is a work of the end of the Ming Dynasty that depicts later wakō. Most of the later wakō were Chinese, but in this scroll, all the wakō are depicted like Japanese, with the wakō pirates to the right and the Ming military to the left.

Yoshimochi's opposition to the tributary system, but it was resumed during the time of the sixth shōgun, Ashikaga Yoshinori 足利義教. In the tributary trade system, all costs, such as for accommodation and transportation, were provided by the Ming Dynasty, so it was quite profitable for Japan. In particular, the large amount of copper coins that were imported to Japan had a great impact on the Japanese currency in circulation[18].

With the decline of the bakufu in the late 15th century, actual authority over the trade gradually shifted to the Hosokawa family, who were cooperating with merchants in Sakai 堺, and the Ōuchi family, who were cooperating with merchants in Hakata 博多. These two families competed intensely over trade, causing them to clash in Ningbo in 1523 (**Ningbo Incident** 寧波の乱). The Ōuchi family, which emerged victorious, started to monopolize the trade with Ming, but the tally trade ended with the family's defeat in the mid-16th century. Along with these changes, the activities of the wakō intensified again[19], until they were finally suppressed when Toyotomi Hideyoshi 豊臣秀吉 issued his Piracy Prohibition Edict 海賊取締令.

---

[18] Japan exported items including arms such as swords, spears, and armor; craft items such as fans and folding screens; and minerals such as copper and sulfur. In addition to copper coins, imported items included silk, high-quality fabrics, porcelain and chinaware, books, and calligraphic works and paintings, all of which were called karamono〈唐物〉 (imported goods from China) and highly prized.

[19] The wakō during this period are referred to as "later wakō" as opposed to the "early wakō" that used to be active during the 14th century. The later wakō actually included many Chinese smugglers as well. They traded in Japanese silver and Chinese silk, while engaging in piracy around an extensive area.

Meanwhile, on the Korean peninsula, **Yi Seong-gye** 李成桂 (1335-1408), a general who had gained fame by repelling wakō, overthrew the Goryeo Dynasty in 1392 and established the **Joseon Dynasty** 朝鮮 (1392-1910). The dynasty also asked for diplomatic relations with Japan, as well as the suppression of wakō activities, to which Ashikaga Yoshimitsu responded favorably. Thus, diplomatic relations between the two countries were established. Unlike Japan's trade with Ming China, the **trade between Japan and Joseon** 日朝貿易 involved from the start not only the bakufu but also shugo, kokujin, and merchants. The flourishing trade led the Joseon Dynasty to establish a system to regulate trade relations through the **Sō family** 宗氏 in Tsushima. The trade was suspended temporarily due to the **Ōei Invasion** 応永の外寇[20], but it continued to be actively conducted until the 16th century[21].

The main imports from Joseon Korea were textiles, particularly **cotton** 木綿 cloth, which had a great impact on people's lifestyles such as clothing[22]. However, the trade between Japan and Korea also gradually declined following the Disturbance of the Three Ports 三浦の乱 (Sanpo Incident) that occurred in 1510[23].

The Ryūkyū Islands and Ezogashima

In the Ryūkyū 琉球 Islands, three polities – Sanhoku 山北, Chūzan 中山, and Sannan 山南 (collectively called Sanzan 三山) were established and fought for dominance. However, in 1429, **Shō Hashi** 尚巴志 (1372-1439), the ruler of Chūzan, united the three polities and established the **Ryūkyū Kingdom** 琉球王国. The kingdom opened diplomatic relations with countries like Ming China and Japan, and was active in overseas trade. Ryūkyū ships reached as far as the islands of Java and Sumatra, and the Indochina peninsula, in the south and actively engaged in intermediary trade among East Asian countries under the Ming policy forbidding private people from conducting foreign trade. The Ryūkyū Kingdom flour-

---

[20] Wakō activities began to increase following the death of Sō Sadashige〈宗貞茂〉 of Tsushima, who had undertaken active efforts to suppress the wakō and promote trade between Japan and Korea. This increase led Joseon forces to attack Tsushima, which they considered to be the main wakō base, in 1419.

[21] The Joseon Dynasty opened three ports to trade with Japan, namely Pusanpo (Busan)〈富山浦（釜山）〉, Naeipo (Jepo)〈乃而浦（薺浦）〉, and Yeompo (Ulsan)〈塩浦（蔚山）〉. Japanese settlements were established in these ports and in the capital Hanseong (Hanyang, present-day Seoul)〈漢城（漢陽）〉 to welcome Japanese envoys and trade with Japan.

[22] Exports from Japan included not only minerals, such as copper and sulfur, and crafts, but also sappanwood (dye) and fragrant wood (incense) that was acquired through trade with the Ryūkyū Islands. Imports included the traditional Buddhist scriptures (Tripitaka〈大蔵経〉).

[23] A variety of privileges had been granted to the Japanese residents of the three ports. However, when these privileges were gradually reduced, the disgruntled Japanese started a riot in response, only to be suppressed.

SHURI CASTLE
This castle flourished as the palace of the Ryūkyū Kingdom from the 14th or 15th century until the Ryūkyū Disposition〈琉球処分〉 of 1879. Based on the style unique to Ryūkyū culture, it reflects a rich cosmopolitan influence, incorporating architectural styles from both China and Japan. It was destroyed by fire in 1945 during the Battle of Okinawa and reconstructed in 1992, only to burn down in 2019.

ished as Naha (那覇), the outer harbor of Shuri (首里), the capital, became a major international port.

In the meantime, the Japan Sea trade between the Kinai region and Tosaminato (十三湊) in Tsugaru (津軽) had already been quite active by the 14th century, bringing to Kyōto products of the North Sea such as salmon and kombu seaweed. People in Honshū (本州) gradually began to find their way to the southern part of Hokkaidō (北海道). In Hokkaidō, which was called **Ezogashima** (蝦夷ヶ島) at the time, they began building settlements around ports or forts (Dōnan Jyūni Tate (道南十二館), or 12 Forts of Southern Hokkaidō)[24] along the coastal areas. Those people, called Wajin (和人), expanded their sphere of influence under the rule of the powerful Andō family (安藤（安東）氏) in Tsugaru.

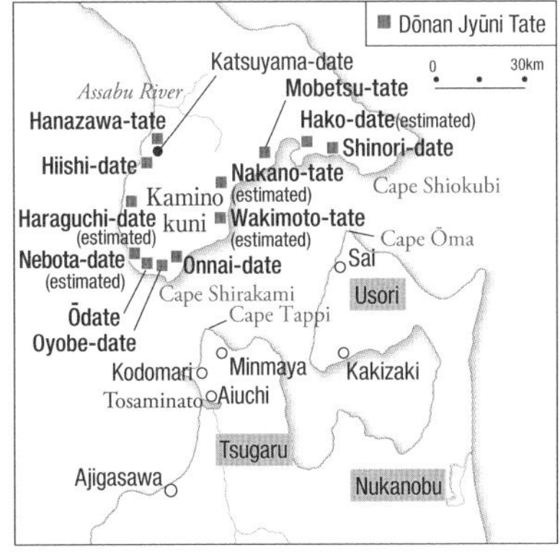

DŌNAN JYŪNI TATE AND THEIR ENVIRONS
All but Mobetsu-tate〈茂別館〉 and the Kakizaki family's Hanazawa-tate〈花沢館〉 were captured by Koshamain.

The Ainu (アイヌ) people, who had lived in Hokkaidō since early times and made their living through fishing, hunting, and trading, engaged in trade with the Wajin. The Wajin grew to encroach upon the Ainu, who finally rose in revolt under the great chieftain **Koshamain** (コシャマイン) (?-1457) in 1457. While they managed to capture most of the Wajin settlements at one point, the revolt was soon suppressed by the Kakizaki (Takeda) (蠣崎（武田）氏)

[24] A total of 390,000 Chinese coins, buried around the time between the end of the 14th century and the early 15th century, were unearthed in the vicinity of one of the twelve forts, the Shinori-date〈志苔館〉, which was located in Hako-date〈函館〉. This speaks to the economic prosperity enjoyed by the area.

family that ruled Kaminokuni(上之国)[25]. In the wake of the revolt, the Kakizaki family came to control the Wajin settlements in the southern Hokkaidō region. In the Edo period, the family gained the position of daimyō(大名), and changed its name to Matsumae(松前氏).

2 The Decline of the Bakufu and the Rise of Commoners

The Evolution of Sō Villages

In the latter half of the Kamakura period, in the Kinki(近畿) region and surrounding areas several villages spontaneously emerged within estates and public lands, which were the basic administrative units at the time. This type of village gradually became more common in various areas during the Nanbokuchō upheavals. These self-sustaining and autonomous villages, managed by farmers, were called **sō**(惣) or **sōson**(惣村) (sō village).

Such villages were comprised of not only the headmen, who were long-established farmers, but also newly-emerged small-scale farmers. They gradually united tightly through village shrine rituals[26], collaborative agricultural work, and defense of their village during conflicts. These villagers were also known as **sōbyakushō**(惣百姓).

Sō villages were managed by leaders called otona(おとな(長·乙名)) or satanin(沙汰人), in accordance with decisions made by a village committee called **yoriai**(寄合). Villagers also stipulated **sō okite**(惣掟) (village laws, also called sonpō(村法) or mura okite(村掟)), which were rules that they had to keep; moreover, they wielded police authority by themselves (jigekendan(地下検断) or jikendan(自検断)) to keep order within the village. The villages managed common lands (iriaichi(入会地)), like mountains and fields, that were necessary for agricultural production, as well as water for irrigation[27]. The practice of **jigeuke**(地下請) (also called murauke(村請) or hyakushō-uke(百姓請)), where the annual taxes for the lord were collected by the village and paid together, also gradually became widespread.

The sō village farmers, bound together with a strong sense of solidarity, at times formed **ikki**(一揆) seeking the dismissal of corrupt local agents or estate managers, or tax relief

---

[25] There have been excavations at the ruins of the Katsuyama-date〈勝山館〉fort (built in Kaminokuni-chō〈上ノ国町〉, Hiyama-gun〈檜山郡〉, Hokkaidō by Takeda Nobuhiro〈武田信広〉, progenitor of the Kakizaki family, after the Koshamain War〈コシャマインの戦い〉). Discoveries include not only the remains of a warrior residence and an artisan's workshop, and burial sites of both Wajin and Ainu people, but also numerous artifacts including ceramics made in Japan and China, as well as Ainu bone and antler artifacts.

[26] A group of farmers called **miyaza**〈宮座〉performed the religious rituals at the shrine, and played a major role in uniting the sō village.

[27] Village committees at times imposed their own taxes on villagers in order to cover the costs necessary to manage the village.

in the wake of natural disasters like flooding or drought. They frequently employed direct action, confronting the estate proprietor with a petition (gōso 強訴), or having everyone abandon their farmland and run away to other estates or the wilderness (an action called chōsan 逃散)[28].

Among the leading farmers in sō villages there were many who became warriors by establishing lord-retainer ties with shugo or other elites[29], which gradually made it difficult for estate proprietors or jitō to control the land.

The Shaking of the Bakufu, and Tsuchi Ikki

The era of Ashikaga Yoshimochi (1386-1428), who succeeded Yoshimitsu, was a relatively stable time because the power balance between the shōgun and the powerful shugo was maintained[30]. However, in aiming to strengthen shōgunal authority, the sixth shōgun, **Ashikaga Yoshinori** 足利義教 (1394-1441), governed in a more autocratic fashion. In 1438, Yoshinori dispatched forces to the Kantō region to suppress Ashikaga Mochiuji 足利持氏 (1398-1439), the rebellious Kamakura Kubō, and defeated him the following year (Eikyō Rebellion 永享の乱)[31]. Since Yoshinori continued to crack down on powerful shugo even after this, in 1441 he was assassinated by one of them, **Akamatsu Mitsusuke** 赤松満祐 (1373-1441), triggering the Kakitsu War 嘉吉の変. The Akamatsu family was crushed by the bakufu army that same year, but from this point on the shōgun's authority was greatly shaken.

Around this time, **tsuchi ikki** 土一揆 (**famer ikki**, also called tokusei ikki 徳政一揆) became more frequent, particularly in the Kinki region[32]. Such ikki consisted of farmers under the bond of sō villages, a segment of the urban-dwelling population, and destitute

---

[28] When pursuing group action, sō villages often united based on their estate or town to form larger, stronger groups called sōshō〈惣荘〉 or sōgō〈惣郷〉. In some cases, sō villages under different proprietors united outside of the estate/town framework.

[29] People who gained warrior status by establishing a lord-vassal relationship with a shugo or other powerholder, while paying taxes to an estate proprietor as a farmer, were called jizamurai〈地侍〉 (rural warriors).

[30] In 1416, Uesugi Zenshū〈上杉禅秀〉, the former Kantō Kanrei, rose in revolt by taking advantage of an internal dispute in the Kamakura-fu, but was suppressed (Uesugi Zenshū Rebellion〈上杉禅秀の乱〉).

[31] Ashikaga Yoshinori took advantage of a conflict between the Kamakura Kubō, Mochiuji, and the Kantō Kanrei, Uesugi Norizane〈上杉憲実〉, to support the latter and destroy the former. After this incident, in 1440 Yūki Ujitomo〈結城氏朝〉 raised an army supporting a child of the late Mochiuji's, but this too was suppressed (Yūki Incident〈結城合戦〉). Afterwards, Ashikaga Shigeuji〈足利成氏〉, another son of Mochiuji's, became Kantō Kubō; however, he too fell into conflict with the Uesugi family, and in 1454 had Uesugi Noritada〈上杉憲忠〉 assassinated, triggering the Kyōtoku Rebellion〈享徳の乱〉. This set off the Sengoku period in the Kantō region.

[32] Since most of the tsuchi ikki demanded tokusei (debt relief), they are also called tokusei ikki. The one that occurred in Harima Province〈播磨国〉 in 1429 included a political demand to expel a retainer of the shugo family (the Akamatsu family) from the province.

SHŌCHŌ NO TOKUSEI IKKI[1]

In the ninth month of Shōchō 1 [1428], farmers throughout the region rose up. Calling for debt cancellation, they destroyed sakaya (breweries), dosō (warehouses), temples, and more, despoiled whatever goods they wished, tore up all the debt contracts, and so on. The Kanrei[2] suppressed the uprising. As a cause of the ruin of our country, nothing could exceed this. There has never been such an uprising of farmers since the dawn of Japan[3].

[1] Source: *Daijōin Nikki Mokuroku*〈『大乗院日記目録』〉, original in kanbun.
[2] Refers to Hatakeyama Mitsuie〈畠山満家〉. [3] In other words, the beginning of time.

warriors, who rose up seeking debt relief. In particular, the major ikki calling for debt cancellation that occurred in Kyōto in 1428 (**Shōchō no Tokusei Ikki** 正長の徳政一揆) had a great impact on the central political sphere, since the participants attacked the warehouses and breweries of moneylenders to get hold of pawned items and credit records. In both urban and rural areas, high-interest moneylending by warehouse pawnbrokers and so forth was deeply rooted in the society at the time, so ikki spread across the Kinki region and surrounding areas, resulting in the use of force in various areas to repudiate debt contracts or recover land (shitokusei 私徳政).

In 1441, tsuchi ikki totaling tens of thousands of people occupied Kyōto during the **Kakitsu no Tokusei Ikki** 嘉吉の徳政一揆[33]. Eventually the bakufu acquiesced to their demands and issued a debt cancellation decree. Thereafter, tsuchi ikki frequently rose up crying for debt relief in various areas, and the bakufu also came to issue debt cancellation decrees in a scattershot fashion[34].

The Ōnin War and Kuni Ikki

After the Kakitsu War, the power of the shōgun weakened, contributing to one conflict after another within the shōgunal family and influential shugo families. First, the Hatakeyama and Shiba kanrei families both had internal succession disputes, and then the shōgunal family had its own succession dispute over who would succeed the

[33] Shōchō no Tokusei Ikki took place during the governance of the sixth shōgun, Yoshinori, while Kakitsu no Tokusei Ikki (or Daihajime no Tokusei〈代始めの徳政〉) occurred at the start of the rule of the seventh, Yoshikatsu〈足利義勝〉. In medieval society, there was an understanding that relationships, such as those pertaining to the ownership of land or lending/borrowing money, could be amended when a new ruler came to power. This social concept played a significant role as a backdrop to the Tenka'ichidō no Tokusei〈「天下一同の徳政」〉, which were frequent tsuchi ikki demanding debt cancellation that followed a change in shōgun.

[34] Debt cancellations by the bakufu included many conditional cancellations, whereby the bakufu both protected credit and cancelled debt, under the condition that a 10% or 20% fee (buichisen〈分一銭〉) was paid to the bakufu.

eighth shōgun, **Ashikaga Yoshimasa** 足利義政 (1436-90). On one side was Yoshimasa's brother, Yoshimi 足利義視 (1439-91), and on the other was Yoshimasa's wife Hino Tomiko 日野富子 (1440-96), who backed their son **Ashikaga Yoshihisa** 足利義尚 (1465-89)[35]. Moreover, because **Hosokawa Katsumoto** 細川勝元 (1430-73) and **Yamana Mochitoyo** 山名持豊（宗全） (Sōzen, 1404-73), who were competing over the real power in the bakufu, intervened in these disputes, the conflicts became intensified. This led to the outbreak of the **Ōnin War** 応仁の乱 in 1467, which ushered in the Sengoku period 戦国時代.

The shugo daimyō were largely divided into two factions, between the Hosokawa side (eastern force) and the Yamana side (western force)[36]. The war between these two forces saw Kyōto, which became the central battleground, burned and reduced to ruins. The conflict did not end until 1477, when the two forces, exhausted from fighting, made peace. Although many of the shugo daimyō returned to their home

	Western Force	Eastern Force
Shōgunal Family	**Yoshimi**	**Yoshimasa** — **Yoshihisa**
Hatakeyama Family	**Mochikuni** — **Yoshihiro**	**Mochitomi** — **Masanaga**
Shiba Family	**Yoshikado**	**Yoshitoshi**
Influential Persons in Bakufu	**Yamana Mochitoyo**	**Hosokawa Katsumoto**
Powerful Daimyō	**Ōuchi, Isshiki, Toki, Rokkaku**	**Akamatsu, Kyōgoku, Takeda**

OPPOSING FACTIONS IN THE ŌNIN WAR (C. 1468)

ASHIGARU〈足軽〉 (*SHINNYODŌ-ENGI*〈『真如堂縁起』〉 [ILLUSTRATED SCROLL OF THE FOUNDING OF SHINNYODŌ TEMPLE], PART)
Ashigaru were low-ranking foot soldiers with light equipment enabling them to move quickly. Around the time of the Ōnin War they were extremely active. The picture depicts some of them looting Shinnyodō Temple.

[35] With the onset of the single inheritance system, the status of the heir came to have an absolute advantage over the other sons, which resulted in great conflict over that status. Around this time in particular, the selection of an heir for major figures like daimyō depended not only on the will of the father, but was also strongly influenced by the intentions of the shōgun or retainers. Succession disputes therefore became much more complicated.

[36] In the fifth month of 1467, the eastern force occupied the shōgun's residence and captured Ashikaga Yoshimasa, Yoshihisa and Yoshimi. However, in the eleventh month of 1468 Yoshimi escaped to join the western force, resulting in the bakufu being split in two.

domains, conflict continued in the form of regional struggles that spread across the whole country. Due to these conflicts, bakufu administration, in which powerful shugo participated in governance while residing in the capital, collapsed, and the estate system broke down.

While the shugo daimyō had been occupied fighting in Kyōto, in their home domains deputy shugo or powerful kokujin acquired power, and gradually gained real administrative control over the domains. Meanwhile, in the Kinki region and surrounding areas, some kokujin formed **kuni ikki** 国一揆 (**provincial ikki**)[37] to protect their local order from warfare. For example, in 1485 the **Yamashiro no Kuni Ikki** 山城の国一揆 in the Minami Yamashiro 南山城地方 area forced the two in-fighting camps of the Hatakeyama family to leave the province. With the support of the people in the province, this ikki led to 8 years of autonomy. Such cases illustrate a distinguishing characteristic of the period called **gekokujō** 下剋上, meaning lowers seizing power by overturning their superiors.

Another clear example of gekokujō can be seen in the **Kaga no Ikkō Ikki** 加賀の一向一揆 in 1488. Due to the proselytization efforts of the Honganji 本願寺 monk **Rennyo** 蓮如（兼寿） (Kenju, 1415-99), the Honganji school of the Jōdo Shinshū 浄土真宗 Sect had become widespread in the Kinki, Tōkai 東海 and Hokuriku 北陸 regions. Believers in Kaga Province 加賀国 made ties with kokujin, and together defeated the shugo, Togashi Masachika 富樫政親 (1455?-88). This ikki lasted for about a century, until Oda Nobunaga 織田信長 suppressed the provinces under the control of Honganji Temple.

Agricultural Developments

Agriculture in the Muromachi period was characterized by the development of intensive and diversified farming, which was undertaken in order to improve the productivity of land in relation to the lifestyle needs of commoners. The maintenance and improvement of irrigation and drainage facilities using waterwheels and the like enabled people to raise two or even three crops (**sanmōsaku** 三毛作) a year on the same land. The advancement of selective breeding of rice plants led to the practice of planting early-, mid-, and late-season crops becoming widespread.

For fertilizer, it became common to use cut grasses and ashes together with manure (**shimogoe** 下肥), improving the quality of the soil and contributing to more reliable harvests. People also cultivated such crops as ramie, mulberry, paper mulberry, lacquer

---

[37] Kuni ikki can be differentiated from kokujin ikki because the former involved not only warriors but also local residents. In addition to Yamashiro no Kuni Ikki, Iga Sōkoku no Ikki〈伊賀惣国一揆〉 and Kōga Gunchūsō〈甲賀郡中惣〉 in Ōmi are well known examples. In response to demands from local residents, they sometimes issued their own debt cancellation decrees (zaichi tokusei-rei〈在地徳政令〉).

trees, Chinese indigo, and tea plants to produce materials for handicraft manufacturing. These handicrafts were widely distributed as commodities due to the development of craft industries in farming villages, and the spread of the practice of paying tax in coinage. The increased productivity made farmers wealthy, and the demand for goods increased, leading to the deep penetration of the commodity economy even in villages.

Developments in Commerce and Industry

During the Muromachi period, local industries prospered due to the demand even among farmers, and various kinds of local specialties came to be produced[38].

For salt, in addition to saltpans there was the natural method of sea-salt collection called shizenhama 自然浜 (or agehama 揚浜), as well as a new method called koshiki irihama 古式入浜 (or irihamaenden 入浜塩田), which used the ebb and flow of the tides to bring seawater into salt beds on the shore.

To sell local specialties and acquire money to pay taxes, the number of markets and their frequency increased. Markets were already held three times a month, but after the Ōnin War it became common for them to be held six times a month, a practice called **rokusaiichi** 六斎市[39]. The number of itinerant traders, called renjaku shōnin 連雀商人 or furiuri 振売, greatly increased. There were many female merchants who were highly active in this trade, such as the oharame 大原女 and katsurame 桂女 in Kyōto[40]. Small permanent shops called **misedana** 見世棚（店棚） became routine in larger cities like the capital, and markets dealing only in specialized products, such as rice in Kyōto or fish in Yodo 淀, also began.

Both the kind and number of za 座 (professional guilds) of handicraft manufacturers and merchants also significantly increased. Some of these guilds were active across the country, having received authorization (with the title of "ji'nin" 神人 or "kugonin" 供御人) from major religious institutions or the royal family that allowed them to enjoy exemption

---

[38] Famous local specialties included silk fabric (Kaga and Tango〈丹後国〉 provinces), Mino paper (Mino Province), Suibara paper〈杉原紙〉 (Harima Province), pottery (Mino and Owari provinces), swords (Bizen Province〈備前国〉), deep iron pots (Noto〈能登国〉 and Chikuzen〈筑前国〉 provinces), and broad pots (Kawachi Province〈河内国〉). Swords in particular were forged not only for domestic demand, but also in great quantities as a major export item for trade with Ming China. High-quality silk fabric was produced in Kyōto, and the liquor industry competed to produce quality sake not only in Kyōto, but also in Kawachi, Yamato〈大和国〉, and Settsu〈摂津国〉 provinces.

[39] Estate managers and farmers acquired currency by selling agricultural products at these markets. As a result, many agricultural products that used to be brought to the proprietors as taxes were instead passed to merchants and distributed as commodities.

[40] Oharame were merchants who sold charcoal and firewood, while katsurame belonged to cormorant fishing groups and sold sweetfish. Both of these were active from early times. Additionally, there were many female merchants engaged in selling fish, folding fans, fabrics, and tōfu〈豆腐〉, and some women were involved in the finance industry as well.

SHOPPING ARCADE IN KYŌTO (*RAKUCHŪ RAKUGAIZU BYŌBU*〈「洛中洛外図屛風」〉 [FOLDING SCREEN OF SCENES IN AND AROUND THE CAPITAL], PART)
This image depicts Tachiuri Avenue〈立売通〉 in Kyōto around the end of the Muromachi period. In front of a house stands a shop with a shingle roof, inside of which bows can be seen lined up for sale. On the right side of the river a hawker can also be seen.

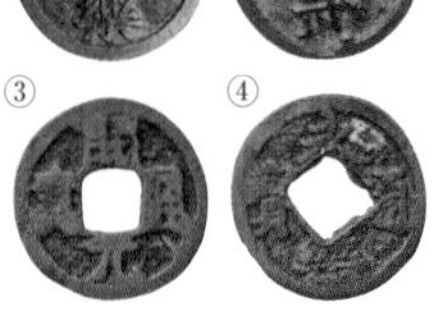

MINSEN AND SHICHŪSEN
During the Muromachi period, Eiraku Tsūhō ①, Kōbu Tsūhō〈洪武通宝〉 ②, Sentoku Tsūhō〈宣徳通宝〉 and other coins were used. The import of Minsen like the Eiraku Tsūhō encouraged the production of inferior privately-minted coins (bitasen〈びた銭〉, ③ & ④).

MUROMACHI-ERA MERCHANTS (LEFT: *ISHIYAMADERA ENGI EMAKI*〈「石山寺縁起絵巻」〉 [ILLUSTRATED SCROLL OF THE FOUDING OF ISHIYAMADERA TEMPLE], RIGHT: *FUKUTOMI ZŌSHI*〈「福富草紙」〉 [THE TALES OF FUKUTOMI])
These merchants sold tokoroten〈心太〉 (gelidium jelly), manjū〈饅頭〉 (steamed buns) and tōfu.

from tolls or monopolies on selling in a certain area[41]. However, after the 15th century, merchants who did not belong to any guild also appeared, while in local areas that lacked patrons new types of guild (called nakama, business associations) also came to increase.

As for the monetary system, along with the Sōsen〈宋銭〉 (Song coins) that had conventionally been used there were also newly-imported coins like the Eiraku Tsūhō〈永楽通宝〉 that were called **Minsen**〈明銭〉 (Ming coins), and with the great increase in demand poorly-made privately-minted coins (Shichūsen〈私鋳銭〉) came to circulate as well. To avoid using bad coins in transactions, high-quality coinage needed to be selected (a process called **erizeni**〈撰銭〉), which inhibited fluid circulation. In response, authorities like the bakufu

---

[41] Tōrokugonin〈灯炉供御人〉 (or imoji〈鋳物師〉, iron casters) had the royal secretariat as their patron and were thus exempt from tolls by the authority of the royal court; they were active across the country. In Ōyamazaki, the aburaji'nin〈大山崎油神人〉 (or aburaza〈油座〉, oil guild), had the Iwashimizu Hachimangū Shrine〈石清水八幡宮〉 as their patron, which gained them a monopoly on selling oil in nearly ten provinces across the Kinai region and areas including Mino, Owari, and Awa〈阿波〉. They also enjoyed a monopoly on purchasing perilla as raw material for their oil. Other famous guilds in Kyōto included the kōjizaji'nin〈麴座神人〉 (malted rice guild), supported by Kitano Shrine〈北野社〉, and the watazaji'nin〈綿座神人〉 (cotton guild), supported by Gion Shrine〈祇園社〉.

REMAINS OF A STOREHOUSE AFTER A FIRE (*KASUGA GONGEN GENKI*〈『春日権現験記』〉 [CHRONICLES OF THE MIRACLES OF THE KASUGA DEITY], PART)
Dosō, together with sakaya, engaged in high-interest moneylending since the end of the Kamakura period. Sometimes they became deputies of estate proprietors and collected taxes on their behalf, thereby amassing great wealth. Their storehouses often burned down, but were quickly reconstructed.

BASHAKU PASSING A CHECKPOINT (*ISHIYAMADERA ENGIEMAKI*, PART)
Ōtsu was close to Kyōto, so from ancient times the number of merchants passing through this checkpoint carrying tax payment items and commodities was substantial. The lower part of the picture shows bashaku passing the checkpoint with payment from estates bound for proprietors in the Kyōto area.

and sengoku daimyō 戦国大名 took measures such as setting the ratio of metals in poor coins and high-quality coins, and issuing **erizeni-rei** 撰銭令 (coin selection laws) that, rather than banning the circulation of bad coins, instead enforced the circulation of other ones[42].

The development of the monetary economy stimulated the activities of moneylenders. At the time, many wealthy merchants like **sakaya** 酒屋 (breweries) were also high-interest moneylenders called **dosō** 土倉, and along with protecting and controlling these the bakufu also imposed business taxes on them.

The prosperity of local industry also led to increased long-distance trade. Merchants engaged in distance transactions frequently made use of a type of promissory note called **saifu** 割符. The transportation networks based on the sea, rivers, and land all developed[43], and cargo vessels were often coming and going on the waters[44].

---

[42] With the decrease in high-quality coins, in the latter half of the 16th century rice and silver also came to be used as currency in western Japan.

[43] The bakufu, religious institutions, nobles and so forth took note of the increase in transportation of people and goods, and established checkpoints at important locations on both land and maritime routes where they imposed tolls or customs. This became a major obstacle to smooth transportation.

[44] According to historical sources like the *Hyōgo Kitaseki Irifune Nōchō*〈『兵庫北関入船納帳』〉 (Records of Cargo Vessels Entering North Hyōgo Checkpoint and Customs Imposed), during one year (1445) the number of cargo vessels bringing various goods into Hyōgo harbor from ports in the Seto Inland Sea〈瀬戸内海〉 reached over 2700.

Wholesalers (**toiya** 問屋) appeared in big cities like Kyōto and Nara, as well as in important transportation hubs like Hyōgo and Ōtsu 大津. Transportation agents called **bashaku** 馬借 or **shashaku** 車借 were active on the routes to Kyōto, conveying great amounts of merchandise.

3 Muromachi Culture

Muromachi Culture

The Muromachi period saw several cultural movements, namely, **Nanbokuchō culture** 南北朝文化, that emerged during the conflict between the two courts; **Kitayama culture** 北山文化, that flourished during the time of Ashikaga Yoshimitsu; and **Higashiyama culture** 東山文化, that developed during Ashikaga Yoshimasa's era.

These cultures were characterized by broadness and integration. With the bakufu situated in Kyōto, warrior culture and courtier culture became integrated, while the active exchange with East Asia brought continental culture and traditional culture together. Moreover, the cultures of the era were connected to the commoners both in urban areas and in the sō villages that grew around this time, contributing to the emergence of a broad cultural foundation.

The integration, and eventual harmonization, of urban and rural culture gradually brought about the emergence of a particular culture unique to Japan. Many of the practices that are today considered representative of traditional Japanese culture – such as Nō 能, Kyōgen 狂言, Cha no Yu 茶の湯 (tea ceremony), and ikebana 生花 (flower arrangement) – were products of the Muromachi period. These were admired and refined by people of the time regardless of where they lived, or whether they were warriors, courtiers, or commoners.

Nanbokuchō Culture

The heightened tension that characterized the turning points of the Nanbokuchō period prompted the creation of historical accounts and military tales. Historical accounts include *Masukagami*, which records the history after the Genpei War 源平争乱 from the viewpoint of courtiers, Kitabatake Chikafusa's ***Jinnō Shōtōki*** 『神皇正統記』 (**Chronicle of the Authentic Lineage of the Divine Sovereigns**), which discusses the principles of royal succession from the perspective of the Southern Court using theories drawn from Ise Shintō 伊勢神道, and *Baishōron* 『梅松論』, which charts the process of the Ashikaga family's rise to power from the perspective of warriors. As for military tales, ***Taiheiki*** 『太平記』 (**Chronicle of the Great Pacification**), a masterpiece that portrays the entirety of the Nanbokuchō upheavals, became extremely popular and continued to be read for generations afterwards.

Further, as can be seen in *Nijō Kawara no Rakusho*〈「二条河原落書」〉 (Lampoon by the Nijō River), renga〈連歌〉 (linked verse) also became popular among both warriors and courtiers, while **Nōgaku**〈能楽〉 **(Nō theatre)** also drew large audiences to performances. **Chayoriai**〈茶寄合〉 **(tea gatherings)**, were also held in various areas, and **tōcha**〈闘茶〉, a contest in which participants competed to identify different types of tea to win prizes, became immensely popular. These new trends were often pioneered by newly-emerged warriors who gained power during the upheavals. These warriors loved to take up new things, a tendency called **basara**〈バサラ〉, a term meaning fancy or luxurious[45].

Kitayama Culture

The third shōgun, Ashikaga Yoshimitsu, built a splendid villa in Kitayama, the northern mountains of Kyōto, and within those grounds stands the **Kinkaku**〈金閣〉 (Golden Pavilion)[iv]. The architectural style of the building represents a compromise between the more traditional shinden-zukuri〈寝殿造〉 style and Zenshūyō〈禅宗様〉, the style seen in Zen〈禅宗寺院〉 Buddhist temples, and because it effectively captures the characteristics of this time, the culture of the era is referred to as Kitayama culture.

The Rinzai〈臨済宗〉 Sect, which spread amongst the higher-ranked warriors during the Kamakura period, further flourished under the support and protection of the bakufu, since Ashikaga Takauji devotedly followed **Musō Soseki**〈夢窓疎石〉, (1275-1351), a monk of the sect. The **Gozan Jissatsu**〈五山・十刹の制〉 (Five Mountains and Ten Monasteries) system[46], which was modelled on the state-sponsored〈官寺〉 temples of the Southern Song, was also almost completed during Yoshimitsu's time. Many of the Five Mountains monks came from China, or had returned from studying there, and brought to Japan not only Zen itself, but also artistic pursuits embodying the spirit of Zen, such as **suibokuga**〈水墨画〉 **(ink wash paintings)**[47] or architectural and gardening styles. These monks enjoyed studying Sogaku〈宋学〉 (Song Neo-Confucianism) and composing Chinese poetry and

---

[45] One of the most well-known basara daimyō〈バサラ大名〉 is Sasaki Dōyo (Takauji)〈佐々木導誉（高氏）〉, a powerful shugo who displayed great talent in renga, nō, Cha no Yu, and ikebana.

[46] Nanzenji Temple〈南禅寺〉 was put at the peak of the Five Mountains system. The Five Mountains of Kyōto consisted of Tenryūji〈天龍寺〉, Shōkokuji〈相国寺〉, Kenninji〈建仁寺〉, Tōfukuji〈東福寺〉, and Manjuji〈万寿寺〉, while the Five Mountains of Kamakura included Kenchōji, Engakuji〈円覚寺〉, Jyufukuji〈寿福寺〉, Jyōchiji〈浄智寺〉, and Jyōmyōji〈浄妙寺〉. The Ten Monasteries were state-sponsored temples that were ranked below the Five Mountains, followed by another rank called the Shozan〈諸山〉. The bakufu appointed managers of the temples called sōroku〈僧録〉, who had the power to appoint chief priests and so on for the temple.

[47] Suibokuga portray nature or people metaphorically through gradations of the ink. The foundations of Japanese suibokuga were laid by the Gozan monks Minchō〈明兆〉, Josetsu〈如拙〉 and Shūbun〈周文〉.

KANZE NŌ-ZU〈観世能図〉(*RAKUCHŪ RAKUGAIZU BYŌBU*, PART)
The painting depicts how Nō was performed in its early years. The performers utilize a real pine tree as a background, and use a passageway that looks much like a real bridge. The location depicted seems to be the bank of the Kamo River〈鴨川〉 in Kyōto.

prose, trends that reached their height around Yoshimitsu's time with authors such as Zekkai Chūshin 絶海中津 (1336-1405) and Gidō Shūshin 義堂周信 (1325-88), now referred to as **Gozan Literature** 五山文学. The Gozan monks also served as bakufu political and diplomatic advisors[48], and played a major role in spreading Chinese culture through such activities as publishing (in what are known as Five Mountain 五山版 editions) Zen sutras and Chinese poetry and prose.

Nō is another artistic product that represents this age. Nō originated from Sarugaku 猿楽 and Dengaku 田楽, which developed as ritual performing arts in ancient times and included various elements of performance. Out of those older traditions, gradually a musical and theatrical form developed that came to be called Nō. Around this time, professional theatre troupes (za 座) that performed Nō under the protection of temples and shrines emerged, and began performing frequently in various locations. In particular, the four groups (Konparu 金春座, Kongō 金剛座, Kanze 観世座, and Hōshō 宝生座) that had Kōfukuji 興福寺 Temple as their patron were renowned as the Yamato Sarugaku Shiza 大和猿楽四座. Under the patronage of Yoshimitsu, **Kan'ami** 観阿弥 (1333-84) and his son **Zeami** 世阿弥 (1363?-1443?), actors and playwrights from the Kanze group, pursued the beauty of refined art, and developed the highly-artistic style of Sarugaku Nō 猿楽能. The two wrote numerous yōkyoku 謡曲 (chants) that served as scripts for Nō plays, and Zeami also wrote treatises such as *Fūshikaden* 『風姿花伝』(花伝書) (also known as *Kadensho*) that explained the essence of Nō.

[48] They not only drafted diplomatic documents, but also traveled to Ming China and Korea as envoys themselves.

Higashiyama Culture

Muromachi culture flowered with the rise of Kitayama culture, and its artistic characteristics pervaded through the lives of the Muromachi people, fully taking root as a new distinct culture in its own right.

After the Ōnin War, Ashikaga Yoshimasa created a villa in the Higashiyama mountains of Kyōto, where, like his predecessor Yoshimitsu, he built a pavilion, the **Ginkaku** 銀閣 (Silver Pavilion). As the villa well represents the cultural characteristics of its age, the culture of the time is called Higashiyama culture. The basic spiritual theme of Higashiyama culture was a simplicity derived from Zen Buddhism and the traditional artistic sense of wabi 侘 (embracing the imperfect and transient) and yūgen 幽玄 (sense of profound mystery conveyed by art). The architectural style seen in the Tōgudō Dōjinsai 東求堂同仁斎 is referred to as **shoin-zukuri style** 書院造[49], and became the model for Japanese-style housing in later times. Shoin-zukuri houses and Zenshūyō-style temples had gardens that also reflected the essence of the Zen spirit[50]. Most representative of these were **karesansui** 枯山水, which symbolically represented nature through combining rocks and sand. Famous examples of this gardening style include those at

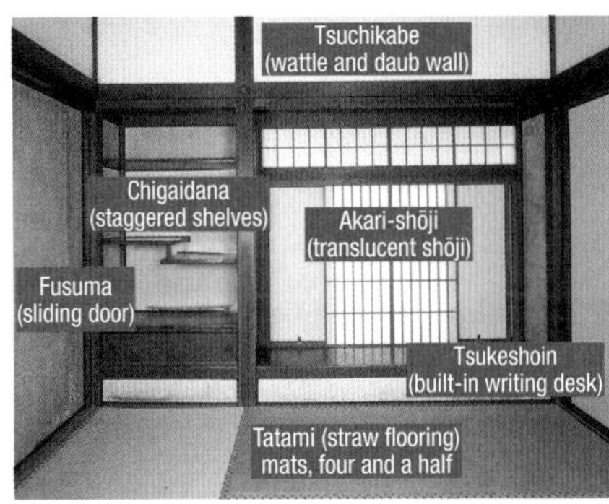

JISHŌJI TŌGUDŌ DŌJINSAI
The Dōjinsai is a small (four-and-a-half mat) room in the Tōgudō that served as Yoshimasa's study. The room is equipped with a 3 shaku〈尺〉(0.9 m) shelf and a tsukeshoin〈付書院〉(built-in writing desk) that is about 1 ken〈間〉(1.8 m) long.

GARDEN OF DAITOKUJI DAISEN-IN
One of the representative karesansui gardens. The garden symbolically depicts the journey of water originating in the gorges and flowing into a river. It is thought to have been created in the early 16th century.

---

[49] The shoin-zukuri style had as its foundation the shinden-zukuri style, and incorporated built-in features such as decorative alcoves, shelves, and writing desks separated from the main room with a shōji〈障子〉. The style was characterized by multiple rooms, with tatami〈畳〉mats on the floor, ceilings installed, and translucent shōji.

[50] Yoshimasa gathered around him many people talented in arts such as kadō or chadō. These figures, called dōbōshū〈同朋衆〉, played a major role in the development of Higashiyama culture. In terms of landscape gardening, outcasts called kawaramono〈河原者〉(senzui-kawaramono〈山水河原者〉) played an important role. One example is Zen'ami〈善阿弥〉, who created the garden at Yoshimasa's Higashiyama villa.

SHŪTŌ SANSUI-ZU〈秋冬山水図〉 (LANDSCAPE OF AUTUMN AND WINTER, BY SESSHŪ)
A painting that consists of two scenes, one of autumn and the other of winter. The picture shown depicts winter. (Length 46.4 cm, width 29.4 cm)

Ryōanji 龍安寺 Temple and Daisen-in 大仙院 (a sub-temple of Daitokuji 大徳寺 Temple).

The establishment of a new housing style encouraged the creation of interior decorations. Kakejiku (calligraphic and pictorial hanging scrolls) and fusumae (paintings on sliding doors), as well as ikebana or handicrafts for the tokonoma 床の間 (alcove for decorative art), all flourished.

In the area of suibokuga, **Sesshū** 雪舟 (1420-1506?), a monk who developed his artistic techniques while visiting Ming China, went beyond the stylistic limitations of Zen painting to create a Japanese style of suibokuga upon his return. As for Yamato-e 大和絵, after the Ōnin War, the **Tosa School** 土佐派[v] was formally established by Tosa Mitsunobu 土佐光信 (?-1522), while Kanō Masanobu 狩野正信 (1434?-1530) and his son Motonobu 狩野元信 (1476-1559) applied traditional Yamato-e techniques to suibokuga, and founded the **Kanō School** 狩野派.

In sculpture, the flourishing of Nō theatre encouraged the development of **Nōmen** 能面 (Nō masks) carving, and as for other crafts, Gotō Yūjō 後藤祐乗 (1440-1512) produced masterpieces of metalwork, while gold lacquer techniques witnessed advancements.

Chadō 茶道 (Cha no Yu) and kadō 花道 (ikebana), two activities considered to be representative of traditional Japanese culture, also have their roots in this era. Murata Jukō 村田珠光 (also known as Shukō, 1423-1502) argued that the spirit of tea should be unified with that of Zen Buddhism, and founded **wabicha** 侘茶, a style of tea ceremony in which one seeks calmness of mind in the tearoom[51]. Meanwhile, ikebana gave rise to a new style called Tatehana 立花 that created, and encouraged appreciation for, flower arrangements to decorate tokonoma[52].

---

[51] Wabicha was further developed by Takeno Jō-ō〈武野紹鷗〉 from Sakai, and was perfected by Sen no Rikyū〈千利休〉.

[52] Ikenobō Senkei〈池坊専慶〉, a monk in Kyōto Rokkakudō〈京都六角堂〉, was known to have been a master of Tatehana ikebana, and his descendants, Ikenobō Sen'ō〈池坊専応〉 in the mid-16th century and Ikenobō Senkō〈池坊専好〉 in the late 16th century, further developed and perfected this style.

On the other hand, courtiers, who had lost their political and economic power, became mainly patrons of traditional culture, dedicating themselves to studying classics and yūsoku kojitsu 有職故実[53]. Scholars like **Ichijō Kaneyoshi** 一条兼良 (also known as Kanera, 1402-81) wrote a number of scholarly texts and commentaries. Moreover, in Shintō thought there were studies of works such as *Nihonshoki* 『日本書紀』. Yoshida Kanetomo 吉田兼倶 (1435-1511) developed Yuiitsu Shintō 唯一神道, which sought to unite Confucianism and Buddhism under Shintō using the theory of Inverted Honji Suijaku 反本地垂迹説 (or Shinpon Butsujaku 神本仏迹説, the notion that Buddhist deities were manifestations of Japanese kami 神).

The Rise of Arts among Commoners

As the status of commoners rose during the Muromachi period, cultural pursuits emerged that not only warriors and courtiers, but also commoners, could enjoy.

Tea ceremonies and renga gatherings were often held among commoners as well, and in addition to the Nō appreciated by the upper classes there was a simpler and more entertaining variety of Nō performed in various areas at local festivals and the like. **Kyōgen** 狂言, satirical comedy performed between Nō programs, became immensely popular amongst commoners, as the themes and language were often based on people's daily lives.

Other entertainments that were popular amongst commoners included kōwakamai 幸若舞 (recitative dance), kojōruri 古浄瑠璃 (narrative musical performance), and ko'uta 小歌 (popular songs), and the *Kanginshū* 『閑吟集』, a collection of ko-uta, was compiled. Commoners also enjoyed **Otogizōshi** 御伽草子, works that frequently combined illustrations with text written in the form of the spoken language of the time, as they could enjoy looking at the pictures even if they could not read.

Renga was a form of collaborative poetry, where waka were divided into upper and lower stanzas, and people collectively completed them by adding stanzas in turns. Nijō Yoshimoto 二条良基 (1320-88), a poet in the Nanbokuchō era, compiled an anthology called the *Tsukubashū* 『菟玖波集』, and produced the *Ōan Shinshiki* 『応安新式』, a set of guidelines for composing renga. After the *Tsukubashū* came to be considered comparable to a royal anthology, the status of renga came to equal that of waka. Further, around the time of the Ōnin War, **Sōgi** 宗祇 (1421-1502) established a style of renga known as **shōfū renga** 正風連歌. He complied the *Shinsen Tsukubashū* 『新撰菟玖波集』 (Newly-selected Tsukuba), and wrote *Minase Sangin Hyakuin* 『水無瀬三吟百韻』

[53] In terms of classics, the *Kokin Wakashū* 〈『古今和歌集』〉 had long been highly regarded in the waka 〈和歌〉 canon, to the point where its interpretations were deemed to be sacred. These interpretations were kept secret, and were only passed on orally to specific people. This oral tradition, called kokin denju 〈古今伝授〉, was systemized by Tō Tsuneyori 〈東常縁〉, and was later further organized by Sōgi.

FURYŪ ODORI (FURYŪ DANCE, FROM *RAKUCHŪ RAKUGAIZU BYŌBU*, PART)
Wearing elaborate costumes and singing songs, people paraded through the streets in a dance. In this period the dance was often performed during Shintō festivals, such as the Gion Matsuri.

(100 Stanzas by Three Poets at Minase) with his disciples. In contrast, Sōkan 宗鑑 (?-1539?) created a freer style of renga called haikai renga 俳諧連歌, and compiled the *Inu Tsukubashū* 『犬筑波集』. The popularity of renga gave rise to professionals called **rengashi** 連歌師 (renga masters). They traveled to many places and worked to spread renga, leading to its popularity among both warriors and commoners in urban and rural areas.

Bon Odori 盆踊り (Bon festival dance), which is still practiced all over Japan, also became popular in this era. During festivals, new years and bon celebrations, people in urban and rural areas used to create elaborate decorations and dance in flamboyant outfits, a custom called furyū 風流. This custom became combined with Nenbutsu Odori 念仏踊り, and gradually became what we know as Bon Odori. One characteristic shared by many of these folk entertainments was that people came together as a community, and enjoyed participating in them together.

The Spread of Culture into Local Regions

As the Ōnin War devastated Kyōto, courtiers escaped one after another into local regions by counting on the daimyō. The local warriors actively welcomed these aristocrats, as they were interested in and admired the culture of the capital. In particular, Yamaguchi 山口, the castle town of the Ōuchi family that was thriving from trade with Ming China, attracted many intellectuals from Kyōto. These intellectuals lectured on classics such as Confucianism and waka, and published texts on these subjects. Similarly, the Kikuchi family in Higo 肥後 and the Shimazu family 島津氏 in Satsuma 薩摩 also invited Keian Genju 桂庵玄樹 (1427-1508)[54], to give lectures on Confucianism. There were also Zen

[54] Genju was highly active in Satsuma, publishing Zhu Xi's〈朱熹〉*Commentary on the Great Learning*〈『大学章句』〉, and establishing the foundations of what later became Satsunan Gakuha〈薩南学派〉(a Neo-Confucianist school).

monks, such as Banri Shūku 万里集九 (1428-?), who traveled around the Chūbu 中部 and Kantō regions, interacting with local people and composing Chinese-style poetry and prose.

In the Kantō region in the mid-15th century, Uesugi Norizane (1410-66), the Kantō Kanrei, revived the **Ashikaga School** 足利学校. The school provided high-level education to many warriors and Zen monks from across Japan, and also collected many texts.

By this time, even in local regions the custom of warriors sending their children to temples for education was well established. Works such as *Teikin Ōrai* 『庭訓往来』 and *Goseibai Shikimoku* 『御成敗式目』 were used as textbooks. Powerful merchants and craftsmen in the cities also needed to be able to read, write, and perform simple arithmetic. Among the merchants in Nara were some involved in publishing a dictionary called *Setsuyōshū* 『節用集』. Furthermore, even among leaders in villages the need to be able to read, write and perform arithmetic to manage their villages increased, and slowly literacy spread.

The Development of New Buddhism

As the power of the court and bakufu declined, and the estate system broke down, older Buddhist sects such as Tendai 天台宗 and Shingon 真言宗 gradually lost influence. By contrast, the sects of Kamakura Buddhism 鎌倉仏教 gained support among warriors, farmers, merchants, and craftsmen, and spread in both towns and farming villages.

The Zen Gozan system lost influence as the bakufu, which had been their patron, declined. On the other hand, other Zen groups (known as **Rinka** 林下[55]) that, seeking more independence, set about proselytizing in rural areas, were increasingly supported by warriors and commoners in various locales, enabling them to expand.

The Nichiren (or Hokke) 日蓮宗（法華宗） Sect, a Buddhist sect that was first based in eastern Japan, gradually extended its influence to Kyōto. **Nisshin** 日親 (1407-88), a monk active around the time of the sixth shōgun, Ashikaga Yoshinori, was known for his combative propagation style, having intense arguments with members of other sects and frequently being persecuted for his behavior. Many wealthy merchants and artisans in Kyōto were Nichiren believers, and in 1532, in what came to be called the **Hokke Ikki** 法華一揆, they fought with the Ikkō Ikki 一向一揆, and formed a self-governing administration. However, in 1536 the Hokke Ikki movement clashed with Enryakuji Temple 延暦寺, which set fire to their temples, forcing the followers to flee Kyōto. This struggle is known as the **Tenbun Hokke Conflict** 天文法華の乱.

As for the Jōdo Shinshū (or Ikkōshū 一向宗) Sect, aside from farmers it was also popular

---

[55] Prominent Rinka temples included Eiheiji〈永平寺〉 and Sōjiji〈総持寺〉 of the Sōtō Sect〈曹洞宗〉, and Daitokuji and Myōshinji〈妙心寺〉 of the Rinzai Sect. As for monks, Ikkyū Sōjun〈一休宗純〉 of Daitokuji is a well-known figure.

among those merchants and workers (mainly in transport and crafting) that made their livelihoods from travelling to various locations, which contributed to its spread. Around the time of the Ōnin War in particular, Rennyo, the head of Honganji Temple, taught that simply believing in the Buddha Amida (阿弥陀仏) was enough to attain rebirth in the Pure Land. He taught using letters written in simple language (**ofumi** (御文)), and organized religious associations (kō (講)) that enabled his teaching to spread in sō villages[56]. Enthusiastic propagation, especially by Rennyo, led Honganji to extend its influence to the Kinki, Tōkai, and Hokuriku regions, and in each of these areas, believers formed a strongly-bonded community. As these communities became powerful, they often came into conflict with daimyō, who were strengthening their control over farming villages, and the resulting clashes and uprisings were called Ikkō Ikki. One of the best examples of this was the Kaga no Ikkō Ikki.

4 The Emergence of the Sengoku Daimyō

Sengoku Daimyō

During the Sengoku period that began with the Ōnin War, powerful local rulers emerged in different regions. In the first half of the 16th century, an internal power struggle – in which the Hosokawa family played a major role – over the leadership of the Muromachi Bakufu continued in the Kinki region[57]. Meanwhile, in other regions, new local authorities emerged that established and controlled their own domains (known as **ryōkoku** (領国（分国）) or bunkoku). These authorities were the **Sengoku daimyō** (戦国大名).

In the Kantō region, after the Kyōtoku Rebellion, the post of Kamakura Kubō was divided into two: Ashikaga Mochiuji's son Shigeuji (1434-97), who became Koga Kubō (古河公方), and Shōgun Yoshimasa's brother Masatomo (足利政知) (1435-91), who became Horigoe Kubō (堀越公方). The Uesugi family, which controlled the post of Kantō Kanrei, also experienced a factional struggle between two branch families, the Yamanouchi (山内氏) and the Ōgigayatsu (扇谷氏). Taking advantage of this unrest, at the end of the 15th century **Hōjō Sōun** (北条早雲) (Ise Sōzui (伊勢宗瑞), 1456?-1519) from Kyōto defeated the Horigoe Kubō and took over Izu. He then advanced into Sagami (相模) and made Odawara (小田原) his base. By the time his son Hōjō (北条氏綱)

---

[56] Rural believers deepened their faith through gatherings in village halls, where paintings and sculptures of Amida sent from Honganji were enshrined.

[57] In 1493, the Hosokawa family deposed the shōgun (Meiō Incident〈明応の政変〉) and assumed control of the bakufu. However, in a later power struggle, the Hosokawa vassal Miyoshi Nagayoshi〈三好長慶〉 came to power, before being supplanted by a vassal of his own, Matsunaga Hisahide〈松永久秀〉.

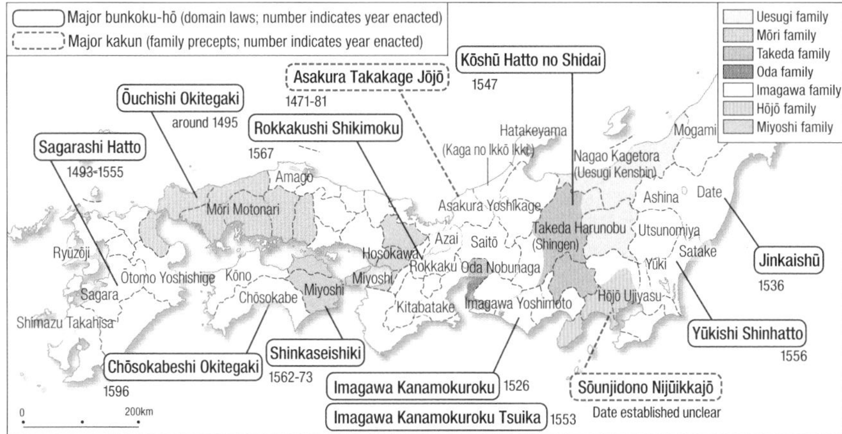

SPHERES OF INFLUENCE OF SENGOKU DAIMYŌ AS WELL AS MAJOR BUNKOKU-HŌ AND KAKUN〈家訓〉(C. MID-16TH CENTURY)

Ujitsuna (1487-1541) and grandson Ujiyasu (北条氏康) (1515-71) were in power, the Hōjō family had become a major daimyō family that controlled a large part of Kantō[58].

In the Chūbu region in the mid-16th century, Kagetora (景虎), from the Nagao family (長尾氏), succeeded the Uesugi as Kantō Kanrei. The Nagao family had controlled the post of deputy shugo under the Uesugi shugo of Echigo (越後国) Province. Kagetora, who changed his name to **Uesugi Kenshin** (上杉謙信) (1530-78), often fought against **Takeda Shingen** (武田信玄（晴信）) (Harunobu, 1521-73), who had expanded his territory from Kai Province to Shinano (信濃国) Province. Among their many battles, Kawanakajima (川中島) in northern Shinano is especially well known. In the Chūgoku (中国) region, the Ōuchi family, which had held power through the post of shugo daimyō, in the mid-16th century lost their domain to their major retainer, Sue Harukata (陶晴賢). He was in turn later defeated by **Mōri Motonari** (毛利元就) (1497-1571), originally a kokujin in Aki (安芸国) Province, who engaged repeatedly in fierce battles against the Amago family (尼子氏) in the San'in (山陰) region.

In Kyūshū, there were two dominant families. One was the Shimazu family, which was based in Satsuma and controlled a large area of southern Kyūshū, and the other was the Ōtomo family (大友氏), which had extended its power in northern Kyūshū centered on Bungo (豊後). In Shikoku (四国), the Chōsokabe family (長宗我部氏), which had unified Tosa (土佐) Province, was advancing into the northern half of the island as well. As for the Tōhoku region, there were a number of relatively small-scale kokujin competing for power, but gradually

[58] After the death of Ashikaga Masatomo, his son Chachamaru〈茶々丸〉became the next Horigoe Kubō. However, after Izu was taken by Hōjō Sōun in 1493, Chachamaru committed suicide in 1498. The Sengoku daimyō Hōjō family is also referred to as the Later Hōjō family〈後北条氏〉, in order to distinguish them from the Hōjō family of the Kamakura Bakufu.

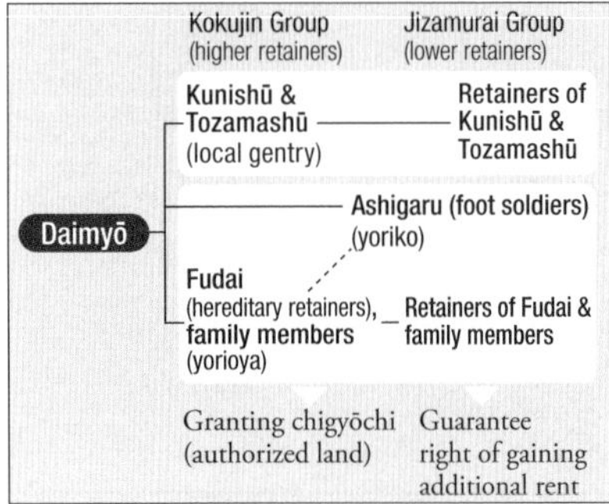

RETAINER CORPS OF SENGOKU DAIMYŌ

from among them the Date (伊達氏) family emerged and grew into a powerful daimyō family.

No small number of Sengoku daimyō had originally been deputy shugo or kokujin. During the Sengoku period, the old authority like that of the shugo was no longer sufficient to rule. In order to maintain power as a Sengoku daimyō it was necessary to gain support from people such as retainers in danger of losing territorial control due to intense conflict, or people in the territory whose livelihoods were threatened. In other words, a Sengoku daimyō needed to function as a military leader as well as a territorial governor[59].

In addition to newly-subjugated kokujin, Sengoku daimyō also recruited jizamurai as retainers. The income of all these vassals was assessed through a uniform standard called **kandaka** (貫高), measured in currency. Instead of guaranteeing the status and income of their retainers, daimyō used kandaka in order to impose a set of military services (**gunyaku** (軍役)) on them. This **kandaka system** (貫高制) became the foundation of the military system of the Sengoku daimyō. Daimyō incorporated jizamurai into their retainer corps by entrusting them to important retainers (**yorioya-yoriko system** (寄親・寄子制)). This new retainer structure enabled group battles utilizing new weapons such as firearms and long spears.

Sengoku Daimyō Territorial Control

The Sengoku daimyō implemented various policies, one after another, to unite and control both their retainer corps and territories. Some established their own laws called **bunkoku-hō** (分国法) (or kahō (家法)). These included laws inherited from bakufu and shugo legal codes, as well as laws that incorporated regulations from kokujin ikki, making them a culmination of medieval laws. There were also many laws that illustrated the new authority wielded by the daimyō, such as **Kenka Ryōseibai-hō** (喧嘩両成敗法), which held both parties responsible in a conflict or fight[60].

[59] By this time, Sengoku daimyō families who used to have shugo posts, such as the Imagawa family〈今川氏〉 and the Takeda family, were ruling their own territories directly without relying on the authority of the bakufu.

[60] The purpose of the Kenka Ryōseibai-hō was to prohibit retainers from settling disputes among themselves through fights. Instead, it stipulated that all disputes be solved through judgement by the daimyō, in the interest of maintaining peace in the territory.

Sengoku daimyō often carried out land surveys (**kenchi** 検地)[61] of their territory, such as land they had newly conquered. The purpose of these surveys was to record in a land register, called **kenchichō** 検地帳, the surface area of cultivated land and the amount of annual tax of each farmer. This system strengthened the direct control of daimyō over farmers[62].

The daimyō needed to produce or procure a large amount of materials including weapons[63]. Therefore, they recruited important merchants and craftsmen and had them control their fellows within each territory. By mobilizing merchants and craftsmen like this, daimyō were able to initiate large-scale projects such as building great castles and castle towns (**jōkamachi** 城下町), developing mines[64], preparing flood control for large rivers[65], and managing irrigation.

Moreover, daimyō attempted to transform their territories into unified economic spheres with a castle town at the center. To this end, in their domains they developed transportation systems including post towns and post horses, and facilitated trade by abolishing checkpoints and building markets. Major retainers had to reside in the castle towns, and merchants and craftsmen also came to settle there. As a result, these towns gradually became political, economic, and cultural centers[66].

---

[61] There were two kinds of self-enumeration used in the land surveys conducted by Sengoku daimyō. In the first type, lords, who were retainers of the daimyō, reported the surface area they ruled as well as the income, and in the other, farmers reported the surface area that they farmed along with their income. This type of self-reporting land survey was called sashidashi kenchi〈指出検地〉.

[62] The amount of annual tax assessed through the land survey was converted into a monetary value and became the base of the kandaka system. The kandaka was used to determine the amount of tax that farmers paid to their lord, as well as the amount of military service that retainers rendered to their daimyō, and the amount of corvée labor required by villages.

[63] The demand for cotton, which was imported from Joseon Korea and Ming China, increased as it came to be used for military clothing and match cords for matchlock guns. Its cultivation quickly spread in various regions such as Mikawa〈三河〉, and greatly changed the clothing lifestyle of commoners.

[64] Sengoku daimyō developed mines and brought about technological innovation in refining and mining. As a result, the production of gold and silver increased drastically. Gold mines in Kai, Suruga〈駿河〉 and Izu, and silver mines in Iwami〈石見〉 and Tajima〈但馬〉, were particularly well-known.

[65] Takeda Shingen invested great effort in flood control works, and built embankments called Shingen-zutsumi〈信玄堤〉 near the confluence of the Kamanashi River〈釜無川〉 and the Midai River〈御勅使川〉.

[66] The following are examples of castle towns that flourished around this time period: Odawara of the Hōjō family, Fuchū〈府中〉 (Shizuoka City〈静岡市〉) of the Imagawa family, Kasugayama〈春日山〉 (Jōetsu City〈上越市〉) of the Uesugi family, Yamaguchi of the Ōuchi family, Bungofunai〈豊後府内〉 (Ōita City〈大分市〉) of the Ōtomo family, and Kagoshima〈鹿児島〉 of the Shimazu family.

City Development and Mercantile Townspeople

During the Sengoku period, farming village markets and cities drastically increased in number, partly owing to the policies of the daimyō to ensure economic development within their territories. As for monzenmachi 門前町 (temple and shrine towns)[67], not only those around major religious institutions but also provincial ones around medium- and small-sized institutions flourished. In areas where the Jōdo Shinshū Sect had a particularly strong influence, communities called **jinaimachi** 寺内町 (towns on temple grounds)[68] were created around temples and meditation halls, where merchants and craftsmen who followed the sect resided.

Many of these markets and towns functioned as **rakuichi** 楽市 (**free markets**) which did not charge fees for **ichiza** 市座 (**sales stands**) or market tax. Daimyō issued free market laws in order to protect these markets, and at times they also set up free markets themselves to promote commercial distribution.

Long-distance trade continued to thrive even during wartime, and both port towns[69] and post towns flourished. In some of these cities, wealthy merchants and craftsmen formed self-governing organizations and carried out municipal administration, creating peaceful and free cities. Representative examples include **Sakai** 堺 and **Hakata** 博多, which were bustling hubs of trade between Japan and Ming China, as well as Hirano 平野 (in Settsu), and Kuwana 桑名 and Ōminato 大湊 (in Ise). The cities of Sakai and Hakata in particular were administered by councils of wealthy merchants and had characteristics of autonomous cities. Sakai's council consisted of 36 members and was called the **Kaigōshū** 会合衆 (also read as Egōshū), while Hakata's had 12 members and was called the **Nengyōji** 年行司.

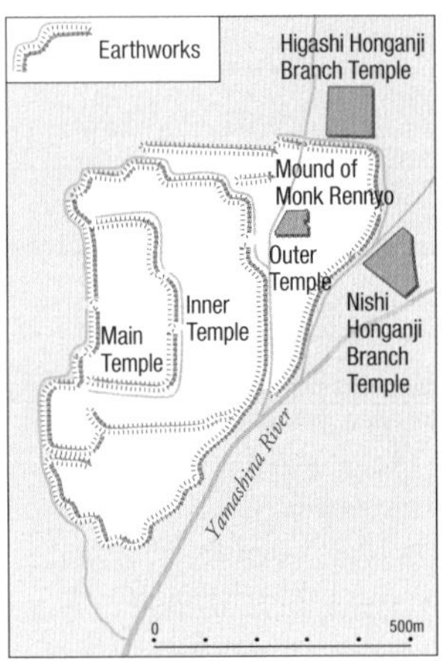

MAP OF YAMASHINA JINAIMACHI〈山科寺内町〉

Even in long-established political centers such as Kyōto, **chō** 町, which were autonomous groups of urban residents, sprang up. At the core of these groups were wealthy mercantile townspeople called **chōshū** 町衆. As with

---

[67] Uji〈宇治〉 and Yamada〈山田〉 (Ise City〈伊勢市〉) of the Ise Grand Shrine〈伊勢神宮〉, and Nagano〈長野〉 of Zenkōji Temple〈善光寺〉 in Shinano are the best-known monzenmachi.

[68] Ishiyama〈石山〉 (Ōsaka) of Settsu, Kanazawa〈金沢〉 of Kaga, Tondabayashi〈富田林〉 in Kawachi, and Imai〈今井〉 in Yamato were well-known jinaimachi. These jinnaimachi were also free markets, but were gradually seized by Sengoku daimyō and lost their privileges.

[69] Besides Sakai and Hakata, other important port towns included Bōnotsu〈坊津〉, Onomichi〈尾道〉, Obama〈小浜〉, Tsuruga〈敦賀〉, Ōtsu, Kuwana, Ōminato, and Shinagawa〈品川〉.

SUMIYOSHI FESTIVAL〈住吉の祭〉(*SUMIYOSHI SAIREI-ZU BYŌBU*〈『住吉祭礼図屏風』〉[FOLDING SCROLL OF SUMIYOSHI SHRINE FESTIVAL], PART)
Rows of two-story warehouses with white walls represent Sakai, a wealthy and prosperous city. The moat defined the town limits. The image shows the costume parade of the Sumiyoshi Festival.

the sō villages, each town established its own **chōhō** 町法 (town laws) in order to protect residents' livelihoods and commercial activities[70]. Several towns could come together to form an organization called chōgumi 町組 (town associations)[71]. Both towns and town associations were autonomously administered by a board called **gachigyōji** 月行事 (also read as gatsugyōji), the members of which were chosen from the mercantile townspeople. After being burned down in the Ōnin War, Kyōto was reconstructed by these townspeople. The Gion Matsuri 祇園祭 was also resuscitated as a town festival of the people.

[70] Sometimes sō villages and chō are together called sonchō kyōdōtai〈村町共同体〉(village-town community), and the system of control based on this community sonchōsei〈村町制〉(village-town system).

[71] In Kyōto, two large urban organizations called Kamigyō〈上京〉and Shimogyō〈下京〉were formed by a collection of town associations (sōchō〈惣町〉).

[i] "建武の新政" has conventionally been rendered as "Kenmu Restoration" in English, reflecting the long-held view that Go-Daigo was attempting to restore a more ancient form of Japanese rulership. More recent scholarship has suggested Go-Daigo's innovations were revolutionary, and that perhaps "Kenmu Revolution" would be more appropriate, but this is controversial, and so the more conventional term is generally more appropriate. A similar debate concerns the "Meiji Restoration" (明治維新), which various scholars refer to as "Meiji Revolution" instead.

[ii] The term "shugo daimyō" eventually gave rise to just "daimyō," a term for regional administrators in the medieval and early modern eras. "Daimyō" is sometimes translated as "warlord" (a powerful military leader) or just "lord" (a master, often belonging to the nobility), especially in popular writing, but these terms are vague and imprecise. As the role and authority of daimyō varied dramatically depending on the time period, to avoid confusion most scholars prefer to just use "daimyō," and this text follows suit.

[iii] "Ikki" (一揆) was originally an ancient term referring to a league of people united for a goal, which often led to some form of uprising. By modern times, "ikki" had come to be associated with uprisings rather than the leagues that caused them, but while in Japanese writing this does not really pose a problem, in English it does because an "uprising" (or a related term like "riot" or "revolt") is an event and by itself, unlike a group of people, lacks agency. Rendering "ikki" as "uprising" in English, although common, therefore changes the meaning. To avoid inaccuracy, therefore, this textbook instead uses "ikki" consistently.

[iv] "Kinkaku" and "Ginkaku" were rendered to be consistent with the Japanese text, but in English are almost always called "Kinkakuji" or "Golden Pavilion" and "Ginkakuji" or "Silver Pavilion" (since their primary function was not as religious institutions, "pavilion" is more appropriate than "temple"). Note that these are not their proper names, which are Rokuonji (鹿苑寺) and Jishōji (慈照寺), respectively.

[v] The Japanese term "派" is inclusive and has no direct English equivalent, and so this textbook uses "school," "group" or "faction" depending on what is most appropriate for the context in question. Generally, "school" is most suitable for literary, artistic and philosophical contexts; "faction" for political and military ones; and "group" for other situations. Note that "流," in the sense of a style of art etc., is also rendered as "school" in this text.

The Early Modern Era

Chapter

6

The Establishment of the Bakuhan System

1 The Oda and Toyotomi Regimes

European Advances into East Asia

While Japan was undergoing the Sengoku (戦国時代) period from the second half of the 15th century into the 16th century, the countries of Europe were moving beyond the Renaissance (ルネサンス) and Reformation (宗教改革) towards becoming modern societies. In order to compete with the Islamic world, they began to advance into the non-European world, aiming to propagate Christianity and expand overseas trade[1]. This led to what is called the **Age of Discovery** (大航海時代), where various regions of the world began increased exchange, with Europe as the hub.

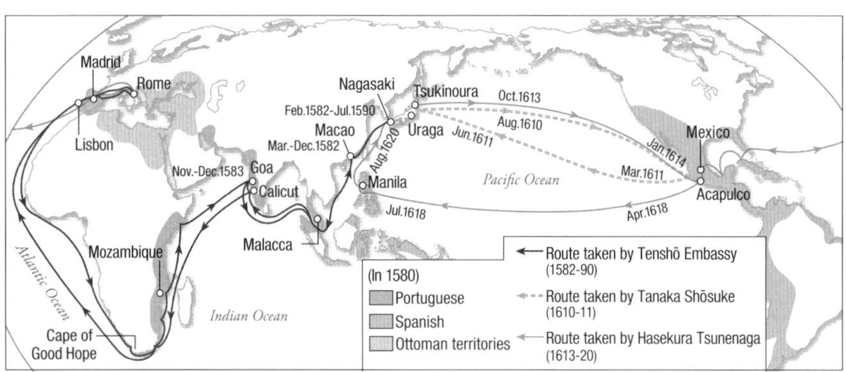

WORLD AT END OF 16TH CENTURY, AND TRAFFIC OF JAPANESE

---

[1] In 1492, the Italian Columbus〈コロンブス〉, with support from Queen Isabella〈イサベル〉 of Spain, crossed the Atlantic and arrived in the West Indies, while in 1498 the Portuguese Vasco da Gama〈ヴァスコ＝ダ＝ガマ〉 rounded the southern edge of the African continent, and reached Calicut on the west coast of India. The first circumnavigation of the earth was achieved by the Portuguese Magellan〈マゼラン〉 at the beginning of the 16th century. Magellan led a Spanish fleet around the southernmost tip of the American continent and crossed the Pacific to arrive in the Philippines, and then continued further westward to finish the voyage.

The leaders of this age were Spain (España) and Portugal, the two kingdoms on the Iberian peninsula. Spain, having colonized parts of the Americas, crossed the Pacific to reach East Asia around the mid-16th century and occupied the Philippines, where it founded Manila as a base. Portugal made Goa on the west coast of India its base, and moved eastward, establishing another base in Macao in China.

In East Asia at the time, the **Ming Dynasty** (明) was continuing its **Sea Ban Policy** (海禁政策) that prohibited private trade, but the peoples of Japan, Korea, the Ryūkyū (琉球) Islands, Vietnam, and the region of China on the East China Sea, widely engaged in cross-border transit trade. The Europeans came to be involved in this trade as part of the world trade network.

The Nanban Trade and Christianity

In 1543, a Chinese wakō (倭寇) vessal with Portuguese on board drifted ashore at **Tanegashima Island** (種子島), located south of Kyūshū (九州)[2]. This was the first time for Europeans to come to Japan. Tanegashima Tokitaka (種子島時堯) (1528-79), the lord of the island, bought firearms from the Portuguese and had his retainers learn both the use and manufacture of these weapons. Thereafter, the Portuguese began to visit ports in Kyūshū almost every year to trade with Japan. A Spanish ship also arrived in Hirado (平戸) in Hizen (肥前国) Province in 1584, inaugurating trade between Spain and Japan. In Japan at the time

Iwami Ginzan Silver Mine

The Iwami Ginzan〈石見銀山〉 Silver Mine and its Cultural Landscape in Ōda City〈大田市〉, Shimane Prefecture〈島根県〉, was listed as a UNESCO World Heritage Site in 2007. Also called Ōmori Ginzan〈大森銀山〉, it used to be also known abroad as one of the major silver mines of the world. It began to thrive after a merchant from Hakata named Kamiya Jutei〈神屋（谷）寿禎〉 introduced a refining method called cupellation from Korea in the first half of the 16th century. Because of this technical improvement, the Iwami Ginzan flourished from the second half of the 16th century to the beginning of the 17th century, and many Spanish and Portuguese came to Japan by ship to buy its silver. The Portuguese in particular sought Japanese silver in order to compete with the Spanish, who were using silver from the Potosi silver mine in South America for their trade in East Asia.

Cupellation eventually spread to silver mines throughout Japan, and as a result, the annual silver production in Japan amounted to about 200 tons around the beginning of the 17th century, which was one third of the gross production of silver worldwide. After that, however, the silver production gradually decreased, and Iwami Ginzan's role as a silver mine came to an end around the mid-17th century.

---

[2] Another theory argues that this occurred in 1542.

ARRIVAL OF NANBANJIN, AND NANBANJI (*NANBAN BYŌBU*〈『南蛮屏風』〉 [FOLDING SCREEN OF SOUTHERN BARBARIANS], PART)
Christian missionaries, thinking that it was crucial for the sake of propagation to observe Japanese customs and lifestyle, ardently studied the Japanese language and culture. Many of the churches (Nanbanji) they built were renovated Buddhist temples, while newly-built ones followed Japanese architectural styles, with wood construction and tile-roofing〈瓦葺〉.

the Portuguese and Spanish were called Nanbanjin 南蛮人 (southern barbarians), leading to the term **Nanban trade** 南蛮貿易.

The Portuguese and Spanish brought goods such as Chinese raw silk, firearms, and gunpowder, and traded them for things like Japanese **silver** 銀, which had been produced in dramatically increased quantities since around the middle of the 16th century[3]. Among the Sengoku daimyō 戦国大名, muskets were quickly embraced as the most advanced weapon. The use on battlefields of ashigaru 足軽 (foot soldiers) equipped with firearms brought about a shift away from cavalry-focused tactics, and also triggered the redesign of castles as defensive structures.

The Nanban trade was intrinsically bound up with Christian missionary activities. In 1549, **Francis Xavier** フランシスコ＝ザビエル (1506?-52), a Jesuit イエズス会 missionary aiming to propagate Christianity in Japan[4], arrived in Kagoshima and embarked on missionary activities under the protection of daimyō such as Ōuchi Yoshitaka 大内義隆 (1507-51) and Ōtomo Yoshishige 大友義鎮（宗麟） (Sōrin, 1530-87).

Xavier was followed by other missionaries who sought to propagate their faith through activities such as building "Nanbanji" 南蛮寺 (churches), "collegios" コレジオ (training schools

---

[3] The main trading ports were Hirado, Nagasaki〈長崎〉 and Bungofunai〈豊後府内〉 (present-day Ōita City〈大分市〉), and many merchants from Kyōto〈京都〉, Sakai〈堺〉, Hakata〈博多〉 and other places participated in the trade.

[4] In Europe at the time, Protestantism was gaining influence after the Reformation, while Catholic forces sought to regain dominance. Many Catholic orders, one of which was the Society of Jesus, put effort into missions in Asia. In Japan, Christianity was variously known as Kirishitanshū〈キリシタン宗〉, Tenshukyō〈天主教〉 (faith in the Lord) or Yasokyō〈耶蘇教〉 (faith in Jesus), and so on.

for missionaries), and "seminarios" (セミナリオ) (seminaries)[5]. Portuguese ships docked in the territories of daimyō who permitted missionary activities, so daimyō hoping to trade with the Portuguese protected such activities. Some of these daimyō were even baptized themselves, and are called **Kirishitan daimyō** (キリシタン大名) (Christian daimyō). In 1582, three such Christian daimyō – Ōtomo Yoshishige, Arima Harunobu (有馬晴信) (1567?-1612), and Ōmura Sumitada (大村純忠) (1533-87) – dispatched an embassy (**Tenshō Ken'ō Shisetsu** (天正遣欧使節)) consisting of young men to visit the Pope in Rome, on the recommendation of the Jesuit missionary Valignani (ヴァリニャーニ) (1539-1606)[6].

Oda Nobunaga's Unification Project

The first daimyō to embark on the unification of the country was **Oda Nobunaga** (織田信長) (1534-82) from Owari Province (尾張国). In 1560, Nobunaga defeated Imagawa Yoshimoto (今川義元) (1519-60) at the Battle of Okehazama (桶狭間の戦い). In 1567, he achieved victory over the Saitō (斎藤氏) family of Mino (美濃), whereupon he settled in Gifu Castle (岐阜城) and started to use seals bearing the term "Tenkafubu" (天下布武) (literally "govern by force," but metaphorically "govern by warrior virtue"), revealing his intention to rule the country[7]. In the following year, he entered Kyōto with **Ashikaga Yoshiaki** (足利義昭) (1537-97), who had been exiled from the Kinai region, and installed him as the shōgun. This was Nobunaga's first step towards unification.

At the Battle of Anegawa (姉川の戦い) in 1570, Nobunaga defeated both the Azai (浅井氏) family of Ōmi (近江) Province and the Asakura (朝倉氏) family of Echizen (越前国) Province. The following year, he burned down Enryakuji (延暦寺) Temple on Mt. Hiei (比叡山), thereby subjugating the greatest religious authority of the time. In 1573, he drove Yoshiaki, who had been seeking to restore shōgunal authority, out of Kyōto, and put an end to the Muromachi Bakufu (室町幕府). Then, at the **Battle of Nagashino** (長篠合戦), which occurred in Mikawa (三河) Province in 1575, he deployed abundant firearms against the formidable Takeda Katsuyori (武田勝頼) (1546-82), who had emphasized cavalry tactics, and achieved a crushing victory. The next year, he initiated construction of the stately **Azuchi Castle** (安土城) in Ōmi.

Nobunaga's efforts were resisted by the Ikkō Ikki (一向一揆), based in Jōdo Shinshū (浄土真宗) temples and jinaimachi (寺内町) in various areas across the country, and headed by Ishiyama Honganji (石山本願寺)

---

[5] Xavier was followed by other missionaries such as the Portuguese Gaspar Villela〈ガスパル＝ヴィレラ〉 and Luis Frois〈ルイス＝フロイス〉, whose proselytizing efforts led to the rapid spread of Christianity. The number of believers around 1582 was said to have reached 115,000 in the areas of Hizen, Higo〈肥後〉 and Iki〈壱岐〉, 10,000 in Bungo〈豊後〉, and 25,000 in and around the Kinai region〈畿内〉.

[6] The embassy consisted of four boys: Itō Mancio〈伊東マンショ〉, Chijiwa Miguel〈千々石ミゲル〉, Nakaura Juliao〈中浦ジュリアン〉, and Hara Martinho〈原マルチノ〉. They journeyed by way of Goa and Lisbon, arrived in Rome to meet Pope Gregory XIII〈グレゴリウス 13 世〉, and returned to Japan in 1590.

[7] In this period, the term "tenka" referred to not only the world or a whole country, but also the Kinai region. Nobunaga may have used it in the latter sense.

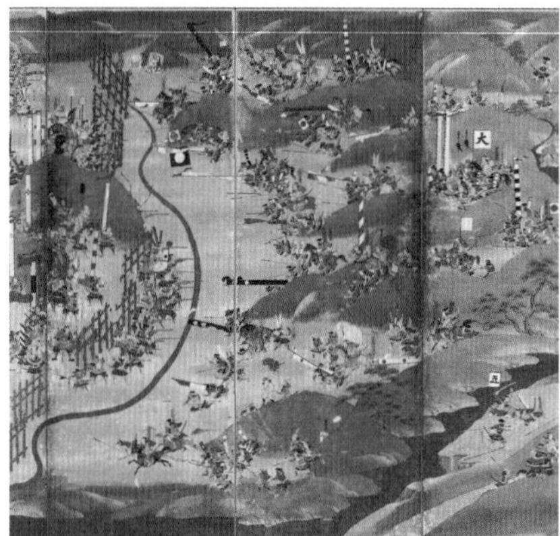

MUSKET TROOPS IN ACTION (*NAGASHINO KASSENZU BYŌBU*〈『長篠合戦図屏風』〉, [FOLDING SCREEN OF THE BATTLE OF NAGASHINO], PART)
At the Battle of Nagashino, the Oda and Tokugawa joint forces fully utilized the power of firearms to defeat the Takeda cavalry.

Temple in Ōsaka 大坂. However, Nobunaga succeeded in vanquishing the Ikkō Ikki in Ise-Nagashima 伊勢長島 in 1574, and pacified them in Echizen Province the following year. In 1580, he finally forced the Ishiyama Honganji Temple to surrender[8].

Nobunaga was able to flexibly deploy massive military power due to policies such as demanding that his retainers settle in castle towns 城下町. Not only was he a skillful military commander who defeated daimyō one after another, but he was intent on overcoming conventional political and religious systems and authorities. His economic policies were also noteworthy. One was to discontinue, throughout his territories, the self-reporting land surveys and checkpoints that had been implemented by other daimyō. Another was to militarily dominate the city of Sakai, which had been flourishing as an autonomous city, and put it under his control, thereby seizing the economically thriving Kinai region. He also issued a **rakuichi-rei** 楽市令 (free market edict) for the castle town of Azuchi permitting free economic activities for merchants and craftsmen there. In short, Nobunaga's economic policies placed much emphasis on towns and encouraged industry and commerce.

In this way, through control of Kyōto and domination of the Kinki, Tōkai 東海 and Hokuriku 北陸 regions, Nobunaga was on his way towards unifying the country. However, his aggressive approach to politics invited a backlash, and in 1582, while resting in Honnōji 本能寺 Temple in Kyōto on his way to wage war against the Mōri 毛利氏 family, he was assassinated by Akechi Mitsuhide 明智光秀 (1528?-82), one of his own vassals (**Honnōji Incident** 本能寺の変).

Toyotomi Hideyoshi's Unification of the Country

Nobunaga's vision of unification was realized by **Toyotomi (Hashiba) Hideyoshi** 豊臣（羽柴）秀吉 (1537-98). Born in Owari, Hideyoshi gradually proved his talents while serving Nobunaga, who promoted him to one of his major retainers. Hideyoshi avenged his

[8] Kennyo (Kōsa)〈顕如（光佐）〉, the head of Honganji Temple, called out to followers across Japan to take up arms against Nobunaga in 1570, and fought a series of battles called the Ishiyama War〈石山戦争〉 that lasted for 11 years. Ultimately, Kennyo surrendered and left Ishiyama Honganji.

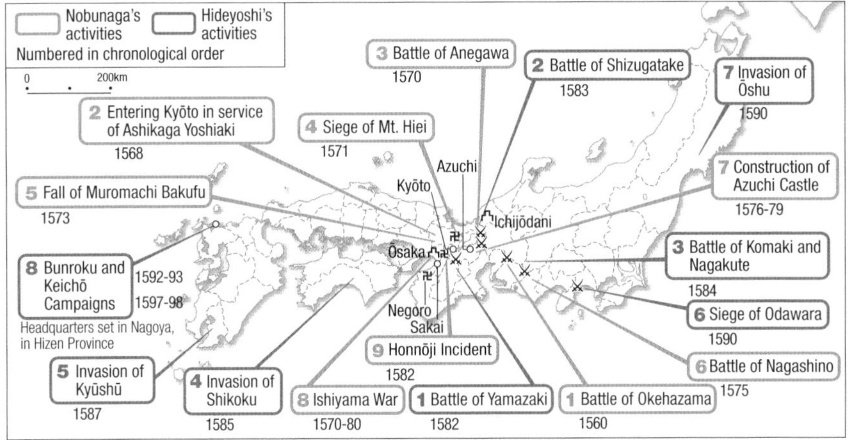

ACTIVITIES BY NOBUNAGA AND HIDEYOSHI

master by destroying Akechi Mitsuhide, who had vanquished Nobunaga, at the Battle of Yamazaki 山崎の合戦 in Yamashiro Province 山城国 in 1582. In the following year he defeated Shibata Katsuie 柴田勝家 (?-1583), another major retainer of Nobunaga's, at the Battle of Shizugatake 賤ヶ岳の戦い. These actions established him as Nobunaga's successor. In that same year, Hideyoshi started to build the magnificent **Ōsaka Castle** 大坂城 on the former site of the Ishiyama Honganji Temple, a location with excellent access by both land and waterway. In 1584, he fought against the joint forces of Oda Nobukatsu 織田信雄 (1558-1630, Nobunaga's second son) and Tokugawa Ieyasu 徳川家康 at the Battle of Komaki and Nagakute 小牧・長久手の戦い, but ended up reconciling with them.

These events prompted Hideyoshi to depend not only on military power, but also to make use of traditional authority to achieve unification. In 1585, he was appointed **kanpaku** 関白 by the court, and conquered Shikoku 四国 by defeating Chōsokabe Motochika 長宗我部元親 (1538-99). The next year he was appointed daijōdaijin 太政大臣 (supreme minister) and granted the new clan name **Toyotomi** 豊臣. After becoming kanpaku, Hideyoshi proclaimed that he was entrusted with the right to rule Japan by the tennō. He ordered all of the daimyō across Japan to agree to a truce, and compelled them to give him the right to determine their territories[9]. In 1587, Hideyoshi went on an expedition to attack Shimazu Yoshihisa 島津義久 (1533-1611) in Kyūshū for having violated this rule, and forced him to surrender. Then, in 1590, he defeated Hōjō Ujimasa 北条氏政 (1538-90) and his son Ujinao 北条氏直 (1562-91) in Odawara (Siege of Odawara 小田原攻め), subjugated daimyō in the Tōhoku region such as Date Masamune 伊達政宗 (1567-1636), and completed the unification of the country.

[9] This policy was also called the Sōbuji-rei〈惣無事令〉(Truce Edict).

TENSHŌ ŌBAN, MINTED 1588
Also called Hishi Ōban〈菱大判〉(large coin with diamond seal) because it has a paulownia seal stamped in a diamond design.

In 1588, Hideyoshi received Go-Yōzei Tennō 後陽成天皇 (r. 1586-1611) at his newly-constructed **Jurakutei** 聚楽第 mansion in Kyōto. He took full advantage of that occasion to have many daimyō swear loyalty to the tennō and himself. By doing so, Hideyoshi established a new political order by skillfully making use of the tennō's authority.

The financial foundation of the Toyotomi regime was its enormous **kurairichi** 蔵入地 (directly-controlled lands). Having important mines such as Sado 佐渡, Iwami Ōmori 石見大森 and Tajima Ikuno 但馬生野 under its control, it minted coins such as the Tenshō Ōban 天正大判 oval gold coin. Further, the Toyotomi government directly managed major cities like Kyōto, Ōsaka, Sakai, Fushimi 伏見 and Nagasaki, and put wealthy merchants under their control, utilizing these economic resources for politics and military affairs[10].

However, like the Oda regime, the Toyotomi regime also had an autocratic side. As a result, it was not able to establish an effective central administration. It was only later in his life that Hideyoshi established a system in which he discussed important political matters with the Go-Tairō 五大老 (five senior counselors), who were five powerful daimyō, and shared administrative tasks among the Go-Bugyō 五奉行 (five magistrates), consisting of five of his closest retainers[11].

Land Surveys and the Sword Hunt

The main policies of the Toyotomi regime were land surveys (**kenchi** 検地) and the sword hunt (**katanagari** 刀狩). Hideyoshi carried out numerous land surveys in his newly-acquired territory. Collectively, his series of land surveys are known as the **Taikō Kenchi** 太閤検地[12]. The Taikō Kenchi instituted a set of standardized units – chō 町, tan 段, se 畝, and bu 歩[13] – for measuring land surface, and standardized **kyōmasu** 京枡 as a unit of volume instead of the

---

[10] Hideyoshi made use of the talents and power of merchants including Sen no Rikyū〈千利休〉and Konishi Ryūsa〈小西隆佐〉(father of Yukinaga〈小西行長〉) in Sakai, and Shimai Sōshitsu〈島井宗室〉and Kamiya Sōtan〈神屋宗湛〉in Hakata.

[11] The Go-Bugyō consisted of Asano Nagamasa〈浅野長政〉, Mashita Nagamori〈増田長盛〉, Ishida Mitsunari〈石田三成〉, Maeda Gen'i〈前田玄以〉and Natsuka Masaie〈長束正家〉. As for the Tairō, there were originally six of them: Tokugawa Ieyasu, Maeda Toshiie〈前田利家〉, Mōri Terumoto〈毛利輝元〉, Kobayakawa Takakage〈小早川隆景〉, Ukita Hideie〈宇喜多秀家〉, and Uesugi Kagekatsu〈上杉景勝〉. Only after the death of Kobayakawa Takakage did they come to be called the Go-Tairō.

[12] Taikō is a honorific title for a former kanpaku.

[13] Previously, the bu was commonly defined as an area of 6 shaku〈尺〉by 5 sun〈寸〉(about 197 cm square), and the tan as consisting of 360 bu. However, the Taikō Kenchi redefined the bu as 6 shaku by 3 sun (about 191 cm square), and the tan as consisting of 300 bu.

conventional unit, masu 枡, that had been variably defined. Village surveys of the surface area and grade of farmland and residential land were carried out, and used to determine **kokudaka** 石高 (or muradaka 村高; estimated agricultural yield measured in rice)[14]. In this way, the kokudaka system 石高制, in which the productivity of the country was measured in terms of rice value, was established. The Taikō Kenchi also resolved the problems with the estate system, under which multiple people claimed rights over the same parcel of land. Instead, farmland and residential land was recorded in a kenchichō 検地帳 (land cadaster) under the farmer actually cultivating it (**icchi issakunin** 一地一作人, or "one parcel of land, one cultivator" policy). Consequently, the farmers' rights to the fields they were actually cultivating came to be legally protected, but at the same time this incurred a tax burden according to each land's assessed productivity[15].

Having completed the unification in 1591, Hideyoshi ordered the daimyō throughout the country to submit a **kenchichō** 検地帳 (also called gozenchō 御前帳) as well as a **kuniezu** 国絵図 (domain map) of their territories on the pretext that these were to be submitted to the tennō. Thus, an administrative structure was formally realized in which every daimyō's kokudaka was officially defined, with the result that he was obliged to provide military service according to the productivity of his territory.

The purpose of the sword hunt was to confiscate weapons from farmers and clarify their status. Under the estate system, farmers had often had weapons such as swords that they took full advantage of during various ikki. In order to prevent such ikki from occurring and have the farmers concentrate on farming, Hideyoshi issued the **Katanagari-rei** 刀狩令 (Sword Hunt Edict) in 1588, and confiscated weapons from them[16].

Next, in 1591, Hideyoshi enacted the **Hitobarai-rei** 人掃令 (Population Census Edict) which prohibited changing one's occupation, for example, a warrior (bushi) becoming

---

[14] Farmland was evaluated and given a grade such as good, fair, poor, or bad, and its productivity was measured in terms of yield of rice crop. For example, 1 tan of good farmland had a productivity of 1 koku〈石〉 5 to〈斗〉 worth of rice crop (1 koku = 10 to, where 1 to is equivalent to about 18.039 kg), while 1 tan of fair farmland had a productivity of 1 koku 3 to, and so forth. The productivity of 1 tan was called kokumori〈石盛〉 (or todai〈斗代〉), and the yield obtained by multiplying the kokumori by the land surface was the kokudaka. In the Taikō Kenchi, the muragiri〈村切〉 (demarcation of borders between villages) was also carried out in parallel with the land survey.

[15] The amount of tax commonly imposed was two-thirds of the rice crop, to be collected by the local lord. This method was called "two for the lord, one for the farmer〈二公一民〉."

[16] The enactment of this law largely deprived the sō villages〈惣村〉 of military power, but their manner of autonomous community management was maintained even after the implementation of the Taikō Kenchi. The practice of the murauke system〈村請〉, where the entire village took responsibility for the batch delivery of annual taxes based on the muradaka〈村高〉 (productivity of the village), also continued into the Edo period〈江戸時代〉.

a merchant or farmer, or a farmer becoming a merchant or an artisan. In the following year, Kanpaku Toyotomi Hidetsugu 豊臣秀次 (1568-95, Hideyoshi's nephew) re-enacted the Hitobarai-rei of the previous year to secure the manpower for troops to be dispatched to the Korean peninsula. This comprised a country-wide census of the number of households and a headcount, divided into three occupational categories: warrior, merchant, and farmer. This resulted in the cementing of status and occupation, and for this reason the Hitobarai-rei is also called the Mibuntōsei-rei 身分統制令 (Status Control Edict). The differentiation of status based on occupation – warrior, merchant, and farmer – was thus implemented through policies such as land surveys, the sword hunt and the population census, resulting in the separation of warriors and farmers (**heinō bunri** 兵農分離).

Hideyoshi's Foreign Policy and the Invasion of Korea

At first, Hideyoshi permitted Christian missionary activities. However, in 1587, while on his expedition to Kyūshū, he learned that the Christian daimyō Ōmura Sumitada had donated Nagasaki to the Jesuit order. Hideyoshi responded first by instituting an approval system for daimyō wishing to convert to Christianity. Immediately afterwards, he issued the **Bateren Tsuihō-rei** バテレン（宣教師）追放令 (Missionary Expulsion Edict) and drove the missionaries out of Japan[17]. However, on the other hand in 1588 Hideyoshi enacted the **Kaizoku Torishimari-rei** 海賊取締令 **(Piracy Prohibition Edict)** to prohibit piratical activities (such as those of the wakō), and strengthen maritime control while encouraging wealthy merchants in Kyōto, Sakai, Nagasaki and Hakata to conduct trade with South Asia (i.e., the Nanban trade). Consequently, his measures to remove Christian missionaries were not very effective, because the Nanban trade and missionary activities were inextricably linked[18].

International relations in East Asia in the second half of the 16th century were undergoing a change from the long-standing order centered on China, due to the decline of the Ming Dynasty. Hideyoshi, having completed the unification of Japan, saw this situation as a chance to create a new regional order centered on Japan. He demanded submission and tribute from the Portuguese viceroy's office in Goa, the

---

[17] Takayama Ukon〈高山右近〉, the lord of Akashi Castle〈明石城〉 in Harima〈播磨〉, refused to abandon his belief, and had his territory confiscated. However, commoners were not prohibited from having Christian faith, on the basis of "it should be at their own discretion."

[18] In 1596, a Spanish ship, *San Felipe*, drifted to Tosa〈土佐〉. During exchanges between its crew and the Japanese, some crew members stated that Spain was using missionaries as a means of territorial expansion (*San Felipe* Incident〈サン＝フェリペ号事件〉). This led to Hideyoshi's decision to arrest 26 missionaries and believers (the "26 Martyrs of Japan〈26聖人殉教〉"), and execute them in Nagasaki. Behind this incident lay the rivalry between the Spanish Franciscan order and the Society of Jesus in their missionary activities in Japan.

Spanish viceroy's office in Manila, and Formosa 高山国 (Taiwan).

In 1587, Hideyoshi, through the Sō 宗氏 family in Tsushima 対馬, demanded tribute from Korea, as well as the provision of guides for Japanese troops he intended to send to Ming China. Upon rejection by Korea, Hideyoshi established a headquarters at Nagoya 名護屋 in Hizen Province, and in 1592 dispatched a force of over 150,000 warriors to Korea (**Bunroku Campaign** 文禄の役). After landing at Busan 釜山, the Japanese force swiftly occupied Hanseong 漢城 (present-day Seoul) and Pyongyang 平壌 owing much to the power of their weaponry, such as guns, but were gradually overwhelmed by the Korean navy led by **Yi Sun-sin** 李舜臣 (1545-98), resistance from the Korean volunteer army, and Ming troops sent to assist Korea. Therefore, the Japanese forces ceased fighting, and asked Hideyoshi to make peace with the Ming Dynasty. However, due to Hideyoshi's insistent attitude, the negotiations did not succeed[19].

BUNROKU AND KEICHŌ CAMPAIGNS

In 1597, Hideyoshi again sent more than 140,000 warriors to Korea (**Keichō Campaign** 慶長の役), but the Japanese forces did not fare well from the start, and withdrew in the following year when Hideyoshi died from illness. The **invasion of Korea** 朝鮮侵略 that spanned almost seven years in total involved many people in Korea and caused them a great deal of damage[20]. In Japan, the enterprise cost an enormous sum in war expenses as well as military manpower, and contributed to the decline of the Toyotomi regime.

---

[19] During the peace negotiations beginning from 1593, the Japanese commanders in Korea, who wanted to reach an agreement as soon as possible, decided not to relay to the Ming Dynasty some of Hideyoshi's demands: namely, his demand for the marriage of a Ming princess to the tennō, a Korean prince to be a hostage in Japan, and the cession of the southern part of Korea. When it came to Hideyoshi's knowledge, on the occasion of receiving an envoy from the Ming in 1596, that his demands had not been properly conveyed, he was infuriated and broke off the negotiations.

[20] In Korea, these two invasions were called Imjin Waeran and Jeong-yu Waeran〈壬辰・丁酉倭乱〉.

2 Momoyama Culture

Momoyama Culture

The era of the Oda and Toyotomi regimes is called the **Azuchi-Momoyama period** 安土・桃山時代 because their castles were built in these locations. Likewise, the culture of this period is known as **Momoyama culture** 桃山文化[21]. The openness that characterized the times gave rise to a fresh, extravagant and luxurious culture that flourished under a unified authority wherein wealth and power were concentrated after Japan had suffered years of civil strife. The culture reflected the tastes and economic power of the daimyō, who had emerged as new rulers, and of the leading merchants, whose great wealth was derived from profits made from war and trade. The power enjoyed by the Buddhist temples, the bearers of many cultural traditions, declined due to Nobunaga and Hideyoshi. Consequently, the Buddhist color waned in the culture of the era, giving rise to many paintings and sculptures characterized by realism and dynamic representation.

Furthermore, inspired by the contact with European culture that began with the arrival of the Portuguese, the culture of the era also embraced diversity.

The Art of the Momoyama Period

Momoyama culture is symbolized by castle architecture (**jōkaku kenchiku** 城郭建築). Castles of this time were built on flat land, with stone foundations supporting a main structure with a multi-layered keep, and multiple compounds surrounded by earth mounds and moats[22]. Major castles, such as Azuchi Castle, Ōsaka Castle, and Fushimi Castle 伏見城, were built to be grand and magnificent to symbolize the power that achieved unification. The residential areas inside castles employed the **shoin-zukuri style** 書院造. As interior decoration, walls, sliding screens and folding screens were painted with gorgeous **dami-e** 濃絵 (paintings using blue and green colors applied to gold foil). These pictures painted on interior fixtures were generally called **shōhekiga** 障壁画. Fretwork was carved on transoms. Genre pictures with motifs such as the everyday life and customs of townsfolk were also frequently produced.

---

[21] Hideyoshi built Fushimi Castle and lived there in his later years. Later, peach trees (momo〈桃〉) were planted on the castle ruins, giving rise to the name Momoyama.

[22] Many medieval castles were mountain castles that served as fortresses at time of war. The castles in the Momoyama period, on the other hand, were built on hills or flatland out of consideration of convenience for ruling territories. The castles of this time thus had a dual function, being military bases on the one hand, and the residences and offices of the lords on the other.

HIMEJI CASTLE〈姫路城〉(SHIRASAGI CASTLE〈白鷺城〉)
Ikeda Terumasa〈池田輝政〉, who became the lord of the castle after the Battle of Sekigahara〈関ヶ原の戦い〉, started large-scale construction that was completed in 1609. It stands on flatland with a total area of about 1.875 km^2, and has a magnificent main complex composed of a keep and associated quarters (the keep and west wing still remain).

KARAJISHI-ZU BYŌBU〈「唐獅子図屏風」〉(FOLDING SCREEN OF LIONS, PART, BY KANŌ EITOKU)
A pair of six-panel folding screens. It depicts with strong and dynamic brushstrokes male and female lions majestically swaggering among golden clouds. This work had been kept by the Mōri family until the Meiji period〈明治時代〉. (Height 224 cm, width 453 cm.)

Kanō Eitoku 狩野永徳 (1543-90) from the Kanō School 狩野派, the dominant school of shōhekiga, blended the suibokuga 水墨画 that became popular during the Muromachi period 室町時代 and the traditional indigenous Yamato-e 大和絵, and perfected a new genre of decorative painting characterized by rich coloring, strong brushstrokes, and grandiose composition. Together with his disciple, **Kanō Sanraku** 狩野山楽 (1559-1635), Eitoku created many such works of shōhekiga. Other artists, such as Kaihō Yūshō 海北友松 (1533-1615) and **Hasegawa Tōhaku** 長谷川等伯 (1539-1610), left decorative works rich in bright colors, as well as masterpieces of suibokuga.

In the world of sculpture, the influence of Buddhist sculpture waned. Transom sculpture (**ranma chōkoku** 欄間彫刻) became popular, and many works were made with strong decorative elements, examples being furnishings adorned with maki-e 蒔絵, and decorative metal fittings on buildings. Several kinds of books were also published after the introduction of typography (**katsuji insatsujutsu** 活字印刷術) through Japan's invasion of the Korean peninsula[23].

---

[23] During the Keichō era〈慶長年間〉(1596-1615), several books were published using wooden type printing by order of Go-Yōzei Tennō (Keichō royal editions〈慶長勅版〉).

TSUKUBUSUMA SHRINE〈都久夫須麻神社〉**, MAIN HALL**
A building with hip-and-gable roof using hinoki bark thatching. It was part of Fushimi Castle and was transferred to this location. A taste for opulence characteristic to the Momoyama culture is evident especially in the karahafu gable〈唐破風〉 and doors with luxurious openwork carving.

The Lifestyle of the Mercantile Townspeople

The wealthy **chōshū**〈町衆〉 (mercantile townspeople) in cities such as Kyōto, Ōsaka, Sakai and Hakata also actively participated in the culture of the time. **Sen no Rikyū**〈千利休〉 (1522-91) from Sakai set out the principles for tea ceremony and established chadō〈茶道〉, the way of tea. The wabicha〈侘茶〉 style perfected by Rikyū emphasized the spirit of simplicity and tranquility, representing a divergent element within the flamboyant Momoyama culture. Tea ceremony, being patronized by Toyotomi Hideyoshi and other daimyō, enjoyed tremendous popularity[24]. This led to the creation of numerous masterpieces: tea rooms, tea ware, and tea house gardens. The arts of flower arrangement (kadō〈花道〉) and incense appreciation (kōdō〈香道〉) also developed during this time.

Popular entertainment also thrived. In addition to the Nō〈能〉 theater established in the Muromachi period, Kabuki Odori〈かぶき踊り〉 (Kabuki dance), started by Izumo no Okuni〈出雲阿国〉 (dates unknown) in Kyōto in the early 17th century, became widely popular. This **Okuni Kabuki**〈阿国歌舞伎〉 gave rise to Kabuki performance by women[25]. Similarly popular was **Ningyō Jōruri**〈人形浄瑠璃〉 (puppet theater), which was performed with the accompaniment of a musical instrument called shamisen〈三味線〉 that originated in the Ryūkyū Islands. The

---

[24] In 1587, Hideyoshi held a tea ceremony in Kitano〈北野〉 in Kyōto (Grand Kitano Tea Ceremony〈北野大茶湯〉), in which he had not only tea masters such as Sen no Rikyū, Imai Sōkyū〈今井宗久〉, and Tsuda Sōgyū〈津田宗及〉 participate, but also commoners, regardless of their status and wealth. Tea ceremony was popular among daimyō, and some military leaders even became tea masters, including Oda Urakusai〈織田有楽斎〉 (Nobunaga's younger brother Nagamasu〈長益〉), Kobori Enshū〈小堀遠州〉, and Furuta Oribe〈古田織部〉.

[25] The word "Kabuki" derived from "kabuku〈「傾く」〉" (to lean or sway, implying extraordinariness), and those who walked around in strange costumes were called kabuki-mono〈かぶき者〉 at that time. Kabuki performance by women (Onna Kabuki〈女歌舞伎〉) was later banned by the Edo Bakufu〈江戸幕府〉, and its subsequent alternative, boys' Kabuki (Wakashu Kabuki〈若衆歌舞伎〉), was then also banned. Hence, from the mid-17th century onward, Kabuki has been performed only by adult male actors (Yarō Kabuki〈野郎歌舞伎〉).

commoners also liked Ryūtatsu-bushi 隆達節, a genre of ditty to which melody was provided by Takasabu 高三隆達 Ryūtatsu (1527-1611), a merchant from Sakai. Bon Odori 盆踊り was widely performed in many places.

OKUNI KABUKI (*KOKUJO KABUKI EKOTOBA* 〈『国女歌舞伎絵詞』〉 [ILLUSTRATED SCROLL OF KABUKI], PART)
The woman on the stage ringing a handbell is Okuni.

As for clothing, people usually wore **kosode** 小袖 (short-sleeved kimono). Men often donned hakama 袴 trousers with a sleeveless robe (kataginu 肩衣), an ensemble called kamishimo 裃 that served as simplified formal wear. Women's everyday wear was kosode without hakama. Both men and women began putting their hair up. People ate three meals a day instead of the previous two (morning and evening). Courtiers and warriors used rice for daily meals, whereas most of the commoners lived on miscellaneous grains. In farming villages, housing was typically a one-story house with thatched roof. Cities such as Kyōto started to see two-story structures as well as an increase in tiled roofs.

Nanban Culture

As the Nanban trade and missionary activities expanded, some commoners began to take an interest in Nanban fashion. The missionaries introduced practical sciences such as astronomy, medicine, and geography, along with oil painting and techniques for copper engraving. Japanese artists created **Nanban Byōbu** 南蛮屏風 (Nanban themes painted on folding screens) inspired by Western art. Typography using metal type was also introduced by the Jesuit Alessandro Valignano, along with a printing press. As a result,

NANBANJIN TORAIZU BYŌBU 〈『南蛮人渡来図屏風』〉 (FOLDING SCREEN OF THE ARRIVAL OF NANBANJIN, PART)
A pair of six-panel folding screens. It depicts Spanish or Portuguese led by a *capitan* (captain) walking down the street towards a Nanbanji (church). The party includes many black followers. Inside the church, a Jesuit in black vestments and Japanese lodgers are also seen. (Height 163.5 cm, width 362.5 cm)

NIFON NO
COTOBA TO
Hiſtoria uo narai xiran to
FOSSVRV FITO NO TAME-
NI XEVA NI YAVA RAGVETA-
RV FEIQE NO MONOGATARI.

IESVS NO COMPANHIA NO
Collegio Amacusa ni voite Superiores no go men-
qio to xite core uo fan ni qizamu mono nari,
Go xuxxe yori M.D.L.XXXXII.

AMAKUSA EDITION OF *HEIKE MONOGATARI* (THE TALE OF THE HEIKE)

translations of Christian literary works and religious books using Roman characters, and Japanese dictionaries and classics, were printed (**Christian editions** キリシタン版, **Amakusa editions** 天草版)[26]. The Nanban culture was short-lived because of the Edo Bakufu's sakoku 鎖国政策 policy, but its influence endures today in some of the names of clothing and food[27].

3 The Establishment of the Bakuhan System

The Establishment of the Edo Bakufu

Tokugawa Ieyasu 徳川家康 (1542-1616) had wielded power in the Tōkai region in alliance with Oda Nobunaga. However, under the Toyotomi regime, in 1590 he was made to move to the Kantō region where, after the fall of the Hōjō family, he became a daimyō with a territory of around 2,500,000 koku 石 under his rule. Ieyasu, in his position as the head of the Go-Tairō, consolidated his power following the death of Hideyoshi.

A conflict began to surface between Ieyasu and one of the members of the Go-Bugyō, **Ishida Mitsunari** 石田三成 (1560-1600), who was trying to maintain the Toyotomi regime. In 1600, Mitsunari raised an army, setting up Mōri Terumoto (1553-1625), one of the Go-Tairō, as their leader. This "Western Force" was opposed by an "Eastern Force" consisting of Ieyasu and other daimyō who supported him, such as Fukushima Masanori 福島正則 (1561-1624) and Kuroda Nagamasa 黒田長政 (1568-1623). The two forces clashed with each other at Sekigahara (**Battle of Sekigahara** 関ヶ原の戦い).

Having achieved victory in this decisive battle, Ieyasu punished various daimyō of the Western Force[28]. Then, in order to justify his authority over all the daimyō, in 1603 he received the title of Seii Taishōgun 征夷大将軍, whereupon he established a bakufu in **Edo** 江戸. This marked the beginning of the **Edo period** 江戸時代. As the ruler of the country, Ieyasu put major mines around Japan, such as Sado, under his direct control, and

---

[26] Such publications included the Amakusa editions of *Heike Monogatari*〈『平家物語』〉 and *Isoho Monogatari*〈『伊曽保物語』〉, as well as *Nippo Jisho*〈『日葡辞書』〉 (Japanese-Portuguese dictionary).

[27] Japanese words of Portuguese origin still used today include: *kasutera*〈カステラ〉 (sponge cake, from *castelo*), *kappa*〈カッパ〉 (raincoat, from *capa*), *karuta*〈カルタ〉 (cards, from *carta*), *konpeitō*〈コンペイトウ〉 (sugar candy, from *confeito*), *shabon*〈シャボン〉 (soap, from *sabão*), *pan*〈パン〉 (bread, from *pão*), *rasha*〈ラシャ〉 (a kind of wool textile, from *raxa*) and *juban*〈ジュバン〉 (underwear for kimono, from *gibão*).

[28] Daimyō such as Ishida Mitsunari and Konishi Yukinaga were executed in Kyōto, while 93 families of various daimyō who sided with the Western Force forfeited their positions and domains worth 5.06 million koku in total. Mōri Terumoto had his domains reduced from 1.2 million koku to 370,000 koku, and Uesugi Kagekatsu had his reduced from 1.2 million koku to 300,000 koku.

sent diplomatic letters to Vietnam, the Philippines, and Cambodia, seeking friendly relations. Further, Ieyasu demonstrated his authority as a ruler by ordering various daimyō to contribute to the construction of Edo Castle 江戸城 and its surrounding urban area, while also having them create a domain map and gōchō 郷帳 (statistical account)[29] for each domain.

However, **Toyotomi Hideyori** 豊臣秀頼 (1593-1615), despite being reduced to a mere daimyō – of Settsu 摂津, Kawachi 河内, and Izumi 和泉 with a total holding of 600,000 koku – had inherited his father Hideyoshi's position in name, and still held Ōsaka Castle. To show the daimyō that the shōgun post was a hereditary office held by the Tokugawa family, Ieyasu resigned his position as shōgun in 1605 and had his son, **Tokugawa Hidetada** 徳川秀忠 (1579-1632), appointed as his successor. While Ieyasu moved to Sunpu 駿府, he effectively stayed in power as **Ōgosho** 大御所 (a retired shōgun). Taking advantage of an inscription on a temple bell at Hōkōji 方広寺 Temple (constructed by the Toyotomi family) in Kyōto as a pretext, he attacked and destroyed the Toyotomi forces in the **Siege of Ōsaka** 大坂の役 (Winter Siege of Ōsaka and Summer Siege of Ōsaka) between 1614 and 1615.

The Bakuhan System

In 1615, after the Siege of Ōsaka, the bakufu issued a decree permitting each daimyō to have only one castle per domain (**Ikkoku Ichijō-rei** 一国一城令), and also enacted the **Buke Shohatto** 武家諸法度 **(Regulations Concerning Bushi Households)**[30] to keep a tight rein on the daimyō[31]. After the death of Ieyasu, the second shōgun, Tokugawa Hidetada, issued documents in 1617 confirming the land rights of daimyō, courtiers, and temples and shrines. By doing so, he demonstrated his authority over all the land in the country.

---

[29] Following the Keichō era, the creation of domain maps and gōchō (registers that recorded the total yield of each village within a district before compiling the records for the domain as a whole) took place during the Shōhō, Genroku and Tenpō eras〈正保・元禄・天保年間〉 as well.

[30] Ieyasu ordered Sūden〈崇伝〉, a monk of Konchi-in〈金地院〉 at Nanzenji Temple〈南禅寺〉, to draft these regulations, and had them issued in the name of Shōgun Hidetada. They were based on the Kenmu Shikimoku〈建武式目〉 and other laws such as bunkoku-hō〈分国法〉. Even after Iemitsu, the regulations were reissued every time the shōgun changed, with slight revisions added.

[31] A daimyō referred to a bushi with a kokudaka of over 10,000 koku, who had become a vassal of the shōgun. Daimyō were classified into **shinpan**〈親藩〉, **fudai**〈譜代〉, and **tozama**〈外様〉 categories depending on how close or distant their relations were to the shōgun. Shinpan were daimyō who belonged to the Tokugawa family, such as the **Sanke**〈三家〉, or the three privileged branches (of the three domains of Owari〈尾張〉, Kii〈紀伊〉, and Mito〈水戸〉). Fudai referred to daimyō who were originally hereditary retainers of the Tokugawa family, while tozama were those who had become followers of the Tokugawa family around the time of the Battle of Sekigahara. As for the allocation of domains to daimyō, shinpan and fudai were placed in strategic locations, while powerful tozama lords were placed in areas as remote as possible.

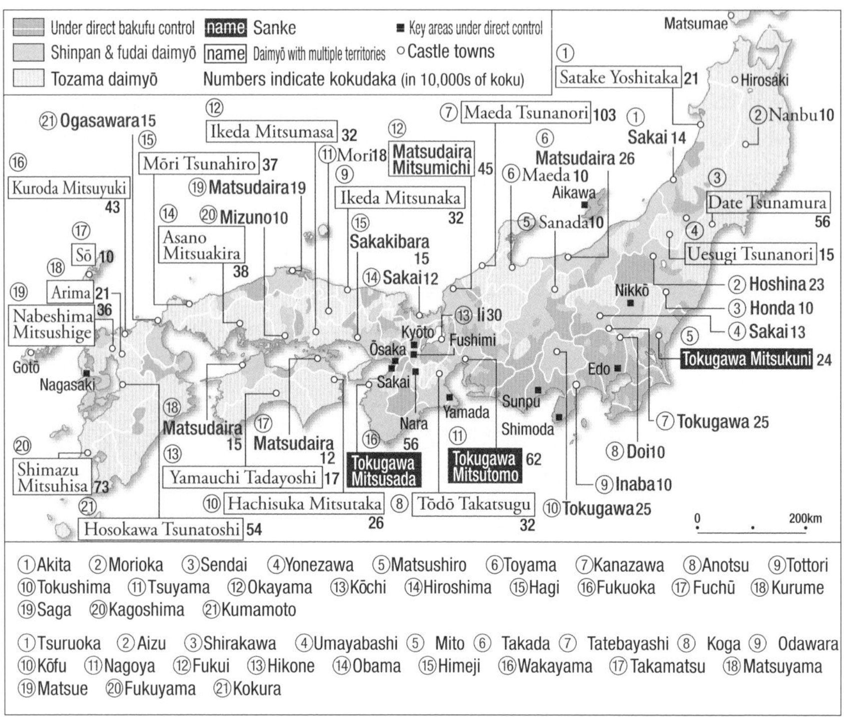

REGIONAL ASSIGNMENT OF DAIMYŌ (C. 1664, COLORS INDICATE APPROXIMATE DIVISIONS)

Moreover, in 1619 he deprived Fukushima Masanori of his position and property for violating the Buke Shohatto. By doing so, he emphasized the importance of complying with those laws, but he was also displaying the shōgunal power to punish even a tozama daimyō (daimyō who had not supported Ieyasu before Sekigahara) who had long rendered distinguished service. Hidetada passed his post as shōgun to **Tokugawa Iemitsu** (徳川家光) (1604-51) in 1623, and continued to lay the foundations for the authority of the bakufu as a retired shōgun.

Following Hidetada's death in 1632, the third shōgun, Tokugawa Iemitsu, also punished the Katō (加藤氏) family, a tozama daimyō family of Higo Province, shoring up the authority of the bakufu in Kyūshu. Furthermore, in 1634, Iemitsu went up to Kyōto at the head of a force of over 300,000 men. This was a display of his military leadership by imposing uniform military service (**gunyaku** (軍役)) on all the daimyō. Depending on their **kokudaka** (石高), a daimyō kept a standing army of a fixed number of troops, took part in battles on the order of the shōgun in wartime, and was tasked with construction projects such as repairing Edo Castle or river work in times of peace.

In 1635, Tokugawa Iemitsu issued a new version of the Buke Shohatto (called the **Kan'ei-rei** 寛永令), and strictly ordered the daimyō to observe these laws. The edict also obliged the daimyō to alternate their residence between Edo and their home domain every year, a system called **Sankin Kōtai** 参勤交代 (alternate attendance system)[32], while forcing the wives and children of the daimyō to remain in Edo. Thus, the lord-vassal relationship between the shōgun and the daimyō was established by the time of the third shōgun, Tokugawa Iemitsu. This system of rule over the land and people, in which the shōgun (the **bakufu** 幕府) and the daimyō (the **han** 藩, or domains) held powerful rights, is called the **bakuhan system** 幕藩体制.

The Structural Organization of the Bakufu and Domains

Bakufu revenues were based on the income from the major mines such as Sado, Izu 伊豆, Tajima Ikuno, and Iwami Ōmori, in addition to the annual land tax from as much as 4 million koku (around the end of the 17th century) of land under the bakufu's direct control. The bakufu also controlled commerce and trade by directly controlling major cities such as Edo, Kyōto, Ōsaka, Nagasaki, and Sakai, while seizing the right to mint coinage as well. The bakufu retained an overwhelming military force, consisting of **hatamoto** 旗本 and **gokenin** 御家人[33] who were in the direct service of the shōgun, as well as military service that was imposed on the daimyō.

Bakufu administration had been carried out by close attendants during the time of Ieyasu and Hidetada, but by the time of the third shōgun, Iemitsu, it had been reorganized. The **toshiyori** 年寄, senior retainers who had played a central part in the administrative system, became known as **rōjū** 老中 (elders) who were responsible for supervising state affairs. A provisional supreme post called tairō 大老 (great counselor) was temporarily assigned to take part in a council just when important decisions were required, such as when the shōgun changed. Various additional positions were established with their own official duties: wakadoshiyori 若年寄 (junior counselors), who assisted the rōjū and

---

[32] It was stipulated that the daimyō should alternate between residing for a year in Edo and a year in their home domain. However, the alternation occurred every half a year for daimyō in the Kantō region. The Sankin Kōtai system led to the development of transportation, and Edo grew into a metropolitan city. For the daimyō, however, it was a heavy duty that incurred large expenditures, as they were required to maintain a residence in Edo for their wives and children, not to mention the cost of traveling to and from Edo with many accompanying retainers.

[33] Both were retainers in the direct service of the shōgun (jikisan〈直参〉, or immediate retainers) with an income of less than 10,000 koku. Hatamoto were entitled to have an audience with the shōgun, while gokenin were not. According to a survey carried out in 1722, there were 5205 hatamoto and 17,399 gokenin. They lived in Edo, held positions according to their kokudaka and abilities, and bore the burden of military service.

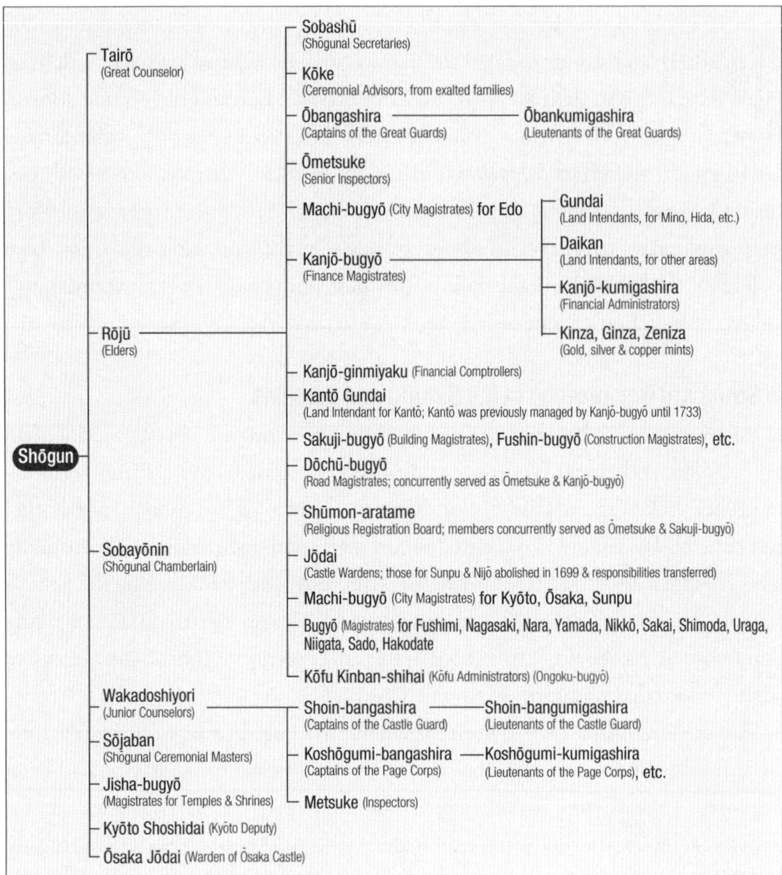

ORGANIZATIONAL STRUCTURE OF EDO BAKUFU

supervised the hatamoto; ōmetsuke (senior inspectors), who monitored the daimyō; and metsuke (inspectors), who monitored the hatamoto and gokenin; as well as the **San-Bugyō**[34], or three magistrate posts of jisha-bugyō (magistrates for temples and shrines), machi-bugyō (city magistrates), and kanjō-bugyō (finance magistrates). In principle, these positions were held by several of the fudai daimyō (allied daimyō, who had followed Ieyasu before Sekigahara) and the hatamoto, with the affairs each handled being rotated monthly (**tsukiban kōtai**). Simple lawsuits were decided inde-

[34] The death of Sūden of Konchi-in, who had single-handedly overseen the administration of temples and shrines as the shōgun's close advisor, triggered the institutionalization of the duties of the jisha-bugyō. Jisha-bugyō were directly under the shōgun and were appointed from among fudai daimyō, wheareas kanjō-bugyō and machi-bugyō were under the rōjū and were appointed from the hatamoto.

pendently by a single office, but cases pertaining to the jurisdictions of several offices were decided at the **Hyōjōsho** 評定所 (bakufu high court) as the rōjū and the San-Bugyō conferred on the matter.

In terms of local administrative organizations, the **Kyōto Shoshidai** 京都所司代 (Kyōto deputy) was an important office that controlled the royal court and monitored the daimyō of the western provinces. **Jōdai** 城代 (castle wardens) and **machi-bugyō** 町奉行 were appointed in major cities such as Kyōto, Ōsaka, and Sunpu, while other magistrates (so-called ongoku-bugyō 遠国奉行) were appointed in Fushimi, Nagasaki, Sado, and Nikkō 日光. Moreover, local intendants were assigned to manage the land under the bakufu's direct control: **gundai** 郡代 for areas including Kantō 関東, Hida 飛騨, and Mino, and **daikan** 代官 for the rest of the lands. The local intendants were in turn supervised by the kanjō-bugyō.

The domains of the daimyō and their own governments were collectively called **han** 藩. In the early Edo period, daimyō would at times grant lands to powerful bushi within their domain and allow them to govern the people therein, a system called **jikata-chigyō** 地方知行制. However, the daimyō gradually strengthened their control over their entire domains[35]. They incorporated even the powerful bushi into their corps of retainers, who were required to gather and reside in the castle towns, and had them take part in domain administration by appointing them to posts such as karō 家老 (house elders) or bugyō (magistrates). By the mid-17th century, the jikata-chigyō system was no longer practiced in most domains. Instead, daimyō came to adopt the **hōroku system** 俸禄制度[36], in which the annual tax from the land under the domain's direct control (managed by local intendants) was paid to their vassals, in rice, as their salary. Thus, the daimyō strengthened their control over their land and people, and the domains, through consolidating their administrative organization, established their authority.

The Tennō and the Royal Court

When he helped Go-Mizuno'o Tennō 後水尾天皇 (r. 1611-29) ascend the throne in 1611, Tokugawa Ieyasu demonstrated the extent to which his authority had reached. The royal court had to bow to the wishes of the bushi even in matters such as the tennō's

---

[35] The Ikkoku Ichijō-rei issued in 1615 had the effect of weakening the powerful bushi based in branch castles within the domain who could challenge the daimyō.

[36] The main source of domain revenue was the annual rice tax, nearly half of which was provided to the daimyō's retainers as their salary. There were rare cases where some retainers earned more than 10,000 koku, but most of them had a stipend of only a few hundred, or a few dozen, koku. Low-ranking warriors, such as ashigaru, were paid in a ration for a number of people, or in wages in ryō〈両〉. For rations, 5 gō〈合〉 (cups) of rice per day was provided for one person's sustenance.

abdication and enthronement. Furthermore, following the enactment in 1613 of the Kugeshū Hatto 公家衆法度 (Regulations for Court Nobles)[37], in 1615 Ieyasu issued the **Kinchū Narabini Kuge Shohatto** 禁中並公家諸法度 (Regulations Concerning the Royal Household and Court Nobles), through which he clearly showed his standards for managing the royal court. In addition to having the Kyōto Shoshidai and others monitoring the court, the bakufu allowed the kanpaku (open only to the Sekke 摂家 [regental families, i.e. Sekkanke 摂関家]) and top three ministers 三公 to take the initiative in supervising the court, under the guidance of the **buke tensō** 武家伝奏 (bakufu liaisons to the court)[38].

The bakufu established a system to regulate the life and conduct of the tennō and courtiers to prevent them from exerting their own power or from being exploited by daimyō[39]. In 1620, the bakufu also took advantage of the marriage between Tokugawa Hidetada's daughter, Masako 和子 (Tōfukumon-in 東福門院, 1607-78), and Go-Mizuno'o to expand their authority throughout the country. It henceforth required the royal court to have consent from the bakufu in exercising its remaining authority, namely over appointment of official positions, changing of the era name, and changing of the calendar.

In 1629, Go-Mizuno'o, who had been in poor health, suddenly abdicated without asking the bakufu's consent, an event triggered by the **Purple Robe (Shie) Incident** 紫衣事件[40]. The abdication was subsequently approved by the bakufu, since the new tennō, Meishō Tennō 明正天皇 (r. 1629-43)[41], was Hidetada's grandchild. However, the bakufu ordered the

---

[37] The Kugeshū Hatto prescribed that court nobles were obliged to inherit their family's specialization and to serve as kinri-koban〈禁裏小番〉(who performed shift duty watching over the royal palace). The family specialization for the Shirakawa〈白川家〉and Yoshida families〈吉田家〉was Shintō affairs, while for the Tsuchimikado family〈土御門家〉it was Onmyōdō〈陰陽道〉, and for the Asukai family〈飛鳥井家〉it was kemari〈蹴鞠〉(kickball).

[38] Two courtiers were selected to be buke tensō, and received an allowance from the bakufu. Acting as liaisons between the court and the bakufu, they maintained contact with the Kyōto Shoshidai and conveyed the bakufu's instructions to the court.

[39] Estates owned by the royal family (kinrigoryō〈禁裏御料〉), court nobles (kugeryō〈公家領〉) and monzeki temples (monzekiryō〈門跡領〉) were all limited to the necessary minimum. Royal progresses were in principle not approved until the end of the Edo period, the last of them having taken place during the Keian era〈慶安年間〉(1648-52). Courtiers were not allowed to even leave Kyōto for Daigo〈醍醐〉or Yoshino〈吉野〉to see cherry blossoms without reporting it through the buke tensō.

[40] The Kinchū Narabini Kuge Shohatto stipulated whether the head monks of temples were permitted to wear purple robes. When the rules were not met with compliance, in 1627 the bakufu made an issue of Go-Mizuno'o granting the right to wear such robes without consulting it. This led to Takuan〈沢庵〉(of Daitokuji Temple〈大徳寺〉), among others, protesting and being punished. The incident clearly demonstrated that the bakufu's regulations took precedence over royal approval.

[41] She was the first female tennō in 859 years, since Shōtoku Tennō〈称徳天皇〉in the Nara

Sekke and the buke tensō to impose strict control over the royal court. As such, a basic framework was established to control the court, initiated in Ieyasu's time and maintained until the end of the Edo period.

The Ban on Christianity, and the Situation of Temples and Shrines

Initially, the bakufu tolerated Christianity. However, the propagation of Christianity became strongly recognized as a threat that could invite invasion from Spain and Portugal, and there was also the possibility of Christians banding together for their faith. This led the bakufu to issue a ban on Christianity within the territories directly under its control in 1612. The bakufu imposed this prohibition (**Kinkyō-rei** 禁教令) throughout the country the following year and forced the believers to convert to Buddhism. Thereafter, the bakufu and the domains severely persecuted Catholic missionaries and believers by executing or expelling them[42]. Many of the followers converted, but some of them refused to submit to persecution, becoming martyrs or secretly holding on to their faith as underground Christians (kakure 隠れキリシタン kirishitan).

In 1637, the **Shimabara Rebellion** 島原の乱 (1637-38) occurred. This was an ikki composed of farmers and powerful local magnates against the Matsukura 松倉氏 family of Shimabara Castle 島原城, and the Terasawa 寺沢氏 family of Amakusa 天草 Domain, who had imposed severe taxes and oppressed Christians during a famine. The Shimabara peninsula and the Amakusa Islands had once been the domains of two Christian daimyō, Arima Harunobu and Konishi Yukinaga (1558-1600). Consequently, there were many of their former vassals (rōnin, masterless bushi) as well as Christians among the rebels. The rebel forces, numbering about 30,000 and led by Masuda (Amakusa Shirō) Tokisada 益田（天草四郎）時貞 (1623?-38), occupied the abandoned Hara 原城 Castle. The bakufu mobilized a force of some 120,000, consisting of daimyō forces in the Kyūshū region and others, and finally quashed this ikki the following year in 1638.

After the Shimabara Rebellion, in order to root out Christians the bakufu intensified the enforcement of ebumi 絵踏 (making people step on Christian images), which had been conducted since before the rebellion, particularly in regions that had many believers such as the northern part of Kyūshū. In addition, the bakufu established

---

period〈奈良時代〉. Another female tennō later in history was the older sister of Momozono Tennō〈桃園天皇〉, Go-Sakuramachi Tennō〈後桜町天皇〉 (r. 1762-70), who took the throne following his sudden death.

[42] In 1614, over 300 Christians including Takayama Ukon were banished to Manila or Macau. Ukon arrived in Manila along with his family and received a warm welcome from the Spanish governor of Manila. However, he died of illness before long. Additionally, in 1622, 55 missionaries and believers were executed in Nagasaki (Great Genna Martyrdom〈元和の大殉教〉).

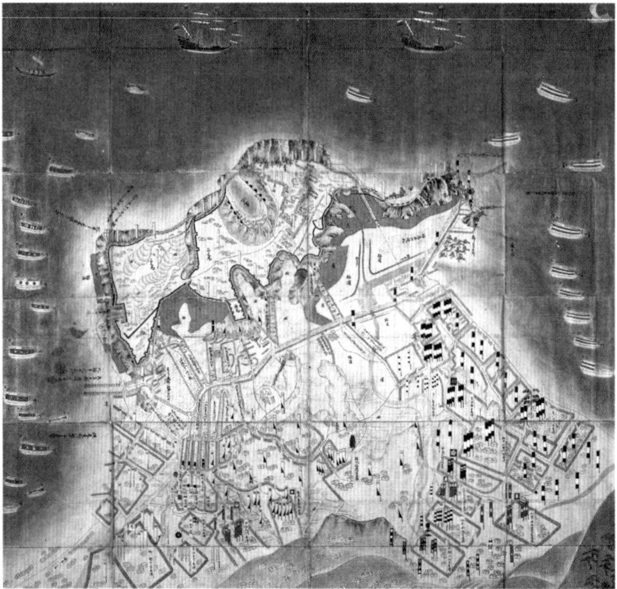

BAKUFU FORCES BESIEGING HARA CASTLE (*KAN'EI 15 HIZEN SHIMABARAJIN NO ZU*〈寛永十五年肥前島原陣之図〉 [ILLUSTRATION OF THE SHIMABARA SIEGE IN HIZEN IN 1638]) The Shimabara Rebellion turned into an unexpectedly large-scale uprising in which Dutch vessels also bombarded Hara Castle from the sea. The painting depicts two Dutch ships at the top.

the **terauke system** (寺請制度), in which temples were required to reveal which households had registered with them. **Shūmon-aratame** (宗門改め) (inspection of one's registration at a Buddhist temple) was conducted, enforcing conversion to Buddhism. Through such measures, the bakufu kept a watchful eye out for Christianity.

To prevent people from believing in religions prohibited by the bakufu, such as Christianity and the Fuju-fuse (不受不施派) School of the Nichiren (日蓮宗) Sect[43], everyone, even bushi and Shintō priests, had to register at a temple (**jidan system** (寺檀制度)) and receive a terauke certificate to prove it. However, not all religions other than Buddhism were suppressed, and Shintō, Shugendō (修験道), and Onmyōdō[44] were seen as conforming to Buddhism and were thus approved.

In cases where a monzeki temple (a temple headed by a child of a royal branch family or the Sekkanke) was the head temple of a sect, the bakufu regarded them as part of the royal court and put them under bakufu control. Moreover, the bakufu issued the **Jiin Hatto** (寺院法度) (temple regulations) which guaranteed the position of the head temple of each sect while requiring them to organize their respective branch temples

[43] It was a subsect of the Nichiren Sect that refused to accept charity from, or give any to, non-believers, while also believing in the supremacy of religion over the bakufu's power.

[44] People relied on Shugenja〈修験者〉 (yamabushi〈山伏〉, or mountain ascetics) for prayers and divinations when such needs were not met by the monks of their family temples.

(honmatsu system) 本末制度[45]. In 1665, the **Shoshū Jiin Hatto** 諸宗寺院法度 (Temple Regulations for Each Sect) was issued to uniformly control all monks of Buddhist temples regardless of the sect. In the same year the **Shosha Negi Kannushi Hatto** 諸社禰宜神主法度 (Regulations for All Shrines, Deputy Priests and Head Priests) was also enacted to control shrines and priests, under the supervision of the Yoshida courtier family.

In the case of Shugendō, the Shōgoin Monzeki 聖護院門跡 Temple of the Tendai 天台系 Sect (Honzan 本山派 School) and the Daigoji Sanbōin Monzeki 醍醐寺三宝院門跡 Temple of the Shingon 真言系 Sect (Tōzan 当山派 School) were made the head temples of their respective sects, with practitioners under their control. As for Onmyōdō, the Tsuchimikado courtier family were put in charge of all of the practitioners.

Foreign Relations in the Early Edo Period

In 1600, the Dutch ship *Liefde* リーフデ号 drifted ashore at Bungo. At that time, two countries had been gaining power in Europe: the Netherlands, which had become independent from Spain in the latter half of the 16th century, and England, which had developed a woolen textile industry. Both countries established East India Companies 東インド会社 in an attempt to make forays into Asia. Tokugawa Ieyasu invited the *Liefde*'s second mate, Jan Joosten ヤン＝ヨーステン（耶揚子） (Yayōsu, 1556-1623), and its English navigator, William Adams ウィリアム＝アダムズ（三浦按針） (Miura Anjin, 1564-1620), to Edo and made them his advisors on foreign affairs and trade. From then on, the Dutch in 1609 and the English in 1613 gained the bakufu's permission to trade with Japan[46], establishing trading posts at **Hirado** 平戸 in Hizen. Ieyasu also tried to resume diplomatic relations with Ming China through Joseon Korea and the Ryūkyū Kingdom, although the Ming Dynasty turned this down.

Ieyasu was also eager to develop trade with Spain, and sent Tanaka Shōsuke 田中勝介 (dates unknown), a Kyōto merchant, to the Spanish territory of Mexico (Nueva Espana, or New Spain), seeking to establish trade relations[47]. In 1613, Date Masamune, the lord of Sendai Domain 仙台藩, dispatched his retainer Hasekura Tsunenaga 支倉常長 (1571-1622) to Spain in order to open direct trade with Mexico, but he could not achieve his goal of

---

[45] In addition to making use of various Buddhist sects that had developed in Japan since the medieval era, the bakufu also approved the **Ōbaku Sect**〈黄檗宗〉 of Zen Buddhism, which was introduced by Ingen Ryūki〈隠元隆琦〉, a monk from Ming China, in the mid-17th century.

[46] The Dutch and the English were called Kōmōjin〈紅毛人〉 ("red-haired people"), to distinguish them from the Nanbanjin. Their religion was Protestant, rather than Catholic, Christianity.

[47] There had been no traffic with Spain since the *San Felipe* Incident in 1596. However, an opportunity arose when a former governor-general of Luzon, Rodrigo de Vivero y Aberrucia〈ドン＝ロドリゴ〉, was cast ashore at Kazusa〈上総〉 in 1609. Trade relations resumed when Ieyasu sent him back to New Spain in 1610, providing a ship for him. Tanaka Shōsuke and others who accompanied him on this journey are said to have been the first Japanese to travel to the Americas.

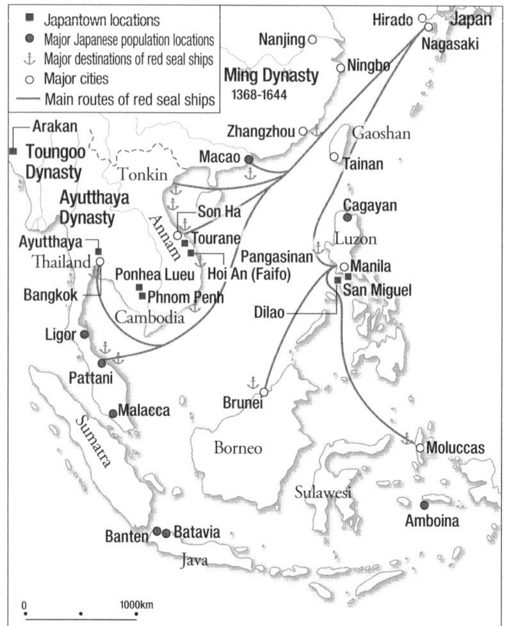

MAJOR DESTINATIONS OF RED SEAL SHIPS, AND JAPAN TOWNS

establishing a trade relationship (**Keichō Mission to Europe** 慶長遣欧使節).

At that time, Portuguese merchants were gaining an enormous profit by importing Chinese **raw silk** 生糸 (white thread) to Nagasaki through their trading base of Macao. However, the bakufu established the **itowappu system** 糸割符制度 in 1604 by granting a monopoly to purchase imported raw silk thread in bulk to a group of select merchants called itowappu nakama 糸割符仲間, putting an end to the exclusive benefits gained by the Portuguese merchants[48].

Japanese continued to travel overseas as they had under the Toyotomi regime, with many merchant ships making voyages to destinations such as Luzon in the Philippines, Tonkin and Annam (Vietnam), Cambodia, and Thailand. The bakufu granted red seal permits 朱印状 to merchants allowing them to sail abroad. Trade ships that carried official red seal permits were called **shuinsen** 朱印船, or red seal ships[49]. As red seal trade 朱印船貿易 started to thrive, more Japanese migrated abroad, forming autonomous Japan towns (**Nihonmachi** 日本町) in various places across Southeast Asia. Some of the Japanese who went overseas

---

[48] In the itowappu system, a group of select merchants from Kyōto, Sakai, and Nagasaki established a guild called itowappu nakama, which decided the price of imported raw silk thread every spring in order to buy it in bulk at a set price, distributing it among the members of the guild. As merchants in Edo and Ōsaka were later added to the group, they were called gokasho-shōnin〈五カ所商人〉 (merchants of the five cities).

[49] Among those engaged in the red seal trade were daimyō such as Shimazu Iehisa〈島津家久〉 and Arima Harunobu, and merchants like Suetsugu Heizō〈末次平蔵〉 of Nagasaki, Sueyoshi Magozaemon〈末吉孫左衛門〉 of Settsu, and Suminokura Ryōi〈角倉了以〉 and Chaya Shirōjirō〈茶屋四郎次郎〉 of Kyōto. Imported goods were mainly from Asia and included raw silk, silk fabrics, sugar, deer hide, and shark skins, but goods like woolen cloth came from Europe. Silver, copper, and iron were the main exports from Japan, and the value of Japanese silver exports at the time accounted for as much as one third of the world's silver production.

became influential there, such as Yamada Nagamasa (山田長政) (?-1630)[50] who held an important position in the court of the Ayutthaya Kingdom (アユタヤ朝) (1351-1767).

The Sakoku Policy

While the foreign trade was flourishing and the bakuhan system became solidified, the bakufu began to impose restrictions on trade and overseas travel by Japanese. The first reason for these restrictions was the prohibition of Christianity.

The second reason was to give the bakufu a monopoly on trade to secure exclusive benefits. The bakufu attempted to keep trade under its control out of fear that the daimyō of the western provinces engaged in trading might become too rich and powerful. Consequently, in 1616, the arrival of all foreign vessels except Chinese ships was restricted to the ports of **Hirado** (平戸) and **Nagasaki** (長崎), followed by Spanish ships being prohibited from coming to Japan altogether in 1624[51]. Subsequently in 1633, all Japanese ships except **hōshosen** (奉書船)[52] were prohibited from travelling overseas. In 1635, the bakufu forbade Japanese to go abroad, or Japanese living abroad to return. It also made Nagasaki the only port that Chinese ships could call at instead of ports all around Kyūshū, where they had previously been allowed to visit[53].

After quashing the Shimabara Rebellion, the bakufu placed a ban on the arrival of Portuguese ships in 1639. In 1641, the Dutch trading post at Hirado was moved to **Dejima** (出島) in Nagasaki. Dejima was put under close surveillance by the Nagasaki bugyō (長崎奉行), and open communication between the Dutch and Japanese was forbidden. It was in this way that the so-called **sakoku** (鎖国)[54] of Japan began. Thereafter, for more than 200 years Japan broke off all relations with other countries except for the Dutch trading post, the private merchant ships from China, Joseon (朝鮮) Korea, the Ryūkyū Kingdom (琉球王国), and the Ainu (アイヌ) people. It was possible for the bakufu to control foreign relations because

---

[50] Yamada Nagamasa, from Sunpu, was the head of a Japan town in Ayutthaya, the capital of the Ayutthaya Kingdom (Thailand). He later became the governor or Ligor〈リゴール〉 (present-day Nakhon Si Thammarat), but died from poisoning during political turmoil.

[51] Meanwhile, the English had already withdrawn, having closed their trading post in 1623 after losing out to the Dutch.

[52] Hōshosen refers to a ship that was travelling abroad, carrying not only a red-seal permit but also an official letter of permission called rōjū-hōsho〈老中奉書〉 (official permit issued by rōjū).

[53] The bakufu gave up restoring official diplomatic relations with China, and decided instead to engage in private trade with Chinese merchant ships in Nagasaki.

[54] A German physician, Engelbert Kaempfer〈ケンペル〉, pointed out in his *History of Japan*〈『日本誌』〉 that Japan was closed off from the world, only maintaining a connection with the Netherlands through Nagasaki. When Shizuki Tadao〈志筑忠雄〉, a former Dutch interpreter, translated *History of Japan* in 1801, he rendered this as "sakoku" (closed country). The term has continued to be used until the present.

the Japanese economy at the time did not require ties with overseas economies.

Thus, the bakufu was able to strengthen its control over the country through the sakoku policy by establishing a monopoly on trade, limiting overseas influence on industry and culture, and achieving the suppression of Christianity.

The Nagasaki Trade

Under the sakoku policy, Nagasaki became the single port open to foreign trade, with the only trading vessels coming to Japan being limited to Dutch and Chinese ships. The Dutch, seeking only trade benefits, ran the trading post at Dejima as a branch of the Dutch East India Company that they had established in Batavia (present-day Jakarta)[55]. The bakufu made use of Nagasaki as a gateway for importing European goods, and was able to learn about matters abroad from the **Dutch news reports** オランダ風説書[56] submitted by the chief executive officers of the Dutch trading post each time Dutch ships arrived in Nagasaki.

In China, the Ming 明 Dynasty founded by the Han Chinese collapsed in the mid-17th century, and was replaced by the **Qing** 清 **Dynasty** (1636-1912), established by the Manchu 満州民族 people from northeastern China. Once the turmoil caused by the dynastic change settled down, the volume of trade in Nagasaki continued to grow

NAGASAKI-KŌ NO ZU (ILLUSTRATION OF THE PORT OF NAGASAKI, BY MARUYAMA ŌKYO〈円山応挙〉)
This painting depicts the port of Nagasaki during the latter half of the 18th century. Mt. Inasa〈稲佐山〉 is depicted at the top of the painting, while the flag of the Netherlands can be seen on the fan-shaped Dejima at the bottom. The Dutch vessel at the upper left is being towed by numerous small boats.

---

[55] Dutch ships brought to Japan such articles as Chinese raw silk, woven goods (including silk fabrics, woolen cloth, and cotton fabrics), medicines, sugar, and books. When the value of gold rose in Europe during the 1660s, gold coins began to be exported instead of silver.

[56] Since 1633, Dutch missions to Edo had been systemized and dispatched regularly. There were 167 of these missions in total, with one taking place every year up until the 150th time.

every year[57]. The increasing volume of imports had led to an excessive outflow of silver which the bakufu sought to curb. In 1685 the bakufu placed limits on the value of imports from trading with Dutch and Chinese ships[58], and in 1688, it limited the annual number of ships arriving from Qing China to 70 ships in total. The following year, the Chinese Quarter (**Tōjin Yashiki** 唐人屋敷) was established to restrict where Chinese were able to live in Nagasaki.

Joseon Korea, the Ryūkyū Islands, and Ezochi[i]

Tokugawa Ieyasu, in contrast to the Toyotomi regime, achieved peace with Joseon Korea. In 1609, the **Sō family** 宗氏 that ruled Tsushima Domain concluded the **Kiyū Treaty** 己酉約条 with Korea. This treaty formed the basis of the relationship between Korea and early modern Japan. A Japanese settlement (**Wakan** 倭館) was established in Busan, and the Sō family was granted a privileged position in terms of diplomatic relations between Korea and Japan[59]. Joseon Korea sent some 12 delegations to Japan, and from the fourth delegation they came to be referred to as **Chōsen Tsūshinshi** 朝鮮通信使[60]. Over half of these missions were sent to Japan ostensibly to offer congratulations on the ascension of a new shōgun.

The Ryūkyū Kingdom had been conquered in 1609 by an army under Shimazu Iehisa (1576-1638) of Satsuma 薩摩, whereupon it was placed under the rule of Satsuma Domain. Satsuma seized the commerce and trade rights of the kingdom, in addition to establishing its control over farming villages by carrying out land surveys there. Furthermore, it invested the Shō 尚氏 family of the Ryūkyū Kingdom with the kingship, with a holding worth a little over 89,000 koku, and had them continue the tributary 朝貢貿易

[57] Imports included raw silk, silk fabrics, and books from China, cotton fabrics and woolen cloth from Europe, and sugar, sappanwood, fragrant wood, animal hide, and animal horns from South Asia. Japan mostly exported silver, copper, and marine products.

[58] The itowappu system was temporarily abolished in 1655, to be replaced by direct, free trade based on competitive bidding. However, the itowappu system was brought back in 1685, and the bakufu limited the value of imports from trading with Dutch ships to 3,000 kan〈貫〉 of silver and with Chinese ships to 6,000 kan of silver (1 kan = approx. 3.75 kg) per year.

[59] The Sō family was granted the privilege to monopolize the trade with Korea. The family established a lord-vassal relationship with its retainers by sharing the trade profits with them. Since Tsushima had limited arable land, trade profits were granted instead of territory.

[60] The first Joseon mission to Japan consisted of about 300 to 500 members. This mission and the two that followed were dispatched in order to bring back Koreans that had been taken captive during the invasions of Korea. The first envoy brought back 1,240 captives, while the second brought back 321, and the third, 146. The title tsūshinshi (literally "communication envoys"), which began to be used after the fourth mission, signified that these were missions aimed at building friendly relations based on mutual trust.

RYŪKYŪAN MISSIONS TO EDO (*RYŪKYŪ CHŪZAN-Ō RYŌSHISHA TOJŌ GYŌRETSU ZU* 〈琉球中山王両使者登城行列図〉 [ILLUSTRATION OF THE PROCESSION OF THE RYŪKYŪ KING'S DELEGATION TO EDO CASTLE], PART)

1710 procession. A musical performance given while marching consisted of wind and percussion instruments such as the ryōban〈両班〉 (wooden clappers), tonrō〈銅鑼〉 (gongs), tonchie〈銅角〉 (brass instruments), kuiha〈喇叭〉 (trumpets), and ku〈鼓〉 (hand drums) that are depicted in the painting. It must have been a rare type of sound for the spectators.

WAJIN ADVANCES (C. 1669)

trade with China as an independent kingdom[61]. The Ryūkyū envoy sent to pay tribute to China traveled by land from the port of Fujian 福建 to Beijing 北京. At the same time, the Ryūkyū Kingdom sent the bakufu a mission of gratitude (**shaonshi** 謝恩使) each time the king changed as well as a mission of congratulations (**kei-gashi** 慶賀使) whenever the shōgun changed[62]. As such, the Ryūkyū Kingdom maintained dual foreign relations with both the bakufu and China.

The Kakizaki family 蠣崎氏, who had power over Wajin settlements 和人地 in the southern part of Ezogashima 蝦夷ヶ島 (Hokkaidō), changed its name to the **Matsumae family** 松前氏 in the early modern period. In 1604, Tokugawa Ieyasu guaranteed the family's exclusive rights to trade with the Ainu people of the island, and it ruled the region as a domain. Trade with Ainu communities outside of Wajin settlements, such as at river basins or around the wide expanse of Ezochi, was conducted at trading posts called **akinaiba** 商場 or **basho** 場所[63],

---

[61] In addition to making the Ryūkyū Kingdom offer brown sugar (a local product) as payment, Satsuma Domain also had the kingdom deliver Chinese products it gained from the tributary trade with Ming (and later Qing) China.

[62] Ryūkyūan missions to Edo were made to parade wearing exotic costumes and hairstyles, with flags and musical instruments adding to the effect, so that it would seem as if the Ryūkyūans were "foreigners" paying tribute to the shōgun.

[63] The lord-vassal relations that the Matsumae family established with its retainer corps involved

CEREMONIAL VISIT OF AINU PEOPLE (*EZO KOKUFŪ ZUE*〈『蝦夷国風図絵』〉[ILLUSTRATION OF CUSTOMS OF EZO], PART)
Matsumae Norihiro〈松前矩広〉, lord of Matsumae Domain, is seated on a raised platform to the left. At a formal reception of Ainu visitors (shown on the right), Norihiro wears a daimon〈大紋〉(type of ceremonial dress for warriors of the fifth or higher rank).

and profits from this trade were provided to retainers. In 1669, an Ainu rebellion led by Shakushain シャクシャイン (?-1669) broke out against Matsumae Domain, but it ended with the latter's victory with the help of Tsugaru 津軽藩 Domain. As a result of **Shakushain's Revolt** シャクシャインの戦い, the Ainu were forced into complete submission to Matsumae Domain. In addition, by the first half of the 18th century, many of the trading posts were subcontracted to Wajin merchants (**basho ukeoi system** 場所請負制度)[64].

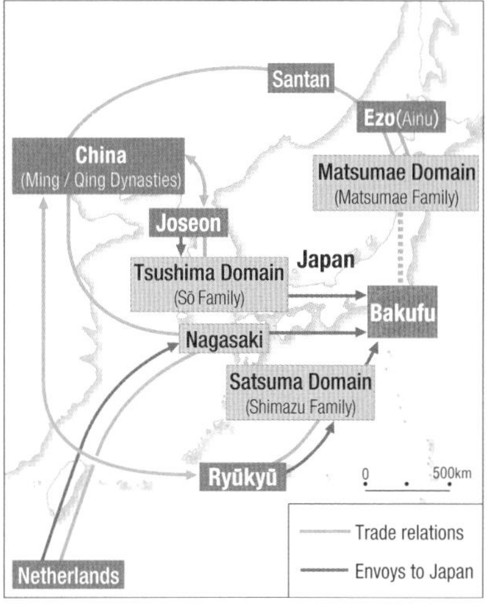

DIPLOMATIC ORDER CENTERED ON JAPAN

In summary, the bakufu carried on relations with foreign countries and peoples through four gateways – Nagasaki, Tsushima, Satsuma, and Matsumae. Following the dynastic change in China from Ming to Qing, two diplomatic orders started to coexist in East Asia: one being the traditional tributary system centered on China, and the other being the diplomatic order centered on Japan through these four gateways.

---

granting the latter trading rights with the Ainu in place of territory. This system is known as the "trade territory" system〈商場知行制〉.

[64] By this time, most Ainu people had already lost their status as independent traders and were instead utilized by Wajin merchants at fishing grounds and other places. The Wajin would sometimes cheat the Ainu people in trade or exploit them.

Kan'ei Culture

The culture of the early Edo period had derived from Momoyama culture, but new trends started to appear around the Kan'ei (寛永期) era (1624-1644) as the bakuhan system stabilized.

In terms of scholarship, Confucianism became popular, starting with the **Shushigaku** (朱子学) that Zen monks of the Five Mountains (五山) had studied during the Muromachi period. The bakufu and the domains adopted Shushigaku because it placed much emphasis on the hierarchical order, exemplified by the distinction between lords and vassals, and between fathers and sons. **Fujiwara Seika** (藤原惺窩) (1561-1619), who had been a Zen monk of Shōkokuji (相国寺) in Kyōto, returned to secular life and worked on promoting studies of Shushigaku. His student, **Hayashi Razan** (林羅山) (Dōshun (道春), 1583-1657), was recruited by Ieyasu, and Razan's descendants (the **Hayashi/Rin family** (林家)[ii]) served the bakufu for generations as Confucian scholars responsible for scholarship and education.

In architecture, mausoleum architecture (**reibyō kenchiku** (霊廟建築)) flourished, most notably at Nikkō Tōshōgū (日光東照宮) which enshrined Ieyasu, and the **gongen-zukuri style** (権現造) was widely used for shrine construction. These buildings were decorated with splendid ornamental carvings in the manner of Momoyama culture. In addition, the **sukiya-zukuri style** (数寄屋造) developed from the shoin-zukuri (書院造) style that incorporated tea house aesthetics in a manner resembling a thatched hut. The **Katsura Rikyū** (桂離宮) (Katsura Imperial Villa) in Kyōto is a representative example of this architectural style.

KATSURA RIKYŪ

This was a villa built by Royal Prince Hachijō Toshihito〈八条宮智仁親王〉, the younger brother of Go-Yōzei Tennō. Shown on the right in the photo is the Old Shoin〈古書院〉 that faces the pond, with the Middle Shoin〈中書院〉 to its left and the New Palace seen diagonally next to the Middle Shoin. These buildings were all constructed in the sukiya-zukuri style that incorporates tea rooms.

HIKONE BYŌBU〈『彦根屛風』〉(HIKONE FOLDING SCREEN)
A six-panel folding screen representative of genre painting in the Kan'ei era. On the left is an indoor scene in which men and women are shown playing the shamisen, enjoying a traditional Japanese board game using dice, and focusing on love letters. On the right, a man and women are depicted standing outdoors as they chat. Their costumes and hairstyles show the popular trends of the time. The painter is unknown; the work is a national treasure. (Length 94 cm, width 271 cm)

IROE KACHŌMON FUKABACHI〈『色絵花鳥文深鉢』〉(DEEP BOWL WITH PICTURES OF BIRDS AND FLOWERS IN OVERGLAZE ENAMELS, SAKAIDA KAKIEMON STYLE)
This bowl was made with an overglaze painting technique in which figures are painted on white porcelain already fired once, using red, blue, green, and other pigments, which will then be fired again. It is called akae (red-painting) ware due to red being its predominant color. (Diameter 30.3 cm, height 21.4 cm)

As for painting, **Kanō Tan'yū** 狩野探幽 (1602-74) of the Kanō School made his name and became an official painter for the bakufu. However, his descendants merely imitated his style. Meanwhile, in Kyōto, Tawaraya Sōtatsu 俵屋宗達 (dates unknown) created a new style of decorative painting based on the Tosa 土佐派 School of painting, becoming one of the founders of the Rinpa 琳派 School that flourished during the Genroku 元禄期 era. **Hon'ami Kōetsu** 本阿弥光悦 (1558-1637), an upper-class merchant of Kyōto, was well-known as a multi-talented man of culture. He created superb works of calligraphy and lacquerware, as well as excellent tea bowls in the Raku 楽焼 ware style of pottery.

At the time of the Bunroku and Keichō campaigns in Korea, manufacturing techniques such as climbing kilns and ceramics painting were passed on by Korean potters whom many daimyō brought back with them to their domains. This resulted in kickstarting the production of local ceramic ware around the provinces in the Kyūshū and Chūgoku 中国 regions. Famous examples include Arita ware 有田焼 (of the Nabeshima 鍋島氏 family), Satsuma ware 薩摩焼 (of the Shimazu family), Hagi ware 萩焼 (of the Mōri family), Hirado ware 平戸焼 (of the Matsura 松浦氏 family), and Takatori ware 高取焼 (of the Kuroda 黒田氏 family). In Arita in particular, **porcelain** 磁器 was produced, and **Sakaida Kakiemon** 酒井田柿右衛門 (dates unknown) perfected the creation of **akae ware** 赤絵[65] using an overglaze painting technique.

In terms of literature, the foundation for a new popular culture developed. Kanazōshi 仮名草子, printed books that focused on moral lessons and ethics, appeared, and the Teimon School of haikai poetry 貞門俳諧, established by Matsunaga Teitoku 松永貞徳 (1571-1653) in Kyōto, also became popular, as haikai 俳諧 diverged from renga 連歌 to stand on its own.

4 The Structure of Bakuhan Society

Social Classes and Society

Under the bakuhan system, the bushi, who comprised the ruling class, monopolized not only politics and military affairs, but also matters of learning and knowledge. They enjoyed various privileges such as **myōji** 苗字 **(surnames)** and **taitō** 帯刀 **(wearing a sword)**. The structure of the bushi class consisted of various ranks with the shōgun 将軍 at the top, followed by the daimyō, hatamoto, gokenin, and so forth, with hierarchy and loyalty to one's master being strictly enforced. The royal family, court nobles, and high-ranking monks and Shintō priests were equivalent to bushi as members of the ruling class.

In bushi families, women were required to focus on household matters. Bushi were organized around the family of their master. Through social ranks and law and order they controlled their society, which was comprised of various groups or communities such as villages, towns, guilds, and associations.

On the other hand, the controlled classes that accounted for the majority of the population consisted mainly of three ranks: **hyakushō** 百姓 **(farmers)**[iii], who engaged mainly in agriculture, as well as small-scale businesses in forestry or fishing; **shokunin** 職人 **(artisans)**, who worked on various types of handicraft; and **iemochi chōnin** 家持町人 **(home-owning townspeople)**, the merchants who worked mainly in the trade, finance, and logistics/transportation businesses. This social order is therefore sometimes called shi-nō-kō-shō 士農工商 (bushi, farmer, artisan, merchant).

In early modern times, the peripheral areas of villages and towns contained many small groups that consisted of people of the same social rank. Examples of such groups

---

[65] A type of overglaze painting technique that employs red as its predominant color while using a great deal of pigments to paint with various colors.

DIFFERENCES OF RANK SEEN IN CLOTHING AND FOOD (*RŌNŌ YAWA*〈『老農夜話』〉, PART)
Depicted are meal tables of (from left) nobles, warriors, farmers, merchants, monks, and artisans. Note the differences in table size and height, number of dishes, garments, hairstyles, and so on for the person of each rank.

included: religious practitioners, such as general monks and Shintō priests, as well as Shugenja and Onmyōji(陰陽師); intellectuals, such as Confucian scholars and medical doctors; entertainers, like puppeteers, actors, and professional storytellers; and manual laborers called hiyō(日用). Among these, the lowest ranks were the kawata(かわた) and hinin(非人). Kawata were gathered close to castle towns, where they formed kawata machimura(かわた町村) (kawata towns and villages) separate from the hyakushō, and engaged in agriculture and handicrafts such as the production of leather goods and straw-work. Some of them even ran wholesale businesses that traded leather with remote areas. However, under the control of the bakufu and daimyō, they were forced to process dead livestock and conduct prison administration, and were called derogatory names like "eta(えた)."

Hinin referred to beggars(乞食) who formed a group after being driven from villages and towns. However, there were many who became hinin due to experiencing famine, poverty or punishment. They would work as guards in villages and towns, or were involved in entertainment, cleaning, and begging. Kawata and hinin were distinguished from other ranks by their specific garments, hairstyles, and residential areas, and were an object of disdain.

These social classes were organized by large groups or associations, such as bushi households, hyakushō villages, chōnin towns, and shokunin guilds. Each person belonged to a household, and was socially ranked based on that household or the group to which it belonged. In bushi households, or the households of some powerful hyakushō and chōnin, the head of the household (kachō(家長)) wielded great authority. In principle, this position, along with the family's wealth and property, was inherited by the eldest son. Family members aside from the head were considered less important, and moreover, in this type of household women were eliminated from succession[66].

---

[66] In the event that there were no male heirs, or male heirs were born but deemed incompetent, the family could adopt a son in order to continue the line. Female succession also occurred.

Villages and Hyakushō

The greatest elements structuring early modern society were **villages**（村） and **hyakushō**（百姓）. After the long medieval era, villages were formed centering on settlements consisting of hyakushō residences, which developed into a small society that encompassed a broad area including farmlands, plains, mountains and shores. Relatively autonomous organizations emerged to support the small-scale businesses and lifestyles of hyakushō, and became a vital foundation for the bakuhan system which depended upon agricultural production. Villages were directly overseen at the country level for the first time, due to the land surveys and the policy of heinō bunri (separation of warriors and farmers) implemented by the Toyotomi regime. The division of sō villages by **muragiri**（村切） (**village borders**) and the rapid development of cultivated land from the end of the medieval era gave rise to new villages. By the end of the 17th century, the number of villages in the whole country had reached as high as sixty-three thousand[67].

Most of these villages were farming villages organized based on agriculture, but there were also fishing villages, mountain villages, and even zaigōchō（在郷町）[68], which resembled small towns. Villages varied widely by region, such as in their size of crop yield and number of households, but while each village had its own particular characteristics they also shared some similar features, as will be seen.

Villages were managed by honbyakushō（本百姓） (titled farmers), especially the village officials known as **murakata sanyaku**（村方三役）, which were divided into **nanushi**（名主） (village headman, also called shōya（庄屋） or kimoiri（肝煎）), and **kumigashira**（組頭） **/ hyakushō-dai**（百姓代） (farmer representatives). These officials jointly and independently handled tasks such as common land（入会地） use, management of irrigation water, management of fields and mountains, road maintenance, public peacekeeping, and disaster prevention[69]. The expenses required for such tasks were called murairiyō（村入用）, and were borne by the villagers collectively. Village administration was based on **sonpō**（村法） (village law, also called muraokite（村掟）), and those who disobeyed the law faced sanctions such as ostracization. The bakufu, various daimyō and hatamoto depended on the autonomous administration of these villages. For the first time, they were able to oversee the villagers and have them assign and collect the

---

[67] The total kokudaka at the end of 17th century was about twenty-five million koku, while the average per village was about four hundred koku.

[68] Zaigochō referred to villages around castle towns or roadsides that were urbanized based on regular markets.

[69] When undertaking rice-planting, rice-reaping, threshing, or roof covering, villagers concentrated their labor in group work called yui〈結〉 or moyai〈もやい〉, and supported each other's labor and lives.

land tax and other various taxes themselves[70]. This system is called the **murauke** 村請制 **(subcontracting village taxation) system**. Villagers organized several households into **gonin-gumi** 五人組 that were collectively responsible for the payment of land tax and the prevention of crimes.

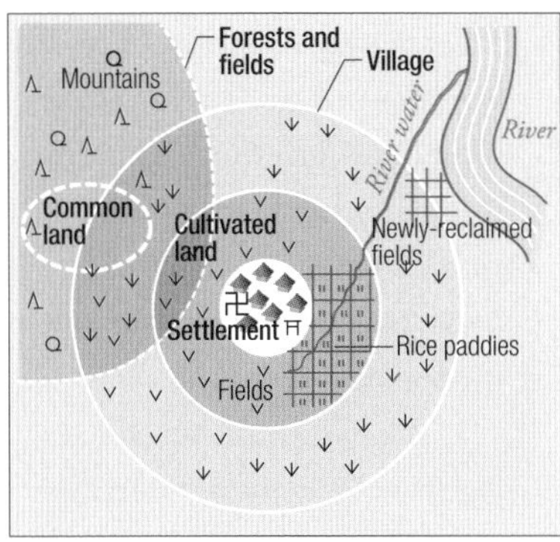

VILLAGE STRUCTURE
A village consisted of three parts. The center was the settlement made up of hyakushō residences. Outside this were the cultivated farmlands, and then forests and fields including common land. Residences and cultivated lands were subject to taxation.

Villages had their own social hierarchy. In the farming villages, the **honbyakushō** 本百姓[71] were the proper constituent members of the village community. They owned their own houses and fields for which kokudaka had been calculated, and which were recorded as registered land in the land registry. They were obligated to pay taxes, and were able to participate in village administration. The **mizunomi** 水呑 (or mudaka 無高) were landless villagers who engaged in farming under a landowner or performed daily work as a laborer. There were also people who served as subordinates of influential honbyakushō, such as nago 名子, hikan 被官, or fudai 譜代. Further, there also existed hierarchical relations based on bloodlines, such as head family and branch family, and relations based on work, such as that of amimoto 網元 (fishing masters) and amiko 網子 (fishers) in fishing villages. Villages also built temples and shrines, and invited monks and Shintō priests for them. These institutions supported the connections among the villagers, as well as their faith[72].

The main responsibility imposed on honbyakushō was the annual tax (**hontomononari** 本途物成) which was charged based on their registered property such as rice fields, farms and houses. As standard practice, 40-50% of their kokudaka was paid to their lord in rice or coinage (shikōrokumin 四公六民: four for the lord, six for the people; or gokōgomin 五公五民: five for the lord, five for the people)[73]. Aside from the annual tax, there were other responsibilities. One was **komononari** 小物成 **(miscellaneous tax)**, which was imposed on the use of fields, mountains, rivers and seas, and on side businesses

---

[70] The same principle applied in cases where several lords took control in one village at the same time (a situation called aikyū 〈相給〉).

[71] When a hyakushō family lost their head, the widow could occasionally act as the head of the family.

[72] Apart from hyakushō, villages often included some religious people such as monks and Shintō practitioners, as well as artisans and merchants.

[73] There were two ways of determining the annual tax rate (called men 〈免〉). One was kemihō 〈検見法〉, which based the rate on the yield for the year, and the other was jōmenhō 〈定免法〉, which used a fixed rate for a certain time period.

other than agriculture. Others included the takagakarimono 高掛物 (additional tax), which was imposed based on agricultural yield; **kuniyaku 国役 (provincial corvée)**, meaning labor duties involving engineering work at rivers across the territory; and tenmayaku 伝馬役 (supplying horses to post stations), which was a duty imposed on villages near highways and required the provision of carriers and horses for transportation. In sum, a heavy burden was placed on the small-scale hyakushō who made up the majority of the population.

The bakufu attempted to stabilize the small businesses of hyakushō while keeping them away from involvement in the monetary economy, in order to ensure the collection of the various taxes. To this end, in 1643 the bakufu issued a permanent prohibition on the sale of arable land (**Denpata Eitai Baibai no Kinshi-rei 田畑永代売買の禁止令**), and followed this in 1673 with a restriction on parceling up estates (**Bunchiseigen-rei 分地制限令**) in order to prevent the subdivision of fields due to inheritance. The free cultivation of commercial crops, such as tobacco, cotton, and rapeseed, was prohibited[74]. As is evident from the ordinances issued to villages after the Kan'ei famine 寛永の飢饉 of 1641-42, the bakufu regulated even the particulars of daily life and labor[75].

Some of the powerful hyakushō in villages had a lifestyle similar to that of bushi, but most hyakushō usually dressed in tight-sleeved clothing of hemp or cotton, and mainly ate a mixed-grain diet including wheat, foxtail millet, and barnyard grass, while rice was rarely eaten. Their dwellings were simple affairs with thatched roofs of grass and straw. Whether in terms of food, clothing, or housing, the life of most hyakushō was a poor one.

Towns and Chōnin

In the early modern era, many more cities were built than in the medieval era. First and foremost was the castle town (**jōkamachi 城下町**). Bushi who had previously lived in farming villages as resident proprietors were forced to move into the castle towns by the Toyotomi regime's heinō bunri policy. Many merchants and craftsmen (artisans in various trades) also settled in castle towns, where they could enjoy the privileges of freely engaging in business and being exempted from property taxes.

The core of a castle town was the district containing the residence of the shōgun or daimyō. Other residential areas were clearly distinguished by rank: **bukechi 武家地 (warrior district)**, **jishachi 寺社地 (temple and shrine district)**, **chōninchi 町人地 (townspeople district)**,

[74] This prohibition was called "Denpata katte-zukuri no kin〈「田畑勝手作りの禁」〉." Recently whether or not this policy actually existed has come into question.

[75] Among such regulations, "Keian no Furegaki〈「慶安の触書」〉," understood to have been issued by the bakufu in 1649, is famous, but its existence has been debated.

and kawata machimura[76]. Among these, the core and bukechi, which contained various administrative and military facilities as well as the residences of retainers and ashigaru, occupied a majority of the castle town. The jishachi contained an assortment of temples and shrines, beginning with particularly powerful ones, which were required to regulate religion within the territory.

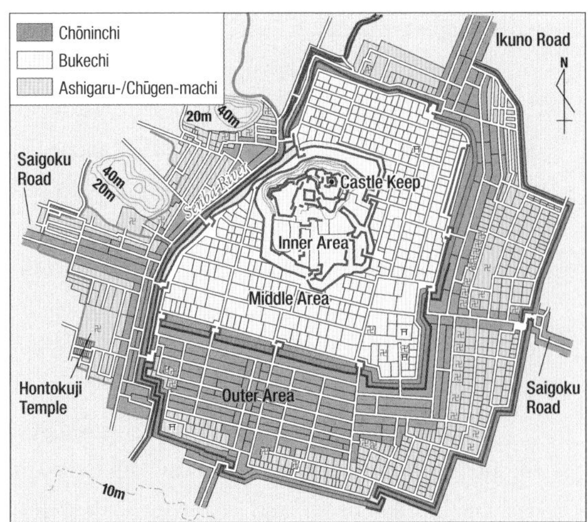

HIMEJI CASTLE TOWN
The inner area〈内曲輪〉, with the castle keep at its center, was surrounded by the middle〈中曲輪〉 and outer areas〈外曲輪〉, the majority of which consisted of the bukechi. Most of the temples can be seen in the eastern part of the outer area, and to the west the residences of the ashigaru and chūgen (bushi attendants), called ashigaru-/chūgen-machi〈足軽町／中間町〉. The chōninchi was concentrated in the southern part of the outer ring and also extended along the roads.

The chōninchi, also known as the machikata 町方, was where merchants and craftsmen resided and engaged in business and production. Although small in scale, this district played an important role as the pivotal center of distribution and economy connecting the domain to the rest of the country. Within the chōninchi were many small communities called **chō** 町 (town). These chō had an autonomous structure similar to that of the villages, and supported the lives and business activities of the resident merchants and craftsmen. Residents who owned houses within a chō were called **chōnin** 町人 **(townspeople)**[77]. The chō were managed based on **chōhō** 町法 **(town law**; also called **chō'okite** 町掟**)** primarily by the **nanushi** 名主 (or **toshiyori** 年寄**, town headman**) and the gachigyōji 月行事 (monthly delegate), who represented the chōnin. Since the chō lacked any rice fields or farms, chōnin were exempt from the heavy annual tax burden imposed on hyakushō. However, they were required to fulfill roles supporting town functions, such as maintaining the water and sewer systems, as well as roads and bridges, cleaning the castle district and moats, engaging in fire and disaster prevention, and keeping the peace. They either performed these roles directly, through labor service known as chōninsoku 町人足, or by

[76] In some of the castle towns like the three great cities, official pleasure quarters were established.
[77] In many towns, the number of home-owning chōnin was actually rather small. In contrast to villages and hyakushō, however, all residents of a chōninchi were usually called chōnin.

paying money instead.

Moreover, people of various social ranks resided in the chō. These included **jigari** 地借 (**land tenants**), who rented a plot of land wholly or partly and built their own residence on it; **shakuya** 借家 (**tenants**; also called **tanagari** 店借), some of whom rented a whole residence but most of whom rented part of a terrace house; and servants or employees who lived in merchant houses. Aside from needing to pay rent for land or housing, jigari and shakuya had little burden, but on the other hand they were not allowed to participate in the management of the chō. Aside from castle towns, there were port towns, temple towns, post towns, and mining towns, but in all of them chō served as the basic foundation of society.

These merchants and artisans were engaged in various professions and had different interests. Depending on their occupation they formed business associations called nakama 仲間, kumiai 組合, or kō 講, and as a result society in the chōninchi had a complicated structure. To maintain control, the bakufu and han focused on appointing machi-bugyō for the castle towns, and to order the chōninchi in particular they appointed town elders and leading wholesalers from among the influential chōnin to assist the magistrates.

Agriculture

Agriculture in early modern times was characterized by small-scale operations that used advanced skills, and were comprised of small families centered on married couples that invested intense effort in farming small plots of land in order to increase the yield per field. The bakufu and daimyō made these highly-productive operations, and the villages that supported them, a foundation for the generation of social wealth. To this end, they conducted land surveys to ascertain the situation of these operations and the increase in cultivated land.

From the early 17th century, the bakufu and daimyō began large-scale work on flood control as well as irrigation to improve the water supply system[78]. They also utilized the economic might of merchants to develop shallow coastal areas, lakes and marshes, and wastelands into new fields (**shinden kaihatsu** 新田開発)[79]. They then had

[78] Well-known examples include the irrigation canal of Hakone〈箱根用水〉, which originated from Lake Ashi〈芦ノ湖〉, and that of Minumadai〈見沼代用水〉, which was diverted from the Tone River〈利根川〉.

[79] From the end of the 17th century, powerful town merchants invested funds in developing new fields in various places. These fields were called chōnin ukeoi shinden〈町人請負新田〉. Bizen Kojima Bay〈備前児島湾〉 and the Ariake Sea〈有明海〉 are good examples of places where new fields were reclaimed from tidal flats. Shimousa Tsubakinoumi〈下総椿海〉 is a good example of lake-bottom reclamation.

hyakushō move to the newly-developed land and form villages there. As a result, the amount of cultivated land in the whole country had nearly doubled by around the start of the 18th century, contributing to an increase in the annual tax.

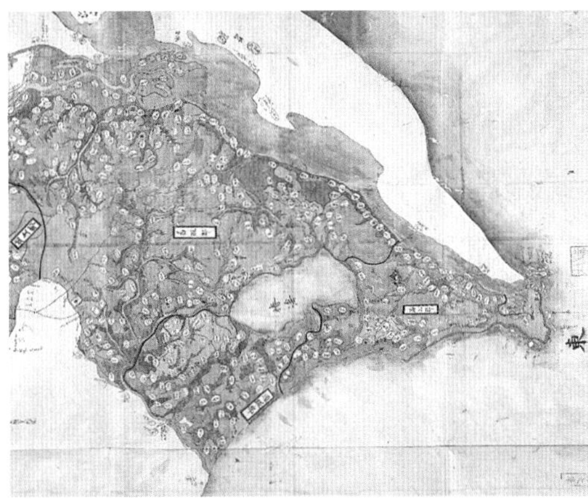

TSUBAKINOUMI DEPICTED ON A DOMAIN MAP OF JAPAN
This domain map of Shimousa shows a lake called "Tsubakinoumi," the size of which was considered to be three times that of Lake Suwa 〈諏訪湖〉 in Shinano〈信濃〉. Edo chōnin, with funding support from the bakufu, undertook reclamation of the area. Construction was completed in 1673, and resulted in the creation of 18 new villages.

Agricultural tools developed in various forms depending on their use in cultivation, weeding or harvesting. Tools included hand tools like spades, hoes, and sickles, and those that employed the animal power of cows or horses like small plows. Such tools were made of iron, and were produced and repaired by smiths from castle towns who went to villages.

Basic fertilizers were manure and karishiki (刈敷). Karishiki was cut grass obtained from within the village or shared land nearby. As for crops, the most important was rice, most of which was used to pay the annual tax, but various other crops were produced based on the conditions of the local area. Such crops included mixed grains used for sustenance (wheat, foxtail millet, barnyard grass, and buckwheat), hemp and cotton for making garments, vegetables and fruits for the nearby castle town, commercial crops such as mikan and tea for distant locations like Edo and the Kinai region, and mulberry for sericulture.

Villages played an indispensable role in agricultural operations by hyakushō, such as water supply work (e.g. waterways and reservoirs), the maintenance and management of common lands, and collaborative labor (**yui** (結)) in planting and harvesting rice.

Forestry and Fishery

In a country where most of the land is mountainous, it is not surprising that many villages and castle towns were deeply connected to the mountains. First of all, mountains provided abundant lumber necessary for architecture and construction work. In particular, mountain areas with quantities of fine timber were directly controlled by the bakufu and daimyō, which made use of lumbered trees to build castle districts and bushi residences. Large amounts of wood were also transferred to common-

LOGGING LARGE TREES IN KISO (*KISO-SHIKI BATSUBOKU UNZAI ZUE*〈「木曽式伐木運材図絵」〉[ILLUSTRATIONS OF KISO-STYLE TIMBER PRODUCTION], PART)
A scene depicting the logging of large trees such as Japanese cypress in the mountains of Kiso. The soma cut through the roots, after which laborers pulled it down together.

ers. In some domains such as Owari and Akita 秋田, timber cut from the mountains and forests directly controlled by the domain was commercialized and became famous, like **Kiso hinoki** 木曽檜 and **Akita sugi** 秋田杉. In villages that had timber-producing mountains, skilled forestry workers called soma and daily laborers engaged in transporting timber lived as hyakushō.

Part of the mountain was shared land for the village, or common land used jointly by several villages. In these areas, karishiki for fertilizer, and fodder for horses and cows was gathered, along with various types of plants for use in hyakushō food, housing or clothing. Mountains were also the source of firewood and charcoal which represented almost the entirety of energy sources before the spread of fossil fuels. Vast amounts of firewood and charcoal were sold in the nearest castle town.

Fishery in the early modern period, which aimed at catching fish and shellfish to provide the main source of animal protein, as well as fertilizer called gyohi 魚肥, developed in many respects. A wide variety of fishing methods, fishing tools and fishing boats were used in the ocean, rivers, lakes and marshes. There were improvements in fishing methods, mainly **amiryō** 網漁 **(net fishing)**, and developments in fishing grounds in coastal areas. Since the end of the medieval era, amiryō techniques were spread across the country by fishermen from the Kinai region, such as Settsu, Izumi and Kii. Fish and shellfish were consumed by fishermen, sold in towns as fresh fish, or preserved via salt or sun-drying. In particular, dried abalone and dried bonito spread across the whole country. In fishing villages along the coast, fishing grounds were occupied by fishermen, especially powerful people like amimoto who made deals with the wholesalers in the castle towns. The funds from wholesalers in castle towns and the three great cities (Edo, Ōsaka and Kyōto) played a major role in fishery and the distribution of seafood.

The Handicraft and Mining Industries

The early modern era was also an age of artisans. Artisans owned their own tools and production workplaces, and took apprentices. Although small in scale, they were independent craftsmen. Handicrafts in the early modern era, like agriculture, concentrated on advanced skills and technology that employed specialized tools of various sorts.

At the dawn of the early modern age, artisans referred only to workers like carpenters, sawyers, and gunsmiths in the service of the bakufu or daimyō, who were engaged in such tasks as construction (of castle districts, bushi residences, temples, and shrines), city-building, mine management, and weapon production. These artisans lived in towns and villages, provided technical labor to the bakufu or daimyō without charge, and in return were exempted from the duties imposed on hyakushō and chōnin.

In the middle of the 17th century, in response to demand from the population, many kinds of handicraft production developed rapidly in the city. Artisans engaged in this production formed groups and associations based on their profession, and had settled in cities as tenants by the end of the 17th century.

On the other hand, there were artisans such as carpenters in the villages as well. Aside from that, small handicraft businesses also emerged early on. Typical examples included textiles like hemp and cotton, papermaking, and sake brewing. Cotton techniques were introduced from Korea at the end of the Sengoku period, whereupon cotton, together with hemp, quickly became established as typical garment materials for commoners. Cotton production was done by female laborers in villages, mainly using the traditional jibata 地機 (back-tension loom, also called izaribata いざり機). The production of washi 和紙 (handmade Japanese paper) most commonly used paper mulberry, and along with the **nagashisuki** 流漉 **(shaking and spreading pulp)** technique, spread to villages throughout the country. Washi was produced in vast amounts, and became essential for conducting administration and management, as well as recording and transferring information. It also contributed greatly to the development of learning and culture. These village handicrafts were regarded as work done by hyakushō during intervals in farming.

As for the mining industry, new refining and drainage techniques were introduced from overseas from the end of the medieval era through the beginning of the early modern era. There were also innovations in steelmaking technology. Areas competed with each other to develop mines producing gold, silver, and copper, which in turn led to the development of many mining towns in various regions[80]. Silver in particular reached a production level prominent on the world scale, and became the main

[80] Major mines included the Iwami, Ikuno〈生野〉 and Innai〈院内〉 silver mines. The gold and silver mines of Sado Aikawa〈佐渡相川〉, and the Ashio〈足尾〉, Besshi〈別子〉, and Ani〈阿仁〉 copper mines were also well known.

PICTURE OF TENBIN TATARA〈天秤たたら〉
Air was blown into the central furnace by pairs of bellows, generating intense heat that refined iron to produce tamahagane of high purity.

trading commodity in East Asia.

In the latter half of the 17th century, the production of gold and silver rapidly decreased, but conversely the production of copper increased. The increase in copper was a response to the demands for coinage, and this metal became the largest export in the Nagasaki trade. In the case of iron, iron sand was gathered for **tatara seitetsu** (たたら製鉄) (**tatara furnaces**), mainly in the Chūgoku and Tōhoku regions. Tamahagane (玉鋼) (high-quality steel made from iron sand) produced in those places spread across the country as a commercial item, and was used for making various tools.

Iron tools used in mines, such as hammers and various chisels, and mining technologies such as drilling, measuring, and draining, were adapted as excavation techniques for other work, such as flood control, and digging reservoirs or irrigation canals. As a result, large-scale cultivation around riverbeds and coastal strips became possible, greatly contributing to the development of agricultural and handicraft production.

Commerce

Originally, merchants referred to those who ran a small business, acquiring stock with their own funds and selling directly to the buyer. This type of merchant was commonly seen in many places since the medieval era. When transportation and distribution came to be safely conducted during the peaceful times at the beginning of the early modern era, a prominent role came to be played by **gōshō** (豪商)[81]. These were wealthy merchants who had abundant funds, means of transportation such as ships and horses, and storage facilities like warehouses. They were based in cities such as Sakai, Kyōto, Hakata, Nagasaki, and Tsuruga (敦賀), and achieved great wealth by taking advantage of the price difference between areas before the organization of the red

---

[81] These people were also referred to as early wealthy merchants. Famous examples were Suminokura Ryōi and Chaya Shirōjirō of Kyōto, Sueyoshi Magozaemon of Settsu Hirano〈摂津平野〉, and Imai Sōkun〈今井宗薫〉 of Sakai.

seal trade and transportation systems. However, as overseas trading became limited under the sakoku policy, and domestic transportation on land and water came to be organized, the gōshō rapidly declined.

In the latter half of the 17th century, the distribution of commodities across the country came to be controlled by **toiya** 問屋 (**wholesalers**) who were based in the three great cities and castle towns. Toiya contracted products from **nakagai** 仲買 (**brokers**) at the production location, and sold them wholesale to nakagai in the city with a handling fee. The nakagai at the point of origin consigned goods in stock to a remote toiya, while the nakagai in the cities purchased goods in stock from the toiya and markets in the cities, and gained a profit by selling them to bushi families and **kouri shōnin** 小売商人 (**retail dealers**). Kouri shōnin were merchants who purchased goods from the nakagai in the market, and then sold those to consumers. These dealers took various forms, ranging from permanent stores and streetside stalls to **furiuri** 振売 (**peddlars**), who carried around products to sell. Toiya and nakagai formed business associations called nakama or kumiai based on towns or production areas, which established their own regulations (**nakama okite** 仲間掟) and attempted to monopolize sale rights.

Translators' Notes

[i] "Ezo" (蝦夷) was a term that referred to the far northeastern peoples, and also came to refer to Hokkaidō (which was also known as Ezogashima). "Ezochi" (literally "lands of the Ezo"), on the other hand, referred to not only Hokkaidō but also its environs or the far northeastern region as a whole.

[ii] This family is referred to by both readings in Japanese, but in English scholars overwhelmingly use "Hayashi." To avoid confusion, in this textbook both readings are retained.

[iii] "Hyakushō" (百姓) is often rendered in English as "farmers" or "peasants," both of which may be suitable in some Japanese historical contexts but not in others. Like "bushi," "hyakushō" was an old term that used to be used in a more inclusive and flexible manner, but became more solidly defined in the Edo period as a social class. Therefore, in the part of this text concerned with ancient Japan they are rendered as "farmers," but in the part covering the Edo period, when they become a distinct, recognized social class, they are rendered as "hyakushō" to avoid confusion. When discussing modern Japan, when the Edo social system has ended, they are once again rendered as "farmers." Note that this is different from how the text handles "chōnin," which were a distinct group but not an official social class. Also see the note for "農民" in Chapter 2, Section 3.

Chapter

7

The Evolution of the Bakuhan System

1 The Stabilization of Bakufu Administration

The Establishment of Peace and Order

In the fourth month of 1651, the third shōgun 将軍, Tokugawa Iemitsu 徳川家光, died. In the eighth month, his son, **Tokugawa Ietsuna** 徳川家綱 (1641-80), succeeded him at the age of eleven to become the fourth shōgun. In 1662, with the final destruction of the Ming 明 Dynasty by the **Qing** 清[1], China managed to establish a new social order after nearly half a century of upheaval. Consequently, peace returned to East Asia as a whole, while within Japan as well after the Shimabara Rebellion 島原の乱 internal conflict ceased to occur.

With the consolidation of the bakufu 幕府 administrative system, and the young Shōgun Ietsuna being supported by his uncle **Hoshina Masayuki** 保科正之 (1611-72, the lord of Aizu Domain 会津藩) and the fudai daimyō 譜代大名, the social order came to be stabilized. In an era of lasting peace, the most pressing political issue became how to deal with rōnin 牢人 (masterless bushi), who hoped for conflict, and "kabukimono" 「かぶき者」 (groups of flamboyant rogues), who were outside the social order. After the **Keian Rebellion** 慶安の変, an uprising by

GREAT MEIREKI FIRE (*EDO KAJI ZUKAN*〈『江戸火事図巻』〉, PART)
This picture depicts members of a fire brigade (bushi), wearing masks and trying to extinguish the fire with fans attached to long poles, as well as wheeled coffers. The damage increased because people tried to escape with their household goods in such coffers which caused the roads to be blocked. As a result, they were later banned.

[1] In 1662, with the death of Zheng Chenggong (Koxinga)〈鄭成功（国姓爺）〉, who had resisted the Qing in Taiwan, and the collapse of Zhu Youlang (Prince of Gui)'s〈朱由榔（桂王）〉 Ming regime, the Qing Dynasty secured its rule.

military strategist Yui Shōsetsu 由井（比）正雪 (1605?-51), broke out in the 7th month of 1651, the bakufu **eased the prohibition on matsugo yōshi** 末期養子禁止の緩和 (the practice of a daimyō adopting a son on the former's deathbed)[2] in order to prevent an increase in rōnin, and strengthened its control over the rōnin and kabukimono living in Edo 江戸.

In 1657, the **Great Meireki Fire** 明暦の大火 broke out and caused tremendous damage to Edo Castle and the city itself. In 1663, after the city had been repaired, Ietsuna, now an adult, issued a revised version of the Buke Shohatto 武家諸法度. At the same time, he **forbade junshi** 殉死の禁止 (the practice of a bushi committing suicide upon the death of his lord), and obligated bushi to serve their new master when the previous one died[3]. In the following year, he issued ryōchi ategaijō 領知宛行状 (certificate guaranteeing territory) to all the daimyō to make them recognize the shōgun's authority, while ordering that land surveys be conducted on all bakufu territories to secure bakufu finances.

As for the domains, the burden of military duties was lightened due to the enduring peacetime, and after the Kan'ei famine 寛永の飢饉, there were efforts to stabilize internal politics and develop domain economies. Various daimyō promoted capable retainers as advisors, and organized the administrative structures in their domains, thereby strengthening their authority. Furthermore, they tried to stabilize domain finances by increasing agricultural production through flood control work on rivers and the development of new fields. However, they made little leeway due to the great expenses resulting from Sankin Kōtai 参勤交代 and construction work obligations. Daimyō in several domains recruited Confucian scholars as advisors and reformed their administrations on that basis. Examples include **Ikeda Mitsumasa** 池田光政 (1609-82) of Okayama 岡山藩, Hoshina Masayuki of Aizu, **Tokugawa Mitsukuni** 徳川光圀 (1628-1700) of Mito 水戸藩, and **Maeda Tsunanori** 前田綱紀 (1643-1724) of Kaga 加賀藩[4].

---

[2] It had previously been uncommon for a daimyō without an heir to have a deathbed appointment of an adopted son approved. However, after the rebellion, this was permitted for daimyō under 50 years of age.

[3] The code clearly stated that the relationship between shōgun and daimyō, and between daimyō and their retainers, was hereditary in nature, and vassals served not their master individually but rather their master's household. Consequently, gekokujō〈下剋上〉 became impossible.

[4] Ikeda Mitsumasa established Shizutani Gakkō〈閑谷学校〉, a local school (gōkō〈郷校〉, or gōgaku〈郷学〉), and recruited Kumazawa Banzan〈熊沢蕃山〉. Banzan was given preferential treatment and founded another school, Hanabatake Kyōjō〈花畠教場〉. Hoshina Masayuki (a brother of Shōgun Iemitsu) studied Shushigaku〈朱子学〉 under Yamazaki Ansai〈山崎闇斎〉 and produced numerous writings. Tokugawa Mitsukuni established the Shōkōkan〈彰考館〉 (historical bureau) in Edo, and launched the compilation of *Dai Nihonshi*〈『大日本史』〉 (Great History of Japan). Mitsukuni also had Zhu Zhiyu〈朱舜水〉, a leading Confucian scholar and Ming refugee, play a significant role in the project. Maeda Tsunanori invited some Shushigaku scholars such as Kinoshita Jun'an to promote academic learning.

The Genroku Era

In the late 17th century, the fifth shōgun, **Tokugawa Tsunayoshi** (徳川綱吉) (1646-1709), came to power against a backdrop of political stability and economic prosperity during the **Genroku era** (元禄時代). Tsunayoshi's governance was assisted by the tairō (大老) Hotta Masatoshi (堀田正俊) (1634-84), but after the latter's assassination, he was replaced by **Yanagisawa Yoshiyasu** (柳沢吉保) (1658-1714), the shōgun's chamberlain (側用人).

In 1683, due to the new shōgun taking office, the Buke Shohatto was re-issued. Article 1, which had formerly stated, "Devote yourself to civil and martial pursuits," was changed to "Devote yourself to civil and martial pursuits, loyalty, filial piety, and courtesy." This revision was intended to demand that bushi, above all else, be loyal to their masters (**chū** 忠), venerate their ancestors (**kō** 孝), and maintain the social order through courtesy (**reigi** 礼儀). This notion of civil order was based on Confucianism. Tsunayoshi, who had studied under the Shushigaku scholar Kinoshita Jun'an (木下順庵) (1621-98), embraced Confucianism: he established **Yushima Seidō** (湯島聖堂) (a prominent Confucian academy) and appointed Hayashi Hōkō (林鳳岡) (1644-1732; also called Nobuatsu (信篤)) as its chief administrator[5]. In addition to maintaining social order based on courtesy, Tsunayoshi revised the longstanding policy towards the tennō and the royal court. He restored several courtly rituals at the earnest request of Reigen Tennō (霊元天皇) (r. 1663-87), such as the Daijōe (大嘗会) (harvest ceremony after enthronement), and increased the royal estates, establishing a more harmonious relationship between the court and the bakufu[6].

Tsunayoshi was also devoted to Buddhism. In 1685, he issued the **Shōrui Awaremi no Rei** (生類憐みの令) **(Edict on Compassion for Living Beings)**, which forbade killing living beings and was in effect for more than 20 years. Commoners found this edict bothersome, but began especially to treat dogs better, resulting in the disappearance of a rough atmosphere with wild dogs marauding around the streets. Moreover, under the influence of Shintō, Tsunayoshi issued the **Bukki-rei** (服忌令) **(Edict on Mourning and Other Taboos)**[7], propagating a public phobia of death and bloodshed. In this way, the

---

[5] Tsunayoshi transferred the Confucian temple and the private school that Hayashi Razan〈林羅山〉 had established at Ueno Shinobugaoka〈上野忍ヶ岡〉 to Yushima. He then had the Hayashi/Rin family〈林家〉 organize it into a center of learning, resulting in the Seidō Gakumonjo〈聖堂学問所〉.

[6] In 1687, the Daijōe was held for the first time in 221 years, and in 1694, the Kamo Aoi Matsuri〈賀茂葵祭〉 was resumed after an interval of 192 years. Thereafter, courtly rituals came to be gradually revived. Around this time, rituals for royal messengers visiting the bakufu came to be considered significant. In 1701, the lord of Akō Domain〈赤穂藩〉, Asano Naganori〈浅野長矩〉, stabbed Kira Yoshinaka〈吉良義央〉, a hatamoto〈旗本〉 responsible for managing rituals related to the royal court, in Edo Castle. This resulted in Asano being ordered to commit seppuku〈切腹〉. In the following years, his former retainers took revenge on Kira by killing him (Akō Incident〈赤穂事件〉).

[7] The Bukki-rei, issued in 1684, stipulated the number of days of absence from work due to

value of elevating oneself by inflicting pain and death on others through military force – which had endured since the Sengoku period 戦国時代 – was, along with the kabukimono, repudiated entirely. Instead of emphasizing military power, increasingly one's social status, knowledge of courtesy, and administrative skill as an official came to be valued.

Under Tsunayoshi's rule, bakufu finances also underwent significant change. The revenue from mining, which had been relatively prosperous, dropped due to the decrease in gold and silver production at mines such as Sado gold mine 佐渡金山, hurting bakufu income. Moreover, expenses dramatically increased due to the reconstruction costs for Edo Castle and its environs after the Great Meireki Fire, and the building cost of temples and shrines during the Genroku era, driving the bakufu's finances to the edge of collapse.

In order to increase bakufu revenues, Kanjō-Ginmiyaku 勘定吟味役 (auditing officer) **Ogiwara Shigehide** 荻原重秀 (1658-1713, later kanjō-bugyō 勘定奉行) proposed reminting the coinage, which Tsunayoshi approved. The bakufu increased its revenues significantly by issuing low-quality coins with a lower amount of gold content. However, the drop in currency value caused an inflation which afflicted people's daily lives. Moreover, a great eruption of Mt. Fuji 富士山 in 1707 caused serious damage to surrounding areas such as Suruga 駿河 and Sagami 相模 due to volcanic ash[8].

The Politics of the Shōtoku Era

After Tsunayoshi's death, the sixth shōgun, Tokugawa Ienobu 徳川家宣 (1662-1712), attempted to reform bakufu politics. To this end he abolished the Shōrui Awaremi no Rei, dismissed Yanagisawa Yoshiyasu, and promoted the Shushigaku scholar **Arai Hakuseki** 新井白石 (1657-1725) and his chamberlain Manabe Akifusa 間部詮房 (1666-1720). This is known as **Shōtoku politics** 正徳の政治. However, Ienobu died just three years after succeeding to the post of shōgun. As his successor, the seventh shōgun Tokugawa Ietsugu 徳川家継 (1709-16), was still just three years old, bakufu administration continued to depend on officials like Arai Hakuseki.

Given the sequence of young and short-lived shōguns, Hakuseki endeavored to

---

mourning that someone could take when they had a close family member who had died. This edict exerted a significant influence on society. Some workers, such as kawata〈かわた〉 (also called chōri〈長吏〉) who were responsible for dealing with dead cows and horses, despite performing an essential job for society came to be seen as impure and were called "eta〈えた〉." Social discrimination against them intensified.

[8] The bakufu ordered all the domains to collect the provincial corvée in cash (shokoku takayaku/kuniyaku kin〈諸国高役（国役）金〉), requiring 2 ryō〈両〉 for every 100 koku〈石〉 in revenue, in order to repair the areas damaged by the volcanic ash. This amounted to 490 thousand ryō.

elevate the status and authority of the shōgunal post rather than the personality of individual shōguns. To do so, he strengthened the ties between the bakufu and the royal family by establishing **Kan'in no Miyake** 閑院宮家[9], a branch of the royal family, and by arranging the marriage of Ietsugu and a two-year old royal princess. Hakuseki placed emphasis on family and social status, and revised the clothing codes to make status clear at a glance.

When Korean envoys 朝鮮通信使 arrived on the occasion of Ienobu becoming shōgun, Hakuseki took the opportunity to simplify the reception protocol, criticizing earlier receptions for envoys as excessive. Moreover, he demanded that diplomatic correspondence from Korea, which had previously been addressed to "His Excellency the Tycoon of Japan," henceforth be addressed to the "King of Japan," in order to clarify the position of shōgun as a powerholder representing the country[10].

As for financial matters, Hakuseki tried to stabilize prices by minting **Shōtoku Koban** 正徳小判 coins that, unlike the Genroku Koban 元禄小判 with a lower gold content, had the same amount of gold as the older Keichō Koban 慶長小判. However, the changes in currency just led to social disruption. Moreover, as a considerable amount of gold and silver was exported through the Nagasaki trade 長崎貿易, in 1715 he issued the **Kaihaku Goshi Shin-rei** 海舶互市新例 (also called the Nagasaki Shin-rei 長崎新令 and Shōtoku Shin-rei 正徳新令) limiting the amount of trade[11].

2 Economic Development

The Evolution of Agricultural Production

During the hundred years following the latter half of the 17th century, Japan's economic production, centered on agriculture and manufacturing based on small-scale management, expanded, while logistic networks were established, connecting in particular the three great cities. This resulted in the maturation of early modern society

[9] There were only three branches (miyake〈宮家〉, or shin'nōke〈親王家〉) of the royal family: Fushimi〈伏見〉, Katsura〈桂〉, and Arisugawa〈有栖川〉. Consequently, many royal princes and princesses were ordained and entered monzeki temples〈門跡寺院〉. The bakufu therefore paid to establish the Kan'in branch as an exceptional case.

[10] The change in form of address was due to the lesser connotation of "tycoon" in comparison to "king." The eighth shōgun, Tokugawa Yoshimune〈徳川吉宗〉, and subsequent shōguns resumed using the title "tycoon" out of respect for conventional custom.

[11] Based on estimates that one quarter of Japan's gold and three-quarters of its silver had been exported since the start of the Edo period, Hakuseki limited the number of trading vessels and export amounts as follows: for the Qing, up to 30 vessels per year with 6000 kan〈貫〉 worth of silver, and for the Dutch, up to 2 vessels per year with 300 kan worth of silver.

in terms of both economy and culture.

Agricultural technology also advanced, with the invention of new tools: **bicchū-guwa** 備中鍬, an iron hoe to plow soil more deeply; **senba-koki** 千歯扱 for threshing; **tōmi** 唐箕 and **sengoku-dōshi** 千石簁 for grain separation; and **fumi-guruma** 踏車, a treadwheel for irrigation. These new tools spread wildly across various villages. However, large-scale agriculture employing larger tools did not evolve. In terms of fertilizer, to deal with the shortage of karishiki 刈敷 caused by the development of new fields, shimogoe 下肥 (human and animal manure) was widely used in fields around cities, while in communities that produced **commercial crops** 商品作物 like cotton the use of **kinpi** 金肥 (consisting of small dried sardines, oil cake, grit, etc.) from distant regions became common.

Various texts on agricultural techniques were also circulated. Already in the first half of the 17th century, *Seiryōki* 『清良記』, a book explaining new cultivation techniques and agricultural knowledge, was produced, and by the end of the century, Miyazaki Yasusada 宮崎安貞 (1623-97)'s ***Nōgyō Zensho*** 『農業全書』 (**Compendium of Agriculture**), the first systematic work on agriculture, was published. After the turn of the 19th century, many agricultural books were produced based on the conditions of each area and widely read. Examples include *Nōgu Benriron* 『農具便利論』 and *Kōeki Kokusankō* 『広益国産考』, both by Ōkura Nagatsune 大蔵永常 (1768-1860?).

Due to the development of new fields and technical innovations, the kokudaka 石高 significantly expanded. The total area of fields and paddies, which had been 1.64

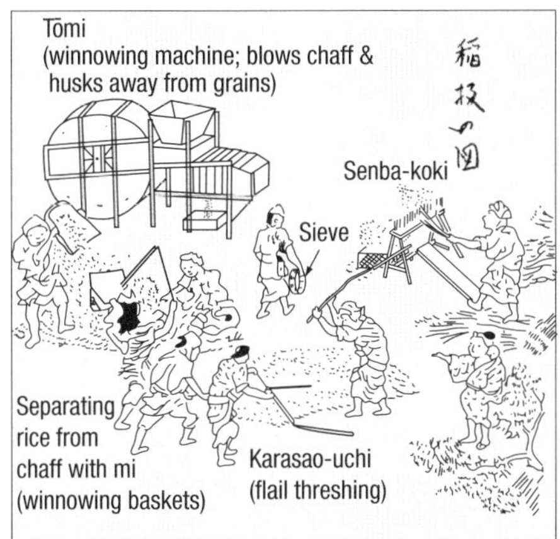

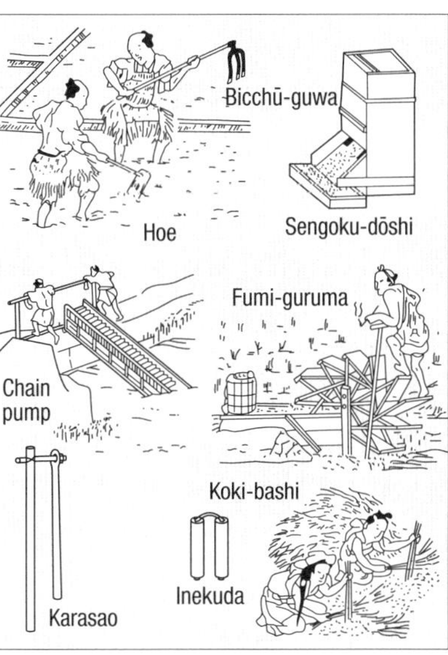

FARM WORK AND FARM TOOLS

Bicchū-guwa were used for the preliminary plowing, and sengoku-dōshi for grain separation. Water pumps based on the traditional Chinese chain pump were replaced by smaller fumi-guruma, and koki-bashi〈扱箸〉 for threshing were replaced by senba-koki. The upper left picture from the *Rōnō Yawa*〈『老農夜話』〉 depicts the threshing and conveying process.

million chōbu (町歩) at the beginning of the Edo period, exploded to 2.97 million by the early 18th century (1 chōbu = approximately 1 ha). Thus, the annual tax revenues of the bakufu and daimyō increased considerably.

The bakufu and daimyō tried to accumulate monetary revenue by selling rice (collected as tax) in large cities, and furthermore, they attempted to increase tax revenues through the promotion of commercial crop production. At the end of the 17th century, as a market network was established across the country, and as urban areas like the three great cities and castle towns developed, the consumption demand diversified among not only bushi but also other groups, especially city-dwellers, resulting in the production of commercial goods thriving in many areas. Since these commercial goods were traded through toiya (問屋) and markets in castle towns and local towns, villages gradually came to be involved in the distribution of goods with distant regions.

In villages, landowners sold surplus rice as a commercial good, and common hyakushō had greater opportunities to gain wealth through producing commercial crops such as mulberry, hemp, cotton, rape, paper mulberry, various vegetables, tobacco, tea and fruits. Moreover, under the promotion of the daimyō, all across the country areas came to develop their own local specialties suited to their climate: safflower in the Dewa Murayama (Mogami) region (出羽村山（最上）地方), tea in Suruga and Yamashiro Uji (山城宇治), common rush in Bingo (備後), aidama (藍玉) (indigo plants) in Awa (阿波), brown sugar in Satsuma (薩摩) (from the Ryūkyū (琉球) Islands), hōshogami (奉書紙) (thick quality paper) in Echizen (越前), grapes in Kai (甲斐), and mandarin oranges in Kii (紀伊).

The Development of Various Industries

Besides agriculture, other industries also developed significantly. In the forestry industry, at the end of the 17th century some timber merchants from Hida (飛騨) and Kii began to work as contractors, cutting wood in Mutsu (陸奥) and Dewa (出羽), as well as in Ezochi (蝦夷地). They sold the timber in large cities like Edo and Kyōto to make considerable fortunes. As this type of lumber business became widespread across the country, wealthy merchants dealing in timber came to be seen in various areas. Meanwhile, some regions like Kumano (熊野), Izu (伊豆), and Shimousa (下総) produced high-quality charcoal as tribute for the bakufu or daimyō, or for sale in the three great cities and castle towns. With the improvement of woodworking tools and the spread of lacquering techniques, wooden tableware and commodities were produced in large quantities[12].

In the fishing industry, fishing methods were improved, and new fishing grounds

[12] Woodworkers called "kijishi〈木地師〉" lived in many rural communities throughout the country where they made wooden commodities.

were developed around coastal areas. Sardines and herrings were processed to make dried sardines and oil cake, which were transported across the country, starting with the Kansai region, as fertilizer indispensable for raising commercial crops like cotton. Aside from that, fishing rods were used to catch red snappers in the Seto Inland Sea 瀬戸内海 or skipjack tuna in Tosa 土佐, while whaling using nets and harpoons thrived in the waters off Kii, Tosa, Hizen 肥前 and Nagato 長門. From the end of the 17th century, tawaramono 俵物 (dried fishery products such as abalone, sea slug and shark fin) and konbu 昆布 came to replace copper as a main export good to China, and the fishing industry expanded in the coastal areas of Ezochi and Mutsu in order to obtain these.

SKIPJACK FISHING (FROM *MIE-KEN SUISAN ZUKAI*〈『三重県水産図解』〉 [ILLUSTRATED GUILD TO SKIPJACK FISHING])
The picture depicts skipjack fishing in Shima〈志摩〉. In Satsuma, Tosa and Izu Provinces, dried bonito flakes became a local specialty and were transported across the country, contributing to the development of Japanese food culture along with shōyu.

In the salt industry, **irihama enden** 入浜塩田, a cultivation method that required advanced engineering, further developed, and salt production spread to various regions beginning with the coastal areas of the Seto Inland Sea.

As for textiles, specialized textiles came to emerge in various areas, including cotton in Kawachi 河内, hemp in Ōmi 近江, and bleached cotton in Nara 奈良. Although textiles like silk and pongee were produced in large quantities in farming villages as well, luxurious textiles like kinran 金襴 (gold brocade) and donsu 緞子 (satin damask) were produced exclusively in Kyōto's **Nishijin** 西陣 district, using **takabata looms** 高機 which required advanced skills. Nevertheless, by the middle of the 18th century, other regions, like Kiryū 桐生 in Kōzuke 上野, also began to produce quality silk textiles.

The production of porcelains increased significantly with the spread of pottery techniques introduced by Korean potters who had been taken to Japan during Toyotomi Hideyoshi's 豊臣秀吉 military campaigns. In Arita 有田 in Hizen, porcelains came to be produced from the first half of the 17th century under the patronage of Saga Domain 佐賀藩, and became a major export item for traders in Nagasaki. Afterwards, under the patronage of Owari Domain 尾張藩, porcelain production thrived in other areas such as Seto in Owari and Tajimi 多治見 in Mino 美濃, and came to increase elsewhere as well. In communities

SHIMOUSA NO KUNI SHŌYU SEIZŌ NO ZU《『下総国醤油製造之図』》
(ILLUSTRATION OF SHŌYU PRODUCTION IN SHIMOUSA PROVINCE)
Shimousa was an area in eastern Japan that had been known for agricultural products for centuries, including shōyu. The raw materials (soy beans, wheat, salt) were processed for preservation in large quantities for fermentation and aging; moromi, the fermented product, was pressed to make shōyu. The finished shōyu was barreled and labeled as a commodity, mainly for distribution to Edo.

surrounding castle towns, inexpensive pottery was produced in large quantities.

As for the brewing industry, sake brands produced in the **Fushimi** 伏見 and **Nada** 灘 areas established their fame from the mid-Edo era, and sake retailers developed in many regions. Meanwhile, shōyu 醤油, the production of which had begun earlier in western Japan, came to be well-known as extensive amounts were produced across the country, starting in **Noda** 野田 and **Chōshi** 銚子 in the Kantō region, whereupon it became one of the mainstays of Japanese cooking ingredients like katsuobushi 鰹節.

The Organization and Development of Transportation Networks

The transportation network began to be organized during the unification of the country under the Toyotomi regime, and was completed under the Edo Bakufu. The whole network connected the three great cities of Edo, Ōsaka, and Kyōto with the various castle towns across the country. Within this network, five major routes (the **Gokaidō** 五街道) were put under the bakufu's direct control as main roads. These routes, which had Nihonbashi 日本橋 in Edo as their starting point, were the Tōkaidō 東海道 (which connected the three great cities), Nakasendō 中山道, Kōshū-dōchū 甲州道中, Nikkō-dōchū 日光道中, and Ōshū-dōchū 奥州道中. From the mid-17th century, they were managed by **Dōchū Bugyō** 道中奉行 (Main Route Supervisors).

Main subroutes called **waki kaidō** 脇街道 (or wakiōkan 脇往還)[13] were also organized across the country. Along these routes, numerous **shukueki** 宿駅 (post stations)[14] were established, as were facilities like **ichirizuka** 一里塚 (mile stones), bridges, ferry ports, and sekisho 関所 (checkpoints)[15]. Shukueki were even set up in the central areas of castle towns along the main roads, while other shukueki became small towns (called **shukuba-machi** 宿場町) and served as local hubs for goods distribution.

The top priority for land transportation was given to official use, such as by the bakufu, daimyō or hatamoto. The service of coolies and horse transportation for such business was often requisitioned at no charge, or for half the regular fee. This service was called **tenmayaku** 伝馬役[16], the fees for which were borne by the chōnin and hyakushō of a shukueki or the neighboring villages. Shukueki were normally equipped with a **toiyaba** 問屋場 (**relay station**), where toiya (wholesale merchants and shippers) and officials like toshiyori 年寄 (supervisors) and chōzuke 帳付 (accountants) worked overseeing tenmayaku and conveying official documents and goods (**tsugi bikyaku** 継飛脚)[17]. Shukueki also had lodgings for daimyō and the like (**honjin** 本陣 and **waki honjin** 脇本陣), and inns for common travelers.

By the middle of the early modern era, the land transportation network was increasingly used for the transport of commercial goods as well as just for official purposes like Sankin Kōtai and bakufu or daimyō goods. Roads and shukueki developed further as commoner pilgrimages to famous temples and shrines became popular. In

---

[13] Major waki kaidō routes included Ise Kaidō〈伊勢街道〉, Hokkoku Kaidō〈北国街道〉, Chūgoku Kaidō〈中国街道〉, and Nagasaki Kaidō〈長崎街道〉.

[14] For example, along the stretch of the Tokaidō from Shinagawa〈品川〉 to Ōtsu〈大津〉, 53 shukueki were established, and on the stretch from Ōtsu to Ōsaka there were four; while on the Nakasendō from Itabashi〈板橋〉 to Moriyama〈守山〉, 67 shukueki were established.

[15] Major checkpoints were situated at such locations as Hakone〈箱根〉 and Arai〈新居〉 on the Tokaidō; Usui〈碓氷〉 and Kiso-Fukushima〈木曽福島〉 on the Nakasendō; Kobotoke〈小仏〉 on the Kōshū-dōchū; and Kurihashi〈栗橋〉 on the Nikkō-dōchū and Ōshū-dōchū. At such checkpoints, presenting one's tegata〈手形〉 (travel permit) was mandatory. At checkpoints in the Kantō region in particular, "the entry of guns and the departure of women〈「入鉄砲に出女」〉" was strictly checked.

[16] From the mid-17th century, it became standard practice to provide each shukueki on the Tokaidō with 100 coolies and 100 horses; each shukueki on the Nakasendō with 50 coolies and 50 horses; and each shukueki on the Kōshū-dōchū, Nikkō-dōchū and Ōshū-dōchū with 25 coolies and 25 horses. Communities that had to supply coolies and horses to meet a tenmayaku requisition order for official duty were called sukegō〈助郷〉, and the individuals in charge of executing such an order were called sukegō-yaku〈助郷役〉.

[17] Following the tsugi bikyaku system, daimyō devised their own form, daimyō bikyaku〈大名飛脚〉. Eventually, machi bikyaku〈町飛脚〉 evolved for the use of chōnin, leading to hikyaku toiya〈飛脚問屋〉, who were brokers that handled the transfer of letters, money and parcels.

particular, improvements in the mail system using hikyaku 飛脚 (couriers) made the swift and accurate conveyance of information possible across the country[18]. For land transportation, kago 駕籠 (palanquins), cattle and horses, and daihachi-guruma 大八車 (two-wheeled carts) were mainly used. In the Chūbu region, long-distance transport of commercial goods using horses and cattle developed, but carriage services connecting remote destinations did not[19].

For moving a large amount of goods at a reasonable cost, water transportation, utilizing the sea, rivers and lakes, was a better alternative than land transportation. From the early 17th century, the river transport network in inland areas was improved. **Suminokura Ryōi** 角倉了以 (1554-1614), a wealthy merchant from Kyōto, maintained the Kamo 鴨川 and Fuji 富士川 rivers, and established a waterway by excavating other rivers such as the Takase 高瀬川 River. Large rivers functioned as the main transportation routes for timber: logs were carried to the rivers where they were made into rafts that could be used to transport other goods as well. On rivers like the Yodo 淀川, Tone 利根川, and Shinano 信濃川, and on lakes like Biwa 琵琶湖 and Kasumigaura 霞ヶ浦, boat transportation using small boats, or mid-size boats like Takasebune 高瀬舟, developed as a way to carry goods and people. Harbor towns called kashi 河岸 were established in many regions as transportation hubs connecting the land and water transportation networks.

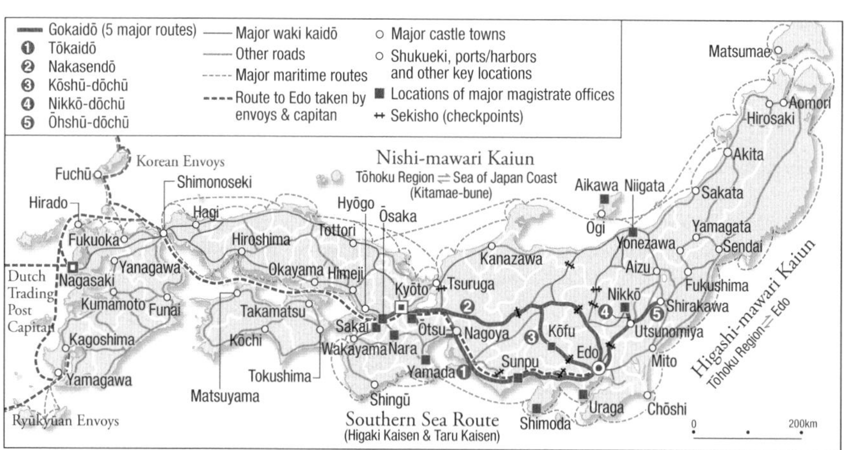

EDO-ERA TRANSPORTATION NETWORKS

---

[18] Such information included bakufu edicts (ofuregaki〈御触書〉), the market indexes of commodities like rice, and reports on social calamities (like disasters and ikki) and foreign affairs.

[19] There were many oxcarts and daihachi-guruma in Edo, but these were not used for long-distance transportation.

As for sea transportation, in the first half of the 17th century transport services like **Higaki Kaisen** 菱垣廻船 began ferrying goods between Ōsaka and Edo, using large cargo vessels (that later took their name). In the late 17th century, **Kawamura Zuiken** 河村瑞賢 (1618-99), a merchant from Edo, improved the **Higashi-mawari Kaiun** 東廻り海運 (east circuit sea route) and **Nishi-mawari Kaiun** 西廻り海運 (west circuit sea route), the two major sea transportation routes (which had as their starting point the port of Sakata 酒田, in Dewa), and in so doing established a country-wide sea transportation network based around Edo and Ōsaka. Along these sea routes, numerous port towns thrived. In the early 18th century, **Taru Kaisen** 樽廻船, a shipping service connecting Ōsaka and Edo that specialized in carrying sake barrels, started operation. Taru Kaisen ships, which were exceptionally fast, and carried not only sake but also various goods in barrels at reasonable fees, frequently competed with Higaki Kaisen. Both services operated on a regular basis to carry large quantities of goods like cotton, oil and sake from Ōsaka to Edo. Later on the Higaki Kaisen went into decline, and by the end of the early modern era Taru Kaisen enjoyed an overwhelming position. Meanwhile, from around the end of the 18th century, other sea transport services, such as **Kitamae-bune** 北前船 in the Sea of Japan and Utsumi-bune 内海船 from around Owari Bay, developed to connect distant destinations.

Currency and Finance

Regularly issuing currency that would be accepted throughout the country was one of the most important roles of the bakufu. The first gold and silver coins minted to the same standard and quality in Japan were the Keichō Kin-gin 慶長金銀, which Tokugawa Ieyasu 徳川家康 had minted in large quantities at **Kinza** 金座 (**gold mints**) and **Ginza** 銀座 (**silver mints**) around 1600. Kinza were founded in Edo and Kyōto, and coins like koban 小判 and ichibukin 一分金 were minted under the master, Gotō Shōzaburō 後藤庄三郎 (dates unknown). The first Ginza, meanwhile, were founded in the Fushimi and Sunpu regions, but later transferred to Kyōto and Edo, and minted coins of fixed weight (**shōryō kahei** 秤量貨幣, also known as hyōryō kahei) like chōgin 丁銀 and mameitagin 豆板銀[20]. At the beginning of the early modern era, the country's monetary system was unstable because of the circulation of various currencies, including imported coins and coins of poor quality[21]. However, in the Kan'ei era 寛永期, mints called **Zeniza** 銭座 were established in about ten locations across the country, including Edo and Sakamoto 坂本 in Ōmi, to mint large quantities of **Kan'ei Tsūhō** 寛永通宝 copper coins which were issued throughout the country. By the mid-17th century, the "three coins"

---

[20] Eventually, Kinza and Ginza were integrated into Edo.

[21] Other coins that were used included ware-sen〈われ銭〉(broken coins), kake-sen〈欠け銭〉(mutilated coins), namari-sen〈鉛銭〉(lead coins), and privately-minted coins〈私鋳銭〉.

(Year Minted)	1 monme = 3.75 g
1600 Keichō koban	
1695 Genroku koban	
1710 Hōei koban	
1714 Shōtoku koban	
1716 Kyōhō koban	
1736 Genbun koban	
1819 Bunsei koban	
1837 Tenpō koban	
1859 Ansei koban	Weight of 1 koban
1860 Man'en koban	Gold content

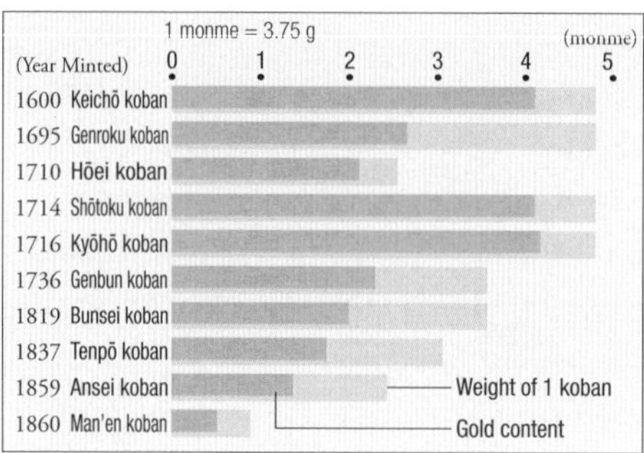

TRANSITION IN GOLD CONTENT IN GOLD COINS

The gradual decrease in the ratio of gold content eloquently demonstrates the difficulties in the bakufu's finances. Tokugawa Tsunayoshi decreased the gold content from 84% in the Keichō koban to 57% when minting the Genroku koban. As the issuing of this lesser-quality currency led to an extreme hike in prices, Arai Hakuseki restored the gold content in the Shōtoku koban to the same level as that of the Keichō koban. The extremely small amount of gold in the Man'en koban（万延小判）was the result of the bakufu's efforts to counter a massive gold drain, caused by the opening of ports, through currency recasting.

Koban   Chōgin

Ichibugin   Isshugin

Kan'ei Tsūhō

Mameitagin   Hansatsu

MAJOR FORMS OF CURRENCY

(**sanka**) – gold, silver, and copper[22] – had spread
三貨
throughout the country, and fueled a dramatic development in the distribution of goods.

However, while in eastern Japan the gold coin was used as the base for transactions and monetary calculations (**kinzukai**), in western Japan the silver
金遣い
coin was used instead (**ginzukai**). On top of this
銀遣い
issue, the exchange ratio among the three coins was always unstable due to changes in the market, and as a result it was not until the New Currency Act of 1871 that the Japanese mon-
新貨条例
etary system was finally unified. Moreover, from the latter half of the 17th century, each domain issued **hansatsu** (domain paper money) for use within its own territory,
藩札
particularly the castle towns. In some regions, merchants issued small-value amounts of private currency to supplement the three coins when the latter ran short.

---

[22]   Monetary units were ryō（両）, bu（分）, and shu（朱）for gold coins; kan（貫）, monme（匁）, fun（分）, rin（厘）and mō（毛）for silver coins; and kan and mon（文）for copper coins. Initially, silver coins were used as the fixed-weight currency, meaning that in a given exchange, the weight of the coins was used to determine the value. Later, the exchange rate was officially set at 1 gold ryō to 4 copper kanmon（貫文）(i.e., 4000 copper mon coins), weighing 60 monme of silver, but the actual rates depended on current market values.

The widespread use of currency was promoted by the economic activities of **ryōgaeshō** 両替商 **(money changers)**[23], who weighed and exchanged the three coins, in the three great cities and the castle towns. Particularly influential ryōgaeshō in Ōsaka and Edo called **hon-ryōgae** 本両替 supported the finances of the bakufu and domains through account-keeping, exchanges and loans.

The Development of the Three Great Cities

The development of agriculture and other industries formed country-wide networks of markets for goods distribution around each castle town and port. These networks comprised what we could call a national market. At the centers of these networks were the three great cities (**santo** 三都) of Edo, Ōsaka and Kyōto, which came to rank among the most prosperous cities in the late 17th-century world[24].

In **Edo**, known as the "foyer of the shōgun" 「将軍のお膝元」, were concentrated the various bakufu facilities as well as the residences for each domain, starting with the daimyō residences (hantei 藩邸), and the residences of the hatamoto and gokenin 御家人. A large number of bushi 武士 and their families, including many retainers and servants, resided there as well. The chōninchi 町人地 were crowded with many structures[25], where various types of merchants, artisans and hiyō 日用 (or hiyatoi 日雇, day laborers) gathered together, making Edo the greatest center of consumption in Japan.

Ōsaka, on the other hand, was called the "kitchen of the realm" 「天下の台所」, and was a large commercial center in western Japan as well as a distribution hub for goods from across the country. Various domains, mostly from western Japan or along the Sea of Japan, had **kurayashiki** 蔵屋敷 (warehouse facilities)[26] in Ōsaka where they could obtain currency by selling their nengumai 年貢米 (rice collected as annual tax) or **kuramono** 蔵物 (regional specialties) through merchants called **kuramoto** 蔵元 or **kakeya** 掛屋[27]. Additionally, various

---

[23] Particularly well-known ryōgaeshō included the one Mitsui Takatoshi〈三井高利〉started along with his textile store in the three great cities; Tennōjiya〈天王寺屋〉, Hiranoya〈平野屋〉and Kōnoike〈鴻池〉in Ōsaka; and Mitani〈三谷〉and Kajimaya〈鹿島屋〉in Edo.

[24] The population of Edo's city districts in the first half of the 18th century was estimated to be about 500,000. If the population of bushi households and religious institutions were added to this figure, the total population is estimated to have reached one million. Meanwhile, Ōsaka's population was about 350,000, and that of Kyōto was about 400,000.

[25] Until the mid-17th century, the number of chō in Edo was around 300, but by 1713 it had increased to 933, and by 1745 it had reached 1678 before stabilizing.

[26] Aside from Ōsaka, kurayashiki warehouses were also set up in towns under the direct control of the bakufu, such as Edo, Nagasaki and Ōtsu.

[27] In a kurayashiki, the person responsible for managing trade was called kuramoto, and the person in charge of account-keeping was called kakeya. Often, the same merchant played both roles.

KURAYASHIKI IN ŌSAKA (*SETTSU MEISHO ZUE*〈『摂津名所図会』〉[ILLUSTRATIONS OF FAMOUS PLACES IN SETTSU], PART)
Kurayashiki warehouses for various domains were located in Nakanoshima〈中之島〉, Ōsaka and its vicinity. Domains sent their local products (kuramono), like rice, from their region to Ōsaka, where they sought to exchange it for money.

products (**nayamono**〈納屋物〉) sent from many regions were actively traded and transported from Ōsaka to Edo and other destinations. The bakufu installed officials, including the Ōsaka Jōdai〈大坂城代〉 and Ōsaka Machi-bugyō〈大坂町奉行〉, in order to control Ōsaka and western Japan.

Kyōto had been the location of the residences of the royal family and nobility since ancient times, and also had within it and in the surrounding area numerous head temples for various Buddhist sects[28] as well as major Shintō shrines. The bakufu recognized the significance of controlling Kyōto in order to make use of the authority of the royal court to control the numerous sects and the many temples and shrines across the country. On top of this, many influential merchants, such as gofukuya〈呉服屋〉 (textile merchants) and ryōgaeshō, were based in the city, and many advanced manufacturing businesses developed, including **nishijin-ori**〈西陣織〉 **(textiles)**, **kyōzome**〈京染〉 **(dyeing)**, and **kyōyaki**〈京焼〉 (porcelains). The bakufu installed the Kyōto Shoshidai〈京都所司代〉 and Kyōto Machi-bugyō〈京都町奉行〉 to control the royal court, nobility, and religious institutions, as well as to administer the Kinai〈畿内〉 region and surrounding provinces.

---

[28] Examples of head temples include Ninnaji〈仁和寺〉 and Tōji〈東寺〉 (Shingon Sect〈真言宗〉); Shōren-in〈青蓮院〉, Myōhō-in〈妙法院〉 and Shōgo-in〈聖護院〉 (Tendai Sect〈天台宗〉); Higashi Honganji〈東本願寺〉 and Nishi Honganji〈西本願寺〉 (Jōdo Shinshū Sect〈浄土真宗〉); Chion-in〈知恩院〉 (Jōdo Sect〈浄土宗〉); and Nanzenji〈南禅寺〉, Shōkokuji〈相国寺〉, Daitokuji〈大徳寺〉 and Myōshinji〈妙心寺〉 (Rinzai Sect〈臨済宗〉).

Developments in Commerce

With the establishment of a country-wide market and thriving sea transportation, various kinds of syndicates of toiya merchants, such as the **Tokumi-toiya** 十組問屋 in Edo and the **Nijūshikumi-toiya** 二十四組問屋 in Ōsaka, were formed in order to ensure the safety of goods transportation between Edo and Ōsaka, offer collective insurance, and establish a monopoly over distribution channels. The range of such merchants' activities spread across the country. Among these merchants were some major ones who originally came from Ōmi, Ise, or Kyōto, where they specialized in dealing with textiles, cotton, or tatami 畳, but also increasingly engaged in exchanging money. These merchants, one prominent example being the Mitsui family 三井家, began to set up branch stores in the three great cities and various castle towns. Some urban toiya merchant groups cooperated with influential farmers (gōnō) to take charge of the production and distribution of goods in farming village communities, and also lent money and raw materials to hyakushō. This contributed to the organization of farming village manufacturers into a systemized contract domestic industry (**toiyasei kanai kōgyō** 問屋制家内工業).

In the first half of the 18th century, associations consisting of merchants (those who were not toiya or middlemen) or artisans also came to be officially recognized, resulting in their economic activities becoming consolidated and autonomous enough to resist intervention from the bakufu or domains.

On top of that, wholesale markets (**oroshiuri ichiba** 卸売市場), which functioned as con-

ECHIGOYA GOFUKU-TEN (TEXTILE SHOP) **IN SURUGA-MACHI**
In 1673, the Mitsui family opened Echigoya Gofuku-ten〈越後屋呉服店〉in Edo-honmachi〈江戸本町〉(in today's Chūō-ku, Tōkyō), and later, in 1683, transferred it to Suruga-machi〈駿河町〉. Its store policy was "Payment in cash (silver) only, no credit."

RICE MARKET OF DŌJIMA (*NANIWA MEISHO ZUE*〈『浪花名所図会』〉[ILLUSTRATIONS OF FAMOUS PLACES IN NANIWA], PART)

This picture shows the rice trade in Dōjima, Ōsaka (today's Kita-ku, Ōsaka), in the 18th century. During the Genroku era (1688-1704), the rice market that opened in Dōjima Shinchi〈堂島新地〉 exclusively dealt in rice transactions, such as rice collected as annual tax for daimyō.

necting venues between production areas and toiya or middlemen, developed in the three great cities and castle towns, and played a role as economic hubs connecting urban and rural areas. Well-known markets included, in Ōsaka, the rice market of **Dōjima**〈堂島〉, the fish market of **Zakoba**〈雑喉場〉, and the vegetable market of **Tenma**〈天満〉; and in Edo, the fish market of **Nihonbashi**〈日本橋〉 and the vegetable market of **Kanda**〈神田〉[29].

3 Genroku Culture

Genroku Culture

In the Genroku era, with political stability in East Asia and the consolidation of bakufu rule at home, Japan's economy experienced dramatic growth and cultural developments flourished. The key players in the cultural sphere, who had formerly been limited to wealthy elites like court nobles, priests, bushi and privileged chōnin, came to be diversified and include common chōnin, local merchants and influential hyakushō as well. The culture of this period is called **Genroku Culture**〈元禄文化〉.

One of the most distinctive features of this culture was the maturity of Japan's native culture due to the decline of influence from abroad that resulted from the

[29] Other well-known markets include the Atsuta〈熱田〉 fish market of Nagoya〈名古屋〉 and the vegetable market of Biwa-jima〈枇杷島〉.

sakoku policy. Another characteristic was how in the relatively peaceful and stable society of the time learning came to be valued, including not just Confucian studies but also scientific disciplines such as astronomy. Thirdly, serving as the context behind the broader acceptance of literature, arts and crafts, performing arts, and so forth, was the improved production of paper and developments in printing and publishing technology and distribution networks.

Genroku Literature

Due to the amicable relationship between the court and bakufu, waka (和歌) became popular among bushi, with daimyō receiving poetic instruction from courtiers. Besides waka, the most popular literary works in the Genroku era were produced by chōnin in the Kansai region, with representative authors being **Ihara Saikaku** (井原西鶴) (1642-93), **Matsuo Bashō** (松尾芭蕉) (1644-94), and **Chikamatsu Monzaemon** (近松門左衛門) (1653-1724).

Saikaku, a merchant in Ōsaka, first learned haikai (俳諧) poetry from Nishiyama Sōin (西山宗因) (1605-82) of the Danrin School (談林派) and achieved some fame, before turning to write novels called **ukiyozōshi** (浮世草子). He broke new literary ground by depicting, against a colorful backdrop of the customs of the real world, people surviving on their own talents while caught up in desire for lust or money[30].

Bashō was a poet from Iga (伊賀). In contrast to the eccentric style of the Danrin School, he established the **Shōfū School of haikai** (蕉風（正風）俳諧), distinguished by a style informed by the aesthetics of yūgen kanjaku (幽玄閑寂) (sense of profound mystery and tranquility) represented by sabi (さび) (simplicity) and karumi (かるみ) (plainness). He also produced travel writings like *Oku no Hosomichi* (『奥の細道』) (Narrow Road to the Deep North), in which he scrutinized humanity and nature. Even local farming communities warmly welcomed Bashō and his entourage, and supported their literary activities.

Chikamatsu, who came from a bushi family, wrote plays for Ningyō Jōruri (人形浄瑠璃) and Kabuki (歌舞伎) performance. In his works, he portrayed the suffering of people caught in dilemmas between duty and affection, inspired by contemporary society and historical events. Chikamatsu's plays[31], which were performed by puppeteers like Tatsumatsu (辰松八郎兵衛)

[30] Saikaku's works include amorous stories like *Kōshoku Ichidai Otoko*〈『好色一代男』〉(The Life of an Amorous Man), warrior stories such as *Budō Denraiki*〈『武道伝来記』〉(Transmission of the Martial Arts), and chōnin stories like *Nippon Eitaigura*〈『日本永代蔵』〉(The Japanese Family Storehouse) and *Seken Munesan'yō*〈『世間胸算用』〉(Worldly Mental Calculations).

[31] Chikamatsu's works include domestic plays like *Sonezaki Shinjū*〈『曽根崎心中』〉(The Love Suicides at Sonezaki), set in contemporary society, and epic plays dealing with historical events like *Kokusen'ya Kassen*〈『国性（姓）爺合戦』〉(The Battles of Koxinga), which depicts the efforts of a vassal of the former Ming Dynasty, modeled on Koxinga〈鄭成功〉, to rebuild the dynasty.

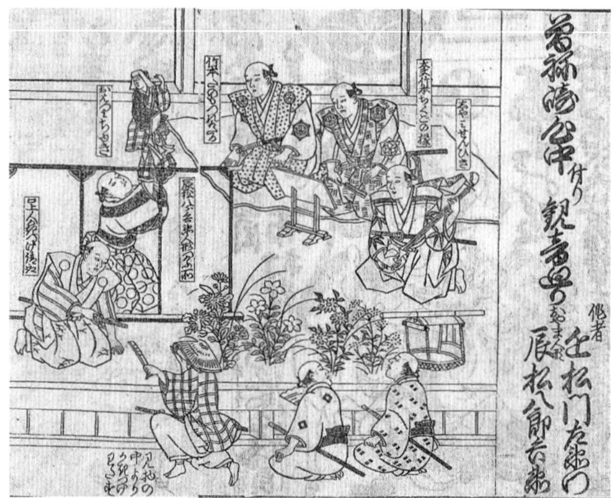

KŌJŌ BANZUKE〈口上番付〉 (PLAYBILL) **FOR *SONEZAKI SHINJŪ***
(FROM *MUGIKOGASHI*〈『牟芸古雅志』〉)
This scene depicts Tatsumatsu Hachirobē performing with a puppet. In the background on the right, a Jōruri narrator〈浄瑠璃語り〉 and a shamisen player〈三味線弾き〉 can be seen.

Hachirobē (?-1734) with narration by reciters like **Takemoto Gidayū** 竹本義太夫 (1651-1714), were deeply evocative. The narration techniques later evolved into a distinct musical art form known as **Gidayū-bushi** 義太夫節.

Around this time, Kabuki[32] also developed as a form of popular theatre. In contrast to Nō 能 and Kyōgen 狂言 plays, which were performed mostly for bushi society, Kabuki enjoyed such wide appeal that it had its own **shibaigoya** 芝居小屋 **(permanent theatres)** in Edo and the Kansai region. Celebrated Kabuki actors of the era included, in Edo, Ichikawa Danjūrō 市川団十郎 I (1660-1704), known for his heroic performance (**aragoto** 荒事), and in Kansai, Sakata Tōjūrō 坂田藤十郎 (1647-1709), who excelled at melodramatic performance (**wagoto** 和事), and Yoshizawa Ayame 芳沢あやめ I (1673-1729), a noted example of a specialist in female roles.

The Evolution of Confucianism

Confucianism grew in relevance in tandem with the stability of the bakuhan system. This was because the fundamental tenets of Confucianism, which articulated the social role for each class, and emphasized social hierarchy while respecting loyalty and filial piety, were well-suited to the needs of contemporary society. In particular, Shushigaku (Cheng-Zhu Neo-Confucianism), with its emphasis on Taigi Meibunron 大義名分論, was embraced by the bakufu and domains as a set of principles to maintain the social structure.

Nangaku 南学 (or Kainan-gakuha 海南学派), which was said to have originated in Tosa Province during the Sengoku period, and was developed by Tani Jichū 谷時中 (1598?-1649), was one leading Shushigaku school, producing scholars like **Yamazaki Ansai** 山崎闇斎 (1618-82) and

---

[32] In the early Edo period, aiming to prevent moral corruption the authorities banned Kabuki performed by first women, and then by young men. Ultimately, only Kabuki plays performed by adult men were allowed.

Nonaka Kenzan 野中兼山 (1615-63). Ansai, in particular, interpreted Shintō teachings from a Confucian framework, laying the foundation for what later became called **Suika Shintō** 垂加神道[33].

In contrast to Shushigaku, **Nakae Tōju** 中江藤樹 (1608-48) and his disciples like **Kumazawa Banzan** 熊沢蕃山 (1619-91) studied **Yangming learning** 陽明学, which originated from the Ming intellectual Wang Yangming 王陽明 (1472-1528), and criticized the social order from the perspective of chikō gōitsu 知行合一 (concept of the fundamental unity of thought and action) to correct the contradictions in society. The revolutionary character of these ideas led the bakufu to regard the Yangming scholars with suspicion[34].

Meanwhile, scholars like **Yamaga Sokō** 山鹿素行 (1622-85)[35] and **Itō Jinsai** 伊藤仁斎 (1627-1705), who were not satisfied with Neo-Confucianism teachings from abroad, established the **Kogaku (Ancient Learning) School** 古学派 to advocate a return to the classics of Confucius and Mencius. **Ogyū Sorai** 荻生徂徠 (1666-1728), an intellectual who succeeded Jinsai in the Kogaku School, and who was also interested in politics and economics, warned of the dangers of urban expansion and argued that bushi needed to focus on farming. He founded the **Keiseiron School** 経世論 of thought, which studied governance from a concrete perspective.

Sorai was valued by Yanagisawa Yoshiyasu and Shōgun Tokugawa Yoshimune, and served as a political advisor during the Kyōhō Reforms 享保の改革. **Dazai Shundai** 太宰春台 (1680-1747), one of Sorai's disciples, further developed Keiseiron, advocating that bushi pursue commerce and make profit through monopolies.

The Evolution of Various Fields of Study

The developments in Confucianism had a significant influence on other fields of

---

[33] Suika was an alias of Ansai. Suika Shintō had a strongly moralistic character, and was based on the teachings of various Shintō branches, including Ise Shintō〈伊勢神道〉, Yuiitsu Shintō〈唯一神道〉, and Yoshikawa Shintō〈吉川神道〉, the last of which was developed by Yoshikawa Koretari〈吉川惟足〉. The Kimon School〈崎門学〉, consisting of Ansai and his disciples, held that the kami〈神〉 and the virtue of the tennō were one and the same, a concept that later became the basis of Sonnōron〈尊王論〉 (ideology celebrating the tennō).

[34] Banzan criticized Confucian studies that accepted without question the moral authority of ancient China, leading to the bakufu imprisoning him in Koga〈古河〉, Shimousa, where he died of illness. In his major works such as *Daigaku Wakumon*〈『大学或問』〉 (Discussions on *The Great Learning*), he criticized bakufu policy by arguing that bushi needed to focus on farming.

[35] Yamaga Sokō criticized Shushigaku and argued, in his work *Seikyō Yōroku*〈『聖教要録』〉 (Essentials of Sagely Confucianism), for a return to the teachings of the ancient sages, which resulted in the bakufu exiling him to Akō Domain. When the Ming Dynasty, which had been emblematic of traditional China, was replaced by the Qing Dynasty, Sokō wrote *Chūchō Jijitsu*〈『中朝事実』〉 (The Reality of the Central Realm), which instead defined Japan as the "center of the world."

study in terms of rational and pragmatic thought. Arai Hakuseki wrote ***Tokushi Yoron*** 『読史余論』 (Lessons from History), in which he presented his own historical perspective on transitions in the court and bakufu through careful periodization.

In the field of natural science, practical disciplines like **honzōgaku** 本草学 **(herbal medicine**, encompassing natural history)[36], agricultural science and medicine developed, with works such as **Kaibara Ekiken** 貝原益軒 (1630-1714)'s *Yamato Honzō* 『大和本草』 (Japanese Herbal Medicine) and **Miyazaki Yasusada's** 宮崎安貞 *Nōgyō Zensho* (Compendium of Agriculture) being widely read. The demands of land surveying and commercial transactions fueled the development of **wasan** 和算 **(Japanese mathematics)**[37], and **Seki Takakazu** 関孝和 (1640?-1708) accomplished significant work in the areas of algebraic expression and the calculation thereof, as well as in the calculation of the constant *pi*. In the field of astronomy and the study of the calendar, **Shibukawa Harumi** 渋川春海 (Yasui Santetsu 安井算哲, 1639-1715) became a disciple of the Tsuchimikado 土御門家 family in Kyōto, and revised the existing calendar to draw up a new Japanese one (**Jōkyō Calendar** 貞享暦). Recognizing his achievement, the bakufu established the Tenmonkata 天文方 (Astronomical Bureau) and appointed Shibukawa as its head[38].

Studies of Japanese literature also developed around this time. Toda Mosui 戸田茂睡 (1629-1706) argued that it was absurd to regulate words that could not be used in waka (sei no kotoba 制の詞), and advocated for the legitimacy of using colloquial language. **Keichū** 契沖 (1640-1701), who studied the *Man'yōshū* 『万葉集』, authored *Man'yō Daishōki* 『万葉代匠記』 (Commentary on the *Man'yōshū*), in which he supported Mosui's arguments with numerous examples, and criticized the established convention of interpreting waka from a moralistic perspective. **Kitamura Kigin** 北村季吟 (1624-1705) studied literary classics such as *Genji Monogatari* 『源氏物語』 and *Makura no Sōshi* 『枕草子』 to try and uncover the authors' intent. These classical studies developed into a search for the ancient intellectual world, and eventually evolved into Kokugaku 国学 (native studies).

The Art of the Genroku Era

In the field of art, influential chōnin in the Kansai region, inheriting the culture of the Kan'ei era, produced increasingly refined works.

---

[36] "Honzō" refers to herbal ingredients for medicine. Originally, honzōgaku was a field of study that researched the medical effects of plants, animals and minerals, but gradually its natural history elements became more pronounced.

[37] In the early Edo period, wasan became widely known among commoners through Yoshida Mitsuyoshi's〈吉田光由〉math text, *Jinkōki*〈『塵劫記』〉.

[38] The Tenmonkata was a bureau in charge of calendar-making, and produced numerous talented individuals.

KŌHAKU BAIZU BYŌBU〈『紅白梅図屏風』〉(RED AND WHITE PLUM BLOSSOM FOLDING SCREEN, BY OGATA KŌRIN, PART)
Two panels in a pair. Kōrin's distinctive emphasis on overall tone is well-expressed with a detailed yet subtle rendering of the white plum tree on the left and the red one on the right, painted in an arrangement formed by the stream. (Height 156 cm, width 172.5 cm)

MIKAERI BIJINZU〈見返り美人図〉(BEAUTY LOOKING BACK, BY HISHIKAWA MORONOBU)
A representative beauty painting by Moronobu, a machi-eshi〈町絵師〉(chōnin painter). It exquisitely depicts a beauty in a slightly turned pose. (Height 63 cm)

IRO-E FUJIHANA-MON CHATSUBO〈色絵藤花文茶壺〉(TEA-LEAF JAR WITH WISTERIA DESIGN, BY NONOMURA NINSEI)
Nonomura Seiemon〈野々村清右衛門〉, who built a kiln in front of Omuro Ninnaji Temple〈御室仁和寺〉 in Kyōto, named himself Ninsei ("Nin〈仁〉" from Ninnaji, and "sei〈清〉" from Seiemon). This pot, one of his major works, was made for tea ceremonies. (Height 29 cm)

In painting, in addition to the Kanō School(狩野派), which was patronized by the bakufu and daimyō, other painters were also active. **Tosa Mitsuoki**(土佐光起) (1617-91), who belonged to the Tosa School which represented one branch of the Yamato-e(大和絵) tradition, was patronized by the court. **Sumiyoshi Jokei**(住吉如慶) (1599-1670) and his son **Gukei**(住吉具慶) (1631-1705) left the Tosa School(土佐派) to establish the Sumiyoshi School(住吉派), and become, as the Kanō School painters had already been, official painters serving the bakufu, in which capacity they produced many works. In Kyōto, **Ogata Kōrin**(尾形光琳) (1658-1716) established the **Rinpa School**(琳派), which adapted the decorative techniques of Tawaraya Sōtatsu(俵屋宗達). Kōrin was also known for his excellent maki-e(蒔絵) lacquer designs. In Edo, **Hishikawa Moronobu**(菱川師宣) (?-1694), from Awa(安房) Province, began to produce **ukiyoe**(浮世絵) prints that captured the feel

RIKUGI-EN (DESIGNATED A "SPECIAL PLACE OF SCENIC BEAUTY〈特別名勝〉" BY BUNKYŌ WARD, TŌKYŌ)
Yanagisawa Yoshiyasu spent eight years creating this garden at a residence he had received from Shōgun Tokugawa Tsunayoshi. Yoshiyasu named it himself.

YATSUHASHI MAKI-E RADEN SUZURIBAKO〈八橋蒔絵螺鈿硯箱〉 (YATSUHASHI MAKI-E INKSTONE CASE WITH MOTHER-OF-PEARL, BY OGATA KŌRIN)
One of the major works of Ogata Kōrin, who was the son of the proprietor of the textile store Kariganeya〈雁金屋〉 in Kyōto, and who with his younger brother, Kenzan, left many splendid paintings and laquer works. The design is based on Yatsuhashi〈八橋〉 and Kakitsubata〈カキツバタ〉, depicted in *Ise Monogatari*〈『伊勢物語』〉. The box consists of two parts: the upper part is an ink stone case, while the lower part is for paper. (Height 14.5 cm)

of urban culture by depicting beauties and famous actors. Because these prints were available cheaply, they became immensely popular.

In the field of pottery, in Kyōto **Nonomura Ninsei** 野々村仁清 (dates unknown) developed **Kyō ware** 京焼, by utilizing **iro-e** 色絵 techniques based on **Uwa-etsuke overglazing** 上絵付法. **Ogata Kenzan** 尾形乾山 (1663-1743), Kōrin's younger brother, followed this style to produce elegant decorative works. As for dyeing, **Miyazaki Yūzen** 宮崎友禅 (dates unknown) established **Yūzenzome** 友禅染 techniques to add exquisite patterns on plain textiles like rinzu 綸子 (silk satin damask) and chirimen 縮緬 (silk crepe).

In landscape gardening, as shōgunal visits to daimyō residences became more frequent, daimyō built beautifully-decorated stroll gardens. Kōraku-en 後楽園, located at the Koishikawa 小石川 residence in Mito Domain, reflected the influence of Zhu Zhiyu (Shu Shunsui, 1600-82), and Rikugi-en 六義園, at the residence of Yanagisawa Yoshiyasu, is one of the most splendid gardens that still survives today.

Chapter

8

The Waning of the Bakuhan System

1 Reforms by the Bakufu Regime

The Kyōhō Reforms

In 1716, with the death of the seventh shōgun, Tokugawa Ietsugu 〈徳川家継〉, at the age of almost seven[i], the main lineage of the Tokugawa family came to an end. **Tokugawa Yoshimune** 〈徳川吉宗〉 (1684-1751), who as the lord of Kii Domain 〈紀伊藩〉 headed one of the three collateral Tokugawa families, succeeded him as the eighth shōgun. During his twenty-nine year rule, Yoshimune carried out reforms of various aspects of bakufu administration, which came to be called the **Kyōhō Reforms** 〈享保の改革〉.

Yoshimune brought an end to the system of governance by the shōgun's chamberlain 〈側用人〉, which had been practiced since Tokugawa Tsunayoshi's 〈徳川綱吉〉 time. Instead, Yoshimune sought to have bakufu policy reflect his will through newly-installed shōgunal attendants (called goyōtoritsugi 〈御用取次〉). In order to put his policies into practice, Yoshimune recruited many talented individuals[1], such as Ōoka Tadasuke 〈大岡忠相〉 (1677-1751), a hatamoto 〈旗本〉, or Tanaka Kyūgu 〈田中丘隅〉 (?-1751)[2], the head of a shukueki 〈宿駅〉. Yoshimune also employed Confucian scholars such as Ogyū Sorai 〈荻生徂徠〉 or Muro Kyūsō 〈室鳩巣〉 (1658-1734), and spearheaded reforms himself.

One of the most significant issues addressed by the reforms was financial reconstruction. In 1719, the bakufu issued the **Mutual Settlement Promotion Edict** 〈相対済し令〉[3], which aimed at discouraging people from filing loan-related lawsuits (kanekuji 〈金公事〉) by

---

[1] For hatamoto recruits, salary was determined according to one's post. The post of ōbangashira 〈大番頭〉 received a salary of 5000 koku, the posts of ōmetsuke 〈大目付〉, machi-bugyō 〈町奉行〉, and kanjō-bugyō 〈勘定奉行〉 each received a salary of 3000 koku, and so on. A supplementary stipend system (**tashidaka no sei** 〈足高の制〉) was implemented for cases where one's position was higher than the base salary to which one was normally entitled.

[2] Tanaka was the head of the Kawasaki shuku 〈川崎宿〉 on the Tōkaidō 〈東海道〉. He studied under Sorai, and wrote a jikata-sho 〈地方書〉 (local administrative guide) called *Minkan Seiyō* 〈『民間省要』〉 (Essentials for Local Administration). He was recruited by Yoshimune and contributed to governance.

[3] From the latter half of the 17th century, further Aitai Sumashi-rei were issued several times. In 1718, thirty-six thousand lawsuits were filed with the Edo Machi-Bugyōsho, of which more than 90% were loan-related lawsuits.

instead promoting settlements among the concerned parties. The bakufu also issued sumptuary edicts (ken'yaku-rei〈倹約令〉) to decrease expenditures, and implemented a temporary tax called **agemai**〈上げ米〉 that entailed collecting 100 koku〈石〉 per 10,000 koku from each daimyō's〈大名〉 rice revenue. They compensated for this by reducing the burden of Sankin Kōtai〈参勤交代〉[4]. The bakufu more harshly punished corruption among their territorial administrators, while at the same time changing the tax assessment system from kemihō〈検見法〉 to **jōmenhō**〈定免法〉 in order to increase the tax rate and therefore revenues. In addition, the bakufu turned their attention to wealth creation through the production of commercial crops, such as cotton, that had been expanding in their territories in western Japan, and in so doing sought to increase the revenue from those farmlands. The bakufu also promoted the development of new fields (**shinden kaihatsu**〈新田開発〉)[5] with help from merchant capital, and encouraged increases in the amount of rice production.

With these financial initiatives, the rice production of the bakufu territories was increased by more than 10%, and together with the annual revenue accrued, the bakufu's financial situation was relatively ameliorated. Yoshimune, who became known as the "kome kubō"「米公方」 (rice lord), aiming to ensure the financial security of the

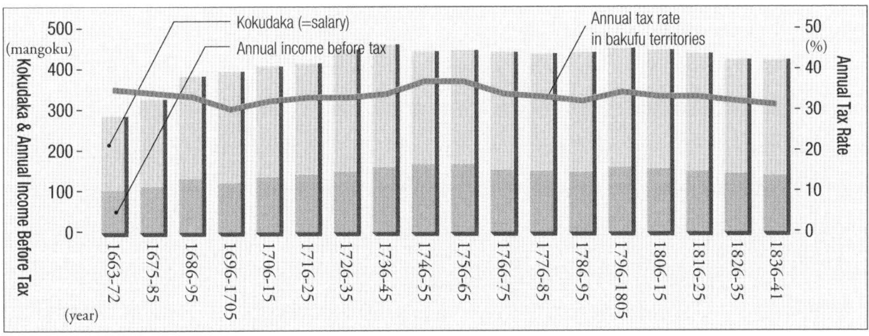

TOTAL KOKUDAKA IN BAKUFU TERRITORIES AND ANNUAL TAX RATE
Initially, the sum of all kokudaka (agricultural yield; basis for one's salary) in bakufu territories was a little under 3 million koku; this amount increased gradually, and in the Genroku era〈元禄期〉 (1688-1704) it rose to about 4 million koku. From the Kyōhō era (1716-36) until the Bakumatsu era (at the end of the Edo period) the figure stayed at around 4.4 million koku. The annual tax rate began fairly high, but gradually decreased over time. It rose again due to the effects of the Kyōhō Reforms, and reached a peak in the Hōreki era〈宝暦期〉 (1751-64) before decreasing again. It temporarily rose again under the Kansei Reforms〈寛政の改革〉, but then fell again.

[4] For nine years from 1722 to 1730, the obligatory stay in Edo mandated by the Sankin Kōtai system was halved. The income per year from the agemai amounted to 187,000 koku, more than 10% of the bakufu's revenue.

[5] At Nihonbashi〈日本橋〉, in Edo, the bakufu erected a kōsatsu〈高札〉 (official bulletin board) about the development of rice fields to encourage the cooperation of wealthy merchants. Famous examples of new field areas at the time include Iinuma Shinden〈飯沼新田〉, Shiunjigata Shinden〈紫雲寺潟新田〉, Musashino Shinden〈武蔵野新田〉, and Minuma Daiyōsui Shinden〈見沼代用水新田〉. The additional rice harvest from the new rice fields amounted to 200,000 koku.

MACHI-BIKESHI (*HIKESHI SEN-KUMI NO ZU ŌEMA* 〈火消千組之図大絵馬〉[VOTIVE TABLET ILLUSTRATION OF SEN-KUMI FIRE BRIGADE])
Fire brigades were divided into 47 units. Among them, the units with the names "He〈へ〉," "Ra〈ら〉," and "Hi〈ひ〉" were renamed, respectively, as "Hyaku〈百〉," "Sen〈千〉," and "Man〈万〉" for the sonority.

bushi by stabilizing the rice price, officially recognized the rice market of Dōjima 堂島 in Ōsaka. He also promoted the development of new industries, including the cultivation of sweet potatoes, sugar cane, wax trees, and ginseng, and eased the embargo on Western books translated into Chinese[6].

Seeing the improvement in the financial situation, in the fourth month of 1728 Yoshimune ordered a shōgunal excursion to Nikkō 日光 Shrine for the first time in 65 years, showcasing the power of the shōgun while claiming he was following a precedent set by Tokugawa Ieyasu 徳川家康. He abolished the agemai, which had been considered a "shameful practice" of the shōgun, and returned the Sankin Kōtai system to its previous form.

The second pillar of the reforms was city planning for Edo, which was carried out by Ōoka Tadasuke, now a machi-bugyō. Even after the Great Meireki Fire 明暦の大火, Edo had continued to repeatedly suffer from major fires. To make the city more fire resistant, Ōoka established various fire prevention measures, such as hirokōji 広小路 (broadened streets) and hiyokechi 火除地 (fire barrier zones), and organized **machi-bikeshi** 町火消 (town fire brigades)[7] to strengthen the firefighting system which had previously depended mainly on jōbikeshi 定火消 (bakufu-managed firefighting squads). A suggestion box (**meyasubako** 目安箱) was set up in front of the conference chamber in order to collect public feedback, in response to which was then established the **Koishikawa Yōjōsho** 小石川養生所, a hospital for the poor.

By the end of his rule, Yoshimune had achieved numerous administrative reforms.

---

[6] Yoshimune recruited Aoki Kon'yō〈青木昆陽〉 to spread the cultivation of sweet potatoes as an emergency crop for relief from the poor harvests. He also had Aoki and Noro Genjō〈野呂元丈〉 learn Dutch, which laid the foundations for the flourishing of Rangaku〈蘭学〉 (Dutch, i.e. Western, learning).

[7] For organizing the machi-bikeshi, the chō〈町〉 in Edo were divided up to form a total of 47 (and later, 48) groups, following i/ro/ha〈「いろは」〉 name order. At first, the fire-fighting system was facilitated by chōnin sokuyaku〈町人足役〉 (town laborers), but these were soon replaced by tobi-ninsoku〈鳶人足〉 (laborers specializing in construction).

He enacted the ***Kujikata Osadamegaki*** (公事方御定書) (Rulebook for Public Officials) to promote more rational judicial decisions based on precedent. He also ordered the compilation of the *Ofuregaki Kanpō Shūsei* (御触書寛保集成) (Kanpō-Era Collection of Bakufu Ordinances), a categorical collection of all bakufu ordinances issued since 1615, and at the same time, the archiving of the bakufu's administrative documents. Thereafter, updating the compilation became one of the bakufu's ongoing responsibilities. To keep the Tokugawa family's position secure, Yoshimune also had his second son Munetake (宗武) (1715-71) and fourth son Munetada (宗尹) (1721-64) establish, respectively, the Tayasu (田安家) and Hitotsubashi (一橋家) branch families[8], while attempting to maintain a cooperative relationship with the court.

Social Transformation

Following the Kyōhō Reforms, the latter half of the 18th century marked a significant turning point in the bakuhan system.

In the villages, some of the wealthy hyakushō serving as village officials like nanushi (名主) or shōya (庄屋) started to engage in agricultural work themselves (**jinushi tezukuri** (地主手作))[9]. They accumulated rice fields and farmlands around their villages as collateral for loans to impoverished hyakushō, thereby becoming **jinushi (landowners)** (地主). These landowners then rented their land to tenant farmers to collect rent fees. They became the leading village players in commercial crop production as well as in the logistics and finance markets, and played principal roles in communal economic activities, becom-

NIHONBASHI, ASA NO KEI〈日本橋「朝之景」〉(MORNING VIEW AT NIHONBASHI, FROM *53 STATIONS ON THE TŌKAIDŌ* 〈東海道五十三次〉, BY UTAGAWA HIROSHIGE〈歌川広重〉)
A daimyō's procession is passing Nihonbashi. The kōsatsu is visible on the left, while in the foreground are some fish peddlers carrying fresh stock from Uogashi〈魚河岸〉, Nihonbashi's fish market.

---

[8] The Tayasu and Hitotsubashi branch families were, together with the Shimizu branch family〈清水家〉 that began with Tokugawa Shigeyoshi〈徳川重好〉, the second son of the ninth shōgun Ieshige, called the **Sankyō**〈三卿〉.

[9] Jinushi tezukuri referred to a land management system in which poor farmers were recruited as indentured servants.

ing known as **gōnō** 豪農. Meanwhile, small-scale hyakushō who lost their land had to work as tenant farmers, or become indentured servants or day laborers, the latter often being pushed into Edo or neighboring urban areas and becoming more involved in the monetary economy. For these reasons, communal society, which had been based on a self-sufficient economy, radically shifted, and the conflict between gōnō, serving as village administrators, on the one hand, and the small-scale hyakushō and tenant farmers on the other, intensified. As a result, **murakata sōdō** 村方騒動 **(village disturbances)**, in which these hyakushō denounced corruption by village officials and demanded more democratic, fair communal governance, occurred frequently across the country.

In urban areas, the chō, which functioned as the foundation of society, changed drastically. In particular, in the three great cities and the central chōninchi in the castle towns, the number of homeowners decreased, and most of the dwellings came to be occupied by land tenants, shop tenants, or the servants of merchants. In the uranagaya 裏長屋 (backstreet row houses)[10] within the chō, and on the outskirts of the castle towns, there were many poor commoners who were migrant workers, or who worked as botefuri 棒手振 (peddlers) or day laborers. These city dwellers lived in paltry row houses, supporting themselves with meager wages. Their daily lives were easily wrecked in the event of price inflation, famine or natural disaster.

Ikki and Riots

Under the murauke 村請制 system, hyakushō suffered from a heavy burden including the annual tax and labor obligations. When their daily life and agricultural production were threatened due to bakufu or domain governance, hyakushō would come together as a village and unite against their lords, often taking direct action to demand reform. Such movements were called **hyakushō ikki** 百姓一揆[11].

From the latter half of the 17th century, **daihyō-osso ikki** 代表越訴型一揆[12], in which representatives of each village appealed directly to their lord, became more frequent. By the end

[10] Uranagaya, also called Uradana〈裏店〉, referred to poor row houses described as "ku-shaku, ni-ken〈「九尺二間」〉" (tiny rented house, 2.7 m wide by 3.6 m deep), which, as the name indicates, were usually small, run-down houses.

[11] Ikki in the early 17th century still showed a degree of continuity from those in medieval times, including violent revolts involving local elites (powerful former warriors who remained in villages even after the separation of warriors and farmers) against bakufu rule, or the desertion of entire villages. The total number of confirmed hyakushō ikki incidents, including those that broke out in the early Meiji period, amounts to about 3700.

[12] There were many cases in which ikki leaders, such as Sakura Sōgorō〈佐倉惣五郎〉of Shimousa〈下総〉or Haritsuke Mozaemon〈磔茂左衛門〉of Kōzuke〈上野〉, were mythologized as self-sacrificing heroes (**gimin**〈義民〉).

of the century, large-scale **sōbyakushō ikki**(惣百姓一揆)[13] that reached across broad areas were occurring across the country. The hyakushō who participated in these ikki demanded the repeal of new taxes and increases in the annual tax, called for the abolition of the monopoly system, and resorted to violence, destroying the residences of merchants and village administrators who co-operated with bakufu and domain policies.

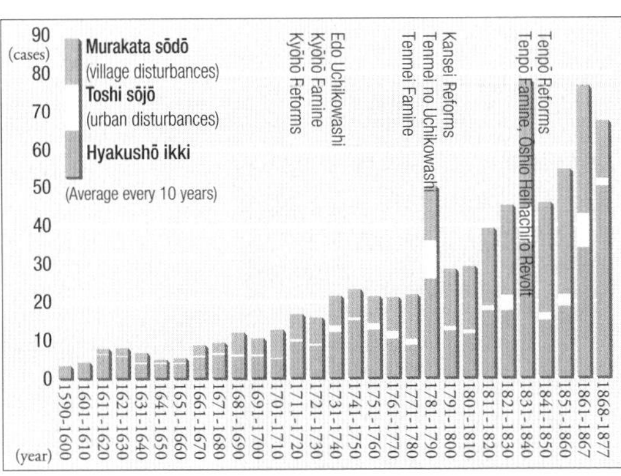

INCIDENT RATE OF HYAKUSHŌ IKKI

KARAKASA RENPANJŌ〈傘連判状〉(UMBRELLA COVENANT)

In 1754, officials of 11 villages in a hatamoto's territory in Hitachi〈常陸〉signed and affixed their seals to this oath demanding the dismissal of the administrator.

At times, bakufu or domain authorities accepted some of the demands made by an ikki, but in most cases they suppressed the uprising by force, and punished the leaders severely. However, in spite of such harsh suppression, hyakushō ikki became more frequent, and particularly at times of poor harvests and serious famines, numerous uprisings would occur simultaneously across the country. In 1732, western Japan was afflicted by unstable weather and great numbers of insects, mainly locusts or leafhoppers, resulting in a poor harvest and great famine that stretched across the whole country (**Kyōhō Famine**(享保の飢饉)). The lives of the commoners were grievously affected. In the following year, a riot (**uchikowashi**(打ちこわし)) broke out in Edo, and the stores of the powerful rice merchants were destroyed by a mob that accused them of being responsible for the soaring rice prices.

A famine that had its origin in cold weather in 1782 was worsened by the erup-

---

[13] Ikki that spread to encompass an entire domain were called "zenhan ikki〈全藩一揆〉." Well-known examples of such are the Kasuke Sōdō〈嘉助騒動〉in Matsumoto Domain〈松本藩〉in Shinano〈信濃〉in 1686, and the Genbun Ikki〈元文一揆〉in Iwaki Taira Domain〈磐城平藩〉in Mutsu〈陸奥〉in 1738.

TENMEI FAMINE (*TENMEI KIKIN NO ZU*〈『天明飢饉之図』〉[ILLUSTRATION OF THE TENMEI FAMINE], PART)
From 1782 to 1787, a serious famine spread across the country in the wake of long periods of rain, the eruption of Mt. Asama, and cold weather.

tion of Mt. Asama 浅間山 the following year, and consequently lasted for several years. In the Tōhoku region in particular, many people starved to death (**Tenmei Famine** 天明の飢饉)[14]. This led to many hyakushō ikki all across Japan, with violent riots occurring in various cities, including Edo and Ōsaka.

The Tanuma Era

Yoshimune was succeeded by the ninth shōgun, Tokugawa Ieshige 徳川家重 (1711-61), and then the tenth, Tokugawa Ieharu 徳川家治 (1737-86). During Ieharu's time, **Tanuma Okitsugu** 田沼意次 (1719-88), who had been promoted from shōgunal assistant to rōjū 老中 in 1772, held the real reins of power for a dozen or so years. This time came to be called the **Tanuma era** 田沼時代. To rebuild the bakufu's finances, which had again fallen into difficulties, Tanuma not only resorted to tax increases, but also fueled economic activity in the private sector, in order to use the profit this generated as part of the finances of the administration. For this purpose, Tanuma widely endorsed the establishing of **kabunakama** 株仲間, guilds formed by merchant and artisan associations in both urban and rural areas[15], and in so doing increased business tax revenues such as unjō 運上 (license fees) and myōga 冥加 (charter fees). He also attempted to standardize the currency system based on the gold standard, by establishing a fixed numeric value for silver coins[16].

Tanuma also actively carried out the development of new fields through reclamation of large swamp areas like Inba-numa 印旛沼 and Tega-numa 手賀沼[17], with financial support from merchants in Edo and Ōsaka. He also accepted the proposal outlined in *Aka Ezo Fusetsukō* 『赤蝦夷風説考』 (An Investigation into Rumors from Red Ezo) by **Kudō Heisuke** 工藤平助 (1734-1800), a doctor from Sendai Domain 仙台藩, and dispatched **Mogami Tokunai** 最上徳内 (1755-1836)

---

[14] Victims of the famine were especially numerous in the domains of the Mutsu region. In Tsugaru Domain〈津軽藩〉 and the surrounding area, well over a hundred thousand people starved to death, and in some villages the entire population perished.

[15] As part of these policies, guilds like the Dōza〈銅座〉 (copper guild), Shinchūza〈真鍮座〉 (brass guild), and Chōsen Ninjinza〈朝鮮人参座〉 (ginseng guild) were established under bakufu monopoly.

[16] The most famous coin minted under the new currency system was the **Nanryō Nishu Gin**〈南鐐二朱銀〉, which was minted in large quantities from 1772. "Nanryō" meant high-quality silver, and this silver coin had a value of 2 shu〈朱〉 of gold.

[17] The work was almost completed, but failed due to the flooding of the Tonegawa River〈利根川〉.

NANRYŌ NISHU GIN, OBVERSE (LEFT) **AND REVERSE** (RIGHT)
The engraving states: "8 pieces of this coin have a value of 1 koban〈小判〉."

TRADE IN NAGASAKI (*RANKAN EMAKI*〈「蘭館絵巻」〉 [ILLUSTRATED SCROLL OF THE DUTCH TRADING POST], PART)
Nagasaki officials are shown calculating the value of merchandise with traders from the Dutch trading post.

to Ezochi to research the possibilities for developing the area and engaging in commerce with Russians[18]. The focus of Tanuma's policies was extensively improving bakufu finances while taking advantage of merchants' financial power. Stimulated by these policies, various spheres of academic studies, culture and art flourished in the private sector. On the other hand, among the bakufu officials corruption and nepotism became rampant, and the decay in traditional warrior morals and discipline came in for severe criticism.

As for the royal court, there occurred a scandal called the **Hōreki Incident** 宝暦事件 (1758) in which a restorationist group of nobles and Takenouchi Shikibu 竹内式部 (1712-67) were severely punished by the regental families. Following the sudden death of Go-Momozono 後桃園天皇 Tennō (r. 1770-79) in 1779, Kōkaku Tennō 光格天皇 (r. 1790-1817), from the Kan'in no Miyake 閑院宮家 line, succeeded to the throne.

In 1784, against a backdrop of frequent hyakushō ikki and riots triggered by the Tenmei Famine, Tanuma Okitomo 田沼意知 (1749-84), a son of Tanuma Okitsugu, who was a bakufu junior counselor 若年寄, was stabbed to death within Edo Castle[19]. Thereafter, Tanuma rapidly lost political influence, and was dismissed from the post of rōjū not long after Tokugawa Ieharu's death. Many of his policies were abolished.

---

[18] The trade policy of Nagasaki was also changed, to aim at the export of copper and crops packed in straw bags, and the import of gold and silver for minting.

[19] Sano Masakoto〈佐野政言〉, who stabbed Okitomo, was praised by commoners as a "yonaoshi daimyōjin〈「世直し大明神」〉" (righteous revolutionary).

2 The Culture of the Hōreki and Tenmei Eras

Hōreki-Tenmei Culture

In the mid-18th century, with the development of the commercial economy, many wealthy hyakushō and chōnin, as well as the now-urbanized bushi, became the bearers of culture across a broad range of areas including learning, philosophy and art. Small schools like terakoya〈寺子屋〉 (schools offering elementary education) were established across the country, driving up literacy even among commoners, and increasing the number of readers. In response, many kinds of books and printed materials came to be produced, and along with the movement of goods and people, information distribution intensified. Furthermore, as the contradictions in the bakuhan system became more readily apparent, modern rationalism and new ideologies that criticized bakufu administration came to emerge.

The Dawn of Western Learning

By the 18th century, the mounting criticism engendered by the realities of the waning bakuhan system fueled the rise of new intellectual movements that sought to break away from the old system. Under the sakoku〈鎖国〉 policy, it was difficult to acquire or study Western knowledge, but at the beginning of the 18th century pioneers, such as the astronomer Nishikawa Joken〈西川如見〉 (1648-1724) or the scholar Arai Hakuseki〈新井白石〉[20], explained world geography, goods and customs. Moreover, Shōgun Tokugawa Yoshimune eased the restrictions on importing Chinese translations of Western books, and had scholars like **Aoki Kon'yō**〈青木昆陽〉 (1698-1769) and **Noro Genjō**〈野呂元丈〉

KAITAI SHINSHO
The original book was a 1734 Dutch translation of *Tabulae Anatomicae*, written by the German physician Johan Adam Kulum and published in 1722. The picture is the frontispiece. The frontispiece and anatomical charts were drawn by Odano Naotake〈小田野直武〉, a bushi of Akita Domain〈秋田藩〉 who learned drawing from Hiraga Gennai.

---

[20] Giovanni Battista Sidotti〈シドッチ〉, an Italian missionary, smuggled himself onto Yakushima〈屋久島〉 in 1708 in order to propagate Christianity. He was arrested and confined in the Kirishitan Yashiki〈キリシタン屋敷〉 in Koishikawa, Edo, until he died five years later. Hakuseki, based on knowledge he acquired by interrogating Sidotti, wrote *Sairan Igen*〈『采覧異言』〉 (Sights and Strange Words) and *Seiyō Kibun*〈『西洋紀聞』〉 (Record of Things Heard about the West).

(1693-1761) learn Dutch. This was the intellectual context in which Western learning began with Rangaku, meaning Dutch studies.

Among the fields that made early efforts to incorporate Western learning was the practical science of medicine[21]. Its crowning achievement came in the form of the 1774 publication of the anatomical text *Kaitai Shinsho* 「解体新書」 (New Text on Anatomy), translated by **Maeno Ryōtaku** 前野良沢 (1723-1803) and **Sugita Genpaku** 杉田玄白 (1733-1817). This was followed by the work of Ōtsuki Gentaku 大槻玄沢 (1757-1827) and Udagawa Genzui 宇田川玄随 (1755-97)[22], whereupon Western learning proliferated across various fields. **Inamura Sanpaku** 稲村三伯 (1758-1811), a disciple of Gentaku, compiled ***Haruma Wage*** 「ハルマ和解」, a Dutch-Japanese dictionary, and **Hiraga Gennai** 平賀源内 (1728-79) researched physics based on the scientific knowledge he acquired in Nagasaki[23].

Meanwhile, the southern expansion of Russia triggered studies of geography and maps of both Japan and the world. Consequently, Western learning laid the foundations for the practical exploration of science and knowledge in various fields.

The Rise of Kokugaku and Sonnō Thought

The philological study of Japanese classics, initiated in the Genroku 元禄時代 era by scholars like Keichū 契沖, proceeded from the 18th century with work on *Kojiki* 「古事記」 and *Nihonshoki* 「日本書紀」, evolving into **Kokugaku** 国学, which sought to understand the ways of ancient Japan (kodō 古道). Scholars like **Kada no Azumamaro** 荷田春満 (1669-1736) and his disciple **Kamo no Mabuchi** 賀茂真淵 (1697-1769) endeavored to study ancient Japanese thought, and rejected the influence of foreign thought, including Confucianism and Buddhism, let alone Western learning. **Motoori Norinaga** 本居宣長 (1730-1801), the son of a merchant in Ise 伊勢, studied under

---

[21] In the field of medicine, in opposition to the contemporary trend which valued Yuan〈元〉 and Ming〈明〉 medical practices, the Koihō〈古医方〉 (Classical Medical School) emphasized a return to Han〈漢〉 methods and clinical practice. Around the mid-18th century, Yamawaki Tōyō〈山脇東洋〉 dissected the cadavers of executed criminals and observed the internal organs to compile *Zōshi*〈『蔵志』〉, Japan's first anatomy text.

[22] Ōtsuki Gentaku wrote *Rangaku Kaitei*〈『蘭学階梯』〉 as a Dutch introductory text, and established the Shirandō〈芝蘭堂〉 in Edo, educating numerous disciples there. Meanwhile, Udagawa Genzui translated a Western internal medicine text, producing *Seisetsu Naika Sen'yō*〈『西説内科撰要』〉 (Essentials of Western Internal Medicine).

[23] Hiraga Gennai was born in Takamatsu Domain〈高松藩〉 as the son of an ashigaru〈足軽〉. He interacted with Dutch and Chinese in Nagasaki, and studied honzōgaku〈本草学〉. Later on he went to Edo, where he conducted experiments with electricity using an electrostatic generator (erekiteru〈エレキテル〉), and invented a thermometer and incombustible cloth, which amazed people. A polymath, he also wrote plays and satirical novels. Through reading Dutch books, he acquired Western painting techniques, and taught these skills in Akita where he was invited to develop copper mines.

Kamo no Mabuchi, and endeavored to enhance Kokugaku, including philosophically. He produced *Kojiki-den*『古事記伝』 (Commentary on *Kojiki*), in which he argued for a return to Japan's native spirit and severely criticized what he termed "karagokoro"「漢意」 (foreign mindset). Unlike the Confucianists, who were unable to overcome established conventions, Kokugaku scholars sharply criticized contemporary politics and society. Meanwhile, the blind Kokugaku scholar Hanawa Hokiichi 塙保己一 (1746-1821) dedicated himself to collecting and preserving classic works, establishing the foundation for what later developed into Japanese historical and literary studies[24].

Sonnō 尊王論 (reverence for the tennō) thought, which was connected to Confucianism, advocated respect for the tennō as the sole ruler atop the bakuhan system, and played a key role in **Mitogaku** 水戸学[25]. It was in this context that in the mid-18th century the Kokugaku scholar Takenouchi Shikibu was expelled from Kyōto for lecturing courtiers on Sonnō thought (Hōreki Incident), and Yamagata Daini 山県大弐 (1725-67), a military strategist, was executed for allegedly plotting a coup due to his accusations of bakufu corruption and calls for Sonnō Sekiha 尊王斥覇 (revere the tennō, and reject the hegemon) in Edo (**Meiwa Incident** 明和事件, 1767). However, Sonnō thought itself, as the notion that the shōgun was entrusted to rule by the tennō, was embraced by many as a way to advocate for bakufu authority through respect for the royal court[26].

Intellectual Developments among Commoners

In the early 18th century, **Ishida Baigan** 石田梅岩 (1685-1744), a Kyōto chōnin, founded **Shingaku** 心学 **(learning of the mind)**, in which he added Buddhist and Shintō concepts to Confucian moral precepts, and employed simple language to lecture on ethics to commoners, primarily chōnin. Shingaku, which emphasized the role of chōnin and hyakushō in society and their value as people, was spread across the country by Baigan's

[24] In the Kansei era (1789-1801), Hanawa Hokiichi established the Wagaku Kōdansho〈和学講談所〉 (Academy for Japan Studies) with financial support from the bakufu to compile and publish works like the *Gunsho Ruijū*〈『群書類従』〉 (Collection of Historical Documents).

[25] Mitogaku had its origin in the compilation of the *Dai Nihonshi*〈『大日本史』〉 (Great History of Japan) in Mito Domain. The school, which combined a Shushigaku〈朱子学〉 core with Kokugaku and Shintō concepts, advocated reverence for the tennō and the established feudal order. Early Mitogaku embraced the notion of Sonnō Sekiha – the tennō who rules with virtue is superior to the hegemon who rules with power – derived from the Shushigaku principle of Taigi Meibun〈大義名分論〉 (moral relations among benevolent superiors and loyal subordinates).

[26] In the Kansei era, Takayama Hikokurō〈高山彦九郎〉 traveled across the country propagating Sonnō thought. His followers, like Gamō Kunpei〈蒲生君平〉 and Rai San'yō〈頼山陽〉, also advocated Sonnō ideas through their writings. The first shōgun to actually receive political designation from the court, however, was Tokugawa Iemochi〈徳川家茂〉 in 1863.

CHILDREN ATTENDING A SHINGAKU LECTURE (*ZEN KUN* 〈『前訓』〉 [ELEMENTARY INSTRUCTION]) Children listen to a master's lecture in a Shingaku lecture hall in Kyōto in the late 18th century. There are many children sitting upright, listening to lectures on morals and behavior for daily living delivered in simple language. The seats for boys and girls are divided by a curtain.

disciples like Teshima Toan 手島堵庵 (1718-86) and Nakazawa Dōni 中沢道二 (1725-1803).

By the mid-18th century, several intellectual movements emerged that substantially criticized the basic ethos of feudal society and sought reform. In particular, **Andō Shōeki** 安藤昌益 (?-1762), a physician from Hachinohe 八戸 in Mutsu, wrote *Shizen Shin'eidō* 『自然真営道』 (The Way of Nature and Labor), in which he described an ideal natural society in which everyone farmed and sustained themselves, in order to criticize the class system and society in which the bushi exploited the farmers.

Confucian Education and the School System

Facing these new intellectual currents, the bakufu strongly encouraged the education of the bushi class based on Confucian teaching. It was in this context that, during the Kansei Reforms, the bakufu established Shushigaku as orthodox thought, and transformed the Hayashi/Rin family's 林家 private school into an official bakufu academy, called the Shōheizaka Gakumonjo 昌平坂学問所, in order to recruit talented intellectuals who could shore up the legitimacy of bakufu rule. Meanwhile, by the late 18th century, intellectual movements thrived, including the **Kogaku School** 古学派, the **Secchūgaku** 折衷学派 (**eclectic**) **School**, which adopted a balanced approach, and the **Kōshōgaku** 考証学派 (**documentary evidence**) **School**, an empirical school derived from Secchūgaku.

Domains across the country established **hankō** 藩校 (domain schools, also called hangaku 藩学) for the education of bushi and their children. Initially, most hankō taught Confucianism, first and foremost of the Shushigaku variety, as well as martial arts, but gradually they incorporated Rangaku and Kokugaku as well, and introduced class management systems based on the age and proficiency levels of their students.

In some domains, **gōkō** (or gōgaku) were established with domain funding to educate bushi and commoners. One of the earliest examples of these was the Shizutani Gakkō, founded in Shizutani Village in Okayama Domain by Lord Ikeda Mitsumasa in the late 17th century. Another was the **Kaitokudō** in Ōsaka, established in the first half of the 18th century with financial support from the chōnin. Around the time of the Kansei Reforms, the school, headed by Nakai Chikuzan (1730-1804), was teaching the chōnin Shushigaku and Yangming learning, and produced unorthodox chōnin scholars such as **Tominaga Nakamoto** (1715-46) and **Yamagata Bantō** (1748-1821)[27].

Meanwhile, at the individual level, various private schools were established by bushi, scholars and chōnin alike to teach Confucianism, Kokugaku, Rangaku, and so on. As for schools teaching Confucianism, major examples include the Kogidō, founded in Kyōto by Itō Jinsai in the latter half of the 17th century, and the Ken'enjuku, which was started by Ogyū Sorai in Edo in the first half of the 18th century. Other prominent schools included the Suzunoya, founded in Matsusaka Domain in Ise by the Kokugaku scholar Motoori Norinaga, and the Shirandō, begun in Edo by the Rangaku scholar Ōtsuki Gentaku.

In terms of elementary education for commoners, numerous **terakoya** were opened in urban and rural areas alike. Terakoya were managed by people like village officials, Buddhist monks, Shintō priests, or wealthy chōnin. Terakoya teachers used published texts to impart practical knowledge like reading, writing, and arithmetic using an abacus, as well as subjects like bakufu law and morality. Such teachers included masterless bushi and women. Education for girls also proliferated, based on texts like *Onna Daigaku* (Great Learning for Women), which was compiled from Kaibara Ekiken's writings for instructing women how to behave. Such education for commoners contributed greatly to the development of commoners' culture in the latter half of the early modern period.

Literature and Art

Literature in the mid-Edo period came to focus on familiar political and social matters, and with the spread of publishing and commercial booklenders (kashihon'ya), came to be widely enjoyed by commoners.

In fiction, as ukiyozōshi became less popular, kusazōshi, works with attractive illustrations, and **sharebon**, books that portrayed the pleasure quarters in Edo, pro-

[27] Both Tominaga and Yamagata were skeptical about established teachings, such as Confucianism and Buddhism, from a rationalist perspective.

KŌSHODŌ〈耕書堂〉(*EHON AZUMA ASOBI* 〈『画本東都遊』〉 [ILLUSTRATED BOOK OF AMUSEMENTS IN EDO])
Tsutaya Jūzaburō〈蔦屋重三郎〉 ran the bookshop Kōshodō, and published various books such as the kibyōshi of Koikawa Harumachi〈恋川春町〉 and the sharebon of Santō Kyōden, as well as pictures by Kitagawa Utamaro or Tōshūsai Sharaku. In 1791, due to having published Santō Kyōden's sharebon, half of his fortune was confiscated.

liferated. **Kibyōshi** 黄表紙, works featuring satirical drawings, also sold well. During the Kansei Reforms, sharebon and kibyōshi came to be strictly regulated, leading to **Santō Kyōden** 山東京伝 (1761-1816), one of the most popular authors of these genres, being punished. As for haikai 俳諧, Buson 蕪村 (1716-83) in Kyōto composed picturesque verses, while Karai Senryū 柄井川柳 (1718-90) established **senryū** 川柳, which satirized various social affairs and customs through the style of haiku 俳句, as a literary genre. Along with senryū, **kyōka** 狂歌 also became popular. Its representative authors included Ōta Nanpo 大田南畝 (Shokusanjin 蜀山人, 1749-1823) and Ishikawa Masamochi 石川雅望 (Yadoya no Meshimori 宿屋飯盛, 1753-1830). Some of these works sharply satirized rulers, or offered ironic commentary on society.

In Jōruri 浄瑠璃, Takeda Izumo II 竹田出雲（2世） (1691-1756) in the early 18th century, and Chikamatsu Hanji 近松半二 (1725-83) who emerged in the Tenmei era, both left exemplary works. As for Kabuki 歌舞伎, which had been popular, mainly in Edo, since the latter half of the 18th century, the Edo Sanza 江戸三座 (three major Edo theatres) – Nakamura-za 中村座, Ichimura-za 市村座, and Morita-za 森田座 – flourished. As Kabuki gradually overtook Jōruri in popularity, the latter survived as Uta Jōruri 唄浄瑠璃 (narrative music, also called Zashiki Jōruri 座敷浄瑠璃), performed in rooms without puppets, in styles such as Icchū-bushi 一中節, Tokiwazu-bushi 常磐津節, and Kiyomoto-bushi 清元節.

Painting

Ukiyoe 浮世絵, which were established by Hishikawa Moronobu 菱川師宣 at the end of the 17th century, were first produced as illustrations for books, but by the mid-18th century became an independent artistic genre with the multicolor prints (**nishiki-e** 錦絵) of **Suzuki Harunobu** 鈴木春信 (1725?-70). With the development of woodcut techniques and the printing business, ukiyoe entered a golden age. In the Kansei era, major artists emerged one after another: **Kitagawa Utamaro** 喜多川歌麿 (1753?-1806) produced numerous pictures of beautiful women, and **Tōshūsai Sharaku** 東洲斎写楽 (dates unknown) fully utilized the ōkubie 大首絵 (close-up portraiture) style to make many distinctive works depicting Kabuki actors and Sumō 相撲 wrestlers.

In traditional painting, the Maruyama 円山派 School, begun by **Maruyama Ōkyo** 円山応挙 (1733-95), valued sketching from reality, and adapted perspective to produce naturalistic works that appeared three-dimensional. Meanwhile, bunjinga 文人画, a style of painting inspired by Ming and Qing 清 styles, proliferated and became popular among some intellectuals. **Ike no Taiga** 池大雅 (1723-76) and Buson in the late 18th century were major artists of this style[28].

Western-style painting, which had been introduced by Westerners at the beginning of the early modern era, had declined, but revived with the rise of Rangaku and the import of painting implements and artistic techniques through Nagasaki. By the late 18th century, **Shiba Kōkan** 司馬江漢 (1747-1818) and **Aōdō Denzen** 亜欧堂田善 (1748-1822) were among those active in Western-style painting. Kōkan also produced copperplate engravings (**dōbanga** 銅版画) using techniques he learned from Hiraga Gennai[29].

GOJŌ "CHI"〈五常「智」〉(THE FIVE VIRTUES: WISDOM, BY SUZUKI HARUNOBU)
A nishiki-e printed in 1767. The picture, one of a series that depicts the five virtues of Confucianism, shows a girl practicing her handwriting with a female teacher. The text in the upper right reads: "Wisdom. If born into a world that follows the Way, it can only be that, if you know one thing, you will know all things."

[28] Bunjinga were works created by literati or scholars who were not specialist artists. As Chinese artwork of this style, known as "nanga〈南画〉," were frequently made by literati or scholars, the term carried the same meaning in Japan. *Jūben Jūgizu*〈「十便十宜図」〉(Ten Conveniences and Ten Goods), a set of collaborative works by Ike no Taiga and Buson, is particularly famous.

[29] In this context, in Akita Domain an original type of painting emerged that combined Japanese and Western styles, called Akita Ranga〈秋田蘭画〉.

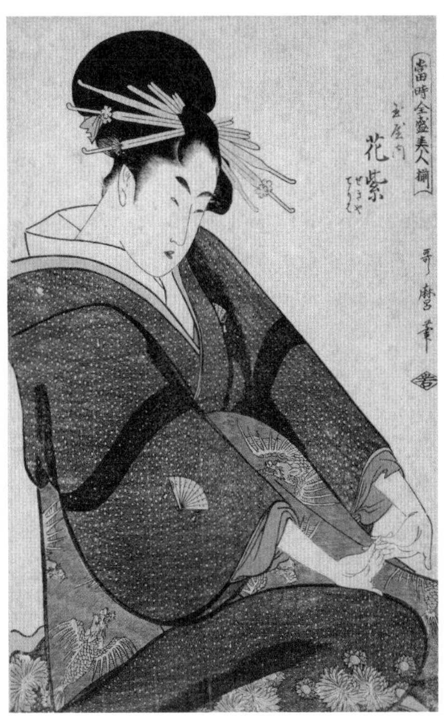

TŌJI ZENSEI BIJIN ZOROE: TAMAYAUCHI HANA-MURASAKI〈当時全盛美人揃「玉屋内花紫」〉(ARRAY OF PRESENT-DAY BEAUTIES: COURTESAN HANA-MURASAKI OF THE TAMAYA, BY KITAGAWA UTAMARO)

One of a series of portraits of beauties of the pleasure quarters. The picture portrays the woman's sensual posture, and vividly renders the designs of her kimono〈着物〉and obi〈帯〉. The beautiful image is powerful enough to make one forget the harsh reality such women faced.

SANDAI-ME ŌTANI ONIJI NO YAKKO EDOBĒ〈三代目大谷鬼次の奴江戸兵衛〉(ŌTANI ONIJI III IN THE ROLE OF THE SERVANT EDOBĒ, BY TŌSHŪSAI SHARAKU)

A scene from the play *Koi Nyōbō Somewake Tazuna*〈「恋女房染分手綱」〉performed in 1794. With his ōkubie technique, Sharaku depicts a yakko (servant of a bushi household) trying to steal money, with an expression that almost suggests he understands the actor's personality.

JŪBEN JŪGIZU, CHŌBENZU〈釣便図〉(FISHING CONVENIENCES, BY IKE NO TAIGA AND BUSON)

Length, breadth 17.9 cm.

3 The Decline of the Bakufu and the Dawn of Modern Japan

The Kansei Reforms

In the mid-17th century, a series of イギリス革命 upheavals shook England (1640-60), while at the end of the 18th century, the American War of Independence アメリカ独立革命 (1775-83) and the French Revolution フランス革命 (1789-99) occurred. Russia began to pursue the development of Siberia, while the westward expansion of the United States (US) led to its advancement into the Pacific Ocean by the early 19th century.

The world was dramatically entering the modern age. Against this backdrop, vessels from Russia, the United Kingdom (UK) and the US began to appear in the waters around Japan, forcing the bakufu to confront the shifting global situation and change its foreign policy.

In the fifth month of 1787, the year after Tanuma Okitsugu's resignation, a number of destructive riots broke out in more than 30 major cities including Edo and Ōsaka – **Tenmei no Uchikowashi** 天明の打ちこわし (Tenmei Riots). The riots in Edo were especially violent, with many businesses like those of rice merchants destroyed, leaving the bakufu stunned. To deal with the dire situation, **Matsudaira Sadanobu** 松平定信 (1758-1829)[30], the lord of Shirakawa Domain, was appointed rōjū to serve as the advisor to the eleventh shōgun, Tokugawa Ienari 徳川家斉 (1773-1841).

Sensing the threats both from within the country as well as from abroad, Sadanobu reviewed the policies of the Tanuma era and began to carry out administrative reforms. He improved the bakufu's financial situation, by revitalizing farming villages endangered by famine; restored peace and order in Edo, which had been damaged by the riots; and implemented diplomatic strategies to deal with the foreign powers, first and foremost Russia. These reforms carried out by Sadanobu are termed the **Kansei Reforms** 寛政の改革.

First of all, to revive the devastated villages, Sadanobu restricted the flow of hyakushō migrating from areas suffering from severe population decline – in particular, Mutsu and the provinces of the northern Kantō region – to seek work outside their home provinces. He also approved loans made to hyakushō across the country to restore arable land, and, in order to prepare for famines, he had each area establish rice

[30] Sadanobu was a son of Tayasu Munetake and thus a grandson of the 8th shōgun, Tokugawa Yoshimune. After his retirement, Sadanobu wrote *Kagetsu Zōshi* 〈『花月草紙』〉, a collection of essays, and *Uge no Hitokoto* 〈『宇下人言』〉, an autobiography.

storehouses (shasō 社倉 and gisō 義倉) to store rice for emergencies (a system called **kakoimai** 囲米).

Another pillar of the Kansei Reforms was urban policy. In Edo, which had suffered severely from the riots, wealthy merchants, mainly those in the money-changing business, were recruited by the bakufu[31] to use their financial power to carry out reforms. First, in order to stabilize prices, an order was issued to cut the prices of rice and commodities, while financial support was offered as incentive to people without jobs to return to farming villages (**Kyūri Kinō-rei** 旧里帰農令). Next, to ensure public safety, a thorough population census was conducted, and at the same time a labor camp was established on Ishikawajima 石川島 to forcibly accommodate the mushukunin 無宿人 (drifters). In the camp, people were registered and trained to practice a profession. In Edo, each chō was ordered to cut its expenses, 70% of the savings (**shichibu tsumikin** 七分積金) from which were then invested in the newly-established Edo Machi Kaisho 江戸町会所 (City Savings Association) to use for saving rice and monetary reserves to assist the poor in the event of famine or natural disaster.

To ease the burdens on bakufu officials responsible for administrative reform, and on the hatamoto and gokenin who served as deputies for bakufu territories, Sadanobu issued a debt cancellation edict (**Kien-rei** 棄捐令), and had the **fudasashi** 札差 – financial agents who handled rice and so forth – waive the loans they had made[32]. He also ordered the hatamoto to devote themselves to martial training, and issued the **Kansei Igaku no Kin** 寛政異学の禁 (Kansei Prohibition of Heterodox Learning). With this edict, Sadanobu reestablished Shushigaku as orthodoxy, and, in 1790, he prohibited the Yushima Seidō 湯島聖堂 from studying or lecturing on other disciplines of knowledge. He also promoted the recruitment of people through examinations. The inability of the Hayashi / Rin family to produce people of talent led Matsudaira to appoint other intellectuals as official

LECTURE AT THE SEIDŌ GAKUMONJO (*SEIDŌ KŌSHAKUZU* 〈聖堂講釈図〉)
In the Yushima Seidō academy, a lecture by a Confucian scholar (ozashiki kōshaku 〈御座敷講釈〉) was held every month, and bushi, mainly direct retainers to the bakufu, attended.

[31] Those merchants were called Kanjōsho Goyōtashi 〈勘定所御用達〉 (Shōgunal Purveyors), and numbered ten.

[32] A loan office was established to provide financial assistance to hatamoto through providing low-interest loans.

Confucian scholars, such as Shibano Ritsuzan 柴野栗山 (1736-1807), Bitō Jishū 尾藤二洲 (1747-1813) and Okada Kansen 岡田寒泉 (1740-1816)[33].

At the same time, Sadanobu issued an edict strictly restricting private publishing (**Shuppan Tōsei-rei** 出版統制令) in order to suppress satire and criticism of the administration, as well as to protect public morals. He banned the works of Hayashi Shihei 林子平 (1738-93), such as *Sangoku Tsūran Zusetsu* 『三国通覧図説』 (Illustrated Description of Three Countries) and *Kaikoku Heidan* 『海国兵談』 (On the Military Defense of Maritime Countries), arguing that they constituted criticism of the bakufu's coastal defense policy. He also prohibited the publication of kibyōshi and sharebon as immoral books, and punished their publishers[34]. Even in farming villages, social morals were strictly enforced; popular plays, for instance, were often banned.

Although the Kansei Reforms appeared to improve social order and reestablish bakufu authority temporarily, they also provoked public fury due to their strict controls and sumptuary edicts. Moreover, the bakufu had to deal with issues emerging in the court. In 1789, the court requested the bakufu's permission to grant the title of daijō tennō 太上天皇 to Kōkaku Tennō's father, Royal Prince Kan'in no Miya Sukehito 閑院宮典仁親王 (1733-94). However, Sadanobu refused. When the bakufu liaisons 武家伝奏 to the court, on behalf of the courtiers, continued to press the issue, in 1793 Sadanobu accused them of failing to stand with the bakufu, and had them punished. This incident came to be called **Songō Ikken** 「尊号一件」 (Honorary Title Incident). Due to a conflict with Shōgun Ienari over his handling of the incident, Sadanobu was left with no choice but to resign after having served as a rōjū for just over six years. The incident also heralded the end of the cooperative relationship between the bakufu and the court. While the bakufu continued to function as the administration until the end of the Edo period, the authority of the tennō became increasingly significant as the period drew to a close.

Like the bakufu, various individual domains also suffered from financial crises resulting from the devastation of farmland and poor tax revenues. In order to deal with the crisis, especially during the Kansei era (1789-1801) many daimyō took up the lead themselves, aiming to overcome financial difficulties and consolidate their authority by tightening regulations, encouraging thriftiness in their domains, and reforming their administrations. To revitalize farming villages, domains worked to encourage the

---

[33] These three figures were called the "Three Savants of the Kansei Era〈「寛政の三博士」〉." Eventually, Okada Kansen was transferred to a deputy post, and Koga Seiri〈古賀精里〉 was appointed his successor. After seven years, the Yushima Seidō became an official school and was renamed the Shōheizaka Gakumonjo.

[34] Those who were punished included Santō Kyōden, an author of sharebon, Koikawa Harumachi, an author of kibyōshi, and Tsutaya Jūzaburō, a publisher.

production of regional specialties, and strengthen their monopoly thereof (**senbaisei**). Moreover, they established hankō to recruit capable human resources. Those daimyō whose reforms met with great success, such as Hosokawa Shigekata (1720-85) of Kumamoto Domain, Uesugi Harunori (1751-1822) of Yonezawa Domain, and Satake Yoshimasa (1775-1815) of Akita Domain, were held in high esteem.

Threats to the Sakoku Policy

Another issue Matsudaira Sadanobu needed to tackle was how to deal with foreign threats, particularly that of Russia. In 1789, a riot broke out among the Ainu on Kunashiri (Kunashir). The riot was suppressed by Matsumae Domain, but the bakufu was concerned about the possibility of a coalition between the Ainu and Russia. It was precisely at this time, when the bakufu was especially wary of Russia, that in 1792 **Adam Laksman** (1766-96?), a Russian envoy, arrived in Nemuro to return Japanese castaways to their home country[35], and demanded a trade agreement with Japan. Laksman's demands to be permitted to enter Edo Bay prompted the bakufu to order various domains to reinforce the coastal defenses of Edo Bay and Ezochi.

By this time, Russians had already landed on Etorofu (Iturup) and been trading with the Ainu there. Then in 1798, the bakufu sent an expedition led by **Kondō Jūzō** (1771-1829) and **Mogami Tokunai** to explore the island and erect a signpost stating "Etorofu of Great Japan." The idea was to clearly demarcate the border with Russia as outside the island. In 1800, the bakufu dispatched 100 members of the Hachiōji Guards (Hachiōji Sennin Dōshin) to settle in Ezochi, and in 1802 put Eastern Ezochi

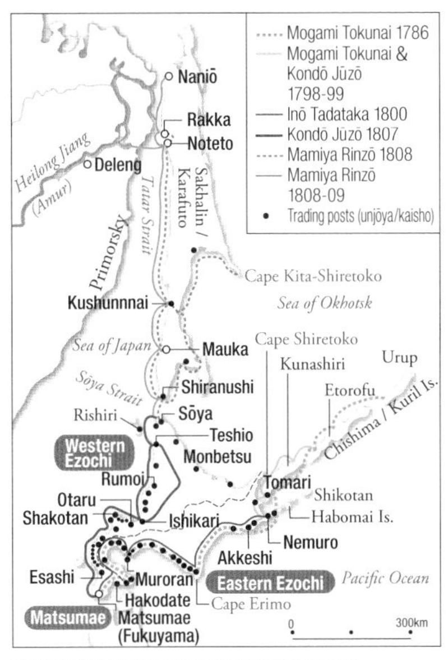

EXPEDITION MAP OF NORTHERN TERRITORY

[35] Daikokuya Kōdayū〈大黒屋光太夫〉, a boatman from Ise, encountered a storm and was shipwrecked on the Aleutian Islands. He was rescued there by Russians, and went to the Russian capital, St. Petersburg, where he was received by Empress Catherine the Great〈エカチェリーナ２世〉. He was then taken back to Japan. Based on Kōdayū's account of his journey, Katsuragawa Hoshū〈桂川甫周〉 wrote *Hokusa Bunryaku*〈『北槎聞略』〉.

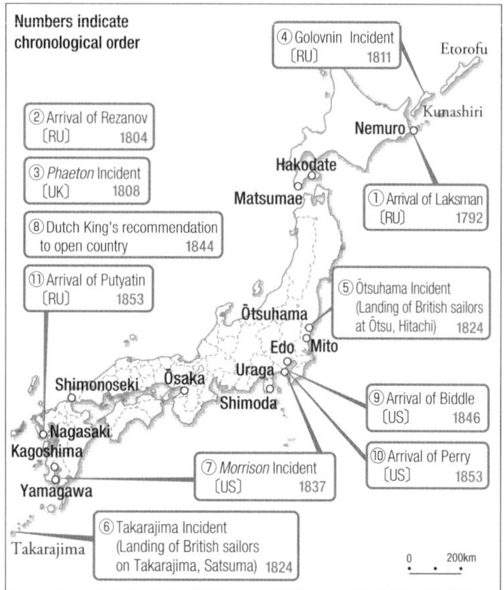

MAP SHOWING ARRIVALS OF FOREIGN SHIPS FROM GREAT POWERS

under its perpetual control, incorporating the Ainu inhabitants as Wajin (和人)[36].

In 1804, **Nikolai Rezanov** (レザノフ) (1764?-1807), a Russian envoy, landed in Nagasaki with the entrance permit that Laxman had brought back to Russia, but the bakufu impolitely dismissed him, resulting in the Russian vessel attacking Sakhalin (Karafuto (樺太)) and Etorofu. As a cannon firefight with a foreign country was unprecedented, the bakufu was shaken by this development. Consequently, the bakufu further strengthened coastal defenses, and in 1807, put Matsumae Domain and the entirety of Ezochi under its direct jurisdiction, with the **Matsumae Bugyō** (松前奉行) responsible for the whole territory, and each of the domains in the Tōhoku (東北) region responsible for providing guards[37]. In the following year, the bakufu sent **Mamiya Rinzō** (間宮林蔵) (1775?-1844) to explore Sakhalin and the coast across the sea channel. Later, when the relationship with Russia improved in the wake of the **Golovnin Incident** (ゴローウニン事件)[38], the bakufu restored Matsumae Domain in Ezochi in 1821.

On top of the foreign tensions in the northern territories, what stunned the bakufu even more was the intrusion of the HMS *Phaeton*, a British frigate, into Nagasaki Bay in 1808. The ship, seeking to capture an enemy Dutch vessel, sailed into the bay and took Dutch representatives hostage to demand supplies of fuel and

---

[36] The bakufu implemented a policy of assimilation regarding the Ainu, making them follow Japanese customs and appointing their chiefs as magistrates.

[37] In the case of Aizu Domain, to prepare for Russian attacks they dispatched troops to Ezochi, which trained on the coasts as gunners, and built batteries for artillery training.

[38] In 1811, Vasily Golovnin, a Russian naval captain, landed on Kunashiri and was captured by Japanese guards. He was sent to Hakodate〈箱館〉 in Matsumae Domain, where he was imprisoned. In retaliation, the following year Russia detained Takadaya Kahē〈高田屋嘉兵衛〉, a merchant from Awaji〈淡路〉 Province who had discovered an Etorofu sea route. Kahē was returned in 1813, and with his help Golovnin was released, thereby settling the incident.

food, whereupon it departed (***Phaeton* Incident**(フェートン号事件))[39]. Shortly after the incident, the bakufu ordered both Shirakawa and Aizu(会津藩) Domains to guard the coast of Edo Bay.

As British and American vessels continued to appear sporadically in neighboring waters, the bakufu ordered daimyō across the country to build forts and deploy cannon along the coast. Formerly, the bakufu had maintained a policy of providing food, water and fuel to foreign vessels in order to prevent conflicts between crews and residents, but in 1825, it issued the **Ikokusen**(異国船打払令) **Uchiharai-rei** (**Foreign Vessel Exclusion Edict**, also called the **Muninen**(無二念打払令) **Uchiharai-rei**), and ordered that foreign ships be repelled[40]. The bakufu now faced foreign powers that existed outside of the conventional diplomatic order structured by the four gateways, and which possessed military might. It thus assumed that these new powers, like the UK and Russia, were enemies.

The Bunka and Bunsei Eras

After Matsudaira Sadanobu's resignation from the rōjū post, Tokugawa Ienari, the eleventh shōgun, continued in office during the Bunka(文化期) and Bunsei(文政期) eras. Even after he passed the position to Tokugawa Ieyoshi(徳川家慶) (1793-1853) in 1837, Ienari continued to wield real power as the Ōgosho(大御所) (retired shōgun; hence the term **Ōgosho Seiji**(大御所政治), government by Ōgosho). During the approximately fifty years of Ienari's rule, the simple and frugal ethos of the Kansei Reforms continued to be embraced until the Bunka era (1804-18). However, by the dawn of the Bunsei era (1818-30), the circulation of low-quality coinage proliferated, leading to the bakufu becoming affluent despite soaring prices, and the shōgun and ladies of the Ōoku(大奥) (women's quarters in Edo Castle) led luxurious lives. The flourishing economic activity of merchants fueled many cultural activities among commoners, mainly in urban areas.

However, while the wealthy farmers and landowners became more powerful, many hyakushō lost their land, and the amount of ruined farmland increased. In the farming villages surrounding Edo, mushukunin and bakuto(博徒) (gamblers) contrib-

---

[39] In the early 19th century, the UK was at war with France. After Napoleon I〈ナポレオン1世〉 conquered the Netherlands, the UK had begun to capture Dutch military bases in Asia. Accused of failing in his duty by not preventing the incident, Matsudaira Yasuhide〈松平康英〉, the Nagasaki bugyō, took responsibility by committing suicide. Furthermore, the daimyō of Saga Domain〈佐賀藩〉, who was responsible for the defense of Nagasaki, was also punished.

[40] Ships from China, Korea, or the Ryūkyū Islands were not subject to the exclusion, while Dutch ships were to be repelled from ports except Nagasaki. In 1811, the bakufu changed the reception venue for the Korean envoys (Chōsen Tsūshinshi〈朝鮮通信使〉) from Edo to Tsushima〈対馬〉. This change in protocol, called Ekichi Heirei〈易地聘礼〉, was done not only for financial reasons, but also because of rising opposition to the conventional treatment of Korea as possessing equal status to Japan.

uted to social unrest, and in 1805 the bakufu established the **Kantō Torishimari Shutsuyaku** 関東取締出役 **(Kantō Regulatory Patrol**, a sort of police)[41] to deal with criminals. Moreover, 1827 witnessed the development of **yoseba kumiai** 寄場組合 (communal policing associations), in which the villages in a region would cooperate to maintain public order for the region irrespective of if the land belonged to the bakufu, temples and shrines, or private landowners.

The Ōshio Heihachirō Revolt

After the Tenmei Famine, the climate during the Kansei, Bunka and Bunsei eras was relatively favorable, and agricultural production stabilized. However, during the Tenpō 天保年期 era (1832-33), crop harvests deteriorated dramatically to less than half of the previous amount. This resulted in rice shortages across the country, triggering a severe famine (**Tenpō Famine** 天保の飢饉). Rural and urban communities alike were filled with destitute people, hyakushō ikki and riots were rampant, and neither the bakufu nor the domains could find effective measures to resolve the situation.

The famine in 1836 was especially harsh, leading to ikki in the Gunnai 郡内地方 region of Kai 甲斐国 Province and Kamo 加茂郡 District in Mikawa 三河国 Province, both of which had already been suffering from serious rice shortages[42].

The famine had a serious impact in Ōsaka as well, causing many to starve to death. While wealthy merchants made great profits by buying up rice, the Ōsaka Machi-bugyō left the starving without any relief measures, and despite the rice shortage continued to ship large quantities of rice from Ōsaka to Edo. Seeing this situation, **Ōshio Heihachirō** 大塩平八郎 (1793-1837), a former yoriki 与力 (assistant magistrate) in the Ōsaka Machi-bugyō's office as well as a Yangming scholar, took up arms by mobilizing his followers and commoners to relieve the poor[43]. However, his uprising was suppressed in just half a day (**Ōshio Heihachirō Revolt** 大塩の乱). This revolt, which had been plotted

---

[41] Members of the Kantō Torishimari Shutsuyaku were chosen from officials serving magistrates in the Kantō region. Initially, there were eight members, who worked in pairs. They patrolled the eight provinces comprising the Kantō region, and arrested mushukunin and bakuto regardless of which authority managed the area they were in.

[42] The movements in the Gunnai and Kamo regions were hyakushō ikki, the former consisting of some 10,000 participants across some 80 villages, and the latter about 12,000 people across some 240 villages. Both movements, which were large-scale ikki that broke out in territories under the bakufu's direct control, dealt significant blows to the bakufu's authority.

[43] Ōshio, who had retired, established a private school called Senshindō〈洗心洞〉in his residence, gathered together disciples, and taught Yangming philosophy. To aid the poor, he sold his collection of books for more than 660 ryō〈両〉, which he then divided among the poor before launching his revolt.

ŌSHIO HEIHACHIRŌ REVOLT
(*DESHIO HIKISHIO KANZOKU MONJŪKI* 〈『出潮引汐奸賊聞集記』〉 [RECORD OF THE RISE AND FALL OF A REBEL], PART)
Ōshio Heihachiro and his followers are shown pulling hand-made cannons, waving flags and setting fires.

by a former official and occurred in Ōsaka, a major city under the bakufu's direct administration, left the bakufu and domains stunned.

The impact of the uprising spread across the country and fueled further unrest. For instance, Ikuta Yorozu 生田万 (1801-37), a Kokugaku scholar, attacked a jinya 陣屋 (bakufu encampment) in Kashiwazaki 柏崎 in Echigo 越後 Province, claiming he was a disciple of Ōshio (**Ikuta Yorozu Revolt** 生田万の乱). Hyakushō ikki sympathizing with Ōshio's revolt also broke out[44].

On top of the domestic unrest, the bakufu also faced foreign threats. In 1837, the *Morrison*, an American merchant ship, sailed to Uraga 浦賀 to return seven Japanese castaways and seek a trade agreement with Japan. However, following the Ikokusen Uchiharai-rei, the bakufu repelled the ship (***Morrison* Incident** モリソン号事件).

This incident prompted **Watanabe Kazan** 渡辺崋山 (1793-1841) to write ***Shinkiron*** 『慎機論』 (**Arguments for Restraint during Crises**), and **Takano Chōei** 高野長英 (1804-50) to write ***Bojutsu Yume Monogatari*** 『戊戌夢物語』 (**An Account of a Dream in 1838**). Both scholars' works criticized bakufu foreign policy. However, in the following year the bakufu severely punished both authors (**Bansha no Goku** 蛮社の獄**, imprisonment of scholars of Western learning**)[45].

Shortly thereafter, news of the First Opium War アヘン戦争 (1840-42) reached the bakufu.

---

[44] Edo also suffered social instability due to the rice shortages, but the bakufu established shelters and gave rice and money to the poor as charity to prevent riots beforehand.

[45] Watanabe Kazan, a karō 〈家老〉 (house elder) of Tahara Domain 〈田原藩〉 in Mikawa Province, was punished with permanent house arrest, and Takano Chōei, a physician from Mizusawa 〈水沢〉 in Mutsu Province, was sentenced to life imprisonment. Eventually, both committed suicide. Both had belonged to an intellectual circle called the Shōshikai 〈尚歯会〉, the other members of which were arrested at the same time. However, the other members were later judged not guilty, and released.

The Tenpō Reforms

Facing these domestic and external threats, after the death of Tokugawa Ienari in 1841 the bakufu, under the leadership of the rōjū **Mizuno Tadakuni** 水野忠邦 (1794-1851), undertook the **Tenpō Reforms** 天保の改革 to shore up its authority.

Following the policies of the Kyōhō and Kansei Reforms, Tadakuni issued sumptuary edicts, prohibiting even the shōgun and ladies of the Ōoku from consuming luxurious commodities or wearing ostentatious clothes. Commoners' lifestyles were also strictly regulated[46]. Moreover, the Edo census control 人別改め was intensified, hyakushō were forbidden from migrating in search of jobs, and an order to make people who had drifted to Edo return to their farms (**Hitogaeshi no Hō** 人返しの法)[47] was issued, in an attempt to revitalize farming villages devastated by the Tenpō Famine. The land reclamation work on Inba-numa 印旛沼 swamp through drainage also resumed.

Tadakuni concluded that the primary cause for the soaring prices was the monopoly held by the kabunakama guilds, such as Tokumi Toiya 十組問屋, on commodity distribution in markets in the Kansai region. Consequently, he ordered the dissolution of the guilds (**Kabunakama no Kaisan** 株仲間の解散). In carrying out this dissolution, the bakufu expected that prices would be stabilized through free trade among non-guild merchants in Edo and local merchants in the surrounding areas. However, the real reason for the price increases was the decline in the influx of commodities from the production regions into the western markets. As a result, the dissolution order just compounded the problem by reducing commodity imports into Edo[48]. As the high prices also increased the financial burden on the hatamoto and gokenin, the bakufu issued another debt cancellation edict, and made financers like the fudasashi offer low-interest loans. The severe restrictions on lifestyle and the continuing recession increased public dissatisfaction.

Meanwhile, in order to relieve the financial burden of Kawagoe 川越藩 Domain, which had been responsible for the coastal defense of Sagami Bay 相模湾, in 1840 the bakufu

---

[46] Expensive sweets and cuisine were also banned. The number of yose〈寄席〉(Japanese vaudeville) theatres in Edo was reduced from 211 to 15, the three great Kabuki theatres〈歌舞伎（三座）〉were relocated to the vicinity of Asakusa, and actors were ordered to put on amigasa〈編笠〉(braided straw hats) when walking outside. Authors of ninjōbon〈人情本〉(romantic novellas and erotica), like Tamenaga Shunsui〈為永春水〉, were also punished.

[47] The order expelled many mushukunin and rōnin〈浪人〉from Edo, which resulted in the farming villages around Edo becoming less safe.

[48] Crops and commodities bound for the markets of the western regions were often bought up by Utsumibune〈内海船〉(also called Bishū Kaisen〈尾州廻船〉) in Shimonoseki or other places in the Seto Inland Sea before they arrived at their destinations. The basic distribution networks had begun to break down. Consequently, ten years after the dissolution order, the kabunakama were permitted to reform again.

ordered an exchange of territories among Kawagoe, Shōnai 庄内藩, and Nagaoka 長岡藩 Domains[49]. However, the order was rescinded due to opposition from the inhabitants. The fact that the bakufu had decided to make the exchange but was unable to enforce its order demonstrated the independent power domains could exert against the bakufu.

In 1843, Shōgun Ieyoshi attempted to renew the bakufu's authority by making a pilgrimage to Nikkō for the first time in 67 years, but this backfired. The immense expenses worsened the financial crisis, and the forced mobilization of people provoked anger among the farmers.

That same year, Mizuno Tadakuni attempted to stabilize bakufu finances and strengthen the country's defenses by issuing the **Jōchi-rei** 上知令 (**Requisition Edict**, also called Agechi-rei), that would put the lands around Edo and Ōsaka – amounting to half a million koku in value – under the direct control of the bakufu. Although he had prepared alternative lands for compensation, the fudai daimyō and hatamoto were staunchly opposed and the order could not be carried out. Tadakuni had to resign his rōjū post, which also resulted in the cancellation of the Inba-numa reclamation project. The failure of the reforms clearly demonstrated how the bakufu's authority had declined.

The Transformation of the Economy

The bakuhan system, which was based on collecting rice taxes from crop production, had begun to break down across the country, a fact that had become increasingly obvious by the time of the Tenpō Famine. By the mid-19th century, the population of Hitachi and Shimotsuke 下野国 Provinces, in the northern Kantō region, had fallen by about 30% from what it had been in the Kyōhō era (1716-36), resulting in the ruination of much farmland. On the other hand, in some regions where agricultural production increased, such as Suō 周防 and Satsuma 薩摩, the population had grown by about 60%.

Meanwhile, mainly in the Kinai 畿内 region, hyakushō or local merchants in areas of agricultural production sought free distribution for rapeseed, cotton, and kinpi 金肥, in opposition to the monopoly on distribution enjoyed by the kabunakama and the like in Ōsaka. This resulted in a major dispute (called kokuso 国訴 or kuniso, a plea for commercial respite) involving a range of provinces and districts.

All these changes in the social and economic structure constituted threats to the bakuhan system, which depended on villages and hyakushō. Countermeasures were

---

[49] The territorial exchange, known as **Sanpō Ryōchigae**〈三方領知替え〉, aimed to relocate Kawagoe Domain to the wealthy Shōnai Domain, Shōnai Domain to Echigo Nagaoka Domain, and Echigo Nagaoka Domain to Kawagoe Domain.

PRODUCTION OF YŪKIJIMA〈結城縞〉(*OWARI MEISHO ZUE* 〈「尾張名所図会」〉 [ILLUSTRATIONS OF FAMOUS SITES IN OWARI])
By the mid-Edo period, the production of cotton textiles had spread across the country. Yūkijima, shown in the picture, was a high-grade product made by using advanced technology to interweave fine cotton threads and silk threads. This production thrived in western Owari from the early 19th century. The image depicts many women at takabata〈高機〉 looms in a textile factory.

clearly needed. Attempts were made to recover farmland and revitalize communities in various regions, such as through **Ninomiya Sontoku** [二宮尊徳] (or Kinjirō [（金次郎）], 1787-1856)'s financial reconstruction proposals (**Hōtoku Shihō** [報徳仕法]) or the **Seigaku** [性学] (a philosophy combining morals and economics) teachings of **Ōhara Yūgaku** [大原幽学] (1797?-1858). However, with funding from urban merchants, in many villages the production, processing, and transportation of commercial crops and manufactures were already well organized. Many forms of commerce and profession had developed, while the number of poor farmers making their living from day labor was increasing, all of which depleted the farming population that the bakufu counted on. Agricultural reform alone was insufficient to rescue the bakuhan system from crisis.

On top of this, by the early 19th century some local landowners and merchants began operating cottage industries. Some implemented specialized production processes for handicraft production, and recruited yet more people away from agriculture. This form of production, namely **proto-factory production** [工場制手工業], began to spread by the Tenpō period (1830-44), examples being the cotton textile industry in the Ōsaka and Owari [尾張] regions, and the silk textile industry in the northern Kantō regions such as Kiryū [桐生] and Ashikaga [足利][50].

As a means of absorbing the profits generated by these new economic activities, **domain-run industries** [藩営工業] and **domain monopolies** [藩専売制], which had already been seen to some extent, spread across the country, becoming a significant focus for domain financial reform.

The Rise of the Royal Court and Powerful Domains

As domestic and foreign threats (naiyū gaikan [「内憂外患」]) became increasingly serious, the bakufu's power weakened and it became unable to assert its authority, prompting a turn to

[50] Proto-factory production had already been seen in the first half of the Edo period in the sake brewing industry in Itami〈伊丹〉, Ikeda〈池田〉, and Nada〈灘〉 in the Settsu region〈摂津〉.

the higher authority of the tennō and court, and the potential thereof to bring unity to the country[51].

In the court itself, the notion of seeking the restoration of courtly rule took root, including with Kōkaku Tennō. While the court nobles suffered financial difficulties and sought additional income by issuing various certifications[52], calls for the restoration of royal authority began to spread in society.

Many daimyō, particularly among the tozama, sought ways to secure their independence from bakufu authority. They recruited capable individuals, even from among the mid- and lower-ranking bushi, and carried out reforms in order to restore their finances and strengthen their domain's power. In Kagoshima 鹿児島 (Satsuma) Domain, **Zusho Hirosato** 調所広郷 (1776-1848), who was promoted from a lower-ranking bushi, started carrying out reforms from 1827. He was able to effectively shelve the enormous debts owed to merchants in the three great cities, strengthened the monopoly on brown sugar, a specialty of the three islands of Amami 奄美三島 (Ōshima 大島, Tokunoshima 徳之島, and Kikaijima 喜界島), and expanded trade with the Ryūkyū Kingdom[53]. As a result, the domain's finances improved. The daimyō, **Shimazu Nariakira** 島津斉彬 (1809-58), built a **reverberatory furnace** 反射炉, a shipyard, and a glass factory in Kagoshima. His successor, Shimazu Tadayoshi 島津忠義 (1840-97), built a spinning mill under the direction of British engineers, and purchased Western weapons from Thomas Glover グラヴァー (1838-1911), a foreign merchant living in Nagasaki, to enhance the domain's military power.

REVERBERATORY FURNACE BUILT BY SAGA DOMAIN (REPRODUCTION BASED ON RESEARCH)
Building on its success creating a cannon factory in 1850, Saga Domain finished constructing a reverberatory furnace in 1854. It cast cannon for bakufu commissions. The furnace emits smoke as metal melted by the intense heat is poured into a cannon mold.

---

[51] In 1825, Aizawa Yasushi ‹会沢安› (Seishisai ‹正志斎›) wrote *Shinron* ‹『新論』› (New Theses) which outlined a view of a polity headed by the tennō.

[52] These certifications recognized religious practitioners like Shintō priests and Onmyōji ‹陰陽師›, artisans, and artists such as kemari ‹蹴鞠› players or calligraphers.

[53] The bakufu had maintained a monopoly on the tawaramono ‹俵物› trade with China through the port of Nagasaki. Opposing this monopoly, Satsuma Domain purchased crops from ships leaving Matsumae bound for Nagasaki, and smuggled the crops to China via the Ryūkyū Islands to make a profit. This development was yet more evidence of the weakening of bakufu authority.

In Hagi (Chōshū) Domain 萩（長州）藩, **Murata Seifū** 村田清風 (1783-1855), settled the domain's great debts, and improved the monopoly on paper and wax. He also established the **Koshinikata** 越荷方 (Domain Trading Office) to purchase commodities bound for the Kansai area, from merchant ships like Kitamae-bune 北前船 bound for Shimonoseki Bay, thereby gaining profits through consignment sales that enabled him to resolve the domain's financial troubles.

Meanwhile, in Saga (Hizen) Domain 佐賀（肥前）藩, the daimyō **Nabeshima Naomasa** 鍋島直正 (1814-71) made efforts to rebuild the rice tax payment (honbyakushō 本百姓) system. He introduced the **kindensei** 均田制 (**equal field system**), granted a payment moratorium to farmers on land under direct domain control, and made city-dwelling landowners return part of their landholdings to the domain. He also improved the domain's finances by promoting the monopoly on ceramics, and sought to strengthen the domain's power through introducing a Western-style military industry, building a **cannon factory** 大砲製造所 equipped with a reverberatory furnace.

In Kōchi (Tosa) Domain 高知（土佐）藩, a group of reformers called Okozegumi 「おこぜ組」 attempted to improve the financial situation through budget austerity. On the other hand, in Mito Domain, despite the efforts of the daimyō, **Tokugawa Nariaki** 徳川斉昭 (1800-60), reform attempts failed due to opposition from conservatives in the domain.

Aside from the major domains like Satsuma, Chōshū, Tosa, and Hizen (collectively termed **Satchōtohi** 薩長土肥) which succeeded in their reforms, some other domains – such as Uwajima Domain 宇和島藩, under Date Munenari 伊達宗城 (1818-92), or Fukui (Echizen) Domain 福井（越前）藩, under Matsudaira Yoshinaga 松平慶永 (or Shungaku 春嶽, 1828-90) – also succeeded in enhancing domain authority. They did this through having capable low-to-mid-ranking bushi take up key roles in administration, and through tightening the relationship between the administration and, on the one hand, merchants in the three great cities, and on the other, local merchants and landowners. By taking flexible moves in response to social changes, these domains were able to establish themselves as powerful domains (**yūhan** 雄藩) in western Japan with a strong voice in the political turmoil at the end of the Edo period.

At the end of this period, the bakufu also ordered the deputy **Egawa Tarōzaemon** 江川太郎左衛門 (or Tan'an 坦庵, 1801-55), to build a reverberatory furnace in Nirayama 韮山, in Izu 伊豆. These Western-style industries established by the bakufu and powerful domains would later become models for government industries after the Meiji Restoration 明治維新.

4 Kasei Culture

Kasei Culture

The culture that had briefly flourished in numerous forms during the Hōreki and Tenmei eras underwent a decline due to the restrictions imposed by the Kansei Reforms. However, at the dawn of the 19th century it began to experience a revival. The cultural trends that blossomed during the long rule of Tokugawa Ienari, the 11th shōgun, particularly during the Bunka and Bunsei eras, lasted until the Tenpō Reforms, and became known as **Kasei culture** 化政文化.

Against a backdrop of the prosperity of the three great cities, most especially Edo, the Kasei era witnessed the apex of chōnin culture centered on commoners, including those of lower social rank. This culture spread across the country in tandem with the flow of information, due to various factors, including the development of urban areas, country-wide interaction among merchants and intellectuals, the spread of publishing and education, and the development of transportation networks. Cultural pursuits became increasingly sophisticated as urban life matured.

Trends in Learning and Thought

In the intellectual domain, from the late 18th century several reform movements emerged that confronted the instability of the bakuhan system. These critically examined politics and society from the perspective of overcoming the problems, and sought practical methods to reform the established system.

Among the people familiar with the real conditions of urban and rural areas, there emerged intellectuals who actively discussed how to rejuvenate and improve the feudal system. **Kaibo Seiryō** 海保青陵 (1755-1817) criticized the bushi bias against commerce, and argued that domain finances should be replenished through the promotion of industries that would develop commercial activity. **Honda Toshiaki** 本多利明 (1743-1820) advocated enriching the country (fukoku) through trade with Western countries and the development of Ezochi, while **Satō Nobuhiro** 佐藤信淵 (1769-1850) promoted mercantilism based on nationalizing industry and trade.

In the first half of the 19th century, under the leadership of the Mito Domain daimyō Tokugawa Nariaki, **Mitogaku** 水戸学 scholars like Fujita Yūkoku 藤田幽谷 (1774-1826) and his son Tōko 東湖 (1806-55), and Aizawa Yasushi (1782-1863) argued for Sonnō Jōi 尊王攘夷 (revere the tennō and expel the barbarians). This later Mitogaku exerted significant influence on the intellectual climate and political movements at the end of the early modern era.

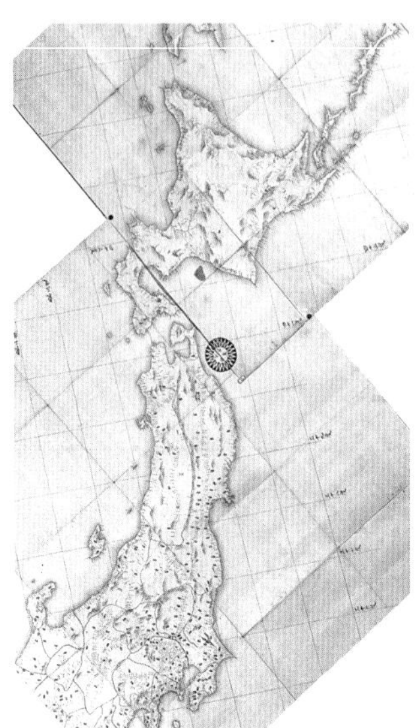

DAI NIHON ENKAI YOCHI ZENZU (MAPS OF JAPAN'S COASTAL AREA, PART)
Inō Tadataka took 17 years to survey every coast across the country, starting from Ezochi. After his death, his disciples completed the map project. Compared with current maps, the precision of Inō's maps is still remarkable.

As for Kokugaku, after the death of Motoori Norinaga, **Fukko Shintō** 復古神道 (restorationist Shintō, which aimed at a return to ancient ways) was popularized by **Hirata Atsutane** 平田篤胤 (1776-1843). Even after Atsutane's death, his disciples worked to propagate his thought, particularly among bushi, wealthy farmers, and Shintō priests in the Chūbu 中部 and Kantō regions. Eventually it developed into a significant type of thought that proved influential in politics at the end of the Edo period, when the country faced internal and external crises[54].

As the early 19th century progressed, many intellectuals and scholars emerged among the wealthy farmers and merchants across the country. These figures played an important role in the cultural activities of the late Edo period; their activities included undertaking evidence-based historical studies of their families and communities, interacting with urban intellectuals through poetry (kanshi 漢詩, waka 和歌, and haikai) circles, and participating in Hirata Atsutane's Fukkō Shintō movement as disciples. Among these intellectuals, **Inō Tadataka** 伊能忠敬 (1745-1818), a merchant of Sahara 佐原 in Shimōsa Province, studied at the Tenmonkata 天文方 (Astronomical Bureau) and was commissioned by the bakufu to carry out a coastal survey across the country, completing *Dai Nihon Enkai Yochi Zenzu* 「大日本沿海輿地全図」 (Maps of Japan's Coastal Area).

As for Western learning, the bakufu had one of its astronomers, Takahashi Yoshitoki 高橋至時 (1764-1804) revise the calendar based on the Western calendar system, resulting in the Kansei Calendar 寛政暦. Within the Tenmonkata, the bakufu also established the **Bansho Wage Goyō** 蛮書和解御用 (Western Book Translation Office)[55], and had its officials, particularly Yoshitoki's son Takahashi Kageyasu 高橋景保 (1785-1829), translate Western books. Shizuki Tadao 志筑忠雄 (1760-1806), a former Dutch interpreter, wrote *Rekishō Shinsho* 『暦象新書』 (New Treatise on Calendrical Phenomena), in which he introduced the universal gravitation 万有引力説 theory of Newton ニュートン (1642-1727) and the heliocentric 地動説 theory of Copernicus コペルニクス (1473-1543).

---

[54] At the end of the Edo period, women activists like Matsuo Taseko〈松尾多勢子〉from the Ina District〈伊那郡〉in Shinano also emerged.

[55] Near the end of the Edo period, the Bansho Wage Goyō became the Bansho Shirabesho〈蕃書調所〉, which later served as a precursor for universities in the modern era.

Western learning, however, did not become linked to intellectual or political movements that criticized the bakufu, due to suppression by the authorities as seen in the Siebold Incident (シーボルト事件) in 1828[56] or the Bansha no Goku during the Tenpō era (1830-44). Instead, it leaned towards more practical learning, with the introduction of Western civilization limited to science and technology in disciplines such as medicine, military sciences, and geography[57].

Education

From the Kasei to Tenpō eras, many schools were newly established across the country by scholars. Famous examples included the Kangien (咸宜園), a school founded by the Confucian scholar Hirose Tansō (広瀬淡窓) (1782-1856) in Hita (日田) in Bungo (豊後) Province; the **Tekiteki Saijuku** (適々斎塾（適塾）) (also called Teki Juku), begun in Ōsaka by the Rangaku scholar **Ogata Kōan** (緒方洪庵) (1810-63); and the Shōkason Juku (松下村塾), established in Hagi in Nagato (長門) Province in the Tenpō era by the uncle of **Yoshida Shōin** (吉田松陰) (1830-59). In the Bunsei era, with interest in Rangaku increasing, **Philipp Franz von Siebold** (シーボルト) (1796-1866), a German physician working for the Dutch trading post, established a clinic and school (called **Narutaki Juku** (鳴滝塾)) in a suburb of Nagasaki, where he educated students like Takano Chōei. These private schools attracted students from across the country, many of whom were active from the end of the Edo period to the early Meiji period.

Literature

In the Bunka era, **kokkeibon** (滑稽本), colorful stories describing the lives of commoners with a humorous touch, became popular. Notable authors of these included **Shikitei Sanba** (式亭三馬) (1776-1822) and **Jippensha Ikku** (十返舎一九) (1765-1831). **Ninjōbon** (人情本), which portrayed love affairs, were also popular among commoners, but their most representative author, **Tamenaga Shunsui** (為永春水) (1790-1843), was punished during the Tenpō Reforms. In contrast to these illustrated books, **yomihon** (読本) (vernacular novels) had few illustrations and narrated historical events and legends. This genre was begun by **Ueda Akinari** (上田秋成) (1734-1809) in Ōsaka, while the works of **Kyokutei Bakin** (曲亭馬琴) (1767-1848) – with their stories of kanzen chōaku (勧善懲悪) (good being rewarded and evil punished)[ii] and inga ōhō (因果応報)

---

[56] In 1828, when departing from Japan, Siebold was permanently expelled for attempting to take maps of the country abroad, which was forbidden. Those involved, including Takahashi Kageyasu who supplied maps to Siebold, were punished. After returning to Europe, Siebold wrote books including *Nippon*〈「日本」〉, and became the leading European scholar of Japan studies.

[57] Sakuma Shōzan〈佐久間象山〉, an advocate for ending the sakoku policy, argued for "Eastern ethics, Western arts [technologies]."

ASAHINA KOBITO-SHIMA ASOBI 〈朝比奈小人嶋遊〉 (ASAHINA'S TRIP TO THE ISLAND OF DWARFS, BY UTAGAWA KUNIYOSHI)
Asaina Saburō〈朝夷三郎〉, the third son of Wada Yoshimori〈和田義盛〉, a warrior of the Kamakura period, was renowned for his bravery, and gained tremendous popularity among commoners as "Asahina," depicted in yomihon and Kabuki plays. In 1847, a huge papier-mâché figure of Asahina was set up in Asakusa, and became a sensation. The image above depicts Asahina as a giant looking down at the procession of a tiny daimyō.

MEISHO EDO HYAKKEI: ŌHASHI ATAKE NO YŪDACHI 〈名所江戸百景「大はしあたけの夕立」〉 (ONE HUNDRED FAMOUS VIEWS OF EDO: SUDDEN SHOWER OVER SHIN-ŌHASHI BRIDGE AND ATAKE, BY UTAGAWA HIROSHIGE)
The Ōhashi (or Shin-Ōhashi〈新大橋〉) Bridge over Sumida River〈隅田川〉 connected Edo's downtown (in the foreground) with the mist-shrouded Fukagawa〈深川〉 district where Ofunagura〈「御船蔵」〉 Pier (the bakufu naval base, also called Atake〈安宅〉) was located. The image depicts people bustling across the bridge, caught in a sudden shower.

FUGAKU SANJŪ ROKKEI: KANAGAWA OKI NAMIURA 〈富嶽三十六景「神奈川沖浪裏」〉 (THIRTY-SIX VIEWS OF MT. FUJI: THE GREAT WAVE OFF KANAGAWA, BY KATSUSHIKA HOKUSAI)
Boats carrying fresh fish to Edo are racked by great waves.

(karmic retribution) – gained a great reputation[58].

In the genre of haikai, **Kobayashi Issa** 小林一茶 (1763-1827), a hyakushō from Shinano, established a style emphasizing the fortitude of commoners through his depiction of people's everyday life in villages. As for waka, poets of the Keien School 桂園派 like Kagawa 香川景樹

[58] Bakin's magnum opus, *Nansō Satomi Hakkenden*〈「南総里見八犬伝」〉 (Legend of the Eight Dog Warriors of the Southern Satomi), was of grandiose scale, based on themes of kanzen chōaku and inga ōhō.

Kageki (1768-1843) sought to establish a more plain poetic style in the period between the Kasei and Tenpō eras, but their efforts remained on the fringes. On the other hand, Ryōkan 良寛 (1758-1831), a Buddhist monk in Echigo, portrayed everyday life with an original style.

There was also Suzuki Bokushi 鈴木牧之 (1770-1842), from Echigo, who interacted with Edo intellectuals like Santō Kyōden and Kyokutei Bakin, and published *Hokuetsu Seppu* 『北越雪譜』 (Snow Stories of North Etsu Province), which introduced the nature and lifestyle of Echigo's snow country.

Art

As travel became more frequent among commoners and various places became known for spots to visit, nishiki-e landscape paintings were produced in profusion. Prints by **Katsushika Hokusai** 葛飾北斎 (1760-1849) and **Utagawa Hiroshige** 歌川広重 (1797-1858) became popular and sold well due to affordable prices. Through the end of the Edo period, painters like Utagawa Kuniyoshi 歌川国芳 (1797-1861) produced works that satirized social and political trends. After the sakoku policy was lifted, many of these ukiyoe were introduced overseas, and greatly influenced European impressionist artists like Monet モネ (1840-1926) and van Gogh ゴッホ (1853-90).

In the area of traditional painting, **Goshun** 呉春（松村月溪） (Matsumura Gekkei, 1751-1811) achieved an original style, departing from the Maruyama School 円山派 to form the Shijō School 四条派. Depicting landscapes with subtle brushstrokes, the school proved popular among the wealthy merchants of the Kansai region. Meanwhile, bunjinga reached its heyday in the Kasei era with the emergence of Tanomura Chikuden 田能村竹田 (1777-1835) in Bungo Province, Tani Bunchō 谷文晁 (1763-1840) in Edo, and Buchō's disciples, notably Watanabe Kazan[59].

Popular Culture Comes of Age

During the Bunka and Bunsei eras, performing arts and entertainments orientated around commoners thrived in urban communities, beginning with the three great cities: **shibaigoya** 芝居小屋 (permanent public theaters) attracted large crowds, the sakariba 盛場 (entertainment districts) had shacks and booths with spectacles, acrobats and storytellers, and many **yose** 寄席 opened in chōninchi. Kabuki enjoyed immense popularity; actors like Ichikawa Danjūrō 市川団十郎 VII (1791-1859), as well as Onoe 尾上, Sawamura 沢村 and Nakamura 中村 were fan favorites, and there were talented playwrights, especially Tsuruya Nanboku 鶴屋南北

[59] There were also women painters of bunjinga, like Ema Saikō〈江馬細香〉, the daughter of a physician serving the lord of Ōgaki Domain〈大垣藩〉 in Mino〈美濃国〉.

(1755-1859)[60]. Plays became known throughout the country through publications and nishiki-e, and through provincial tours of actors from the three great cities. In this context, **murashibai** 村芝居 (village plays), which imitated Kabuki plays and were performed mainly by young people in rural communities, became an important source of entertainment for villages, alongside religious festivals. The unique costumes, make-up, props and elocution employed in Kabuki had a significant influence on popular culture.

Major temples and shrines organized fairs (**ennichi** 縁日), exhibitions of holy statues (**kaichō** 開帳)[61], or lottery events (**tomitsuki** 富突, or tomikuji 富くじ) to attract crowds, in order to accumulate funds for the repair and operation of establishments. Tourist activities among commoners like hot spring sojourns and sightseeing became widespread[62]. Religious travel, such as visiting temples and shrines (**jisha sankei** 寺社参詣) like Ise Grand Shrine 伊勢神宮, Zenkōji 善光寺 Temple, or the Konpira Shrine 金毘羅宮 in Sanuki 讃岐 Province, or pilgrimages (**junrei** 巡礼) to sacred places, was also popular. There were many types of events that entertained people. These included seasonal events – such as Gosekku 五節句 (five seasonal ceremonies), Higan-e 彼岸会 (Buddhist equinox festivals), Urabon-e 盂蘭盆会 (Buddhist ancestor festival), the agricultural ceremonies of Himachi 日待 and Tsukimachi 月待, and **Kōshinkō** 庚申講 **(a nocturnal Buddhist ceremony)**[63] – as well as popular entertainments by traveling performers, such as monkey shows, manzai 万歳 (two-men comic acts), and blind minstrels like goze 瞽女 and zatō 座頭.

---

[60] At the end of the Edo period, the playwright Kawatake Mokuami〈河竹黙阿弥〉gained popularity with his shiranami-mono〈白浪物〉(thief plays), which featured thieves as protagonists.

[61] Kaichō refers to the exhibition of sacred Buddhist statues that were usually preserved inside temples. Dekaichō〈出開帳〉, where statues were conveyed to other places such as Edo or Kyōto, also came to be frequently held as cities developed. The kaichō of Zenkōji Temple in Shinano Province was particularly well known.

[62] Sugae Masumi〈菅江真澄〉, a Kokugaku scholar from Mikawa, travelled around the Tōhoku region for forty years, and wrote *Sugae Masumi Yūranki*〈『菅江真澄遊覧記』〉(Records of Sightseeing by Sugae Masumi) based on his observations during the journey.

[63] During Himachi, people stay inside at night and offer sake to the deities while awaiting the sunrise on the following day. Tsukimachi is similar but involves awaiting the moonrise. Kōshinkō occurs on the evening of every sixtieth day in the sexagenary cycle, and involves people staying up together all night in the belief that this prevents a shortening of one's lifespan when the three worms inhabiting one's body report one's sins to the lord of Heaven. Numerous Kōshintō〈庚申塔〉(Kōshin statues or markers) were erected across the country.

Performance Entertainment

Kabuki and Sumō were the most representative popular entertainments among commoners. Kabuki overtook Ningyō Jōruri in popularity around the Genroku era, even in Edo. In 1714, Eshima〈絵島〉, a servant in the Ōoku serving the mother of Tokugawa Ietsugu, the 7th shōgun, was accused and punished for having an affair with a Kabuki actor, which resulted in the Yamamura-za〈山村座〉, one of the major Kabuki theatres, being abolished. After the scandal, Edo was left with three major Kabuki theatres – Nakamura-za〈中村座〉, Ichimura-za〈市村座〉, and Morita-za〈森田座〉 – which flourished. Lesser theatres were Miyako-za〈都座〉, Kiri-za〈桐座〉 and Kawarazaki-za〈河原崎座〉, and there were also temporary performances called miyachi shibai〈宮地芝居〉 held in venues like Yushima Tenjin Shrine〈湯島天神〉.

In the first half of the early modern era, Sumō was an entertainment held exclusively for bushi like daimyō and hatamoto. In response to an increasing demand among commoners for Sumō, in 1744 the bakufu approved seasonal Sumō tournaments. Tournaments were mainly held in Kyōto in the summer, in Ōsaka in the autumn, and in Edo in the winter and spring. They usually lasted ten days under fair weather. Sumō wrestlers from the three great cities or castle towns would gather to participate in tournaments. Particularly in the Tenmei and Kansei eras, the tournaments were immensely popular due to many strong participants, notably the two yokozuna〈横綱〉 (champions), Tanikaze〈谷風〉 and Onogawa〈小野川〉, and other wrestlers like Raiden〈雷電〉, making this the first heyday of Sumō tournaments. In 1791, the first Sumō tournaments in the presence of the shōgun were held in the Fukiage Gardens〈吹上庭〉 of Edo Castle. Subsequent tournaments continued to be held in the shōgun's presence, bestowing a dignity and authority upon Sumō as a form of entertainment.

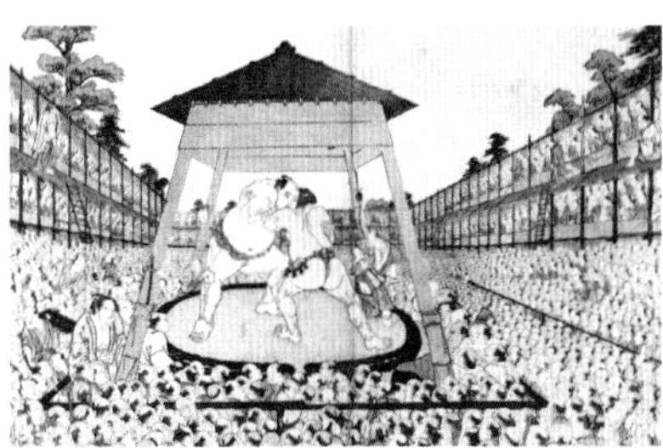

SUMŌ PERFORMANCE
Professional sumō tournaments with admission charges, which were held to raise funds for the maintenance of temples and shrines as well as bridges, were called "kanjin zumō〈勧進相撲〉." Such tournaments came to be approved by the end of the Genroku era, and later recognized by the bakufu as a legitimate profession.

Translators' Notes

[i] The Japanese text states that Tokugawa Ietsugu died at the age of almost eight, because in traditional Japanese age reckoning a child is age one at birth. However, by Western age reckoning a child is age zero at birth, and so in English he would be said to have died at the age of almost seven.

[ii] "Kanzen chōaku" (勧善懲悪) is a literary trope of good deeds ultimately being rewarded and evil deeds being punished, akin to what would be called in English "poetic justice," but since the latter sounds confusing to non-native speakers this textbook uses a more literal rendering.

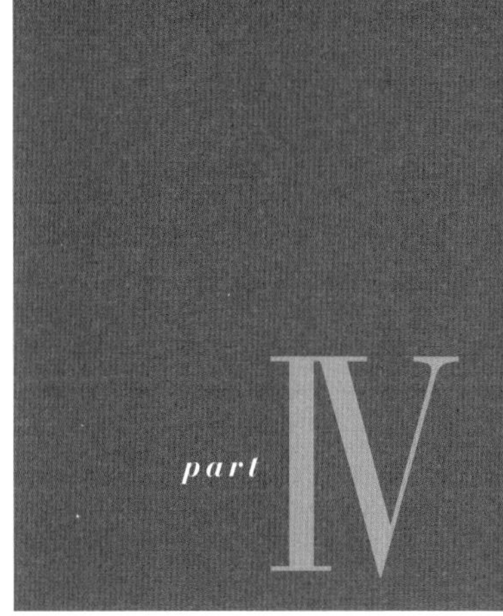

The Modern & Contemporary Eras

Chapter

9

The Establishment of a Modern State

1 Opening the Country, and Upheavals at the End of the Edo Period

Opening the Country

In the latter half of the 18th century, the first **Industrial Revolution** 産業革命 began in the United Kingdom (UK), setting off a wave of industrialization that spread across various European nations and the United States (US). The great powers of the West, having acquired vast industrial and military power, embarked on a race to acquire colonies, seeking foreign markets and sources of raw materials. In particular, they now undertook full-scale advances into Asia.

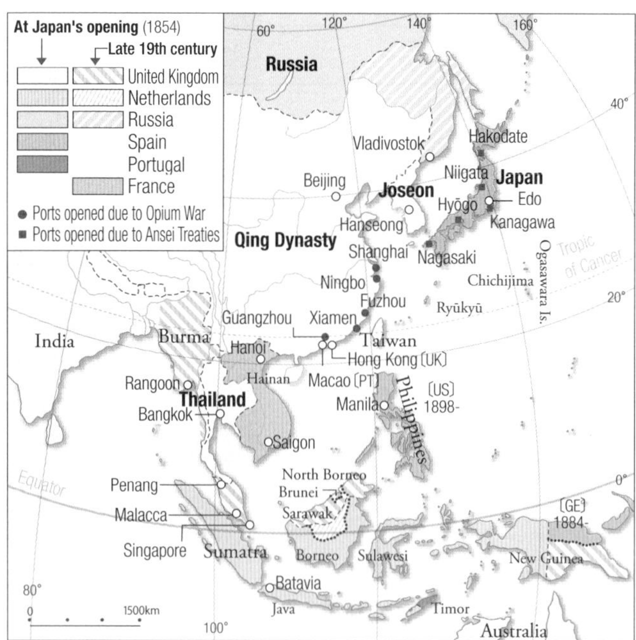

ENCROACHMENTS ON ASIA BY THE GREAT POWERS

Having been defeated in the **First Opium War** アヘン戦争 (1840-42), the Qing 清 Dynasty signed the **Treaty of Nanjing** 南京条約 (1842) with the UK, which forced it to cede Hong Kong and further open Chinese markets to foreigners. When news of the Qing Dynasty's defeat reached Japan, in 1842 the bakufu 幕府 relaxed the Foreign Vessel Exclusion Edict 異国船打払令 and issued the **Edict for the Provision of Firewood and Water** 天保の薪水給与令, which arranged for the provision of firewood, water, and food to foreign vessels that drifted ashore in Japan.

However, even after the King of the Netherlands sent a letter to the bakufu in 1844 advising that the country open its borders, the bakufu, lacking a comprehensive understanding of the world situation, refused, and continued the sakoku 鎖国体制 policy.

The US strongly desired the opening of Japan to serve as a port of call for its trading vessels and whaling vessels in the North Pacific Ocean. In 1846, Commodore **James Biddle** ビッドル (1783-1848) of the East India Squadron entered the Uraga 浦賀 Channel and requested that Japan open to trade, but the bakufu refused. After the US extended its borders to the Pacific Coast by capturing California from Mexico in 1848, trade between the US and China increased even more, and with it the US desire to open Japan.

In the sixth month of 1853, Commodore **Mathew C. Perry** ペリー (1794-1858) of the East India Squadron, who had called at Naha 那覇 in the Ryūkyū Kingdom 琉球王国 in the fourth month, appeared off the coast of Uraga with four warships (the "Black Ships" 黒船), and presented a letter from President Fillmore フィルモア (1800-74) demanding the opening of Japan. The bakufu, caught unprepared by Perry's forceful stance, was pressured into officially accepting the letter, and managed to make him leave by promising to have a reply ready the following year. Not long after, in the seventh month the Russian

PERRY'S ARRIVAL IN YOKOHAMA
In the second month of 1854, Perry came ashore at Yokohama〈横浜〉and went to the appointed meeting place. He was accompanied on both sides by 500 marines and sailors, lined up in a dignified manner, and was met at the entrance of the meeting place by the Japanese representatives, who were bearing flags and banners. This picture is a lithograph illustrating the scene.

envoy **Yevfimiy Putyatin** (プチャーチン) (1804-83) also came to Nagasaki (長崎), and requested both the opening of the country to trade and the demarcation of borders.

In the first month of 1854, Perry returned with a fleet of seven ships and strongly pushed the bakufu to conclude a treaty. The bakufu gave into this show of force, and in the third month signed the **Japan-US Treaty of Peace and Amity** (日米和親条約)[1], which decided the following: 1) Japan was to supply American vessels with necessary fuel and food; 2) Japan was to assist ships and sailors in distress; 3) Japan was to open the ports of Shimoda (下田) and Hakodate (箱館), and a consul was permitted to be stationed; and 4) Japan was to unilaterally grant most favored nation[2] status to the US. Subsequently, the bakufu would sign similar treaties of peace and amity with the UK, Russia[3], and the Netherlands, thereby radically departing from the sakoku policy that had lasted for more than 200 years.

Meanwhile, following the arrival of Perry in 1853, chief rōjū (老中首座) **Abe Masahiro** (阿部正弘) (1819-57), decided to depart from established policy by reporting the situation to the royal court, and holding a meeting for the daimyō (大名) and bakufu retainers to offer their opinions in an attempt to involve the whole country's leadership in policy-making. However, instead these measures just increased the authority of the court and strengthened the influence of the daimyō, and became a trigger for changing the government. The bakufu also appointed new people to the administration[4], involved Tokugawa Nariaki (徳川斉昭) (former lord of Mito Domain (水戸藩)) in governance, ordered the construction of battery emplacements in Edo Bay due to the need to improve defenses, and implemented a series of reforms such as repealing the ban on construction of large vessels (**Ansei Reforms** (安政の改革)).

The Impact of Opening the Ports

Townsend Harris (ハリス) (1804-78), who, under the Kanagawa Treaty, came to Japan in

---

[1] The treaty is also known as the Kanagawa Treaty〈神奈川条約〉, as it was signed close to Kanagawa, a post town on the Tōkaidō〈東海道〉.

[2] This meant that were Japan to conclude a treaty with another nation that included clauses granting it more favorable treatment than the US, then those clauses would automatically be applied to the US as well.

[3] The Russian envoy Putyatin revisited Japan after Perry, and in Shimoda concluded the **Treaty of Commerce and Navigation between Japan and Russia**〈日露和親条約〉. Under this treaty, three ports were opened (Nagasaki was added to Shimoda and Hakodate). Regarding the demarcation of borders, Etorofu〈択捉島〉 and everything south of it was determined to belong to Japan, while Urup〈得撫島〉 and everything north of it was determined to belong to Russia. The status of Sakhalin was left undetermined (as before).

[4] The bakufu gained the cooperation of Lords Matsudaira Yoshinaga〈松平慶永〉 of Echizen〈越前〉, Shimazu Nariakira〈島津斉彬〉 of Satsuma〈薩摩〉, and Date Munenari〈伊達宗城〉 of Uwajima〈宇和島〉.

THE US-JAPAN TREATY OF AMITY AND COMMERCE

Article 3. In addition to the ports of S[h]imoda and Hakoda[te], the following ports and towns shall be opened on the dates respectively appended to them, that is to say:

Kanagawa, on the (4th of July, 1859)...
Nagasaki, on the (4th of July, 1859)...
N[i]gata, on the (1st of January, 1860)...
H[yō]go, on the (1st of January, 1863)....
....Six months after the opening of Kanagawa the port of S[h]imoda shall be closed....
In all the foregoing ports and towns American citizens may permanently reside....

Americans may freely buy from Japanese and sell to them any articles that either may have for sale, without the intervention of any Japanese officers in such purchase or sale, or in making or receiving payment for the same....

Article 4. Duties shall be paid to the government of Japan on all goods landed in the country, and on all articles of Japanese production that are exported as cargo, according to the tariff hereunto appended. ....

Article 6. Americans committing offenses against Japanese shall be tried in American consular courts, and when guilty shall be punished according to American law. Japanese committing offenses against Americans shall be tried by the Japanese authorities and punished according to Japanese law.

*Of the fourteen articles, Article 3 covered free trade; the supplementary appendix referred to in Article 4 deprived Japan of tariff autonomy; and Article 6 recognized the consul's right to jurisdiction over their citizens (extraterritoriality), therefore arbitrarily stripping Japan of its right to try crimes committed by Americans.

1856 as the first Consul General of the US stationed in Shimoda, strongly urged the bakufu to conclude a treaty of commerce. **Hotta Masayoshi** 堀田正睦 (1810-64), chief rōjū and responsible for the negotiations with Harris, sought royal approval to sign a treaty, but Jōi 攘夷 sentiment was strong within the court, and he failed to receive approval from Kōmei Tennō 孝明天皇 (r. 1846-66).

However, in 1858, after the Qing Dynasty concluded the Treaty of Tianjin 天津条約 with the UK and France following the results of the first half of the Second Opium War アロー戦争 (or Arrow War, 1856-60), Harris warned of the threat from the UK and France, and used this to push the bakufu to sign a treaty of commerce. This resulted in **Ii Naosuke** 井伊直弼 (1815-60), the bakufu's tairō 大老 (great counselor), concluding the **US-Japan Treaty of Amity and Commerce** 日米修好通商条約 without royal approval, in the sixth month that same year.

The treaty stipulated the following: 1) Japan was to open the ports of Kanagawa, Nagasaki, Niigata 新潟, and Hyōgo 兵庫[5], and allow trading in the cities of Edo and Ōsaka 大坂; 2)

---

[5] As Kanagawa was a busy post town with frequent traffic, ultimately the nearby town of Yokohama was opened instead. Shortly after the opening of Yokohama port, Shimoda was closed. Hyōgo finally obtained approval to open a port in 1867, which became modern-day Kōbe, while Niigata opened in 1868.

commerce was to be conducted on the premise of free trade; and 3) foreign settlements were to be built in the treaty ports, and travelling within Japan was to be banned for ordinary foreigners. There were also other articles that marked the agreement as an unequal treaty: 4) Japan was to recognize consular jurisdiction (領事裁判権) over Americans staying in Japan (**extraterritoriality** (治外法権)); and 5) Japan would not have the right to set its tariffs, with tariffs instead being determined by mutual agreement (**loss of tariff autonomy** (関税自主権の欠如)). Subsequently, the bakufu also concluded similar treaties with the Netherlands, Russia, the UK, and France (**Ansei Five-Power Treaties** (安政の五カ国条約)).

Foreign trade began in 1859 in the three ports of Yokohama (Kanagawa), Nagasaki, and Hakodate. Trade goods were exchanged between foreign and Japanese merchants (exporters were called urikomishō (売込商), and importers hikitorishō (引取商)) in the foreign settlements by using silver coins. The amount of trade in Yokohama was by far the largest, and the most transactions were conducted with British merchants, as in the US the Civil War (南北戦争) (1861-65) had broken out.

Japan exported many agricultural and marine products, both unprocessed and processed, with examples being raw silk, tea, silkworm egg paper and seafood. Imports included factory-produced textile products, such as wool and cotton fabrics, and military equipment, such as guns and warships. Exports came to greatly exceed imports, which resulted in prices rising, as well as prompting major changes in domestic industry. For example, the production of raw silk expanded since it had become the primary export. On the other hand, an influx of cheap manufactured cotton goods put pressure on the hand-spinning and cotton industries that had been developing in farming villages.

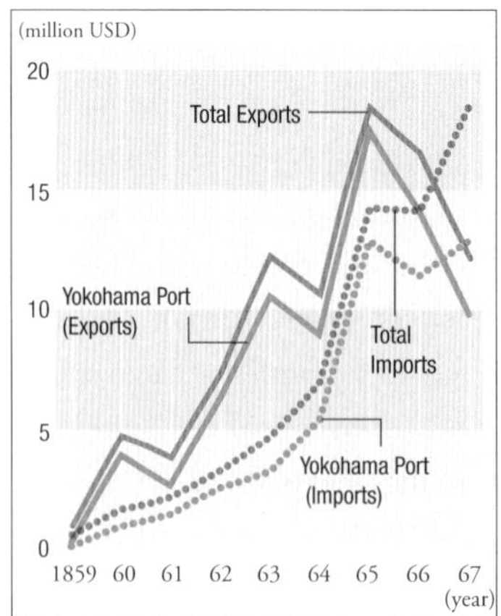

TRANSITION IN VALUE OF IMPORTS AND EXPORTS

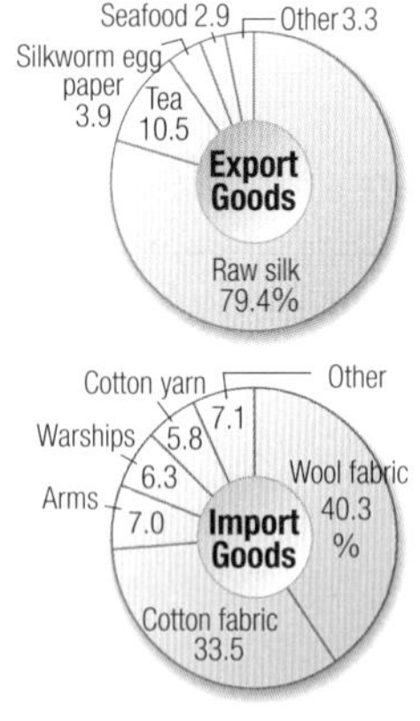

PROPORTIONS OF MAIN IMPORTS AND EXPORTS (1865)

The bakufu attempted to regulate trade on the grounds of controlling the prices, and to this end in 1860 issued a decree requiring five key products, including raw silk and rapeseed oil[6], be exported through Edo wholesalers (**Law Requiring Five Products be Circulated through Edo** 五品江戸廻送令). However, this did not prove effective due to opposition from both local merchants who handled exports, and the great powers which insisted on freedom of trade.

Furthermore, a great outflow of gold coins from Japan occurred due to the difference in the ratios of gold and silver used in coinage in Japan versus foreign countries[7]. The bakufu sought to prevent this by recasting the coinage (**Man'en coin recasting** 万延貨幣改鋳), which substantially reduced the quality, but the drop in real coin value spurred price increases and put a strain on the lives of the populace. These developments resulted in increased antipathy towards trade, which in turn contributed to the rise of violent **Jōi movements** 攘夷運動[8].

The Kōbu Gattai Policy and Sonnō Jōi Movements

Around the time when Harris was seeking the conclusion of a treaty of commerce, a **shōgunal succession issue** 将軍継嗣問題 had arisen because the thirteenth shōgun, **Tokugawa Iesada** 徳川家定 (1824-58), had no heir. Seeking a wise and capable person, some daimyō, including Matsudaira Yoshinaga (also known as Shungaku 春嶽) of Echizen Domain and Shimazu Nariakira of Satsuma Domain, favored **Tokugawa Yoshinobu** 徳川慶喜 (1837-1913, son of Tokugawa Nariaki). As Yoshinobu hailed from the Hitotsubashi 一橋家 branch family, this group was called the Hitotsubashi faction. Opposing it stood a group which favored someone closer to the main Tokugawa bloodline. Made up mainly of fudai daimyō 譜代大名,

[6] Rapeseed oil was known as "mizu abura〈水油〉" (water oil) for its colorless and transparent qualities, and was mainly used for lighting lamps.

[7] While the exchange rate of gold to silver was 1:15 in the West, the ratio in Japan was just 1:5. Foreigners would bring foreign silver coins (yōgin〈洋銀〉) into Japan and exchange them for the cheaper Japanese gold coins, resulting in more than 100,000 ryō〈両〉 in gold coinage leaving the country.

[8] In 1860, Henry Heusken〈ヒュースケン〉, a Dutch-American who had served as an interpreter for Harris, was murdered in Edo by a rōshi〈浪士〉 (voluntarily masterless bushi) from Satsuma Domain. The following year, the British legation, temporarily located on the grounds of Tōzenji Temple〈東禅寺〉 in Takanawa〈高輪〉, was attacked by a group of rōnin from Mito Domain (Tōzenji Incident〈東禅寺事件〉). In 1862, a British person was killed at Namamugi〈生麦〉, near the post station of Kanagawa, for crossing in front of the retinue of Shimazu Hisamitsu〈島津久光〉, who was on his way home from Edo (**Namamugi Incident**〈生麦事件〉). Later that same year, the British legation, under construction at Gotenyama〈御殿山〉 in Shinagawa〈品川〉, was attacked and burnt down by a group including Takasugi Shinsaku〈高杉晋作〉, Inoue Kaoru〈井上馨〉, and Itō Hirobumi〈伊藤博文〉 (Burning of the British Legation Incident〈イギリス公使館焼打ち事件〉). The Namamugi Incident later became the cause of the Anglo-Satsuma War〈薩英戦争〉.

this group supported Tokugawa Yoshitomi 徳川慶福 (1846-66) of Kii 紀伊藩 Domain, and thus was called the Nanki 南紀派 (literally "southern Kii") faction. Ii Naosuke, who was the daimyō of Hikone 彦根藩 Domain and had been appointed tairō in 1858, belonged to the Nanki faction. Thus, while pushing through the treaty of commerce, he also decided that the next shōgun would be Yoshitomi (who became **Tokugawa Iemochi** 徳川家茂, the fourteenth Tokugawa shōgun).

The conclusion of the treaty in spite of royal disapproval angered Kōmei Tennō, and was strongly criticized by the daimyō of the Hitotsubashi faction and shishi, who were bushi that supported Sonnō Jōi 尊王攘夷 ideology. Ii responded by forcefully suppressing the courtiers and daimyō who opposed him, and executing many of their retainers (**Ansei Purge** 安政の大獄)[9]. In 1860, a group of rōnin, mainly from Mito Domain, indignant over the severe suppression, assassinated Ii outside the Sakurada 桜田門 Gate of Edo Castle (**Sakuradamon Incident** 桜田門外の変).

In the wake of this incident, Andō Nobumasa 安藤信正 (1819-71), a rōjū who had become the central figure in the administration, carried out a policy called **kōbu gattai** 公武合体, which attempted to reconcile the court (kō 公) with the bakufu (bu 武). This resulted in the orchestration of a marriage between Kōmei Tennō's younger sister, Kazu no Miya 和宮 (1846-77), and Shōgun Tokugawa Iemochi. This political marriage was criticized by Sonnō Jōi advocates, and in 1862 Andō stepped down after himself being wounded by Mito rōnin in an assassination attempt outside Edo Castle's Sakashita Gate 坂下門 (Sakashitamon Incident 坂下門外の変). Against this backdrop, Satsuma Domain, a tozama 外様 domain with close ties to both the court and bakufu, took action. Shimazu Hisamitsu (1817-87, brother of Shimazu Nariakira), who was the father of the Satsuma daimyō, Shimazu Tadayoshi 島津忠義

SAKURADAMON INCIDENT
On the 3rd day of the 3rd month in 1860, a group consisting of seventeen shishi from Mito Domain and one from Satsuma Domain attacked Ii Naosuke outside of the Sakurada Gate as he was heading towards the castle in heavy snow. The illustration shows Naosuke being pulled out of his palanquin, moments before being beheaded.

[9] Tokugawa Nariaki, Tokugawa (Hitotsubashi) Yoshinobu, and Matsudaira Yoshinaga were either ordered to resign or be suspended, while the bushi Hashimoto Sanai〈橋本左内〉(of Echizen Domain) and Yoshida Shōin〈吉田松陰〉(of Chōshū Domain) were arrested and executed.

(1840-97), traveled to Edo (while escorting a royal messenger) to demand reforms of bakufu governance from his domain's own perspective on kōbu gattai.

The bakufu acquiesced to the demands of Satsuma Domain and revised the administrative system, creating several new posts: Matsudaira Yoshinaga was appointed **Seiji Sōsaishoku** 政事総裁職 **(Chief Administrator)**, Tokugawa Yoshinobu was made **Shōgun Kōkenshoku** 将軍後見職 **(Shōgunal Guardian)**, and Matsudaira Katamori 松平容保 (1835-93) of Aizu 会津藩 Domain became **Kyōto Shugoshoku** 京都守護職 **(Military Commissioner for Kyōto)**[10].

In Kyōto, after Shimazu Hisamitsu had left, representatives of Chōshū 長州藩 Domain (which officially espoused **Sonnō Jōi ideology** 尊王攘夷論[11], advocated by its lower-ranking bushi) conspired with radical courtiers to make the court summon the shōgun to Kyōto and push the bakufu to enact a Jōi policy. Lacking any alternative, the bakufu issued a decree for each domain to implement Jōi on the tenth day of the fifth month in 1863. Beginning from the designated day, Chōshū Domain put the Jōi policy into practice by firing upon foreign ships passing through the straits of Shimonoseki 下関.

In response to movements by the Sonnō Jōi faction (led by Chōshū Domain), the domains of Satsuma and Aizu decided to act. On the 18th day of the eighth month in 1863, these two domains, in collaboration with courtiers supporting kōbu gattai, took power in the court, and banished Chōshū groups as well as radical courtiers like **Sanjō Sanetomi** 三条実美 (1837-91) from Kyōto (**8/18 Coup** 八月十八日の政変)[12]. In an attempt to regain its influence, in the following year, 1864, Chōshū Domain, after witnessing the Ikedaya Incident 池田屋事件 underway[13], advanced upon Kyōto, but was defeated by a coalition of forces from several domains, including Aizu, Kuwana 桑名, and Satsuma (**Kinmon/Hamagurigomon Incident** 禁門の変／蛤御門の変).

---

[10] The bakufu also adopted a Western system for its armed forces and relaxed the stipulations of the Sankin Kōtai system〈参勤交代制〉(Bunkyū Reforms〈文久の改革〉).

[11] Sonnō Jōi ideology was a strand of Mitogaku〈水戸学〉at the end of the Edo period that merged Sonnō and Jōi thought; its leading proponents were Fujita Tōko〈藤田東湖〉and Aizawa Yasushi〈会沢安〉. However, after the conclusion of the commerce treaties without court approval, it developed an anti-bakufu stance and transformed into a movement calling for pragmatic political reform. Those who supported this ideology came to be called the Sonjō faction〈尊攘派〉.

[12] Around the same time, a magistrate's office at Gojō〈五条〉in Yamato Province〈大和〉was attacked by a group seeking to implement Sonnō Jōi, including the courtier Nakayama Tadamitsu〈中山忠光〉and Yoshimura Toratarō〈吉村虎太郎〉, a bushi from Tosa Domain (Tenchūgumi Incident〈天誅組の変〉). Another incident occurred when bushi formerly belonging to Fukuoka Domain〈福岡藩〉, such as Hirano Kuniomi〈平野国臣〉, also attacked a magistrate's office at Ikuno〈生野〉in Tajima Province〈但馬〉, lifting the spirits of their supporters (Ikuno Incident〈生野の変〉).

[13] The Ikedaya Incident was an event in 1864 in which the Shinsengumi〈新選組〉, a special police force led by Kondō Isami〈近藤勇〉and operating under the command of the Military Commissioner for Kyōto, wounded and killed members of the Sonjō faction at the Ikedaya Inn in Kyōto.

Immediately after this incident, the bakufu mobilized forces from various domains and launched the (First) **Chōshū Expedition** 長州征討. The great powers, seeking a chance to strike back at the Jōi faction sabotaging trade, organized a joint fleet – mainly British, but with support from Dutch, French, and Americans – and attacked the battery emplacements at Shimonoseki (**Bombardment of Shimonoseki** 四国艦隊下関砲撃事件). Seeing these developments, the Chōshū leaders suppressed the Sonnō Jōi faction within the domain, and adopted a more deferential attitude towards the bakufu. Consequently, the bakufu's expeditionary forces withdrew without engaging in battle. Satsuma Domain had already experienced being bombarded in 1863 by British ships, which had invaded Kagoshima 鹿児島湾 Bay in retaliation for the Namamugi Incident (**Anglo-Satsuma War** 薩英戦争). In short, it had become evident that repelling the foreigners was impossible. In 1865, the great powers, in order to pressure the bakufu to gain royal approval for treaties, sent a fleet into the waters off Hyōgo. Negotiations with the bakufu proceeded in the following year, leading to the signing of an **agreement for tariff revision** 改税約書[14] which increased the inequality in trade.

From around this time, Henry パークス Smith Parkes (1828-85), the British consul-general, realized the powerlessness of the bakufu, and began to anticipate the establishment of a **coalition polity of powerful domains** 雄藩連合政権 centered on the tennō. Satsuma Domain,

CAPTURE OF BATTERY EMPLACEMENT AT SHIMONOSEKI BY THE FOUR POWERS
The cannon on the emplacement were bronze Western-style ones made by Chōshū Domain. Although Jōi ideology asserted the primacy of sword combat, according to British records the main causes of British casualties were bullets/shells and arrows, not swords or spears.

[14] The tariff rate (ad valorem tax at 20% on average) determined at the conclusion of the commerce treaties was changed to a uniform 5% ad valorem tax, which was more favorable to the foreign nations. Other regulations hindering free trade were also abolished.

having experienced the Anglo-Satsuma War, also shifted its policy towards the UK in order to advance modernization, and governance of the domain was taken over by lower-ranking reformist bushi 武士 such as **Saigō Takamori** 西郷隆盛 (1827-77) and **Ōkubo Toshimichi** 大久保利通 (1830-78). On the other hand, the French consul-general, Léon Roches ロッシュ (1809-1900), remained steadfast in support of the bakufu, and continued to provide both financial and military assistance.

The Development of Movements to Overthrow the Bakufu

The utter defeat at Shimonoseki prompted even supporters of the Sonnō Jōi faction in Chōshū Domain, including **Takasugi Shinsaku** 高杉晋作 (1839-67) and **Katsura Kogorō** 桂小五郎 (later known as Kido Takayoshi 木戸孝允, 1833-77), to realize that the expulsion of foreigners was impossible. Although the domain had tentatively submitted to the bakufu, at the end of 1864 Takasugi and his supporters, commanding the **Kiheitai** 奇兵隊 **(a volunteer militia)**[15] that Takasugi had established beforehand, raised troops and regained control of the domain from conservative forces. Working together with wealthy farmers and village officials within the domain, they transformed the domain's policy from one of acquiescence to working to overthrow the bakufu, and, by approaching the UK, focused on strengthening their military under the leadership of Ōmura Masujirō 大村益次郎 (1824-69).

The bakufu had ordered Chōshū Domain to reduce its territories as compensation for the first expedition, but the domain, having changed its policy, was reluctant to comply. As a result, the bakufu declared a Second **Chōshū Expedition** 長州征討, but Satsuma Domain, having changed direction regarding opening the country, secretly adopted a supportive stance towards Chōshū. In 1866, Satsuma and Chōshū, through the mediation of Sakamoto Ryōma 坂本龍馬 (1835-67) and Nakaoka Shintarō 中岡慎太郎 (1838-67) from Tosa Domain 土佐藩, signed a secret military alliance (**Satchō Coalition** 薩長連合 or **Satchō Alliance** 薩長同盟), and solidified their anti-bakufu stance. Consequently, the Second Chōshū Expedition turned out badly for the bakufu forces, and when Shōgun Tokugawa Iemochi, who had been commanding the campaign from Ōsaka Castle, suddenly died, the bakufu used his death as an excuse to halt hostilities[16].

The price increases and political conflicts triggered by the opening of the country

---

[15] Takasugi Shinsaku proposed the formation of the Kiheitai to the domain leadership. In 1863, he took the initiative to organize the group by recruiting volunteers regardless of their birth or social class, in contrast to regular domain forces. Subsequently, various militias, including farmers and merchants, were organized in Chōshū Domain, and became the fighting units for the anti-bakufu movement.

[16] Kōmei Tennō died suddenly at the end of 1866. Although he had advocated for Jōi, he had not been in favor of overthrowing the bakufu, and had supported kōbu gattai. His sudden death was therefore a great blow to the bakufu.

to the West increased social anxiety and had a negative impact on people's lives. The Kokugaku 国学 -derived Sonnō ideology had spread even into farming villages, and ikki by farmers demanding social reform (**yonaoshi ikki** 世直し一揆, **social reform ikki**) broke out. Distrust of the authorities was clearly evident in the riots that had occurred in Ōsaka and Edo during the expedition.

Popular religions, later collectively termed Kyōha Shintō 教派神道 (sectarian Shintō) and including such groups as Tenrikyō 天理教 in Yamato, Kurozumikyō 黒住教 in Bizen 備前, and Konkōkyō 金光教 in Bitchū 備中[17], had already existed for some time. However, they rapidly spread in this period, along with the popularization of pilgrimages to Ise Grand Shrine 伊勢神宮 (**okage-mairi** 御蔭参り) – two trends that showed a response to people's wish to be saved from a desperate situation in a time of crisis. In 1867, ***Ee ja nai ka*** ええじゃないか, a movement characterized by enthusiastic dancing, developed among people in the Tōkai 東海 and Kinai 畿内 regions, and, as a social movement anticipating reform, temporarily disrupted the bakufu's rule.

The Collapse of the Bakufu

Tokugawa Yoshinobu, who became the fifteenth shōgun after the death of Iemochi, made efforts to rebuild the bakufu administration with aid from France. However, in 1867, Satsuma and Chōshū, having formed an alliance the previous year, finally made the decision to overthrow the bakufu by force. Tosa Domain, on the other hand, continued to support kōbu gattai, and two bushi from the domain, Gotō Shōjirō 後藤象二郎 (1838-97) and Sakamoto Ryōma, worked with the former lord Yamauchi Toyoshige 山内豊信（容堂） (also known as Yōdō, 1827-72) in advising the shōgun to act in advance of the anti-bakufu faction and return authority to the tennō[18]. Yoshinobu accepted this advice, and on the 14th day of the 10th month he submitted to the court a memorial offering to restore political authority to the tennō (**Taisei Hōkan no Jōhyō** 大政奉還の上表).

On the same day, however, Satsuma and Chōshū, in collusion with the courtier **Iwakura Tomomi** 岩倉具視 (1825-83), managed to obtain a secret royal edict to overthrow the bakufu. The anti-bakufu faction had been forestalled by Yoshinobu's memorial, but on the 9th day of the 12th month, backed by Satsuma forces, it carried out a coup at the court, and issued the **Ōsei Fukko no Daigōrei** 王政復古の大号令 (**Decree for Restoration of Royal Rule**), establishing a new tennō-centered government. So it was that the history of the Edo Bakufu, which had lasted for over 260 years, came to a close. The new government abolished not only the position of shōgun, but also within the court

---

[17] Tenrikyō, Kurozumikyō, and Konkōkyō were respectively founded by Nakayama Miki〈中山みき〉, Kurozumi Munetada〈黒住宗忠〉, and Kawate Bunjirō〈川手文治郎〉.

[18] The plan was to have the shōgun return authority to the court for the time being, and then establish a coalition government of domains led by the Tokugawa under the court.

those of sesshō 摂政 and kanpaku 関白, and established three government offices (sanshoku 三職), namely those of chief executive (sōsai 総裁), legislature (gijō 議定), and councilors (san'yo 参与). The san'yo posts were filled by bushi representing Satsuma and other influential domains, creating a coalition government of powerful domains[19].

On the evening of the coup, the **Kogosho Conference** 小御所会議 was held by the sanshoku. It was decided that Tokugawa Yoshinobu was to resign the post of Inner Minister 内大臣[i] and return part of his land to the court (jikan nōchi 辞官納地, stripping of titles and land). Opposing this decision, Yoshinobu withdrew from Kyōto to Ōsaka Castle, determined to confront the new government militarily.

Technology and Culture in the Final Years of the Bakufu

From around the time of Perry's arrival, the bakufu and various domains sought to modernize by adopting Western technology. Their initial aim was to introduce military technology that had existed in the West before the Industrial Revolution, examples being the construction of battery emplacements and reverberatory furnaces, production of cannons, and building of Western-style sailing ships. Within the bakufu, these efforts were led by Egawa Tarōzaemon 江川太郎左衛門 (also known as Tan'an 坦庵), a land intendant (daikan 代官).

After the opening of the ports, the bakufu founded the **Bansho Shirabesho** 蕃書調所 **(Institute for the Study of Barbarian Books)**[20] and the Kōbusho 講武所 in Edo, the former for the purpose of teaching Western knowledge and translating diplomatic documents, and the latter for instruction in military arts, including the use of Western firearms. In Nagasaki, naval training began under the supervision of Dutch instructors, and in conjunction with this, a shipyard (Nagasaki Steel Works 長崎製鉄所), equipped with machine tools capable of manufacturing and repairing steamship engines, was also constructed. This was the first case when machine manufacturing technology was introduced to Japan after the Industrial Revolution. The bakufu and various domains, including

---

[19] Those appointed to san'yo posts included Saigō Takamori and Ōkubo Toshimichi from Satsuma, and Gotō Shōjirō and Fukuoka Takachika〈福岡孝弟〉 from Tosa, shortly to be joined by Kido Takayoshi and Hirosawa Saneomi〈広沢真臣〉 from Chōshū.

[20] The institute subsequently developed into the Yōsho Shirabesho〈洋書調所〉 (Institute for the Study of Western Books) and then later the Kaiseijo〈開成所〉 (Institute for Western Studies). Through this process, the study of Western learning, which had previously focused on medicine and other natural sciences, came to include subjects such as philosophy, politics, and economics. Under the Meiji government, the Kaiseijo became Kaisei School〈開成学校〉, and eventually Tōkyō University. As for medicine, the Shutōjo〈種痘所〉 (Vaccination Center; later to become Igakusho〈医学所〉, the Institute of Medicine) was also established.

Satsuma and Chōshū, also sent students to study abroad[21]. The first example was Katsu Kaishū〈勝海舟〉 (also known as Yoshikuni〈義邦〉, 1823-99) and his crew, who had received naval training and sailed the *Kanrin-maru*〈咸臨丸〉 across the Pacific in 1860 after the ratification of the US-Japan Treaty of Amity and Commerce. Although these students and other learners of Western studies originally aimed to introduce military technology and medical science, as their understanding of Western civilization deepened their interests grew to encompass fields such as science, technology, politics, law, and economics.

In the Keiō era〈慶応期〉 (1865-68), the bakufu invited a French advisory group, proceeded with the construction of a shipyard in Yokosuka (Yokosuka Steel Works〈横須賀製鉄所〉), and trained an army with new equipment. Aside from this, foreign missionaries and journalists came to the open port of Yokohama, and they too played a role in the introduction of Western culture. Among the missionaries were some who actively introduced Western culture to Japanese through English studies, such as the American James Curtis Hepburn〈ヘボン〉 (1815-1911), or Guido Verbeck〈フルベッキ〉 (1830-98). This led to a gradual shift in thinking, away from Jōi ideology and towards the view that Japan should pursue modernization based on the West.

2 The Meiji Restoration and "Fukoku Kyōhei"

The Boshin War and the Founding of the New Government

In the first month of 1868, the bakufu forces under Tokugawa Yoshinobu advanced towards Kyōto from Ōsaka Castle, but were defeated by the forces of the new government at the **Battle of Toba-Fushimi**〈鳥羽・伏見の戦い〉. Yoshinobu retreated to Edo, and the new government promptly dispatched a force (Tōseigun〈東征軍〉) to pursue him as an enemy of the court[22]. However, ultimately the bakufu forces surrendered Edo Castle bloodlessly in the fourth month of the same year, due to negotiations between Katsu Kaishū, who was Yoshinobu's delegate, and Saigō Takamori, the Tōseigun staff officer. The Tōseigun

---

[21] Nishi Amane〈西周〉 and Tsuda Mamichi〈津田真道〉, instructors at the Yōsho Shirabesho, went to study in the Netherlands, while Fukuzawa Yukichi〈福沢諭吉〉 accompanied the bakufu delegation to the US and Europe. Many people from Chōshū, such as Itō Hirobumi and Inoue Kaoru, and Satsuma, such as Mori Arinori〈森有礼〉, went to study in the UK.

[22] Wealthy farmers and merchants joined the Tōseigun, also known as the Kangun〈官軍〉 (Court Army), leading volunteer corps which they organized themselves. One notable group was the Sekihōtai〈赤報隊〉 led by Sagara Sōzō〈相楽総三〉 and his colleagues, which marched eastward down the Tōsandō〈東山道〉 circuit announcing in bakufu territories that the annual taxes would be halved under the new order, earning support from farmers. However, after the new government was established, Sagara and others were executed as members of a false Kangun.

went on to defeat several resisting domains in the Tōhoku 東北 region that had formed the **Ōuetsu Reppan Dōmei** 奥羽越列藩同盟 **(Alliance of Mutsu** 陸奥**, Dewa** 出羽 **and Echigo** 越後**)**, and in the ninth month captured Aizu Wakamatsu Castle 会津若松城, considered the core of the resistance. In the fifth month of the following year (1869), the bakufu's navy, which, under the command of Enomoto Takeaki 榎本武揚 (1836-1908) had made Goryōkaku 五稜郭 Fort in Hakodate their base, also surrendered. With this achievement, the consolidation of the country under the new government was almost complete[23]. This civil war, which had lasted for about a year and a half, is known as the **Boshin War** 戊辰戦争.

While the war was still raging, the new government had proceeded with political reforms. It began by reforming foreign relations through announcing to other nations, in the first month of 1868, that royal governance had been restored and the tennō had regained sovereignty over diplomacy. Subsequently, in the third month, the **Gokajō no Seimon** 五箇条の誓文 **(Charter Oath**, but literally "Five-Article Oath") was promulgated, setting forth the new government's fundamental principles of state policy, including respect for open discussion and amity with foreign nations through opening the country. The document emphasized the tennō's direct rule through its format, in which the tennō, at the head of the courtiers, lords and other officials, made a pledge to the deities.

In the following fourth (intercalary) month that same year, the new government issued a constitution (the Seitaisho 政体書) and reorganized the government structure. State authority was concentrated in a central government body known as the Dajōkan 太政官, and in imitation of the US Constitution the separation of powers doctrine was adopted. High-ranking government posts were to be replaced every four years by holding

THE CHARTER OATH

1. Deliberative Assemblies shall be widely held, and all political matters decided by public discussions.
2. Classes both high and low shall unite as one in vigorously carrying out policies to govern the nation.
3. All commoners, no less than civil and military officials, shall each be allowed to pursue their mission so there may be no discontent.
4. Foul customs of the past shall be ridden of, and all is to be based on the righteous path of the world.
5. Seek knowledge throughout the world in order to enhance the foundations of imperial rule.

---

[23] People at the time used the term "Go-Isshin〈御一新〉" (renewal), in the sense of a political renewal, as well as the term "Ishin〈維新〉" (restoration) derived from ancient Chinese when referring to the collapse of the bakufu and the establishment of a new government. As a historical term, however, **Meiji Ishin**〈明治維新〉 (**Meiji Restoration**) refers to the period of drastic change from the arrival of Perry's "Black Ships" to either Haihan Chiken or the Satsuma Rebellion〈西南戦争〉.

an election among officials[24], and with the implementation of other systems the polity took on a form resembling the modern political systems of Western nations. Furthermore, in conjunction with taking control of the Kantō region, the government changed the name of Edo to Tōkyō in the seventh month, and carried out an enthronement ceremony for Meiji Tennō 明治天皇 (r. 1867-1912) a month later. In the ninth month, the era name was changed to **Meiji** 明治 and the **Issei Ichigen** 一世一元の制 (one reign, one era name) **system** was introduced. In the following year, 1869, the capital was moved from Kyōto to Tōkyō.

Meanwhile, on the day after the promulgation of the Charter Oath, the government issued the **Five Public Notices** 五榜の掲示 for commoners nationwide. The contents included emphasis on Confucian ethics governing the relations between lord and vassal, father and son, and husband and wife, and renewed the prohibitions on conspiracies, direct petition movements, and Christianity, all of which were continuations of the bakufu's policies towards the commoners.

The Abolition of Domains and Establishment of Prefectures

During the Boshin War, the new government had reorganized territory confiscated from the bakufu into prefectures, with strategic areas being designated "fu" 府 and others "ken." 県 In the former domains, however, the system of governance by daimyō continued as before. In the pursuit of political consolidation, the government set a policy of gradually implementing direct rule over these domains. In the first month of 1869, Kido Takayoshi, Ōkubo Toshimichi and others orchestrated **Hanseki Hōkan** 版籍奉還 **(the return of lands and people to the court)**[25] by the four daimyō of Satsuma, Chōshū, Tosa and Hizen. Subsequently, many other domains followed suit. In the sixth month, while ordering the remaining domains to also conduct Hanseki Hōkan, the government established hereditary stipends (karoku 家禄) for former daimyō, equal to one tenth of their annual tax revenue, in place of the kokudaka 石高 system. The government had the ex-daimyō govern their former domains by appointing them as domain

---

[24] The distinction between legislature and administration in the Dajōkan was not clearly defined, and elections among officials were only held once. The legislative organ consisted of an upper assembly (composed of administrative offices and councilors) and a lower assembly (composed of delegates from each prefecture and domain). In the following year, the lower assembly was reorganized into the Kōgisho〈公議所〉, and later on became the House of Representatives (Shūgi'in〈集議院〉).

[25] The "han〈版〉" in "hanseki〈版籍〉" referred to the domain lands, while "seki〈籍〉" meant the population registers: thus, the people. Therefore, nominally Hanseki Hōkan referred to the domain lords returning their territory and people to the tennō, and in this way the new government took control over the whole country.

governors (chihanji知藩事).

Although this change separated the hereditary stipends of the governors from the finance of the domains, in practice the old daimyō structure remained in place, and the domains retained autonomy over taxation and the military as before. For this reason, the new government imposed high annual tax rates on the limited land it had under its direct control (the fu and ken prefectures), which led to a series of protests against the administration. Simultaneously, in the domains public dissatisfaction rose in response to taxation systems that had not changed from the Edo period.

Furthermore, veterans of various militias in Chōshu, starting with the Kiheitai, opposed the reorganization of the domain and were ultimately suppressed by force.

Ultimately, the new government decided to completely abolish the system of domains. In 1871, after enhancing its military power through recruiting a corps of royal guards called Goshinpei御親兵 from the domains of Satsuma, Chōshū and Tosa, it carried out a policy known as **Haihan Chiken廃藩置県 (Abolition of Domains and Establishment of Prefectures)**. All of the domains were summarily abolished, and replaced by prefectures[26]. The domain governors were dismissed from their posts and ordered to move to Tōkyō, while a **prefectural governor** (**fuchiji**府知事 or **kenrei**県令) was dispatched from the central government to take their positions in the local administration. Thus concluded the political consolidation of the country.

At the same time, the central administration was also reorganized. With the return of land and people under Hanseki Hōkan, the Dajōkan system founded under the Seitaisho was revised, and, under the new doctrines of Saisei Icchi祭政一致 (unity of religion and politics) and direct rule by the tennō, the government restored the form of the Taihō大宝令 Code. In imitation of the Code, the Jingikan神祇官 (Department of Shrines) was established alongside the Dajōkan, with the various ministries being set up under the latter. During bureaucratic reforms carried out after the abolition of the domains, a tricameral system was introduced, under which the Dajōkan was divided into the Houses of the Center (Sei-in正院), Left (Sa-in左院), and Right (U-in右院)[27]. The ministries were then placed under the

[26] Initially there was 1 shi〈使〉 (Kaitakushi〈開拓使〉), 3 fu〈府〉 (Tōkyō, Ōsaka and Kyōto) and 302 ken〈県〉, but by the end of the year the ken prefectures had been rearranged into 72. After further mergers among regions, by 1888 the system consisted of 1 dō〈道〉 (meaning Hokkaidō〈北海道〉), 3 fu and 43 ken.

[27] The Dajōkan's House of the Center was the highest organ of state power, and consisted of the councilors and the three ministers (supreme minister, and ministers of the left and right). The House of the Left functioned as the legislature and advised the central house, while the House of the Right gathered the ministers and vice-ministers of each ministry to discuss ministry affairs. The Department of Shrines was later relegated to a ministry, and the Department of Civil Affairs was abolished.

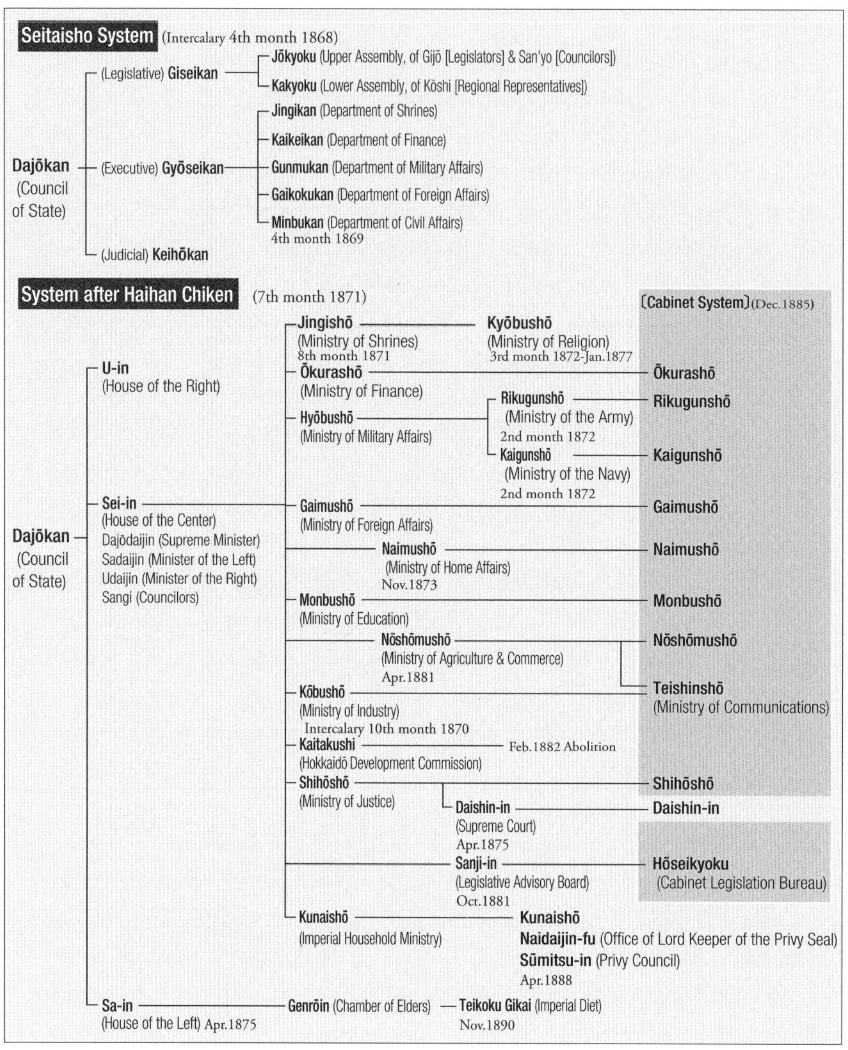
Seitaisho System (Intercalary 4th month 1868)
Dajōkan (Council of State)
(Legislative) Giseikan
Jōkyoku (Upper Assembly, of Gijō [Legislators] & San'yo [Councilors])
Kakyoku (Lower Assembly, of Kōshi [Regional Representatives])
(Executive) Gyōseikan
Jingikan (Department of Shrines)
Kaikeikan (Department of Finance)
Gunmukan (Department of Military Affairs)
Gaikokukan (Department of Foreign Affairs)
Minbukan (Department of Civil Affairs)
4th month 1869
(Judicial) Keihōkan
System after Haihan Chiken (7th month 1871)
〔Cabinet System〕(Dec.1885)
Dajōkan (Council of State)
U-in
(House of the Right)
Sei-in
(House of the Center)
Dajōdaijin (Supreme Minister)
Sadaijin (Minister of the Left)
Udaijin (Minister of the Right)
Sangi (Councilors)
Sa-in
(House of the Left) Apr.1875
Jingishō
(Ministry of Shrines)
8th month 1871
Kyōbushō
(Ministry of Religion)
3rd month 1872-Jan.1877
Ōkurashō
(Ministry of Finance)
Ōkurashō
Hyōbushō
(Ministry of Military Affairs)
Rikugunshō
(Ministry of the Army)
2nd month 1872
Rikugunshō
Kaigunshō
(Ministry of the Navy)
2nd month 1872
Kaigunshō
Gaimushō
(Ministry of Foreign Affairs)
Gaimushō
Naimushō
(Ministry of Home Affairs)
Nov.1873
Naimushō
Monbushō
(Ministry of Education)
Monbushō
Nōshōmushō
(Ministry of Agriculture & Commerce)
Apr.1881
Nōshōmushō
Kōbushō
(Ministry of Industry)
Intercalary 10th month 1870
Teishinshō
(Ministry of Communications)
Kaitakushi
(Hokkaidō Development Commission)
Feb.1882 Abolition
Shihōshō
(Ministry of Justice)
Shihōshō
Daishin-in
(Supreme Court)
Apr.1875
Daishin-in
Sanji-in
(Legislative Advisory Board)
Oct.1881
Hōseikyoku
(Cabinet Legislation Bureau)
Kunaishō
(Imperial Household Ministry)
Kunaishō
Naidaijin-fu (Office of Lord Keeper of the Privy Seal)
Sūmitsu-in (Privy Council)
Apr.1888
Genrōin (Chamber of Elders)
Teikoku Gikai (Imperial Diet)
Nov.1890

STRUCTURE OF CENTRAL GOVERNMENT IN EARLY MEIJI PERIOD

House of the Center. Together with a few court nobles including Sanjō Sanetomi and Iwakura Tomomi, the new government was controlled by powerful young figures mainly from the former domains of Satsuma and Chōshū, who, along with some from Tosa and Hizen, became councilors (sangi 参議) or filled various ministry posts (such as kyō 卿 and taifu 大輔)[28]. In this way, the foundations of an administration that later came to be known as the **Meiji oligarchy** 藩閥政府[ii] were largely set in place.

The new government, having achieved national unity through Hanseki Hōkan in 1871, dispatched a large-scale diplomatic mission in the same year, in which many officials led by Iwakura Tomomi travelled to Western nations (Iwakura Mission 岩倉使節団). In their absence, the caretaker government led by Saigō Takamori focused on making major domestic reforms until 1873, such as implementing an **education system** 学制 and **conscription** 徴兵制, and **reforming the land taxation system** 地租改正.

As for the military, the Goshinpei, which had been organized as a force directly under the government before the abolition of the domains, was titled the Konoehei 近衛兵 (Royal Guard) and assigned to protect the tennō. While domain forces had been disbanded along with the domains, part of them were reassigned to **garrisons** 鎮台 that were established in various places under the Ministry of Military Affairs (Hyōbushō 兵部省) to respond in the event of revolts or ikki. In 1872, the ministry was divided into the Ministry of the Army (Rikugunshō 陸軍省) and the Ministry of the Navy (Kaigunshō 海軍省).

That same year, the government, aiming to establish a modern army, released a **conscription proclamation** 徴兵告諭, on the basis of which in the first month of 1873 it issued a **conscription ordinance** 徴兵令 which enacted the policy of levée en masse. Consequently, a unified military personnel system was established in which every male who had reached the age of twenty was selected, regardless of social class, to serve in the army for a period of three years[29].

A police system was also founded around the same time. In 1873, the newly-established **Ministry of Home Affairs** (Naimushō 内務省), which was responsible for promoting

---

[28] Important posts were filled by Saigō Takamori, Ōkubo Toshimichi, and Kuroda Kiyotaka〈黒田清隆〉of Satsuma Domain; Kido Takayoshi, Itō Hirobumi, Inoue Kaoru, and Yamagata Aritomo〈山県有朋〉from Chōshū Domain; Itagaki Taisuke〈板垣退助〉, Gotō Shōjirō, and Sasaki Takayuki〈佐佐木高行〉of Tosa Domain; and Ōkuma Shigenobu〈大隈重信〉, Ōki Takatō〈大木喬任〉, Soejima Taneomi〈副島種臣〉, and Etō Shinpei〈江藤新平〉of Hizen Domain〈肥前藩〉.

[29] The foundation of a modern army based on levée en masse was the brainchild of Ōmura Masujirō from Chōshū, and was realized by Yamagata Aritomo, commander of the Kiheitai, after Ōmura was assassinated. The conscription ordinance allowed exemptions from military service for individuals who were the heads or heir of a family, bureaucrats, students, and those who paid a substitution fee of 270 yen〈円〉. As a result, most of the men who actually served in the military were second-born or later sons from farming villages.

development of new industries and supervising local districts, was also put in charge of managing police administrations across the country. Subsequently, in 1874, the **Metropolitan Police Department** (Keishichō 警視庁) was founded in Tōkyō.

Equality among the Four Classes

At the same time that national consolidation was underway, the abolition of the early modern class system was also being carried out. The master-servant relationship between the domain lords and their retainers was dissolved as a consequence of Hanseki Hōkan, whereupon the lords, along with the court nobility, were organized into a new class called **kazoku** 華族 (peers), while their retainers and the former retainers of the bakufu formed the **shizoku** 士族 (military) class. Meanwhile, the hyakushō and chōnin who belonged to the nō 農, kō 工 and shō 商 classes collectively became **heimin** 平民 (commoners), and were permitted to have surnames, while also being granted the freedom to marry people of the kazoku or shizoku class, and move between places or occupations, resulting in **shimin byōdō** 四民平等 **(equality among the four classes)**. As for people belonging to the outcaste groups, in 1871 terms such as eta えた or hinin 非人 were abolished, and they came to be legally treated the same as commoners. In 1872, an integrated reorganization of family registries[30] based on the new class system of kazoku, shizoku and heimin was conducted (**Jinshin Koseki** 壬申戸籍). Through these reforms in the class system, although there was discrimination between sexes, a sense of people being citizens[iii] sharing the same social obligations was created.

However, the government continued to provide hereditary stipends (although the amount decreased) to members of the kazoku and shizoku classes, while also paying special stipends (shōtenroku 賞典禄) for people who rendered meritorious service for the Restoration. These two stipends were together known as **chitsuroku** 秩禄 and became a heavy burden, amounting to up to thirty percent of the country's total expenditure. In 1873, the government issued the **Chitsuroku Return Law** 秩禄奉還の法 which offered a lump-sum payment to those who volunteered to cancel receiving their stipends. This was followed in 1876 by the government converting the stipends of each recipient into bonds called **kinroku kōsai shōsho** 金禄公債証書, which amounted to between five and fourteen years' worth of annual payments, and completely abolishing the chitsuroku (**chitsuroku shobun** 秩禄処分). Coupled with the **Haitō-rei** 廃刀令 **(Sword Abolishment Edict)** issued in the same year, this

---

[30] In the beginning of the Meiji period the demographic composition of the country, as of 1873, was 2,829 kazoku, 1,548,568 shizoku, 343,881 sotsu〈卒〉 (lower-ranking former bushi such as ashigaru〈足軽〉 were in this class for a period), 31,106,514 commoners (comprising 93.4% of the total population), and 298,880 people in other categories (monks, Shintō priests, etc.), for a total of 33,300,672 people.

stripped the shizoku class of its major privileges.

Because the shizoku had originally received small stipends, the government bonds they received were of correspondingly low value[31], and except for those who were successfully able to change their occupations to bureaucrats, police officers, teachers and so on, the majority struggled to make a living. Many of them started new businesses by using their bonds as capital, but lacking experience, many of them were ruined (leading to the proverb "**shizoku no shōhō**" 士族の商法," meaning to venture into business unprepared and fail). The government carried out measures to offer relief to the shizoku (**shizoku jusan** 士族授産), such as providing business loans and launching development projects on Hokkaidō, but in most cases these were unsuccessful.

Land Taxation Reform

In order to proceed with modernization, stabilization of the economy was essential. The new government's major financial resource was the annual land tax that had remained unchanged since the days of the Edo Bakufu. The amount of this tax varied among each former domain, and also fluctuated yearly depending on the size of the rice harvest. The government also faced financial difficulties in the form of debts that it had inherited from the domains upon their abolition. While the government cancelled some of these debts, there remained a pressing need to reform the land and taxation system with the aim of stabilizing state finances.

The first step in these reforms began in 1871, when farmers were permitted to grow whatever crops they deemed fit for their land. The permanent prohibition on the sale of arable land was lifted in the following year, and land ownership was officially approved by the issuing of **land title certificates** (**chiken** 地券). In principle, these certificates were granted to those who had paid the former annual land tax (landowners and independent farmers), and the old land tenure system based on the right to collect annual taxes (chigyō 知行) was dissolved. Based on this certificate system, in July 1873 the **Land Tax Reform Ordinance** 地租改正条例 was promulgated, heralding the start of a land tax reform (**chiso kaisei** 地租改正) that had nearly reached completion by 1881. The main components of the reform were: 1) changing the taxation basis from the unstable harvest rates to a constant land value; 2) changing the payment method from in kind to cash, with a tax rate set at 3% of the land value; and 3) having the holder of the land title certificate be liable for paying the tax.

---

[31] Although those who had received smaller stipends were granted government bonds with relatively large payments and high interest rates, the amount of government bonds in 1876 was still low for the shizoku, who only received an average of 500 yen per person, while the kazoku received on average more than 60,000 yen per person.

Consequently, the land tax came to be collected uniformly in cash on a nationally standardized basis irrespective of whether the harvest was good or not. With a modern tax system now in place, the financial base of the government was secure for the time being. Furthermore, with land ownership by landowners and independent farmers established, as the shift to paying tax in cash was implemented the commodity economy began to penetrate into farming villages. On the other hand, the land tax reform had not been intended to decrease the amount of tax income compared to the former annual land tax, and so farmer **ikki** 一揆 seeking tax relief broke out in various regions. In 1877, the land tax rate was reduced to 2.5%. Additionally, common land such as mountains, forests and plains that had been shared by farmers, and so could not be proven to be owned by any individual, was confiscated by the state, and discontent towards this policy also contributed to the ikki.

Promoting Development of New Industries

In an effort to realize **Fukoku Kyōhei** 富国強兵 **(enrich the country and strengthen the military)**, the government put emphasis on **Shokusan Kōgyō** 殖産興業 **(promotion of developing new industries)**. It began by abolishing remnants of the Edo system such as shekisho 関所, shukueki 宿駅, and the sukegō 助郷 system; dissolving monopolies enjoyed by the kabunakama 株仲間 guilds; lifting restrictions regarding social class; and organizing land ownership. In this way, the government sought to lay the foundations for free economic activity. Under the supervision of foreign government advisors (known as **oyatoi gaikokujin** お雇い外国人, literally "hired foreigners"), the administration began to run modern industries in an effort to develop them.

Led by the **Ministry of Industry (Kōbushō** 工部省**)**, founded in 1870, railroads were constructed to connect open ports to major cities, starting with the first railway between Shinbashi 新橋 and Yokohama in 1872, and followed by a line from Kōbe 神戸 to Kyōto via Ōsaka. The government also requisitioned industries previously managed by the bakufu, such as mines in regions like Sado 佐渡 and Ikuno and the Nagasaki Shipyard 長崎造船所, and industries previously managed by the domains, such as coal mines in Takashima 高島 and Miike 三池 and the Hyōgo Shipyard 兵庫造船所, and turned all of them into state-owned enterprises. With the aim of modernizing military defenses, arsenals were built in Tōkyō and Ōsaka to manufacture artillery, and the government endeavored to expand the Yokosuka Shipyard 横須賀造船所 founded by the former bakufu.

As for communication, in 1871 a state-run **postal system** 郵便制度[32] to replace the hik- 飛脚

---

[32] Japan signed the General Postal Union Treaty〈万国郵便連合条約〉(later Universal Postal Convention) in 1877, and the telephone was imported that same year.

INTERIOR OF TOMIOKA SILK MILL
Construction of the Tomioka Silk Mill commenced in 1871, and it began operating the following year. Many of the female factory workers were daughters of the shizoku class who had applied from all around the country, and were known as the "Tomioka Kōjo〈富岡工女〉" (Tomioka Factory Girls). The machinery was imported from France, and the Western-style structure built using bricks remains to this day.

yaku (couriers) was established based on a proposal by **Maejima Hisoka**〈前島密〉 (1835-1919), and soon a nationwide flat rate was adopted. In 1869, the first **telegraph line**〈電信線〉 was built between Tōkyō and Yokohama, and was extended to Nagasaki and Hokkaidō in five years' time. A link to Western nations was also established by a submarine cable between Nagasaki and Shanghai〈上海〉. In marine transportation, the government had domestic companies monopolize shipping in the coastal areas and along the shorelines of the country. It also granted considerable privileges to the shipping company **Mitsubishi**〈三菱〉 (**Mitsubishi Mail Steamship Company**〈郵便汽船三菱会社〉), run by **Iwasaki Yatarō**〈岩崎弥太郎〉 (1834-85) of Tosa, in order to secure a means of military transportation in emergencies.

On the other hand, the government also modernized private industries, putting particular emphasis on the expansion of silk production, the major export product at the time, in an attempt to reduce the trade deficit. In 1872, the **Tomioka Silk Mill**〈富岡製糸場〉 was built as a **state-owned model facility**〈官営模範工場〉 in Gunma Prefecture〈群馬県〉, introducing and promoting the latest technology from France while also training female factory workers.

The Ministry of Home Affairs also played a major role in the promotion of industries. Along with managing state-owned model facilities for reeling and spinning[33], the Ministry also encouraged the improvement of roads to facilitate transportation by rickshaws, carts and carriages. In agriculture and stock farming, the Komaba School of Agriculture〈駒場農学校〉 and Mita Botanical Experiment Yard〈三田育種場〉 were founded to introduce Western technology.

In order to develop the northern regions, in 1869 the government renamed Ezochi〈蝦夷地〉

[33] In 1877, the first National Industrial Exhibition〈内国勧業博覧会〉 was held in Ueno〈上野〉, organized by an office installed under the Ministry of Home Affairs.

Hokkaidō(北海道) and established the **Kaitakushi**(開拓使) **(Hokkaidō Development Commission)**[34]. Seeking to adapt the American plantation system and stockbreeding technology, the government recruited Dr. William S. Clark(クラーク) (1826-86) and founded Sapporo Agricultural College(札幌農学校) in 1876. Further, in 1874, as part of the measures carried out to relieve the shizoku class, the **tondenhei (military settler) system**(屯田兵制度) was implemented to, along with land development, prepare the north for defense against Russia[35].

Regarding currency, in 1871 the **New Currency Act**(新貨条例) was enacted, based on the gold standard, and with the introduction of the decimal system coinage was minted in new units called **Yen**(円), **Sen**(銭) and **Rin**(厘). However, the actual currency used at the time was silver coins in the open ports and predominantly paper money within Japan proper. In the following year, new government paper currency was produced to replace the previous notes (Dajōkan-satsu)(太政官札)[36] that were issued immediately after the Restoration.

Bōekigin

Dajōkan-satsu

Minbushō-satsu

New paper money (Meiji Tsūhō-satsu)

National bank paper money

CURRENCY IN THE EARLY MEIJI PERIOD
The new government issued fiat money such as the Dajōkan-satsu immediately after its establishment, and subsequently in 1872 it issued new paper money that had been printed in Germany. The Dajōkan-satsu, Minbushō-satsu, and other banknotes of the former domains were exchanged with the new paper currency.

---

[34] The Kaitakushi was an office under the direct supervision of the Dajōkan. The head office was initially established in Tōkyō, but in 1871 was relocated to Sapporo. After the development project ended in 1882, the Kaitakushi was dissolved and three prefectures (Hakodate〈函館〉, Sapporo and Nemuro〈根室〉) were established, but in 1886 these too were abolished and replaced by the Hokkaidō Government〈北海道庁〉.

[35] Behind the scenes of the development project, the traditional lifestyles, customs and beliefs of the Ainu culture were gradually disappearing. In 1899 the government issued the Hokkaidō Former Aborigines Protection Act〈北海道旧土人保護法〉, but this did not help prevent the Ainu culture and way of life from being lost. Later on, in 1997, the Ainu Cultural Promotion Act〈アイヌ文化振興法〉 was issued.

[36] When the new government was first established it had few financial resources, and therefore requisitioned three million ryō from merchants such as Mitsui〈三井組〉 and Ono-gumi〈小野組〉 in Kyōto, and Kōnoike〈鴻池〉 in Ōsaka, while also issuing fiat money such as the Dajōkan-satsu and Minbushō-satsu〈民部省札〉.

The intent was to unify the paper currency, but the new notes were **fiat money** 不換紙幣 that were not convertible to gold or silver coinage.

To resolve this situation, the government attempted to issue **convertible banknotes** 兌換銀行券 that could be exchanged to gold coinage with the help of the private sector, such as merchants and landowners. To this end the **National Bank Act** 国立銀行条例[37], initiated by **Shibusawa Eiichi** 渋沢栄一 (1840-1931), was promulgated in 1872, and the First National Bank was founded in the following year. However, management proved difficult and immediate implementation of the conversion system was not possible.

In the process of promoting new industries, private entrepreneurs such as Mitsui and Iwasaki (Mitsubishi) were granted privileges from the government. These entrepreneurs obtained monopolistic profits in areas such as finance, trade, and shipping, and came to be called **seishō** 政商 (**political merchants**).

"Civilization and Enlightenment"

The Meiji government, aiming to achieve Fukoku Kyōhei, promoted modernization through adopting Western civilization. It took the lead in incorporating all manner of Western phenomena, from industrial technology and social systems to academic studies, thought, and even lifestyles. A movement called **Bunmei Kaika** 文明開化 (literally "civilization and enlightenment") emerged in the early Meiji period, and spread mainly in the major centers through journalism and the like, gradually coming to influence to some extent the manners and customs of the general public.

In the area of thought and philosophy, the ways of thinking and old conventions based on Confucianism and Shintō came to be dismissed as obsolete, supplanted by modern occidental philosophies such as liberalism and individualism[38], and the **theory of natural rights** 天賦人権の思想[39] became influential. Books that described these new ideas associated with enlightenment became popular and played a major role in changing

---

[37] Modelled on the American banking system, the term "national" is used in the context of a bank founded based on national law, not in the sense that it is state-run. The National Bank Act required that issued banknotes were convertible to gold or silver coinage.

[38] In the beginning of the Meiji period, British and American philosophies of liberalism and utilitarianism became accepted, as the works of John Stuart Mill and Herbert Spencer〈スペンサー〉 were popularly read, becoming the mainstream of modern philosophy at the time. Subsequently, Charles Darwin's〈ダーウィン〉 theory of evolution was also introduced. Nakae Chōmin〈中江兆民〉 (from Tosa), who had studied in France, introduced the concept of a social contract by way of Jean-Jacques Rousseau〈ルソー〉, and became a leading theorist of the Freedom and People's Rights Movement〈自由民権運動〉. Around the same time, political ideologies of nationalism were also introduced from Prussia.

[39] Natural rights is a concept asserting that all people are born with fundamental rights as human beings. This became one of the leading ideas driving the Freedom and People's Rights Movement.

Japanese thinking. Examples include *Seiyō Jijō* 『西洋事情』 (Conditions in the West), *Gakumon no Susume* 『学問のすゝめ』 (Encouragement of Learning), and *Bunmeiron no Gairyaku* 『文明論之概略』 (Outline of a Theory of Civilization), by **Fukuzawa Yukichi** 福沢諭吉 (1834-1901), *Self Help* 『西国立志編』 by Samuel Smiles スマイルズ (1812-1901), and *On Liberty* 『自由之理』 by John Stuart Mill ミル (1806-73), the latter two being translated by **Nakamura Masanao** 中村正直 (1832-91).

In terms of education, in 1872, a year after the establishment of the **Ministry of Education** (**Monbushō** 文部省), a national **education system** 学制 was promulgated modelled on the French system. The government adopted a utilitarian approach to education, seeing its purpose as fostering each citizen to enable them to live independently, broaden their knowledge, and make their own fortunes. Accordingly, it emphasized the development of **primary education** 小学校教育, and aimed to establish a system that provided education to everyone regardless of gender[40]. For advanced education, in 1877 the government established the **University of Tōkyō** 東京大学 by combining various schools that had originated from the Kaiseijo and Igakusho founded by the bakufu, and many foreign instructors were recruited to teach there. Specialized schools were also founded for teacher training, women's education[41], and technical education.

Although the development of the education system was mainly directed by the government, private schools such as Keiō Gijuku 慶応義塾, founded by Fukuzawa Yukichi in 1868, and Dōshisha 同志社, founded by Niijima Jō 新島襄 (1843-90) in 1875, were also established and provided their own distinctive curriculums.

The reforms of the Meiji Restoration also brought about great changes in the religious sphere. In 1868, the government launched a policy of banning the Shintō-Buddhist syncretism that had endured since ancient times (**Shinbutsu Bunri-rei** 神仏分離令, literally "**Separation Order of Kami and Buddhas**") and declared Shintō the state religion, as it had adopted the standpoint of fusing politics and religion through the restoration of rule by the tennō. This led to a brief craze across the nation for Haibutsu Kishaku 廃仏毀釈, meaning abolishing Buddhism and destroying Buddhist images. At the same time, however, this law also stimulated Buddhist monks to awaken from complacency. In 1870, the government issued a royal rescript entitled **Daikyō Senpu** 大教宣布の詔

---

[40] The education system divided the country into 8 university districts, with each district having 1 university and 32 secondary schools. The regulations stipulated that each secondary school district was to have 210 primary schools, and therefore originally 53,760 primary schools were planned for construction across the nation, one primary school having been calculated to provide for 600 people out of the population at the time. However, the plan's degree of standardization was so far from reality as to be impractical and did not suit the actual conditions of people's lives. As a result, it was revised in the Education Order〈教育令〉of 1879.

[41] In 1872, the first women's school was founded in Tōkyō, and a teacher training school for women was also subsequently established.

no Mikotonori (Propagation of the Great Doctrine), while also organizing systems for Shintō Shrines and determining national holidays[42] in an effort to situate Shintō in the center of national consciousness.

As for Christianity, the new government initially maintained the bakufu's prohibition of the religion, and so underground Christians living around Nagasaki, such as in Urakami 浦上 and the Gotō Islands 五島列島, were persecuted. However, after strong protests from the Western powers, in 1873 the notices declaring the prohibition were finally removed, and the religion came to be tacitly tolerated[43].

Missionaries of various denominations, who had heretofore been involved in businesses such as education and medicine since the end of the Edo period, took this opportunity to start actively propagating their beliefs among Japanese.

Since the end of the bakufu, foreign newspapers had been translated under the supervision of the authorities, and this continued to be done by former bakufu retainers even during the dawn of the Meiji period, which, along with the development of letterpress printing[44], led to the launch of all sorts of **daily newspapers** 日刊新聞 and **magazines** 雑誌, primarily in Tōkyō. In addition to reporting, these publications engaged in criticism of political issues, and ushered in new forms of discourse, with books for academic study and self-cultivation becoming popular. Moreover, scholars of Western learning such as Mori Arinori (1847-89), Fukuzawa Yukichi, Nishi Amane (1829-97), Katō Hiroyuki 加藤弘之 (1836-1916), and Nishimura Shigeki 西村茂樹 (1828-1902) formed an academic association called the **Meirokusha** 明六社 in 1873. They began publishing a journal, *Meiroku Zasshi* 『明六雑誌』, from the following year, as well as holding lecture gatherings, through which they advocated eliminating feudal ideologies and promoted modern thought.

In the twelfth month of 1872, the government decided to change the calendar to follow that of Western countries. The old lunisolar calendar was abolished and replaced by the **solar calendar** 太陽暦, with changes such as one day being divided into 24 hours, and later, Sundays being set as holidays. This resulted in changes to long-practiced events

---

[42] One national holiday was the Kigen Festival〈紀元節〉(February 11 in the modern calendar), which honored the day of Jinmu Tennō's〈神武天皇〉enthronement (first day of the year in the lunar calendar) according to *Nihonshoki*〈『日本書紀』〉, and another was the Tenchō Festival〈天長節〉(November 3 in the modern calendar), which honored Meiji Tennō's birthday.

[43] The underground Christians of Urakami came into the open in 1865 when they confessed their beliefs to a French missionary who was visiting Ōura Church〈大浦天主堂〉upon its completion. However, the new government, having adopted Shintō as the state religion, arrested the Urakami Christians and exiled them to other domains (Urakami Incidents〈浦上教徒弾圧事件〉).

[44] The modern development of letterpress printing began in 1869 after Motoki Shōzō〈本木昌造〉successfully introduced technology to mass produce lead moveable type.

GINZA SCENE, EARLY 1880S
The two-story brick buildings and pavements that had been built as national projects, gas lights along the sidewalks, horse-drawn trams, and rickshaws all catch the eye. Pedestrians wearing Western clothing also stand out.

and customs[45].

The influence of the Bunmei Kaika movement was especially pronounced in the major urban centers like Tōkyō. The custom of wearing **Western clothing** 洋服 began with government officials and police officers and gradually spread into the private sector, while a hairstyle called **zangiri-atama** ざんぎり頭 (“**cropped head**”) became a symbol of the movement. Aside from newspapers, traditional multicolor prints (nishiki-e 錦絵) were frequently printed. Brick buildings appeared along Ginza Avenue in Tōkyō, conveniences like gas lights and horse-drawn trams became city attractions, and eating beef hot pot became popular.

In the countryside, lifestyles changed more slowly, but gradually the wave of modernization reached these areas too, bringing changes like the development of transportation and the spread of newspapers. On the other hand, old artwork and traditional performing arts came to be neglected, resulting in the loss of much valuable cultural heritage.

Diplomatic Relations in the Early Meiji Period

In foreign affairs, the most pressing issue for the Meiji government was revising the unequal treaties that it had inherited from its predecessor. At the end of 1871, a delegation headed by Minister of the Right Iwakura Tomomi was dispatched to the US and Europe (**Iwakura Mission** 岩倉使節団)[46]. The initial objective was to negotiate with the powers, beginning with the US, but while this was unsuccessful, the mission was able to visit various modern Western nations and thoroughly observe their political and industrial developments before returning to Japan. From 1876, Minister of

---

[45] The third day of the 12th month of 1872 by the lunar calendar was converted to January 1, 1873 by the solar calendar.

[46] The Ansei Treaties permitted negotiation for revisions from 1872. The mission's purpose was thus to hold overtures for the revision of these conventions, and to examine the various Western systems and cultures. The participants were a large group of some 50 people, including Iwakura Tomomi as ambassador, Kido Takayoshi, Ōkubo Toshimichi, Itō Hirobumi, and Yamaguchi Naoyoshi〈山口尚芳〉 as vice envoys, and others. They were also accompanied by some 60 students who were to study abroad, including five young women such as Tsuda Umeko〈津田梅子〉 and Yamakawa Sutematsu〈山川捨松〉.

Foreign Affairs Terashima Munenori 寺島宗則 (1832-93) negotiated with the US and was nearly successful in recovering Japanese autonomy over tariffs, but failed due to opposition from the UK and Prussia.

IWAKURA MISSION
On the 12th day of the 11th month of 1871, the mission set sail from Yokohama, and returned in 1873. This photograph was taken in San Francisco. From right to left: Ōkubo Toshimichi, Itō Hirobumi, Iwakura Tomomi, Yamaguchi Naoyoshi, and Kido Takayoshi.

As for neighboring countries, the government sent a delegation to Qing China in 1871 to conclude the **Sino-Japanese Friendship and Trade Treaty** 日清修好条規[47], which stipulated the mutual opening of ports and recognition of consular jurisdiction.

The Ryūkyū Kingdom was in a complex situation in which it was nominally a client state of the Qing Dynasty but in practice had been controlled since the Edo period by the Shimazu family of Satsuma Domain. The Meiji government undertook a policy of officially making the kingdom Japanese territory, and in 1872 it was reconfigured into **Ryūkyū Domain** 琉球藩 under the direct control of the government, with King **Shō Tai** 尚泰 (1843-1901) as han-ō 藩王 ("domain king"). However, the Qing Dynasty did not approve of this development, and strongly protested by asserting its suzerainty.

In 1871, the Mudan Incident 琉球漂流民殺害事件 occurred in Taiwan when Ryūkyūan fishermen who drifted there after a shipwreck were massacred by aborigines. As the Qing Dynasty refused to take responsibility for the killings and offer compensation, the Meiji government, pressured by the military and shizoku, dispatched a military expedition to Taiwan in 1874 (**Taiwan Expedition** 台湾出兵). Following arbitration by the UK, the Qing Dynasty recognized the dispatch as legitimate and paid de facto compensation. In 1879, the Japanese government formally abolished Ryūkyū Domain and the Ryūkyū Kingdom, and established Okinawa Prefecture 沖縄県 (**Ryūkyū Disposition** 琉球処分)[48].

When the Meiji government had been founded, it had called on Joseon Korea to establish diplomatic relations. However, Korea, which had adopted an isolationist policy, refused to open official negotiations, expressing discontent with Japan's attitude.

---

[47] This was the first equal treaty that Japan concluded, but it was not ratified until 1873 because the government was not satisfied with the terms.

[48] Although the Ryūkyū Kingdom was reconfigured into Japanese territory as Okinawa Prefecture, the former systems such as those for land ownership, taxation and regional administration were maintained, and elections for members of the House of Representatives were not held until 1912. Since the economic disparity with the mainland was substantial, and the general income of Okinawa residents was low, the number of people migrating to work elsewhere in Japan or overseas was by no means small.

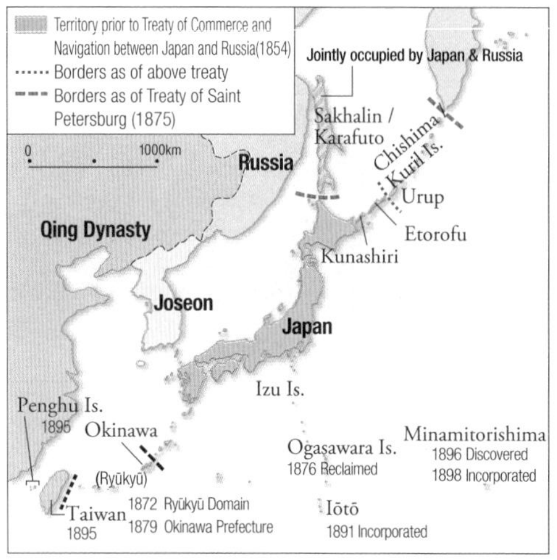

JAPANESE TERRITORY IN EARLY MEIJI PERIOD

In 1873, the leaders of the caretaker government, Saigō Takamori and Itagaki Taisuke (1837-1919), advocated a punitive expedition to Korea (**Seikanron** 征韓論), but this was not realized due to staunch opposition from Ōkubo Toshimichi and others who had returned from the Iwakura Mission[49]. Subsequently, in 1875, in the wake of the **Ganghwa Island Incident** 江華島事件[50], Japan put pressure on Korea, and in the following year the **Japan-Korea Treaty of Amity** 日朝修好条規（江華条約） (also called the **Treaty of Ganghwa Island**) was signed, bringing about the opening of Korea[51].

The possession of Sakhalin was another issue, having been unresolved with Russia since the end of the Edo period. Since the Japanese government was preoccupied with the development of Hokkaidō, in 1875 the **Treaty of Saint Petersburg** 樺太・千島交換条約 was signed, whereby Japan renounced its rights over Sakhalin in exchange for possession of the Kuril Islands 千島列島.

As for the southern regions, in 1861 the bakufu had dispatched officials to the **Ogasawara Islands** 小笠原諸島, where Westerners had been settling, to assert control over the territory, but soon withdrew. In 1876, the Ministry of Home Affairs established a branch office there and resumed governance. Thus, the Japanese boundaries were set internationally on both the northern and southern extremities[52].

---

[49] The caretaker government had provisionally come to the conclusion to adopt a plan to send Saigō Takamori to Korea to pressure the country to open relations, and resort to military action in the event that Korea refused. However, top officials returning to Japan from the Iwakura Mission, such as Ōkubo Toshimichi and Kido Takayoshi, were against this plan, arguing that the development of domestic affairs should be prioritized. Ōkubo's side won the debate, and Saigō's side resigned from their posts in response.

[50] An incident where the Japanese gunboat *Un'yō* 〈雲揚〉 provoked Korean forces on Ganghwa Island, close to the capital city of Hanseong〈漢城〉.

[51] The Japan-Korea Treaty of Amity was an unequal treaty which opened the ports of Busan〈釜山〉, Incheon〈仁川〉 and Wonsan〈元山〉, and agreed to grant Japan privileges such as consular jurisdiction and exemption from tariffs.

[52] After confirming that no other country owned the Senkaku Islands〈尖閣諸島〉 and Takeshima〈竹島〉, they were incorporated as Japanese territory in January 1895 and January 1905, respectively.

Resistance to the New Government

Among the shizoku who had joined government forces during the Boshin War, no small number felt dissatisfied with the new government for not reflecting their views in its policies. This discontented group supported the argument for an expedition to Korea in 1873, and when this plan was unsuccessful, political figures who had supported it, including Saigō Takamori, Itagaki Taisuke, Gotō Shojirō, Etō Shinpei (1834-74) and Soejima Taneomi (1828-1905) all resigned their posts (**Political Crisis of 1873** 明治六年の政変). Led by these figures, against the backdrop of dissatisfaction by the shizoku, a political movement criticizing the government began in the following year. This upheaval left Ōkubo Toshimichi, who took the post of Naimukyō 内務卿 (Lord of Home Affairs), in charge of the government.

Itagaki, Gotō and others established the Aikoku Kōtō 愛国公党 (Public Party of Patriots) and submitted to the House of the Left a **Petition for Establishing a Popularly-Elected Chamber** 民撰議院設立の建白書. This document, which was drafted with the help of intellectuals who had returned from the UK, criticized the negative influence of arbitrary bureaucracy and called for the establishment of a national assembly to govern the country based on public opinion. The petition was published in newspapers and caused a great public stir, igniting the **Freedom and People's Rights Movement** 自由民権運動.

On the other hand, there were some conservative members of the shizoku who, dissatisfied with the loss of their old privileges amid the rapid reforms, led anti-government uprisings, even though they had contributed to establishing the new government in the first place.

In 1874, Etō Shinpei, another of the former councilors who had supported an expedition to Korea, was greeted by disaffected shizoku in Saga 佐賀, his home region, and became the head of the Seikantō 征韓党, a group that launched a rebellion against the government (**Saga Rebellion** 佐賀の乱). Furthermore, in 1876 when the rights to carry swords and receive stipends were abolished, a group called the Keishintō 敬神党 (also known as Shinpūren 神風連), made up of disaffected shizoku in Kumamoto 熊本 who called for restoring Jōi ideology, started a rebellion and attacked the Kumamoto garrison. In response to this incident, other armed uprisings by disaffected shizoku occurred, such as the Akizuki Rebellion 秋月の乱 in Fukuoka Prefecture 福岡県, and the rebellion led by former councilor Maebara Issei 前原一誠 (1834-76) in Hagi 萩, Yamaguchi Prefecture 山口県. However, all of these uprisings were suppressed by government forces.

Moreover, in 1873, many ikki by farmers known as **ketsuzei ikki** 血税一揆 (**blood tax ikki**) erupted due to resentment towards the increased burdens caused by the introduction of conscription and the establishment of primary schools under the new education system. In 1876, large-scale farmer ikki broke out against the land tax reforms because the tax was to be based on land value determined by assessing the average amount of rice prices in the past, even though prices had since declined (**anti-land tax reform ikki** 地租改正反対一揆)[53].

In 1877, farmer dissatisfaction was alleviated somewhat by a reduction in land tax, but at this same juncture the largest rebellion by shizoku broke out in Kagoshima Prefecture, centered on students at private military academies founded by Saigō Takamori, who had resigned his post and returned home. Seeing this rebellion break out under Saigō's leadership, disaffected shizoku from across Kyūshū rebelled against the government, but after half a year government forces were able to suppress all of them (**Satsuma Rebellion** 西南戦争[iv]). With this rebellion drawing to a close, uprisings by disaffected shizoku finally ceased.

The Founding of a Constitutional State and the First Sino-Japanese War

The Freedom and People's Rights Movement

Stimulated by Itagaki Taisuke and other statesmen submitting their Petition for Establishing a Popularly-Elected Chamber, debate on freedom and people's rights rapidly increased. In 1874, Itagaki returned to his home in Tosa and gathered fellow advocates such as Kataoka Kenkichi 片岡健吉 (1834-1903) to form the **Risshisha** 立志社 (**Self-Help Society**). In the following year, intending to create a national-level organization for people's rights groups like his, which played a key role, he founded the **Aikokusha** 愛国社 (Patriot Society) in Ōsaka. In response to these movements, the government also decided to gradually shift towards constitutionalism[54]. In April 1875, it issued the **Promulgation for the Gradual Establishment of Constitutional Government** 漸次立憲政体樹立の詔, and in tandem established the Genrōin 元老院 (Chamber of Elders) as a legislative advisory board, the Supreme Court 大審院 as the highest judicial body, and the **Assembly of Prefectural Governors** 地方官会議, which was composed of governors from both the fu and ken prefectures. Under the Genrōin, it was decided to begin drafting a constitution from the following

---

[53] Starting in Ibaraki Prefecture〈茨城県〉, farmer ikki followed in the prefectures of Mie〈三重〉, Aichi〈愛知〉, Gifu〈岐阜〉 and Sakai〈堺〉. The government dispatched the military to suppress all of them.

[54] In early 1875, the three statesmen Ōkubo Toshimichi, Kido Takayoshi, and Itagaki Taisuke met in Ōsaka, where they decided on policies aimed at gradually forming a national assembly by adopting Kido's ideas (Ōsaka Conference〈大阪会議〉). Although Kido had left the government due to opposing the Taiwan Expedition, he and Itagaki temporarily returned to office after the meeting.

year (1876)[55]. On the other hand, the government also enacted laws, such as the **Defamation Law** 讒謗律 and the **Press Ordinance** 新聞紙条例 in June 1875, to crack down on people's rights activists who frequently criticized them via newspapers and magazines.

As ikki by shizoku and farmers gradually ceased from 1876-77, the government moved to reform its system of local governance by issuing what became known as the **Three New Laws on Local Governments** 地方三新法 in 1878: the Law for the Reorganization of Counties, Wards, Towns, and Villages 郡区町村編制法[56]; the Regulations for Prefectural Assemblies 府県会規則[57]; and the Regulations for Local Taxes 地方税規則[58]. This resulted in the local administrative system being overhauled, enabling public opinion to be incorporated to a certain degree via assemblies.

During the Satsuma Rebellion, the Risshisha, at the forefront of the people's rights movement, had attempted to submit a petition to Meiji Tennō requesting the establishment of a national assembly headed by Kataoka Kenkichi (**Risshisha Petition** 立志社建白), but the government rejected this. After this, an incident occurred where several members of the society attempted to join the rebel forces, which led the movement to temporarily decline. However, in the wake of a revival convention of the Aikokusha, which had been disintegrating, held in Ōsaka in 1878, the movement grew again, and expanded beyond just the shizoku, gaining supporters among landowners, city merchants and craftsmen, and members of prefectural assemblies[59].

In March of 1880, the **Kokkai Kisei Dōmei** 国会期成同盟 (**League for the Establishment of a National Assembly**) was founded under a decision made during the Aikokusha's third

---

[55] After several revisions, the draft constitution by the Genrōin was completed in 1880 as the "Draft of the National Constitution of Japan〈「日本国憲按」〉." However, Iwakura Tomomi and other statesmen argued that it did not suit Japan's "kokutai" ("national polity" or "national essence"), causing it to be abandoned.

[56] The standardized administrative divisions of large wards〈大区〉and small wards〈小区〉, introduced after Haihan Chiken, were discontinued, and the former administrative units of counties, towns, and villages were restored in their place. Regarding administrative units within prefectures, urban districts were wards (ku〈区〉) and the remaining areas were counties (gun〈郡〉); under the counties, towns and villages that had existed since the Edo period were designated as subsidiary units of local governments.

[57] Although some assemblies based on elections had already begun to be established in local areas at the discretion of the governors, this regulation approved them on a nation-wide basis and established universal regulations for them. Prefectural assemblies were granted some rights pertaining to deliberating prefectural budgets.

[58] Various complex taxes that had been collected, such as prefectural taxes and residential taxes, were combined into local taxes with the aim of building prefectural finances.

[59] In 1879, books introducing people's rights concepts, such as Ueki Emori's *Minken Jiyūron*〈「民権自由論」〉(On People's Rights and Freedom), were published, and greatly stimulated the spread of the movement.

convention held at the end of the previous year. A petition calling for the establishment of a national assembly was addressed to the tennō, and signed by representatives of various political associations[60] across Japan that belonged to the League. The League attempted to submit the petition to the Dajōkan, Genrōin, and so forth. However, the government did not accept this petition, and issued the **Public Assembly Ordinance** (集会条例) in April, restricting the activities of these political associations. The League held its second convention in Tōkyō in November that same year, but there was no consensus on what direction the movement should take. In the end, it was decided that each association would produce a draft constitution and bring them to a meeting in October of the following year (1881). Later on, some members held another meeting at which they decided to form a liberalist political party. In October 1881, led by members of this group, the **Jiyūtō** (自由党) (**Liberal Party**) was founded, and Itagaki Taisuke was appointed the leader.

The government, after the assassination of its most influential leader, Ōkubo Toshimichi, in 1878, lacked powerful leadership, and was divided upon seeing the rise of the Freedom and People's Rights Movement. Ōkuma Shigenobu (1838-1922) proposed implementing a British-style parliamentary cabinet system in short order, but was staunchly opposed by Minister of the Right Iwakura Tomomi and Itō Hirobumi (1841-1909). During this period, a **scandal over disposal of state-owned property by the Kaitakushi** (開拓使官有物払下げ事件)[61] occurred, agitating media criticism of the government. In October 1881, the government dismissed Ōkuma for ostensibly being involved with this tide of public opinion. The government then decided on the basic principles for establishing a Kintei Kenpō (欽定憲法) (Imperial Constitution)[62], and issued the **Edict on the Establishment of a National Assembly** (国会開設の勅諭), pledging to organize a parliament in 1890. Consequently, this **Political Crisis of 1881** (明治十四年の政変) resulted in a Satchō (Satsuma and Chōshū) oligarchy being formed around Itō Hirobumi and others, and steps towards establishing a constitutional monarchy with great authority invested in the monarch.

Many private proposals for constitutions were also drafted by citizens. After the

---

[60] Political groups in people's rights movements across Japan, pioneered by Risshisha in Tosa, were called "political associations" (seisha〈政社〉).

[61] In 1881, it was reported that the head of the Kaitakushi in Hokkaidō, Kuroda Kiyotaka from the former Satsuma Domain, was attempting to sell state-owned property belonging to the Kaitakushi to people from the same domain at an extremely low price. This developed into a scandal, and the sale was cancelled as a result of the political crisis that same year.

[62] In contrast to a civil constitution which is based on national consensus, this term refers to a constitution established by the tennō.

Kōjunsha (交詢社) Club, a social organization founded by Fukuzawa Yukichi, announced its "Private Draft (「私擬憲法案」) of the Japanese Constitution" in 1881, people's rights advocates such as **Ueki Emori** (植木枝盛) (1857-92) similarly created many of their own[63]. At the same time, there was great discussion about people's rights ideas in general[64].

When the time for opening the national assembly had been decided, the **Rikken Kaishintō** (立憲改進党)[v] (**Constitutional Progressive Party**, hereafter Kaishintō) was founded in 1882. Appointing Ōkuma Shigenobu as its leader, the party advocated the implementation of a British-style parliamentary system, in opposition to the Jiyūtō which called for the adoption of French-style radical liberalism. The Jiyūtō, carrying on the legacy of the Risshisha and Aikokusha, was mainly based in rural areas, whereas the Kaishintō was supported by urban businessmen and intellectuals.

The government, meanwhile, similarly formed a conservative party called the Rikken Teiseitō (立憲帝政党) (Constitutional Imperial Party) that included Fukuchi Gen'ichirō (福地源一郎) (1841-1906) and a number of other conservatives in 1882. However, the party failed to become a force to compete with the various people's rights factions, and was disbanded the following year.

Matsukata Finance

During the Satsuma Rebellion, the government, in need of military funds, issued more fiat paper currency. Meanwhile, in the wake of legal reforms in 1876 that ended the obligation for banks to convert paper money to coinage, numerous national banks were founded by merchants or landowners, or by kazoku or shizoku who invested their

---

[63] From around the time that the Kōjunsha Club announced their draft for a constitution, a movement sprang up in various areas as people announced their own drafts. Today, these drafts are collectively referred to as "**shigi kenpō**〈「私擬憲法」〉" ("**private draft constitutions**"). The Kōjunsha draft advocated a parliamentary cabinet system and a system of collective responsibility for ministers of state. Ueki Emori's "Draft Constitution of Oriental Greater Japan〈「東洋大日本国国憲按」〉," on the other hand, was a radical proposal that included extensive assurance of human rights, a powerful unicameral parliament, and the rights to resistance and revolution. Risshisha's "Draft of the Constitution of Japan〈「日本憲法見込案」〉" was part of this same movement. Other than these, there were also proposals such as the Itsukaichi Draft Constitution〈五日市憲法草案〉, drafted by a study group consisting of young people from farming villages in the suburbs of Tōkyō.

[64] Nakae Chōmin published *Min'yaku Yakukai*〈『民約訳解』〉, a partial Japanese translation of and commentary on *Du contrat social* by Jean-Jacques Rousseau. Katō Hiroyuki, meanwhile, in *Jinken Shinsetsu*〈『人権新説』〉 (A New Theory of Human Rights) criticized the theory of natural rights, embraced by people's rights groups, from a Social Darwinist perspective. This in turn triggered counterarguments, such as Baba Tatsui's〈馬場辰猪〉 *Tenpu Jinken-ron*〈『天賦人権論』〉 (Theory of Natural Human Rights) and Ueki's *Tenpu Jinken-ben* 〈『天賦人権弁』〉(Argument for Natural Human Rights).

government bonds[65]. These banks also began issuing large numbers of nonconvertible paper currency. These two factors combined caused rampant inflation that lowered the value of paper money against the silver coins used in foreign trade. As a result, government revenues – which mainly consisted of land taxes, paid at fixed amounts in paper currency – effectively declined, leading to a financial crisis. Furthermore, the amount of bullion coin reserves (gold and silver) had bottomed out around 1867 since imports were continuously exceeding exports.

In response to this situation, in 1880 **Ōkuma Shigenobu** 大隈重信 took the lead in financial and currency reform by raising the brewery tax and formulating plans for selling off state-owned factories[66]. In the following year, **Matsukata Masayoshi** 松方正義 (1835-1924), the new minister of finance, adopted a policy of fiscal restraint, seeking to increase government revenue by raising taxes while drastically decreasing expenditures other than military spending. The government followed deflationary policies by using the surplus revenue to dispose of fiat paper currency, while also accumulating bullion coins, and in 1882 it established the **Bank of Japan** 日本銀行 as a central government bank[67]. The Bank of Japan began issuing banknotes that were convertible to silver in 1885, when the value of silver coins and paper money had almost become equal, and conversion to silver for government paper currency began from the following year, finalizing a **silver standard** 銀本位 monetary system[68].

BANK OF JAPAN'S FIRST CONVERTIBLE BANKNOTE
Under the Convertible Banknote Regulations, the Bank of Japan issued four banknotes that were convertible to silver: 100 yen, 10 yen, 5 yen, and 1 yen.

However, the severe financial austerity and deflationary policies also resulted in sig-

---

[65] The establishment of national banks was discontinued after the 153rd National Bank had been founded in 1879.

[66] In 1880, the government announced the **Guidelines for the Disposal of Factories** 〈工場払下げ概則〉 in order to dispose of some state-owned enterprises that had been suffering from substantial losses. However, since the focus was on recovering invested funds, there were few takers, and it was only after the guidelines were abolished in 1884 that enterprise disposal picked up steam.

[67] In 1883, the National Bank Act was amended, depriving national banks of the right to issue banknotes and thereby converting them into ordinary private banks.

[68] If paper currency could be converted into gold or silver coinage, then the international value of the currency could be stabilized. Paper currency was circulated domestically, but paying for the excessive imports of the time required the conversion of those bills into silver and gold that then flowed overseas. Thus, it was to be expected that the amount of domestic coinage would decrease and prices drop, which would then automatically have the effect of decreasing imports and increasing exports.

nificant drops in commodity prices, such as for rice and silk cocoons, leading to a severe recession across the country. Moreover, as the land tax had to be paid at a fixed amount, the higher taxes meant that the burden on farmers increased substantially, resulting in many independent farmers being forced to abandon their land and become **tenant farmers** (小作農). Landowners cultivated part of their land and lent the rest to these farmers, collecting a large share of these high tenant fees in crops produced. The landowners would also run other businesses, such as moneylending and liquor shops, collecting more land that was pledged as collateral for loans. Some farmers who lost their land moved into cities to become urban poor, and this, combined with the struggles of lower-ranking shizoku also becoming more severe, led to greater social unrest.

The Reorganization of the People's Rights Movement

The economic difficulties encountered by the rural areas under Matsukata's financial reforms also greatly affected the people's rights movement. Among the landowners and farmers who supported the campaign, a large number withdrew from activities due to financial hardship and declining living standards, while on the other hand, there were also some who became more politically radicalized for those same reasons.

Under these circumstances, in 1882 the government revised the Public Assembly Ordinance and banned political parties from establishing branch offices, while also adopting conciliatory measures such as funding Jiyūtō leader Itagaki Taisuke's trip to Europe. Criticism of Itagaki's trip arose even from within his own party, while the Kaishintō launched a barrage of criticism against him[69], causing the people's rights movement to lose its united leadership. Meanwhile,

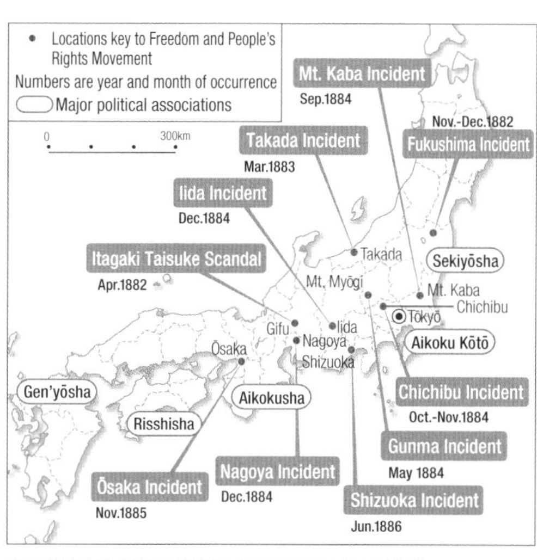

POLITICAL UPRISINGS INVOLVING JIYŪTŌ MEMBERS

[69] Itō Hirobumi, Inoue Kaoru and other members of the government seeking to moderate the people's rights movement, arranged a trip to Europe – funded in secret by Mitsui – for members of the Jiyūtō including Itagaki Taisuke and Gotō Shōjirō. The Kaishintō criticized the Jiyūtō by questioning the source of its travel funding, but was countered by the Jiyūtō which exposed the relationship between Ōkuma Shigenobu and Mitsubishi.

SUPPRESSION OF SPEECH (*TÔBAÉ,* ISSUE 22)
Immediately after the promulgation of the Safety Preservation Law, the government revised the Press Ordinance and slightly relaxed its control, although fundamentally nothing changed. This illustration, by French artist Georges Ferdinand Bigot, depicts journalists advocating people's rights being arrested by a police officer.

in some local areas Jiyūtō members and farmers took direct action, protesting against the government suppression and heavy taxes imposed during the recession. The **Fukushima Incident** 福島事件 at the end of the year was followed by a series of political revolts occurring in the Kantō, Hokuriku 北陸, and Tōkai regions, such as the Takada Incident 高田事件, Gunma Incident 群馬事件, and Mt. Kaba Incident 加波山事件. In 1884, approximately three thousand farmers in the Chichibu 秩父 region of Saitama 埼玉県 Prefecture, calling themselves the Konmintō 困民党 (Distressed People's Party), rose in revolt, seeking a reduction of mounting debts. Bolstered by supporters, they attacked loan sharks, police officers, and local government officials, prompting the government to go so far as to dispatch the army to suppress them (**Chichibu Incident** 秩父事件).

Although not all of these incidents had been led by members of the Jiyūtō[70], the aftermath nevertheless fractured the confidence in the party's leadership, and coupled with a lack of funds, the party was dissolved after the Mt. Kaba Incident. Similarly, the Kaishintō also essentially dissolved after its major leaders, notably Ōkuma Shigenobu, left the party. In 1885, an incident occurred where a group including Ōi Kentarō 大井憲太郎 (1843-1922), who had belonged to a leftist faction of the former Jiyūtō, was arrested in Ōsaka. They had been preparing to travel to Korea, where they were planning to

[70] The Fukushima Incident was a protest movement led by farmers that broke out when the governor, Mishima Michitsune〈三島通庸〉, attempted to impose a labor statute upon them, irrespective of their economic difficulties, to fund prefectural roads. Although the Fukushima Jiyūtō〈福島自由党〉only supported this protest through indirect means such as lawsuits, Mishima used this as a pretext to arrest many of their members, such as Kōno Hironaka〈河野広中〉. This incident therefore became known as the first of many cases where the Jiyūtō was associated with radicalism. The Chichibu Incident was another case where former members of the party were indirectly involved.

overthrow the conservative government (**Ōsaka Incident** 大阪事件)[71]. Oscillating repeatedly between radicalization and being suppressed, the people's rights movement gradually fell into decline.

However, as the date of the opening of the national assembly grew closer, members of the people's rights movement prepared to regroup. In 1887, a movement called the **Petition on the Three Major Affairs** 三大事件建白運動[72] began in the wake of the minister of foreign affairs, Inoue Kaoru, failing to negotiate for a revision of the unequal treaties. The movement eschewed differentiation between former members of the Jiyūtō and Kaishintō, instead calling for unity under a common purpose (daidō danketsu 大同団結) while awaiting the opening of the assembly. Even after the government promulgated the **Safety Preservation Law** 保安条例 at the end of the same year, which expelled many people's rights supporters from Tōkyō, the movement continued, mainly in the Tōhoku region, carrying on towards rebuilding the party in the wake of the enactment of the Meiji Constitution in 1889.

The Establishment of the Meiji Constitution

The government had already decided during the political crisis of 1881 to establish a constitution that would grant itself and the tennō great authority, but in the following year it dispatched **Itō Hirobumi** 伊藤博文 and some other statesmen to Europe in order to conduct research on the constitutions of various nations. Itō mainly studied German constitutional theory under political scientists such as Rudolf von Gneist グナイスト (1816-95) at the University of Berlin and Lorenz von Stein シュタイン (1815-90) at the University of Vienna, and returned to Japan in the following year to begin preparations for the establishment of the constitution and the national assembly.

In 1884, reforms began with the enactment of the **Kazoku Law** 華族令[73], which expanded the kazoku category to include, in addition to the former aristocratic families and daimyō, individuals who had made contributions to the nation. This laid the foundation for creating the future upper house (House of Peers 貴族院). In the following year, the

---

[71] After the Imo Incident 〈壬午軍乱〉 in 1882, members of the Jiyūtō, notably Itagaki Taisuke, supported reformists in Korea such as Kim Ok-gyun 〈金玉均〉 and attempted to domestically reform the country.

[72] The Three Major Affairs refer to demands for 1) a reduction in land taxes, 2) freedom of speech and assembly, and 3) recovery from diplomatic failures by concluding equal treaties. Representatives with petitions from all over Japan carried out fierce lobbying against various governmental agencies.

[73] The kazoku were divided into the five ranks of kō 〈公〉 (duke), kō 〈侯〉 (marquis), haku 〈伯〉 (count), shi 〈子〉 (viscount), and dan 〈男〉 (baron). The qualifications for each rank were defined by internal regulations.

Dajōkan system was abolished and replaced by the **Cabinet System** 内閣制度.

Under this new system, the heads of each ministry were not only directly responsible to the tennō as ministers of state for the duties of their own ministries, but would also directly participate in national administration under the prime minister as members of the cabinet. Furthermore, the Imperial Household Ministry (Kunaishō 宮内省) and its minister, responsible for the affairs of the royal household, were placed outside of the cabinet's purview, while the Lord Keeper 内大臣 of the Privy Seal, who advised the tennō and was responsible for keeping the Tennō's Privy Seal 天皇御璽 and the State Seal of Japan 日本国璽, was relocated within the household. Although the first prime minister, Itō Hirobumi, concurrently held the post of imperial household minister, the distinction between the household and the government was nevertheless clearly distinguished under the new system.

Local administrative reforms were carried out mainly by **Yamagata Aritomo** 山県有朋 (1838-1922), advised by German consultant Albert Mosse モッセ (1846-1925). The **City, Town and Village Systems** 市制・町村制[74] were promulgated in 1888, followed by the establishment of the **Prefectural and County Systems** 府県制・郡制[75] in 1890. Although local areas were still under the strict control of the central government, the implementation of these systems constructed a framework of local autonomy that depended on influential people in each region.

The government's drafting of the constitution had been proceeding in secret since the end of 1886, under the leadership of Itō and other statesmen such as Inoue Kowashi 井上毅 (1843-95), Itō Miyoji 伊東巳代治 (1857-1934), and Kaneko Kentarō 金子堅太郎 (1853-1942), with the assistance of the German advisor Hermann Roesler ロエスレル (1834-94). The constitutional draft was examined thoroughly by the **Privy Council** (Sūmitsuin 枢密院)[76] in the presence

---

[74] Municipalities with a population of 25,000 or more people were defined as cities (shi〈市〉), which were administrative divisions equal to counties (gun), while former towns and villages were largely merged to make new towns and villages. City mayors were appointed by the minister of home affairs, who made his choice from a list of candidates recommended by the respective city council. City governance was carried out by the city auxiliary councils. Mayors of towns and villages were unpaid honorary posts, and were chosen by the respective local council through election.

[75] County mayors and county auxiliary councils were the administrative organs, and the county councils were decision-making bodies whose members were selected by votes from the town or village councilors, as well as through an internal selection carried out among major landowners. The prefectural assemblies also adopted an indirect election process based on votes from county council members.

[76] The Privy Council was established in 1888 as a body to advise the tennō on matters regarding particular laws, spending, treaties, and so forth, such as the Constitution and election laws. Subsequently, its authority was clarified in Article 56 of the Constitution.

CONSTITUTION OF THE EMPIRE OF JAPAN

Article 1 The Empire of Japan shall be reigned over and governed by a line of Emperors unbroken for ages eternal.

Article 3 The Emperor is sacred and inviolable.

Article 4 The Emperor is the head of the Empire, combining in Himself the rights of sovereignty, and exercises them, according to the provisions of the present Constitution.

Article 8 The Emperor, in consequence of an urgent necessity to maintain public safety or to avert public calamities, issues, when the Imperial Diet is not sitting, Imperial ordinances in the place of law.

Article 11 The Emperor has the supreme command of the Army and Navy.

Article 12 The Emperor determines the organization and peace standing of the Army and Navy.

Article 29 Japanese subjects shall, within the limits of law, enjoy the liberty of speech, writing, publication, public meetings and associations.

Article 33 The Imperial Diet shall consist of two Houses, a House of Peers and a House of Representatives.

Article 55 The respective Ministers of State shall give their advice to the Emperor, and be responsible for it.

Article 70 When the Imperial Diet cannot be convoked, owing to the external or internal condition of the country, in case of urgent need for the maintenance of public safety, the Government may take all necessary financial measures, by means of an Imperial Ordinance.

of the tennō, and the **Constitution of the Empire of Japan** 大日本帝国憲法 (also known as the Meiji Constitution 明治憲法) was proclaimed on February 11, 1889.

The constitution, as a **Kintei Kenpō** 欽定憲法 which, nominally, the tennō had decided upon and bestowed to the citizenry himself, granted the tennō and the government immense authority. According to the constitution, the tennō, regarded as sacred and inviolable, was the supreme leader who assumed full sovereignty, possessing a great amount of power that could not be delegated to parliament, such as the right to appoint and dismiss civilian and military officials[77]; supreme command over the army and navy (military operations, tactics, etc.); and the right to declare war, conclude peace, and ratify treaties (altogether called **Tennō Taiken** 天皇大権, the Tennō's Prerogatives). Among these powers, supreme command over the army and the navy was independent of the cabinet, and these services reported directly to the tennō (**independence of military high command authority** 統帥権の独立).

[77] The government promulgated the Imperial University Ordinance〈帝国大学令〉in 1886, which clearly stated the position of universities as training schools for government officials. In the following year, a system for higher civil-service examinations〈文官高等試験の制〉was implemented, laying the foundation for the modern Japanese bureaucracy.

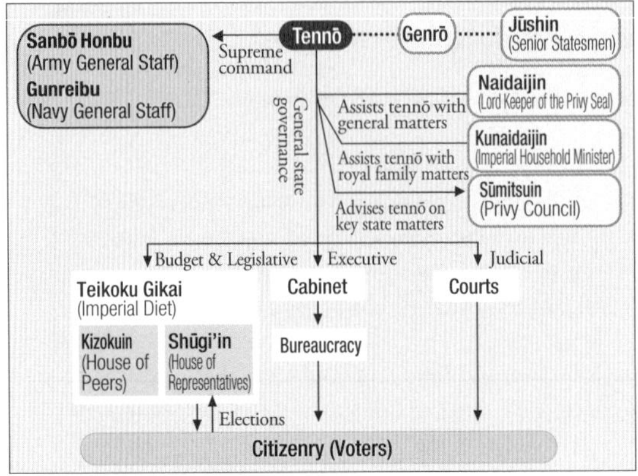

STATE STRUCTURE UNDER CONSTITUTION OF THE EMPIRE OF JAPAN

Under the tennō's sovereignty, the three powers – the legislature, the executive, and the judiciary – were separated, with each of these bodies being expected to assist the tennō. However, the government proper was far more powerful than parliament, the authority of which was restricted by various regulations[78], and each minister owed their responsibilities not to parliament but solely to the tennō.

The **Imperial Diet** 帝国議会 was composed of the **House of Peers (Kizokuin** 貴族院**)**[79] and the **House of Representatives (Shūgi'in** 衆議院**)**, which possessed an equal amount of power. The legislative power of the House of Representatives, however, was substantively restricted by the presence of the House of Peers, which was comprised of members of the kazoku as well as imperial appointees (chokusen-gi'in 勅選議員). However, despite many regulations, budgets and laws could not be approved without the consent of the Diet. Consequently, the government came to make compromises with the Diet (especially the House of Representatives), and the influence of political parties came to gradually increase.

Under the new system, the Japanese people, who were referred to in the Constitution as "subjects" (shinmin 「臣民」), were granted rights – within the scope of the law – to the inviolability of property, freedom of religion, and freedom of speech, the press, assembly, and association. The path towards participation in politics was also opened through deliberation over budgets and law bills in the Diet. So it was that Japan became the first modern constitutional country in Asia. At the same time as the promulgation

---

[78] It was stipulated (in Article 67 of the Constitution) that the Diet did not have the authority to reduce the budget for matters specified as the Tennō's Prerogatives in the Constitution without the consent of the government. Additionally, if the budget failed to pass, the government possessed the right to reuse the budget from the previous year.

[79] The House of Peers was composed of the following: members of the royal family, members of the kazoku who either held hereditary status or were selected internally, and people appointed by the tennō (chokunin-gi'in〈勅任議員〉). This latter category included chokusen-gi'in (people chosen for service to the nation or for expertise) and one of the highest taxpayers from each prefecture.

of the Constitution, the Parliamentary Law 議院法, the House of Representatives Election Law 衆議院議員選挙法, and the House of Peers Decree 貴族院令 were all issued. The **Imperial Household Law** 皇室典範[80], which stipulated matters such as royal succession and regency, was also established.

Compiling Legal Codes

The compilation of legal codes in the manner of Western nations began from the first year of the Meiji period. The French legal scholar Gustave Boissonade ボアソナード (1825-1910) was invited to draft various laws modelled on French law, and in 1880, the Penal Code 刑法[81] and the Code of Criminal Procedure 治罪法 were established in advance of the Constitution. Subsequently, the compilation of the Civil Code 民法 and the Commercial Code 商法 was rushed because of the need to revise the unequal treaties, and in 1890 both of these, along with the revised Civil Procedure Code 民事訴訟法 and Criminal Procedure Code 刑事訴訟法, were promulgated. Thus, the political framework for the country as a nation of laws was finally organized.

Regarding the Civil Code, although the bulk of it had been promulgated in 1890, criticism from legal scholars erupted even before its enactment. They argued that its implementation would destroy traditional Japanese ethics such as family values, and this prompted a major controversy (**Civil Code Controversy** 民法典論争)[82]. As a result, during the third Diet session of 1892, the enforcement was postponed, along with that of the Commercial Code, on the premise that they would be revised. In 1896 and then 1898, the Civil Code was issued anew with significant modifications. The new Civil Code that resulted from this process granted great power to the head of a household (koshu 戸主) to exercise over his family (Rights of the Head of the Household 戸主権), and maintained the succession of family headship, ensuring that the patriarchal family system endured.

---

[80] While the Constitution was announced to the public, via an official gazette, the Imperial Household Law was not, for it was regarded as "a matter with which subjects should not dare interfere."

[81] A regulation was added stating that crimes against the tennō or the royal family, such as high treason, lèse-majesté, and criminal insurrection, would be severely punished.

[82] In 1891, an Imperial (Tōkyō) University professor, Hozumi Yatsuka〈穂積八束〉, authored an article entitled "Minpō Idete Chūkō Horobu〈「民法出デヽ忠孝亡ブ」〉" (Loyalty and Filial Piety Shall Perish if the Civil Code is Enacted) for a law journal, in which he heavily criticized Boissonade's Civil Code.

The Diet in the Early Years

With Japan's first ever general election for the House of Representatives[83] to be held in 1890, the former people's rights faction began to regroup. In an effort to counter this, Prime Minister Kuroda Kiyotaka (1840-1900) had already announced immediately after the promulgation of the Constitution that the government would adopt a policy of **transcendentalism** (**chōzenshugi** 超然主義), meaning that the government would maintain a distance from political parties and not be swayed by their interests. However, the former people's rights faction won an overwhelming victory in the election, and in the first parliamentary session of the Diet so-called "**people's parties**" (**mintō** 民党) such as the Rikken Jiyūtō 立憲自由党 (Constitutional Liberal Party, which changed its name to "Jiyūtō," Liberal Party, the following year) and the Kaishintō gained the majority of seats in the House of Representatives[84].

When the first session began, the First Yamagata Aritomo Cabinet, which adopted a transcendentalist position, was attacked on budget issues by the people's parties, which called for government spending cuts and relief for the burden on the populace[85]. The government was, however, successful in gaining approval of the budget by convincing some members of the Jiyūtō to change their support[86]. In the second session, the First Matsukata Masayoshi Cabinet clashed with the people's parties and dissolved the House of Representatives. Upon the second general election in 1892, the Matsukata Cabinet tried to ensure the victory of pro-government candidates through aggressive **electoral interference** 選挙干渉, mainly carried out by Minister of Home Affairs Shinagawa Yajirō 品川弥二郎 (1843-1900). Despite these efforts, the cabinet failed to capture the lead from the people's parties, and Matsukata resigned after the end of the third parliamentary session.

---

[83] Under the House of Representatives Election Law that was promulgated along with the Constitution, the franchise was limited to men of the age of twenty-five or older who paid at least 15 yen in direct tax (i.e., land and income tax; business tax was added later). Therefore, those with the right to vote comprised a little more than one percent of the whole population, consisting of upper- and middle-class farmers and the higher-class urban residents. On the other hand, eligibility to run as a candidate was limited to men of thirty years or older who met the same tax-paying qualifications as voters.

[84] At the first parliamentary session, the Rikken Jiyūtō gained 130 seats and the Kaishintō 41, giving them together a majority of the total number of 300 seats. At the time, opposition parties like these were referred to as mintō, while pro-government parties were called ritō〈吏党〉.

[85] The demands were for the government to cut administrative spending, then reduce land taxes and revise land prices.

[86] In his explanation of the budget, Yamagata argued for the need to strengthen the army and navy to protect what he called the "sovereignty line〈「主権線」〉," meaning Japan's borders, as well as the "profitable line〈「利益線」〉," which included areas like Korea.

The next administration formed was the Second Itō Hirobumi Cabinet, also known by the name "All Meritorious Leaders" (Genkun Sōde 「元勲総出」)[87]. Itō made an overture to the Jiyūtō, the most dominant of the people's parties, and with the help of an edict issued by the tennō[88], in 1893 he was successful in expanding naval armaments. However, the other people's parties, such as the Kaishintō, opposed this cooperation between the Jiyūtō and the government, and formed a coalition with the Kokumin Kyōkai 国民協会 (National Association), a former pro-government party (ritō), and criticized the government for its problems regarding revision of the unequal treaties[89]. The government and the House of Representatives continuously clashed until the sixth parliamentary session, which ended just before the First Sino-Japanese War 日清戦争.

Revision of the Treaties

The revision of the unequal treaties that the bakufu had signed with the Western nations was an important issue for the government, which was concerned with realizing national independence and achieving Fukoku Kyōhei. Among the treaty terms, the government was particularly eager to **abolish consular jurisdiction** 領事裁判権（治外法権）の撤廃 (extraterritoriality) and **restore tariff autonomy** 関税自主権の回復.

After seeing his predecessors Iwakura Tomomi and Terashima Munenori fail in negotiations, in 1882 Minster of Foreign Affairs **Inoue Kaoru** 井上馨 (1835-1915) changed tactics and held preliminary meetings in Tōkyō with representatives of the great powers. Then, from 1886, he turned these into official conferences. As a result, by 1887 a revised plan that essentially abolished consular jurisdiction, in exchange for allowing foreigners to travel freely and reside within Japan, was basically approved by the Western countries.

However, the abolishment of consular jurisdiction was accepted on the condition that Japan compile Western legal codes and appoint foreign judges to more than half of the seats in trials involving foreign defendants. Criticism that this condition would violate Japanese sovereignty arose within the government, coupled with antagonism

---

[87] The cabinet contained many political figures from Satsuma or Chōshū who were known as "meritorious leaders" for their great contributions during the Meiji Restoration.

[88] An edict telling the Diet to cooperate with the government was issued, stating that to cover the costs of warship construction the tennō himself would be offering 300,000 yen per year for six years, to be saved from cutting household costs, and that civil and military officials would pay one tenth of their salaries.

[89] This coalition was called the "hard-line diplomatic faction〈対外硬派連合〉." In 1896, after the end of the First Sino-Japanese War, the Shinpotō〈進歩党〉(Progressive Party) was formed largely by those groups, with the exception of the Kokumin Kyōkai.

towards what was seen as Inoue's extreme attitudes of Westernization[90], which he had adopted to stimulate the negotiations. These objections built up to become a torrent of opposition against the revisions from both within and outside the administration[91], and finally resulted in Inoue cancelling negotiations and resigning from his post.

The next minister of foreign affairs, Ōkuma Shigenobu, began negotiating separately with nations that were in favor of revising the unequal treaties, and eventually signed revised treaties with the US, Germany, and Russia. However, when word got out that, while not reflected in the text of the treaties, an agreement had been made accepting the inclusion of foreign judges in the Supreme Court, a storm of opposition erupted from within the government and the populace at large. After an incident in 1889 in which Ōkuma was wounded by a young member of a radical militaristic group called the Gen'yōsha〈玄洋社〉, negotiations were discontinued yet again.

The UK, which was initially the biggest obstacle in treaty revision, shifted its policies and became more friendly to Japan due to concern over Russia expanding into East Asia by way of the latter's plans to construct the Trans-Siberian Railway. The UK adopted a supportive attitude towards opening discussion for a revised treaty based on, in principle, mutual equality. Aoki Shūzō〈青木周蔵〉, the new minister of foreign affairs, began negotiations for this revision, but due to the **Ōtsu Incident**〈大津事件〉[92] in 1891 he too resigned.

After this, the Second Itō Cabinet's foreign affairs minister, **Mutsu Munemitsu**〈陸奥宗光〉 (1844-97), was able, with the help of the Jiyūtō, to suppress domestic opposition to the revision, and successfully concluded the **Anglo-Japanese Treaty of Commerce and Navigation**〈日英通商航海条約〉 – which abolished consular jurisdiction, raised tariff rates, and included a mutually equal most favored nation clause – just before the outbreak of the First Sino-Japanese War in 1894.

Revised treaties were subsequently ratified with other Western nations, all of

---

[90] In an effort to gain an edge in the negotiations for treaty revision, Inoue had the **Rokumeikan**〈鹿鳴館〉 built in Hibiya〈日比谷〉, Tōkyō in 1883 as a salon to welcome and entertain foreign dignitaries, utilizing it on many occasions (Rokumeikan Diplomacy).

[91] In 1886, an incident had occurred in which a British steamship heading from Yokohama to Kōbe sank in a storm. The captain had abandoned his Japanese passengers, who died, but was judged by the British Consul as not negligent (***Normanton* Incident**〈ノルマントン号事件〉), fanning resentment among the public against the unequal treaties.

[92] An incident in which the Tsesarevich of Russia was injured by Tsuda Sanzō〈津田三蔵〉, a policeman on guard who had slashed him with his saber, in Ōtsu City in Shiga Prefecture〈滋賀県〉 during the Tsesarevich's return from sightseeing at Lake Biwa〈琵琶湖〉. The Japanese government at the time (the First Matsukata Cabinet), fearful of making relations with Russia worse, pressured the court to sentence the criminal to death for high treason (a crime against the royal family). However, the chief justice, Kojima Koretaka〈児島惟謙〉, rejected this and sentenced Tsuda to life imprisonment instead, thereby defending the independence of the judiciary.

which came into effect from 1899. The remaining issue, the restoration of tariff autonomy, was eventually achieved under Minister of Foreign Affairs **Komura Jutarō** 小村寿太郎 (1855-1911) in 1911. Thus, half a century after the opening of the country, Japan was finally able to obtain in treaties an equal position to the great powers.

The Korean Problem

Since Japan had made Korea open its borders by concluding the Japan-Korea Treaty of Amity in 1876, a pro-Japanese faction had been emerging within that nation. However, in 1882 troops supporting the Daewongun 大院君（李昰応） (Yi Ha-eung, 1820-98) rose in revolt against his political opponents, the maternal relatives of King Gojong 高宗 (1852-1919), the Min 閔氏 family, who had been attempting to establish stronger ties with Japan. Public riots also broke out in response to this uprising, and the Japanese legation was surrounded (**Imo Incident** 壬午軍乱). Although the revolt itself ended in failure, the Min-dominated government distanced itself from Japan after this incident, and began to shift towards relying on the Qing Dynasty.

Against this change of policies, pro-Japanese reformists (the Enlightenment Party 独立党) such as Kim Ok-gyun (1851-94), who sought to modernize Korea by creating bonds with Japan, attempted a coup d'état with the support of the Japanese legation upon seeing the results of the Sino-French War 清仏戦争 in 1884, which they understood as an opportunity for reforms (**Gapsin Coup** 甲申事変). This effort, however, failed when reinforcements arrived from Qing China. In an effort to repair Sino-Japanese relations, which had deteriorated significantly due to this incident, in the following year (1885) the Japanese government dispatched Itō Hirobumi to Tianjin, where he concluded the **Tianjin Convention** 天津条約 with Li Hongzhang 李鴻章 (1823-1901) who had full diplomatic power to negotiate for the Qing Dynasty. Under this agreement, both Japan and Qing China were to withdraw their military forces from Korea, and were obliged to give prior notification in the event that they sent troops to the peninsula in the future. Consequently, clashes between the two nations were avoided for a time.

In the wake of the two incidents on the peninsula, Japanese influence on Korea had significantly declined, while encroachments by the Qing Dynasty expanded. At the same time, public opinion in Japan towards Qing China and Korea became increasingly hostile.

In the midst of these times, Fukuzawa Yukichi published "**Datsu-A Ron**" 「脱亜論」 (**Leaving Asia**) in March 1885. The article argued that Japan should deny solidarity with other Asian countries, leaving Asia to join the Western powers; and moreover, that it should use military force to deal with the Qing Dynasty and Korea. This too contributed to building momentum for an armed confrontation.

FUKUZAWA YUKICHI, "DATSU-A RON"[1]

Taking today's diplomatic policies into consideration, we no longer have time to wait for the enlightenment of our neighbors in order to work together towards the development of Asia. On the contrary, we must leave the ranks of Asian nations and join the civilized nations of the West. As for how we should deal with China and Korea, there is no need to offer special treatment just because they are our neighbors; rather, we should simply follow the manner of the Westerners in dealing with them. One who cherishes a bad friend cannot avoid gaining his notoriety. We must erase from our hearts our bad friends in Asia.

[1] *Jiji-Shinpō*〈『時事新報』〉 editorial, 16 March 1885

The First Sino-Japanese War and the Triple Intervention

After the conclusion of the Tianjin Convention, the Japanese government, seeking to increase its influence over Korea, began to strengthen its military power[93]. At the same time, it intensified its conflict with the Korean government, which was using the military backing of the Qing Dynasty to counter Japanese economic expansion on the peninsula[94].

In 1894, a major farmer uprising (**Donghak Peasant Rebellion** 甲午農民戦争（東学の乱）[vi])[95] broke out in Korea, primarily led by followers of a Korean religion called Donghak 東学, and demanding lower taxes and the expulsion of Japanese. Witnessing this, and receiving a request for help from the Korean government, the Qing Dynasty dispatched its military to the peninsula, and informed Japan as per the stipulation in the Tianjin Convention. In response, the Japanese government also dispatched troops to the peninsula, and the threat of war prompted the peasants to seek reconciliation with the Korean

[93] Prior to this, in 1878 the army had established the Army General Staff Office〈参謀本部〉 and strengthened the Supreme Command Staff〈統帥部〉. In 1882, it had issued the **Imperial Rescript to Soldiers and Sailors**〈軍人勅諭〉 which stressed the loyalty of the military to the tennō as the supreme commander〈「大元帥」〉, while foreshadowing the involvement of military personnel in political matters. Thereafter, the Japanese military went on to strengthen its capabilities with the aim of effectively fighting foreign wars. For instance, in 1888 the army's organizational units were changed from garrisons, which were focused on domestic security, to divisions.

[94] From 1889 to the following year, a regional governor in Korea prohibited exports of grains, such as soybeans, to Japan with the **Grain Export Ban Act**〈防穀令〉. The Japanese government responded by forcing the Koreans to abolish the law, and sought compensation for the period during the ban, a demand that was only met in 1893 after it had fired off an ultimatum.

[95] Donghak (literally "Eastern learning") was a Korean religious movement that emerged in opposition to Seohak〈西学〉 (literally "Western learning," but especially Christianity). The farmer uprising, led by Donghak leaders, grew to become a movement that took over the southern part of the Korean peninsula.

government. However, tensions between Japan and China were further fueled by disagreement over domestic reforms in Korea, and brought the two nations to the brink of war. The UK, which was initially critical of Japan dispatching troops, changed its position to one of support after signing the Anglo-Japanese Treaty of Commerce and Navigation, creating a more favorable international situation for Japan. In August 1894, Japan declared war against the Qing Dynasty, and the **First Sino-Japanese War** (日清戦争) began.

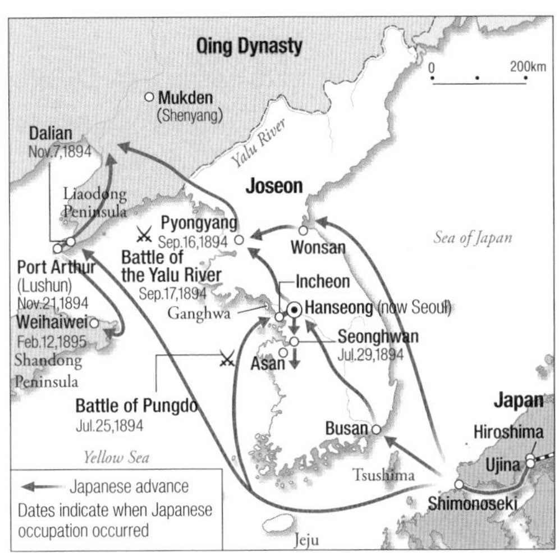

OUTLINE MAP OF THE FIRST SINO-JAPANESE WAR

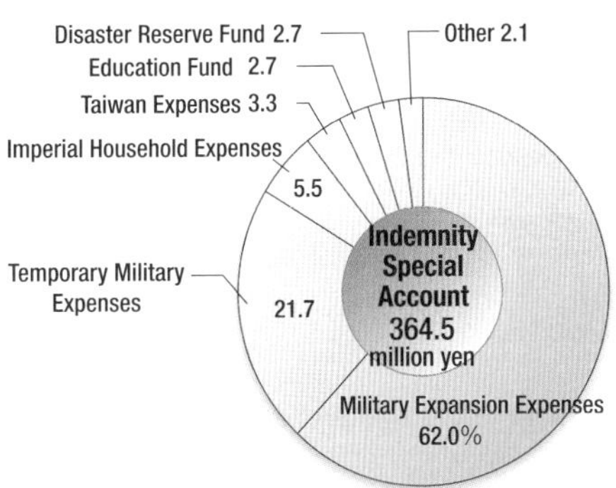

USE OF INDEMNITY FROM THE FIRST SINO-JAPANESE WAR

With the additional indemnity of 30 million Kuping Taels for returning the Liaodong peninsula, the total sum of compensation amounted to 230 million Kuping Taels, equal to approximately 356 million yen at the time. A special account was created which generated a further 8.5 million yen as investment income, producing a grand total of approximately 364.5 million yen.

Upon the outbreak of war, the political parties ceased criticizing the government, and began approving any war-related budgets and bills in the Diet[96]. The war proceeded greatly in the favor of Japan, which enjoyed superiority in the training and discipline of its armed forces and employed standardized modern armaments. Japanese forces drove the Qing army from Korea, captured the Liaodong peninsula (遼東半島), defeated the Qing's Beiyang Fleet (北洋艦隊) in the Battle of the Yalu River (黄海海戦), and occupied their naval base, Weihaiwei (威海衛). The war ended in a Japanese victory, and in April 1895, the **Treaty of Shimonoseki** (下関条約) was signed between Japanese representatives Itō Hirobumi and Mutsu Munemitsu and the Qing repre-

[96] The financial cost of the First Sino-Japanese War amounted to more than 200 million yen, which was over twice the state's revenue at the time.

sentative Li Hongzhang.

The treaty stipulated that the Qing Dynasty was to: 1) recognize the independence of Korea; 2) cede to Japan the Liaodong peninsula, Taiwan, and the Pescadores 澎湖諸島 (Penghu Islands); 3) pay Japan a war indemnity of 200 million Kuping Taels (equivalent to about 310 million yen at the time); and 4) open the ports of Shashi 沙市, Chongqing 重慶, Suzhou 蘇州 and Hangzhou 杭州.

However, the cession of the Liaodong peninsula alarmed Russia, which had been attempting to expand its influence in East Asia. Recruiting France and Germany to its side, Russia demanded that Japan return the peninsula to Qing China (**Triple Intervention** 三国干渉). The Japanese government, ascertaining that it had no chance to resist the pressure from three major powers, acquiesced. At the same time, the government shifted towards further expanding its armed forces, against a backdrop of rising hostility towards Russia among the population, as evidenced by slogans like "Gashin Shōtan" 「臥薪嘗胆」 (endure hardship to achieve future revenge).

After returning the Liaodong peninsula, the Japanese government focused on the governance of its newly-acquired territory, **Taiwan** 台湾[97]. In 1895, Kabayama Sukenori 樺山資紀 (1837-1922), chief of the Navy General Staff, was appointed governor-general of Taiwan 台湾総督, and suppressed the strong resistance of the Taiwanese by force.

4 The Russo-Japanese War and International Relations

The Birth of the Rikken Seiyūkai

The victory in the First Sino-Japanese War and the Triple Intervention greatly influenced the relationship between the government and the political parties. The Jiyūtō openly supported the Second Itō Hirobumi Cabinet, approved of Itagaki Taisuke being minister of home affairs, and approved the new budget for military expansion.

[97] The governor-general of Taiwan was appointed from among army generals or lieutenant generals, or navy admirals or vice-admirals, and wielded great authority over the executive, legislature, and judiciary, as well as the military. From 1898, under then-governor-general Kodama Gentarō〈児玉源太郎〉, Gotō Shinpei〈後藤新平〉 worked on developing the civil administration, and began conducting land surveys in order to modernize the land system. Measures to promote local industries were also implemented, such as can be seen from the founding of the Bank of Taiwan and the Taiwan Sugar Company. Rule over Taiwan proceeded through appeasing the local wealthy classes, such as landowners and merchants, but there were others such as poor farmers who continued to resist Japanese rule, frequently triggering anti-Japanese armed revolts. The Japanese authorities confronted these movements by thoroughly suppressing them, and continued to control the country until 1945.

The Second Matsukata Masayoshi Cabinet, which succeeded Itō's in 1896, similarly collaborated with the Shinpotō, and Ōkuma Shigenobu was accepted as minister of foreign affairs, and similarly pushed forward with strengthening the military. However, the Third Itō Cabinet, formed in 1898, became disenchanted with the Jiyūtō after it struggled in the general election, prompting the cabinet to abandon this tie and turn back to transcendentalism. In response to this development, the Jiyūtō and the Shinpotō merged to form the **Kenseitō** 憲政党 (**Constitutional Party**). The emergence of a joint political party holding an absolute majority in the House of Representatives resulted in Itō's resignation, as he no longer had the initiative to manage the Diet. This led to the First Ōkuma Cabinet (**Wai-Han Cabinet** 隈板内閣) taking its place, as the first administration formed by members of a political party[98].

However, the Ōkuma Cabinet ran into trouble immediately after its establishment due to conflicts between members of the former parties. Tensions reached a high point when the education minister, Ozaki Yukio 尾崎行雄, resigned in the wake of the so-called Republican Speech Affair 共和演説事件[99], and the government became divided over his succession. The Kenseitō split into the Kenseitō (composed of former Jiyūtō members) and the Kenseihontō 憲政本党 (True Constitutional Party, composed of former Shinpotō members), and thus concluded the cabinet's short life of merely four months.

The Second Yamagata Cabinet, which replaced it, gained the support of the Kenseitō, enabling it to pass a bill increasing the land tax. Moreover, in order to prevent political parties from exercising influence over government officials, in 1899 the government carried out a **revision of the Civil Service Appointment Ordinance** 文官任用令改正[100]. In 1900, it also took steps to prevent political parties from abusing their power over the military, by issuing the **Military Ministers to be Active-Duty Officers Law** 軍部大臣現役武官制, which specified that only an active-duty general or lieutenant-general could serve as

[98] All positions except for the army and navy ministers were filled by members of the Kenseitō, with Ōkuma as prime minister and Itagaki as minister of home affairs.

[99] Ozaki had criticized the plutocratic system, stating that "If Japan were to become a republic, Mitsui or Mitsubishi would be worthy candidates for the presidency." Although he had stated beforehand that this would never happen, criticism flared up against him from the royal household, the Privy Council, the House of Peers, and even from people within the ruling party who had been associated with the former Jiyūtō.

[100] Eligibility requirements were established even for high-ranking officials, such as vice-ministers, who had not previously had regulations governing their appointment. The intention was to restrict political parties from exercising their power to grant these posts to individuals with no experience or knowledge in the field as bureaucrats. The Civil Service Reprimand Ordinance〈文官懲戒令〉 and the Civil Service Status Ordinance〈文官分限令〉 were also enacted at the same time to further secure the position of government officials other than ministers, and sought to shield them from the influence of political parties.

army minister, and only an active-duty admiral or vice-admiral as navy minister. The cabinet also enacted the Security Police Law 治安警察法 to tighten restrictions over political and labor movements.

The Kenseitō turned against Yamagata after these policies were unveiled. In 1900, the party approached Itō, who had been planning to form his own party, and disbanded to join with government officials in Itō's camp, creating the **Rikken Seiyūkai** 立憲政友会 (**Association of Friends of Constitutional Government**, hereafter Seiyūkai) with Itō as leader. Itō organized his fourth cabinet in the same year, but was forced to once again resign after tiring of opposition from the House of Peers, whereupon he was replaced by the First **Katsura Tarō** 桂太郎 (1847-1913) Cabinet in 1901.

Hereafter, the political world was divided into two major groups. On one side was a coalition comprised of the military, officials, and aristocrats, and led by Katsura, a Chōshū oligarch who had succeeded Yamagata; on the other was the Seiyūkai, led by **Saionji Kinmochi** 西園寺公望 (1849-1940), who had succeeded Itō. Yamagata and Itō retired from the political front lines due to age, but continued to exert great influence over future cabinets – and in particular, wielding the right to appoint the prime minister – from behind the scenes as unofficial aides to the tennō, known as **genrō** 元老 (**elder statesmen**).

The Scramble for Concessions and the Anglo-Japanese Alliance

The Western powers, having learned of the weakness of the Qing Dynasty from the outcome of the First Sino-Japanese War, hurriedly set to work securing their own spheres of influence within China (the **scramble for concessions** 中国分割). First of all, in 1898 Germany leased Jiaozhou Bay 膠州湾 on the Shandong peninsula 山東半島, followed by Russia, which leased Port Arthur 旅順 (Lushun) and Dalian 大連, also on the peninsula. The UK then leased the Kowloon peninsula 九龍半島 and Weihaiwei, and in the following year France leased Guangzhou Bay 広州湾. The great powers viewed these concession territories as strategic bases around which to carry out projects, such as building railroads. The US was not directly involved in the scramble for concessions, but it officially annexed Hawaii in 1898 and proceeded to occupy the Philippines. However, in the following year US Secretary of State John Hay ジョン＝ヘイ (1838-1905) made a proposal regarding China in which he argued for an "Open Door Policy 門戸開放" and equal opportunity for the great powers, including Japan, with freedom of trade within the spheres of influence of each country[101].

In 1900, an anti-foreign group known as the Boxers 義和団 (Yihetuan) began to

[101] In 1823, US President James Monroe〈モンロー〉had articulated what became later known as the Monroe Doctrine〈モンロー宣言〉, which declared that the US opposed any European intervention in the Americas, and that in exchange it would not meddle with European affairs. The US had long abided by this position, but the Open Door Policy marked a shift in diplomatic strategy.

spread rapidly across China. Under the slogan "Support the Qing, exterminate the foreigners," (「扶清滅洋」) they attacked foreigners in various areas, and laid siege to the legations of the great powers in Beijing (北京) in what became known as the **Boxer Rebellion** (義和団事件)[vii]. The Qing government also sided with this movement, and declared war against the great powers (**North China Incident** (北清事変)). The powers, including Japan, responded by sending an allied force that drove the Boxers from Beijing and forced the Qing government to surrender. In the following year, the Boxer Protocol (北京議定書)[102] was signed between China and the allied powers.

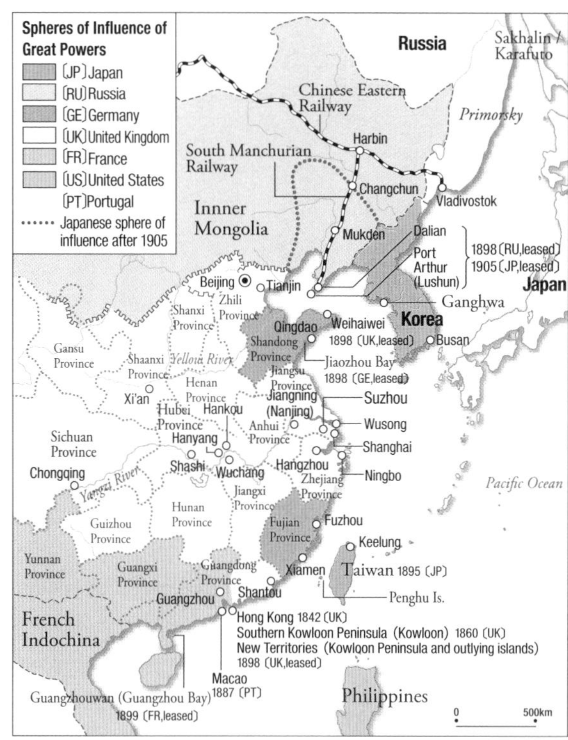

SCRAMBLE FOR CONCESSIONS BY GREAT POWERS

The defeat of the Qing Dynasty also affected the foreign policy of its client state, Korea, where, having gained support from Russia, a rivalry with Japan developed and led to the formation of a pro-Russian government[103]. In 1897, in order to compete with Japan, the new administration renamed the country the **Empire of Korea** (大韓帝国), while

[102] Through this protocol, the great powers forced the Qing government to pay a grand sum in compensation, and to approve of extraterritorial rights within the legation quarters in the capital, Beijing, as well as the stationing of guards for the legations.

[103] Not long after the Triple Intervention, the pro-Japanese government led by the Daewongun quickly crumbled due to Queen Min and pro-Russian members of the government. The Daewongun had originally come to power through the Japanese army's occupation of the royal palace, which had also become a direct cause of the First Sino-Japanese War. In an attempt to reestablish the Daewongun's administration anew, the Japanese resident minister, Miura Gorō (三浦梧楼), had then ordered his legation guards to reoccupy the palace, leading to the assassination of Queen Min. With his queen murdered, King Gojong then fled to the Russian legation and formed a pro-Russian administration.

SOLDIERS OF THE ALLIED FORCE DURING THE NORTH CHINA INCIDENT
From left: soldiers of the UK, the US, Russia, British India, Germany, France, Austria, Italy, and Japan.

the king declared himself an emperor.

Russia, meanwhile, used the Boxer Rebellion as an opportunity to essentially occupy northeastern China (Manchuria (満州)), and forced the Qing Dynasty to recognize its monopolistic interests in that region. As Japan's interests within Korea would be threatened if Manchuria, being connected to the peninsula, was under Russian control, the Japanese government began to change its formerly cooperative policy towards Russia. Although there were still a few in the government, including Itō Hirobumi, who favored a **Russo-Japanese entente** (日露協商論) with a plan to "trade Manchuria for Korea[104]," (「満韓交換」) the Katsura Cabinet decided to adopt a hawkish attitude toward Russia, and ally with the UK to defend Japanese interests in Korea through force. Thus, in 1902 the Anglo-Japanese Treaty of Alliance[105] (日英同盟協約) was concluded between the two countries (**Anglo-Japanese Alliance** (日英同盟)).

Since Russia continued to station troops in Manchuria even after the alliance was signed, the Japanese government began preparations for war while continuing to conduct negotiations with Russia. Within Japan, some individuals led pacifist and anti-war campaigns, including the Christian Uchimura Kanzō (内村鑑三) (1861-1930); and the socialists Kōtoku Shūsui (幸徳秋水) (1871-1911) and Sakai Toshihiko (堺利彦) (1870-1933), who founded the Heiminsha (平民社) (Commoners' Society) and published the *Heimin Shinbun* (『平民新聞』) (Commoners' Newspaper). Initially the general public was not especially in favor of

[104] "Manchuria" is the old name for the three provinces that make up the northeastern region of China. The entente aimed to ensure Japanese superiority in Korea in exchange for granting Russia the freedom to develop Manchuria.

[105] The treaty stipulated that the two countries would mutually recognize the independence, and maintain the territorial integrity of, China and Korea; recognize their special interests in China as well as the political, commercial and industrial interests of Japan within Korea; promise strict neutrality if their ally were in a war against another country, and to enter in support if a third country were to join the war on the opposing side.

war either, but gradually became inclined in that direction as groups such as the Tairo Dōshikai 対露同志会 (Anti-Russian League) loudly called for a decisive showdown[106].

The Russo-Japanese War

In early 1904, negotiations between Japan and Russia broke down, and the two nations declared war in February, beginning the **Russo-Japanese War** 日露戦争. Japan had a substantial advantage in the conflict because it had gained financial support from the US and the UK, two countries that opposed Russia's occupation of Manchuria. In early 1905, after a siege lasting more than half a year and costing many lives, Japanese forces captured Port Arthur. In March, Japan seized victory in the Battle of Mukden 奉天会戦, and went on to triumph in May at the Battle of Tsushima 日本海海戦, at which the Japanese Combined Fleet defeated the Russian Baltic Fleet, which had only arrived after sailing around the world from Europe.

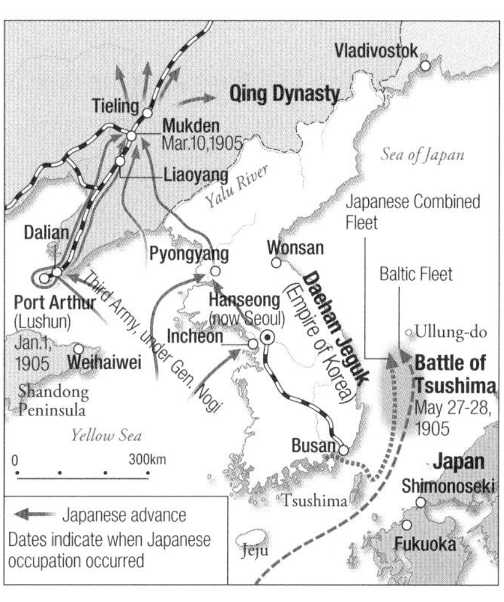

OUTLINE OF RUSSO-JAPANESE WAR

However, Japan lacked the resources to conduct a long-term war[107], while Russia too was incapable of continuing due to the outbreak of a domestic revolutionary movement. Consequently, in September 1905, with the mediation of US President Theodore Roosevelt セオドア＝ローズヴェルト (1858-1919), Japanese representative Komura Jutarō and Russian represen-

---

[106] Groups such as the Tairo Dōshikai (founded in 1903) and the Seven Professors〈七博士〉(including Tomizu Hirondo〈戸水寛人〉of Tōkyō Imperial University) aggressively clamored for war, while journalists such as Kuroiwa Ruikō〈黒岩涙香〉of the *Yorozu Chōhō*〈『万朝報』〉(Morning News) and Tokutomi Sohō〈徳富蘇峰〉of the *Kokumin Shinbun*〈『国民新聞』〉(People's Newspaper) helped evoke the idea within the public. After the war had begun, poet Yosano Akiko〈与謝野晶子〉published an anti-war poem entitled "Kimi Shinitamaukoto Nakare〈「君死にたまふこと勿れ」〉" (Thou Shalt Not Die) in the literary magazine *Myōjō*〈『明星』〉(Bright Star).

[107] The Russo-Japanese War, with the introduction of new armaments such as machine guns and quick-firing artillery, was a full-scale modern conflict of technology and industrial resources. Japanese supplies of weapons, ammunition, and troops quickly reached their limits. On top of that, out of the 1.7 billion yen in the military budget, approximately 1.3 billion yen relied upon domestic and foreign bonds (600 million and 700 million, respectively), while nearly 320 million was covered by raising taxes, a sum similarly close to the limits of what the public could afford.

tative Sergei Witte (ウィッテ) (1849-1915) concluded a peace treaty (**Treaty of Portsmouth** (ポーツマス条約)). The treaty stipulated that Russia: 1) fully acknowledge Japan's interests in, and rights to supervise, Korea; 2) cede the leasehold rights (from the Qing Dynasty) for Port Arthur and Dalian, and the railway line south to Changchun (長春), with all of their attendant concessions, to Japan; 3) transfer the southern part of Sakhalin (サハリン（樺太）) (below the 50th parallel north), and adjacent islands, to Japan; and 4) approve Japanese fishing rights in waters adjacent to Primorsky (沿海州) and the Kamchatka (カムチャツカ) peninsula. The Japanese public, which had supported the war effort while enduring casualties and high tax increases, burst into outcry against the peace treaty as it lacked any indemnity. The backlash intensified to such an extent that a national rally in opposition to the treaty, held on the day of the signing, turned into a riot (the **Hibiya Incendiary Incident** (日比谷焼打ち事件)).

International Relations after the Russo-Japanese War

After the conclusion of the war, Japan sought to secure for continental expansion the territory that it had acquired through its victory. In 1905, the Japanese government made the informal Taft-Katsura Agreement (桂・タフト協定) with the US, and revised the Anglo-Japanese Alliance with the UK, gaining approval from both countries of Japan making Korea a protectorate. Against this backdrop, in the same year Japan concluded the Japan-Korea Treaty of 1905 (第２次日韓協約) (Second Japan-Korea Convention)[108], which deprived Korea of diplomatic sovereignty, and established the **Office of the Resident-General** (統監府) in the city of Hanseong, a commission to manage Korean diplomacy under Itō Hirobumi, who was appointed the first resident-general.

SEOUL HEADQUARTERS OF THE ORIENTAL DEVELOPMENT COMPANY
The Oriental Development Company was established to exploit natural resources and develop industries in Korea. It also bought land that was confiscated by the land survey projects, and invested in managing land ownership.

In 1907, Korean Emperor Gojong protested this state of affairs by sending secret emissaries to the Second Peace Conference (第２回万国平和会議) held at The Hague in the Netherlands, but his appeals were ignored by the Western powers (**The Hague Secret Emissary Affair** (ハーグ密使事件)). This incident gave Japan

[108] The Japan-Korea Treaty of August 1904 (First Japan-Korea Convention〈第１次日韓協約〉), signed during the Russo-Japanese War, required the Korean government to employ financial and diplomatic advisors recommended by Japan, and to consult with the Japanese government regarding any important diplomatic matters.

the opportunity to force the emperor to abdicate, and conclude the Japan-Korea Treaty of 1907 第3次日韓協約 (Third Japan-Korea Convention), which handed over Korean domestic sovereignty and disbanded the Korean army. This prompted the **Righteous Army Movement** 義兵運動, which had previously been a loose group sporadically resisting Japanese colonization, to grow into a large-scale movement due to the involvement of ex-soldiers. In 1909, the Japanese government dispatched reinforcements and suppressed this movement, but in the midst of these events, former resident-general Itō Hirobumi was assassinated by a Korean nationalist named An Jung-geun 安重根 (1879-1910) at Harbin Railway Station. In 1910, after having made preparations such as stationing the Kenpeitai 憲兵隊 (military police corps) there, Japan forced Korea to conclude the Japan-Korea Annexation Treaty 韓国併合条約, thereby bringing about the **annexation of Korea** 韓国併合, colonizing the country. The city of Hanseong was renamed Gyeongseong 京城 and the **Office of the Governor-General of Korea** 朝鮮総督府 was established there as a governmental agency, with the army minister Terauchi Masatake 寺内正毅 (1852-1919) appointed the first governor-general. Initially, the governor-general was a post restricted to active-duty military personnel, while important positions in the police were filled by Japanese military police officers.

Under the office of the governor-general, a nationwide survey of Korean land and ownership (**land survey projects** 土地調査事業) was conducted in order to create a basis for imposing land taxes. Vast arable lands and forests were confiscated during this process for reasons such as unclear ownership[109], and some of these were sold off to the **Oriental Development Company** 東洋拓殖会社 and Japanese landowners.

Meanwhile, Japan's expansion into Manchuria also accelerated during this period. In 1906, the **Office of the Kwantung Governor-General** 関東都督府 was set up in Port Arthur to administer the **Kwantung Leased Territory** 関東州 (the southern Liaodong peninsula including Port Arthur and Dalian), and the semi-governmental **South Manchurian Railway (Mantetsu)** 南満州鉄道株式会社（満鉄） was established in Dalian. The South Manchurian Railway also managed the former Chinese Eastern Railway, which had been ceded from Russia and ran between Changchun and Port Arthur, and coal mines and other facilities along the railway lines. In this way, it provided an important foothold for Japanese economic expansion in the region. The US, which was interested in the Manchurian market, objected to this situation. In favor of the Open Door Policy, it opposed Japan's monopoly on special interests in southern Manchuria[110], and consequently Japan-US

[109] As a result, many Korean farmers who had lost their land suffered from poverty, and some of them migrated to Japan in search of new jobs.

[110] In 1905, American railroad executive Edward Henry Harriman〈ハリマン〉 proposed joint management of the railways in Manchuria, but the Japanese government refused. Later, in 1909, the US government proposed to the other powers that the railways be neutralized.

relations rapidly deteriorated[111]. In Qing China as well, demands for the return of those interests also grew. Against this backdrop, Japan, through cooperation with the UK and Russia under, respectively, the renewed Anglo-Japanese Alliance and the four Russo-Japanese Agreements 日露協約 (1907-16), was able to push global society to recognize its interests in Manchuria[112].

In 1911, the **Xinhai Revolution** 辛亥革命 broke out in China against the autocratic system and non-Han rule. By the end of the year the Qing Dynasty was collapsing, giving rise to the **Republic of China** 中華民国 with **Sun Yat-sen** 孫文 (1866-1925), a revolutionary leader responsible for the Three Principles of the People 三民主義, as its provisional president[113]. These developments prompted the Japanese army and some in government to propose military intervention in China in order to secure Japanese interests in southern Manchuria, but the government instead adopted a policy of non-intervention in light of the intentions of the Western powers as well as its domestic economic situation.

The Kei-En (Katsura-Saionji) Era

The First Katsura Tarō Cabinet remained in power for some time, only resigning at the end of 1905 in the wake of the Russo-Japanese War's conclusion. The Seiyūkai, which had been in opposition all this time, gained the support of influential people in the provinces by pledging to expand railways and ports. 1906 saw the party's president, Saionji Kinmochi, forming a cabinet for the first time and passing the Railway Nationalization Act 鉄道国有法. The cabinet also initially recognized the Nihon Shakaitō 日本社会党 (Japan Socialist Party) when it was formed in the same year[114]. However, despite winning a major victory in the 1908 general election, Saionji's policies had ground to a halt

---

[111] Another factor was the intensification of anti-Japanese exclusion movements in the US, especially in California, where incidents occurred such as the refusal to permit Japanese children to enroll in public schools in San Francisco in 1906.

[112] Japan and Russia quickly established closer ties when they agreed on matters such as confirming their respective spheres of influence in Manchuria and Inner Mongolia〈内蒙古〉.

[113] Sun Yat-sen was soon pressured to cede his position of provisional president to the warlord Yuan Shikai〈袁世凱〉. Thereafter, the political situation in China continued to be unstable, with various warlords in different regions, some with the backing of the powers, competing with each other.

[114] In 1901, during the rise of labor movements after the First Sino-Japanese War, figures such as Abe Iso'o〈安部磯雄〉, Katayama Sen〈片山潜〉, Kōtoku Shūsui, and Kinoshita Naoe〈木下尚江〉 formed the first socialist party in Japan, the Shakai Minshutō〈社会民主党〉 (Social Democratic Party). The party was immediately ordered to disband due to the Security Police Law. In 1907 the Nihon Shakaitō was also officially ordered to disband after a fierce internal struggle saw members who were in favor of direct action (such as Kōtoku Shūsui) win the party initiative over members in favor of parliamentary policies (such as Katayama Sen).

大逆罪の判決
▽幸徳秋水等廿四名は死刑
▽有期懲役は僅に二名のみ

NEWSPAPER ARTICLE REPORTING THE JUDGMENT IN THE HIGH TREASON INCIDENT (*TOKYŌ ASAHI SHINBUN*, 19 JANUARY 1911)

due to the 1907 depression, and he yielded the government to Katsura once more.

The Second Katsura Cabinet issued the Boshin Imperial Rescript (戊申詔書) that same year, and promoted the Local Improvement Movement (地方改良運動), which was mainly supervised by the Ministry of Home Affairs. The movement reorganized old towns and villages, which in many cases were based on Edo-period village communities, as administrative units in order to improve their tax sustainability. As a result, the property of former villages was absorbed into newborn towns and villages, and the old village youth associations were accordingly reorganized into new ones, strengthening ties with the Ministry of Home Affairs and Ministry of Education. Local military reserve associations were similarly modified to become affiliates of the Imperial Local Military Reserve Association, founded in 1910.

After the **High Treason Incident** (大逆事件) in 1910[115], the Katsura Cabinet began to crack down on socialists and anarchists. This began the "winter years" (「冬の時代」) for socialists, who were prevented from conducting activities until the First World War (第一次世界大戦). On the other hand, the cabinet also worked to alleviate certain social concerns by implementing polices such as the Factory Act (工場法) in the following year. After imposing annexation on Korea, Katsura resigned in 1911, handing the reins back to Saionji.

In this way, power passed back and forth between Katsura and Saionji for more than ten years, and so the era became known as the **Kei-En era** (桂園時代), a term produced from a Chinese character from each of their surnames.

---

[115] Triggered by the arrest of socialist activists who had been assembling bombs for use in a plan to assassinate the tennō, the Second Katsura Cabinet ordered a round-up of hundreds of socialists and anarchists nationwide, 26 of whom, including Kōtoku Shūsui, were charged with high treason. In the following year, all 26 were found guilty and 12 of them were sentenced to death, despite most having had no direct involvement in the conspiracy. It was during this time that a department for thought crime called the Special Higher Police 〈特別高等課〉 (often shortened to Tokkō 〈特高〉) was established within the Metropolitan Police Department.

5 Modern Industrial Development

The Industrial Revolution

The first half of the 1880s witnessed economic deflation and recession in the wake of Matsukata finance. However, as exports came to exceed imports and the silver standard was established, prices stabilized, interest rates fell, and stock trading took off, leading to an economic recovery. From 1886 to 1889, there was a boom in launching businesses, particularly in the railway and spinning industries (referred to as the "**rise of entrepreneurship**" 企業勃興)[116] , and an industrial revolution fully utilizing machinery took off in Japan. This boom ended due to a concentration in payments for stocks, which led to a lack of funds among financial institutions, coinciding with a bad harvest the previous year and raw silk exports dropping by half (the Depression of 1890 1890年恐慌). At this juncture, the Bank of Japan created an infrastructure to provide funds to industry through ordinary banks.

The government, having received substantial reparations from China after the victory in the First Sino-Japanese War, sought to jumpstart postwar management by investing these funds, and pushed for armament expansion while revising policies for finance and trade. In 1897, the government enacted the **Currency Law** 貨幣法 and used part of the reparations as reserve money to adopt the **gold standard** 金本位制 in line with Western countries, in order to stabilize the value of money and promote trade[117]. The government also set out to create specialized banks[118] that supplied funds to particular fields in the industry.

After the war, entrepreneurship took off once more in areas such as railways and spinning, resulting in **capitalism** 資本主義[119] becoming firmly established, especially in the

---

[116] For the five years from 1885 to 1890, the total sum of business capital in Japan rapidly increased from 7.77 million yen to 77.53 million yen in industry, and from 25.59 million yen to 103.63 million yen in the transportation business.

[117] At that time, the value of silver against gold was continually dropping, so the use of the silver standard had the effect of increasing exports and decreasing imports against Western nations on the gold standard. However, Japan was put at a disadvantage when it came to capital imports from gold standard countries. Due to the decline in silver values, the amount of gold contained in 1-yen coins was changed from 1.5 grams to 0.75 grams by the New Currency Act.

[118] Banks were established such as Nihon Kangyō Ginkō〈日本勧業銀行〉(Japan Bank for the Promotion of Industry), Nihon Kōgyō Ginkō〈日本興業銀行〉(Industrial Bank of Japan), the Bank of Taiwan, and agricultural-industrial banks for each prefecture.

[119] An economic system in which the mainstream of economic activities are represented by capitalists, meaning individuals who own the means of production such as factories, machinery,

textile industry. However, this also led to another depression occurring in 1900 due to overproduction.

The scale of trade expanded along with the development of industrialization, but an increase in imports of raw materials, such as cotton, and heavy industrial products, such as machinery and iron, led to an import surplus. **Trading companies** 商社, exemplified by Mitsui Trading Company 三井物産会社[viii], played a major role handling these goods, and the **Yokohama Specie Bank** 横浜正金銀行, a specialized bank, actively financed trading activities.

Additionally, under the shipping encouragement policy 海運業奨励政策[120], many new sea lanes were opened during this period by Japanese shipping companies like Nihon Yūsen Kaisha 日本郵船会社 (NYK)[121].

Spinning, Silk-Reeling, and Railways

The industrial revolution in Japan was centered on the spinning industry which produced cotton yarn. From the final years of the Edo Bakufu, cotton cultivation and the production of cotton yarn and textiles temporarily declined in the face of pressure from the influx of British cotton products. However, a shift to using imported cotton yarn as raw material and the incorporation of the flying shuttle 飛び杼[122] to improve handlooms led to gradual increases in cotton textile production, centered on the cottage industry in farming villages. The recovery of the cotton textile industry created an environment for the spinning industry to rise, as it was the supplier of raw yarn. However, many mills

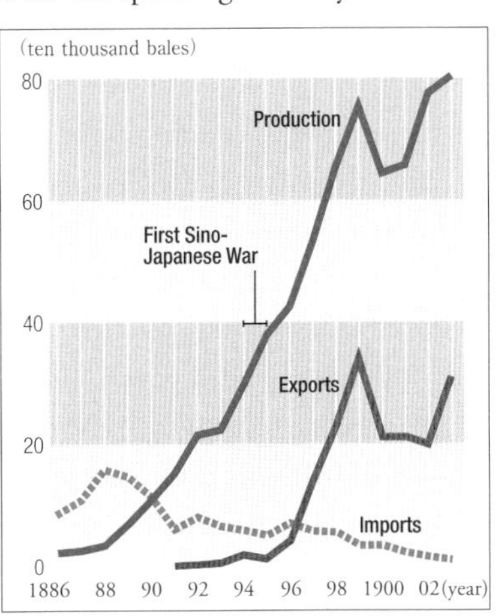

CHANGES IN PRODUCTION, IMPORTS, AND EXPORTS OF COTTON YARN

---

and raw materials, and employ paid workers for the purpose of gaining profit.

[120] In 1896, the government promulgated the **Shipbuilding Promotion Act** 〈造船奨励法〉 and the **Navigation Promotion Act** 〈航海奨励法〉. These acts issued subsidies for companies building steel ships and launching foreign routes, with the aim of saving foreign exchanges and securing warships in the event of conflict.

[121] NYK was formed in 1885 through the merger of Mitsubishi and a semi-governmental company, Kyōdō Shipping 〈共同運輸会社〉. The line established a Bombay route to India in 1893, and routes to Europe, the Americas, and Australia by 1896.

[122] A device that makes the shuttle carrying the weft move back and forth by pulling a cord. It was invented by John Kay of England in 1733, and was introduced to Japan through the Vienna World's Fair in 1873, whereupon it became widespread.

ŌSAKA COTTON SPINNING COMPANY
The company became highly successful by introducing the most modern spinning machinery from the UK as well as electric lights for operating on a day and night shift rotation.

struggled to operate efficiently at the small scale (2,000 spindles) promoted by the government. In contrast, in 1883 Shibusawa Eiichi founded the **Ōsaka Cotton-Spinning Company** (大阪紡績会社) that successfully managed large-scale operations (10,000 spindles) by using imported spinning machines and steam engines. This success prompted merchants, mainly in Ōsaka, to launch businesses, and led to a rapid increase in **mechanical production** (機械制生産) as well as a decline in cotton yarn production by hand spinning or Garabō (ガラ紡) throstle spinning[123]. By 1890, the amount of cotton yarn being produced exceeded the amount imported. From around the time of the First Sino-Japanese War, exports of cotton yarn to China and Korea rapidly increased, and by 1897 exports exceeded imports.

After the Russo-Japanese War, major spinning companies solidified their dominant market position through mergers and produced great amounts of cotton textiles with large imported power looms, while making further advances into Korean and Manchurian markets by forming sales associations. Meanwhile, the rural cotton textile industry, which was based on cottage industry production mainly using handlooms, began to see a trend in workshops transforming into small factories through adopting the small power looms invented by **Toyoda Sakichi** (豊田佐吉) (1867-1930) and other innovators. By 1909, the amount of exported cotton fabrics had exceeded those imported.

Although exports of cotton yarn and cotton textiles continued to mount throughout this period, the excess of imports in cotton trade actually increased because raw cotton was dependent upon imports from countries such as China, India, and the US. For this reason, the **silk-reeling industry** (製糸業) played a vital role because it was able to generate foreign income by exporting raw silk, which was derived from Japanese cocoons.

Because raw silk had been Japan's major export product since the final years of

[123] Garabō throstle spinning employed a simple spinning machine, invented by Gaun Tokimune〈臥雲辰致〉 and awarded the first prize at the First National Industrial Exhibition〈内国勧業博覧会〉. The device spread mainly in Aichi Prefecture after it was adapted to run on water-wheel power instead of manual operation. However, it went into decline in the 1890s due to the increase in large machine-based spinning factories.

the bakufu, silk-reeling rapidly developed to become Japan's leading export industry to the West. At first, the **zaguri silk reeling machine** (座繰製糸), a simple mechanism based on hand-reeling, was popular. However, soon small factories utilizing **machine silk-reeling** (器械製糸)[124], which improved conventional methods through studying imported machinery, began to be built one after another in rural areas such as Nagano (長野) and Yamanashi (山梨) prefectures. The number of silkworm farmers supplying cocoons as raw materials also correspondingly increased. As exports increased, production by machine silk-reeling had come to surpass zaguri silk-reeling by the end of the First Sino-Japanese War. The power loom was introduced in the silk textile industry, and the production of habutae (羽二重) silk for export mounted in popularity. After the Russo-Japanese War, raw silk exports further increased, mainly to the US, and by 1909 Japan had exceeded China to become the largest exporter of raw silk in the world.

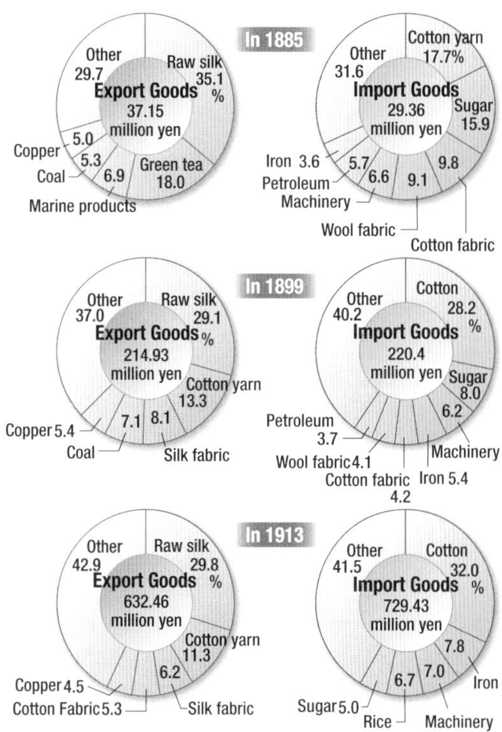

BREAKDOWN OF IMPORTED AND EXPORTED GOODS

In the railway industry, the **Nihon Railway Company** (日本鉄道会社), founded in 1881 mainly by kazoku investors, received governmental support and encountered great success, triggering a boom in railway entrepreneurship among merchants and landowners. As a result, the total operating length of private railways had exceeded that of national lines by 1889 when the state-run Tōkaidō Line (東海道線) (Shinbashi to Kōbe) was completed. Beginning with the Nihon Railway Company completing lines between Ueno

[124] Machine silk-reeling was considerably different from the zaguri silk-reeling that had spread in the final years of the Edo period. Silk-winding machines were all connected by a single shaft and rotated manually or by water-wheel (and later by steam engine), with multiple employees working simultaneously.

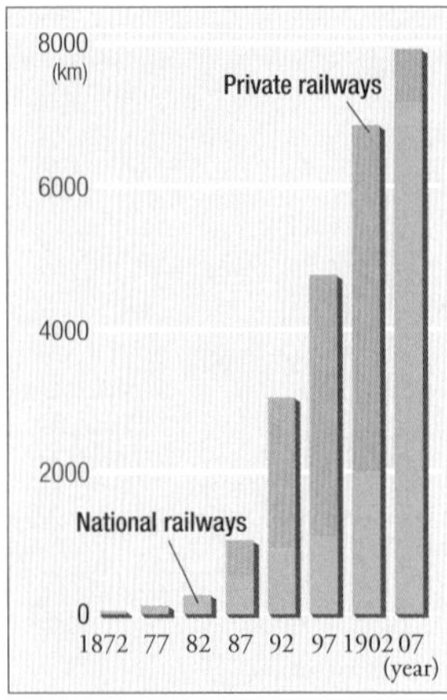

GROWTH OF THE RAILWAY SYSTEM

and Aomori in 1891, other private railways such as the Sanyō Railway 山陽鉄道 and the Kyūshū Railway 九州鉄道 also began to construct major lines, and cities spanning from Aomori 青森 to Shimonoseki were connected after the First Sino-Japanese War. In 1906, however, no sooner had the Russo-Japanese War ended than the First Saionji Cabinet issued the **Railway Nationalization Act** 鉄道国有法. The act was motivated by consideration of the military value of railways, and sought to unify and manage them on a national scale. Seventeen private railways running major lines were purchased and nationalized. Many investors who earned large amounts of capital in this way began investing in heavy industry.

The Formation of Heavy Industry

From 1884, state-run enterprises with the exception of railways and military factories began to be privatized one after another (**disposal of state-owned enterprises** 官営事業払下げ). In particular, **seishō** 政商 such as Mitsui, Mitsubishi (Iwasaki), and Furukawa 古河 acquired rich mines where they automated operations, such as by introducing winch machinery, and contributed to increasing coal and copper exports. With the mining industry as their revenue base, these merchants grew to become the so-called **zaibatsu** 財閥 (**financial conglomerates**). In the Chikuhō 筑豊 area of northern Kyūshū, the successful introduction of the steam pump for drainage purposes helped develop coal mining, and after the First Sino-Japanese War the Chikuhō coalfield became the largest coal-producing area in Japan.

However, Japanese heavy industry saw little development in the private sector apart from the growth of shipyards, notably the Mitsubishi Nagasaki Shipyard 三菱長崎造船所, due to the Shipbuilding Promotion Act issued after the First Sino-Japanese War. Steel, a key raw material, still depended upon imports. In its haste to expand the military, the government increased the number of state-run military factories, and also established the **Yahata Steelworks** 八幡製鉄所 in 1897 in northern Kyūshū, close to the aforementioned Chikuhō coalfield, with the aim of domestically producing steel to provide a base for supporting heavy industry. The Yahata Steelworks began operation by introducing German technology in 1901, but while production became stable from around the time of the Russo-Japanese War, it was unable to meet domestic demand.

After the end of the Russo-Japanese War, the government expanded its sales of bonds in foreign countries and increased various taxes in order to carry out postwar management centered on further expansion of the military. Under the protection of the government, private heavy industry companies also began to develop. In the steel industry, Yahata Steelworks launched a series of projects in order to expand operations[125], while private steel companies such as **Japan Steelworks** (日本製鋼所) began to be established. Shipbuilding technology, which had retained an important position in Japanese policies, reached world standards. In the field of machine tools (i.e., machinery for creating machines), **Ikegai Ironworks** (池貝鉄工所) was successful in domestically producing high-precision lathes that were equivalent to those of advanced nations. Meanwhile, an **electrical power industry** (電力事業) also developed as hydroelectric power generation got fully underway, and electric lighting came to spread in the larger cities.

YAHATA STEELWORKS
Construction of the steelworks was partly funded with reparations from the First Sino-Japanese War. Building of the factory itself began from 1897, and steel production started from 1901. The photograph above was a commemorative one taken when Itō Hirobumi visited the site in 1900.

Zaibatsu such as Mitsui and Mitsubishi diversified into various fields – primarily finance, trade, transport, and mining – and began to form concerns (コンツェルン) (enterprise partnerships) that controlled multiple enterprises through stockholding[126].

The role of colonies in the Japanese economy grew after the Russo-Japanese War, with soybean meal imports from Manchuria, rice imports from Korea, cotton fabric exports to both, and shipments of rice and raw sugar from Taiwan all increasing.

---

[125] In return for Japanese government loans to the Hanyehping Company〈漢冶萍公司〉, one of China's greatest iron manufacturers, Yahata Steelworks was able to acquire iron ore from the Daye iron mines〈大冶鉄山〉 (in Hubei Province〈湖北省〉) at a low price.

[126] Mitsui Zaibatsu began by forming the Mitsui Gōmei Company〈三井合名会社〉 in 1909, and the other zaibatsu – Yasuda〈安田〉, Mitsubishi, and Sumitomo〈住友〉 – also started creating their own holding companies through to the early 1920s. These holding companies were directly controlled by relatives of the founders, and owned shares of many businesses under their respective zaibatsu umbrella. Aside from the four major zaibatsu, there were also small- to medium-sized ones founded by entrepreneurs such as Furukawa Ichibē〈古河市兵衛〉, Asano Sōichirō〈浅野総一郎〉, and Kawasaki Shōzō〈川崎正蔵〉.

Although this period saw an increase in Japanese exports of products such as raw silk and cotton fabrics, imports of raw cotton, military equipment, and materials for heavy industry also increased, and as a result the trade balance suffered from major deficits nearly every year. On top of that, the interest payments for foreign debts also piled up, and consequently Japan's balance of international payments gradually drifted into dangerous territory.

Agriculture and Farmers

In contrast to industry, the development of agriculture was slower, and remained focused on small-scale management with rice cultivation first and foremost. Although the yield per area gradually increased due to the introduction of **selective breeding**[127] 品種改良 and purchased fertilizers such as soybean meal, the supply of rice regularly failed to keep pace with population growth.

At the same time, however, farmers came to be deeply involved in the commodity economy that had grown out of the development of trade and domestic industry, and the production of clothing at home decreased. While the production of some crops such as cotton, hemp, and rapeseed declined due to the influx of low-cost imports, the cultivation of mulberry (for silk worms) and **silk farming** 養蚕 were stimulated by the increase in raw silk exports.

The percentage of land under tenancy began to rise from the 1880s due to the deflationary policies of Matsukata finance, and continued to go up throughout the 1890s. Poorer farmers were forced to become tenant farmers, while large landowners ceased farming themselves and moved to a **sharecropping system**, 寄生地主制 where their income depended on farm rent. As farm rent was paid in kind and the land tax in cash at a fixed amount, these landowners benefitted from an increase in income as rice prices rose. They used their rent income to

Average annual rate	Tenant farms (%)	Owned farms (%)
1873	27.4	72.6
1883-84	35.9	64.1
1892	40.2	59.8
1903	43.6	56.4
1912	45.4	54.6
1922	46.4	53.6
1932	47.5	52.5
1940	45.9	54.1

TRANSITION IN RATIO OF TENANT FARMING

[127] The government established an agricultural experiment station in 1893 and launched projects for improving crops such as rice plants.

start businesses or invest in stock or government bonds, gradually deepening their involvement in capitalism. On the other hand, tenant farmers who struggled to make their payments had to send their sons and daughters to work in factories or start side jobs in order to make ends meet for their families.

RICE PLANTING
Rice planting was traditionally done as a group until mechanization methods began to increase in the 1970s.

After the Russo-Japanese War, as the land tax and indirect taxes increased, a decline in agricultural productivity and rising poverty in farming villages became a significant social problem. It was for this reason that, in an effort to alleviate the situation, the government launched the **Local Improvement Movement** 地方改良運動 to promote nationwide exemplary villages that were successful in cooperative projects.

The Dawn of Social Movements

Along with the growth of factory-based industry, the number of wage earners also increased. At the time, the majority of factory workers were employed in the textile industry, where most of them were women[128]. Many of these women workers (called jokō 女工 or kōjo 工女, "factory girls") were the daughters of tenant farmers who had left home to work in order to help their families' struggling finances. Bound to the factories by pre-wage borrowing and dormitory systems, they were made to work long hours in poor conditions at wages significantly lower than in the West. In the spinning industry, work was divided into two shifts to enable day and night operations, and in the silk-reeling industry, working hours were about 15 hours per day, and sometimes even 18. The number of skilled male workers in heavy industry was still limited, with many male laborers outside the factories working in the mining and transportation industries[129].

During the industrialization era around the time of the First Sino-Japanese War,

---

[128] In 1900, out of a total of 390,000 factory workers, around 240,000, or nearly 60%, were employed in the textile industry. Of this latter number, 88% were women.

[129] The miserable conditions of workers during the industrialization era were reported in the magazine *Nihon-jin*〈『日本人』〉 (The Japanese) in 1888, which covered the terrible situation of workers in the Takashima coal mine〈高島炭鉱〉 (Nagasaki Prefecture, managed by Mitsubishi), causing a sensation. Other sources include Yokoyama Gennosuke's〈横山源之助〉 *Nihon no Kasō Shakai*〈『日本之下層社会』〉 (The Lower Strata of Japanese Society) in 1899, and the Ministry of Agriculture and Commerce's *Shokkō Jijō*〈『職工事情』〉 (Factory Worker Conditions) in 1903.

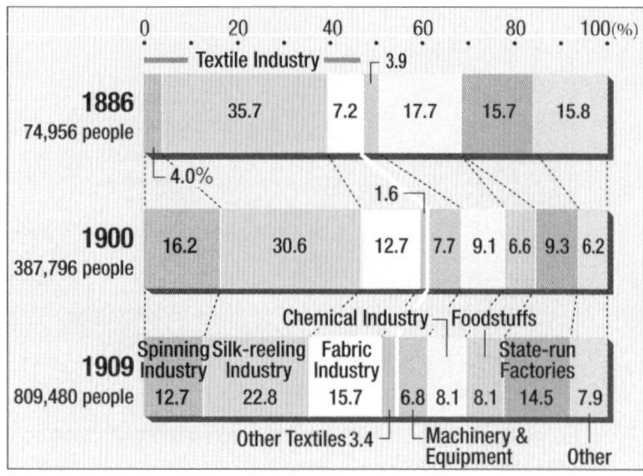

DETAILED STATISTICS ON FACTORY WORKERS
Data collected from factories with more than ten workers.

labor strikes (ストライキ) came to be launched by factory workers demanding improvements in working conditions and better wages, and in 1897 more than 40 such strikes occurred nationwide. In the same year, Takano Fusatarō (高野房太郎) (1868-1904), Katayama Sen (1859-1933) and other activists, influenced by the labor movement in the US, formed the **Association for the Promotion of Labor Unions** (労働組合期成会). The group took a leading role in the labor movement, and inspired the organization of labor unions such as the Ironworkers' Union (鉄工組合) and the Japan Railway Workers' Reform Society (日本鉄道矯正会). In this way, a movement developed in which workers, and particularly skilled workers, came to unite and oppose capitalists. Meanwhile, in 1891 mining pollution from the Ashio Copper Mine (足尾銅山) (in Tochigi Prefecture (栃木県)) caused severe damage to fishing and farming communities around the Watarase River (渡良瀬川) basin (**Ashio Copper Mine Pollution Incident** (足尾鉱毒事件)), and developed into a major social problem for over 15 years.

It was in response to this rising labor movement that the government enacted the **Security Police Law** (治安警察法) in 1900, which cracked down on the labor movement by restricting workers' rights to organize and strike. On the other hand, the government also sought to relieve tension between laborers and capitalists by improving working conditions from a social policy perspective[130], and began working towards issuing the **Factory Act** (工場法). This act, which was the first law for the protection of workers in Japan, was finally passed in 1911 after much opposition from capitalists, but was deeply flawed[131] and had its implementation delayed until 1916.

---

[130] Behind this decision was the fear that deteriorating living standards among working families would lower the quality of soldiers and thus adversely affect Japanese military power.

[131] Maximum working hours for children and women were set at 12, and late-night work was prohibited. The scope of this law only applied to factories which hired 15 or more workers, industries such as silk-reeling were allowed a limit of 14 hours, and the spinning industry was permitted limited late-night work.

Tanaka Shōzō and the Ashio Copper Mine Pollution Incident

In 1877, Furukawa Ichibē bought the Ashio Copper Mine, which had been close to abandonment by the end of the Edo period. Six years later, the amount of profit generated by copper smelting there had amounted to more than ten times the price for which the site was purchased. However, the rapid growth resulted in great hazards being foisted upon the farming and fishing communities living at the lower reaches of the Watarase River basin. From the middle of the 1880s, rumors spread that there would always be dead fish floating on the surface of the water when the color of the river turned milky blue. This was the result of toxic pollution from the copper mine flowing into the river. To make matters worse, the great flood of 1896 affected the whole valley, stretching across four prefectures including Gunma, and greatly harming crops and livestock, all of which affected the health of local people.

From 1897, villagers from the stricken areas would head to Tōkyō in large groups in their straw capes and sandals to petition the government. However, after several failed attempts, dozens of these protestors were arrested for fighting with police in 1900. In the Diet, a politician in the House of Representatives, Tanaka Shōzō〈田中正造〉 from Tochigi Prefecture, urged the government to issue a demand to halt the mine operations. Tanaka also collaborated with intellectuals such as Kinoshita Naoe in order to arouse public opinion in favor of suspending operations. In response to this, the government also set up an investigation committee for mining pollution and ordered the copper mine to take precautions to prevent the outflow of toxic pollution, but ultimately did not order the company to halt operations. In 1901, Tanaka resigned and attempted to appeal directly to the tennō, but failed. In 1907, to alleviate the damage and flooding the government decided to build a retention basin and dissolve Yanaka Village〈谷中村〉, located in Tochigi Prefecture close to the Watarase River's confluence with the Tone River〈利根川〉. The villagers were to be relocated, but Tanaka remained in the village with other locals who were dissatisfied with this decision, and stayed there to protest against the government until his death in 1913.

6 The Evolution of Modern Culture

Meiji Culture

In order to compete with the Western powers, the new Meiji government had set out to modernize itself through adopting Western culture and technology under slogans such as "Fukoku Kyōhei," "Shokusan Kōgyō" and "Bunmei Kaika." However, in contrast to the rapid influx of material culture, changes in mindset occurred much more slowly, and modernization proceeded more rapidly in cities than in farming villages. In this way the culture of the Meiji period was characterized by a unique dualism in which new and old, Western and Eastern components were all mixed up together.

In the early Meiji period modernization was largely led by the government, but from mid-Meiji the spread of education, and remarkable developments in transportation, communication, and publishing, fueled a rise in public awareness that resulted in the public nurturing modern culture themselves.

Thought and Religion

The intellectual trends toward introducing **Enlightenment** 啓蒙主義 and other Western thought that had begun under Bunmei Kaika were succeeded by the Freedom and People's Rights Movement. However, in the wake of the Korean problem from the late 1870s, some people's rights activists shifted towards advocating for Japan's **kokkenron** 国権論 **(national rights)**. The conflict between Westernization and national rights intensified as the treaty revision issue came to the forefront. Debates occurred between those who favored **democratic Westernization** 平民的欧化主義, like Tokutomi Sohō (1863-1957), and advocates of **modern ethnic nationalism** 近代的民族主義, like Miyake Setsurei 三宅雪嶺 (1860-1945), Shiga Shigetaka 志賀重昂 (1863-1927), and Kuga Katsunan 陸羯南 (1857-1907)[132].

The victory in the First Sino-Japanese War had a decisive impact in shifting the direction of trends in Japanese intellectual culture. As soon as the war broke out, Tokutomi switched to supporting overseas expansion, and Takayama Chogyū 高山樗牛 (1871-1902) too justified Japan's military advance into the Asian continent by advocating **Nihonshugi** 日本主義 **(Japanism)** in the magazine *Taiyō* 『太陽』 (The Sun). Even Kuga Katsunan, who had criticized the government for participating in the scramble for concessions, turned to favor a hardline policy towards Russia due to the Russian

FRONT COVERS OF INAUGURAL ISSUES OF *KOKUMIN NO TOMO* AND *NIHON-JIN* MAGAZINES
The total annual circulation of newspapers and magazines in Japan by 1890 had almost doubled to 190 million copies in a period of three years. Half of the copies were issued in Tōkyō.

[132] Sohō founded the Min'yūsha〈民友社〉 society and published *Kokumin no Tomo*〈『国民之友』〉, a magazine in which he criticized the government's Westernization policies, aimed at enabling revision of the unequal treaties, as aristocratic Westernization, arguing instead for a democratic Westernization that would improve life and expand freedom for the general public. Setsurei and Katsunan similarly focused on the welfare of the people but also emphasized the independence of the state and nationality as its preconditions. Setsurei and his group founded the Seikyōsha〈政教社〉, which published the magazine *Nihon-jin*, while Katsunan with others published the newspaper *Nihon*〈『日本』〉.

occupation of Manchuria after the Boxer Rebellion. Socialists and some Christian groups opposed these ideological trends, but **nationalism** 国家主義 favoring overseas expansion had already become the mainstream of Japanese intellectual culture before the Russo-Japanese War.

However, once Japan had joined the ranks of the great powers through its victory in the Russo-Japanese War, a strong sentiment arose among the population that Japan had finally achieved its national goals since the Meiji Restoration. This prompted increased questioning of nationalism. In farming villages, a tendency to prioritize the interests of local communities over national interests emerged. In urban areas too, among the younger generations some moved away from nationalism and politics to instead pursue practical profits, while others lamented over the meaning of life.

In order to counter these trends, in 1908 the government issued the **Boshin Edict** 戊申詔書 which, to raise national morale to support the country now that it had become a great power, called for the public to be diligent, frugal, and respective of the royal family.

In the religious sphere, there were conflicts between the traditional beliefs of Shintō and Buddhism on the one hand and Christianity from the West on the other. Although government efforts to establish Shintō as Japan's state religion in the early Meiji period had failed, government-approved sects, collectively termed **Kyōha Shintō** 教派神道 (**Sectarian Shintō**), spread among the general public. Buddhism, which had suffered greatly for a time due to the anti-Buddhist **Haibutsu Kishaku** 廃仏毀釈 movement, also recovered due to the efforts of figures like Shimaji Mokurai 島地黙雷 (1838-1911) who went to great lengths to fully separate Buddhism from Shintō.

Christianity spread among young intellectuals, partly due to the influence of foreign instructors[133], such as William Smith Clark and Leroy Lansing Janes ジェーンズ (1838-1909), who had come to Japan in the early Meiji period. Among them, Uchimura Kanzō, Ebina Danjō 海老名弾正 (1856-1937), and Nitobe Inazō 新渡戸稲造 (1862-1933) became active as proponents of Christianity and modern Western philosophy. In addition to missionary activities, Christian churches, motivated by humanitarianism, made contributions in education, welfare, and the **prostitution abolition movement** 廃娼運動. However, as nationalism intensified, the religion also came under pressure from various directions.

The Spread of Education

As a result of great effort invested in the spread of primary education under the new education system, promulgated in 1872, the school enrollment rate for **compulsory** 義務教育

[133] Clark taught at Sapporo Agricultural College while Janes taught at the Kumamoto School of Western Learning〈熊本洋学校〉.

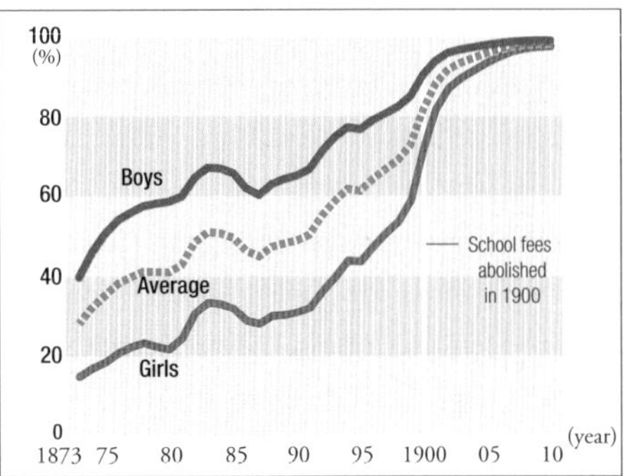

RISE IN SCHOOL ENROLLMENT RATE FOR COMPULSORY EDUCATION

education steadily rose. However, the system encountered criticism from both inside and outside the government for its uniform and coercive nature which ignored the reality of each region, and so in 1879 it was abolished and replaced by the **Education Order** 教育令. This order substantially relaxed the compulsory education requirement, abolishing the nationally standardized school district system and specifying towns and villages as the administrative unit responsible for establishing primary schools, while transferring their management to regional government.

The sudden shift from compulsion to non-interference caused great confusion, and led to the Education Order being quickly amended the following year, emphasizing the government's responsibility for supervising primary education.

After much trial and error, the **School Orders** 学校令 were promulgated under Minister of Education **Mori Arinori** 森有礼 in 1886, establishing an education system consisting of primary schools, middle schools, normal schools (which trained teachers), imperial universities, and other institutions[134]. For the primary schools (ordinary and higher), the Primary School Order 小学校令, revised in 1890, clarified that compulsory primary education was to be 3 to 4 years for ordinary schools, and 2 to 4 years for higher schools[135]. Later, in 1907, compulsory primary education was extended to 6 years.

At the same time, the education policy gradually turned to emphasize nationalism. The **Imperial Rescript on Education** 教育に関する勅語, promulgated in 1890, emphasized that allegiance and patriotism were the fundamentals of school education[136]. In 1903, it

[134] The orders issued for imperial universities, normal schools, middle schools, and primary schools were collectively called the School Orders. Primary, middle and normal schools were each divided into two subgroups, ordinary and higher. Later on, ordinary middle schools and higher middle schools became middle schools and higher schools, respectively. Meanwhile, Tōkyō University, the only public university at the time, was reorganized to become the Imperial University (later renamed Tōkyō Imperial University again in 1897).

[135] In 1892, school enrollment stood at 70% for boys and 36% for girls. As school fees were abolished for students of compulsory school age in 1900, the enrollment rate in 1902 exceeded 90%.

[136] In 1891, the Christian Uchimura Kanzō refused to bow and show respect to a copy of the Imperial Rescript on Education with the tennō's signature at a reading ceremony held at the First Higher Middle School〈第一高等中学校〉. Being a teacher there, he was forced to resign from his post, in what became called the "Uchimura Kanzō Lèse-Majesté Incident〈内村鑑三不敬事件〉."

was decided that primary school textbooks were to be limited to those written by the Ministry of Education (**government-approved textbooks** (国定教科書)), further strengthening the state's control over education.

Public institutions of higher education also continued to expand. Along with Tōkyō Imperial University, Kyōto Imperial University was founded in 1897, and subsequent years also saw the founding of Tōhoku Imperial University and Kyūshū Imperial University[137]. In the private sector, Keiō Gijuku and Dōshisha were followed by schools like Tōkyō Senmon Gakkō (東京専門学校) (later renamed Waseda (早稲田大学) University), founded by Ōkuma Shigenobu, which developed a unique style different from that of the public schools.

Developments in Science

Modern academic studies began in the early Meiji period in the form of studying abroad or learning from scholars invited from Europe or the US. Gradually, Japanese came to be able to carry out specialized research and educate students in each field by themselves.

In economics, British economics, which supported laissez-faire policies and free trade, was introduced first, and later, German theories of protectionism and social policy became mainstream. In legal studies, Gustave Boissonade was invited from France to take the lead in compiling law codes, but after the Civil Code controversy German law became predominant. Similarly, in philosophy German philosophy, and especially German idealism, took center stage. Even in the fields of Japanese history[138] and Japanese literature, scientific research based on Western research methodologies renewed the existing research done by Kokugaku scholars[139].

In the natural sciences, modern scientific technology from the West was intro-

---

[137] From the Taishō period to the early Shōwa period, further imperial universities were established in Hokkaidō, Gyeongseong (Korea), Taipei〈台北〉(Taiwan), Ōsaka, and Nagoya〈名古屋〉. The schools were collectively called the "Nine Imperial Universities〈「9帝大」〉."

[138] In the field of Japanese history, historical perspectives were reinvigorated by the appearance of private works of civilization history such as Taguchi Ukichi's〈田口卯吉〉 *Nihon Kaika Shōshi*〈『日本開化小史』〉 (A Short History of Japanese Civilization). At the Historiographical Institute〈史料編纂掛〉 at Tōkyō Imperial University, compilation projects of primary source documents were systematically conducted, such as *Dai Nihon Shiryō*〈『大日本史料』〉 (Chronological Source Books of Japanese History) and *Dai Nihon Komonjo*〈『大日本古文書』〉 (Old Documents of Japan).

[139] There were times when scientific research clashed with traditional thought. In 1891, a professor at the Imperial University, Kume Kunitake〈久米邦武〉, argued that "Shintō is an outdated custom of heaven worship," and was consequently forced to resign from his position the following year.

duced to accelerate the Fukoku Kyōhei and Shokusan Kōgyō policies. By the end of the Meiji period, Japanese research had reached world-class standards, and original contributions in fields such as seismology came to be recognized.

Journalism and Modern Literature

From the 1880s to 1890s, public opinion increased with developments in the Freedom and People's Rights Movement, tensions in Asia, and revision of the unequal treaties. It was in this context that newspapers featuring political commentary, called **ōshinbun** 大新聞 (literally "large newspapers") began to be published. These newspapers, each with its own political slant, played a major role in spreading political ideas among the public, while also contributing to the production and dissemination of modern literature through their own dedicated literary writers and contributors. On the other hand, **koshinbun** 小新聞 (literally "small newspapers"), which inherited the tradition of kawaraban 瓦版 (slate prints), were popular newspapers which mainly featured news and entertainment and helped revive gesaku 戯作文学 literature.

Magazines, which first gained ground with *Meiroku Zasshi* in the early Meiji period, came into their own in the latter half of the 1880s with the launch of *Kokumin no Tomo* (The Public's Friend) and *Nihon-jin*, among others. In the later years of the Meiji period, **general interest magazines** (sōgō-zasshi 総合雑誌) such as *Taiyō* and *Chūō Kōron* 『中央公論』 (Central Review) began to be published.

As for literature, **gesaku literature** 戯作文学, a popular literary genre from the Edo period, continued to be widely read in the early Meiji period. Meanwhile, political literature was produced by activists in order to publicize their opinions on matters such as people's rights or national rights[140].

In 1885, Tsubouchi Shōyō 坪内逍遙 (1859-1935) published an essay criticizing the kanzen chōaku 勧善懲悪 (good being rewarded and evil punished) themes of gesaku literature and the prioritizing of political ideology over everything else in political literature. In this essay, *Shōsetsu Shinzui* 『小説神髄』 (The Essence of the Novel), Tsubouchi instead argued, drawing on Western literary theories, that literature focus on people's psychology or social conditions and be written in an objective and realistic manner (a movement called shajitsushugi, **realism** 写実主義). *Ukigumo* 『浮雲』 (The Drifting Cloud), a novel by Futabatei Shimei 二葉亭四迷 (1864-1909), brought Shōyō's ideal to fruition. It was written in vernacular Japanese,

[140] Notable works of gesaku literature include *Aguranabe*〈「安愚楽鍋」〉 (The Beef Eater) by Kanagaki Robun〈仮名垣魯文〉, which depicted many aspects of society during the Bunmei Kaika movement. Political literature included works such as *Keikoku Bidan*〈「経国美談」〉 (Inspiring Tales of Statesmanship) by Yano Ryūkei〈矢野龍溪〉, who was also a politician in the Kaishintō, and *Kajin no Kigū*〈「佳人之奇遇」〉 (Unexpected Encounters with Beauties) by Tōkai Sanshi〈東海散士〉.

SHŌSETSU SHINZUI (THE ESSENCE OF THE NOVEL)

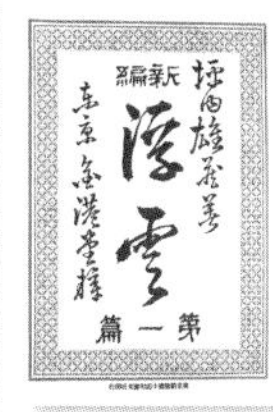

UKIGUMO (THE DRIFTING CLOUD)

KONJIKI YASHA (THE GOLDEN DEMON)

WAKANASHŪ (COLLECTION OF YOUNG GREENS)

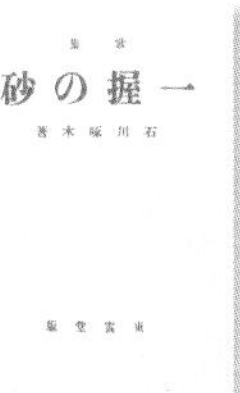

ICHIAKU NO SUNA (A HANDFUL OF SAND)

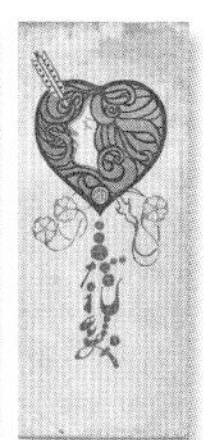

MIDARE-GAMI (TANGLED HAIR)

called **genbun itchi-tai** 言文一致体 (a style reflecting the "unification of the spoken and written language"). Writers belonging to the Ken'yūsha 硯友社[141], such as Ozaki Kōyō 尾崎紅葉 (1867-1903), similarly embraced realism while promoting writing for the masses. By contrast, Kōda Rohan 幸田露伴 (1867-1947) decided to pursue Shōyō's emphasis on valuing the human mind, and wrote idealistic novels based on Eastern philosophy.

Around the period of the Sino-Japanese War, **romantic** ロマン主義 literature, which focused upon the dynamics of sentiments and individuality, became popular in Japan as a counter movement to enlightenment and rationalism. The literary magazine *Bungakukai* 『文学界』 (Literary World), published by writers such as Kitamura Tōkoku 北村透谷 (1868-94), was the platform for this trend that saw the birth of novels by Mori Ōgai 森鷗外 (1862-1922) and Izumi Kyōka 泉鏡花 (1873-1939), as well as poetry such as new verse (shintaishi 新体詩) by Shimazaki Tōson 島崎藤村 (1872-1943) and passionate tanka 短歌 by Yosano Akiko (1878-1942)[142]. Higuchi Ichiyō 樋口一葉 (1872-96), who wrote stories on the sorrows of women at the bottom of the social scale, was also under the influence of romanticism. Meanwhile, Masaoka Shiki 正岡子規 (1867-1902) became known as a reformist of traditional literature through his innovative haiku 俳句 and revival of Man'yō-style waka 万葉調和歌[143].

---

[141] The Ken'yūsha (Friends of the Inkstone) was formed mainly by Ozaki and Yamada Bimyō〈山田美妙〉, and published the magazine *Garakuta Bunko*〈『我楽多文庫』〉(Miscellanea) circulated among group members.

[142] Shimazaki Tōson established the new verse form through writing *Wakanashū*〈『若菜集』〉(Collection of Young Greens). Yosano Akiko published her works in the literary magazine *Myōjō*, run by her husband, Yosano Tekkan〈与謝野鉄幹〉. The magazine played a major role in the romantic movement in Japan.

[143] In 1897, the haiku magazine *Hototogisu*〈『ホトトギス』〉(Cuckoo) was founded with the assistance of Shiki, who was bedridden with illness at the time. The editorship was later taken over by his disciple, Takahama Kyoshi〈高浜虚子〉. As for waka, other disciples of Shiki such as Itō Sachio〈伊藤左千夫〉 and Nagatsuka Takashi〈長塚節〉 began attracting attention, and a tanka magazine called *Araragi*〈『アララギ』〉(Japanese Yew) was founded in 1908.

After the First Sino-Japanese War, the social novels of Tokutomi Roka 徳冨蘆花 (Sohō's younger brother), who was an advocate of humanitarianism, came to have a presence in the field. Around the period of the Russo-Japanese War, **naturalism** 自然主義, drawing inspiration from French and Russian works, came to the forefront of Japanese literature. Naturalism attempted to depict the harsh realities of human society in a realistic form, and writers such as Kunikida Doppo 国木田独歩 (1871-1908), Tayama Katai 田山花袋 (1871-1930), Shimazaki Tōson, and Tokuda Shūsei 徳田秋声 (1871-1943), came under the spotlight in this movement. Ishikawa Takuboku 石川啄木 (1886-1912), who began as a romantic poet, also began writing daily life poems which included socialist ideology.

There were also works written to counter the rise of naturalism, such as the novels of Natsume Sōseki 夏目漱石 (1867-1916) which focused upon the inner lives of intellectuals in relation to state and society, and Mori Ōgai's series of historical stories. Moreover, as literary reviews began to be published in newspapers and magazines, not only writers but also critics came to occupy an important position in the literary world.

The Art of the Meiji Period

In the theatre world, Kabuki 歌舞伎 performances were widely appreciated by commoners. In the beginning of the Meiji period, Kawatake Mokuami 河竹黙阿弥 (1816-93) wrote new plays influenced by the latest trends in the Bunmei Kaika movement. The social status of Kabuki rose significantly in the mid-Meiji years with the appearance of many illustrious actors, giving rise to the term "**Dan-Kiku-Sa Trio Era** 団菊左時代[144]." Sōshi 壮士芝居 (agitator) theatre, by activists like Kawakami Otojirō 川上音二郎 (1864-1911), incorporated people's rights ideology in topical plays, which together with dramatizations of popular literary works around the time of the First Sino-Japanese War came to be called **Shinpageki** 新派劇 (New-school Drama). After the Russo-Japanese War, modern drama from the West was translated and performed by Tsubouchi Shōyō's Bungei Kyōkai 文芸協会 (Literary Arts Society) and the Jiyū 自由劇場 (Free) Theatre of Osanai Kaoru 小山内薫 (1881-1928), and came to be referred to as **Shingeki** 新劇 (New Drama) in contrast to Kabuki and Shinpageki.

Western music in Japan began with performances by military bands. This was followed by songs put to Western melodies by the educator Isawa Shūji 伊沢修二 (1851-1917) for use in primary school education. In 1887, the **Tōkyō Music School** 東京音楽学校 was founded and marked the beginning of higher music training in Japan, graduating composers such as Taki Rentarō 滝廉太郎 (1879-1903). The traditional Nō 能 theatre form was also revived during the mid-Meiji period.

---

[144] In the 1890s, Ichikawa Danjūrō IX〈9代目市川団十郎〉, Onoe Kikugorō V〈5代目尾上菊五郎〉, and Ichikawa Sadanji I〈初代市川左団次〉 became stars and created the golden age of Kabuki during the Meiji period.

As was the case with education and music, the development of fine arts in Meiji Japan was dependent upon government support. The government began by founding the **Technical Art School** (工部美術学校) where foreign instructors taught Western fine arts. However, this educational policy changed to focus on traditional fine arts instead under the influence of the American professor Ernest Fenollosa (フェノロサ) (1853-1908) and Okakura Tenshin (岡倉天心) (1862-1913). The Technical Art School was closed down, and in 1887 the **Tōkyō School of Fine Arts** (東京美術学校) was established, where Western art was excluded as a subject. With such government support, painters such as Kanō Hōgai (狩野芳崖) (1828-88) and Hashimoto Gahō (橋本雅邦) (1835-1908) were able to create exceptional Japanese paintings. One of the reasons why the Japanese government became inclined towards protecting traditional fine arts was that Japanese art had come to be highly regarded in Europe at the time.

Western painting, pioneered by Takahashi Yuichi (高橋由一) (1828-1907), consequently experienced a temporarily decline, but gradually regained popularity through the founding of the **Meiji Fine Arts Society** (明治美術会), Japan's first Western painting society, by Asai Chū (浅井忠) (1856-1907), and the return of Kuroda Seiki (黒田清輝) (1866-1924), who had been studying in France. In 1896, the Department of Western Painting was established at the Tōkyō School of Fine Arts, and with the founding of the **Hakuba-kai** (白馬会) **(White Horse Society)** by Kuroda and others, the style became mainstream.

Traditional Japanese art also developed through competition among many art organizations such as the **Japan Art Institute** (日本美術院) run by Okakura Tenshin. Both tradi-

READING **(LEFT) AND** ***LAKESIDE*** **(RIGHT), BY KURODA SEIKI**

Kuroda traveled to France at the age of seventeen. Two years later, he changed his specialization from law to painting, and studied for another ten years. After he returned to Japan, he taught at the newly-established Department of Western Painting at the Tōkyō School of Fine Arts. On *Reading*〈「読書」〉, which was awarded a prize in France, his signature is in Japanese on the bottom left, whereas on *Lakeside*〈「湖畔」〉, which he produced after returning to Japan and which depicts a more Japanese scene, his signature is in the same place but in roman letters. This demonstrates how Kuroda sought to represent Japan while studying with Westerners, and conversely wanted to utilize his achievements as a person who studied abroad when back in Japan.

UMI NO SACHI〈海の幸〉(FRUITS OF THE SEA)
This painting by Aoki Shigeru〈青木繁〉, whose mentors included Kuroda Seiki, was displayed at the Hakuba-kai Exhibition of 1904. The painter uses the sea of the Mera region〈布良〉 of Bōshū Province〈房州〉 (present-day Chiba Prefecture〈千葉〉) as a motif and illustrates a group of fishermen carrying large fish by applying a rhythmic structure, dynamic techniques, and brown colors.

RŌEN (AGED MONKEY, BY TAKAMURA KŌUN; HEIGHT 90.9 CM)

tional and Western art were promoted by the Ministry of Education, which from 1907 began to hold the **Ministry of Education Fine Arts Exhibition** (文部省美術展覧会) (known as Bunten (文展)) where artists from different groups could present their works at the same venue.

In sculpture, traditional wood carving led by Takamura Kōun (高村光雲) (1852-1934) and Western-style sculpting and casting led by Ogiwara Morie (荻原守衛) (1879-1910), who had studied in the US and France, contributed to developing the field through competition, before settling down to coexist in the same manner as painting had done with the opening of Bunten. The craftworks industry also adopted Western methods, and began producing new kinds of pottery, cloisonné enamel, glasswork, and lacquerware, of which pottery and cloisonné enamel were also exported overseas. Meanwhile, in architecture too full-fledged Western buildings began to be built, and by the end of the Meiji period buildings using reinforced concrete were being constructed.

Modernization in Lifestyle

During the Meiji period, a Western style of living came to be adopted mainly in urban areas, in government offices, companies, schools and the military, where people worked or studied in buildings with glass windows, used tables and chairs, wore Western clothing, and went by the clock.

By the end of the 1880s, electric lights were being used in the central areas of major cities. Public transportation began with the opening of railways in the early Meiji years, followed by horse-drawn trams in the 1880s, and streetcars started running in Kyōto in the 1890s. From around 1900, major dry goods stores (which primarily sold silk drapery) in large cities began to imitate American department stores, using show windows and display stands to retail to a large customer base.

YAMAGATA-SHIGAIZU〈山形市街図〉(VIEW OF YAMAGATA CITY, BY TAKAHASHI YUICHI)
Mishima Michitsune〈三島通庸〉, who became governor of Yamagata Prefecture in 1876, founded a district where governmental agencies such as prefectural government buildings, schools, and police stations adopting Western architecture were built in order to physically portray Bunmei Kaika.

In this way, lifestyles gradually evolved to become a mixture of Japanese and Western styles. One example was the notion of the sokuhatsu束髪 (Western hairstyles), which replaced the nihongami日本髪 (Japanese hairstyles) for women and became widespread due to their convenience.

In farming and fishing villages, oil lamps spread, and rickshaws and police officers in Western clothing became commonplace. The availability of imported thread and chemical dyes allowed people a wider range of options for kimono着物, and the wealthy could use a mail order system to purchase merchandise from department stores. However, everyday life in rural regions did not undergo major changes. Even the old lunar calendar was used alongside the solar calendar due to its connection to traditional farming and fishing methods.

The Transformation of Tōkyō

In 1890, people living in cities with populations over 100,000 comprised only 6% of the whole Japanese population. By 1908, this number had risen to 11%. When the City of Tōkyō was officially established in 1889, its population was 1.1 million, but by 1908 that number had almost doubled to 2.1 million. Roads and waterworks projects to improve the city's appearance as a capital were carried out under the Tōkyō City-Ward Reform Ordinance 〈東京市区改正条例〉 (issued in 1888), and in 1899, Japan saw its first modern water supply system begin operation with the opening of the Yodobashi Purification Plant〈淀橋浄水場〉.

By 1904, horse-drawn trams had disappeared as streetcar networks, introduced the previous year, expanded. The Kōbu Railway〈甲武鉄道〉 (later to become the JR Chūō Line〈中央線〉) began electric train operations between Iidamachi〈飯田町〉 and Nakano〈中野〉, and began the custom of commuting to work on electric trains.

The Marunouchi〈丸の内〉 District came to be called "Icchō (one block) London〈「一丁ロンドン」〉" as buildings were constructed one after another by Mitsubishi, which had acquired land sold off by the Ministry of the Army. In 1911, the Imperial Theatre 〈帝国劇場〉 was completed, and car rental businesses were launched to take ladies and gentlemen to the theatre. By this time, the spread of electric lights and gas infrastructure had reached half of the households in the city.

Hibiya Park, opened in 1903, was often used as a venue to celebrate victories such as the capture of Port Arthur and the Battle of Tsushima in the Russo-Japanese War, but also became the setting of the Hibiya Incendiary Incident. In 1911, streetcar strikes occurred after the city purchased the company. This exemplified how dissatisfaction among members of the lower strata of society was on the rise.

MARUNOUCHI BUSINESS OFFICE DISTRICT

[i] "Naidaijin" (内大臣) is a term used for two very different positions, the first being a role in the court often translated as "Inner Minister," and the second, after 1885, a position in the Meiji political system usually rendered as "Lord Keeper of the Privy Seal." This textbook uses both of these translations, depending on which of these two positions is being discussed.

[ii] While the Japanese term (藩閥政府) is literally "domain clique government," in English scholarship it is usually referred to as the "Meiji oligarchy." Although less specific than "domain clique government," this rendering (oligarchy meaning a type of government run by a small, exclusive group) does accurately convey the type of political system at work.

[iii] Usually "kokumin" (国民) is translated as "public" or "citizens" in more specific contexts or as "people" or "populace" in broader ones. In this textbook usually "public" is used, except in 1) cases like this one where a sense of shared responsibilities makes "citizen" a better translation, and 2) cases where a more general term is required, whereupon "people" (which has a more inclusive meaning of everyone in an area, etc.) and occasionally "populace" (which is also general but is more suitable when discussing the population and so forth) are used instead.

[iv] Technically, the Japanese term "西南戦争" would be rendered in English as the "Southwest War," but this is vague, and English historiography has instead consistently called this event the "Satsuma Rebellion," which is why this textbook has followed suit.

[v] In English, Japanese political parties are referred to in one of three ways: a Japanese short form (e.g. Jimintō), an English translation (e.g. Liberal Democratic Party), or an English acronym (e.g. LDP). Prewar parties are almost always referred to by Japanese short form (e.g. Seiyūkai), and since party names can be quite long and acronyms may be confusing for Japanese speakers, this textbook primarily uses the Japanese short form for all Japanese political parties. English translations are also provided the first time that a party is mentioned.

[vi] Although elsewhere in the text "農民" is rendered as "farmer," this movement in Korea is overwhelmingly referred to in English with the term "peasant." "Donghak Peasant Revolution" is also quite frequent in English, but "Donghak Peasant Rebellion" is most common and so is used in this textbook.

[vii] The Yihetuan (義和団) became known in English as "Boxers" because they practiced Chinese martial arts, which English-speakers at the time called "Chinese boxing." In China they are also popularly called Yihequan (義和拳), but while "Yihetuan" and "Yihequan" both occasionally appear in English the most common term has always remained "Boxers." The event is not called "incident" because of its great scale, and is instead commonly known as the "Boxer Rebellion."

[viii] Mitsui was usually known in the prewar era as "Mitsui Trading Company" in English, but the company also occasionally used "Mitsui & Co." The latter became the official English name for the company after it was reconstituted in 1959. This textbook uses "Mitsui Trading Company" for the prewar era since it was the most common English name used by the company at that time.

Chapter

10

The Two World Wars and Asia

1 Japan and the First World War

The Taishō Political Crisis

In 1911, amidst a worsening national financial situation, the Second Saionji Kinmochi 西園寺公望 Cabinet was formed. However, the cabinet found itself in a difficult position amidst various demands. The ruling party, the Rikken Seiyūkai 立憲政友会 (Association of Friends of Constitutional Government, hereafter Seiyūkai), demanded an aggressive fiscal policy, while commercial interests called for tax cuts, the navy sought the implementation of its shipbuilding plan[1], and the army wanted expanded divisions[2]. With the passing of Meiji Tennō 明治天皇 in July 1912, Taishō Tennō 大正天皇 (r. 1912-26) ascended to the throne. Around this time, **Minobe Tatsukichi** 美濃部達吉 (1873-1948), a professor at Tōkyō Imperial University 東京帝国大学, published *Kenpō Kōwa* 『憲法講話』 (Lectures on the Constitution), in which he set out the Tennō Organ Theory 天皇機関説 (i.e. that the tennō was an organ of the state) and party cabinet theory, ushering in an era of heightened national interest in politics. Meanwhile, the genrō 元老 Yamagata Aritomo 山県有朋 appointed a Chōshū 長州 clique senior military officer, Katsura Tarō 桂太郎, as both Taishō Tennō's Lord Keeper of the Privy Seal 内大臣 and Grand Chamberlain 侍従長.

The Second Saionji Cabinet did not take a clear stance in response to the Xinhai 辛亥革命 Revolution and the fall of the Qing 清 Dynasty in China. It prioritized the expansion of the navy, but Yamagata disapproved of the cabinet's position and strongly urged the creation of a further two divisions for the army. When Saionji refused this request due to financial difficulties, the army minister, Uehara Yūsaku 上原勇作 (1856-1933), responded by unilaterally submitting his resignation to the tennō, and at the end of 1912 the rest of the cabinet resigned.

---

[1] In the Imperial Defense Policy〈帝国国防方針〉 of 1907, the navy set a long-term objective of having eight battleships and eight armored cruisers in what was referred to as the **Eight-Eight Fleet**〈八・八艦隊〉.

[2] The reasons for the army's demand for an additional two divisions were to 1) place a permanent division in Korea, which had been annexed in 1910; 2) take precautions against the increasing cooperation of Russia and Outer Mongolia〈外蒙古〉, which had declared independence from the Qing Dynasty immediately after the outbreak of the Xinhai Revolution; and 3) secure Japan's various concessions in Inner Mongolia〈内蒙古〉, adjacent to southern Manchuria〈南満州〉.

The genrō appointed Katsura to be the next prime minister, but there was an immediate outcry that were the Lord Keeper of the Privy Seal and Grand Chamberlain to become prime minister this would upset the boundaries between the royal institution and the government. **Ozaki Yukio** 尾崎行雄 of the Seiyūkai and **Inukai Tsuyoshi** 犬養毅 (1855-1932) of the Rikken Kokumintō 立憲国民党 (Constitutional National Party, hereafter Kokumintō) joined forces with influential opposition party members, journalists, members of commerce and industry, and the urban commoners to form what spread into a nationwide movement to "dispel cliques and defend constitutional government" 「閥族打破・憲政擁護」 (the **First Movement to Defend the Constitution** 第一次護憲運動). Katsura attempted to maintain his cabinet by establishing a new party[3] distinct from the Seiyūkai that could break away from conventional genrō politics. However, the Seiyūkai and the Kokumintō submitted a vote of no confidence to the Diet, which was soon surrounded by supporters of the movement, and the cabinet resigned in February 1913 after serving just a little over fifty days in office. This series of events came to be called the **Taishō political crisis** 大正政変.

After Katsura, Admiral Yamamoto Gonbē 山本権兵衛 (1852-1933), from Satsuma 薩摩, organized a cabinet with the Seiyūkai as the ruling party. The Yamamoto Cabinet carried out an administrative reorganization and revised the Civil Service Appointment Ordinance 文官任用令, enabling party members to become high-ranking officials. It also expanded the scope of the Military Ministers to be Active-Duty Officers Law 軍部大臣現役武官制 to make eligible generals/admirals and lieutenant-generals/vice-admirals who were on reserve or retired[4]. These changes sought to increase political party influence on the government and military. However, in 1914 public protests broke out again due to the discovery of the **Siemens Scandal** シーメンス事件, a corruption case involving high-ranking naval officers and the import of foreign-made warships and weapons, forcing the cabinet to resign.

Observing the situation, the genrō, notably Yamagata and Inoue Kaoru 井上馨, quickly moved to appoint Ōkuma Shigenobu 大隈重信, who was popular with the press and the public, as the next prime minister[5]. The Second Ōkuma Cabinet commenced with the Dōshikai as the ruling party. The party only held a minority in the House of Representatives compared to the Seiyūkai, but by involving the youth and adopting popular election tactics it won an overwhelming victory over its rival in the 1915

[3] Together with secessionists from the Kokumintō, the new party, Rikken Dōshikai ⟨立憲同志会⟩ (Association of Allies of the Constitution, hereafter Dōshikai) was reconfigured under Katō Takaaki's ⟨加藤高明⟩ leadership after Katsura's death in late 1913.

[4] The reason for modifying the stipulation that only active officers of the appropriate rank were eligible to become army or navy minister was to attempt to limit military influence on the cabinet. No actual appointments based on this modification were made.

[5] Ōkuma had resigned from politics, but Yamagata and the other genrō hoped that Ōkuma's appointment would quiet the backlash against domain cliques and deliver a blow to the Seiyūkai.

general election. The pending issue of expanding the army by two divisions was then passed by the Diet.

Around the time of the Taishō political crisis, the international environment surrounding Japan was changing dramatically. As can be seen by Japan's annexation of Korea (韓国併合) in 1910 and the recovery of tariff autonomy in 1911, various pending issues dating from the start of the Meiji period (明治時代) had been resolved. Accordingly, the Meiji oligarchy (藩閥) that had once led the nation had disintegrated into political parties, bureaucrats, and military factions.

The First World War

On the European continent at the dawn of the 20th century, conflict escalated between the **Triple Alliance** (三国同盟) – consisting of Germany (which had been expanding its armaments and pursuing an aggressive international policy), Austria-Hungary, and Italy – and the Franco-Russian Alliance (露仏同盟). To prepare for a possible confrontation with Germany, the UK signed the Entente Cordiale[i] (英仏協商) (Anglo-French Agreement) with France in 1904. Meanwhile, Russia, due to its defeat in the Russo-Japanese War (日露戦争), pivoted from East Asia to advancing into the Balkan peninsula, and signed the Anglo-Russian Entente (英露協商) with the UK in 1907. This resulted in the formation of the **Triple Entente** (三国協商) of the UK, France and Russia, representing a shift in the balance of power vis-à-vis the Triple Alliance. Due to the Anglo-Japanese Alliance (日英同盟) and the Russo-Japanese Agreement (日露協約), Japan stood aligned with the Triple Entente.

In a corner of the Balkan peninsula referred to as the "powder keg of Europe," (ヨーロッパの火薬庫) in June 1914 the heir to the throne of Austria-Hungary was assassinated by a pro-Russian Serb (Sarajevo Incident) (サライエヴォ事件). This ignited a war between the two countries that by August had expanded into a war between Germany and Russia. With France and the UK entering the war as allies of Russia, what began as a struggle for hegemony among the imperial powers became a total war[6] that lasted for more than four years: the **First World War**[7][ii] (第一次世界大戦).

---

[6] A form of war that utilizes to the maximum extent the nation's military, political, economic, and human capabilities. On the other hand, a nation was at times pressured to make democratic changes in its political or economic systems in order to gain the cooperation of the public.

[7] Initially, the German side occupied the dominant position in the conflict, but as the country suffered from a British naval blockade it resorted to unrestricted submarine warfare〈無制限潜水艦作戦〉. The US entered the war on the side of the Triple Entente in 1917, shifting the balance in its favor. In the following year, a revolution occurred in Germany resulting in the collapse of the imperial government, and in November an armistice was made with the Allied powers〈連合国〉.

Japan's Advance on China

When the UK declared war on Germany, the Second Ōkuma Cabinet entered the war using the pretext of the Anglo-Japanese Alliance[8], under the leadership of Minister of Foreign Affairs Katō Takaaki (1860-1926). In 1914, Japan captured the German base of Qingdao and German concessions in Shandong, and also occupied part of the German territories north of the equator in the South Sea Islands.

In 1915, Katō oversaw the issuing of the **Twenty-One Demands**[9] to the Yuan Shikai (1859-1916) government, which included handing over the German concessions in Shandong, reinforcement of Japan's south Manchurian and

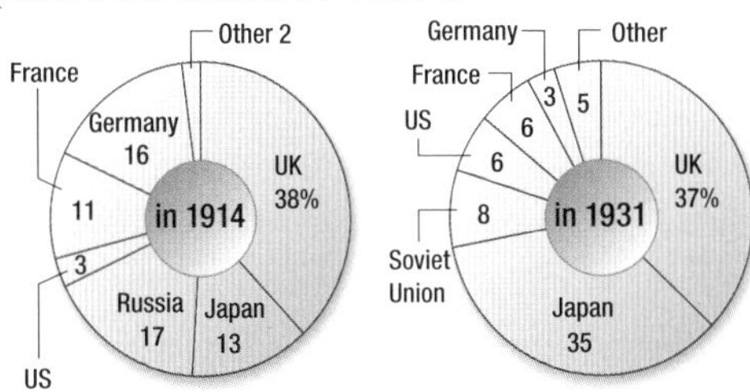

COMPARISON OF INVESTMENTS IN CHINA BY THE GREAT POWERS

THE TWENTY-ONE DEMANDS

Group 1, Article 1. The Chinese Government engages to give full assent to all matters upon which the Japanese Government may hereafter agree with the German Government, relating to the disposition of all rights, interests and concessions, which Germany, by virtue of treaties or otherwise, possesses in relation to the Province of Shantung.

Group 2. The Japanese Government and the Chinese Government, with a view to developing their economic relations in South Manchuria and Eastern Inner Mongolia, agree to the following articles:

Article 1. The two Contracting Powers mutually agree that the term of lease of Port Arthur and Dalny[1] and the terms of the South Manchurian Railway and the Antung-Mukden Railway, shall be extended to 99 years.

Group 5, Article 1. The Chinese Central Government to engage influential Japanese as political, financial, and military advisers.[2]

[1] According to a treaty made with Russia and the Qing Dynasty after the Russo-Japanese War, the Port Arthur and Dalian lease was to expire in 1923.

[2] This demand was withdrawn after strong opposition from China.

---

[8] The British Foreign Ministry and others were reluctant for Japan to enter the war. However, Japan declared war on Germany without an agreement with the UK regarding the scope of Japanese military actions.

[9] Each article in the Twenty-One Demands was a compilation of opinions from officials in the Ministry of Foreign Affairs, army, and navy responsible for dealing with issues in China. Japan dispatched a fleet to China while the army took advantage of a troop turnover in Manchuria to pressure China and issue an ultimatum. The Chinese public strongly opposed this development, and marked May 9, when Yuan Shikai's government accepted the demands, as a day of national humiliation.

east Inner Mongolian interests, and approval of Japanese-Chinese joint management. In May 1915, an ultimatum was issued and a majority of the demands were accepted[10]. Katō's foreign policies received criticism from all directions. Even Yamagata, the genrō who had appointed Ōkuma as prime minister, expressed his disapproval to Hara Takashi 原敬 (1856-1921), president of the Seiyūkai (the opposition party at the time), stating that "It is a capital mistake to include even the most nonsensical, futile articles in detail in a list of demands."

Behind the Ōkuma Cabinet's diplomacy was Ōkuma's notion that truly opening the country (kaikoku shinshu 「開国進取」) necessarily incorporated national expansion, while the cabinet sought to suppress Yuan Shikai's government and gradually came to clearly show support for revolutionary forces in the south. By contrast, the Terauchi Masatake 寺内正毅 Cabinet provided large economic loans (**Nishihara Loans** 西原借款) to the Duan Qirui 段祺瑞 (1865-1936) administration, a northern military clique that had succeeded Yuan Shikai, with the intention of securing Japanese interests through this administration.

The government also undertook preparations for postwar peace negotiations. In 1916, the Second Ōkuma Cabinet concluded the Fourth Russo-Japanese Agreement, reconfirming both countries' special interests in the Far East 極東. During the Terauchi Cabinet that followed, leveraging the UK's request for dispatching Japanese warships to the Mediterranean Sea, a secret agreement was made with the UK, France, and other powers to support Japan's claims at the postwar peace conference to the German territories in Shandong and the South Sea Islands. Meanwhile, the US was wary of Japan's advance on China and sought to ensure stability in the Pacific upon entering the First World War. As a result, an official diplomatic note was signed by Special Ambassador Ishii Kikujirō 石井菊次郎 (1866-1945) and Secretary of State Lansing ランシング (1864-1928) in 1917. Known as the **Lansing-Ishii Agreement** 石井・ランシング協定[11], it stated that both parties pledged to uphold China's territorial integrity and the Open Door Policy, and also recognized Japan's special interests in China due to its geographic proximity.

As the war dragged on, the **Russian Revolution** ロシア革命 erupted in 1917, launched by laborers and soldiers who opposed the imperial government and the continuation of the war. This led to the formation of the world's first socialist state (later known

[10] Although the demands comprising Group 5, which required the Chinese government to appoint Japanese advisors, were deleted, the remaining demands were concluded on May 25, 1915 in the form of two treaties, namely, the Treaty on Shandong Province and the Treaty on Southern Manchuria and Eastern Inner Mongolia. The second treaty enabled Japan to extend the lease on Port Arthur〈旅順〉, Dalian〈大連〉, and the South Manchurian Railway territory, that it had gained from Russia, for 99 years.

[11] The agreement was dissolved after the Washington Naval Conference〈ワシントン会議〉established the Nine-Power Treaty〈九カ国条約〉.

as the Soviet Union (ソヴィエト連邦). The Soviet administration, led by Lenin (レーニン) (1870-1924) and his Bolshevik (ボリシェヴィキ) Party (later the Communist Party) called for all warring nations to abide by the fundamental principles of peace without annexations or indemnities, and the right of self-determination. In the following year, 1918, the Bolshevik government signed a separate peace treaty with Germany and Austria-Hungary (Treaty of Brest-Litovsk (ブレスト＝リトフスク条約)), and withdrew from the war.

Fearing the collapse of the Eastern Front and the birth of a socialist state, the UK, France, and other Allies intervened in the Russian Civil War and urged Japan to dispatch troops as well. After an invitation from the US to participate in a joint allied expeditionary force to rescue the Czechoslovak Legions in Siberia, the Terauchi Cabinet dispatched troops to Siberia and northern Manchuria in August 1918 (**Siberian Intervention** (シベリア出兵)). After the war ended the Allies withdrew from Russia, but Japanese forces remained until 1922[12].

The Wartime Economic Boom

The First World War resolved the recession and financial crisis that had plagued Japan from the end of the Meiji period. Japan exported munitions to the Allies, notably the UK, France and Russia, as well as cotton textiles to Asian markets in the wake of the European powers withdrawing from the region, and raw silk to the US market, which was experiencing a wartime economic boom. The upshot of this was a highly favorable balance of trade for Japan[13].

Due to a global shortage of ships, the shipping and shipbuilding industries experienced an unprecedented boom. Japan became the third largest maritime power, after the UK and the US, and so-called **funanarikin** (船成金) (people made newly rich through the shipping industry) multiplied. In the iron and steel industry, the expansion of the Yahata (八幡製鉄所) Steelworks, the establishment of the Anshan Iron and Steelworks (鞍山製鉄所) (a subsidiary of the Manchurian Railway Company (南満州鉄道株式会社)), and the founding of various private companies occurred in rapid succession. In the areas of chemicals, dyes and fertilizers, there was a sudden rise in the chemical industry due to the lapse in German imports. Meanwhile the electric power industry, which had already begun to expand before the war, saw large-scale hydroelectric power generation get underway, successful long-distance power transmission between Inawashiro (猪苗代) and Tōkyō, the extension of electric lighting to agricultural areas, and the increasing transition of industries from steam power to

---

[12] War expenditure for the dispatch of troops reached one billion yen. The resulting casualties were 3,000 fatalities and over 20,000 injured.

[13] In 1914, Japan was a debtor nation by 1.1 billion yen, but by 1920 it had become a creditor nation to the amount of 2.7 billion yen.

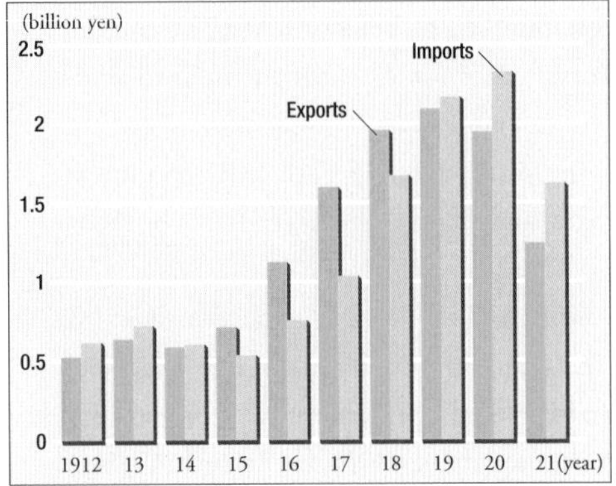

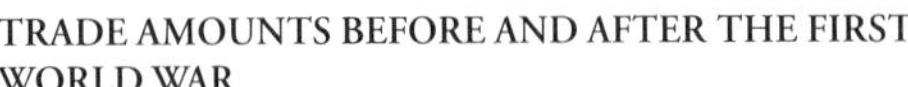
TRADE AMOUNTS BEFORE AND AFTER THE FIRST WORLD WAR

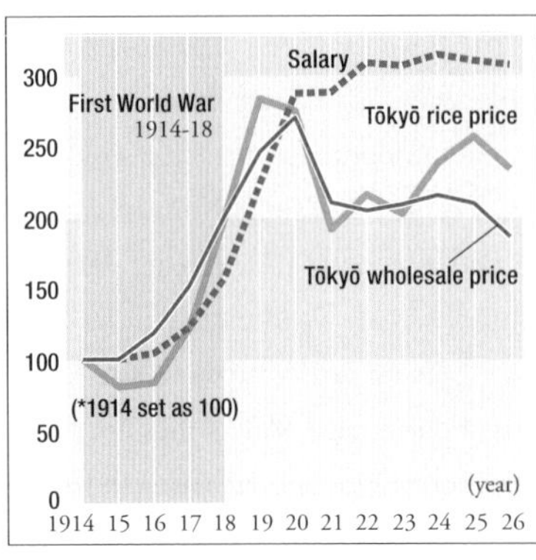

PRICE INDEX AFTER START OF THE FIRST WORLD WAR

electric power, all of which fueled domestic production of electrical machinery.

As a result, the heavy chemical industry came to account for 30% of industrial output. Stimulated by increased exports, the textile industry also became very active, prompting a rapid expansion of Japanese-owned cotton-spinning mills in China (**zaikabō** 在華紡).

Due to the rapid industrial progress, industrial (factory) output came to exceed agricultural output. The number of factory workers before the war had increased by 150% to over 1.5 million by the end. Development of the heavy chemical industry caused the number of male workers to double, nearing female employment figures. Yet even then the number of people employed in industry was less than half of the number employed in agriculture.

The **wartime economic boom** 大戦景気 was unprecedented, but its base was ultimately superficial. While capitalists benefitted and gave rise to many **narikin** 成金 (**newly rich**), many more people suffered from soaring prices. Moreover, in contrast to the dramatic industrial growth, agricultural development remained stagnant.

The Establishment of Party Cabinets

The rise of the popular movement triggered by the Taishō political crisis had a significant effect on political thought. Voices calling for the democratization of politics gradually increased, perhaps best exemplified by **Yoshino Sakuzō** 吉野作造 (1878-1933) advocating government rooted in the people (**minponshugi** 民本主義)[14] in 1916. However, that

[14] While "minponshugi" is a translation of "democracy," it was distinct from democracy proper in the sense of popular sovereignty. It adopted elements of democracy within the framework of the Meiji Constitution〈明治憲法〉, which stipulated the sovereignty of the tennō, and that, together with Minobe Tatsukichi's Tennō Organ Theory, became the philosophy underpin-

same year, the Second Ōkuma Cabinet resigned, and Terauchi Masatake, a military officer who had served as the first governor-general of Korea, formed a cabinet based on the notion of "national unity."「挙国一致」 Various factions of the ruling party from the previous administration, such as the Dōshikai, came together to form the **Kenseikai** 憲政会 (**Constitutional Party**) in opposition to the new cabinet. Prime Minister Terauchi responded by dissolving the House of Representatives in 1917, and calling a general election, which resulted in the Seiyūkai replacing the Kenseikai as the leading party in the House. The cabinet then brought together representatives from various parties, such as Hara Takashi from the Seiyūkai and Inukai Tsuyoshi from the Kokumintō, to form with the ministers the Temporary Foreign Affairs Investigation Committee 臨時外交調査委員会 to unify diplomatic policy.

The rapid economic development caused by the war led to larger numbers of industrial workers and a more concentrated urban population, which in turn increased the consumption of rice. However, under the restraints of the sharecropping system 寄生地主制, agricultural production remained stagnant while rice prices rose, putting urban workers and lower-class farmers in dire straits. In 1918, with rice needed for the Siberian Intervention, speculation led to rice prices soaring. Riots in Toyama 富山県 in July prompted urban-dwellers, poor farmers, and outcastes to demand lower prices and protest rice hoarding. They attacked rice wholesalers, wealthy merchants, landowners, and rice-milling companies, while clashing with police. These **rice riots** 米騒動[iii] spread nationwide to 38 cities, including Tōkyō and Ōsaka, 153 towns, and 177 villages, while involving approximately 700,000 participants. The government dispatched the military to suppress the situation, and the Terauchi Cabinet, held responsible by the public, resigned.

Seeing the power of popular movements and the public's increasing desire for greater political participation, the genrō Yamagata finally approved party cabinets, and so in September 1918 a cabinet was formed headed by **Hara Takashi** 原敬, president of the Seiyūkai. Although he had been born into the family of a chief retainer of Morioka (Nanbu) Domain 盛岡（南部）藩, Hara was neither a noble nor a member of a domain clique. As a prime minister with a seat in the House of Representatives, he

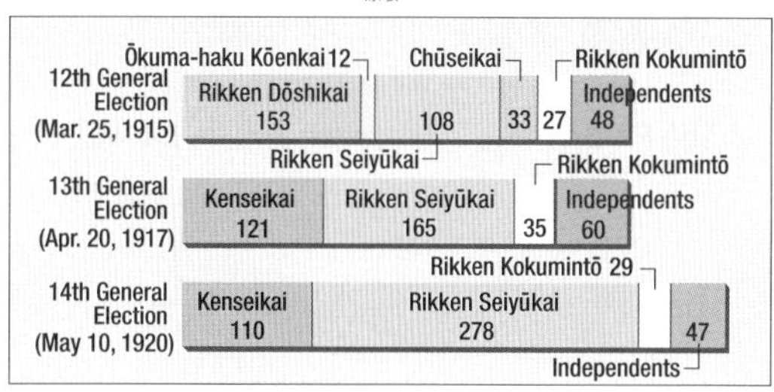

TRENDS IN ELECTION RESULTS

ning "Taishō democracy〈大正デモクラシー〉." Yoshino argued that party cabinets based on universal suffrage should rectify the economic inequality of the lower classes.

was referred to as the "Commoner Prime Minister," 「平民宰相」 and was welcomed by the public. Utilizing the Temporary Foreign Affairs Investigation Committee, Hara initiated foreign policies centered on international cooperation. He was even able to reach a compromise with the US, UK and France pertaining to Japan's Manchurian interests and development policy.

However, the Hara Cabinet took a cautious approach toward instituting social policies and universal suffrage, and went no further than decreasing the tax qualification for the right to vote to three yen or more while introducing a **single-member constituency system** 小選挙区制. A movement calling for universal suffrage gradually intensified, ultimately leading to a mass demonstration of tens of thousands of protesters in 1920. In this social context, opposition parties including the Kenseikai submitted a male universal suffrage bill to the House of Representatives. The government promptly refused it and dissolved the House. The Seiyūkai pledged to fulfill long-awaited, assertive policies such as railroad expansion and an increase in the number of high schools, and with the effect of the single-member constituency system, the party won an overwhelming victory in the general election.

The Seiyūkai may have advocated active policies, but in 1920 a recession after the war caused financial stagnation, and a series of corruption cases involving party members also surfaced. In 1921, Hara was assassinated in Tōkyō Station by a young man indignant about corruption in party politics. Takahashi Korekiyo 高橋是清 (1854-1936) became the party president and formed the succeeding cabinet, but his term was short-lived, and he was followed by Admiral Katō Tomosaburō 加藤友三郎 (1861-1923), who organized his cabinet with the Seiyūkai as the de facto ruling party. The Katō administration was followed by three more non-party cabinets, for approximately two years.

2 The Washington Settlement

The Paris Peace Conference and its Impact

With Germany accepting the terms of peace based on the Fourteen Points 14カ条[15] proposed by US President Wilson ウィルソン (1856-1924), an armistice was signed in November 1918. The following year, a peace conference was held in Paris. As one of the five major Allied Powers, Japan sent Saionji Kinmochi and Makino Nobuaki 牧野伸顕 (1861-1949) as

[15] The Fourteen Points were outlined in a presidential address that Wilson gave to Congress on 18 January, 1918. The main points included the abolishment of secret diplomacy, the complete removal of economic barriers, and the formation of an international peace organization. However, he made no mention of the issue of reparations.

its delegates. The resulting **Treaty of Versailles** ヴェルサイユ条約, signed in June, imposed severe terms on Germany, including substantial reparations, armament limitations, and the ceding of some German territory. At the same time, through the principle of self-determination many independent nations came into being in Eastern Europe, and the **League of Nations** 国際連盟[16] was established as an organization to foster cooperation among nations and find peaceful resolution of international disputes. The new international order based on the Treaty of Versailles came to be referred to as the **Versailles Settlement** ヴェルサイユ体制[iv].

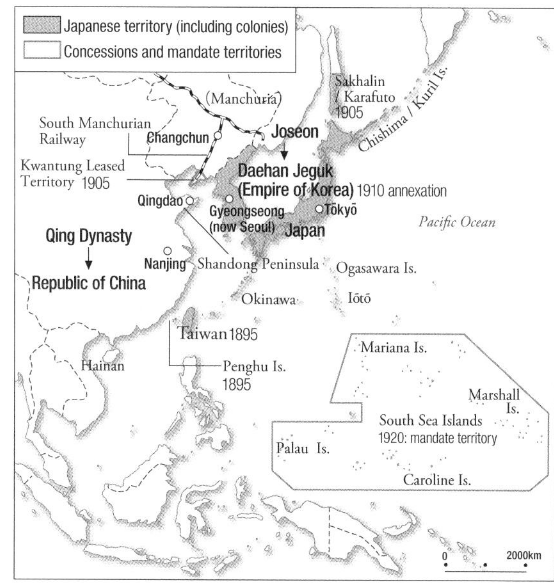

JAPANESE TERRITORY UNDER THE TREATY OF VERSAILLES

As stipulated in the Treaty, Japan gained Germany's concessions in Shandong, and was granted **mandatory rule** 委任統治権 of former German holdings in the South Sea Islands north of the equator[17]. Regarding the Shandong problem, the Republic of China, participating in the conference as one of the Allies, faced opposition, particularly from the US. A request by China to revoke the agreements comprising the Twenty-One Demands and return the former German concessions was also turned down. This prompted the **May Fourth Movement** 五・四運動[18], a nationalist, anti-Japanese movement

[16] The League of Nations was founded in 1920 to establish principles of international law to govern actions among countries, and to promote international cooperation and settle disputes without resorting to war. On the other hand, it also tended to favor maintaining a situation favorable to the victors of the First World War. Japan became a permanent member of the Council of the League, along with the UK, France, and Italy. However, the US, despite initially proposing the concept, was unable to join due to opposition in the Senate.

[17] Another issue raised at the conference by the Japanese delegation was the Racial Equality Proposal. The aim was to address a measure excluding Japanese immigrants in the US, while ensuring that the League of Nations would remain impartial and not just favor the interests of Caucasian peoples. However, the clause was not included in the treaty due to opposition from other nations.

[18] A series of movements that grew out of student protests held in Beijing〈北京〉 on May 4, 1919.

in China involving students, merchants, and laborers, and ultimately led to China's refusal to sign the Treaty.

Just prior to this, against the backdrop of rising international support for self-determination, a Korean independence movement took shape, led by Korean students living in Tōkyō and student/religious groups in Japanese-ruled Korea. With a reading of the Korean Declaration of Independence at Pagoda パゴダ公園 Park (Tapgol タプッコル公園 Park) in Seoul on March 1, 1919, a mass movement for independence spread across Korea (**March First Movement** 三・一独立運動). Although the movement was largely peaceful and nonviolent, the governor-general of Korea mobilized police, military 憲兵 police, and military forces to firmly suppress it. In consideration of international opinion, the Hara Takashi Cabinet undertook revisions to the bureaucratic system, enabling civilian appointees to the positions of governor-general for Korea and Taiwan[19], and also made minor improvements to colonial rule policies, such as abolishing the military police force in Korea.

On the other hand, while Japan participated in the peace conference as one of the victor nations, its diplomats and newspaper reports were shocked by the criticism from China and the US regarding the Shandong problem. It was in this context that Kita Ikki 北一輝 (1883-1937) wrote *Nihon Kaizō Hōan Taikō* 『日本改造法案大綱』 (Fundamental Principles for the Reorganization of Japan) and Ōkawa Shūmei 大川周明 (1886-1957) formed the Yūzonsha 猶存社 (Society of Those Who Remain).

The Washington Naval Conference and Cooperative Diplomacy

German reparations amounted to 132 billion gold marks, but the victorious nations like the UK, France and Italy also struggled to pay their war debts to the US. There was a need for an international economic circulation system in which the US provided aid to Germany to help revive German industry, thereby facilitating smooth reparation payments to the UK, France, and Italy, which could then pay off their debts to the US. Meanwhile, it was also necessary to respond to new situations in East Asia, including Japan's aggressive advance into China during the war, the Soviet administration's moves towards the formation of a federal state, and the increasingly active nationalist movement in China. So in 1921, the US held an international conference, the **Washington Naval Conference** ワシントン会議, to discuss naval disarmament and issues regarding the Pacific and East Asia. America's main objective was to prevent a naval arms race among the US, the UK, and Japan in order to reduce their own financial burden and limit Japanese expansion in East Asia. Japan dispatched Katō Tomosaburō and Shidehara Kijūrō 幣原喜重郎

---

[19] Naval officer Saitō Makoto〈斎藤実〉was appointed governor-general of Korea and Den Kenjirō〈田健治郎〉was made governor-general of Taiwan.

Treaty		Countries Involved	Contents etc.
Treaty of Versailles (Jun. 1919)		27 countries	Established post-WWI order; founding of League of Nations (1920)
Washington Naval Conference	Four-Power Treaty (Dec. 1921)	US, UK, Japan, France	Treaty for peace in Pacific; ended Anglo-Japanese Alliance
	Nine-Power Treaty (Feb. 1922)	US, UK, Japan, France, Italy, Belgium, Portugal, Netherlands, China	Treaty on "China Question" (Chinese sovereignty, Open Door Policy, etc.); related agreement on "Shangdong Question" returned former German territory in Shandong Peninsula to China
	Washington Naval Treaty (Feb. 1922)	US, UK, Japan, France, Italy	Limited number of capital ships countries could own; ten-year moratorium on building capital ships
* Geneva Naval Conference (Jun. 1927)		US, UK, Japan	Sought limits on US, UK & JP auxiliary vessels
Kellogg–Briand Pact (Pact of Paris) (Aug. 1928)		15 countries	Renunciation of war
London Naval Treaty (Apr. 1930)		US, UK, Japan, France, Italy	Limits on owning, and prohibition on building, capital ships extended to 1936; limits on US, UK & JP auxiliary vessel numbers

MAJOR INTERNATIONAL TREATIES AFTER THE FIRST WORLD WAR
In the treaty column, ( ) indicates year and month of signing, * indicates negotiation breakdown.

(1872-1951) as delegates.

At the conference, an agreement was made to maintain the status quo of the Pacific Islands, and the **Four-Power Treaty** (四カ国条約), intended to resolve disputes caused by issues in the Pacific, was concluded among the US, the UK, Japan, and France. The ratification of this treaty in 1921 also involved an agreement to terminate the Anglo-Japanese Alliance.

In 1922, those same four nations, together with China and a further four nations with interests in China, signed the **Nine-Power Treaty** (九カ国条約). This treaty affirmed China's territory and sovereignty, and declared an economic Open Door Policy, with equal opportunity for all nations with interests in China, thereby repealing the Lansing-Ishii Agreement between Japan and the US. That same year, the **Washington Naval Treaty** (ワシントン海軍軍縮条約) was signed by five major powers – the US, the UK, Japan, France, and Italy. The treaty limited the retention of capital ships for each of these nations to a ratio of 5 : 5 : 3 : 1.67 : 1.67, respectively, and further stipulated that replacement warships could not be constructed for ten years, even in the event of deterioration. Within Japan, the navy, and especially the Navy General Staff, insisted on having a fleet that would be 70% of the size of those retained by the UK and the US. However, despite this disapproval, the treaty was signed by the Minister of the Navy, Katō Tomosaburō. During the conference, negotiations were also held between Japan and China, with the UK and the US as intermediaries, resulting in a 1922 agreement by Japan to return the former German concessions on the Shandong peninsula to China.

This series of international agreements, which aimed to prevent future wars and strengthen cooperation among the great powers, resulted in the emergence of a new international order in the Asia-Pacific region known as the **Washington Settlement** (ワシントン体制). The Takahashi Korekiyo Cabinet (Seiyūkai), which took over after the assassination of Hara Takashi, actively accepted the agreements and laid the groundwork for **cooperative diplomacy** (協調外交), which was continued by both the Katō Tomosaburō and Second Yamamoto Gonbē Cabinets. It is likely that this cooperative diplomacy was made possible due to the shift in US policy from Wilson's idealist diplomacy to a more realistic economic diplomacy, as well as the good economic relations between Japan and the US in the 1920s. In 1924, with the formation of Katō Takaaki's Three-Party Pro-Constitution Coalition Cabinet (護憲三派), the Kenseikai returned to power. Up until then the party had been against cooperative diplomacy, which had been developed by foreign ministers from the Seiyūkai, but along with Katō's moderation of policies regarding China, the Kenseikai began to shift towards a coordinated policy called **Shidehara diplomacy** (幣原外交), under Minister of Foreign Affairs Shidehara Kijūrō[20].

While keeping pace with world trends based on justice and peace, Shidehara diplomacy was characterized by an economy-focused diplomatic stance. This approach even advocated a policy of nonintervention regarding China, but it was uncompromising when it came to economic issues, and in the wake of anti-Japanese movements it ultimately failed to stabilize Sino-Japanese relations[21].

Honoring cooperative diplomatic relations resulted in a significant degree of naval disarmament, with the disposal of old ships and the construction of new battleships being cancelled. It also affected the army, with disarmament being carried out by the Katō Tomosaburō Cabinet and the succeeding Katō Takaaki Cabinet, while military

---

[20] Although the withdrawal of troops, except from north Sakhalin, had already been completed in 1922, Minister of Foreign Affairs Shidehara continued to work towards improving relations with the Soviet Union. At the beginning of 1925, diplomatic relations were established with the signing of the Soviet-Japanese Basic Convention〈日ソ基本条約〉. At that time, in exchange for the withdrawal of troops from north Sakhalin, Japan acquired development rights to half of the oil fields in the area.

[21] In 1925, Chinese laborers at a Japanese cotton mill in Shanghai〈上海〉 went on strike, demanding better working conditions. This triggered large-scale anti-imperialist demonstrations by workers and students to spread throughout China (May Thirtieth Movement〈五・三〇事件〉).

equipment was modernized[22].

The Rise of Social Movements

Because the First World War was a total war that mobilized entire nations, in European countries the public increasingly called for more extensive workers' rights and greater political participation. Fueled by the Russian Revolution and the rice riots, social movements also arose in Japan. The rapid industrial development during the war caused a significant increase in the number of laborers, and as the price of commodities rose, labor movements demanding wage increases intensified, and the number of labor disputes 労働争議 multiplied drastically.

In 1912, the **Yūaikai** 友愛会 (Friendly Society) was established by Suzuki 鈴木文治 Bunji (1885-1946) to improve the status of the working class and foster labor unions. It rapidly evolved from a mutual improvement group into a nationwide labor union organization. In 1919 the organization was renamed the Dai Nihon Rōdō Sōdōmei Yūaikai 大日本労働総同盟友愛会 (Greater Japan Friendly Society General Federation of Labor), and the following year it hosted the first May Day 第1回メーデー. In 1921, it was renamed once again to the **Nihon Rōdō Sōdōmei** 日本労働総同盟 **(Japan General Federation of Labor)**, and gradually shifted focus from labor-management cooperation to issues of class struggle. Around this time, there were also frequent **tenant disputes** 小作争議 in farming villages demanding decreases in farm rent. In 1922, Sugiyama Motojirō 杉山元治郎 (1885-1964) and Kagawa Toyohiko 賀川豊彦 (1888-1960) formed the **Nihon Nōmin Kumiai** 日本農民組合 **(Japan Farmers' Union)**, a national organization.

Meanwhile, minponshugi advocate Yoshino Sakuzō organized the **Reimeikai (Dawn Society)** 黎明会 in 1918, and launched a nationwide enlightenment campaign. Declaring that current trends called for peace and cooperation, the Reimeikai had

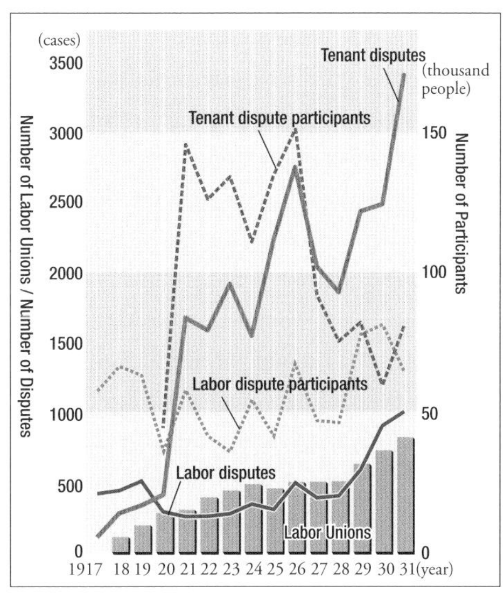

RISE AND FALL OF LABOR AND TENANT DISPUTES

[22] As a result, military spending, which had been close to 50% of national expenditure (general accounts) in 1921, was reduced to less than 30% by 1926.

SEITŌ (BLUESTOCKINGS) **COTERIE**
(FROM *SEITŌ*, FEBRUARY 1912 ISSUE)
New Year's party at Ōmori coast〈大森海岸〉 in Tōkyō on January 21, 1912. Hiratsuka Raichō pictured second from right.

great influence primarily on the intellectual class. Students influenced by Yoshino formed study groups, notably the **Tōdai Shinjinkai** 東大新人会 **(Tōkyō Imperial University New Man Society)**, and gradually deepened ties with labor and agricultural movements.

In such a progressive atmosphere, socialists, who had been enduring their "winter years" 「冬の時代」 since the High Treason Incident 大逆事件, revived their activities as well. In 1920, labor and student activists along with socialists from various factions came together to form the Nihon Shakaishugi Dōmei 日本社会主義同盟 (Japan Socialist League), but it was banned the following year. Academic research on socialism was also restricted, and in 1920 Morito Tatsuo 森戸辰男 (1888-1984), an assistant professor at Tōkyō Imperial University, was suspended for his study on the Russian anarchist Kropotkin クロポトキン (1842-1921). Among the socialist forces, there was opposition between anarchists like Ōsugi Sakae 大杉栄 and communists (Marxist-Leninists) マルクス・レーニン主義 such as Sakai Toshihiko 堺利彦, but the impact of the Russian Revolution resulted in a marked increase in communism affecting the entire social movement. In July 1922, the **Nihon Kyōsantō** 日本共産党 **(Japanese Communist Party, JCP**, hereafter Kyōsantō) was formed, illegally, by Sakai, Yamakawa Hitoshi 山川均 (1880-1958) and others as the Japan branch of the Comintern.

A liberation movement for women, who faced social discrimination, began in 1911 with the founding of the **Seitōsha** 青鞜社 **(Bluestocking Society)** literary group by Hiratsuka Raichō 平塚らいてう（明） (Haru, 1886-1971) and her compatriots. In 1920 the **Shin Fujin Kyōkai** 新婦人協会 **(New Women's Association)** was founded by Hiratsuka and Ichikawa Fusae 市川房枝 (1893-1981), among others. It worked to raise the status of women in society, such as by demanding women's suffrage[23].

Without relying on the government's reconciliation policy, a movement to independently abolish social discrimination against settlements of outcastes (burakumin) was formed at this time under the leadership of Saikō Mankichi 西光万吉 (1895-1970), and

[23] Largely due to the movements prompted by the Shin Fujin Kyōkai (which developed into the Women's Suffrage League〈婦人参政権獲得期成同盟会〉 in 1924), Article 5 of the Security Police Law, which prohibited women from participating in political movements, was amended in 1922, giving women the right to attend political meetings. During this time, activists such as Yamakawa Kikue〈山川菊栄〉 and Itō Noe〈伊藤野枝〉 organized the Sekirankai〈赤瀾会〉 (Red Wave Society) and promoted women's rights from a socialist perspective.

in 1922 the **Zenkoku Suiheisha** 全国水平社 **(National Levelers' Association)** was established.

The Universal Suffrage Movement and the Establishment of the Three-Party Pro-Constitution Coalition

The movement calling for universal male suffrage grew into a mass movement in 1919-20. The government itself had been considering the notion from the time of the Katō Tomosaburō Cabinet, and the Second Yamamoto Gonbē Cabinet, formed in 1923, had decided upon its implementation. However, as a result of the **Great Kantō Earthquake** 関東大震災, and the resignation of the cabinet due to the Toranomon Incident 虎の門事件[24], this did not come to fruition.

In 1924, the genrō Matsukata Masayoshi 松方正義 and Saionji Kinmochi, seeking to select someone distanced from political parties, supported Kiyoura Keigo 清浦奎吾 (1850-1942), chairman of the Privy Council 枢密院, for prime minister. With the exception of the army and navy ministers, all of the cabinet ministers chosen by Kiyoura were from the House of Peers. Seeing this as the emergence of a non-partisan cabinet, the Kenseikai, Seiyūkai, and Kakushin 革新俱楽部 (Reform) Club responded by starting a movement in defense

The Chaos of the Great Kantō Earthquake

On September 1, 1923 at 11:58 a.m., a 7.9-magnitude earthquake with its epicenter in northwest Sagami Bay 〈相模湾〉 struck Japan, causing all the needles of the seismographs at the Central Meteorological Observatory to break off. The earthquake and resulting fires reduced most of Tōkyō and Yokohama 〈横浜〉 to ruins. Moreover, approximately 40,000 people who evacuated to an open space, a former army clothing depot in Tōkyō's Ryōgoku 〈両国〉 area, died from a devastating fire. The number of dead and missing totaled over 100,000. The number of homes completely destroyed, washed away, or burned down reached 570,000, and total damages exceeded 6 billion yen. In the wake of the earthquake, many Korean and Chinese residents were murdered, a unique example in the history of Japan where a natural disaster triggered large-scale killings. Many Koreans were killed due to rumors, behind which likely lurked ethnic discrimination and fears of the resistance to Japanese colonial rule. On the night of 4 September, ten socialists were killed by armed forces guarding the Kameido 〈亀戸〉 police station grounds, and on the 16th, Ōsugi Sakae, Itō Noe, and Ōsugi's nephew were also killed by military police. The use of force and violence by citizens, police and military was on such a scale that such cases cannot be considered exceptional.

---

[24] In 1923, the anarchist youth Nanba Daisuke 〈難波大助〉 fired a shot at Prince Regent Hirohito (later Shōwa Tennō) near the former Toranomon Gate. The Prince Regent was unharmed, but the cabinet took responsibility and resigned. Nanba was executed for high treason the following year.

of constitutional government (**Second Movement to Defend the Constitution** 第二次護憲運動). The Kiyoura Cabinet then gained support from the Seiyūhontō 政友本党 (Orthodox Constitutional Friends Party), which had been organized by critics of the Seiyūkai leader Takahashi Korekiyo. The Diet was dissolved and a general election took place, but Kiyoura suffered a devastating loss to the **Three-Party Pro-Constitution Coalition** 護憲三派.

After the resignation of the Kiyoura Cabinet, Katō Takaaki, president of the Kenseikai (which was now the ruling party), formed a three-party coalition cabinet. Katō thus became the only prime minister appointed through election results under the Meiji Constitution. The Katō Cabinet, which based itself on Minister of Foreign Affairs Shidehara's cooperative diplomacy model, established the **Universal Male Suffrage Law** 普通選挙法 in 1925. As a result, all men over the age of 25 were given the right to vote in elections for the House of Representatives, quadrupling the number of eligible voters[25].

On the other hand, the cabinet also enacted the **Peace Preservation Law** 治安維持法 to punish those organizing or participating in any group seeking to reform the "kokutai" 国体 ("national polity" or "national essence")[26] or rejecting the system of private property. The original intent of this law was to prevent the spread of communist ideology in the wake of the establishment of Japanese-Soviet diplomatic relations (1925), and to prepare for an increase in the political influence of the working class due to the Universal Male Suffrage Law.

Year Promulgated	Cabinet at Time	Year Enacted	Voters			
			National Tax Requirement	Sex & Minimum Age	Total # (in 10K)	Total % of Population
1889	Kuroda Kiyotaka	1890	Over 15 yen	Men, 25	45	1.1
1900	Yamagata Aritomo	1902	Over 10 yen	〃	98	2.2
1919	Hara Takashi	1920	Over 3 yen	〃	306	5.5
1925	Katō Takaaki	1928	No requirement	〃	1240	20.8
1945	Shidehara Kijūrō	1946	〃	Men & Women, 20	3688	50.4

ELECTION LAW REVISIONS
According to the 1889 election laws, a person eligible for election had the same tax payment requirements as a voter, but this was later abolished with the revision in 1900.

Also in 1925, the Seiyūkai appointed Tanaka 田中義一

[25] The thought and social movements of the era from the First Movement to Defend the Constitution until the realization of universal male suffrage are commonly referred to under the term "**Taishō democracy**〈大正デモクラシー〉." Specifically, it can be summarized as comprising calls for expanded civil liberties (speech, press, and assembly) and greater public participation in politics (party politics and universal suffrage).

[26] A form of state structure based upon the distinctive character of national sovereignty. In this case, it refers to the Tennō-sei〈天皇制〉 (Tennō System).

> **PEACE PRESERVATION LAW**
>
> **Peace Preservation Law** (1925)
>
> Article 1. Anyone who organizes a group for the purpose of changing the kokutai or denying the private property system, or anyone who knowingly participates in said group, shall be sentenced to penal servitude or imprisonment not exceeding ten years. ……
>
> **Amended Peace Preservation Law** (1928)
>
> Article 1. Anyone who organizes a group for the purpose of changing the kokutai, or anyone who has served as an officer or other leader of said group, shall be sentenced to death, or indefinite penal servitude, or imprisonment exceeding five years …… Anyone who organizes a group for the purpose of denying the private property system, or anyone who knowingly participates in said group or has committed an act contributing to its objectives, shall be sentenced to penal servitude or imprisonment not exceeding ten years. ……

Giichi (1864-1929), an army officer and leading figure in the army's Chōshū faction, as its president, and with the absorption of the Kakushin Club the Three-Party Pro-Constitution Coalition was dissolved. This resulted in the Kenseikai becoming the Katō Cabinet's sole ruling party. In 1926, Wakatsuki Reijirō 若槻礼次郎 (1866-1949) became the president of the Kenseikai and formed a cabinet after Katō died of illness. At the end of that same year, Taishō Tennō passed away, and Prince Regent Hirohito 裕仁親王 (Shōwa Tennō 昭和天皇, r. 1926-89) ascended to the throne, whereupon the era name was changed to **Shōwa** 昭和.

In 1927, the First Wakatsuki Cabinet resigned after failing to handle a financial crisis 金融恐慌. The Seiyūkai president, Tanaka Giichi, organized the succeeding cabinet, while the Kenseikai, which was now in opposition, merged with the Seiyūhontō to form the **Rikken Minseitō** 立憲民政党 **(Constitutional Democratic Party**, hereafter Minseitō).

In this way, a period of "regular procedures of constitutional government" (**kensei no jōdō**「憲政の常道」)[27] lasted for eight years, beginning with the formation of the First Katō Takaaki Cabinet in 1924, and ending with the collapse of the Inukai Tsuyoshi Cabinet (due to the May 15 Incident 五・一五事件) in 1932. During this time, cabinets alternated between the Seiyūkai and the Kenseikai (later the Minseitō).

---

[27] Conventionally, "kensei no jōdō" may refer to a two-party system, but it is broadly used to refer to a situation where the president of the party with the largest number of seats in the House of Representatives (or the second largest if the majority party is deposed) receives the mandate to organize the cabinet.

3 Popular Culture and the Transformation of Urban Life

Urbanization and Urban Life

As urbanization and industrialization continued to advance after the First World War, **salaried employees** (俸給生活者) (so-called "salarymen" (サラリーマン)), such as office workers, bank employees, and civil servants appeared in great numbers in large cities like Tōkyō and Ōsaka, forming a new middle class. Women employees, such as typists and telephone operators, were called **working women** (職業婦人).

The cityscape and urban life changed drastically while Westernization and modernization marched on. In the metropole, reinforced concrete office buildings like the Marunouchi Building ("Marubiru") (丸の内ビルディング（丸ビル）) appeared, and **bunka jūtaku** (文化住宅) ("cultured residences," meaning houses incorporating some European elements) for the new middle class were built along railway lines extending from the city center to the suburbs. The Dōjunkai (同潤会) Corporation, established in 1924 one year after the Great Kantō Earthquake, built wooden houses and 4-to-5 story apartment buildings in Tōkyō and Yokohama. **Electric lights** (電灯) became widespread in ordinary homes, including those in farming village communities, while in the cities water and gas supply businesses were fully underway. Streetcars, buses, and one-yen taxis provided new means of city transportation, while **subways** (地下鉄) also began operation in Tōkyō and Ōsaka. The number of men wearing Western-style clothing increased. Moga (モガ) (modern girls) with bobbed hair and skirts, and mobo (モボ) (modern boys) outfitted with derby hats and canes, were seen strolling through busy neighborhoods like Ginza (銀座) and Shinsaibashi (心斎橋). In terms of

WOMEN USING JAPANESE TYPEWRITERS
Invented by Sugimoto Kyōta (杉本京太) in 1914, the typewriter became publicly available in 1916, whereupon it spread rapidly and prompted an urgent need to train typists. This image shows the Yokohama Women Typists' Association taking applications from companies looking for typists.

MOGA STROLLING
Moga in American Hollywood fashion take a stroll down Ginza Avenue.

HANSHIN EXPRESS ELECTRIC RAILWAY COMPANY HEADQUARTERS (UMEDA)
In 1920, the first floor of this building was leased to Shirokiya 〈白木屋〉 which sold daily necessities, making it the first terminal department store in Japan. In 1925, the company headquarters were moved, and the lease with Shirokiya was terminated in order to undertake direct management of the Hankyū Market on the second and third floors.

eating habits, "Western foods" such as pork cutlets and curry rice became popular.

Department stores that displayed and sold various products also appeared. In Japan most department stores originated as dry goods stores like Mitsukoshi 三越, but with the emergence of **terminal department stores** ターミナルデパート operated by private railways, emphasis shifted to selling daily necessities like fresh food. A prime example was the Minō-Arima 箕面有馬電気軌道 Electric Railway, established in 1907 (and renamed the Hanshin Express Electric 阪神急行電鉄 Railway in 1918). Based on an idea by Kobayashi Ichizō 小林一三 (1873-1957), residential development was promoted along the railway line in order to increase the number of passengers, while at the same time, the company ran recreational facilities like amusement parks, hot springs, and the all-female Takarazuka theater troupe 宝塚少女歌劇団, along with opening a department store at the Umeda 梅田 terminal.

Meanwhile, the increasing gap between large enterprises and small- or medium-size businesses, and between urban and rural areas, became a problem referred to as a dual structure. Although private consumer spending increased and a mass consumption society emerged, the standard of living among ordinary farmers and the laborers in small- and medium-sized businesses remained low, and the disparity between these demographics and the employees of large businesses expanded.

The Birth of Modern Popular Culture

By 1907, after the Russo-Japanese War, the enrollment rate for elementary schools exceeded 97%, and most people were able to read. By the 1920s, the number of students in middle schools (old system) increased rapidly, and institutions of higher education were also expanded[28]. Against this backdrop, mass media in the form of newspapers, magazines, radio and films developed rapidly, giving rise to modern

---

[28] The number of students in middle school was approximately 170,000 in 1920, and by 1930 this had doubled to about 340,000. The number of higher schools increased with the Higher School Order 〈高等学校令〉 enacted by the Hara Takashi Cabinet in 1918. That same year, the **University Order** 〈大学令〉 was also enacted, enabling (in addition to the imperial universities, which were comprehensive universities) the establishment of colleges and public and private universities. The number of university students increased from about 9,000 in 1918 to about 70,000 in 1930.

COVER ART FOR THE INAUGURAL ISSUE OF *KING*
Launched by Dai Nippon Yūbenkai (Greater Japan Oratorical Society) Kōdansha〈大日本雄弁会講談社〉in 1925, with a mission to become "Japan's most interesting and beneficial" magazine.

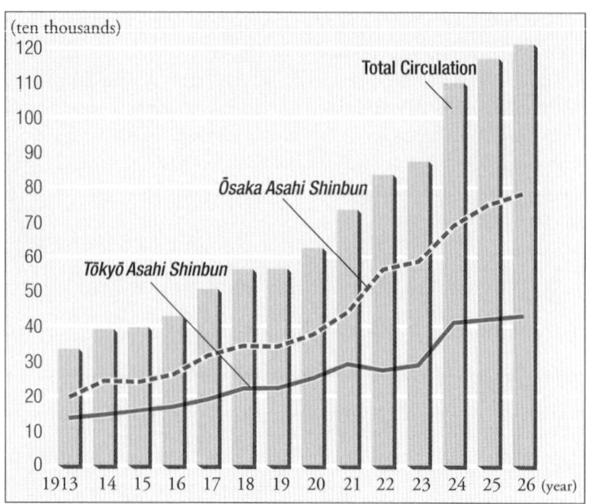

ŌSAKA ASAHI SHINBUN AND *TŌKYŌ ASAHI SHINBUN* NEWSPAPER CIRCULATION

popular culture 大衆文化 among the general public comprised of laborers and salaried workers.

Newspaper and magazine circulation increased dramatically. By the end of the Taishō period, there were newspapers with print runs of over one million copies, such as the *Ōsaka Asahi Shinbun* 『大阪朝日新聞』, *Tōkyō Asahi Shinbun* 『東京朝日新聞』, *Ōsaka Mainichi Shinbun* 『大阪毎日新聞』, and *Tōkyō Nichi Nichi Shinbun* 『東京日日新聞』. General interest magazines such as *Chūō Kōron* 『中央公論』 and *Kaizō* 『改造』 also experienced rapid growth. Weekly magazines like *Sunday Mainichi* 『サンデー毎日』 and *Shūkan Asahi* 『週刊朝日』, women's magazines like *Shufu no Tomo* 『主婦之友』, and even economic magazines for general investors like *Keizai Zasshi Diamond* 『経済雑誌ダイヤモンド』 were also published. It was also around this time that Suzuki Miekichi 鈴木三重吉 (1882-1936) launched the children's literary magazine *Akai Tori* 『赤い鳥』 (Red Bird). In the Shōwa era, **one-yen books** 円本 such as the *Gendai Nihon Bungaku Zenshū* 『現代日本文学全集』 (Complete Works of Contemporary Japanese Literature) and the Iwanami Bunko 岩波文庫 series emerged as pioneers of low-cost, mass-produced publications. The circulation of the popular entertainment magazine *King* 『キング』 also exceeded one million copies.

There were also advancements in radio and movies. **Radio broadcasting** ラジオ放送 began in Tōkyō, Ōsaka, and Nagoya 名古屋 in 1925, and in the following year the broadcast stations were unified to form the Japan Broadcasting Corporation (NHK: Nihon Hōsō Kyōkai 日本放送協会). Radio dramas and live sports commentaries[29] gained popularity, and the

[29] The National Middle School Championship Baseball Tournament〈全国中等学校優勝野球大会〉, which began in 1915, and the Tōkyō Big6 Baseball League〈東京六大学野球〉, which started in 1925, were particularly popular.

broadcasting network expanded nationwide[30]. Films were called "moving pictures," and initially silent films were shown accompanied by performers who provided live narration. During the Taishō period, however, movies developed as popular entertainment and movie companies such as Nikkatsu 日活 and Shōchiku 松竹 started producing films domestically. In the 1930s, the production and screening of sound films called "talkies" トーキー began.

Academia and Art

Numerous developments in science and art occurred during the age of Taishō democracy. Various schools of thought and literature were introduced from Western countries, and while liberal radicalism was emphasized in such venues as the *Tōyō Keizai Shinpō* 『東洋経済新報』 magazine[31], **Marxism** マルクス主義 exerted great influence on the intellectual community. In particular, Kawakami Hajime 河上肇 (1879-1946)'s *Binbō Monogatari* 『貧乏物語』 (A Tale of Poverty), published in 1917, gained a wide readership. Marxism also influenced academic research methods, and in the early Shōwa period debates occurred over how to grasp the nature of Japanese society since the Meiji Restoration[32].

Also at this time, Nishida Kitarō 西田幾多郎 (1870-1945) authored *Zen no Kenkyū* 『善の研究』 (An Inquiry into the Good) and founded his own school of philosophy, and Watsuji Tetsurō 和辻哲郎 (1889-1960), who studied Buddhist art and the history of Japanese thought, wrote *Koji Junrei* 『古寺巡礼』

COVER ART FOR *TAIYŌ NO NAI MACHI* AND THE INAUGURAL ISSUE OF *SHIRAKABA*

Taiyō no nai Machi was a novel based on Tokunaga Sunao's own experience of a labor dispute with the Kyōdō Printing Company in 1926. *Shirakaba* was first published in April 1910, and promoted an anti-naturalist perspective.

[30] In the first year of operation there were 360,000 subscribers, but after the Manchurian Incident〈満州事変〉 people fearing for the safety of soldiers at the front began to listen to regular radio news broadcasts, increasing the number of subscribers to over one million.

[31] Ishibashi Tanzan〈石橋湛山〉, a journalist for *Tōyō Keizai Shinpō*, called for the abandonment of Japanese colonies like Korea and Manchuria, and advocated peaceful economic development, an approach referred to as the "Small Japan Policy〈「小日本主義」〉."

[32] This dispute, referred to as the "debate on Japanese capitalism〈日本資本主義論争〉," had a significant effect on subsequent social science methodology in Japan. On one side was the Rōnōha〈労農派〉 (Labor-Farmer Faction), led by Kushida Tamizō〈櫛田民蔵〉 and Inomata Tsunao〈猪俣津南雄〉, who wrote treatises for the journal *Rōnō*〈「労農」〉; on the other was the Kōzaha〈講座派〉 (Lecture Faction), with Hani Gorō〈羽仁五郎〉, Hattori Shisō〈服部之総〉, and Yamada Moritarō〈山田盛太郎〉, who contributed treatises to *Nihon Shihonshugi Hattatsu-shi Kōza*〈「日本資本主義発達史講座」〉 (Lectures on the History of the Development of Japanese Capitalism) edited by Noro Eitarō〈野呂栄太郎〉.

(Pilgrimages to the Ancient Temples in Nara) and *Fūdo* 『風土』 (Climate and Culture). Meanwhile, Tsuda Sōkichi 津田左右吉 (1873-1961) conducted scientific analysis of *Kojiki* 『古事記』 and *Nihonshoki* 『日本書紀』, and Yanagita Kunio 柳田国男 (1875-1962)'s studies of folklore brought to light the life history of the unknown "common people" (jōmin 「常民」) and established the field of Japanese folklore studies (minzokugaku 民俗学).

In the field of natural science, with imports of dyes and medicines cut off during the First World War, independent research began, and the Institute of Physical and Chemical Research 理化学研究所 (RIKEN) was established in 1917[33]. Moreover, landmark achievements included Noguchi Hideyo 野口英世 (1876-1928)'s research on yellow fever and Honda Kōtarō 本多光太郎 (1870-1954)'s invention of KS steel.

In literature, naturalism was in decline, but with the emergence of many authors such as Mori Ōgai 森鷗外 and Natsume Sōseki 夏目漱石 from the latter half of the Meiji period, the literary world flourished. The **Shirakaba Group** 白樺派 was organized around the literary magazine *Shirakaba* 『白樺』 (White Birch, 1910-23), which advocated humanism and idealism, and consisted of writers like Arishima Takeo 有島武郎 (1878-1923), Shiga Naoya 志賀直哉 (1883-1971), and Mushanokōji Saneatsu 武者小路実篤 (1885-1976), who shared metropolitan and European cultural sensibilities. Also active at this time were Nagai Kafū 永井荷風 (1879-1959) and Tanizaki Jun'ichirō 谷崎潤一郎 (1886-1965), who were known for their aesthetic writing style, and the **Shinshichō Group** 新思潮派, in which Akutagawa Ryūnosuke 芥川龍之介 (1892-1927) and Kikuchi Kan 菊池寛 (1888-1948) played active roles. There was also popular literature that was serialized in newspapers and popular magazines, starting with Nakazato Kaizan 中里介山 (1885-1944)'s long novel *Daibosatsu Tōge* 『大菩薩峠』 (Great Bodhisattva Pass), the historical novels of Yoshikawa Eiji 吉川英治 (1892-1962) and Osaragi Jirō 大佛次郎 (1897-1973), and the detective novels of Edogawa Ranpo 江戸川乱歩 (1894-1965).

With the rise of the socialist and labor movements from the end of the Taishō period to the beginning of the Shōwa period, a **proletarian literary movement** プロレタリア文学運動 also emerged, and magazines such as *Tane Maku Hito* 『種蒔く人』 (The Sower, first published in 1921) and *Senki* 『戦旗』 (Battle Flag, first published in 1928) were launched. These magazines published works that were based on the lives of laborers (proletariats) and followed the theory of class struggle, such as Kobayashi Takiji 小林多喜二 (1903-33)'s *Kani Kōsen* 『蟹工船』 (The Crab Cannery Ship) and Tokunaga Sunao 徳永直 (1899-1958)'s *Taiyō no nai Machi* 『太陽のない街』 (The Street without Sunlight).

In the theater world, Osanai Kaoru 小山内薫 and Hijikata Yoshi 土方与志 (1898-1959) formed

[33] RIKEN was established through financial support from the business world, government subsidies, and donations from the royal household, for the purpose of conducting research in physics and chemistry that could compete with that of Western countries. It later grew to become the RIKEN Konzern.

the Tsukiji Shōgekijō (築地小劇場) (Tsukiji Little Theater) in 1924, which became the center of the **Shingeki movement** (新劇運動) and received a great amount of attention from the intellectual community. The spread of Western music was remarkable, and along with elementary school songs newly-created nursery rhymes came to be frequently sung. Yamada Kōsaku (山田耕筰) (1886-1965) was active in composing and performing professional symphony music.

TENSHŌ 〈転生〉 (REINCARNATION, BY HIRAGUSHI DENCHŪ; HEIGHT 150 CM)

KINYŌ 〈金蓉〉 (CHIN-JUNG, BY YASUI SŌTARŌ)

As for the art world, the Nikakai (二科会) (Second Division Association) and Shun'yōkai (春陽会) (Spring Light Society) artist groups were formed by Western-style artists in opposition to the academism of the Bunten (文展) exhibitions[34]. Artists such as Yasui Sōtarō (安井曽太郎) (1888-1955), Umehara Ryūzaburō (梅原龍三郎) (1888-1986), and Kishida Ryūsei (岸田劉生) (1891-1929) were active at this time. In Japanese painting, Yokoyama Taikan (横山大観) (1868-1958) and others revived the **Japan Art Institute** (日本美術院) and through frequent exhibitions (called Inten (院展)) pioneered a new style of modern painting. In the field of architecture, Tōkyō Station, the most notable work designed by Tatsuno Kingo (辰野金吾) (1854-1919), opened in 1914.

4 An Age of Crisis

From Postwar Depression to Financial Crisis

After the First World War, as European nations underwent recovery more European products reappeared in Asian markets. In contrast to the economic boom experienced

[34] The first Bunten was organized by Makino Nobuaki (minister of education in the First Saionji Cabinet, and the son of Ōkubo Toshimichi 〈大久保利通〉), who, in consideration of opinions from figures in the Ministry of Education and the Tōkyō School of Fine Arts 〈東京美術学校〉, planned an exhibition divided into three categories: Japanese painting, Western painting, and sculpture. Bunten was held many more times, and was renamed the Imperial Academy of Fine Arts Exhibition (Teiten) 〈帝国美術院美術展覧会（帝展）〉 in 1919.

DEPOSITORS RUSHING A BANK
Police maintain order as crowds wait in line to withdraw deposits from the Nakano Bank in Tōkyō in 1927.

during the war, the Japanese economy faced a difficult situation. From 1919, a shift in foreign trade resulted in an import surplus. In the heavy and chemical industries in particular, increased imports put pressure on domestic production. Triggered by a stock market crash in 1920, Japan experienced a **postwar depression** 戦後恐慌 before Europe and the US did. The market price for cotton yarn and raw silk dropped to less than half of its previous value. On top of that, in 1923 the Japanese economy suffered a serious blow due to the Great Kantō Earthquake. Banks became unable to settle accounts, and despite the Bank of Japan providing temporary relief through special loans, progress in clearing bills was hindered by the chronic recession[35].

In 1927, as the Diet deliberated measures for handling the earthquake costs, a verbal gaffe by Minister of Finance Kataoka Naoharu 片岡直温 (1859-1934) revealed the critical situation of several banks. This triggered a wave of bank runs and resulted in a succession of bank closures, in what is known as the **Shōwa Financial Crisis** 金融恐慌. The Wakatsuki Reijirō Cabinet attempted to issue an emergency decree in order to rescue the Bank of Taiwan, which had incurred a great amount of bad debts with the collapse of Suzuki Shōten 鈴木商店[36], but this was rejected by the Privy Council and the cabinet resigned en masse. The newly-established Tanaka Giichi Cabinet (Seiyūkai) declared a three-week **moratorium** モラトリアム (payment postponement 支払猶予令) and obtained a substantial amount of relief loans from the Bank of Japan, finally containing the financial panic that had

---

[35] The government had the Bank of Japan provide a special loan of ¥430.82 million for dishonored bills (earthquake bills〈震災手形〉). As of the end of 1926, ¥206.8 million worth was still left unsettled.

[36] Suzuki Shōten was a general trading company that began as an importer/exporter. During the war, with the support of loans from the Bank of Taiwan, it rapidly expanded into a wide range of businesses and came to rival Mitsui〈三井〉 and Mitsubishi〈三菱〉. However, the company faced bankruptcy during the postwar recession.

by then spread nationwide.

Although there was growth in the heavy and chemical industries related to electrical power generation, such as the electrical machinery and electro-chemical industries, the Japanese economy as a whole in the 1920s was in a chronic recession. The government responded to the recurring panics in the form of bailouts, issuing additional Bank of Japan notes each time. However, this only fended off financial collapse temporarily, and little progress was made on restructuring the economy which had overexpanded during the war. In an environment in which industries were not internationally competitive, resulting in an import surplus, and the **gold embargo** 金輸出禁止 introduced in 1917 remained in place, foreign exchange rates were constantly unstable. In many industrial fields, moves were made to intensify the concentration of businesses, cartel formation, and the export of capital[37]. During this time the zaibatsu expanded their control of industries, largely through the financing and distribution sectors, while also strengthening ties with political parties[38].

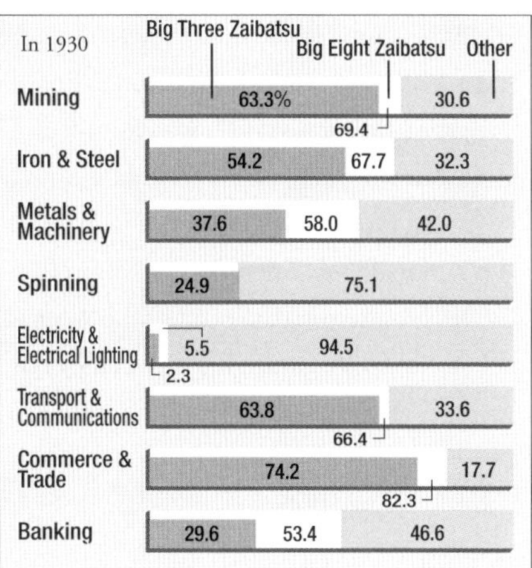

CONCENTRATION OF PAID-IN CAPITAL BY ZAIBATSU, CLASSIFIED BY INDUSTRY

Figures as of end of 1930. The "Big Three" zaibatsu 〈財閥〉 were Mitsui, Mitsubishi, and Sumitomo, while the "Big Eight" also included Yasuda, Asano 〈浅野〉, Ōkura 〈大倉〉, Furukawa 〈古河〉 and Kawasaki 〈川崎〉.

As a result, monopoly capital and financial capital came to occupy a dominant position within the Japanese economy. On the other hand, the number of small- and medium-sized corporations increased due to the surplus labor ousted from large enterprises and agricultural areas.

The Rise of Socialist Movements and a Shift to Aggressive Foreign Diplomacy

After the enactment of the Universal Male Suffrage Law, socialist forces based on labor

---

[37] After the First World War, large Japanese spinning companies built a succession of spinning mills (zaikabō) in China.

[38] As the financial crisis progressed, many small and medium-sized banks were liquidized and/or consolidated, and accounts became concentrated in large banks. Five major banks – Mitsui, Mitsubishi, Sumitomo 〈住友〉, Yasuda 〈安田〉, and Daiichi 〈第一〉 – dominated the industry. Ties between Mitsubishi and the Minseitō, and between Mitsui and the Seiyūkai, were publicly known and played a role in escalating anti-party sentiment.

unions and farmers' unions attempted to reform the social system through the Diet. In 1926, the **Rōdō Nōmintō** 労働農民党 **(Labor-Farmer Party**, or Rōnōtō 労農党), a legal proletarian party (musan seitō 無産政党)[39], was founded. However, intensifying communist influence within the party caused two factions to break away, forming the Shakai Minshūtō 社会民衆党 (Social Democratic Party, or Shamintō 社民党), which favored parliamentarism and pursued a national party line, and the Nihon Rōnōtō 日本労農党 (Japan Labor-Farmer Party), which occupied an intermediate position between the Rōdō Nōmintō and the Shakai Minshūtō.

In 1928, in the first general election held after the enactment of universal suffrage, eight members from the proletarian parties were elected. During the election, the Kyōsantō, which had until now been conducting illegal activities clandestinely, began to operate openly. This alarmed the Tanaka Giichi Cabinet, which, immediately following the election, ordered a mass arrest of the party's members and dissolved affiliated organizations such as the Council 日本労働組合評議会 of Japanese Labor Unions, in what became known as the **March 15 Incident** 三・一五事件. That same year, the Peace Preservation Law was revised to raise the maximum penalty to capital punishment or life imprisonment[40], and

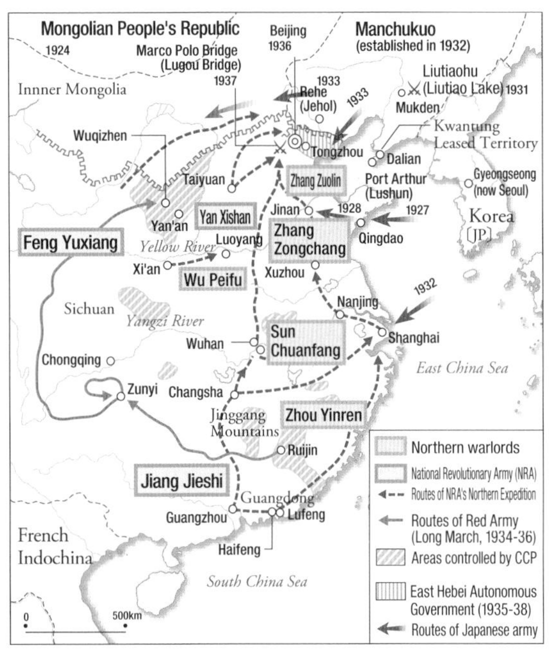

NORTHERN EXPEDITION

---

[39] This term was chosen because the circumstances of the time made it difficult to refer to the party with the term "socialism〈社会主義〉." The Nōmin Rōdōtō〈農民労働党〉 (Farmer-Labor Party), which was established in 1925 as a national proletarian party, was promptly banned on the day of its founding for being affiliated with the Kyōsantō. This led to the formation of the Rōdō Nōmintō, which excluded the Kyōsantō.

[40] Since the Diet refused to approve the revisions to the law, it was revised by emergency imperial decree instead. In contrast to the previous maximum punishments of imprisonment or penal servitude of up to ten years, it now became possible to impose the death penalty or life imprisonment upon organizers or leaders of associations aspiring to alter the "kokutai." Collaborators also came to be subject to punishment.

Special Higher Police (Tokkō) 特別高等課（特高） detachments were established in the prefectural police forces. In 1929, another mass arrest was carried out (**April 16 Incident** 四・一六事件), striking a devastating blow to the Kyōsantō.

During the Tanaka Giichi Cabinet, Japanese diplomacy adopted a more assertive stance in its policy towards China[41]. Seeking to unify the nation, China's National Revolutionary Army advanced north from Guangdong 広東 to the Yangzi 長江 River basin, gaining control over each region as they progressed northward (**Northern Expedition** 北伐)[42].

In response, the Tanaka Cabinet convened the Far East Conference 東方会議 in 1927, gathering diplomats and military officers connected to China. The meeting solidified a policy of acting to assertively protect Japanese interests in Manchuria. In 1927-1928, the Tanaka Cabinet supported the Manchurian warlord Zhang Zuolin 張作霖 (1875-1928), and dispatched **troops to Shandong** 山東出兵 on three separate occasions to counter the National Revolutionary Army, under the pretext of protecting Japanese residents. During the second of these dispatches, a conflict broke out between the National Revolutionary Army and the Japanese forces, the latter of which at one point occupied the Jinan 済南 stronghold (**Jinan Incident** 済南事件).

However, after Zhang Zuolin's forces were defeated by the National Revolutionary Army, a plot was conceived within a faction of the **Kwantung Army** 関東軍[43] to eliminate the warlord and take direct control of Manchuria. In June 1928, the Kwantung Army assassinated Zhang, who was on his way back to Manchuria, by blowing up

---

[41] In an effort to maintain cooperative diplomatic relations with Western nations, the Tanaka Cabinet signed the anti-war Kellogg-Briand Pact〈不戦条約（ケロッグ - ブリアン条約）〉in Paris in 1928. This treaty declared that contracting countries, "in the names of their respective peoples," condemned the use of war as a means of settling international disputes, and moreover renounced war as an instrument of national policy, although upon ratification the following year the Japanese government declared that this part would not apply to Japan because it would infringe upon the sovereignty of the tennō under the Constitution.

[42] The Chinese Nationalist Party〈中国国民党〉(Guomindang)[v], formed by Sun Yat-sen〈孫文〉in 1921, was based in Guangdong Province and extended its control to southern China. The party formed an alliance with the Chinese Communist Party〈中国共産党〉(CCP, founded in 1921), establishing the First United Front〈第 1 次国共合作〉in 1924. Jiang Jieshi〈蔣介石〉(Chiang Kai-shek), who succeeded Sun after the latter's death in 1925, led the National Revolutionary Army and embarked on the Northern Expedition in 1926 in order to defeat the Beiyang Clique and unify China. Jiang advanced northward after having established the Nationalist Government〈国民政府〉in Nanjing〈南京〉.

[43] When the Office of the Kwantung Governor-General〈関東都督府〉was reorganized as the Kwantung Bureau〈関東庁〉in 1919, the army division, renamed the Kwantung Army, became independent. Its mission was to defend the Kwantung Leased Territory on the Liandong peninsula〈遼東半島〉and the South Manchurian Railway, but it also came to take the initiative in advancing into the continent.

HUANGGUTUN INCIDENT
This photo shows the intensity of the explosion that blew up Zhang Zuolin's private coach (June 5, 1928).

his train in a Fengtian 奉天 (Mukden)[vi] suburb (**Huanggutun Incident** 張作霖爆殺事件). At the time, the facts of the incident were not known to the Japanese public, and it was referred to as "**a certain serious incident in Manchuria** 満州某重大事件." Heeding the advice of the genrō 元老 Saionji Kinmochi, initially Prime Minister Tanaka resolved to publicize the facts regarding the event and severely punish those responsible, and reported so to Shōwa Tennō. However, with opposition from cabinet ministers and the army, in the end only the mastermind of the plot, Colonel Kōmoto Daisaku 河本大作 (1883-1955), was suspended from duty. Tanaka's change in policy displeased the tennō, and the cabinet resigned en masse in 1929.

As a result of the Huanggutun Incident, contrary to what the Kwantung Army had planned, Zhang Zuolin's son and successor, Zhang Xueliang 張学良 (1901-2001), aligned himself with the Nationalist Government after assuming control of Manchuria in 1928[44]. Thus, the Nationalists' Northern Expedition came to a close, with China essentially reunified. Nationalist movements in China demanding the abolition of the unequal treaties and the restoration of national rights intensified, and in 1931, the Nationalist Government also adopted a diplomatic policy seeking to have the treaties declared invalid.

The Lifting of the Gold Embargo, and the Great Depression

In the financial world there was an increasing demand to **repeal the gold embargo** 金輸出解禁（金解禁）[45] – returning to the gold standard like the Western nations had done shortly after the First World War – in order to stabilize exchange rates and promote trade. The **Hamaguchi Osachi** 浜口雄幸 (1870-1931) Cabinet (Minseitō), established in 1929, appointed Inoue Junnosuke 井上準之助 (1869-1932), a former governor of the Bank of Japan, as finance minister. The government undertook fiscal austerity measures to reduce prices, and

---

[44] Zhang Xueliang aligned himself with the Nationalist Government, and raised their flag (incorporating a white sun against a blue sky), throughout Manchuria (Northeast Flag Replacement〈易幟事件〉).

[45] The lifting of the gold embargo meant permitting the export of specie (metallic currency such as gold coins and bullion) to pay for imported goods. Freeing the export of gold would also serve to stabilize the exchange rates. Ending the gold embargo also meant resuming gold conversion and returning to the gold standard.

promoted industrial rationalization in order to strengthen international competitiveness. Then, in January 1930, the gold embargo was lifted in an effort to stabilize foreign exchange rates and drastically reorganize the economy[46].

Around the same time that the gold embargo was lifted, the stock market crash that had begun on Wall Street in New York in October 1929 developed into the worldwide **Great Depression** 世界恐慌. This dealt an additional blow to the Japanese economy, which was already struggling with a recession caused by the end of the gold embargo, precipitating a serious crisis in the form of the **Shōwa Depression** 昭和恐慌. Exports decreased sharply, an enormous outflow of specie occurred, many businesses reduced operations or declared bankruptcy, and both wages and workforces were reduced due to industrial rationalization, thereby increasing unemployment. In 1931, the government enacted the **Important Industries Control Law** 重要産業統制法 which permitted the formation of depression cartels in certain industries, a precursor to a more controlled economy.

Rice prices had been sluggish since the 1920s due to an influx of rice from the colonies[47], but with the onset of the Shōwa Depression the cost of rice and other agricultural products plummeted. The price of silkworm cocoons fell significantly due to the decrease in raw silk exports to the US, where use had shrunk due to the Depression. An abundant harvest in 1930 caused the price of rice to fall even more, resulting in "impoverishment despite a bumper harvest." 「豊作貧乏」 By contrast, in the following year the Tōhoku region 東北地方 and Hokkaidō 北海道 both suffered from extremely poor harvests. Due to the depression, opportunities for side jobs decreased and the unemployed from the cities returned to the farms. There was an **agricultural crisis** 農業恐慌 – farmers suffered signif-

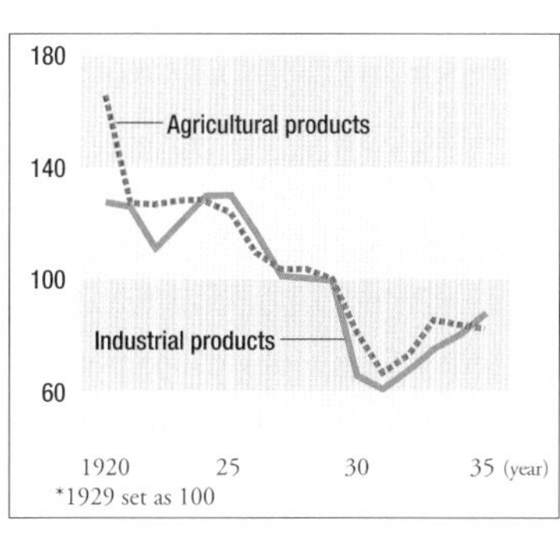

FALL IN PRICES OF INDUSTRIAL AND AGRICULTURAL PRODUCTS

[46] Although the actual JPY-USD exchange rate was valued with a weak yen at approximately ¥100 to $46.50, the gold embargo was lifted at the prewar parity of ¥100 to $49.85, meaning the yen was effectively elevated. In order to preserve international confidence in the yen, the government brought about a strong yen that made Japanese exports expensive, and lifted the gold embargo at the older parity despite the high probability of this causing deflation and a recession in Japan. It was decided that the reduction or elimination of weak, unproductive businesses was necessary to drastically reform the Japanese economy.

[47] Following the rice riots, the government attempted to increase rice production and breeding programs in Korea and Taiwan, and promoted the resulting rice being imported to Japan. At the same time, the use of chemical fertilizers such as ammonium sulfate came into full swing, and domestic rice production also increased.

icant poverty, especially in the Tōhoku region – that resulted in growing numbers of undernourished children, and girls being sold into prostitution.

Under such conditions, there was a sharp increase in labor and tenant disputes, and simultaneously public outcry over incompetent political parties and zaibatsu that were selling yen and buying dollars in anticipation of the gold embargo being reinstated.

The Breakdown of Cooperative Diplomacy

The Hamaguchi Osachi Cabinet revived the policy of cooperative diplomacy, and once more appointed Shidehara Kijūrō as minister of foreign affairs. In an effort to improve relations with China, a customs agreement was concluded between the two countries in 1930, and although it was conditional, China was granted tariff autonomy.

In accordance with the policy of disarmament, in 1930 Japan participated in the London Naval Conference ロンドン海軍軍縮会議. At the conference, the ban on constructing capital ships was extended for a further five years, and quantities for auxiliary vessels (cruisers, destroyers, and submarines) that had been excluded in the Washington Naval Treaty were determined. Japan's request for auxiliary vessel tonnage equivalent to 70% of the British and American levels was approved, but its similar 70% request with regards to heavy cruisers was rejected; nevertheless, the government signed the treaty (**London Naval Treaty** ロンドン海軍軍縮条約).

In response, members of the Seiyūkai, the Naval General Staff Office, and the right wing denounced the government for deciding matters pertaining to military forces despite objections from the Chief of the Naval General Staff, an act they saw as a **violation of military high command authority** 統帥権の干犯[48]. Although the government secured the approval of the Privy Council and the treaty was ratified, in November 1930 Prime Minister Hamaguchi was shot at Tōkyō Station by a right-wing youth. Seriously injured, he resigned in April the following year and died several months later.

---

[48] The tennō retained supreme command of the military, independent from the general affairs of the state overseen by the cabinet, and was aided in military matters through the direct participation of the Chief of the General Staff and the Chief of the Naval General Staff. According to how the Constitution was conventionally understood, decisions regarding military strength fell under Article 12, which dealt with organization of the military and concerning which the tennō was to be advised by the cabinet, as opposed to the tennō's supreme command of the military set forth in Article 11. However, this caused a disagreement with the Naval General Staff Office, which under the Imperial Defense Policy〈帝国国防方針〉was responsible for decisions regarding national military strength. Furthermore, because the treaty required approval from the Privy Council in order to be ratified, the government was forced to confront two national bodies: the Privy Council and the Naval General Staff Office.

5 The Rise of the Military

The Manchurian Incident

While nationalist movements to recover state rights rose in China, in Japan the military and right wing criticized Shidehara Kijūrō's cooperative diplomacy as a weak foreign policy, and caused an uproar over what was called a "**crisis in Manchuria and Inner Mongolia**" 「満蒙の危機」. The Kwantung Army, with an increasing sense of impending crisis, planned to use force to prevent the Chinese national rights-recovery movement from reaching Manchuria, as well as to separate Manchuria from Chinese sovereignty south of the Great Wall 長城, bringing it under Japanese control instead.

A faction of the Kwantung Army led by staff officer Ishihara Kanji 石原莞爾 (1889-1949)[49] caused an explosion along the South Manchurian Railway near Liutiaohu 柳条湖, a location outside Fengtian (Mukden), on 18 September 1931 (**Liutiaohu Incident** 柳条湖事件). This was then blamed on Chinese forces and followed up with military action, sparking the **Manchurian Incident** 満州事変. The Second Wakatsuki Reijirō Cabinet (Minseitō) declared a non-expansion policy, but public opinion and the media, as if caught up with war fever, supported the military's actions. As the Kwantung Army expanded the front line to place all of Manchuria under military control[50], the Wakatsuki Cabinet, having lost confidence in its handling of the situation, resigned.

MAP OF THE MANCHURIAN INCIDENT
Manchuria refers to the three provinces of Fengtian, Jilin〈吉林〉, and Heilongjiang〈黒龍江〉. Manchukuo also incorporated Rehe〈熱河〉 and Xing'an〈興安〉 for a total of five provinces, with Xinjing (Changchun)〈新京（長春）〉 as the capital. The Chinese government referred to this region as "Dongbei" ("Northeast").

---

[49] For some time, Ishiwara had predicted that in the near future a "final world war" would be fought between Japan and the US – as the leaders of the civilizations in the East and West, respectively – in a war of annihilation waged by airplanes, and insisted on preparing for this eventuality by occupying Manchuria.

[50] Japanese military actions in Manchuria heightened the anti-Japanese movement in China, and in 1932, a battle ensued between Japanese and Chinese troops in Shanghai (First Shanghai Incident〈第1次上海事変〉, also known as the January 28 Incident).

In December 1931, a cabinet was formed by Inukai Tsuyoshi, president of the Seiyūkai, and sought direct negotiations with China. However, by the start of the following year the Kwantung Army had occupied the major areas of Manchuria, and in March 1932, the founding of the state of Manchukuo 満州国 was declared, with Aisin-Gioro Puyi 溥儀 (1906-67), who had been the last emperor of the Qing Dynasty, as regent. The US expressed disapproval over this series of actions by Japan, and in response to an appeal from China and a motion from Japan, the Council of the League of Nations appointed the Lytton Commission, headed by the UK's Victor Bulwer-Lytton リットン (1876-1947), to conduct a fact-finding mission at the site of the incident as well as in China and Japan.

The Collapse of Party Cabinets and the Withdrawal from the League of Nations

Prompted by such developments as the London Naval Conference (with its reputed violation of the supreme command authority), the Shōwa Depression, and the Manchurian Incident, a radical **movement for national reconstruction** 国家改造運動 rapidly grew among military and right-wing circles. Young officers in the armed forces along with right-wing activists blamed Japan's predicament on the incompetence and corruption of the ruling class, including the zaibatsu and political parties, and sought to overthrow them in order to create a strong, military-based cabinet and overhaul domestic and foreign policy.

In 1931 there were two abortive coup attempts by young army officers (March Incident 三月事件[51] and October Incident 十月事件[52]), and between February and March of 1932 members of the Ketsumeidan 血盟団 (League of Blood), a right-wing organization led by Inoue Nisshō 井上日召 (1886-1967), assassinated former Finance Minister Inoue Junnosuke and the head of the Mitsui zaibatsu, Dan Takuma 団琢磨 (1858-1932), in what became known as the **Ketsumeidan Incident** 血盟団事件. This was followed by the **May 15 Incident** 五・一五事件 that same year, in which a group of young naval officers entered the prime minister's residence where they shot and killed Prime Minister Inukai.

This series of terrorist activities worried the ruling class, and after the May 15 Incident the genrō Saionji Kinmochi recommended the moderate Admiral Saitō Makoto (1858-1936) for the next prime minister. So it was that, eight years after the

---

[51] The Sakurakai〈桜会〉 (Cherry Blossom Society), a secret society comprised of young army officers led by Hashimoto Kingorō〈橋本欣五郎〉, in collaboration with right-wing leader Ōkawa Shūmei〈大川周明〉 and with the support of several army leaders, planned a coup d'état to establish a military government, but their attempts ended in failure.

[52] With the cooperation of right-wings including Ōkawa, the Sakurakai sought to overthrow party government, and in response to the Manchurian Incident planned a coup to carry out national reform. However, the plot was discovered and ended once again in failure.

end of the Taishō period, party government collapsed, not to be revived until after the Pacific War 太平洋戦争.

With the exchange of the **Japan-Manchukuo Protocol** 日満議定書 [53] in September 1932, the Saitō Cabinet confirmed Japanese recognition of Manchukuo. The Japanese government endeavored to create a fait accompli in an attempt to withstand opposition from the League of Nations, but an emergency General Assembly of the League in February 1933 determined, based on the report by the **Lytton Commission** リットン調査団 [54], that Manchukuo was a Japanese puppet state, and adopted a resolution calling for Japan to rescind its recognition. After the motion passed, Matsuoka Yōsuke 松岡洋右 (1880-1946) and the other Japanese delegates walked out, and in March the Japanese government formally announced its **withdrawal from the League of Nations** 国際連盟からの脱退 (effective from 1935).

JAPANESE-STYLE ENTRANCE OF PRIME MINISTER'S OFFICIAL RESIDENCE AFTER MAY 15 INCIDENT
The nation's prime minister was assassinated in the official residence. The tension surrounding the incident is palpable.

In May 1933, a Sino-Japanese ceasefire agreement 日中軍事停戦協定 (Tanggu Truce 塘沽停戦協定)[55] was concluded, bringing the Manchurian Incident to a close. However, Japan embarked on the management and development of Manchuria, and in 1934 proclaimed Manchukuo a monarchy with Puyi as its emperor. In 1936, Japan withdrew from the Second London Naval Conference, and the London Naval Treaty expired, as did the Washington

[53] Manchukuo confirmed Japanese rights and interests in the country, and accepted the unconditional stationing of the Japanese army there. Moreover, an attached confidential document stipulated that management of the transportation system in Manchuria would be consigned to Japan, and that Japanese officials had to be hired for key positions in the Manchukuo government based on the recommendation and approval of the commander of the Kwantung Army.

[54] The Lytton Report stated that the Japanese military actions did not constitute legal self-defense measures, and that Manchukuo had not been voluntarily established through a genuine independence movement, but on the other hand it also compromised by asserting that China needed to take Japanese economic interests into consideration.

[55] A demilitarized zone was established in the northeastern part of Hebei Province 〈河北省〉 by withdrawing both Chinese and Japanese troops from there, and it was decided that public order would be maintained by the Chinese police.

Naval Treaty, which Japan had already indicated in 1934 that it would not renew. Consequently, Japan was left internationally isolated.

Escape from Crisis

In December 1931, Takahashi Korekiyo, the finance minister of the then just-formed Inukai Cabinet (Seiyūkai), had acted immediately to **reinstate the gold embargo** 金輸出再禁止 and suspend yen-to-gold conversion. In this way, the Japanese economy ultimately came to abandon the gold standard and shift to a **managed currency system** 管理通貨制度. Many industries that had implemented rationalization policies during the depression took advantage of the sharp depreciation of the exchange rate (i.e., the weak yen 円安)[56] to dramatically increase exports. In particular, the export of cotton textiles grew tremendously, and Japan overtook the UK to become the world's leading exporter in this field.

At the time, the world was in turmoil, with the major powers struggling to escape from the Great Depression[57]. The UK adopted protectionist policies, with quotas and high tariffs on imports, and created a closed bloc economy within the British Empire. The UK and the other great powers criticized Japan for taking advantage of the weak yen to expand exports to its own colonies (called social dumping, as wages were decreased to boost exports). Meanwhile, Japan became increasingly dependent on the US for imports such as raw cotton, oil, scrap iron, and machinery.

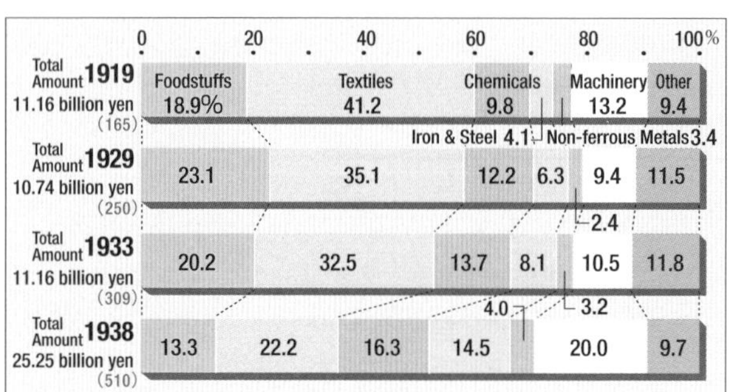

BREAKDOWN OF INDUSTRIAL PRODUCTION VALUE
( ) indicates index realized by price (with 1913 being 100).

On top of the export breakthrough, industry was stimulated by the expansion

[56] In 1932, the foreign exchange rate of the yen dropped to less than half of what it had been when the gold embargo was lifted, and even reached $20 to ¥100 at one point.

[57] In the US, President Franklin D. Roosevelt〈フランクリン＝ローズヴェルト〉, inaugurated in 1933, instituted a series of economic stimulus programs through government spending (the "New Deal〈ニューディール政策〉") to overcome the crisis. In Italy and Germany, meanwhile, totalitarian one-party dictatorships (Fascism and Nazism, respectively) were established, with Benito Mussolini〈ムッソリーニ〉 leading the National Fascist Party〈ファシスト党〉 and Adolf Hitler〈ヒトラー〉 heading the Nazi Party〈ナチ党〉. As for the Soviet Union, it adopted its own centralized economic system through a command economy, under the dictator Joseph Stalin〈スターリン〉 and his theory of "socialism in one country〈一国社会主義〉."

of public finance, especially in the form of deficit bonds issued for military expenditures and rural relief. Around 1933, Japan's production returned to its pre-depression level, ahead of other capitalist nations. In particular, aided by arms production and protectionist policies, there was significant development in the heavy and chemical industries. In 1933, the combined output of the metal, machinery and chemical industries exceeded the textile industry, and by 1938 it accounted for the majority of industrial production value, as the industrial structure shifted from one focusing on light industry to one centered on heavy and chemical industries.

In the iron and steel industry, a large merger combined the Yahata Steelworks with several zaibatsu-affiliated steel companies to form **Japan Iron & Steel Co.** (日本製鉄会社), a national policy (i.e., semi-governmental) company. This enabled Japan to become self-sufficient in steel. In the automobile and chemical industries, **new zaibatsu** (新興財閥) (shinkō zaibatsu) such as Nissan (日産) and Nitchitsu (日窒) emerged, and through ties with the military they expanded into Manchuria and Korea[58]. The established zaibatsu also actively strengthened the heavy and chemical industry sectors.

As movements petitioning for rural relief rose during the agricultural crisis, from 1932 the government commenced emergency relief measures consisting of public works programs, which allowed farmers to earn cash income as day laborers. Furthermore, the government initiated the **Rural Economic Rehabilitation Movement** (農山漁村経済更生運動) in order to help farmers unite and "self-rehabilitate" (jiriki kōsei) (「自力更生」) through the expansion of farm cooperatives.

The Age of "Tenkō"

The surge in nationalism within Japan in the wake of the Manchurian Incident, combined with state suppression, had a substantial impact on the socialist movement, resulting in a large number of people converting (**tenkō**) (転向)[59] away from socialism. The proletarian parties, which continued to fragment, also switched to national socialism, and in 1932 the Nihon Kokka Shakaitō (日本国家社会党) (Japan National Socialist Party) was formed

[58] Aikawa Yoshisuke〈鮎川義介〉 formed the Nissan Concern consisting of subsidiaries such as Nissan Motor and Hitachi, Ltd., and proceeded to advance into Manchuria, supplanting the South Manchurian Railway to monopolize the heavy and chemical industries there. Noguchi Shitagau〈野口遵〉, founder of Nihon Nitrogen Fertilizer Co. (Nihon Chisso Hiryō Kaisha〈日本窒素肥料会社〉, or Nitchitsu), constructed, under Nitchitsu as the parent company, large hydroelectric power stations and electrochemical complexes in northern Korea, and formed the Nitchitsu Concern.

[59] The term "tenkō" generally refers to a change in an individual's ideological position, but during this time it particularly signified abandoning socialist or communist ideology due to violence and oppression imposed by the state.

under the leadership of Akamatsu Katsumaro 赤松克麿 (1894-1955)[60]. The remaining socialists jointly formed the Shakai Taishūtō 社会大衆党 (Social Masses' Party), the largest proletarian party at the time, but that gradually became a national socialist party as well. Furthermore, in 1933 the top leaders of the Kyōsantō, who were in prison at the time, issued a statement announcing their own tenkō, which triggered a mass conversion[61]. The Nihon Musantō 日本無産党 (Japan Proletarian Party), led by Suzuki Mosaburō 鈴木茂三郎 (1893-1970) and others, managed to sustain its socialist beliefs, but was suppressed and disbanded in 1937.

Control over ideas and discourse was intensified, and there was a series of crackdowns not only on communism, but also on liberal and democratic scholarship[62]. The press, moreover, was increasingly dominated by views reflecting the military's ambitions for domestic reform based on national socialism.

The February 26 Incident

The influence of political parties on domestic politics gradually decreased after the May 15 Incident. In contrast, the **military** 軍部 (particularly the army), along with people who favored reform or who opposed established political parties and the status quo[63], gained increasing sway in the political sphere, with the support of some government officials (called kakushin kanryō 革新官僚, "reform bureaucrats") and political party members. The succession of two moderate party cabinets, led by navy Admirals Saitō Makoto and Okada Keisuke 岡田啓介 (1868-1952), further escalated their disapproval. In 1934, the Ministry of the Army distributed a pamphlet entitled "Kokubō no Hongi to Sono Kyōka no Teishō" 「国防の本義と其強化の提唱」 (The Essence of National Defense and Proposals to Strengthen It), which sparked controversy because it revealed the army's willingness to be involved

[60] National socialism aimed to remove the ill effects of capitalism through national social policies; the National Fascist Party and Nazi Party also advocated this stance. The Nihon Kokka Shakaitō sought to create an equal society centered on the tennō, "Ikkun Banmin〈「一君万民」〉" ("one monarch for all subjects"), and supported war from the standpoint of defending national interests.

[61] Two Kyōsantō leaders, Sano Manabu〈佐野学〉 and Nabeyama Sadachika〈鍋山貞親〉, jointly announced their conversion, criticizing policies calling for the abolishment of the Tennō System and opposing wars of aggression that the Comintern had instructed the Kyōsantō to follow; instead, they now advocated the implementation of one-state socialism under the Tennō System and nationalism. This declaration triggered the conversion of most of the imprisoned party members.

[62] In 1933, Kyōto Imperial University professor Takigawa Yukitoki〈滝川幸辰〉, who had been advocating liberal criminal law theory, was suspended from teaching due to pressure from Education Minister Hatoyama Ichirō〈鳩山一郎〉. The members of the university's Faculty of Law all submitted their resignations in protest, but were ultimately defeated (**Takigawa Incident**〈滝川事件〉).

[63] Domestically, these groups aimed at national integration under the tennō, economic planning, and reform of the cabinet and parliamentary systems, while in terms of foreign policy they advocated the abolishment of the Washington Settlement.

in political and economic affairs.

Minobe Tatsukichi's constitutional law theory had been under attack by the right wing for some time, but in 1935 it developed into a political issue (**Tennō Organ Theory Affair** 天皇機関説問題) when Kikuchi Takeo 菊池武夫 (1875-1955), a member of the House of Peers with a military background, criticized the theory for going against the "kokutai."

The Tennō Organ Theory[64] had until then been considered a legitimate theory underpinning the Meiji Constitution. However, this was now challenged by the army, as well as part of the Seiyūkai, the right wing, and other groups such as the military reserve association, which together fueled an intense nationwide denouncement movement. This forced the Okada Cabinet to issue a **Declaration Clarifying the Kokutai** 国体明徴声明 and reject the Tennō Organ Theory. In this way, party politics and the party cabinet system were deprived of their theoretical foundations along with (quasi-democratic) minponshugi.

The army was gaining greater political influence, but within it were two opposing factions. The **Kōdōha** 皇道派 (**Imperial Way Faction**), primarily supported by young officers, sought to take direct action to overthrow the established ruling class and instate rule by the tennō. The **Tōseiha** 統制派 (**Control Faction**), on the other hand, was mostly comprised of mid-level staff officers of the Ministry of the Army and the General Staff Office, and aspired to establish a total war system under tight military control, with the cooperation of reform bureaucrats and zaibatsu[65]. Early in the morning on February 26, 1936, a group of young officers of the Kōdōha who were influenced by the ideology of Kita Ikki[66] led approximately 1,400 troops in an attack on locations including the prime minister's official residence and the Metropolitan Police Department, killing Lord Keeper of the Privy Seal Saitō Makoto, Finance Minister Takahashi Korekiyo, and Inspector General of Military Training Watanabe Jōtarō 渡辺錠太郎 (1874-1936). The troops occupied the administrative core, including the Diet, for four days (**February 26** 二・二六事件

[64] Minobe's "Tennō Organ Theory" understood sovereignty as belonging to the state, which was a juridical body, with the tennō serving as the highest organ of that state and exercising sovereign rights in accordance with the Constitution. This was opposed to the theory advocated by Uesugi Shinkichi〈上杉慎吉〉 and others that held that absolute sovereignty belonged to the sacred and inviolable tennō himself.

[65] The central figures of the Tōseiha were considered to be Nagata Tetsuzan〈永田鉄山〉 and Tōjō Hideki〈東条英機〉, whereas those of the Kōdōha were Araki Sadao〈荒木貞夫〉 and Masaki Jinzaburō〈真崎甚三郎〉. The conflict between the two factions came to the surface in the Aizawa Incident〈相沢事件〉 (1935), in which Major General Nagata was assassinated in the Ministry of the Army offices by Lt. Colonel Aizawa Saburō〈相沢三郎〉 of the Kōdōha.

[66] Kita was a right-wing theorist whose 1923 tract *Nihon Kaizō Hōan Taikō* (Outline Plan for the Reorganization of Japan) discussed a policy of national reform centered on the tennō and the military, and became regarded as a bible for right-wing activists.

Incident). Martial law was declared in the capital. The coup sought to reorganize the state and establish a military government, but the tennō ordered severe punishment for those involved and they were suppressed as a rebel force. Following the incident, the Tōseiha dissolved the Kōdōha and took over leadership within the army, further strengthening the military's political influence. The Hirota Kōki 広田弘毅 (1878-1948) Cabinet that replaced the Okada administration was barely established due to the need to meet military demands regarding the selection of cabinet members, expansion of armaments, and fiscal reform. This occurrence marked the beginning of the military interference that would characterize subsequent cabinets[67].

With both the Washington and London Naval Treaties lapsing in 1936, the Hirota Cabinet drafted the "Kokusaku no Kijun「国策の基準」" (Fundamentals of National Policy), based on the military's **revision of the Imperial Defense Policy** 帝国国防方針の改定[68]. The policy sought to secure Japan's position on the continent while establishing plans for a progressive advance southward, strengthen diplomatic ties with Germany to counter the Soviet Union, and promote a large-scale military expansion plan in Japan[69].

However, facing opposition both from the military, which was dissatisfied with the lack of domestic reform, and political parties that opposed major military expansion, the Hirota Cabinet resigned in January 1937. Ugaki Kazushige 宇垣一成 (1868-1956), a moderate from the army, received an order from the tennō to form a cabinet, but the army, opposing this development, refused to appoint an army minister, leaving Ugaki unable to form an administration. Ultimately, General Hayashi Senjūrō 林銑十郎 (1876-1943) organized a cabinet, and endeavored to achieve coordination between the military and the business world (gunzai hōgō 軍財抱合, or a coalition of mil-

FEBRUARY 26 INCIDENT
The revolt by an "insurgent unit〈「蹶起部隊」〉" early in the morning on February 26 occupied the Diet and Metropolitan Police Department. The Martial Law Headquarters scattered fliers and called for the submission of the "rebel unit〈「反乱部隊」〉." This photo shows troops at Akasaka Sannōshita〈赤坂山王下〉.

---

[67] To placate the army's demands, the Military Ministers to be Active-Duty Officers Law was reinstated in 1936.

[68] In revising the defense policy, because the army insisted on expanding northward ("Northern Expansion Doctrine〈北進論〉," meaning moving against the Soviet Union) whereas the navy sought a southward advance ("Southern Expansion Doctrine〈南進論〉," meaning moving into the South Sea Islands and Southeast Asia), the "Kokusaku no Kijun" mentioned both and compromised.

[69] The navy initiated a major shipbuilding plan, which included the construction of the battleships *Yamato*〈大和〉 and *Musashi*〈武蔵〉.

itary and business interests)[70], but that too proved short-lived. In June that same year, President of the House of Peers **Konoe Fumimaro** 近衛文麿 (1891-1945) formed his first cabinet with great anticipation from all classes, ranging from the genrō and the military to the general public.

6 The Second World War

The Anti-Comintern Pact

Two conditions were required to maintain the order established through the Versailles and Washington Settlements after the First World War. The first was that the global economy remain strong and continue to increase in scale, while the second called for the wide recognition of peacekeeping efforts. However, the first condition crumbled in the wake of the Great Depression, and in the mid-1930s, signs of the collapse of the world order began to emerge. While Japan was instigating the Manchurian Incident that shook the Washington Settlement, Germany established a totalitarian regime (Nazism) in 1933, denounced the Versailles Settlement, and withdrew from the League of Nations. By 1935, Germany had begun the process of rearmament despite this having been prohibited. In Italy, meanwhile, a one-party dictatorship (Fascism) was established, and the country's invasion of Ethiopia in 1935 led to condemnation from the League of Nations. As the Spanish Civil War スペイン内戦 (1936-39) broke out in 1936, Germany and Italy strengthened their ties and formed the **Axis** 枢軸[71].

The Soviet Union's first Five-Year Plan 第1次5カ年計画 (1928-32) promoted heavy industrialization and agricultural collectivization, which rapidly increased the strength of the nation. Recognition of the Soviet Union by the US (1933) and its membership into the League of Nations (1934), moreover, denoted the Soviet Union's heightened position within the international community. In opposition to the international communist movement centered on the Soviet Union, in 1936 the Hirota Cabinet concluded the Anti-Comintern Pact (called the **Japan-Germany Anti-Comintern Pact** 日独防共協定 in Japan) with Germany. The following year, Italy signed the agreement as well (which then became known in Japan as the **Japan-Germany-Italy Anti-Comintern Pact** 日独伊三国防共協定), and also withdrew from the League. Thus, the three nations of Japan, Germany, and Italy,

---

[70] The Tōseiha thought it necessary to foster key industries in order to advance large-scale military expansion.

[71] With the Spanish Civil War in progress, Germany and Italy took the opportunity to strengthen their relationship and formed the Rome-Berlin Axis 〈ベルリン＝ローマ枢軸〉. The term "Axis" denoted a partnership between countries meant to play a "central role in the world."

which had faced international isolation, became united in opposition to the Soviet Union and formed the Axis camp.

The Second Sino-Japanese War

Since 1935 the Kwantung Army had overtly exercised the **North China Buffer State Strategy** 華北分離工作 in order to separate North China[72] from Nationalist Government rule. That same year, the Nationalist Government, with British support, implemented a currency reform aimed at promoting economic unification within China by eliminating the muddled situation caused by regional currencies. Observing this, the Kwantung Army established a puppet government (East Hebei Autonomous Anti-Communist 冀東防共自治委員会 Government) in north China to shore up their separation efforts, and in 1936 the Japanese government also decided to facilitate the separation of North China as a national policy. In response, the anti-Japanese movement aimed at saving China intensified among the Chinese public, and with the occurrence of the **Xi'an Incident** 西安事件[73] in December that same year, the Nationalist Government stopped fighting the Chinese Communist Party, ending the civil war, and set about engaging in full-scale resistance against Japan.

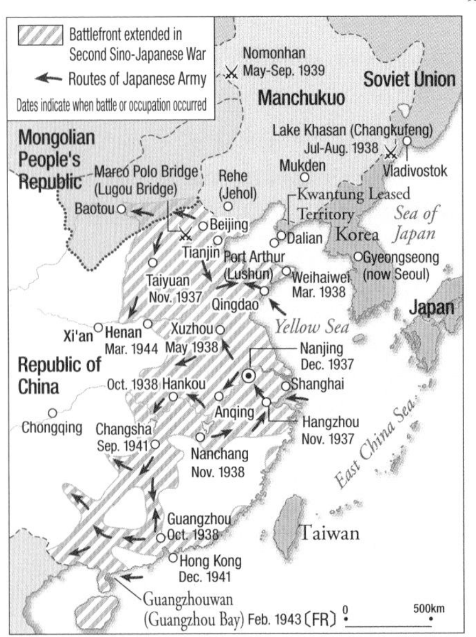

THE SECOND SINO-JAPANESE WAR

On July 7, 1937, not long after the establishment of the First Konoe Fumimaro Cabinet, a clash broke out

[72] The Japanese referred to the five provinces of Chahar〈チャハル〉, Suiyuan〈綏遠〉, Hebei, Shanxi〈山西〉, and Shandong as North China.

[73] After suffering repeated onslaughts from Chinese Nationalist forces, the Chinese Communist troops were forced to abandon their southern base in Ruijin〈瑞金〉 and embarked on the Long March〈長征〉, a difficult trek of over 12,000 km (1934-36), eventually arriving in Yan'an〈延安〉 on the northwestern frontier, where they established a new base for revolution. Zhang Xueliang, who was ordered by the Nationalist Government to attack the Communist forces in Yan'an, detained Jiang Jieshi (who was visiting to urge progress of this strategy), in a suburb of Xi'an, and demanded a suspension of the Chinese Civil War and the establishment of a united anti-Japanese front. After embarking on negotiations with the Chinese Communist Party, Jiang was released, and the civil war halted.

between Japanese and Chinese forces near the Lugou Bridge (盧溝橋) on the outskirts of Beijing (**Marco Polo Bridge Incident** (盧溝橋事件)). A ceasefire was reached locally, but the Konoe Cabinet succumbed to military pressure and changed its initial non-expansion policy by instead dispatching troop reinforcements and expanding the battle line. The Nationalist Government responded with a firm resistance stance, and the ensuing battle thus developed into a full-scale war far greater than what the Japanese side had anticipated – the **Second Sino-Japanese War** (日中戦争)[74]. In August, a battle commenced in Shanghai (Battle of Shanghai, also called the Second Shanghai Incident (第２次上海事変)), and the war spread southward. In September, the Chinese Nationalist Party and Chinese Communist Party declared that they had joined forces once again to form a united front against Japan (Second United Front (第２次国共合作)). Japan continued to dispatch large numbers of troops, and gained possession of Nanjing, the Nationalist Government capital, at the end of the year[75]. The war became an arduous, protracted struggle as the Nationalist Government retreated from Nanjing to Hankou (漢口), and eventually moved further inland to Chongqing (重慶), while continuing to fight.

At that point, Japan switched strategies by suspending large-scale attacks and moving to establish puppet governments in various locations. In January 1938, Prime Minister Konoe declared that Japan would "no longer deal with the Nationalist Government," severing any possibility of obtaining a peaceful resolution through negotiations. That same year, Konoe also proclaimed that the objective of the war was to build a **New Order in East Asia** (東亜新秩序) based on solidarity among Japan, Manchuria and China[76]. Wang Zhaoming (Wang Jingwei, 1883-1944) (汪兆銘（精衛）), a leading figure in the Nationalist Government, secretly escaped from Chongqing, and later in 1940 was

---

[74] Although the Japanese government initially referred to this battle as the "North China Incident〈「北支事変」〉", and then the "China Incident〈「支那事変」〉", it was in actuality already an all-out war. Neither Japan nor China officially declared war, primarily to avoid violating the US Neutrality Act〈中立法〉, which included stipulations for embargoes on weapons and ammunition to belligerent countries.

[75] Before and after the fall of Nanjing, the Japanese Army repeatedly plundered and committed violent acts both inside and outside the city, and killed a large number of Chinese civilians (including women and children) and prisoners, in what became known as the Nanjing Incident〈南京事件〉[vii]. The situation in Nanjing was relayed from early on to the Army Central Headquarters through the Ministry of Foreign Affairs.

[76] This refers to two statements given by Konoe Fumimaro in late 1938, one on November 3 ("Declaration of a New Order in East Asia〈東亜新秩序声明〉") and the other on December 22 ("Declaration of Konoe's Three Principles〈近衛三原則声明〉," the principles being neighborly amity, defense against communism, and economic cooperation). The reason for Japan reaffirming the aim of this unanticipated war around this time was that the UK's policy towards Asia had softened in the context of the ongoing crisis in Europe, making it a good opportunity to draw out pro-Japanese elements within China to establish control over the region.

appointed head of state of a new pro-Japanese Nationalist Government established in Nanjing, with the aim of unifying the puppet governments of various regions. However, the Wang government was weak, and Japan's political strategy to end the war failed, whereas the Nationalist Government received aid from the US, the UK, and others through supply routes ("Enshō Rūto," meaning "Jiang Support Routes" 援蔣ルート) and continued to fight.

Wartime Regulations and Everyday Life

The swift rise in military expenditures, triggered by the large-scale arms expansion budget set by the Hirota Kōki Cabinet, greatly affected public finances, and the rapid increase in imports of military materiel led to a crisis in the balance of payments. As the Second Sino-Japanese War got underway, the First Konoe Cabinet drew up an even greater military budget and embarked on direct economic control, enacting the Temporary Capital Adjustment Act 臨時資金調整法 and Temporary Measures on Imports and Exports Act 輸出入品等臨時措置法, having decided to centrally allocate funds and imported materials to military-related industries. As the controlled economy progressed, the advancement of economic bureaucrats became significant, and among them developed a movement to form close ties with the military in order to build a strong national defense state. With the expanding scope of the war, military expenditures ballooned year after year, resulting in successive tax increases to offset growing finances. Yet the enormous expenditures could not be covered, and public bonds were issued, while the increased number of banknotes fueled inflation.

In April 1938, the **National Mobilization Law** 国家総動員法 was issued, granting the administration authority over the mobilization of manpower and resources required to conduct warfare without the need for approval from the Diet, thereby putting civilian life under full government control. The Electric Power Control Law 電力国家管理法, enacted around the same time, consolidated private electric power companies into a single national policy company, giving the government an opportunity to increase its involvement in private enterprise. While the compulsory reorganization of small and medium-sized businesses progressed, in 1939 the **National Service Draft Ordinance** 国民徴用令, based on

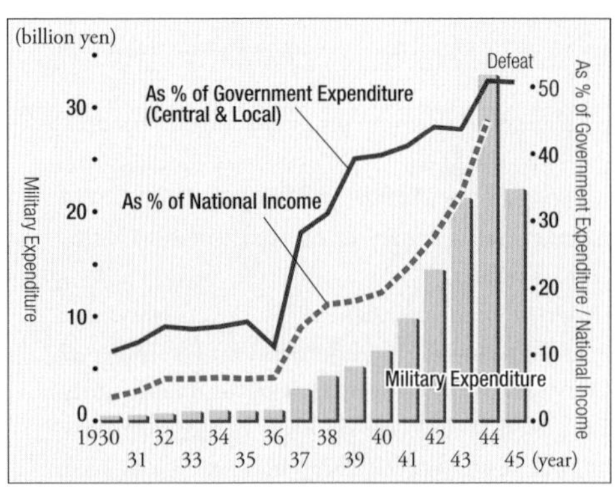

INCREASE IN MILITARY SPENDING AND EXPANSION OF NATIONAL BUDGET

NATIONAL MOBILIZATION LAW

Article 1. In this law, national mobilization refers to the control and utilization of human and material resources in order to most effectively employ the full strength of the nation for the purpose of achieving national defense objectives in times of war.

Article 4. When necessary for national mobilization in times of war, the government may draft civilians to perform national mobilization duties as required by imperial edict.

Article 8. When necessary for national mobilization in times of war, the government may command the production, repair, distribution, transfer, and other dispositions, usage, consumption, possession, and movement of commodities as required by imperial edict.

Article 20. When necessary for national mobilization in times of war, the government may restrict or prohibit the publication of newspapers and other printed materials as required by imperial edict. [Clause 2 omitted]

the National Mobilization Law, marshaled civilians to support the arms industry. Already from 1938 the **Planning Bureau** (企画院)[77] had implemented a material mobilization plan that prioritized munitions production. For this reason, not only new zaibatsu centered on the heavy and chemical industries, but also major companies associated with the established zaibatsu, actively ventured into munitions production and profited greatly through cooperating with this national policy. Plans were also made to expand production capacity in anticipation of an all-out war, but with the pressing demands of immediate military production this remained out of reach. Production of machinery and nonferrous metals continued to rise due to military demand until 1944[78], but with degradation in the quality of raw materials, disruption of high-performance machinery imports, and lack of experience in mass production, the required quality was often unachievable.

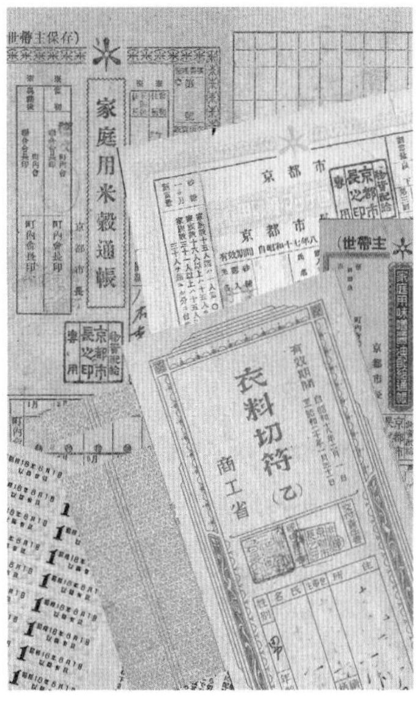

RATION COUPONS FOR HOUSEHOLD GOODS
The introduction of a coupon rationing system for daily necessities made life on the home front even more severe, and was a heavy burden on the lives of the public.

---

[77] The Planning Bureau was established in October 1937 under cabinet control to formulate, draft, and coordinate wartime mobilization efforts, but due to a strong backlash from the business community it was eventually absorbed into the newly-established Ministry of Munitions in 1943.

[78] Arms production increased 640% from 1936 to 1941, and 300% from 1941 to 1944.

In contrast, production and sales of cotton goods for domestic use was prohibited, and severe restrictions were placed on the production and import of consumer goods deemed "nonessential," causing a shortage of daily necessities. In October 1939, the administration issued the **Price Control Ordinance** (価格等統制令), based on the National Mobilization Law, and introduced an official price system that further strengthened government control over the economy. Further, the public was made to reduce consumption, and in 1940 the manufacture and sale of luxury items was prohibited (**July 7 Restrictions** (七・七禁令)), and a **coupon rationing system** (切符制) was instated to limit use of commodities like sugar and matches. The following year, the **rationing system** (配給制) was applied to rice, and eventually extended to clothing, intensifying the government's control over daily necessities.

In agricultural communities, from 1940 the government enforced a **compulsory rice provision system** (供出制), and took measures to promote production, such as restricting tenancy fees and prioritizing rice prices for producers, leading to a reduced share for landowners. Despite these efforts, however, food production began to decrease after 1939 due to a lack of labor and materials, and food shortages became an increasingly critical matter.

With the formation of a wartime regime, thought control grounded in kokutai theory, as well as the suppression of socialism and liberal ideologies, increased in severity[79]. From October 1937, the First Konoe Cabinet launched the **National Spiritual Mobilization Movement** (国民精神総動員運動) to encourage nationalism and militarism, and to generate public cooperation in economizing and saving for the war effort. In order to fully mobilize laborers for the purpose of an all-out war, the Sangyō Hōkokukai (**Patriotic Industrial Association** (産業報国会)) was formed[80] to bring capital and labor organizations together

---

[79] Just before the start of the Second Sino-Japanese War, the Ministry of Education published *Kokutai no Hongi*〈『国体の本義』〉 (Fundamentals of the Kokutai) and distributed it to schools and government offices nationwide in order to instill national sentiment. Moreover, Yanaihara Tadao〈矢内原忠雄〉, a professor at Tōkyō Imperial University who was a researcher of colonial economic policy, was forced out of the university for criticizing the government's continental policy, and his books were banned (Yanaihara Incident〈矢内原事件〉, 1937). There were also cases such as the arrest of Tōkyō Imperial University professor Ōuchi Hyōe〈大内兵衛〉 and others on charges of attempting to organize a popular front (Popular Front Incident〈人民戦線事件〉, 1938).

[80] In 1938, capitalist groups and labor union leaders were assembled to form the Sangyō Hōkoku Renmei〈産業報国連盟〉 (Patriotic Industrial League). Meanwhile, under police guidance, a Sangyō Hōkokukai that integrated labor and capital was established at each company, and a number of existing labor unions were reorganized for this purpose. In 1940, when the League became the Dai Nihon Sangyō Hōkokukai〈大日本産業報国会〉 (Greater Japan Patriotic Industrial Association) and all the labor unions were dissolved, there were approximately 70,000 Sangyō Hōkokukai with a total of 4.18 million members.

to advance national policy. In 1940, the Cabinet Intelligence Bureau 内閣情報局 was established, with the aim of asserting comprehensive control over the mass media – including publishing, theatre, radio, and film – for the war effort.

Wartime Culture

In the 1930s, amidst an environment of strict government control and intensifying nationalism, many people "converted" from Marxism and its influence gradually weakened. There was a resurgence of traditional Japanese thought and culture, a tendency that became even stronger by the late 1930s. *Nihon Rōmanha* 「日本浪曼派」 (Japanese Romantics), a journal launched by Kamei Katsuichirō 亀井勝一郎 (1907-66), Yasuda Yojūrō 保田与重郎 (1910-81), and others, published literary criticism asserting a nationalist and anti-modernist stance. During the Second Sino-Japanese War, totalitarian ideology shaped by kokutai theory and Nazism became mainstream, and "innovative" domestic reform theories developed, such as the New Order in East Asia, Greater East Asia Co-Prosperity Sphere, and Controlled Economy.

In the literary world of the early Shōwa period, two main styles prospered: proletarian literature, which was closely connected to the socialist movement, and the **Shinkankaku 新感覚派 (New Sensationalist) School**, a literary trend represented by writers such as Yokomitsu Riichi 横光利一 (1898-1947) and Kawabata Yasunari 川端康成 (1899-1972) who sought the essence of literature in expressions of subjectivity and sensitivity. However, with the increasing suppression of socialism in the early 1930s, proletarian literature was all but wiped out[81].

Meanwhile, against the backdrop of encroaching war, many established writers quietly continued to produce powerful works, with masterpieces like Shimazaki Tōson's 島崎藤村 *Yoakemae* 「夜明け前」 (Before the Dawn) and Tanizaki Jun'ichirō's *Sasameyuki* 「細雪」 (literally "Light Snowfall," but often called "The Makioka Sisters") emerging. During the Second Sino-Japanese War, war literature, such as Hino Ashihei 火野葦平 (1907-60)'s *Mugi to Heitai* 『麦と兵隊』 (Wheat and Soldiers), which depicted the author's own experience in the military, grew popular. However, Ishikawa Tatsuzō 石川達三 (1905-85)'s *Ikiteiru Heitai* 『生きてゐる兵隊』 (Soldiers Alive), which realistically depicted the lives of Japanese soldiers, was banned, and in 1942, the Nihon Bungaku Hōkokukai 日本文学報国会 (Patriotic Association for Japanese Literature) was established.

---

[81] The shift away from socialism and proletarian literature was depicted in works of tenkō bungaku〈転向文学〉(conversion literature), such as Nakano Shigeharu's〈中野重治〉*Mura no Ie*〈「村の家」〉(The House in the Village) and Shimaki Kensaku's〈島木健作〉*Seikatsu no Tankyū*〈「生活の探求」〉(In Search of Life).

The Outbreak of the Second World War

In Europe, Nazi Germany completely renounced the Versailles Settlement, and after annexing Austria in 1938 moved towards invading Czechoslovakia. It was in this context that Germany appealed to the First Konoe Cabinet to strengthen the Anti-Comintern Pact, proposing a military alliance that positioned the UK and France as potential enemy countries in addition to the Soviet Union. The Konoe Cabinet, however, resigned en masse before concluding the matter, and at the beginning of 1939 a new cabinet was formed by the chairman of the Privy Council, Hiranuma Kiichirō 平沼騏一郎 (1867-1952). The Hiranuma Cabinet was divided over the issue of concluding a military alliance, but in August that year, Germany unexpectedly signed a non-aggression pact with the Soviet Union (German-Soviet Nonaggression Pact 独ソ不可侵条約, or Molotov-Ribbentrop Pact)[82]. Unable to contend with the sudden changes in the international sphere, the Hiranuma Cabinet too resigned en masse.

On September 1, 1939, Germany invaded Poland. The UK and France promptly responded by declaring war on Germany on 3 September, marking the start of the **Second World War** 第二次世界大戦. Following the Hiranuma Cabinet, the succeeding administrations of Abe Nobuyuki 阿部信行 (1875-1953, Army General) and Yonai Mitsumasa 米内光政 (1880-1948, Navy Admiral) were reluctant to form a military alliance with Germany, and continued to maintain a policy of non-intervention in the European

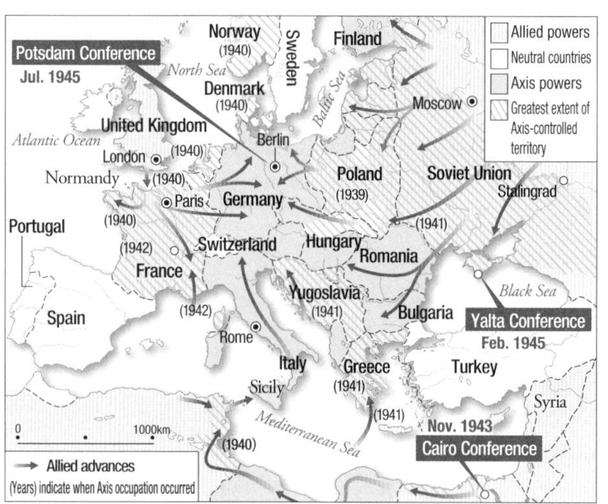

EUROPE DURING THE SECOND WORLD WAR

[82] The Japanese Army, wary of the Soviet Union's moves during the Second Sino-Japanese War, in 1938 fought with Soviet forces on the disputed border of the Soviet Union and Manchukuo in the Battle of Lake Khasan (also known as the Changkufeng Incident〈張鼓峰事件〉). Furthermore, in May the following year Japanese forces engaged Soviet-Mongolian allied forces on the western border of Manchukuo and the Mongolian People's Republic, but suffered heavy damage from the Soviet tank corps (**Nomonhan Incident**〈ノモンハン事件〉, also called the Battles of Khalkhin Gol). The German-Soviet Nonaggression Pact came as a great shock to Japan, which was busy fighting the Soviets at Nomonhan at the time.

war.

On the other hand, from the beginning of the Second Sino-Japanese War Japan's arms industry could not be sustained solely by resources from its own economic zone (the **yen bloc** 円ブロック), which consisted of Japanese colonies and occupied territories in Manchuria and China proper, and as a result it had to rely on imported materials from the Western countries and their respective spheres of influence. However, the US saw maintaining free trade relations with the Asia-North Pacific region as an important matter of national interest, and consequently when Japan embarked on the formation of its New Order in East Asia, the US deemed this a challenge to its own East Asia policies, and trade between the two countries began to decline. Moreover, upon learning that Japan and Germany were taking steps towards concluding a military alliance, in July 1939 the US gave notice that the US-Japan Treaty of Commerce and Navigation 日米通商航海条約 would be terminated. After the treaty expired the following year, it became extremely difficult for Japan to obtain materials for its armaments.

As Germany became overwhelmingly dominant in Europe, with only the UK continuing to resist, in Japan, pushed by the army, there was increasing insistence on strengthening ties with Germany, and, being resolved to a coming war with the US and the UK, on advancing southward into the Western colonies, building the "**Dai Tōa Kyōeiken**" 「大東亜共栄圏」 (**Greater East Asia Co-Prosperity Sphere**), and securing resources such as petroleum, rubber, and bauxite. Although there was opposition within the Diet and among the upper political echelons, this was not powerful enough to turn the tide[83], and ultimately the southward expansion only strengthened the Western powers' economic blockade of Japan.

The New Order and the Tripartite Pact

In June 1940, Konoe Fumimaro retired from the post of chairman of the Privy Council in order to head the **Shintaisei Undō** 新体制運動 (**New Order Movement**). Ostensibly a reform movement, it aimed to break down existing party politics and replace them with a single leading party modeled after the powerful mass organizations of the Nazi and National Fascist Parties, in order to mobilize the whole nation for the war effort under a unified leadership. Political organizations and parties – such as the Seiyūkai,

---

[83] In 1940, Saitō Takao〈斎藤隆夫〉, a member of the Diet from the Minseitō, gave a speech in the House of Representatives harshly criticizing the policies of the military and government regarding the war in China. This incident, known as the Anti-military Speech〈反軍演説〉, led to him being expelled from the Diet due to pressure from the military. Figures in the upper echelons of the political world seen as constituting a "pro-Anglo-American faction" were also attacked by the military and other critics.

Minseitō, and Shakai Taishūto – either willingly dissolved to join the movement, or were forced to do so. In anticipation of Konoe once again becoming prime minister, the Yonai Cabinet was driven to resign by the military.

In July 1940, the Second Konoe Cabinet was formed. However, prior to its formation Konoe had already met with his prospective army, navy, and foreign affairs ministers, and they had resolved to shift from the nonintervention policy regarding the conflict in Europe, strengthen ties with Germany, Italy, and the Soviet Union, and actively proceed with expansion into Southeast Asia and the Pacific in line with the southward advance strategy. This strategy aimed at subjugating colonies belonging to European states that had surrendered to Germany[84], as well as alleviating the war stalemate in China by blocking the "Jiang support routes." Thus, in September, Japanese forces advanced into northern French Indochina while the **Tripartite Pact** 日独伊三国同盟[85] was concluded among Japan, Germany and Italy at almost the same time. In response, the US imposed economic sanctions on Japan, placing embargos on exports such as aviation fuel and scrap iron.

Meanwhile, the New Order Movement came to fruition in October 1940 in the form of the **Taisei Yokusankai** 大政翼賛会 (**Imperial Rule Assistance Association**). However, it was not the party system that had originally been intended, but instead became a government-manufactured command hierarchy with the prime minister as president, prefectural governors as branch heads, and a substructure of village, town and neighborhood associations[86].

In the education sphere, elementary schools were reorganized as **National Schools** 国民学校 in 1941, and promoted "Chūkun Aikoku" 「忠君愛国」 (loyalty and patriotism) through nationalistic education. Similarly, in Korea and Taiwan a policy of "**Kōminka Seisaku**" 「皇民化」政策 (literally

---

[84] These colonies included the Dutch East Indies (Indonesia), as the Netherlands was under German occupation, and French Indochina (Vietnam, Laos, and Cambodia), as France had surrendered to Germany.

[85] The three nations mutually recognized each other's leadership role in the "new order" in Europe and Asia, and pledged to support each other if attacked by a third-party nation. An exclusionary rule existed with regards to the Soviet Union. Because the pact was a military alliance that framed the US as a potential enemy, it triggered a strong backlash from that nation.

[86] Eventually, various associations such as the Dai Nihon Sangyō Hōkokukai, Dai Nihon Fujinkai〈大日本婦人会〉 (Greater Japan Women's Association), Dai Nihon Yokusan Sōnendan〈大日本翼賛壮年団〉 (Greater Japan Imperial Rule Assistance Youth Corps), and Dai Nihon Seishōnendan〈大日本青少年団〉 (Greater Japan Youth Association) were put under the umbrella of the Taisei Yokusankai and played a role in national mobilization during the war. In particular, the Tonarigumi〈隣組〉 (or Rinpohan〈隣保班〉), the smallest of the organizational units, were neighborhood associations consisting of about five to ten households. Their wartime duties included the exchange and distribution of information through circular notices.

"making imperial subjects," meaning Japanization) was implemented, consisting of thorough Japanese language education and so on, and Koreans were pressured by the "Sōshi Kaimei" (創氏改名) policy to change their names to Japanese ones.

The Beginning of the Pacific War

The conclusion of the Tripartite Pact further hardened the US' stance toward Japan. The Second Konoe Cabinet commenced negotiations with the US in an attempt to avoid conflict between the two nations. US-Japan talks that began at the end of 1940 with private citizens developed into formal government-level negotiations between Nomura Kichisaburō (野村吉三郎) (1877-1964) and Secretary of State Cordell Hull (ハル) (1871-1955).

Around the same time, Foreign Minister Matsuoka Yōsuke, who had been visiting Germany and Italy to reinforce the partnership of the Tripartite Pact, concluded the **Soviet-Japanese Neutrality Pact** (日ソ中立条約) in Moscow in April 1941 while returning to Japan. Japan's aims with this agreement were to facilitate advancing the southward expansion policy by not only securing peace in the north, but also rebalancing the deteriorating relationship with the US through forging stronger relations with the Soviet Union.

In June 1941, Germany suddenly invaded the Soviet Union, beginning the Eastern Front (独ソ戦争) of the war. In response to this situation, an Imperial Conference (御前会議)[87][viii] was held on July 2, 1941, and with strong insistence from the military, it was decided to advance southward despite the risk of war with the UK and the US, and, should the opportunity present itself, to move against the Soviet Union (i.e., the northward advance policy)[88]. The Second Konoe Cabinet planned to continue negotiations with the US, and to this end first resigned en masse to remove Foreign Minister Matsuoka, who had an uncompromising stance towards the US. However, immediately after the establishment of the Third Konoe Cabinet, at the end of July the **Japanese invasion of French Indochina** (南部仏印進駐), which had already been planned, was carried out, and in response the US froze Japanese assets in the US and prohibited the export of

---

[87] When an Imperial General Headquarters and Government Liaison Conference〈大本営政府連絡会議〉 was held with the tennō in attendance in order to discuss matters pertaining to war against foreign countries, it was called an Imperial Conference. These conferences were typically attended by representatives of the army and navy like the chiefs of the respective general staffs, as well as the prime minister, the minister of foreign affairs, the minister of finance, the minister of home affairs, and the president of the Planning Bureau.

[88] Consequently, the army devised a plan to occupy Far Eastern Soviet territories like Siberia, and mobilized 700,000 troops in Manchuria under the pretext of carrying out "Kwantung Army Special Maneuvers〈関東軍特種演習〉." However, the plan was aborted after the decision was made in August to advance southward.

petroleum to Japan[89]. The US thus expressed its intent to prevent Japan's advance to the south and plans to create a New Order in East Asia, a view with which the UK and the Netherlands concurred. The Japanese military, feeling a crisis was imminent, asserted that war was the only way to counter Japan being oppressed by "ABCD encirclement 「ABCD 包囲陣」[90]."

The Imperial Conference of September 6 sanctioned the **Guidelines for Executing Imperial Policy** 帝国国策遂行要領 that established early October as a deadline: should diplomatic negotiations prove unsuccessful by that time, then Japan would embark on hostilities against the US (along with the UK and the Netherlands). With the U.S. insisting on a total withdrawal of Japanese troops from China, however, US-Japan negotiations continued through mid-October without a compromise being reached. Prime Minister Konoe strongly desired to continue talks with the US in order to reach an agreement, but he faced opposition from the army minister, Tōjō Hideki (1884-1948), who insisted on ending negotiations and going to war. This ultimately led to the resignation of the Konoe Cabinet on October 16.

Lord Keeper of the Privy Seal Kido Kōichi 木戸幸一 (1889-1977) recommended that Tōjō succeed as prime minister on the condition that the decisions made during the Imperial Conference of September 6 were reconsidered[91]. Thus the Tōjō Hideki Cabinet was formed, with the new prime minister also serving as army minister and home affairs minister. The new government reexamined the decisions from September 6, and continued negotiations with the US for the time being. However, a proposal from the US (the "Hull Note" ハル＝ノート) issued on November 26 sought the complete withdrawal of troops from China and French Indochina, the renunciation of the Wang Jingwei and Manchukuo regimes, and the abrogation of the Tripartite Pact. Since this was perceived by Japan as an ultimatum seeking a return to the situation prior to the Manchurian Incident, a compromise was deemed hopeless. An Imperial Conference on December 1 concluded that negotiations with the US had failed, and solidified the decision to go to war against the US and the UK. On December 8, the Japanese Army landed on the Malay Peninsula, a British protectorate, and the Japanese Navy

---

[89] With domestic oil reserves expected to last only another two years, even within the navy, which had heretofore been reluctant to commence hostilities, the view that immediate action was required to secure oil resources in the south suddenly came to the forefront.

[90] The military conceived of the economic blockade of Japan by (A) America, (B) Britain, (C) China and the (D) Dutch as an alliance set on encircling Japan – the "ABCD encirclement" – and appealed to the public that the country was being unfairly oppressed.

[91] After the death of the last surviving genrō, Saionji Kinmochi, the selection of successive prime ministers was agreed upon at a conference of senior statesmen consisting of former prime ministers and led by Kido Kōichi (grandson of Kido Takayoshi〈木戸孝允〉).

暴戻米英に對して宣戰布告

グアム島わが包圍下 猛火に包

畏し大詔渙發

詔書

今朝來香港猛爆敢

上海在港英艦撃沈

獨伊對米宣戰布

西太平洋全面に亙り

OUTBREAK OF THE PACIFIC WAR
Right: newspaper article reporting on the war between Japan and the US (*Yomiuri Shinbun*, December 8, 1941). Above: US Pacific Fleet in flames after the surprise attack on Pearl Harbor.

launched a surprise attack on Pearl Harbor in Hawaii. Japan declared war on the US and the UK[92], thus commencing the **Pacific War** (太平洋戦争)[93], which became a major theater of the Second World War.

Progress of the War

With Japan's declaration of war on the US, Germany and Italy also declared war on the US in accordance with the Tripartite Pact. The US thus faced a two-front war, fighting in both the European and Asia-Pacific theatres. Consequently, the scope of the conflict expanded across the globe, with the US, UK and Soviet Union referred to as the main **Allied powers** (連合国), and Japan, Germany and Italy the main **Axis powers** (枢軸国).

At the start of the war, the Japanese forces had struck the US Pacific Fleet in Hawaii and the British Eastern Fleet off Malaya. Following this, within the first six months of the war a vast area from Southeast Asia to the South Pacific Ocean was placed under Japanese military administration, including the British colonies on the Malay Peninsula, Singapore, Hong Kong, Burma (Myanmar), the Dutch East Indies

---

[92] The announcement informing the US of the termination of negotiations, which was understood as a de facto declaration of war, was delayed until after the start of the attack on Pearl Harbor, partly because of the military's desire to achieve greater results through a pre-emptive strike. As a result, American public sentiment coalesced under the slogan "Remember Pearl Harbor," and this event sparked intense hostility towards Japan. Beginning in California, 120,313 Japanese-Americans living along the West Coast were relocated to internment camps, but no such measures were taken for Americans of German and Italian descent. In 1988, the US government issued a formal apology and reparations to the internees.

[93] After the outbreak of war with the US, the Japanese government decided to refer to the conflict as the Dai Tōa Sensō 〈大東亜戦争〉 ("Greater East Asia War") in order to include the "China Incident" (Second Sino-Japanese War) as well, and this term was used until Japan's defeat.

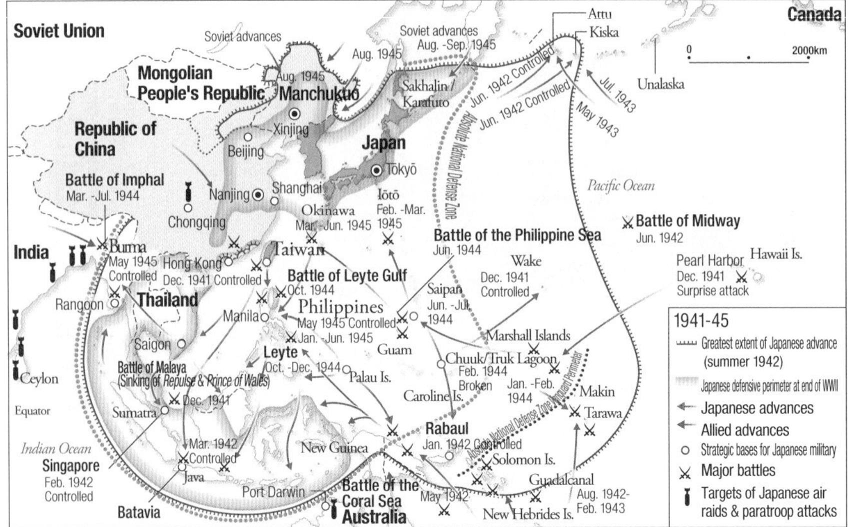

THE PACIFIC WAR

(Indonesia), and the Philippines (a US colony). Many Japanese rejoiced over their military triumphs in the early stage of the war. Initially, Japan articulated the war as a self-defense measure against the threat of the US and the UK, but gradually it became caught up with slogans rallying for the liberation of Asia from Western colonial rule and the creation of the Greater East Asia Co-Prosperity Sphere, and the theatre of war expanded limitlessly[94].

In April 1942, as the nation reveled in its early victories, the Tōjō Hideki Cabinet held the first general election (**Yokusan Senkyo** 翼賛選挙, literally "government support election") in five years, with the aim of establishing a system to support the war effort. The result was government-endorsed candidates acquiring an absolute majority[95], and after the election one united national political association, the Yokusan Seijikai 翼賛政治会 (Imperial Rule Assistance Political Association) was established. Henceforth, the Diet's role was reduced to simply approving proposals made by the government. However,

---

[94] The "Imperial Rescript on the Declaration of War〈「宣戦の詔書」〉," issued on December 8, 1941, explained that the US and the UK had not only intervened in China, hindering Japan's efforts to bring stability to East Asia, but had also threatened even Japan's very existence by severing economic relations, leaving the country no choice but to resort to war as a means of ensuring its self-preservation and self-defense.

[95] Candidates Hatoyama Ichirō, Ozaki Yukio〈尾崎行雄〉, Ashida Hitoshi〈芦田均〉, and Katayama Tetsu〈片山哲〉 were among those not endorsed, and suffered from election interference from police and regional authorities. Only 85 non-endorsed candidates obtained seats in this election, compared to the 381 endorsed candidates who did so.

the Constitution and Diet activities were never formally suspended.

Since the Allies placed priority on defeating Germany first, the movement of military forces into the Pacific Ocean was initially restrained. However, the US was able to soon secure a military advantage, and in June 1942 a decisive battle was fought between the Japanese and American naval fleets in the central Pacific off Midway Island (**Battle of Midway** ミッドウェー海戦). Japan suffered a crushing defeat, losing four aircraft carriers and their aircraft, leaving the country at a serious disadvantage in both naval and aerial warfare. This was a turning point in the war, and by the latter half of the year the US counteroffensive against Japan was firmly underway.

As a result, Japan was forced to revise its strategy, and at an Imperial Conference on September 30, 1943, the decision was made to move the defensive line back to the Absolute National Defense Perimeter 絶対国防圏, a region that included the Chishima 千島列島 (Kuril) Islands, Ogasawara 小笠原, the Mariana and Caroline Islands, West New Guinea, and Burma.

In November 1943, the Tōjō Cabinet held the **Greater East Asia Conference** 大東亜会議 in Tōkyō, inviting representatives from Manchukuo, the Nanjing (Wang Jingwei) regime in China, Thailand, Burma, the Provisional Government of Free India, and the Philippines. The intention was to secure cooperation for the war from occupied areas, and make a show of unity for the Greater East Asia Co-Prosperity Sphere. However, contrary to the pretext of liberating Asia, the top priority of the Japanese occupation rule that replaced the Western powers was to procure resources and labor for the war effort[96], resulting in increasing antipathy and resistance from occupied peoples. In the occupied territories of Southeast Asia, learning Japanese, tennō worship, and shrine worship were imposed without regard for the local culture and lifestyle. Forced mobilization of labor was also used to construct the Burma Railway connecting Thailand and Burma, as well as for civil engineering projects and mining. In Singapore and Malaysia in particular, there were incidents of the Japanese military killing large numbers of Chinese residents (overseas Chinese 華僑) on suspicion of anti-Japanese activities. As a result, Japanese troops had to face organized anti-Japanese movements in various regions, including French Indochina and the Philippines[97].

On the Chinese front, Japanese strategies to prevent the use of Chinese airfields by

---

[96] When Japanese forces first occupied Southeast Asian countries, they were sometimes welcomed by residents as liberators ending Western colonization. However, when military administration was instituted in many of those regions (excluding Thailand and French Indochina), and exploitation and mobilization began, people's opinions changed dramatically.

[97] After the defeat of Japan, these national liberation movements fought against the armies of their mother countries and won independence, ultimately eliminating Western colonial rule in Asia.

US forces, and to connect central and south China, were implemented after the start of the Pacific War. The Chinese Communist Party organized extensive anti-Japanese bases in rural areas of north China ("Liberated Areas"), and carried out guerilla activities. The Japanese Army launched a large-scale operation (referred to by the Chinese side as the "Three Alls Policy" 三光作戦) against the anti-Japanese guerillas, which inflicted a great deal of destruction upon the civilian population[98].

In July 1944, Saipan in the Mariana Islands fell to the US, causing a corner of the Absolute National Defense Perimeter to collapse. Taking responsibility for this failure, the Tōjō Cabinet resigned. The next prime minister was Koiso Kuniaki 小磯国昭 (1880-1950, Army General), who with the support of Admiral Yonai Mitsumasa organized a coalition army-navy cabinet.

Deterioration of Life on the Home Front

After the start of the Pacific War, the government pursued a policy of prioritizing arms production, such as converting private-sector factories to munitions manufacture. People lived thoroughly constrained lives, and were mobilized for the military and labor force. In 1943, humanities students enrolled in universities, higher schools, and vocational schools who were of conscription age were drafted into the military (**student mobilization** 学徒出陣), while remaining students and members of the Women's Volunteer Corps 女子挺身隊 were mobilized to work in arms factories (**labor mobilization** 勤労動員). Furthermore, many Koreans were drafted, and Chinese from occupied territories forcibly moved to the Japanese home islands, to work in mines and construction[99].

Because the number of young men mobilized for the military increased from four to five million, the labor force necessary for domestic production suffered a detrimental shortage. The loss of sea and air superiority made sea transportation from the south difficult, resulting in a shortage of resources such as iron ore, coal, and oil which were essential for munitions production.

A **comprehensive coupon rationing system** 総合切符制 was applied to clothing, but even

[98] Poison gas was also used on the Chinese front, and research on chemical and biological weapons was conducted at Japanese military facilities in Manchuria and elsewhere. In Harbin〈ハルビン〉, Manchuria, a special unit called Unit 731 (led by Lt. General Ishii Shirō〈石井四郎〉) was established to conduct research on biological warfare, and performed experiments on Chinese and Soviet prisoners.

[99] The draft system was enacted in Korea in 1943, and in Taiwan in 1944. However, voluntary military service had already been implemented in 1938, and soldiers were recruited from the colonies. In addition, women from areas including Japan, Korea, China and the Philippines were assembled to work at "comfort facilities" for the Japanese army at the front, and made to serve as "comfort women〈慰安婦〉."

with coupons, items were simply unavailable[100]. Every adult was allotted 2.3 gō (合) (330 g) of rice per day, but this distribution also ran into difficulties and rice was increasingly replaced with **substitutes** (代用食) such as potatoes and flour.

From the latter half of 1944, **air raids on Japan** (本土空襲) intensified, with US bombers flying from airfields on the island of Saipan. Initially the air raids aimed to destroy arms factories, but they soon escalated to indiscriminate bombing using incendiary bombs so the nation would lose the will to fight. In the cities, people demolished buildings and excavated air raid shelters, while munitions factories were relocated to rural areas, people moved to stay with rural relatives, and mass **evacuations of schoolchildren** (学童疎開) from the National Schools began.

MASS EVACUATION OF SCHOOLCHILDREN
Schoolchildren evacuations began in July 1944, and more than 410,000 children were separated from their parents and housed in inns and temples in the countryside.

In the Great Tōkyō Air Raid (東京大空襲) on March 10, 1945, some 300 B-29 Superfortresses dropped approximately 1,700 tons of incendiary bombs on the heavily-populated downtown areas, resulting in an estimated 100,000 people burning to death in one night. Air raids were also carried out against smaller cities throughout the country, resulting in the loss of approximately 2,210,000 homes due to fire, 260,000 dead, 420,000 injured, and the destruction of major production facilities, according to reports by the Air Defense Headquarters of the Ministry of Home Affairs.

Defeat

In October 1944, US forces landed on Leyte Island (レイテ島) in order to recapture the Philippines, and succeeded in doing so after an intense battle[101]. US forces then

---

[100] In a household survey conducted one year after the outbreak of the war, over one-third of the total purchases of grains, and nearly half of all raw fish, dry goods, and vegetables were made on the black market. Moreover, the daily calorie intake per person fell below 2,000 kilocalories in 1942, and had dropped to 1,793 kilocalories by 1945. Among the major powers participating in the Second World War, these figures were extremely low. Even Japanese occupied territories overseas faced a severe economic situation due to military inflation.

[101] The Combined Fleet was defeated by US warships off Leyte, leaving the Imperial Japanese Navy without the capacity for systematic military operations. It was around this time that the navy first employed the Shinpū Tokubetsu Kōgekitai 〈神風特別攻撃隊〉 (Divine Wind Special Attack Unit, often referred to as Kamikaze) to carry out suicide attacks.

The Battle of Okinawa

The US forces, having landed on the central part of Okinawa Main Island, gained control over two nearby airfields and divided the island into north and south. During this juncture, the Japanese military staged an air offensive employing Kamikaze aircraft, but were unable to repel the US fleet from the waters of Okinawa. In preparation for a protracted battle, the Japanese forces defending Okinawa drew American troops inland for a counterattack. This led to a fierce ground battle that enmeshed the island residents, resulting in an enormous number of casualties (including those driven to group suicide) before the end of organized resistance on June 23. According to the Okinawa Prefectural Government National Health Insurance and Relief Division, the number of military and civilian fatalities exceeded 180,000.

captured Iōtō 硫黄島 (Iwo Jima) in March 1945, and proceeded to land on Okinawa Main Island 沖縄本島 that April. After a battle that lasted nearly three months and embroiled the islanders, Okinawa too fell to the US (**Battle of Okinawa** 沖縄戦). Japan's defeat was now inevitable. Immediately after the US landing on Okinawa, the Koiso Kuniaki Cabinet resigned, and Suzuki Kantarō 鈴木貫太郎 (1867-1948), who had long served as the tennō's Grand Chamberlain and enjoyed his trust, organized the succeeding cabinet. In the European theatre, the Allied counteroffensive had begun in 1943. Italy had surrendered in September that same year, followed by the unconditional surrender of Germany in May 1945, leaving Japan completely isolated. The Japanese military continued to call for a decisive battle on the home islands, but the Suzuki Cabinet sought to persuade the Soviet Union to mediate peace negotiations.

However, a summit meeting, the **Yalta Conference** ヤルタ会談, had already taken place among the US, the UK and the Soviet Union in Yalta, a city on the Crimean Peninsula, in February 1945[102]. In July, the three countries held the Potsdam Conference ポツダム会談 in

[102] Prior to this, in 1943, US President Franklin D. Roosevelt, British Prime Minister Winston Churchill〈チャーチル〉, and Chairman of the National Government of the Republic of China Jiang Jieshi held talks in Cairo, Egypt, where the decision was made that the Allied powers would continue fighting exhaustively until Japan's unconditional surrender. They also decided on the policy of handling Japanese territories: Manchuria, Taiwan, and the Pescadores〈澎湖諸島〉 would be returned to China; Korea would become independent; and Japan would also lose the South Sea Islands which were under its mandate. The text of these decisions was termed the Cairo Declaration〈カイロ宣言〉. At the Yalta Conference, in addition to discussing postwar strategies regarding Germany, Roosevelt, Churchill, and General Secretary of the Communist Party of the Soviet Union Joseph Stalin concluded a secret agreement for the Soviets to join the war against Japan two to three months after the surrender of Germany, in exchange for the return of Karafuto (South Sakhalin), transfer of the Chishima Islands (Kuril Islands), and access to Dalian and Port Arthur as free trade ports.

POTSDAM DECLARATION

Article 6. There must be eliminated for all time the authority and influence of those who have deceived and misled the people of Japan into embarking on world conquest, for we insist that a new order of peace, security and justice will be impossible until irresponsible militarism is driven from the world.

Article 10. We do not intend that the Japanese shall be enslaved as a race or destroyed as a nation, but stern justice shall be meted out to all war criminals, including those who have visited cruelties upon our prisoners. The Japanese Government shall remove all obstacles to the revival and strengthening of democratic tendencies among the Japanese people. Freedom of speech, of religion, and of thought, as well as respect for the fundamental human rights shall be established.

Article 12. The occupying forces of the Allies shall be withdrawn from Japan as soon as these objectives have been accomplished and there has been established in accordance with the freely expressed will of the Japanese people a peacefully inclined and responsible government.

Article 13. We call upon the government of Japan to proclaim now the unconditional surrender of all Japanese armed forces, and to provide proper and adequate assurances of their good faith in such action. The alternative for Japan is prompt and utter destruction.

A summary of the other main articles include: (Article 8) the reduction of Japanese territories; (Article 9) the dissolution of military forces; and (Article 11) maintenance of peacetime industry other than the arms industry, and eventual participation in world trade relations.

Potsdam, a Berlin suburb, to discuss issues regarding the postwar settlement in Europe. The US took the opportunity to discuss policies towards Japan with the UK, and in the name of the three powers engaged in war with Japan – the US, the UK, and China – issued the **Potsdam Declaration** (ポツダム宣言), which called for the unconditional surrender of the Japanese armed forces and set the terms for Japan's postwar settlement[103].

The US, having interpreted the Japanese government's response of "mokusatsu" (黙殺) (to keep silent, withhold comment, or ignore) as a rejection of the Potsdam Declaration, dropped two **atomic bombs** (原子爆弾), manufactured for the first time in history, on **Hiroshima** (広島) on August 6, and **Nagasaki** (長崎) on August 9. On August 8, the Soviet Union, in defiance of the Soviet-Japanese Neutrality Pact, declared war on Japan, and promptly invaded Manchuria and Korea[104]. The Japanese Army still insisted on a decisive battle for the home islands, but Shōwa Tennō intervened, making a

[103] US President Truman〈トルーマン〉, Churchill (later replaced by Clement Attlee〈アトリー〉), and Stalin held talks in Potsdam. The subject of discussion was the postwar settlement of Germany.

[104] The Kwantung Army was utterly defeated by the invading Soviet troops, and many Japanese, including Manchukuo settlers, met a tragic end. Even survivors encountered severe hardship during the withdrawal, resulting in many Japanese war orphans being left behind in China.

DEVASTATION OF HYPOCENTERS IN HIROSHIMA (ABOVE) **AND NAGASAKI**
The atomic bomb exploded over the center of Hiroshima City, killing approximately 200,000 people. In Nagasaki, it is estimated that over 70,000 people died. Even today, many people continue to suffer from radiation sickness.

"sacred decision" (seidan 聖断)[ix] to accept the Potsdam Declaration, and on August 14, the government informed the Allies. At noon on August 15, the tennō announced to the nation via radio broadcast that the war was over. On September 2, representatives of the Japanese government and military signed the instrument of surrender on the US battleship USS *Missouri* in Tōkyō Bay, thus bringing the four-year Pacific War to an end.

[i] Most of the alliances (同盟) and ententes (協商) have similar names in English and Japanese, but the agreement between the UK and France is an exception. It was officially called the "Entente Cordiale" in both English and French.

[ii] Normally in English writing out numbers is more formal than just employing Arabic numerals, and thus "First World War" is more formal than "World War I" and therefore more common in academic writing. Similarly, "May Fourth Movement" is more formal than "May 4th Movement," but there are occasionally exceptions, like "May 15 Incident" where English scholars have copied Japanese convention when translating. Note that, for the same reason, while "15th" would technically be more correct in the previous example, it is instead left as "15."

[iii] In English, "騒動" in this context could be rendered in various ways (e.g. disturbance, riot, uprising), but "米騒動," based on the nature of the events, are referred to in English as "rice riots."

[iv] The Versailles Settlement and Washington Settlement have the same type of name in Japanese (体制) but not always in English. The former is almost always "Versailles Settlement," whereas the latter is frequently called "Washington Settlement" but also "Washington System." For ease of understanding, this textbook refers to both as "settlements."

[v] The Chinese Nationalist Party (中国国民党) is often called in English "Guomindang" from the Mandarin Chinese reading of the term "国民党," or "GMD" for short. Similarly, the older reading "Kuomintang" is often shortened to "KMT," and both are used in English by the present-day party in Taiwan. The Chinese Communist Party (中国共産党) is, in the same way, often shortened in English to "CCP," an acronym based on its English title rather than its Chinese one (Gongchangdang). To avoid confusion, this textbook consistently uses "Chinese Nationalist Party" and "Chinese Communist Party."

[vi] "Fengtian" (奉天) was the name of both a city and a province in northeastern China, but while in English the province is always rendered "Fengtian," the city is called not only "Fengtian" but also "Shenyang" or "Mukden."

[vii] This event tends to more frequently be called the "Nanjing Massacre" in English. Note that in Japanese historiography most modern events are consistently referred to as "incidents" (事件), and this should not be misconstrued as reflecting any particular ideological perspective.

[viii] "Gozen kaigi" (御前会議), literally a "Conference Before [His Majesty]" is usually rendered as "Imperial Conference" in English, and this textbook follows suit.

[ix] "Seidan" (聖断), literally "sacred decision" or "sacred judgement," is a special term referring to a decision by a tennō with no direct English equivalent but which is also sometimes rendered as "imperial decision."

Chapter

11

Japan under Occupation

1 Occupation and Reforms

The Establishment of the Postwar World Order

The underlying premise when constructing the postwar order was introspection on the enormous casualties and sacrifices wrought by the Second World War, which had erupted only twenty years after the first one. In discussions during and shortly after the war, the US, the UK, and the Soviet Union decided to establish the **United Nations** 国際連合 (UN), to replace the League of Nations 国際連盟, which had failed to prevent the recurrence of a global war. The UN, which was established in October 1945 with 51 participating nations, installed a **Security Council** 安全保障理事会[1] with five major powers – the US, the UK, France, the Soviet Union, and China – as permanent members, and invested it with great authority to decide on the implementation of measures, including military action, in response to threats to peace.

Furthermore, in light of the mistakes made in the Treaty of Versailles ヴェルサイユ条約, which had imposed vast reparations on the defeated nations, the UN elected instead to reform the states and societies of the defeated nations into peaceful institutions through extended occupation, thereby preventing them from resorting to war again.

In this way, the victorious countries, cooperating through a system centered on the UN and undertaking the occupation of the defeated nations, were expected to give rise to a stable postwar order. However, the US and the Soviet Union, which possessed enormous military and economic power, came to hold overwhelming global influence compared to the Western European countries, which had been exhausted by the two world wars. Moreover, after the war mutual distrust and conflicts of interest between these two superpowers intensified. Subsequently, the postwar world developed around this **US-Soviet conflict** 米ソ対立.

On the other hand, many of the Western colonies had been promised indepen-

[1] The Security Council consists of fifteen members, of which five are permanent and ten are elected. Passing an important resolution requires the approval of nine members, but if any permanent member votes against it, this is called a veto and the resolution cannot be passed.

dence after the war in exchange for wartime cooperation, and this, combined with the destruction of their livelihoods during the conflict, led to the rise of national liberation movements as the war drew to a close[2]. In Korea too there was a growing movement for independence, but with Japan's surrender the peninsula was divided at the 38th parallel north (北緯38度線), with the north occupied by Soviet forces and the south by US forces. Consequently, under divided military rule, the country could not achieve united independence.

Initial Occupation Policies

In line with the Potsdam Declaration (ポツダム宣言), it was decided that Japan would be occupied by the Allies[3]. While Germany, the other defeated nation, was divided and occupied under the direct military rule of four nations (the US, the UK, France, and the Soviet Union), Japan was essentially occupied solely by the US military and was governed indirectly by the Japanese government, which operated under the directives and recommendations of the **General Headquarters, Supreme Commander for the Allied Powers** (連合国軍最高司令官総司令部) (GHQ/SCAP), headed by General **Douglas MacArthur** (マッカーサー) (1880-1964)[4].

The Far Eastern Commission (極東委員会) was established in Washington, D.C. to serve as the supreme organization for determining Allied occupation policy for Japan, while the Allied Council for Japan (対日理事会) was installed in Tōkyō as an advisory organ for the Supreme Commander. Nevertheless, the planning and enforcement of occupation policies was conducted under the direction of the US government[5]. The initial goal of the occu-

---

[2] Among territories occupied by Japan, Indonesia and Vietnam also declared their independence, but their respective imperial suzerains, the Netherlands and France, tried to suppress these movements by force, resulting in intense conflict.

[3] The Soviet Union occupied territory including the northern part of the Korean peninsula, South Sakhalin〈南樺太〉, and the Kuril Islands〈千島列島〉, while the US occupied the southern part of the Korean peninsula, southwestern islands including the Amami〈奄美諸島〉 and Ryūkyū Islands〈琉球諸島〉, and the Ogasawara Islands〈小笠原諸島〉. All these territories were put under military rule. Taiwan was returned to China, and Japanese sovereignty was limited to the four home islands and smaller islands determined by the Allies.

[4] Demands made by the occupying forces to the Japanese government were enacted via direct decree ("Potsdam Decrees〈「ポツダム勅令」〉") without waiting for the enactment of laws, and possessed an extralegal character surpassing even the Constitution. Furthermore, the US government had granted MacArthur the authority to implement direct actions whenever he was not satisfied with the measures taken by the Japanese government.

[5] The status of the US vis-à-vis Japan, which it had pushed to surrender through air raids and the atomic bombs, was exceptional: it could issue interim directives in emergency situations without waiting for a decision from the Far Eastern Commission. Even the Allied Council for Japan – composed of the US, the UK, the Soviet Union and China – did not have much influence, except in the case of agrarian reform.

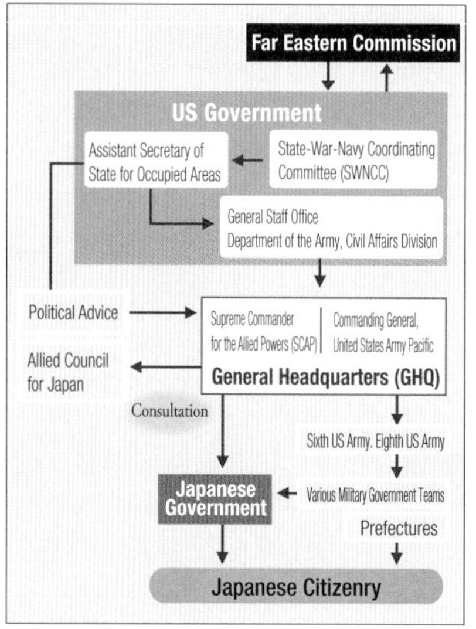

OCCUPATION MANAGEMENT OF JAPAN: CHAIN OF COMMAND

pation was to transform Japanese society through demilitarization and democratization, and to prevent Japan from becoming a threat to the US and East Asia again.

Accompanying the acceptance of the Potsdam Declaration, the Suzuki Kantarō 鈴木貫太郎 Cabinet resigned en masse, enabling Royal Prince Higashikuni no Miya Naruhiko 東久邇宮稔彦 (1887-1990) to form a new one, under which the arrival of Allied occupation forces from the end of August 1945, the prompt disarmament of the former Japanese military, and the signing of the Instrument of Surrender were all smoothly carried out. However, the cabinet, advocating that the "entire nation take responsibility for the war" (Ichioku Sōzange)「一億総懺悔」 and "protect the kokutai" (Kokutai Goji)「国体護持」, took issue with occupation policies, and when in October that same year GHQ ordered the abolition of the Peace Preservation Law 治安維持法 and the Special Higher Police 特別高等警察（特高）, and the immediate release of political prisoners like communists under the **Human Rights Directive** 人権指令[6], while encouraging free discussion about the tennō, the cabinet resigned. Shidehara Kijūrō 幣原喜重郎, well-known by the British and Americans for his cooperative diplomacy, became the next prime minister. In addition to requiring him to liberalize the Constitution, MacArthur also orally instructed Shidehara to carry out **Five Major Reforms** 五大改革: grant women suffrage, encourage the formation of labor unions, liberalize the education system, abolish the secret police, and democratize economic institutions. GHQ also prohibited government support or supervision of the Shintō religion and Shintō shrines under the Shintō Directive 神道指令, and dismantled State Shintō, which had served as the ideological basis for militarism and tennō worship during wartime, thereby separating religion and the state.

The demobilization and disarmament of some 7.89 million army and navy personnel deployed both inside and outside the country proceeded, and the Japanese military was promptly dismantled, ceasing to exist. From September through December

[6] Advances were made in ensuring civil liberties, including freedom of thought and speech, but on the other hand, criticism of the occupying forces was prohibited by the "Press Code〈プレス＝コード〉" (Newspaper Publication Directive〈新聞発行綱領〉), and newspapers and other publications were subject to prior censorship.

The Tōkyō Trials

The Potsdam Declaration had specified that war criminals would face "stern justice," but immediately after the defeat GHQ arrested many prewar and wartime leaders for planning and carrying out wars of aggression, under the category of "crimes against peace" (Class A war crimes). The International Prosecution Section (IPS), established as an office of GHQ, took the lead in selecting the defendants, resulting in 28 suspects being provisionally indicted by the International Military Tribunal for the Far East in April 1946.

The trials concluded in November 1948 with all defendants (excluding two who died from illness and one found mentally unfit) being found guilty, and the seven who received the death penalty (including Tōjō Hideki〈東条英機〉) were executed in December. The phenomenon of individual national leaders being tried as war criminals was almost unprecedented. However, there were differences of opinion among the eleven judges, and along with the majority decision that was read, dissenting opinions were written by Judge Pal〈パル〉 of India and Judge Röling〈レーリンク〉 of the Netherlands.

Aside from the Class A war criminals, more than 5,700 other individuals were prosecuted in trials conducted in Asia by the Netherlands, the UK, and other related countries for violations of international law of war by mistreating prisoners-of-war and civilians (Class B & C war crimes). Of these, 984 were sentenced to death and 475 to life sentences.

1945, GHQ arrested a series of wartime leaders such as top officials and former military officers. Of these, 28 were indicted for Class A war crimes, and were put on trial at the International Military Tribunal for the Far East (極東国際軍事裁判所), often called the **Tōkyō Trials** (東京裁判), that began in May 1946 in Tōkyō.

With the arrests of suspected war criminals ongoing, the issue of the tennō's war responsibility was also discussed at both the domestic and international level. However, in order to avoid the inevitable upheaval that might result from abolishing the Tennō-sei (天皇制) outright, GHQ did not designate the tennō a war crime suspect, and instead thought to use the system as a tool for the occupation. At the beginning of 1946, Shōwa Tennō (昭和天皇) made what came to be called the "Humanity Declaration," (人間宣言) in which he denied that he was a "living deity" (Akitsumikami) (「現御神」).

Moreover, in January 1946 GHQ ordered a **purge of public officials** (公職追放), in which war criminals, military personnel, ultra-nationalists and Imperial Rule Assistance Association (大政翼賛会) leaders were expelled from office. By May 1948, 210,000 leading figures ranging from the political, financial and bureaucratic worlds to journalism, were held responsible for wartime actions and ousted from their positions.

Further, under demilitarization policies, the arms industry was banned and ship ownership restricted, while industrial facilities were dismantled and provided as reparations in kind to nations damaged by the war, including China and countries in Southeast Asia.

Democratization Policies

GHQ considered the zaibatsu (財閥) and the sharecropping systems, which represented the backwardness of the Japanese economy, to be fertile ground for militarism, and made dismantling them a major component of economic democratization. In November 1945, the assets of fifteen zaibatsu – including Mitsui (三井), Mitsubishi (三菱), Sumitomo (住友), and Yasuda (安田) – were ordered frozen and dispersed. In the following year, the **Holding Company Liquidity Committee** (持株会社整理委員会) was established to take over shares and other assets owned by designated holding companies and zaibatsu and sell them to the general public, in an effort to end the control zaibatsu had wielded over enterprises through stock ownership (**zaibatsu dissolution** (財閥解体)). Furthermore, in 1947 the **Antitrust Law** (独占禁止法) prohibited holding companies, cartels or trusts, and the **Law for the Elimination of Excessive Concentration of Economic Power** (過度経済力集中排除法) led to the breakup of large monopolies[7].

GHQ, holding that farmer poverty was one of the main reasons behind Japanese invasions overseas, decided to implement **agrarian reform** (農地改革) to end the sharecropping system and create large numbers of stable, independent farmers. In December 1945, the Japanese government decided to implement the first round of agrarian reform, but this was insufficient to address the sharecropping system, so a second round of agrarian reform began to be carried out in October 1946 under the **Law Concerning Special Measures for the Establishment of Independent Farmers** (自作農創設特別措置法)[8], which was promulgated based on GHQ counsel, and by 1950 was almost completed. All leased land belonging to absentee landowners, and leased land belonging to resident landowners in excess of a set amount

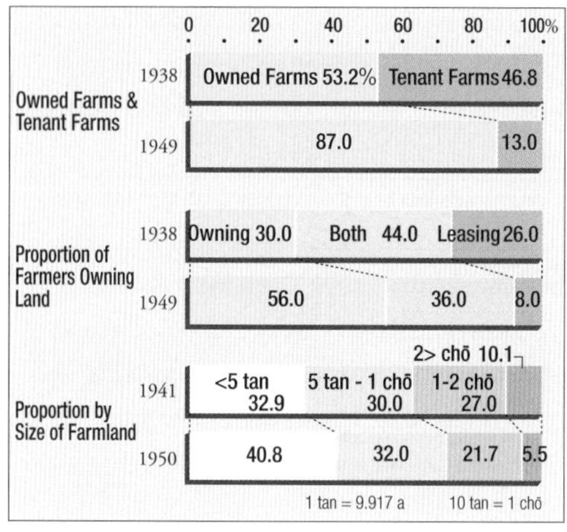

AGRARIAN REFORM

---

[7] In February 1948, 325 enterprises were designated under this law, but due to changes in occupation policy, ultimately only 11, including Japan Iron & Steel Co.〈日本製鉄〉 and Mitsubishi Heavy Industries〈三菱重工〉, were broken up.

[8] In each municipality, a farmland committee〈農地委員会〉 was elected – consisting of 30% landowners, 20% independent farmers, and 50% tenant farmers – which was then responsible for the buying and selling of agricultural land. As for the leased land that remained, the rent became an officially set amount.

(one hectare on prefectural average, four in Hokkaidō), was compulsorily purchased by the state, which then sold it preferentially to tenant farmers at a low price. As a result, tenant farms, which used to comprise nearly half of all farmland, were reduced to ten percent, and the majority of farmers became small independent farmers possessing less than a hectare each, while the large landowners lost their economic power and social prestige[9].

From the perspective of ending the limitations on the local market caused by the low-wage structure, and eliminating the basis for foreign aggression, GHQ labor policies were focused on establishing basic workers' rights and supporting the creation of labor unions. First, in December 1945 the **Labor Union Law** 労働組合法 was enacted, guaranteeing the rights of workers to organize, engage in collective bargaining, and conduct strikes[10]. The next year the **Labor Relations Adjustment Law** 労働関係調整法 was enacted, followed by the **Labor Standards Law** 労働基準法, which stipulated an eight-hour workday, in 1947 (collectively, these were known as the "Three Labor Laws" 労働三法), the same year that the Ministry of Labor (Rōdōshō 労働省) was established.

TEXTBOOK BLOTTED OUT WITH INK
Since new textbooks were not yet available, students were made to blot out inappropriate content with ink. Consequently, some pages were almost useless.

Liberal reform of the education system was another important pillar of democratization. In October 1945, GHQ ordered the deletion of inappropriate passages from textbooks and the expulsion of militaristic teachers from the profession (education purge, kyōshoku tsuihō 教職追放), followed by the temporary banning of moral education, Japanese history, and geography classes[11]. Following recommendations by

[9] The agrarian movement, led by the Nihon Nōmin Kumiai ‹日本農民組合› (Japan Farmers' Union), which was reestablished in 1946, became a driving force for agrarian reform, but weakened after said reform was implemented. Starting in December 1947, agricultural cooperatives ‹農業協同組合 (農協)› were set up in many areas to support agricultural management.

[10] Labor unions continued to be founded in both the private and public sectors, and in 1946 the right-wing Nihon Rōdō Kumiai Sōdōmei ‹日本労働組合総同盟› (Japanese Federation of Trade Unions, often called "Sōdōmei ‹総同盟›") and the left-wing Zen Nihon Sangyō Betsu Rōdō Kumiai Kaigi ‹全日本産業別労働組合会議› (Congress of Industrial Unions of Japan, often called "Sanbetsu Kaigi ‹産別会議›") were created as national organizations.

[11] The Ministry of Education completely revised the contents of the hitherto nationally-mandated textbooks, publishing texts like *Kuni no Ayumi* ‹「くにのあゆみ」› (Path of the Nation) and *Atarashii Kenpō no Hanashi* ‹「あたらしい憲法のはなし」› (The Story of the New Constitution). *Kuni no Ayumi*, the last nationally-mandated history textbook, began with archaeological description rather than national founding myths, but with the school subject becoming "social studies" under the new school system, this text fell out of use.

the United States Education Mission to Japan (アメリカ教育使節団), the **Fundamental Law of Education** (教育基本法), which set out principles such as coeducation and equal opportunity for education, was enacted in 1947, and compulsory education was extended from six years to nine. In accordance with the **School Education Law** (学校教育法) enacted at the same time, the new 6-3-3-4 school system (6 years primary, 3 junior, 3 secondary, and 4 post-secondary) was inaugurated in April. Universities grew in number and became more mainstream, and the number of female university students also increased. In 1948, publicly-elected boards of education were established in each prefecture and municipality, decentralizing educational administration.

The Revival of Party Politics

While democratization policies were being implemented one after another, various political parties were revived or newly established. In October 1945, the Kyōsantō (日本共産党) began to operate as a legal party, led by Tokuda Kyūichi (徳田球一) (1894-1953) and others who had been released from prison on GHQ orders. In November, several new parties emerged: the Nihon Shakaitō (日本社会党) (Japan Socialist Party, JSP, hereafter Shakaitō), which united the former proletarian parties; the Nihon Jiyūtō (日本自由党) (Japan Liberal Party), a successor to the Seiyūkai (立憲政友会) composed largely of members who had not been endorsed during the wartime general election; and the Nihon Shinpotō (日本進歩党) (Japan Progressive Party), a successor to the Minseitō (立憲民政党), that was made up mainly of endorsed members who had belonged to the Dai Nihon Seijikai (大日本政治会) under the Taisei Yokusankai system. Then, in December, the Nihon Kyōdōtō (日本協同党) (Japan Cooperative Party), which advocated cooperation between labor and capital, was formed. However, GHQ did not want former wartime collaborators running as candidates in the upcoming general election, and consequently in January 1946, under the aforementioned purge of public officials, all Diet members who had been endorsed in the wartime election were banned from holding office, throwing the political world into chaos.

In December 1945, the House of Representatives Election Law (衆議院議員選挙法) was substantially revised, and a new election law that recognized **women's suffrage** (女性参政権) for the first time was enacted. Since the right to vote was now given to all men and women over twenty years of age, the number of eligible voters nearly tripled. In April 1946, the first postwar general elections were held: 39 women became members of the Diet, and the Nihon Jiyūtō became the leading party. In May that same year, **Yoshida Shigeru** (吉田茂) (1878-1967), who had been a pro-Anglo-American diplomat in the prewar era, replaced the purged Hatoyama Ichirō (鳩山一郎) (1883-1959), and with the cooperation of the Nihon Shinpotō formed the First Yoshida Cabinet.

The Establishment of the Japanese Constitution

In October 1945, the Shidehara Kiūirō Cabinet had been ordered by GHQ to revise the Constitution, and established the Constitutional Problems Investigation Committee 憲法問題調査委員会 (chaired by Matsumoto Jōji 松本烝治, 1877-1954) within the government. However, since the draft amendments prepared by the committee were conservative ones that still recognized the sovereignty of the tennō, GHQ itself hurriedly prepared an English draft (the "MacArthur Draft" マッカーサー草案)[12] and submitted it to the Japanese government in February 1946, before the Far Eastern Commission got underway. The government slightly corrected it and translated it into Japanese, then published it as their own draft. For procedural reasons, the enactment of the new Constitution took the form of an amendment to the Constitution of the Empire of Japan 大日本帝国憲法, which, after being further revised and passed by the House of Representatives and the House of Peers[13], was promulgated as the **Constitution of Japan** 日本国憲法 on November 3, 1946, and came into effect on May 3, 1947.

The new Constitution was ground-breaking in its clarification of the three principles of **popular sovereignty** 主権在民, **pacifism** 平和主義, and **respect for fundamental human rights** 基本的人権の尊重. The Diet, composed of members directly elected by the citizenry, was made "the highest organ of state power," while the tennō became the "symbol [...] of the unity of the People" with no political power (**Symbolic Tennō-sei** 象徴天皇制). Moreover, the first paragraph of Article 9 **renounced war** 戦争の放棄 as a "means of settling international disputes," and the second paragraph stated that in "order to accomplish [this] aim" military forces "will never be maintained" and "The right of belligerency of the state will not be recognized," something without precedent worldwide.

Following the spirit of the new Constitution, many laws were enacted or substantially revised. The Civil Code, which was amended in 1947 (**new Civil Code** 新民法),

---

[12] In December 1945, the private Constitution Research Group〈憲法研究会〉led by Takano Iwasaburō〈高野岩三郎〉published an "Outline of a Constitution Draft〈「憲法草案要綱」〉," which incorporated the principles of popular sovereignty and a constitutional monarchy, and submitted it to GHQ and the Japanese government. When writing the "MacArthur Draft," GHQ also drew on this draft as a reference.

[13] The GHQ draft did not become the new Constitution as it was. Rather, various additions and corrections were incorporated in the process of government drafting and Diet deliberation. In the draft, the Diet was unicameral, consisting only of the House of Representatives, but due to urging from the Japanese government, the House of Councilors was added, making the system bicameral. Furthermore, when the draft was being revised in the House of Representatives, at the suggestion of Ashida Hitoshi〈芦田均〉the phrase "In order to accomplish the aim of the preceding paragraph" was added to the second paragraph of Article 9 regarding not retaining military forces, thereby leaving room for the retention of a force for the purpose of self-defense.

JAPANESE CONSTITUTION

〔Preamble〕 We, the Japanese people, acting through our duly elected representatives in the National Diet, determined that we shall secure for ourselves and our posterity the fruits of peaceful cooperation with all nations and the blessings of liberty throughout this land, and resolved that never again shall we be visited with the horrors of war through the action of government, do proclaim that sovereign power resides with the people and do firmly establish this Constitution. [...]

Article 1. The Emperor shall be the symbol of the State and of the unity of the People, deriving his position from the will of the people with whom resides sovereign power.

Article 9. Aspiring sincerely to an international peace based on justice and order, the Japanese people forever renounce war as a sovereign right of the nation and the threat or use of force as means of settling international disputes.

In order to accomplish the aim of the preceding paragraph, land, sea, and air forces, as well as other war potential, will never be maintained. The right of belligerency of the state will not be recognized.

Article 11. The people shall not be prevented from enjoying any of the fundamental human rights. These fundamental human rights guaranteed to the people by this Constitution shall be conferred upon the people of this and future generations as eternal and inviolate rights.

Article 25. All people shall have the right to maintain the minimum standards of wholesome and cultured living.

In all spheres of life, the State shall use its endeavors for the promotion and extension of social welfare and security, and of public health.

Article 28. The right of workers to organize and to bargain and act collectively is guaranteed.

abolished the patriarch-headed, household-centered family system, and established a new family system with equal rights for men and women[14]. The Code of Criminal Procedure (刑事訴訟法) was completely revised with a focus on respecting human rights, while the Penal Code (刑法) was partially amended to abolish crimes such as high treason (大逆罪), lèse-majesté (不敬罪), and adultery (姦通罪). 1947 also saw the enactment of the **Local Autonomy Law** (地方自治法), under which prefectural governors and municipal mayors would be publicly elected, and the Ministry of Home Affairs (内務省), which had exercised power over local administration and police, was abolished on GHQ orders. The Police Law (警察法), which stipulated the formation of the National Rural Police (国家地方警察) alongside municipal police forces, was promulgated at the end of 1947 and came into effect the following year.

[14] The right of the head of a household to assert dominion over family members was denied, equal inheritance of property replaced the patriarchal inheritance system, and regulations enabling male dominance in marriage and family relations were abolished.

Daily Life Disruption, and the Rise of Mass Movements

The daily lives of the people had been utterly devastated by the war. Those whose homes had burned down in air raids took shelter from the elements in air-raid shelters or in barracks constructed on burnt-out ruins. Industrial production fell to less than one third of prewar levels. The **demobilization** 復員 and **repatriation** 引揚げ of soldiers swelled the population, and brought with it a sudden increase in the number of unemployed people[15]. 1945 was a year with a record-breaking poor harvest, resulting in severe food shortages[16]. Rice rationing was insufficient, leading to foods such as sweet potatoes and corn being used as substitutes. As delays and non-delivery continued, the urban populace avoided starvation by "**kaidashi**" 買出し ("going shopping," meaning going to farming villages to buy food), using the **black markets** 闇市, and producing their own food at home.

In addition to the extreme shortage of goods, there was an increase in currency being issued due to postwar management and so forth[17], which caused raging inflation.

Demobilization and Repatriation

At the time of Japan's defeat, there were around 3.1 million Japanese soldiers overseas, and around 3.2 million ordinary residents. Thus, nearly 6.3 million Japanese, consisting of residents who had lost their property as well as demobilized soldiers, were to be repatriated to Japan.

Residents of what had been Manchukuo〈満州国〉 faced a particularly tragic situation, with many dying from starvation and disease, while numbers of children were left behind as orphans. The approximately 600,000 soldiers and civilians that surrendered to the Soviet Union were transferred to camps in Siberia, where they were forced to work for years in extreme cold, resulting in more than 60,000 of them dying. Repatriations from the Soviet Union took the longest, lasting until 1956.

China	1,541,329	Okinawa	69,416
Manchuria	1,045,525	Islands Adjacent to Main Japanese Islands	62,389
Korea	919,904	Vietnam	32,303
Taiwan	479,544	Hong Kong	19,347
Former Soviet Union	472,951	Indonesia	15,593
Sakhalin & Kuril Islands	293,533	Hawaii	3,659
Australia	138,843	New Zealand	797
Philippines	133,123	Other	937,461
Pacific Islands	130,968	Total	6,296,685

NUMBERS OF REPATRIATED JAPANESE (AS OF JANUARY 2003, INCLUDING SOLDIERS)

[15] Besides demobilized soldiers and repatriated persons, there were also people rendered unemployed due to the closing of munitions factories and the like.

[16] From an average of 9.11 million tons of rice per year between 1940 and 1944, the total rice yield dropped by more than 30% to 5.87 million tons in 1945.

[17] This was due to the large amounts of temporary military spending immediately following the defeat, as well as factors such as the Bank of Japan increasing its loans to the private sector.

"KAIDASHI" TRAINS
People in need of food got on packed trains headed for farming villages. This photo is from the autumn of 1945, near Hyūga Station〈日向駅〉 on the Sōbu Main Line〈総武本線〉 in Chiba Prefecture.

In February 1946, the Shidehara Cabinet attempted to decrease the amount of money in circulation by blocking deposits and prohibiting the circulation of the old yen that had continued to be used until then (**Emergency Financial Measures Ordinance** 金融緊急措置令), but the effect was only temporary. The First Yoshida Shigeru Cabinet responded to the situation by establishing the Headquarters for Economic Stabilization 経済安定本部, and by adopting in December 1946 the **Priority Production System** 傾斜生産方式, which concentrated materials and funding on key industrial sectors such as coal or steel. In the following January, the Reconstruction Finance Bank 復興金融金庫（復金） was founded to provide funds to vital industries including electric power and shipping.

The crises people encountered in daily life fueled mass movements. Immediately after the war, the struggle for production control, in which workers autonomously undertook business and production, took off. Moreover, a general strike involving key industries was planned for February 1, 1947, focused on public sector employees organized by the Government Employees' Committee for Joint Strike Action 全官公庁共同闘争委員会 with the aim of bringing down the Yoshida Cabinet, but was halted by GHQ order the day before it was to commence.

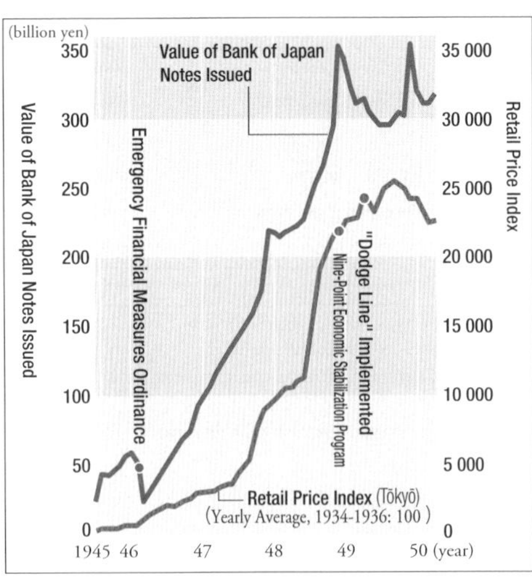

POSTWAR CURRENCY ISSUING AND PRICE INDEX

In April 1947, in order to form a new government under the new Constitution, elections were held for both houses of the Diet. Against a backdrop of the mass movements, the Shakaitō defeated the Nihon

Jiyūtō and the Minshutō 民主党 (Democratic Party) by a small margin, and became the largest party in the House of Representatives. Shakaitō chairman **Katayama Tetsu** 片山哲 (1887-1978) thus became the first prime minister under the new Constitution, and the Shakaitō formed a coalition cabinet with the Minshutō and the Kokumin Kyōdōtō 国民協同党 (National Cooperative Party). GHQ praised the birth of the new cabinet as evidence of Japan taking a "middle path" 「中道」 between conservatism and radicalism, but the cabinet struggled to coordinate policy due to the coalition, and after facing criticism from its left-wing faction over the issue of state control of coal mines, it resigned en masse in the following February. Subsequently, **Ashida Hitoshi** 芦田均 (1887-1959), president of the Minshutō, formed a cabinet under the same three-party coalition, but had to resign in the wake of a major bribery scandal (Shōwa Denkō Incident 昭和電工事件), which involved many people ranging from the political sphere right up to GHQ.

2 From the Dawn of the Cold War to Making Peace

East Asia and the Formation of the Cold War Order

After ending the Second World War with the power of the atomic bomb, the US, with its overwhelming power, inherited the mantle of global leadership from the UK[18]. In the Eastern European countries occupied by the Soviet Union, Soviet-style communist regimes were established, leaving the enormous and powerful Soviet Union ruling over those smaller "satellite states."

In response to this situation, in 1947 US President Truman トルーマン (1884-1972) announced the need for a policy to "contain" the Soviet Union, which became known as the Truman Doctrine トルーマン＝ドクトリン. Through the Marshall Plan マーシャル＝プラン[19] that same year, the US aided the reconstruction and military buildup of Western European countries, thereby demonstrating its intention to confront communist forces in Europe. Thus, two major blocs were formed: the Western Bloc, led by the US and based on capitalism and

[18] Beginning around the end of the Second World War, the US led initiatives to reconstruct a framework for a capitalist world economy, under a fixed exchange rate system – with the US dollar as a reserve currency – and free trade. The establishment of the International Monetary Fund (IMF)〈国際通貨基金〉 and the International Bank for Reconstruction and Development (IBRD, also known as the World Bank)〈国際復興開発銀行〉, as well as the conclusion of the General Agreement on Tariffs and Trade (GATT)〈関税及び貿易に関する一般協定〉 are illustrative examples.

[19] This plan, based on a proposal by US Secretary of State George Marshall〈マーシャル〉, was intended to aid the recovery of all of Europe, but the Soviet Union and Eastern European countries refused to accept it.

liberalism, and the Eastern Bloc, led by the Soviet Union and based on socialism and communism. In 1949, the **North Atlantic Treaty Organization** 北大西洋条約機構 **(NATO)**, a collective defense alliance among the US and Western European countries, was established. The Soviet Union, on the other hand, successfully developed an atomic bomb in 1949. In 1955, the Treaty of Friendship, Cooperation and Mutual Assistance, better known as the **Warsaw Pact** ワルシャワ条約機構 **(Warsaw Treaty Organization)**[i], was established as a collective defense alliance among the Soviet Union and seven Eastern European countries.

From then on, the nuclear-armed Western and Eastern Blocs continued to confront each other militarily, and engaged in an intense rivalry across many areas, including their spheres of influence, armaments, economic power, and ideology. This conflict, known as the **Cold War** 「冷戦」, gradually grew to encompass the entire world, and came to form the backbone of the postwar world order as the "Cold War system." Simultaneously, the credibility of the UN on international security became shaky.

In China, the Chinese Communist Party, with strong support from the farmers, won the civil war against the Chinese Nationalist Party 中国国民党, which was backed by the US, and the founding of the People's Republic of China 中華人民共和国 (PRC), headed by Chairman Mao Zedong 毛沢東 (1893-1976), was proclaimed in Beijing in October 1949. The following year, the Sino-Soviet Treaty of Friendship and Alliance 中ソ友好同盟相互援助条約 was concluded, and China joined the Eastern Bloc. Meanwhile, the defeated Chinese Nationalist Party retreated to the island of Taiwan to continue the Republic of China 中華民国 (ROC) under President Jiang Jieshi 蔣介石 (1887-1975). On the Korean peninsula, in 1948 the Democratic People's Republic 朝鮮民主主義人民共和国 of Korea (North Korea), with Kim Il-Sung 金日成 (1912-94) as premier, was founded in the Soviet-occupied region, and the Republic of Korea 大韓民国 (South Korea), with Rhee Syngman 李承晩 (1875-1965) as president, was founded in the area occupied by the US. Consequently, the division of Korea into north and south became entrenched.

A Shift in Occupation Policy

After it became clear in 1948 that the Communists had the upper hand in the Chinese Civil War, US occupation policy towards Japan changed. The US government decided to restore Japan as a politically stable, industrial nation that would be a major friendly state of the Western Bloc in East Asia[20]. For this reason, GHQ, asserting that the

---

[20] The shift in policy toward Japan was first announced in January 1948, in a speech delivered by Secretary of the Army Kenneth Royall ‹ロイヤル›. In October of the same year, the US government decided to promote Japan's economic recovery, based on the recommendation of diplomat George Kennan ‹ケナン›, one of the key players in US Cold War policy. The plan included a substantial transfer of administrative responsibility to the Japanese government, softening the purge of public officials, fostering private companies, and achieving a balanced budget.

original objectives of the occupation – demilitarization and democratization – had been achieved, changed its policy of holding down Japan's industrial production and instead strongly pushed for an economic recovery.

Japan's reparations to other countries were reduced, and the breakup of corporations under the Law for the Elimination of Excessive Concentration of Economic Power was substantially mitigated. In 1948, at GHQ's direction, the National Public Service Law 国家公務員法 was amended by Cabinet Order 201, depriving government employees, who had been the core of the labor movement, of their right to engage in labor disputes. In the following year, the purge of public officials was gradually lifted.

At the same time that occupation policy shifted, the centrist coalition government headed by Ashida Hitoshi collapsed, and was replaced by the Second Yoshida Shigeru Cabinet, of the Minshu Jiyūtō 民主自由党 (Democratic Liberal Party)[21]. In the general election held in January the following year, the Minshu Jiyūtō secured an absolute majority of seats, stabilizing the conservative government.

GHQ pursued a series of proactive measures to facilitate the revival of the Japanese economy. The Priority Production System, implemented under the Katayama-Ashida Cabinet, aided the recovery of production, but the large-scale fund injection through deficit financing worsened inflation. Thus, in December 1948, GHQ ordered the Second Yoshida Cabinet to implement the **Nine-Point Economic Stabilization Program** 経済安定九原則[22], which included balancing the general budget, enhancing tax collection, restricting credit extension by financial institutions, stabilizing wages, and controlling prices. To realize these goals, in the following year the American banker Joseph Dodge ドッジ (1890-1964) was dispatched to Japan as the financial adviser, where he implemented a series of measures called the "**Dodge Line** ドッジ＝ライン."

In accordance with Dodge's demands, the Third Yoshida Cabinet drafted a budget that did not allow for any deficit, and drastically reduced government expenditure. Next, **a single exchange rate** 単一為替レート of 1 USD = 360 JPY was set, and the Japanese economy linked to the international economy, in order to promote exports in the face of international competition. In 1949, the Shoup Mission, a team of tax specialists led by the economist Carl Shoup シャウプ (1902-2000), was sent to Japan to make recommendations, which resulted in a major overhaul of the tax system, including the adoption of a direct tax system and progressive income tax 累進所得税制.

---

[21] The Nihon Jiyūtō absorbed defectors from the Minshutō, and became the Minshu Jiyūtō. In 1950, it became the Jiyūtō〈自由党〉(Liberal Party).

[22] The program aimed to bring about the recovery, and self-sustainability, of the Japanese economy by stabilizing the value of the yen (by suppressing inflation via a thorough tightening policy) and through strengthening international competitiveness.

MATSUKAWA INCIDENT
Near Matsukawa Station in Fukushima Prefecture 〈福島県〉, loosened track bolts caused a passenger train to overturn, killing crew members. Several members of the Kyōsantō and labor union activists, including from the National Railway Workers' Union, were arrested, but acquitted at the trial.

Although the Dodge Line brought inflation under control, the recession that began in the latter half of 1949 worsened, and many small and medium-sized businesses went bankrupt. This factor, combined with layoffs in both the public and private sectors, caused unemployment to increase dramatically. Laborers – led by the Kyōsantō, the Congress of Industrial Unions of Japan, and the National Railway Workers' Union 国鉄労働組合 – fiercely opposed the forced layoffs, but were eventually defeated. The outcome was partly due to the fact that laborers were suspected of organizing three incidents involving the National Railway – the Shimoyama 下山事件, Mitaka 三鷹事件, and Matsukawa Incidents 松川事件[23] – that occurred that summer.

Japan and the Korean War

In June 1950, North Korea, inspired by the success of the Chinese Communist Revolution, crossed the 38th parallel north and invaded South Korea, intending to unite the peninsula by force. Thus began the **Korean War** 朝鮮戦争.

North Korean forces occupied Seoul and took the southern half of the peninsula by storm, but the US joined the war as part of the United Nations Command 国連軍 and pushed them back[24]. After the Battle of Incheon 仁川 in September 1950 proved a turning point for US forces, they crossed the 38th parallel north and neared the Chinese border. In response, the Chinese People's Volunteer Army entered the war on the North Korean side, and the frontline turned into a stalemate near the 38th parallel north[25].

---

[23] From July to August 1949, several incidents occurred: the mysterious death of Shimoyama Sadanori 〈下山定則〉, first president of Japanese National Railways, who had been carrying out major personnel cuts; an accident caused by a runaway unmanned train at Mitaka Station on the Chūō Line 〈中央線〉; and the derailment and overturning of a train near Matsukawa Station on the Tōhoku Main Line 〈東北本線〉. The government declared that the National Railway Workers' Union and the Kyōsantō were involved in these incidents, which dealt a major blow to the labor movement, but all three incidents remain unsolved.

[24] The UN Security Council, meeting without the Soviet representative, decided to use armed sanction against North Korea for its invasion.

[25] General MacArthur, Commander-in-Chief of the United Nations Command, advocated the bombing of northeast China in order to break the stalemate, but was abruptly removed from command in 1951 by President Truman, who feared an expansion of the war.

Ceasefire negotiations began in July 1951, and in July 1953 the Korean Armistice Agreement was signed in Panmunjom (板門店).

In Japan, when the Korean War broke out GHQ ordered the establishment of the **National Police Reserve** (警察予備隊) in order to fill the military vacuum left after US forces stationed in Japan were mobilized to Korea. The ban on former military personnel was also lifted, enabling them to be recruited into the National Police Reserve. Prior to this, GHQ had ordered the expulsion of Kyōsantō leaders from public office, and with the outbreak of war a "**Red Purge**" (レッドパージ) began, spreading from the mass media to private companies and government offices. In the labor movement, the left-wing Congress of Industrial Unions of Japan lost influence, while the **Nihon Rōdō Kumiai Sōhyōgikai** (日本労働組合総評議会) (**General Council of Trade Unions of Japan**, often called "Sōhyō" (総評)), an anti-Congress organization backed by GHQ, was formed and came to lead the movement[26].

The Peace and Security Treaties

Having become increasingly aware of Japan's strategic value in the Korean War, the US accelerated its efforts to end the occupation and promptly bring Japan into the Western Bloc. US foreign policy consultant John Foster Dulles (ダレス) (1888-1959), among others, paved the way to this goal through measures such as effectively excluding the Soviet Union and some other countries from the peace treaty with Japan (making it a separate peace (単独講和)) and arranging for US troops to be stationed in Japan even after the treaty was concluded.

Some voices within Japan demanded an overall peace (全面講和)[27] with all of the belligerent countries, including the Soviet Union and China, but the Third Yoshida Shigeru Cabinet believed that issues pertaining to the timing of independence and peace depended on the US bases. It thus chose to regain Japanese independence through peace with just the Western nations, and to rely on the US for security thereafter, in exchange for providing facilities. In this way, the Yoshida Cabinet sought to avoid the burden of rearmament and focus its efforts entirely on economic recovery.

In September 1951, a peace conference was held in San Francisco, where the

---

[26] Sōhyō, however, soon changed its position due to the peace treaty issue, and through collaboration with the Shakaitō, adopted a more combative stance in opposition to conservative politics that favored cooperated with the US.

[27] Intellectuals such as Nanbara Shigeru〈南原繁〉 and Ōuchi Hyōe〈大内兵衛〉, as well as the Shakaitō and Kyōsantō, argued for an overall peace. In 1951, the Shakaitō split into two factions, left and right, due to the intensifying conflict within the party over the ratification of the San Francisco Peace Treaty.

San Francisco Peace Treaty (サンフランシスコ平和条約)[ii] was signed between Japan and forty-eight countries[28]. In April of the following year, the treaty came into effect, bringing the occupation of Japan that had lasted for seven years to an end, and restoring the country's sovereignty as an independent nation. While the treaty significantly reduced Japan's liability for reparations to belligerents[29], it also imposed severe territorial restrictions: Korea became independent, Japan had to abandon Taiwan, South Sakhalin, and the Kuril Islands, and the Nansei (南西諸島) (Ryūkyū) and Ogasawara Islands were placed under US administration[30].

SAN FRANCISCO PEACE TREATY

Article 3. Japan will concur in any proposal of the United States to the United Nations to place under its trusteeship system, with the United States as the sole administering authority, Nansei Shoto south of 29°north latitude (including the Ryukyu Islands [...]), Nanpo Shoto south of Sofu Gan (including the Bonin [Ogasawara] Islands [...]) and Parece Vela [Okinotorishima] and Marcus Island [Minami-Torishima]. [...]

Article 6. (a) All occupation forces of the Allied Powers shall be withdrawn from Japan as soon as possible after the coming into force of the present Treaty [...]. Nothing in this provision shall, however, prevent the stationing or retention of foreign armed forces in Japanese territory under or in consequence of any bilateral or multilateral agreements [...].

---

[28] Some countries including the Soviet Union attended the peace conference but did not sign the treaty, while some other countries, such as India and Burma (Myanmar) did not even attend because they were not satisfied with the draft of the treaty. As for China, a major belligerent, neither the People's Republic of China nor the Republic of China was invited. Later, Japan signed the Sino-Japanese Peace Treaty〈日華平和条約〉(often called the Treaty of Taipei〈台北条約〉) with the Republic of China in 1952, followed by peace treaties with India (1952) and Burma (1954).

[29] The San Francisco Peace Treaty stipulated that Japan was obligated to pay reparations for war damage caused to the other belligerents, mainly through rendering service. However, as the Cold War intensified, many belligerents, including the US, abandoned their claims for such reparation. Four countries in Southeast Asia that had been occupied by Japanese forces — the Philippines, Indonesia, Burma, and the Republic of Vietnam (South Vietnam) — concluded reparations agreements with Japan, and by 1976 the Japanese government had paid a total amount of one billion dollars. Payment took the form of providing services, such as construction work, or products, and thus helped Japanese products and companies gain a foothold for entering the Southeast Asian market. Japan also made payments akin to reparations to countries that had not been belligerents, such as Thailand and South Korea.

[30] The Nansei (Ryūkyū) and Ogasawara Islands were originally to be merely put under US trusteeship; however, the US did not actually propose this to the UN, and instead left them under its control. The Amami Islands were returned to Japan in 1953.

On the same day as the peace treaty, the **Security Treaty between the United States and Japan** 日米安全保障条約 (often called the "Anpo 安保条約 Treaty") was signed. This treaty stipulated that US troops would continue to be stationed in Japan after independence to ensure "peace and security in the Far East" and to "contribute" to Japan's defense[31]. Based on this treaty, moreover, the **US-Japan Administrative Agreement** 日米行政協定 was concluded in February 1952, requiring Japan to provide bases (land and facilities) to the stationed US forces and share the cost of stationing them.

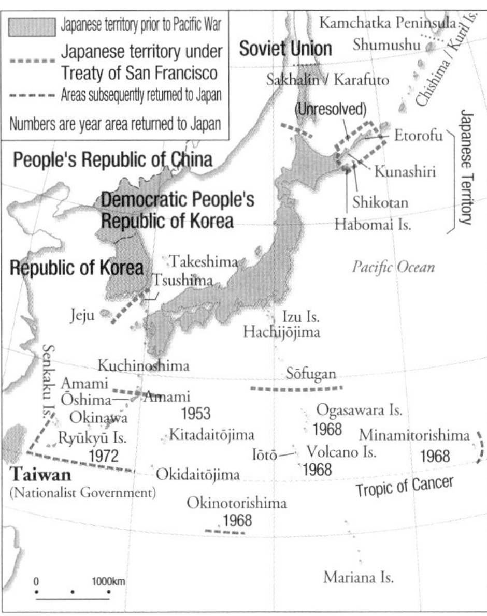

JAPANESE TERRITORY ACCORDING TO SAN FRANCISCO PEACE TREATY

Culture during the Occupation

A series of reforms during the occupation ended state repression of thought and speech, while largely disavowing traditional values and authority. Instead, the occupation authorities spread new ideas of individual liberation and democratization, while US lifestyles and popular culture rapidly flowed into Japan, gradually becoming accepted by the public.

The publishing world grew vibrant, and in spite of a shortage of paper for printing many newspapers and magazines began[32], and promoted democratization.

With the taboo on the Tennō-sei ended, and amidst a rapid revival of Marxism, new fields of research developed in the humanities and social sciences. For example, archaeological research flourished, with the excavation of sites such as Toro 登呂遺跡 and Iwajuku 岩宿遺跡. Studies that criticized Japan's backwardness through comparisons to Western modernity, such as the work of Maruyama Masao 丸山真男 (1914-96) in political science,

[31] According to the treaty, the US had the right to demand any area in Japan for a base if deemed necessary. The definition of "Far East," ostensibly the sphere of action of US forces stationed in Japan, was also left unclear.

[32] General magazines thrived; *Chūō Kōron*〈『中央公論』〉 resumed publication, while new magazines like *Sekai*〈『世界』〉 (World) and *Shisō no Kagaku*〈『思想の科学』〉 (Science of Thought) were launched.

OPENING OF A DANCE HALL (1949, KŌBE)
Ballroom dancing was not only an opportunity for young men and women to develop a closer relationship, but also came to represent the new American culture.

PROFESSIONAL BASEBALL BECOMES POPULAR
The second game of the first All-Star Series that took place in 1951. Kōrakuen Stadium in Tōkyō was completely packed.

Ōtsuka Hisao 大塚久雄 (1907-96) in economic history, and Kawashima Takeyoshi 川島武宜 (1909-92) in the sociology of law, had a major impact on students and intellectuals. In the natural sciences, theoretical physicist **Yukawa Hideki** 湯川秀樹 (1907-81) became the first Japanese Nobel laureate in 1949. That same year, the **Science Council of Japan** 日本学術会議 was founded as an organization to represent scientists of all fields.

Triggered by the destruction of murals in the Main Hall 金堂 of Hōryūji Temple 法隆寺 by fire in 1949, the **Law for the Protection of Cultural Properties** 文化財保護法 was enacted in 1950 to protect cultural properties representing Japan's heritage [33].

In literature, meanwhile, the works of Dazai Osamu 太宰治 (1909-48) and Sakaguchi Ango 坂口安吾 (1906-55) were among those that challenged social norms and conventional realism, shocking a public in a state of lethargy after losing the war. Postwar literature reached a high point with Ōoka Shōhei 大岡昇平 (1909-88) and Noma Hiroshi 野間宏 (1915-91), who expressed their severe wartime experiences through avant-garde techniques adopted from contemporary Western literature.

Simultaneously, a lively and upbeat popular culture thrived among a Japanese public freed from the nightmare of war, despite the hardships of daily life. On the music scene, "Ringo no Uta" 「リンゴの唄」 (The Apple Song) became an enormous hit, followed by the songs of Misora Hibari 美空ひばり (1937-89). Cinema as popular entertainment entered a golden age, with the works of Mizoguchi Kenji 溝口健二 (1898-1956) and Kurosawa Akira 黒澤明 (1910-98) receiving high acclaim both domestically and internationally. Radio broadcasting by NHK, which had been revived under GHQ direction, became immensely popular for its drama and sports, and in 1951 commercial broadcasting also began.

---

[33] In 1968, the Agency for Cultural Affairs 〈文化庁〉 was established to protect traditional cultural properties and safeguard heritage.

[i] In English, the term "Warsaw Pact" is more commonly used and is inclusive in that it refers to the treaty itself (officially the "Treaty of Friendship, Cooperation and Mutual Assistance") as well as the alliance system that resulted (Warsaw Treaty Organization).

[ii] "San Francisco Peace Treaty" is the English rendering closest to the common Japanese name, but "Treaty of San Francisco" is also common. Officially, the treaty was titled the "Treaty of Peace with Japan."

Chapter

12

The Rapid Growth Era

1 The '55 System

The Cold War World

Even after the armistice in the Korean War 朝鮮戦争, the US and the Soviet Union continued a ceaseless arms race, from atomic bombs to hydrogen bombs and then to intercontinental ballistic missiles 大陸間弾道ミサイル (ICBM) able to launch nuclear strikes at distant locations[1]. However, in the midst of an impasse in the nuclear confrontation, in the 1950s a movement to ease the East-West confrontation arose, known as the "**Khrushchev Thaw.**" 「雪どけ」 After the death of the Soviet dictator Joseph Stalin スターリン (1879-1953), Nikita Khrushchev フルシチョフ (1894-1971) laid out a policy for peaceful coexistence between East and West, and in 1959 he visited the US to have a summit meeting with President Eisenhower アイゼンハワー (1890-1969). This was followed by the signing of the Partial Nuclear Test Ban Treaty 部分的核実験禁止条約 (1963) and the Treaty on the Non-Proliferation of Nuclear Weapons 核兵器拡散防止条約 (1968), as well as the start of negotiations on nuclear disarmament.

In the 1960s, multipolarization developed in both the Western and Eastern Blocs, reflecting how the overwhelming positions of the US and the Soviet Union were beginning to decline. The Western Bloc countries continued to recover while relying on the US, but the European Economic Community ヨーロッパ経済共同体 (EEC, 1957) and then European Community ヨーロッパ共同体 (EC, 1967) were formed to promote economic integration and independence. France, led by President Charles de Gaulle ド＝ゴール (1890-1970), pursued an independent diplomatic policy, while West Germany and Japan achieved astonishing economic growth, threatening the US economy. In the Eastern Bloc, meanwhile, the Sino-Soviet confrontation 中ソ対立 came to the surface. China successfully conducted an atomic bomb test in 1964, and launched the Cultural Revolution 文化大革命 in 1966.

A third, non-aligned group of nations also became prominent. In 1955, the **Asian-African Conference** アジア＝アフリカ会議 (Bandung Conference バンドン会議) was held, centered on China and

---

[1] The competition between the US and the Soviet Union expanded to space development, including the launch of the Soviet satellite Sputnik〈スプートニク〉 in 1957 and the first ever moon landing by the American Apollo 11〈アポロ11号〉 mission in 1969.

India[2], with the aim of gathering together newly independent states. In the 1960s, Asian and African countries came to comprise the majority of UN member states.

In Vietnam, French forces withdrew in accordance with the **Indochina Accords** インドシナ休戦協定 (or Geneva Accords ジュネーヴ休戦協定) of 1954. However, civil war continued between North and South Vietnam. From 1965, the US, which supported the South Vietnamese government, began large-scale military intervention, including a **bombing campaign in North Vietnam** 北爆, while North Vietnam and the National Liberation Front of South Vietnam 南ベトナム解放民族戦線 (often called Viet Cong ベトコン) received support from China and the Soviet Union. This conflict became known as the **Vietnam War** ベトナム戦争.

Domestic Reorganization after Regaining Independence

The entry into force of the San Francisco Peace Treaty サンフランシスコ平和条約 in April 1952 meant the revocation of many laws enacted under GHQ orders. The Yoshida 吉田茂 Cabinet proceeded with legislation to suppress labor and social movements, and in July, in the wake of the Bloody May Day Incident 「血のメーデー事件」[3], passed the **Subversive Activities Prevention Law** 破壊活動防止法（破防法）, which aimed at controlling violent subversive activity, with the Public Security Intelligence Agency 公安調査庁 established as an investigative body.

When the peace treaty came into effect, the Coastal Safety Force 海上警備隊 was established, and the National Police Reserve 警察予備隊 was reorganized into the National Safety Force 保安隊. Despite this, US demands that Japan rearm increased, and the Yoshida Cabinet decided to enter a cooperative defense pact. In 1954, the **Mutual Security Agreement** MSA協定 (MSA, a collective term for four agreements including the US-Japan Mutual Defense Assistance Agreement 日米相互防衛援助協定) was signed, obligating Japan to enhance its defensive capabilities in return for receiving aid (such as weapons, produce, etc.) from the US. In July that same year, the government integrated the Coastal Safety Force and National Safety Force to establish the **Jieitai** 自衛隊 **(Self-Defense Forces, SDF)**[4], consisting of three services

---

[2] In 1954, China and India confirmed the "Five Principles of Peaceful Coexistence〈平和五原則〉" as the basis of friendship between the two countries at the meeting between Jawaharlal Nehru〈ネルー〉 and Zhou Enlai〈周恩来〉, and based on these the Asian-African Conference adopted the "Ten Bandung Principles〈平和十原則〉," which called for peaceful coexistence and anti-colonialism.

[3] On May 1, 1952, demonstrators at the main May Day rally entered the Imperial Palace Plaza, which had been prohibited for use. Subsequent clashes between police and demonstrators resulted in a large number of people being injured and some dying. This has also been called the "Imperial Palace Plaza Incident〈皇居前広場事件〉."

[4] The primary mission of the SDF is defense against direct and indirect incursions, but in addition to providing disaster relief they can also be mobilized to maintain public order. The prime minister is the commander-in-chief of the SDF, under whose direction and supervision the minister of defense, a civilian member of the cabinet, presides over military matters.

SUNAGAWA INCIDENT
Sunagawa residents and supporting protestors fiercely resisted the plan to expand the US base in Tachikawa〈立川〉.

REVIEW MARCH AT SELF-DEFENSE FORCES INAUGURATION CEREMONY (JULY 1, 1954)

(Ground, Maritime, and Air) under the direction of the newly-established Defense Agency 防衛庁. Further, under the New Police Law 新警察法[5] in the same year, in order to centralize police organization the municipal police were abolished and replaced by a national police force, which consisted of prefectural police under the control of the National Police Agency 警察庁.

Progressive forces – such as the Shakaitō-saha 社会党左派 and Shakaitō-uha 社会党右派 (Left Socialist Party and Right Socialist Party, respectively; the two parts of the former Shakaitō 社会党), the Kyōsantō 共産党, and Sōhyō 総評 – viewed these moves by the Yoshida Cabinet as a "reverse course" 「逆コース」 to overturn the achievements of the Occupation-era reforms, and responded by organizing an active opposition movement. In particular, movements in opposition to US military bases in Uchinada 内灘 (Ishikawa Prefecture) and Sunagawa 砂川 (Tōkyō), and the **Movement to Ban Atomic & Hydrogen Bombs** 原水爆禁止運動 that was triggered by the *Daigo Fukuryū Maru* Incident 第五福龍丸事件[6], gained momentum throughout the country.

Moreover, as a result of the public official purge being lifted before the peace treaty even came into effect, leading political figures such as Hatoyama Ichirō 鳩山一郎, Ishibashi Tanzan 石橋湛山 (1884-1973), and Kishi Nobusuke 岸信介 (1896-1987) returned to the political sphere, and opposition to Prime Minister Yoshida increased even within the Jiyūtō 自由党.

---

[5] In the field of education as well, the "two education laws〈教育二法〉" enacted in 1954 prohibited political activities and political education by public school teachers, while under the New Board of Education Law〈新教育委員会法〉 boards of education, which had previously been publicly elected, were now appointed by the heads of local government.

[6] In 1954, during a hydrogen bomb test by the US in Bikini Atoll〈ビキニ環礁〉 in the central Pacific, the *Daigo Fukuryū Maru* was exposed to radiation and one crew member died. This triggered a peace movement, and in 1955 the first World Conference against Atomic and Hydrogen Bombs〈原水爆禁止世界大会〉 was held in Hiroshima.

The Establishment of the '55 System

In 1954, as criticism of the Yoshida Cabinet mounted due to a shipbuilding scandal 〈造船疑獄事件〉, the anti-Yoshida faction within the Jiyūtō, including Hatoyama, left to form the Nihon Minshutō 〈日本民主党〉 (Japan Democratic Party) with Hatoyama as leader. At the end of the year, the Yoshida Cabinet resigned, and the Hatoyama Cabinet was formed. Prime Minister Hatoyama once more advocated constitutional revision and rearmament, and launched a platform promoting these policies. On the other hand, the Shakaitō-saha and Shakaitō-uha expanded their influence amidst the growing movement opposing the "reverse course," and the Shakaitō-saha in particular, which had made its position opposing rearmament clear, increased its seats with support from Sōhyō[7].

In the general election held in February 1955, the Shakaitō-saha and Shakaitō-uha together secured one third of the seats – enough to prevent constitutional revision – and were reunited as one Shakaitō in October. In the conservative camp as well, against a backdrop of strong demand from the business community, in November the Jiyūtō and the Nihon Minshutō joined to form the **Jiyū Minshutō** 〈自由民主党〉 (**Liberal Democratic Party**, LDP, hereafter Jimintō), with Prime Minister Hatoyama as its head (an event termed **Hoshu Gōdō** 〈保守合同〉, **Conservative Merger**). In this way, a two-party system emerged in Japan. The conservatives held just under two-thirds of the seats in the Diet, while the progressives occupied about a third. A political system had been established in which conservative and progressive forces competed under the dominance of a conservative party: the **'55 System** (**55-nen Taisei** 〈55年体制〉), which was to endure for nearly 40 years.

The Third Hatoyama Cabinet, which followed the merger, launched the National Defense Council 〈国防会議〉, to promote strengthening defense capabilities (i.e., rearmament), and the Constitution Research Council 〈憲法調査会〉, aimed at constitutional revision. Meanwhile, the government also pursued negotiations with the Soviet Union aimed at restoring diplomatic relations, under the slogan, "an independent foreign policy" (jishu gaikō 〈「自主外交」〉). In October 1956, the prime minister himself visited Moscow and signed the **Japan-Soviet Joint Declaration** 〈日ソ共同宣言〉, normalizing diplomatic relations[8]. As a result, the Soviet

---

[7] A confrontational structure, with conservatives on one hand and progressives on the other, was formed, with conservatives insisting on constitutional revision and a national security policy dependent on the US, while progressives advocated constitutional protection and demilitarized neutrality.

[8] Regarding the Northern Territories〈北方領土〉, Japan had demanded the return of the four islands as its inherent territory, but the Soviet Union asserted that the ownership of Kunashiri〈国後島〉 and Etorofu〈択捉島〉 had already been settled, and consequently a peace treaty was not concluded. The Soviet Union also stated that the return of Shikotan〈色丹島〉 and the Habomai Islands〈歯舞群島〉 to Japan was also to be postponed until after a peace treaty had been signed.

Union, which had up until then been preventing Japan from joining the UN, reversed its position, and Japan **joined the UN** 国連加盟 in December that same year.

The Revision of the US-Japan Security Treaty

The Ishibashi Tanzan Cabinet, which succeeded the Hatoyama Cabinet, was short-lived due to the prime minister falling ill. The subsequent Kishi Nobusuke Cabinet, formed in 1957, confronted progressive forces[9], and, calling for a "new era 「日米新時代」 of US-Japan relations," endeavored to revise the Security Treaty between the United States and Japan to put the two countries on a more equal footing. At first, the US was reluctant to revise the treaty, but after negotiations, the **Treaty of Mutual Cooperation and Security between Japan and the United States of America** 日米相互協力及び安全保障条約 (also called "New Anpo Treaty" 新安保条約) was signed in January 1960. This new security treaty clarified the US obligation to defend Japan, while an annex to the treaty provided for prior consultation regarding military activities, whether in Japan or the "Far East," 「極東」 by US forces stationed in Japan.

Progressive forces, fearing that the new treaty would increase the risk of Japan being caught up in US global strategy, organized a movement against the treaty's revision. In May 1960, the government and ruling party steamrolled a vote on the ratification of the treaty through the House of Representatives, after bringing in police offi-

> **TREATY OF MUTUAL COOPERATION AND SECURITY BETWEEN JAPAN AND THE UNITED STATES OF AMERICA**
>
> Article 4. The Parties will consult together from time to time regarding the implementation of this Treaty, and, at the request of either Party, whenever the security of Japan or international peace and security in the Far East is threatened.
>
> Article 5. Each Party recognizes that an armed attack against either Party in the territories under the administration of Japan would be dangerous to its own peace and safety and declares that it would act to meet the common danger in accordance with its constitutional provisions and processes. […]
>
> Article 6. For the purpose of contributing to the security of Japan and the maintenance of international peace and security in the Far East, the United States of America is granted the use by its land, air and naval forces of facilities and areas in Japan. […]

---

[9] From 1958, the Kishi Cabinet began implementing a nationwide system for evaluating teacher performance, but the Japan Teachers' Union (Nihon Kyōshokuin Kumiai〈日本教職員組合〉, often called Nikkyōso〈日教組〉) fiercely resisted this policy across the country. Furthermore, that same year, anticipating the chaos that would follow the revisions to the Security Treaty, a bill was submitted to the Diet to amend the Police Official Duties Execution Law〈警察官職務執行法（警職法）〉 to strengthen the authority of police officers, but this failed amidst growing opposition from progressives.

cers. The opposition movement, demanding the "protection of democracy," 「民主主義の擁護」 exploded. Enormous demonstrations by progressive elements, led by the People's Council to Stop the Revised Security Treaty 安保改定阻止国民会議 and consisting of the Shakaitō, Kyōsantō, Sōhyō, students belonging to Zengakuren 全学連（全日本学生自治会総連合） (All-Japan Federation of Student Self-Government Associations), and the general public, surrounded the Diet Building day after day (**1960 Anpo Protests** 60年安保闘争). A scheduled visit by the US president was eventually cancelled, but the bill to ratify the treaty was automatically enacted in June without passing a vote in the House of Councilors. After witnessing the treaty entering into force, the Kishi Cabinet resigned en masse.

DEMONSTRATION AGAINST NEW SECURITY TREATY (JUNE 18, 1960)
Protests on an unprecedented scale continued for about a month. Demonstrations and strikes spread in waves throughout the country.

The Stabilization of Conservative Governance

In July 1960, the Ikeda Hayato 池田勇人 (1899-1965) Cabinet, which had taken over from the Kishi Cabinet, called for "tolerance and patience" 「寛容と忍耐」 to avoid directly confronting progressives, while developing economic policies under the mantra of "**income doubling**" (**shotoku baizō** 「所得倍増」)[10] to further advance the rapid economic growth that had already begun. Based on the policy of "separating politics and economics," 「政経分離」 the Ikeda Cabinet, aiming to expand trade with the People's Republic of China despite the countries not having diplomatic relations, concluded a quasi-governmental trade agreement (**LT Trade Agreement** LT貿易)[11] with that country in 1962.

The subsequent cabinet, that of Satō Eisaku 佐藤栄作 (1901-75), began in 1964 and proved to be a long-lasting administration. Supported by the continuing economic growth, it remained in power for seven and a half years. The Satō Cabinet first advanced diplomatic negotiations with Korea, and concluded the **Treaty on Basic Relations between Japan and the Republic of Korea** 日韓基本条約 in 1965. This treaty confirmed the nullification of the treaties and agreements concluded prior to the annexation of Korea 韓国併合 in 1910, recognized the Korean government as "the only legitimate government in Korea," and

---

[10] The Income-Doubling Plan〈国民所得倍増計画〉, which aimed to double the gross national product (GNP) and per capita income over the ten years from 1960 to 1970, was formulated, but actual economic growth proceeded far faster than expected, and the goal was achieved in 1967.

[11] The name of the agreement came from the initials of the individuals negotiating it, namely Liao Chengzhi〈廖承志〉(L) and Takasaki Tatsunosuke〈高碕達之助〉(T).

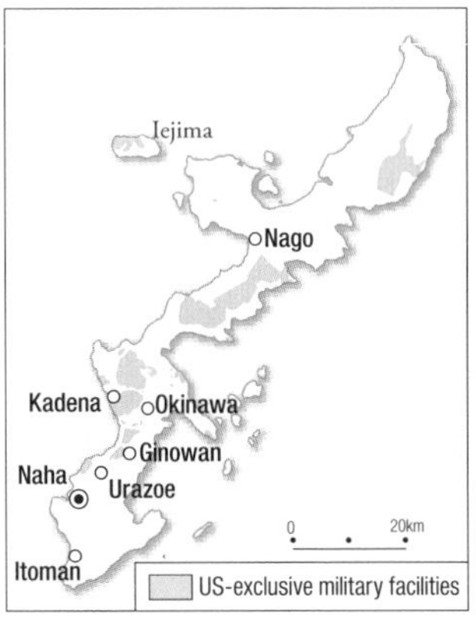

KADENA AIR BASE IN OKINAWA (ABOVE) **AND ITS EXCLUSIVE FACILITIES** (1996)
The photo shows a B-52 landing at Kadena Air Base〈嘉手納基地〉 in 1969. Most of the facilities for exclusive use by the US military were not returned even after Okinawa's reversion to Japan, leaving Okinawan residents feeling dissatisfied and insecure. The area of such facilities comprises some 10.4% of the total area of Okinawa Prefecture, and accounts for approximately 75% of all US-exclusive military facilities in Japan.

established diplomatic relations between the two countries[12].

From 1965, when the US began its full-scale intervention in the Vietnam War, Okinawa 沖縄 and the home Japanese islands became frontline bases for US forces, and the dollar payments related to the war accelerated Japanese economic growth. In Okinawa, the "island of bases" (kichi no shima) 「基地の島」, people had continued campaigns for the island to be returned to Japan, an issue that resurfaced as the Vietnam War intensified[13]. The Satō Cabinet – holding up the **Three Non-Nuclear Principles** 非核三原則 of "not possessing, producing, or permitting [nuclear weapons] to be introduced [to Japan]" – first achieved the return of the Ogasawara Islands 小笠原諸島 in 1968, followed by an agreement at a Japan-US summit (Satō-Nixon Summit) 佐藤・ニクソン会談 the next year that Okinawa would be returned without nuclear weapons. In 1971, the **Okinawa Reversion Agreement** 沖縄返還協定 was signed, and when it came into effect the following year, Okinawa was returned to Japan. The vast US military bases in Okinawa, however, remained.

---

[12] Japan-Korea talks had been continually suspended and restarted since 1952, due to fishery issues and how to handle matters pertaining to the colonial period. However, following the establishment of the Park Chung-hee〈朴正熙〉 administration in 1961, Korea's attitude toward Japan changed and an agreement was reached in the seventh round of talks that started at the end of 1964. Along with the basic treaty normalizing diplomatic relations, four other agreements were signed that covered fishery resources, claims and economic cooperation, the legal status of Korean nationals residing in Japan, and cultural cooperation.

[13] Okinawa was separated from Japan proper following the end of the Second World War, and was placed under the direct control of the US military. Even after the restoration of Japanese independence, Okinawa continued to remain under US authority. However, due to the requisition of land for military bases during the Vietnam War and an increase in crime among US soldiers, the movement calling for Okinawa to be returned to Japan took off.

During this period, the Jimintō continued to hold a stable majority in the Diet, but there were repeated confrontations among its factions over the presidency of the ruling party. As for the opposition parties, the Minshu Shakaitō 民主社会党 (Democratic Socialist Party, DSP; later Minshatō 民社党) split off from the Shakaitō in 1960, the Kōmeitō 公明党[i] was newly formed in 1964, and the Kyōsantō increased its seats. Consequently, the opposition was fragmented into many parties. Additionally, the New Left, a movement largely formed of students criticizing the existing progressive parties, waged campaigns against the Vietnam War and the way universities operated.

2 From Economic Recovery to Rapid Growth

Korean War Special Procurement and Economic Recovery

The Japanese economy had been in a severe recession as a result of the economic stabilization policy known as the Dodge Line ドッジ＝ライン, but it was reinvigorated by the Korean War that broke out in 1950 due to the special procurement demand from the US military for the manufacture of weapons and ammunition, as well as for the repair of vehicles and machinery. Moreover, exports to the US increased amidst the global economic recovery, while production, especially of metals and textile products, expanded. In 1951, due to this **Special Procurement Boom** (Tokuju Keiki 特需景気), industrial production,

	Goods	Services	Total
Year 1 (June 1950-May 1951)	229,995	98,927	328,922
Year 2 (June 1951-May 1952)	235,851	79,767	315,618
Year 3 (June 1952-May 1953)	305,543	186,785	492,328
Year 4 (June 1953-May 1954)	124,700	170,910	295,610
Year 5 (June 1954-May 1955)	78,516	107,740	186,256
Total	974,607	644,129	1,618,736

AMOUNT OF SPECIAL PROCUREMENT CONTRACTS (UNIT: USD 1,000)

	Goods		Services	
1	Weapons	148,489	Building construction	107,641
2	Coal	104,384	Automobile repair	83,036
3	Jute bags	33,700	Cargo handling / warehousing	75,923
4	Automobile components	31,105	Telegraph / telephone	71,210
5	Cotton cloth	29,567	Machinery repair	48,217

CONTRACT AMOUNT OF MAJOR GOODS AND SERVICES (JUNE 1950 – JUNE 1955; UNIT: USD 1,000)

Rank	Year 1 (June 1950-May 1951)	Year 2 (June 1951-May 1952)	Year 3 (June 1952-May 1953)	Year 4 (June 1953-May 1954)	Year 5 (June 1954-May 1955)
1	Trucks	Automobile components	Weapons	Weapons	Weapons
2	Cotton cloth	Coal	Coal	Coal	Coal
3	Blankets	Cotton cloth	Jute bags	Foodstuffs	Foodstuffs
4	Construction steel	Drum cans	Barbed wire	Furniture	Furniture
5	Jute bags	Jute bags	Cement	Dry cell batteries	Cement

RANKING OF MAJOR GOODS CONTRACTS BY YEAR

KOREAN SPECIAL PROCUREMENT DEMAND OVERVIEW

Special procurement demand reached a total of USD 1.619 billion over five years from June 1950. At first, the demand for goods was substantial, but this was gradually surpassed by the demand for services. The goods most in demand were weapons and coal, while for services it was building construction and automobile repair.

Index	Year Prewar Level Surpassed	Year Double Prewar Level Achieved	Year Best Prewar Result Surpassed
Industrial production	1951	1957	1955
Real GNP	〃	1959	1954
Real capital investment	〃	1956	1957
Real personal consumption	〃	1960	1952
Real payments received for exports, etc.	1957	1963	1960
Real payments made for imports, etc.	1956	1961	1959
Real GNP per capita	1953	1962	1957
Real personal consumption per capita	〃	(1964)	1956
Real product per employee	1951	(1962)	—

YEARS IN WHICH MAJOR ECONOMIC INDEXES SURPASSED PREWAR LEVELS (PREWAR CRITERIA: AVERAGE FROM 1934-1936)

GNP and real personal consumption all recovered to their prewar (1934-36 average) levels.

Against this backdrop, the government carried out an aggressive industrial policy. In 1950, the Japan Export Bank (日本輸出銀行)[14] was established to promote exports, and in the following year the Development Bank of Japan (日本開発銀行) was established with the aim of providing industrial funding. In addition, the Enterprise Rationalization Promotion Law (企業合理化促進法) was enacted in 1952 to provide tax incentives for capital investment by corporations. The electric power industry was reorganized in 1951 into a system of nine regional electric power companies, privately owned and operated[15], with each company independently managing everything from power generation to distribution. The Electric Power Development Co. (電源開発株式会社), established in 1952, constructed large-scale hydroelectric power plants in Sakuma (佐久間) and Okutadami (奥只見) to alleviate power shortages. In the shipbuilding industry, a government-led shipbuilding program (Keikaku Zōsen (計画造船)) had been in operation since 1947[16], and in 1956 Japan surpassed the UK to become the world leader in number of ships built. In the steel industry, the first round of rationalization was implemented from 1951 to 1953, although Kawasaki Steel (川崎製鉄) – in defiance of the Ministry of International Trade and Industry (通商産業省) (MITI) policy – built a comprehensive steel plant. In the postwar era, world trade developed under the free trade system led by the US. Japan joined the IMF (International Monetary Fund (国際通貨基金))[17] in 1952, and the GATT (General Agreement (関税及び貿易に関する一般協定)

---

[14] In 1952, operations expanded to include import finance, and it was renamed the Export-Import Bank of Japan〈日本輸出入銀行〉.

[15] Regarding the reorganization of the electric power companies, the plan to continue the prewar system of government management through the Japan Electric Generation and Transmission Company〈日本発送電体制〉 conflicted with the idea of privatizing the electric power industry.

[16] The program aimed at rebuilding the shipping industry and restoring the shipbuilding industry. The plan aimed to supply long-term, low-interest funding to shipping companies, which would enable them to order ships and so create a planned shipbuilding market, ensuring operation of the shipbuilding industry. The shipbuilding program continued in subsequent years.

[17] The IMF, an important organization that supported the international monetary system after the Second World War, was established in 1947 with the aim of stabilizing exchange rates and facilitating international settlements. Member states set their exchange rates against the US dollar, which was interchangeable with gold (fixed exchange rate system〈固定為替相場制〉).

on Tariffs and Trade) in 1955[18].

Serious food shortages continued from wartime into the immediate postwar years, and from 1945 to 1951 emergency food imports were carried out under the GARIOA ガリオア資金 (Government Appropriation for Relief in Occupied Areas Fund 占領地行政救済資金) program. However, thanks to the implementation of agrarian reform, agricultural production rapidly improved, and bumper crops of rice were produced year after year for the first time. In 1955, total rice production was 30% higher than the previous year, enabling rice self-sufficiency. As personal income rose, so too did the level of consumption. According to a public opinion poll conducted by the Prime Minister's Office in 1955, 70% of the public responded that they were no longer worried about having "food to eat," and the food shortages were largely resolved.

Rapid Economic Growth

A major economic boom called the Jinmu Boom 「神武景気」 occurred from 1955 to 1957[19], and in its 1956 *Economic White Paper* 「経済白書」 the Economic Planning Agency 経済企画庁 stated, "**We are no longer in the postwar era** 「もはや戦後ではない」." The Japanese economy shifted from recovery to economic growth led by **technological innovation** 技術革新. In 1968, Japan achieved the second-highest GNP among the world's capitalist nations, following the US, and average annual economic growth from 1955 to 1973 of around 10%.

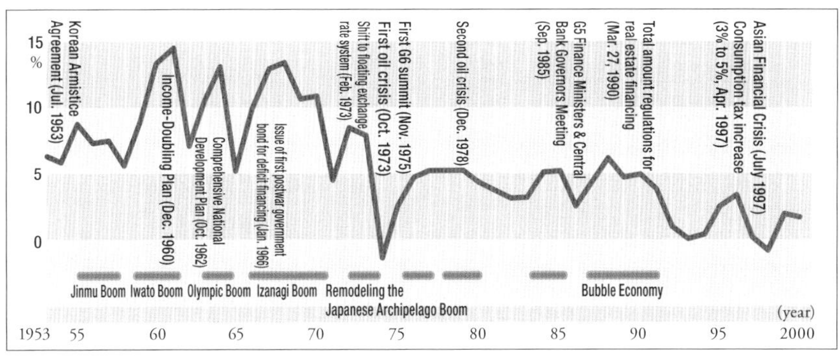

CHANGES IN POSTWAR REAL ECONOMIC GROWTH RATE

[18] The GATT was established along with the IMF in order to expand free trade and lower tariffs with the aim of forming a new international economic order after the end of the Second World War, and came into effect in 1948. Initially there were 23 member states.

[19] It was called the "Jinmu Boom" because it was seen as the greatest economic boom since the reign of the legendary first tennō, Jinmu〈神武天皇〉. Later economic booms were similarly named after the founding myths of the country, examples being the "Iwato Boom〈「岩戸景気」〉" (1958-61) and "Izanagi Boom〈「いざなぎ景気」〉" (1966-70). All these names were superlatives meaning "the greatest economic booms since the dawn of history."

The economic growth was driven by an enormous amount of capital investment by major corporations, which was described at the time as "investment brings investment." In the steel, shipbuilding, automobile, electrical machinery and chemical industries, upgrades were made by incorporating the results of technological innovations from the US, and new industries, such as petrochemicals and synthetic fibers, were developed. The technological innovations spread to small and medium-sized companies, some of which grew into component manufacturers and the like (medium-sized enterprises) rather than just being subcontractors for major corporations[20]. In 1955, the Japan Productivity Center 日本生産性本部[21] was established, launching a productivity improvement movement. The introduction of cutting-edge technology was not just limited to manufacturing processes, but also extended to quality control and labor management, as well as distribution and sales. Moreover, after such innovations were introduced, particular improvements were made to suit the situation in Japan, and **Japanese-style management** 日本的経営 – characterized by lifetime employment, seniority wage systems, and labor-management cooperation – was established. In this way, a low-cost, high-quality mass production system was developed, and exports of Japanese products increased.

As the industrial structure developed, the ratio of primary industries declined while those of secondary and tertiary industries rose. The heavy and chemical industries accounted for two thirds of industrial production, and a shift in energy from coal to petroleum

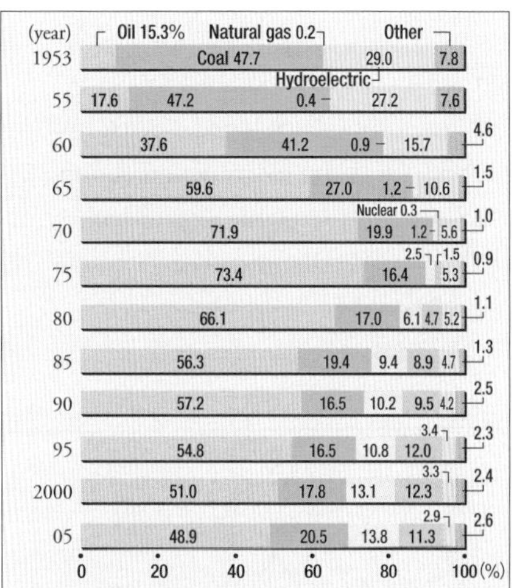

ENERGY SUPPLY AND DEMAND
Following the supply of cheap crude oil from the Middle East, the major energy source shifted from coal to oil. However, after the first oil crisis〈第1次石油危機〉in the early 1970s, the relative amount of oil declined while the weight of natural gas and nuclear power increased.

[20] In 1963, the Small and Medium-sized Enterprise Modernization Law〈中小企業近代化促進法〉and the Small and Medium-sized Enterprise Basic Law〈中小企業基本法〉were promulgated with the aim of improving the structure of small and medium-sized enterprises, including their facilities, technology, and business management.

[21] The Japan Productivity Center was established in 1955 by various business organizations with support from the government. Emphasizing three principles of productivity (labor-management cooperation, unemployment prevention, and the fair distribution of profits), it promoted productivity improvement activities typified by small group activities, such as the "zero defect" (ZD) movement and quality control (QC) circle activities.

Year	1955	1960	1965	1970	1975	1980	1985	1990	1995	2000	2005
Rice	110	102	95	106	110	100	107	100	104	95	95
Wheat	41	39	28	9	4	10	14	15	7	11	14
Soybeans	41	28	11	4	4	4	5	5	2	5	5
Vegetables	100	100	100	99	99	97	95	91	85	82	79
Fruits	104	100	90	84	84	81	77	63	49	44	41
Milk and dairy products	90	89	86	89	81	82	85	78	72	68	68
Meat	100	93	93	89	76	80	81	70	57	52	54
(beef among all meat)	(99)	(96)	(95)	(90)	(81)	(72)	(72)	(51)	(39)	(34)	(43)
Sugar	-	18	31	22	15	27	33	32	31	29	34
Seafood	107	108	100	102	99	97	93	79	57	53	50
Self-sufficiency rate of heat supplied	88	79	73	60	54	53	53	48	43	40	40

TRANSITION IN FOOD SELF-SUFFICIENCY RATE (UNIT: %)
The food self-sufficiency rate was around 80% up until 1960, but it plunged thereafter to below 50% in 1990.

proceeded rapidly: the **energy revolution** (エネルギー革命)[22]. A stable supply of inexpensive crude oil was an important factor facilitating the rapid economic growth. On the other hand, although there were a few exceptions such as rice, food self-sufficiency declined and Japan became increasingly dependant on food imports.

In the industrial sector, workers' wages significantly increased, thanks to improvements in labor productivity through technological innovation, a labor shortage, especially among the younger generation, and the expansion of labor movements adopting the "spring offensive" (「春闘」) (shuntō) approach[23]. In the agricultural sector, meanwhile, farm income increased due to improved agricultural productivity (resulting from the spread of chemical fertilizers, agricultural chemicals, and farming machinery), and policy-based increases in rice prices caused by the food control system and pressure from agricultural cooperatives, as well as an increase in off-farm income[24]. Thus, the income of both laborers and farmers increased. The characteristic features of the prewar period, signified by low-wage laborers and poor farming villages, were significantly improved, and the domestic market continued to expand.

Exports also grew rapidly, supported by the stable international monetary system, based on a fixed exchange rate under a free trade framework, and the import of

[22] The coal industry declined as cheap petroleum became more widespread, and came to be called a "declining industry〈「斜陽産業」〉." In 1960, the Miike Dispute〈三池争議〉, a fierce dispute against mass layoffs at the Mitsui Miike Coal Mine〈三井鉱山三池炭鉱〉, occurred, and ended in a defeat for the miners. Thereafter, coal mines closed one after another in Kyūshū and Hokkaidō.

[23] The "spring offensive," in which labor unions in various industries demand a wage increase in unison under Sōhyō guidance, began in 1955 and gradually took root.

[24] In 1961, the **Agricultural Basic Law**〈農業基本法〉 was enacted, and a large amount of subsidies were provided for agricultural structural improvement projects.

SMALL PASSENGER CAR ASSEMBLY PLANT
In the 1960s, automobile factories adopted the assembly line system. This photo shows an automobile plant in 1970.

inexpensive resources. From the late 1960s, Japan continued to record large **trade surpluses** (貿易黒字). The main export products were steel, ships, automobiles and other heavy and chemical products. Although the automobile industry had previously been considered internationally uncompetitive, in the late 1960s it began exporting vehicles to the US.

Japan adopted the "Outline of Trade and Foreign Exchange Liberalization" (「貿易為替自由化大綱」) in 1960, and in 1963 became a GATT Article XI country. Furthermore, in 1964 the country became an IMF Article VIII country, and joined the OECD (Organization for Economic Cooperation and Development) (経済協力開発機構), implementing **exchange rate and capital liberalization** (為替と資本の自由化)[25]. In preparation for the intensified international competition under the open economic system, large-scale mergers were carried out in the industrial sphere. For example, Mitsubishi Heavy Industries (三菱重工), which had been split into three companies as a result of the dissolution of the zaibatsu (財閥), was re-integrated in 1964, and in 1970 Yahata Iron and Steel (八幡製鉄) and Fuji Iron and Steel (富士製鉄) were merged to form Nippon Steel Corporation (新日本製鉄). Additionally, city banks such as Mitsui, Mitsubishi, Sumitomo (住友), Fuji, Sanwa (三和), and Dai-Ichi Kangyō (第一勧銀) formed **enterprise groups** (kigyō shūdan) (企業集団) through loans to their respective affiliated companies (Six Major Enterprise Groups) (六大企業集団)[26].

The Birth of a Mass Consumption Society

During the era of rapid economic growth (高度経済成長), both the land and society in Japan experienced great changes. Moreover, increased personal income and the advance of urbanization brought about remarkable changes in lifestyle, and the formation of what is

[25] A GATT Article XI country is one to which the provision of Article XI of the agreement is applied. Such countries may not impose import restrictions for the sake of the balance of international payments. An IMF Article VIII country refers to one prohibited from restricting trade payments and capital transfers. Additionally, by joining the OECD, Japan was required to liberalize capital.

[26] An association of various companies characterized by financing from an affiliated bank, cross shareholding, intra-group transactions mediated by the affiliated trading company, and personnel connections such as through presidents' meetings and so on. It was distinct from the prewar zaibatsu.

known as a **mass consumption society**〈大衆消費社会〉.

EXPANDING INDUSTRIAL COMPLEXES (1976, OKAYAMA)

Steelworks and petrochemical complexes were built on the Pacific side of the country, while heavy/chemical industrial zones (collectively the "Pacific Belt Zone"〈太平洋ベルト地帯〉) appeared in the Keiyō〈京葉〉, Keihin〈京浜〉, Chūkyō〈中京〉, Hanshin〈阪神〉, Setouchi〈瀬戸内〉 and Kita-Kyūshū〈北九州〉 regions. The industries and population tended to concentrate in these areas. In 1962, the government issued the New Industrial City Construction Promotion Law〈新産業都市建設促進法〉, and the cabinet approved the Comprehensive National Development Plan〈全国総合開発計画〉 to ease the concentration of industry and population in the major cities and correct regional disparities[27].

In farming villages, as the population outflow to major cities intensified, the agricultural population decreased, and the number of farmers with side jobs rose[28]. In urban areas that saw population inflows, available housing became a serious issue. In suburban areas where land was cheap, unregulated housing development spread ("sprawl"〈スプロール化〉), and clusters of reinforced concrete housing complexes for **nuclear families**〈核家族〉[29], such as 2DK public housing — apartments with two bedrooms, and a dining room/kitchenette — were built next to each other, while the construction of "new towns"〈ニュータウン〉[30] was planned.

---

[27] The Comprehensive National Development Plan aimed for industrial development based on the growth pole strategy, and the New Industrial City Construction Promotion Law designated 15 areas as regional development hubs, including central Hokkaidō, Hachinohe〈八戸〉, Sendai Bay〈仙台湾〉, Toyama-Takaoka〈富山高岡〉, southern Okayama〈岡山〉, Tokushima〈徳島〉, and Ōita〈大分〉. Nevertheless, the concentration of industries in the Pacific Belt Zone continued.

[28] In 1955, the agricultural population comprised just over 40% of the total working population. By 1970, this had fallen below 20%, and the number of type-2 dual-career farmers (those whose main source of income was from a source other than farming) reached 50% of the total number of farmers, giving rise to the term "3-chan farming〈「三ちゃん農業」〉," with three family members – jiichan〈じいちゃん〉 (grandpa), baachan〈ばあちゃん〉 (grandma), and kaachan〈かあちゃん〉 (mom) – farming.

[29] The number of family members per household was about five prior to the rapid growth era, but had fallen to 3.7 by 1970 as the number of nuclear families, consisting of just a couple and their unmarried children, increased.

[30] New towns started with Senri New Town〈千里ニュータウン〉 in Ōsaka Prefecture, followed by others such as Senboku New Town〈泉北ニュータウン〉 (Ōsaka Prefecture) and Tama New Town〈多摩ニュータウン〉 (Tōkyō) being developed.

TV BECAME THE CENTER OF FAMILY LIFE (1956)
Enjoying family time around the black-and-white TV.

PRIVATE CAR (1959)
The spread of private cars heralded the beginning of a mass consumption society.

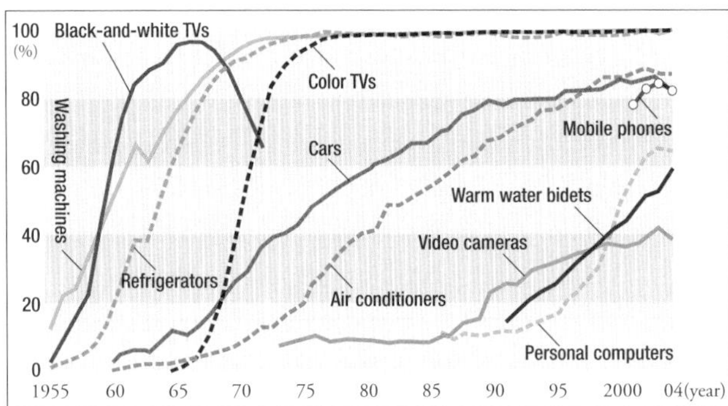

SPREAD OF DURABLE CONSUMER GOODS

Consumer life also underwent significant changes. Television commercials promoted the desire to buy, and people came to feel that "consumption is a virtue."「消費は美徳」 The amount of households with a black-and-white television reached 90% in 1965, and by 1970, 90% of households had a washing machine and refrigerator. Furthermore, from the late 1960s more and more households owned the "3Cs," namely, a car, color television, and cooler (air conditioner)[31].

The spread of durable consumer goods was facilitated by the establishment of mass-production and mass-sale systems by manufacturers and their affiliated distribution networks, as well as by installment sales systems[32]. In the retail industry,

---

[31] "Three Sacred Treasures〈「三種の神器」〉," the term for the treasures that symbolize royal succession in Japanese mythology, was used in this era to refer to the black-and-white television, washing machine, and electric refrigerator, while the 3Cs (named after the English first initial of each), were termed the "New Three Sacred Treasures〈「新三種の神器」〉."

[32] Matsushita Electric〈松下電器〉 (now Panasonic) established an organization of affiliated shops, and Toyota Motor〈トヨタ自動車〉 and Nissan Motor〈日産自動車〉 created a dealer system.

supermarkets grew with their strengths in low prices and wide selection of products (**distribution revolution** 流通革命). In 1972, Daiei ダイエー, founded by Nakauchi Isao 中内㓛 (1922-2005), became the leading company in sales, surpassing the long-established department store Mitsukoshi 三越. People's eating habits became more Westernized, and the consumption of meat and dairy products increased. However, an oversupply of rice and deficits in the Foodstuff Control Special Account 食糧管理特別会計 became an issue, and the **Acreage Reduction Program** 減反政策 for rice was implemented from 1970. Consumption of instant and frozen foods increased, and the food service industry developed.

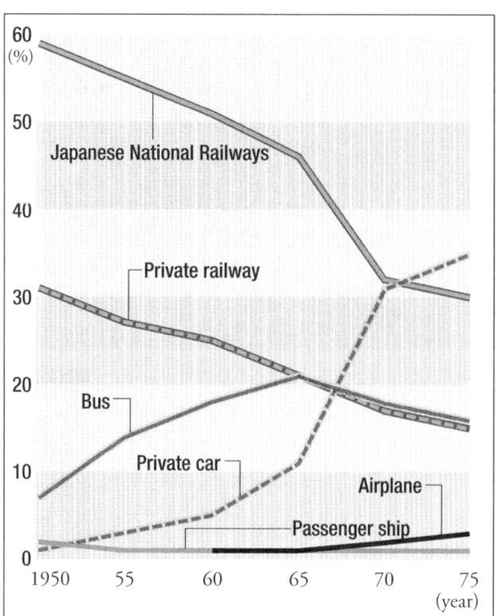

SHIFT IN SHARE OF PASSENGER TRANSPORTATION IN JAPAN BY MEANS OF TRANSPORTATION

The share of transportation by railroads declined from 1950 to the early 1960s, while that of buses and private cars increased. Thereafter, motorization accelerated from the mid-1960s, and the share of public transportation comprised by railroads and buses declined.

Private car ownership increased, and automobiles became a major means of transportation (**motorization** モータリゼーション). In 1965, the Meishin Expressway 名神高速道路 was opened, followed by the Tōmei Expressway 東名高速道路 in 1969. Annual automobile production amounted to about 70,000 vehicles in 1955, but had reached 5.29 million by 1970, and due to improved vehicle performance exports to developed countries, including the US, increased. Electrification of railroads advanced nationwide, and the **Tōkaidō Shinkansen** 東海道新幹線 entered service in 1964, heralding the dawn of the era of high-speed transportation. However, Japan National Railways (JNR) also began to record financial deficits from the same year on a single-year basis[33].

As life became more comfortable, people began to spend their leisure time on family trips and excursions, which fueled the development of the leisure industry. The mass media also developed, and the number of newspapers, magazines and books published increased dramatically. Popular authors included social mystery writer Matsumoto Seichō 松本清張 (1909-92) and historical novel writer Shiba Ryōtarō 司馬遼太郎 (1923-96)[34]. In particular, the circulation of weekly magazines grew by leaps and bounds,

[33] Air transportation also rapidly expanded following the introduction of jet aircraft in 1960.

[34] Their novels were called "middlebrow novels〈「中間小説」〉" because they were positioned between "pure literature" on the one hand and popular novels on the other. During this era, writers such as Mishima Yukio〈三島由紀夫〉, Ōe Kenzaburō〈大江健三郎〉 and Takahashi Kazumi〈高橋和巳〉 found success in the sphere of pure literature.

TŌKYŌ OLYMPICS
In October 1964, the 18th Olympic Games were held in Tōkyō, bringing together athletes from 93 countries and regions. It was the first Olympic Games to be held in Asia.

EXPO IN ŌSAKA
A daily average of about 350,000 people visited the Japan World Exposition held in Ōsaka in 1970.

and weekly comic magazines for boys enjoyed popularity among adults as well[35]. **Television broadcasting** (テレビ放送), which started in 1953, became an essential part of daily life, resulting in the decline of the film industry.

As a result of vast amounts of information from the mass media, Japanese people's lifestyles gradually became more standardized, and some 80-90% of the populace came to consider themselves "middle class" (**middle-class consciousness** (中流意識)). Consequently, "education fever" (kyōiku-netsu 「教育熱」) took hold; the rate of students advancing to secondary school and universities increased, and the popularization of higher education gained momentum[36]. Competition in the entrance examinations became fierce, while the "three nothings" (sanmushugi 「三無主義」) — indolence (mukiryoku 無気力), apathy (mukanshin 無関心), and irresponsibility (musekinin 無責任) — spread among youth, and school disputes broke out at high schools and universities as people demanded the democratization of schools[37].

The development of science and technology was remarkable, and the Nobel Prize in Physics was awarded to Tomonaga Shin'ichirō (朝永振一郎) (1906-79) in 1965 and Esaki (江崎玲於奈)

---

[35] Tezuka Osamu 〈手塚治虫〉, who came to prominence shortly after the Second World War, crafted unique, fully-developed story manga, and laid the foundations for the subsequent rise of manga and anime.

[36] In 1970, the high school enrollment rate reached 82.1% and the university/junior college rate reached 24.2%.

[37] From 1968 to 1969, at universities across the country, including the University of Tōkyō and Nihon University, students protesting unfairness at their institutions barricaded their campuses, resulting in the temporary loss of university functions.

"Leo" Reona (1925-)[ii] in 1973. The government also promoted active policies for scientific and technological development in fields such as nuclear energy[38] and space exploration. In 1964, the **Tōkyō Olympics** (オリンピック東京大会) were held, and in 1970 the **Japan World Exposition** (日本万国博覧会) took place in Ōsaka, both events being grand affairs that displayed Japan's economic and cultural development to the world.

The Strains of Rapid Growth

While Japan achieved rapid economic growth, serious social problems came to light. In the agricultural, mountain and fishing villages, **depopulation** (過疎化) progressed, and the production activities and social life of local communities broke down. On the other hand, overpopulation became a serious problem in large cities, resulting in traffic congestion, noise and air pollution, and a conspicuous shortage of housing and hospitals. Traffic accidents rapidly increased, and about 10,000 lives were lost every year due to this "traffic war." (交通戦争)

Although industrial pollution was serious, measures against pollution were not enacted as the government gave priority to economic growth. Companies continued to release pollutants that destroyed the environment, while victims suffering from diseases caused by pollution were neglected. However, against a backdrop of rising public opinion against pollution, the **Basic Law for Environmental Pollution Control** (公害対策基本法) was enacted in 1967 to regulate seven types of pollution, including air and water pollution, while clarifying the responsibility of business entities, and the national and local governments. A year after the law was amended in 1970, the **Agency for the Environment** (環境庁) was established in order to centralize the pollution administration and various environmental conservation measures that had been implemented. Public opinion and movements by residents against pollution gathered steam, leading to **four major pollution lawsuits** (四大公害訴訟) being filed over diseases caused by pollution: Niigata-Minamata disease (新潟水俣病) (Agano River (阿賀野川) basin), Yokkaichi asthma (四日市ぜんそく) (Yokkaichi City, Mie Prefecture (三重県)), Itai-Itai disease (イタイイタイ病) (Jinzū River (神通川) basin, Toyama Prefecture (富山県)), and Minamata disease (水俣病) (Minamata City, Kumamoto Prefecture (熊本県)). By 1973, all four had ended in victory for the defendants[39].

---

[38] Since the mid-1960s, electric power companies proceeded with the construction of nuclear power plants in various locations with support from the government, which advocated the peaceful use of nuclear power. Especially after the oil crisis, dependence on nuclear power as an alternative energy source increased.

[39] Minamata disease was caused by organic mercury, and Itai-itai disease was caused by cadmium; in both cases the toxic substances came from effluent discharged from factories. Yokkaichi asthma was caused by air pollution from petrochemical complexes.

During this time, human rights issues, such as discrimination against descendants of the burakumin 部落民, also became more serious. In 1946, the National Committee for Buraku Liberation 部落解放全国委員会 had been formed to succeed the Zenkoku Suiheisha 全国水平社 (National Levelers' Association), and in 1955 it was renamed the Buraku Liberation League 部落解放同盟. Resolving this discrimination, however, proved elusive, and based on a 1965 report by the Deliberative Council on Assimilation 同和対策審議会 calling for improvements in living environment and social welfare, in 1969 the Special Measures Law for Assimilation Projects 同和対策事業特別措置法 was enacted[40].

Amidst concern over the strains accompanying rapid growth, **reformist local governments** 革新自治体 emerged in metropolitan areas. In 1967, Minobe Ryōkichi 美濃部亮吉 (1904-84) was elected governor of Tōkyō, and in the early 1970s, local elections were won by candidates endorsed by the Shakaitō, Kyōsantō, and other progressive forces. Many of the governors of Tōkyō, Kyōto, and Ōsaka, as well as mayors in large cities such as Yokohama, came to be progressive leaders 革新首長. Progressive local governments made achievements in welfare policies, such as pollution regulation and the provision of free medical care for the elderly.

[40] The Special Measures Law for Assimilation Projects was succeeded by the Special Measures Law for Regional Improvement〈地域改善対策特別措置法〉 in 1982. Since 1987, a law concerning special measures for financial matters (Chitaizai Toku-hō〈地対財特法〉) has been in effect.

Translators' Notes

[i] Unlike most modern Japanese political parties, Komeitō uses "Komeito" (without the macron) as its official English name rather than a translation.

[ii] Esaki Reona went by the name "Leo Esaki" in Western countries, and there are various awards named after him under this name.

Chapter

13

Turbulent Times for Japan and the World

1 The Path to an Economic Superpower

From the Dollar Crisis to the Oil Crisis

In the late 1960s, the balance of international payments for the US worsened significantly due to the increasing military expenses for the Vietnam War ベトナム戦争, the enormous cost of aid to Western countries, and the rapid increase of exports to the US from other countries such as Japan and West Germany. This also caused a decrease in US gold reserves, prompting the **dollar crisis** ドル危機. As confidence in the US dollar began to waver, in August 1971 President Nixon ニクソン (1913-94), seeking to protect the dollar, suspended the exchange of gold and dollars. He also announced other economic policies, such as imposing a 10% surcharge on imports and a 90-day freeze on wages and prices. In response to countries with surplus balance payments, such as Japan and West Germany, Nixon demanded a major increase in exchange rates (known as the Nixon Shock ニクソン＝ショック). At first, Japan tried to maintain a fixed exchange rate 固定相場 of 360 yen to the dollar, but when Western European countries such as the UK, France, and West Germany shifted to a floating exchange rate 変動相場制 system, it followed suit, and the yen appreciated rapidly.

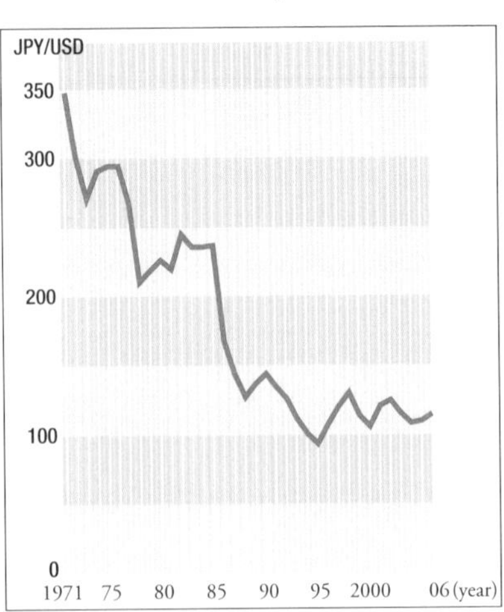

CHANGES IN EXCHANGE RATES (COMPARED TO YEARLY AVERAGE MARKET PRICE IN IMF REPORT)

In this way, the IMF (Bretton Woods) IMF（ブレトン＝ウッズ）体制 system, which had been the axis of postwar world economics, was shaken to the core. At the end of 1971, a meeting of the finance ministers of 10 countries 10カ国蔵相会議 had been held at the Smithsonian Institution スミソニアン博物館 in Washington, D.C., where a fixed exchange rate system, with 308 yen to the dollar, was reintroduced (the Smithsonian Agreement) スミソニアン体制. In 1973, however, dollar instability resurfaced, and so for this reason Japan and the Western countries shifted to a floating exchange rate system.

Meanwhile, in order to end the Vietnam War, Nixon visited China in 1972 to amend the hostile relationship between China and the US, leading to the restoration of diplomatic ties between those nations in 1979. The aim was to make peace with North Vietnam through China, which had regained United Nations representation, replacing Taiwan. In 1973, the **Agreement on Ending the War and Restoring Peace in Vietnam** ベトナム和平協定 (**Paris Peace Accords**) was signed[1].

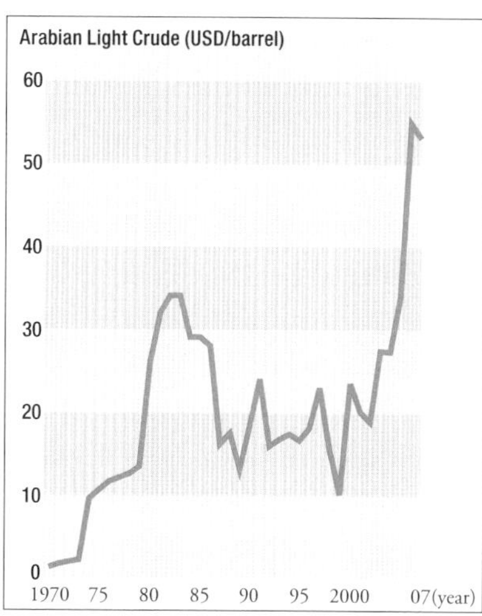

CHANGES IN OIL PRICES (PRICES FROM FIRST FRIDAY OF JANUARY EACH YEAR [EXCEPT FOR FIRST FRIDAY OF FEBRUARY IN 1987], AND FOB PRICES)

In October 1973, at the outbreak of the Yom Kippur War (or Fourth Arab-Israeli War) 第４次中東戦争[2], the Organization of Arab Petroleum Exporting Countries (OAPEC) アラブ石油輸出国機構[3] exercised its "oil strategy," 「石油戦略」 restricting oil exports to countries supporting Israel, such as the US and Japan, and thus causing the price of oil to increase fourfold. This triggered a rise in resource nationalism among Arab oil-producing countries, and brought access to a stable supply of cheap crude oil, a key condition of economic growth, to an end (first **oil crisis** 第１次石油危機). At the time, Japan was the largest importer of crude oil in the world, and since it depended on the Middle East for the bulk of that oil, the blow to the Japanese economy was severe.

---

[1] After losing the backing of the US, South Vietnam collapsed in 1975, and North and South Vietnam were unified as the Socialist Republic of Vietnam. However, other wars, including the Cambodian Civil War and the Sino-Vietnamese War‹中越戦争›, raged one after another on the Indochina Peninsula. These wars produced large numbers of refugees who flowed out to other countries, including Japan (Indochina refugee crisis‹インドシナ難民問題›).

[2] After the Second World War, the Israeli-Palestinian conflict began in the Middle East, and conflicts continued due to the discovery of large oil fields and intervention by the US and the Soviet Union. Jewish people who fled persecution by the Nazis and settled in Palestine had founded Israel in 1948, but this had been opposed by the Arab nations. By this time there had already been three wars between them and Israel, namely the First (or Palestine War‹パレスチナ戦争›), Second (or Suez Crisis‹スエズ戦争›) and Third (or Six-Day War) Arab-Israeli Wars‹第３次中東戦争›.

[3] The Organization of the Petroleum Exporting Countries (OPEC)‹石油輸出国機構› was founded in 1960 by five countries: Iran, Iraq, Saudi Arabia, Kuwait, and Venezuela. Later, other oil-producing nations, including Libya, Indonesia, Algeria, and Equador joined. In 1968, the Arab oil-producing countries of Kuwait, Libya, and Saudi Arabia founded OAPEC.

The prosperity of the world economy changed drastically after 1973, and the world was faced with a grave situation as economic growth rates declined while prices and unemployment increased. In response to this situation, in 1975 the first **G6 Summit** 先進国首脳会議（サミット）[4] was held, bringing together the leaders of six countries – the US, Japan, Germany, the UK, France and Italy – to coordinate economic policies among the developed nations, including economic growth, trade, and currency issues.

The End of Rapid Growth

In 1972, Tanaka Kakuei 田中角栄 (1918-93) formed a cabinet under the slogan "Remodeling the Japanese Archipelago" 「日本列島改造論」. Prime Minister Tanaka visited China in September that same year and announced the **Japan-China Joint Communiqué** 日中共同声明[5], leading to the **restoration of diplomacy between Japan and China** 日中国交正常化. At the same time, he implemented policies under the Remodeling the Japanese Archipelago plan through greatly increasing public investment, such as decentralizing industries and building high-speed transportation networks with highways and shinkansen 新幹線 trains. As a result, speculation on land and stocks occurred, resulting in land prices soaring. Combined with the skyrocketing price of crude oil due to the first oil crisis, this caused rapid inflation,

JAPAN-CHINA JOINT COMMUNIQUÉ

The Japanese side is keenly conscious of the responsibility for the serious damage that Japan caused in the past to the Chinese people through war, and deeply reproaches itself. Further, the Japanese side reaffirms its position that it intends to realize the normalization of relations between the two countries from the stand of fully understanding "the three principles for the restoration of relations" put forward by the Government of the People's Republic of China. The Chinese side expresses its welcome for this. [...]

5. The Government of the People's Republic of China declares that in the interest of the friendship between the Chinese and the Japanese peoples, it renounces its demand for war reparation from Japan.

7. The normalization of relations between Japan and China is not directed against any third country. Neither of the two countries should seek hegemony in the Asia-Pacific region and each is opposed to efforts by any other country or group of countries to establish such hegemony.

---

[4] Canada joined in 1976. The EU Commission came to participate in 1977, and the Soviet Union (now Russia) from 1991.

[5] After the Japan side acknowledged responsibility for the damage caused by the war and expressed its regret, the countries jointly declared an end to the "abnormal state of affairs" between them. Furthermore, Japan recognized the People's Republic of China as the "sole legal Government of China." Consequently, diplomatic relations between Japan and the Nationalist Government in Taiwan were terminated; however, close relations, including trade, continue at the private sector level.

which people called "**crazy prices** 狂乱物価." There was a shortage of daily necessities, partly due to trading companies buying up goods, causing chaos in daily life[6].

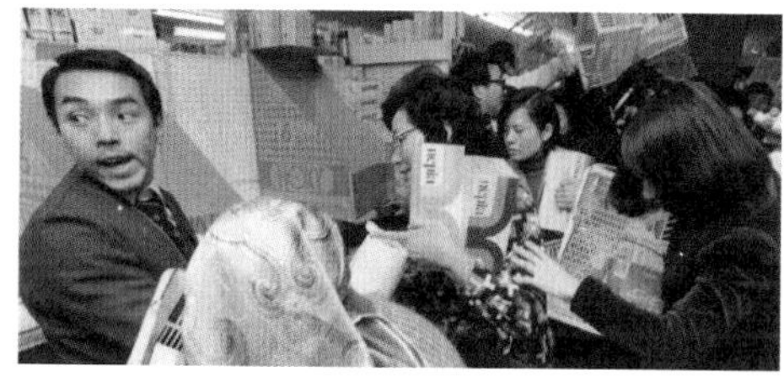

PANIC MASS BUYING AFTER THE OIL CRISIS
The panicked public rushed to stock up on things such as kerosene, detergent, and toilet paper.

The government began to tighten its financial policies, but the inflation persisted, and Japan fell into a deep recession (stagflation スタグフレーション[7]). In 1974 the economy experienced **negative growth** マイナス成長 for the first time in the postwar era, and growth stagnated at 2-5% thereafter. In this way, the period of rapid economic growth 高度経済成長 in Japan came to an end, as the country faced the trilemma of low economic growth, rising prices, and a current account deficit.

The government succeeded in limiting worker wage increases to within the growth of labor productivity, while implementing an economic stimulus package, resulting in 5.1% economic growth in 1976. The current balance also managed to show a surplus for the first time in four years, and the rate of increase in consumer prices stabilized in the single-digit range.

In 1974, the Tanaka Cabinet resigned after suspicions about the prime minister's political funding were revealed (**kinmyaku mondai** 金脈問題, "**gold vein problem**"). The next prime minister, Miki Takeo 三木武夫 (1907-88), promised a "clean government" 「クリーン政治」. Meanwhile, however, in 1976 former prime minister Tanaka was arrested on suspicion of bribery in relation to the purchase of aircraft from the US Lockheed Corporation. The Jimintō 自由民主党 suffered a major defeat in the general election that year, losing its majority in the House of Representatives for the first time since the party's founding. The Miki Cabinet took responsibility for the defeat by resigning, and so in 1976, Fukuda Takeo 福田赳夫 (1905-95) formed a new cabinet.

EX-PRIME MINISTER TANAKA, ARRESTED FOLLOWING THE LOCKHEED SCANDAL〈ロッキード事件〉(JULY 1976)

The Fukuda Cabinet addressed the trade surplus and strong yen recession by expanding domestic demand, and concluded the **Treaty of Peace and Friendship** 日中平和友好条約

[6] Daily necessities such as toilet paper disappeared from the shelves of supermarkets, sending the public into a panic.

[7] "Stagflation" is a term referring to a situation in which both inflation and stagnation exist simultaneously.

between Japan and the People's Republic of China in 1978. The succeeding Ōhira Masayoshi (大平正芳) (1910-80) Cabinet aimed for fiscal reconstruction while facing the second oil crisis in 1979, amidst both internal disputes within the ruling party and the ongoing struggles among conservatives and progressives in the Diet. However, Ōhira passed away suddenly in 1980 while campaigning for the House of Representatives election. The election resulted in the Jimintō regaining a stable majority, and Suzuki Zenkō (鈴木善幸) (1911-2004) became prime minister.

As low economic growth became the norm, the public became more conservative and prioritized a stable and secure lifestyle. While conservative politics regained popularity, however, the cooperative relationship between the socialist and communist parties collapsed as the fiscal administration of municipalities deteriorated, and the progressive local governments disintegrated. In particular, from 1978 to 1979, progressive candidates in gubernatorial elections in Kyōto, Tōkyō, and Ōsaka all met defeat.

Becoming an Economic Superpower

While the world economy stagnated after the first oil crisis, Japan's economy continued to maintain a roughly 5% growth rate by pursuing industries, developing products, and promoting lifestyles that all saved energy. After surviving the second oil crisis, which was triggered by the Iranian Revolution (イラン革命) in 1979[8], the economy was on track to stable growth. While in the early 1980s growth fell to about 3%, this was still relatively high in comparison to the developed Western countries[9].

UNMANNED FACTORIES USING INDUSTRIAL ROBOTS
The development of computers and robots made such factories possible.

Corporations implemented "**streamlined management**" (**genryō** (「減量経営」) **keiei**) by implementing energy-saving methods, reducing their workforces, and increasing part-time workers. They worked towards automated facto-

[8] In Iran, the monarchy, which had been promoting modernization under US support, was overthrown in 1979. It was replaced by a government headed by Khomeini〈ホメイニ〉, a religious leader who advocated Islamic revival. This was the Iranian Revolution, after which the Arab oil-producing nations tripled the price of crude oil.

[9] For example, Japan's annual economic growth rate from 1981 to 1983 was on average 3.2%, whereas the average for OECD (Organization for Economic Co-operation and Development)〈経済協力開発機構〉 nations was 1.4%. During the same era, the unemployment rate in Japan was 2.4%, while the average for OECD nations was 7.7%.

ECONOMIC GROWTH RATE OF JAPAN AND OTHER MAJOR DEVELOPED NATIONS
Although the real growth rate of Japan's economy gradually fell after the two oil crises, it remained relatively high compared to other major developed nations.

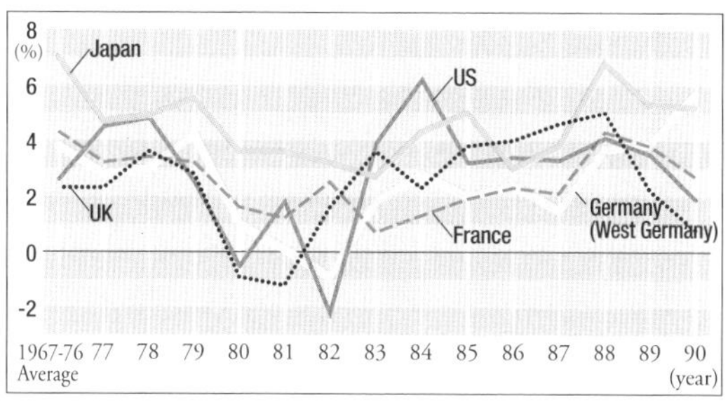

ries and offices through making extensive use of ME (microelectronics) technology, such as computers and industrial robots. In terms of individual industries, resource-intensive industries such as steel, petrochemicals, and shipbuilding stagnated, while energy-saving automobiles and electrical machinery, and high-tech industries, such as semiconductors, IC (integrated circuits), and computers, all experienced growth, mainly through exports[10]. Japan's trade surplus increased dramatically, which caused **trade friction** 貿易摩擦 with Western countries and the appreciation of the yen in the exchange market. The trade friction between the US and Japan over the car industry became particularly serious.

Highways such as the Chūgoku Expressway 中国自動車道, Tōhoku Expressway 東北自動車道, and Kan'etsu Expressway 関越自動車道 were built, and the San'yō Shinkansen 山陽新幹線 was launched in 1975, followed by both the Tōhoku and Jōetsu Shinkansen 東北・上越新幹線 in 1982. In 1998 the completion of the Seikan Tunnel 青函トンネル and the Great Seto Bridge 瀬戸大橋 connected Hokkaidō 北海道, Honshū 本州, Shikoku 四国 and Kyūshū 九州 by road. The New Tōkyō International Airport 新東京国際空港[11] opened in Narita 成田 in 1978; as internationalization progressed, the number of overseas travelers surpassed one million in 1972, and ten million by 1990. In 1994, Kansai International 関西国際空港

"JAPAN BASHING"
In the 1980s, the rapid increase in exports of vehicles to the US caused a heavy blow to the US auto industry, which led to criticism of Japan. The photo shows members of the United Auto Workers of America〈全米自動車労働組合〉protesting by destroying a Japanese car.

---

[10] These sorts of shifts in industrial structure were described as constituting a transition from "heavy industry" to "light industry," or "knowledge-intensive industries."

[11] The New Tōkyō International Airport (now Narita International Airport) is located in the Sanrizuka〈三里塚〉area of Narita City, Chiba Prefecture. The cabinet had decided on its construction in 1966, but building was delayed due to a fierce opposition movement.

Airport[12] opened as well.

In 1955 Japan's share of World GNP amounted to about 2%, but by 1970 this had grown to 6%, and by 1980 to 10%, with Japan having become an "**economic superpower**" (**keizai taikoku**)「経済大国」[13]. Japan's influence in international affairs increased greatly, and in the 1980s it became the world's largest contributor of ODA (**Official** 政府開発援助 **Development Assistance**) to developing countries.

The Bubble Economy and Everyday Life

During the 1980s, Japan's trade surplus with the US increased so dramatically that the US demanded Japanese restrictions on exports like automobiles, as well as **liberalization of agricultural product imports** 農産物の輸入自由化. In 1988 the government decided on the liberalization of imports of beef and oranges, which it implemented in 1991. In 1993, it was also decided to partially liberalize the rice market, but US criticism of Japan intensified, asserting that the country's "unfair" policies and practices were hindering market liberalization.

In Asia, countries such as South Korea, Singapore, Taiwan and Hong Kong continued to show significant economic growth through introducing foreign capital and technology to pursue export-orientated industrialization. These nations were called the Newly Industrializing Economies 新興工業経済地域 (NIES)[14]. This trend spread to China's special economic zones, which were undergoing reform and liberalization, and other ASEAN countries[15]. The resulting economic zone, with "economic superpower"

---

[12] Kansai International Airport, built in southeast Ōsaka Bay off the coast of Senshū〈泉州沖〉, was Japan's first 24-hour international airport. It was managed by a semi-governmental corporation, New Kansai International Airport Co., which was established with investments collected from the national and local governments, as well as the business community.

[13] From the 1980s, Japan's per capita national income (in USD) overtook that of the US, partly due to the impact of yen appreciation. As trade surpluses mounted, Japan became the world's largest creditor nation.

[14] Emerging nations in Asia and Africa that had become independent after the Second World War (and Latin American countries of similar circumstance) struggled to grow economically, and their economic disparity and accumulated debt compared to the industrialized countries in the northern hemisphere became an issue (the "North-South Problem〈南北問題〉"). Since the 1970s, while many emerging nations faced increasingly serious poverty and hunger, some were oil-producing countries that wielded oil strategy to become rich, and some other countries or regions achieved rapid economic growth (becoming called NIES, Newly Industrializing Economies). East Asia became the central region for the development of NIES, and the "Asian Tigers[i]" became particularly well known.

[15] ASEAN is an abbreviation for the Association of South East Asian Nations〈東南アジア諸国連合〉, a regional cooperation organization that was founded in 1967 and consisted of five nations: Indonesia, Singapore, Thailand, the Philippines, and Malaysia. Later, Brunei, Vietnam, Laos,

Japan surrounded by the Asian NIES, became a central hub for the global economy.

In 1985, a meeting of the G5 Finance Ministers and Central Bank Governors (5カ国蔵相・中央銀行総裁会議)[16] was held, at which the **Plaza Accord** (プラザ合意) was signed in agreement to depreciate the US dollar in relation to other currencies. This caused a rapid appreciation of the yen, triggering a recession ("strong yen recession" (円高不況)), especially for the export industries. However, from mid-1987 the economy recovered due to increased domestic demand. The use of computers and telecommunication equipment drove the development of networks of production, distribution and sales, leading to the exponential growth of convenience stores and mass retailers, while the heavy and chemical industries also grew, fueled by aggressive capital investments such as the implementation of ME technologies. Furthermore, tertiary industries such as leisure, travel and dining grew, and the development of a service-based economy gathered steam[17]. The Internet and cellular phones also became widespread from the late 1990s, which had a great impact on people's lives.

This increase in domestic demand, alongside the soaring prices of land and stock, later became known as the "**Bubble Economy**" (「バブル経済」)." Under ultra-low interest policies, funds that had been idling in financial institutions and corporations poured into the real estate and stock markets. On the other hand, extremely long working hours became the norm, and death from overwork (karōshi) among white-collar workers in particular became a serious social issue. Furthermore, as the appreciation of the yen continued, the number of Japanese corporations moving their production bases to other Western and Asian countries increased, causing the production industry in Japan to begin to hollow out.

The Nakasone Yasuhiro (中曽根康弘) (1918-2019) Cabinet, inaugurated in 1982, sought to tighten relations among Japan, the US, and South Korea, while making large increases in defense spending. On the other hand, against a backdrop of a global trend towards neoliberalism (新自由主義) (or neoconservatism), the cabinet promoted **administrative and financial reform** (行財政改革), under the slogan "a final settlement of postwar politics (戦後政治の総決算)." This included rolling back social welfare programs, such as pensions and medical care for the elderly;

Myanmar, and Cambodia joined as well.

[16] This was a meeting of the five greatest economies, namely the US, Japan, Germany, France, and the UK. From 1986, Italy and Canada joined, to make a gathering of seven nations: the G7 Finance Ministers and Central Bank Governors meeting〈7カ国蔵（財務）相・中央銀行総裁会議〉.

[17] As innovation in the industrial structure advanced, in the twenty years between 1970 and 1990 the percentage of the working population employed in primary industry dropped by half to less than 10% of the total, while secondary industry levelled off and the percentage of those employed in the tertiary industry – consisting of commerce, transportation, and other service industries – increased from 50% to 60%.

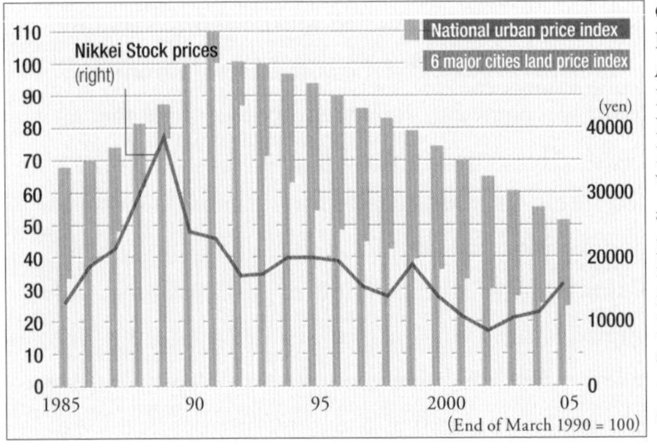

CHANGES IN URBAN PRICE INDEX AND NIKKEI 〈日経〉 **STOCK AVERAGE** (MAJOR CITIES INCLUDE TŌKYŌ, YOKOHAMA, NAGOYA, KYŌTO, ŌSAKA, AND KŌBE)
With the increased demand in office space and improved corporate performance, the price of land and stocks increased, but from around 1987 it began to diverge from real economic performance. However, in the 1990s the price of land and stock fell drastically (asset deflation 〈資産デフレ〉), and the Japanese economy entered a serious recession.

EXCHANGE RATE OF MAJOR CURRENCIES COMPARED TO US DOLLAR (EURO FROM 1999)
The 1985 Plaza Accord ushered in concerted policy efforts by countries to correct US dollar appreciation, which caused the major currencies to rise against the dollar. The Japanese yen and German mark showed particularly dramatic increases.

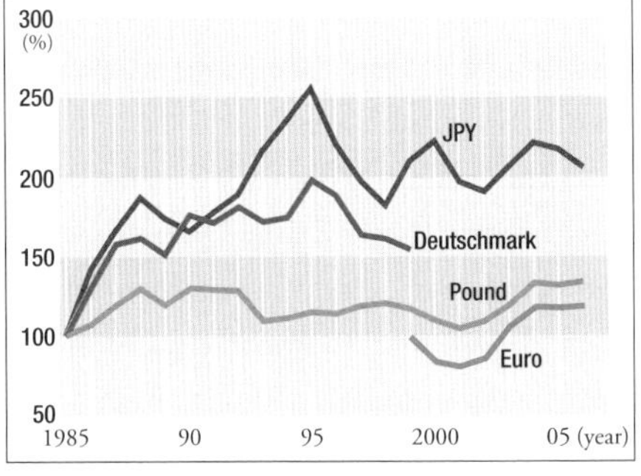

privatizing Nippon 電電公社 Telegraph and Telephone Public Corporation (now NTT), Japan 専売公社 Tobacco and Salt Public Corporation (now JT), and Japan 国鉄 National Railways (now JR); and introducing a large indirect tax. At the same time, the reorganization of labor unions also progressed. In 1987, the Japanese Federation of Private Sector Trade Unions 全日本民間労働組合連合会, which favored cooperation between labor and management, was founded, and in 1989 it merged with Sōhyō 総評 to become the **Japanese Trade Union Confederation** (**Nihon Rōdō Kumiai Sōrengōkai** 日本労働組合総連合会, usually called Rengō 連合). The large indirect tax was realized as **consumption tax** 消費税 under the Takeshita Noboru 竹下登内閣 (1924-2000) Cabinet, and was implemented in 1989.

2 The End of the Cold War, and Transformations in Japanese Society

From the Cold War to Regional Conflicts

By the mid-1970s, the tensions in US-Soviet relations had begun to ease (Détente〈デタント〉), but when the Soviet Union invaded Afghanistan in 1979, the US sharpened its confrontational stance towards the Soviets (the "New Cold War"「新冷戦」). US President Ronald Reagan〈レーガン〉 (1911-2004) significantly expanded the military, but he also implemented large tax cuts and eased regulations to increase corporate vitality[18].

However, the US suffered a hollowing out of its domestic industries, as well as a "twin deficit"「双子の赤字」 (public finances and international balance of payments), becoming the world's largest debtor nation. On the other hand, the Soviet Union also experienced a serious economic crisis, and Mikhail Gorbachev〈ゴルバチョフ〉 (1931-2022), who appeared on the political scene in 1985, attempted to revive the state system (**perestroika**〈ペレストロイカ〉) while pursuing the liberalization of politics and society through the introduction of market principles and information disclosure. Furthermore, the Soviet Union strove to improve relations with the US through assertive diplomacy, which included signing the Intermediate-Range Nuclear Forces (INF) Treaty〈中距離核戦力（INF）全廃条約〉 in 1987 and beginning to withdraw its troops from Afghanistan the following year. Lastly, in December 1989, following top-level meetings between the two countries in the Maltese Islands, the US and the Soviet Union jointly declared the "**end of the Cold War**「冷戦の終結」."

Inspired by the movement towards liberalization in the Soviet Union, one after another East European countries began to abandon socialist systems and break away from the Eastern Bloc (**Revolutions of 1989**〈東欧革命〉). The Berlin Wall〈ベルリンの壁〉, which had been a symbol of the Cold War, was torn down, and East and West Germany were unified in 1990. At the end of 1991, the **Soviet Union collapsed**〈ソ連邦の解体〉[19]. In East Asia as well,

---

[18] The basic tone of economic policy in the developed countries changed substantially around this time, as evidenced by the restraint of the public expenditures, privatization of state-owned companies, and suppression of labor movements that were conducted by the Thatcher〈サッチャー〉 administration in the UK and the Nakasone administration in Japan. Based on neoliberal/neoconservative theory, which criticized conventional policies of creating effective demand〈有効需要創出政策〉 (Keynesian policies〈ケインズ政策〉) and the welfare state, there was a shift towards returning to classic laissez-faire economics and the realization of "small government〈小さな政府〉."

[19] Many member states of the former Soviet Union formed the Commonwealth of Independent States〈独立国家共同体〉 (CIS), a loose association with the Russian Republic (Russian Federation) as its core.

PKO IN CAMBODIA (OCTOBER, 1992)
Here, Self-Defense Forces members assist with constructing National Highway 3.

the Soviet Union and South Korea had established diplomatic relations in 1990, and China and South Korea in 1992, and the East-West confrontation structure fell apart.

In early 1991, after the end of the Cold War, a multinational force led by the US, and backed by a UN resolution, imposed military sanctions on Iraq, which had invaded Kuwait (**Gulf War** 湾岸戦争). Japan, under pressure from the US to "contribute to international society," made a large financial contribution to the multinational force. In light of the global trend to respond to a series of regional conflicts through **United Nations Peace Keeping Operations** 国連平和維持活動 (PKO), for the first time Japan began deploying the Self-Defense Forces 自衛隊 overseas, dispatching them to Cambodia in 1992 to monitor a ceasefire[20]. Moreover, during the Afghanistan War in 2001, Japan enacted the Anti-Terrorism Special Measures Law テロ対策特別措置法 and dispatched the Maritime Self-Defense Forces to the Indian Ocean to carry out oil refueling, and during the Iraq War イラク戦争 in 2003, it provided humanitarian aid under the Law Concerning Special Measures on Humanitarian and Reconstruction Assistance in Iraq イラク復興支援特別措置法.

The Collapse of the '55 System

In 1989, around the time when Shōwa Tennō 昭和天皇 passed away and the **Heisei period** 平成 began, the reality of money politics under the long-term conservative government became clear. That same year, the Takeshita Noboru Cabinet resigned in the midst of the Recruit Scandal リクルート事件, and the subsequent Uno Sōsuke 宇野宗佑 (1922-98) Cabinet was short-lived as well. During the Miyazawa Kiichi (1919-2007) Cabinet that took over from the Kaifu Toshiki 海部俊樹 (1931-2022) Cabinet, which had faced difficulties in responding to the Gulf War, the Sagawa Express Scandal 佐川急便事件 (1992) and construction industry bribery scandal ゼネコン汚職事件 (1993) were brought to light. The cozy relationship that the government and

---

[20] In 1991, after the Gulf War, the Maritime Self-Defense Forces' Mine Warfare Force was dispatched to the Persian Gulf. Despite disagreements over such matters as the unconstitutionality of deploying the Self-Defense Forces overseas, in 1992 the **International Peace Cooperation Law** 〈PKO協力法〉 was enacted under the Miyazawa Kiichi 〈宮沢喜一〉 Cabinet, legalizing Self-Defense Forces overseas deployment for peace-keeping missions. Subsequently, the Self-Defense Forces were dispatched to Mozambique in 1993, Zaire (Democratic Republic of the Congo) in 1994, the Golan Heights in 1996, and East Timor in 2002.

bureaucracy enjoyed with big business faced fierce public criticism.

In June 1993, the Jimintō split[21] and suffered a crushing defeat in the general election for the House of Representatives in the following month. The Miyazawa Cabinet resigned, to be replaced by an anti-Jimintō coalition government of eight other parties, with the exception of the Kyōsantō[22], with Hosokawa Morihiro 細川護熙 (1938-) of the Nihon Shintō 日本新党 (Japan New Party) as prime minister. The governing party had changed for the first time since 1955, 38 years prior, marking the end of the '55 System 55年体制. The traditional conflict between conservative and progressive parties became ambiguous, and an era of unstable coalition politics began.

The Hosokawa Cabinet, which advocated "political reform" (seiji kaikaku) 「政治改革」, reformed the electoral system in 1994 by implementing the combination of 小選挙区比例代表並立制 single-seat constituencies and proportional representation for the House of Representatives. That same year, the subsequent Hata Tsutomu 羽田孜 (1935-2017) Cabinet also ended up being short-lived when the Jimintō and Shakaitō joined forces to make a new coalition, shortly thereafter joined by the Shintō Sakigake (New Party Sakigake), which then formed a government with Shakaitō chairman Murayama Tomiichi 村山富市 as prime minister. The Shakaitō significantly changed its basic platform, moving to accept the US-Japan 日米安保条約 Security Treaty, the Self-Defense Forces, and the consumption tax. On the other hand, the opposition parties, including the Shinseitō (Japan Renewal Party), the Kōmeitō, the Minshatō, and the Nihon Shintō, joined forces in 1994 to form the Shinshintō 新進党 (New Frontier Party).

When the Murayama Cabinet resigned in 1996, Jimintō leader Hashimoto 橋本龍太郎 Ryūtarō (1937-2006) took over the coalition government. Prime Minister Hashimoto issued a joint declaration on the US-Japan Security Treaty system after the end of the Cold War[23], and in the first general election under the new electoral system, held that

---

[21] Secessionists who left the Jimintō to pursue political reform formed the Shinseitō〈新生党〉(Japan Renewal Party, members of which included Ozawa Ichirō〈小沢一郎〉and Hata Tsutomu) and the Shintō Sakigake〈新党さきがけ〉(New Party Sakigake).

[22] The eight parties consisted of seven political parties – the Shakaitō〈社会党〉, Shinseitō, Kōmeitō〈公明党〉, Nihon Shintō, Minshatō〈民社党〉(Democratic Party of Japan), Shintō Sakigake, and the Shakai Minshu Rengō〈社会民主連合〉(Socialist Democratic Federation) – plus the Minshu Kaikaku Rengō〈民主改革連合〉(Democratic Reform Party), which was a faction in the House of Councilors.

[23] It declared that the Guidelines for Japan-US Defense Cooperation〈日米防衛協力指針（ガイドライン）〉would be revised to designate the scope of activities of US forces in Japan as the "Asia-Pacific region," so that the Self-Defense Forces would be able to provide them with logistical support in the event of an emergency occurring around Japan. The new guidelines were agreed upon by both the Japanese and US governments in 1997.

same year, the Jimintō made great strides and was able to form a government by itself again. Meanwhile, the Shakai Minshutō 社会民主党 (Social Democratic Party, the renamed Shakaitō) and the Shintō Sakigake continued to participate in the coalition government in the form of cooperation from outside the cabinet.

Prime Minister Hashimoto established the Fiscal Structural Reform Law 財政構造改革法 in 1997, setting the basic policy for administrative and financial reforms, and raised the consumption tax from 3% to 5%. This consumption tax increase, combined with the currency and financial crises occurring in Asian countries at the time, led the Japanese economy to reenter recession[24].

Prime Minister Hashimoto took responsibility for a loss in the House of Councilors election in 1998[25] and resigned, so a new cabinet was formed by Obuchi Keizō 小渕恵三 (1937-2000). The Obuchi Cabinet endeavored to revitalize the economy with a large budget, while obtaining support to form the government first from the Jiyūtō in early 1999 and then from Kōmeitō in July of the same year, thereby securing a stable majority in both houses of the Diet. The cabinet enacted **legislation on the new Guidelines for Japan-US Defense Cooperation** 新ガイドライン関連法 (such as the Law for Ensuring Peace and Safety in Situations in Areas Surrounding Japan 周辺事態安全確保法) and the Law Regarding the National Flag and National Anthem 国旗・国歌法.

The Japanese Economy during the Heisei Recession

In the early 1990s, the "Bubble Economy" of the late 1980s burst in an instant. Stock prices sharply dropped from early 1990, and in 1991 a recession began. In 1992, land prices began to fall, and the real economic growth rate dropped to 1.3%, hitting less than 1% in 1993, in what is known as the **Heisei Recession** 平成不況[26].

One of the characteristics of the Heisei Recession was a sharp decline in the prices of stock and land (asset deflation 資産デフレ). The stock and land purchased during the bubble in anticipation of it gaining value became bad assets, and financial institutions left

[24] The real economic growth rate in 1997 was −0.4%, which marked the first instance of negative growth since 1974, just after the first oil crisis. However, in 1998 it further dropped to -2.0%.

[25] By the end of 1997, the Shinshintō, beset by a large number of members leaving, had split into six factions, among which the centrist factions, excluding the Jiyūtō (Liberal Party, led by Ozawa Ichirō) and Kōmeitō faction, formed a renewed Minshutō〈民主党〉(led by Kan Naoto〈菅直人〉). In 2003, the Minshutō merged with the Jiyūtō.

[26] The economic growth rate (GNP) from April to June 1992 was −3.3%, but it recovered to −0.1% in the next quarter (July to September) and remained −0.1% in the following quarter (October to December). Although Japan had experienced negative economic growth for two consecutive quarters during the recession following the first oil crisis, this was the first time in the postwar era that it had continued for three.

holding large amounts of such assets deteriorated, resulting in a monetary crunch that then spilled over into recession in the real economy (**compound recession** 複合不況). Although companies attempted to substantially improve management efficiency through restructuring, such as by liquidating businesses, downsizing, and expanding overseas, large numbers of people were left unemployed and job insecurity increased[27]. As a result, consumption declined, prolonging the recession.

At first, the government and the Bank of Japan considered this to be a normal cyclical recession, and attempted to overcome it with increased government spending and low interest rates. However, these policies had no effect. The impact on financial institutions was severe, and from around 1995, housing loan companies began to go bankrupt one after another. In 1997, Hokkaidō Takushoku Bank 北海道拓殖銀行 and Yamaichi Securities 山一証券 went bankrupt, followed by the Nippon Credit Bank 日本債券信用銀行 and the Long-Term Credit Bank of Japan 日本長期信用銀行 in 1998. While public funds were injected into major financial institutions that had gone bankrupt, there continued to be a slew of corporate bankruptcies and restructurings, resulting in significant unemployment.

Corporate production and investment activities suffered as well, a situation compounded by the slump in consumer spending. Consumers began to become increasingly price-conscious, and sales of brand-name goods and luxury items plummeted. In addition, appreciation of the yen pushed the export-led, mass production-orientated industries that had been driving the Japanese economy – such as automobiles, electronics, household appliances, and office equipment – into a serious situation, facing low domestic demand and declining export competitiveness.

Moreover, although in the 1980s Japan had all but closed the gap with the US in terms of new technology, such as new electronics materials and biotechnology, in the 1990s technological innovation in Japan stagnated, and the technological gap widened.

Meanwhile, dramatic advances were realized in information and communication technology, and information networks expanded beyond national borders, making corporate activities borderless. Furthermore, under pressure from the US, Japan proceeded with deregulation and opening its markets to foreign countries. Japanese corporations were more involved in global competition, and underwent large-scale industry restructuring, including international partnerships and mergers.

Facing Contemporary Issues

In 1995, the **Great Hanshin-Awaji Earthquake** 阪神・淡路大震災 and the sarin gas attack on the Tōkyō Subway 地下鉄サリン事件 by the Aum Shinrikyō オウム真理教団 cult occurred. There was also an assault on an elemen-

[27] The unemployment rate in Japan exceeded 4% in 1998 and reached 5% in 2000.

tary school girl by American soldiers in Okinawa, which prompted an upsurge in the social movement by residents demanding a reduction in US military bases. Japan's 20th century thus ended with a string of unprecedented disasters and events.

In April 2000, Koizumi Jun'ichirō 小泉純一郎 (1942-) formed a cabinet under the principle of structural reforms[28]. Prime Minister Koizumi adopted a neo-liberal policy aimed at small government. Along with innovative solutions to the disposal of bad loans, he proceeded with bold privatization and deregulation aimed at eliminating the financial deficit and revitalizing the economy. As a result, the country appeared to have emerged from the period of recession called the "Lost Decade" 「失われた10年」; however, welfare policies regressed, and income and regional disparities grew.

When Prime Minister Koizumi resigned in 2006 after completing his term of office, the premiership rapidly passed through Abe Shinzō 安倍晋三 (1954-2022) to Fukuda Yasuo 福田康夫 (1936-) and then Asō Tarō 麻生太郎 (1940-). In August 2009, almost one year after the global financial crisis ("Lehman Shock" リーマン＝ショック)[29], the Minshutō won a landslide victory over the Jimintō 自民党 in the House of Representatives election. Hatoyama Yukio 鳩山由紀夫 (1947-) formed a cabinet, and a period of government by the Minshutō began. However, the government was unstable, and in the House of Councilors election held in July 2010, under Prime Minister Kan Naoto (1946-) the Minshutō suffered a crushing defeat.

In March 2011 the **Great East Japan Earthquake** 東日本大震災 occurred, and inadequate handling of the response to the disaster contributed to the resignation of the Kan Cabinet. Noda Yoshihiko 野田佳彦 (1957-) then formed a cabinet. However, in the House of Representatives election held in December 2012 the Minshutō suffered another crushing defeat, which led to a coalition government between the Jimintō and Kōmeitō and the beginning of the Second Abe Cabinet.

The population in Japan was 128 million in 2005, but is expected to decline to less than 100 million by 2045, as the birthrate declines and the population ages rapidly. An aging society not only reduces the functioning of families and local communities, but also hinders economic growth due to the smaller working population. Moreover, it causes tax revenue and insurance premiums to decrease, resulting in a serious impact on the social security system that serves as a safety net for the lives of the public.

---

[28] Prime Minister Koizumi visited the Democratic People's Republic of Korea in September 2002 seeking diplomatic normalization, but during the meeting with General Secretary Kim Jong-Il〈金正日〉 a number of issues that had to be resolved came to light, including the abduction of Japanese citizens by North Korea.

[29] This was a world-wide financial crisis triggered by the bankruptcy of Lehman Brothers Holdings Inc., an investment bank in the US, in 2008. Japan suffered from an almost unprecedented economic recession as a result.

Environmental degradation such as global warming and ecosystem destruction is another serious issue. In 1997, the Conference of Parties to the United Nations Framework Convention on Climate Change (UNFCCC) 気候変動枠組条約締約国会議 was held in Kyōto and adopted the **Kyōto Protocol** 京都議定書, which set targets for reducing greenhouse gas emissions by developed countries. The Paris Agreement パリ協定, adopted at the 2015 Conference of Parties to the UNFCCC, called for all nations, including developing countries, to make efforts to reduce greenhouse gas emissions. In the meantime, in 2000 the Basic Law for Establishing a Sound Material-Cycle Society 循環型社会形成推進基本法 was enacted, making recycling of containers, packaging, home appliances and so on a legal requirement. Nuclear power is able to supply a large amount of energy with little greenhouse emission, but confidence in its safety was shaken due to the accident at the "Monju" 「もんじゅ」 fast reactor in 1995, the criticality accident at Tōkaimura 東海村 (Ibaraki Prefecture) in 1999, and the disaster at the Fukushima Daiichi Nuclear Power Plant 福島第一原子力発電所 following the Great East Japan Earthquake of March 11, 2011. This has led to the reexamination of energy policy, including promoting the development of renewable energy.

Further, Japan's international relations have been significantly changing. Relations with other developed countries, such as the US and the members of the European Union, have matured, while economic development has advanced in China and India, in addition to the Asian Tigers and ASEAN countries. In this context, Japan must keep endeavoring to contribute to world peace as well as the improvement of human welfare.

Translators' Notes

[i] While the literal translation of this term "アジアNIES" would be "Asian NIES," in English they have long been called the "Asian Tigers," a term that also gave rise to the concept of a "tiger economy."

A

B

C

H

I

J

K

L

M

N

O

P

Q

R

S

U

Index Japanese

い

う

お

か

き

け

こ

さ

し

す

せ

そ

た

ち

つ

て

と

な

に

ぬ

ね

の

は

へ

ほ

ま

み

む

め

も

や

ゆ

よ

ら

り

る

れ

ろ

わ

所蔵・提供一覧（五十音順）*は提供のみ

朝日新聞社 325, 372, 386, 391, 418, 433, 441
飛鳥園 43下*
明日香村教育委員会 44*
アフロ 453
石橋財団アーティゾン美術館 344上
和泉市久保惣記念美術館 117
一般財団法人南蛮文化館 175左下
犬山城白帝文庫 166
茨城県立図書館蔵（茨城県立歴史館保管）274
ウィングスP.E　宮﨑一雄 38
AC 32左
絵葉書資料館 322
MOA美術館 227上・左下
円覚寺 124右
大阪府立中之島図書館 222
大阪歴史博物館 253
岡谷蚕糸博物館 289
影山光洋撮影 366右
橿原市 30左
株式会社三越伊勢丹ホールディングス 221
株式会社ライトスタッフ 137
かみつけの里博物館 31左上
唐津市教育委員会 18右①②③
観心寺 72右
共同通信社 430右
京都市歴史資料館 94
京都大学考古学研究室 15
京都大学附属図書館 175上
桐生市教育委員会 12⑥
宮内庁京都事務所 192
宮内庁正倉院事務所 57, 62, 63中
慶應義塾図書館 184
公益財団法人川端康成記念会 245下
公益財団法人鍋島報效会 257
公益財団法人日本近代文学館 245下*, 336, 341, 362, 369右
皇居三の丸尚蔵館 114上, 145上, 173下
高知県立埋蔵文化財センター 18左
興福寺 43下
神戸市立博物館（photo：Kobe City Museum/DNPartcom） 20左, 164
神戸新聞社 426左
國學院大學博物館 12①
国立公文書館 190, 201, 256
国立国語研究所 175右下
国立国会図書館 220, 224, 260, 346
国立国会図書館デジタルコレクション 88, 101中, 116, 123, 145下, 243
国立歴史民俗博物館 17*, 19左, 24上, 31右上, 32右, 56, 148
ColBase（https://colbase.nich.go.jp/） 13①②③⑥⑦, 14左, 18右④, 20中, 29, 31左下, 63右, 72左, 81, 83, 90, 96, 101上・下, 111, 120, 150, 227右下, 228下, 233, 244, 245上・中, 262中・下, 343, 344下
埼玉県立さきたま史跡の博物館 28*
堺市 26
堺市博物館 159
佐賀県 21左
桜井市教育委員会 23
慈照寺 149上
島根県教育庁文化財課（古代文化センター） 34*
島根県埋蔵文化財調査センター 20右
市立函館博物館 12②
神護寺 87
真正極楽寺 141
大仙院 149下
高山市教育委員会 13⑧
伊達市教育委員会 16*
田中俊明 27
田中真知郎 43*, 71*
たばこと塩の博物館 262上
千歳市所蔵、北海道立埋蔵文化財センター提供 14中
千葉市立加曽利貝塚博物館 13④⑤
中宮寺 39右上
都久夫須麻神社 174
東京藝術大学（画像提供：東京藝術大学/DNPartcom） 371左
東京国立近代美術館（photo：MOMAT/DNPartcom） 371右

『詳説日本史』著作者　老川慶喜　加藤陽子　五味文彦　坂上康俊　桜井英治　笹山晴生　佐藤　信　白石太一郎　鈴木　淳　高埜利彦　吉田伸之

『詳説日本史』編集協力者　高橋典幸　中家　健　中里裕司　牧原成征

＊五十音順

翻訳監修　近藤成一　Kondo Shigekazu

東京大学名誉教授。放送大学教授。専門は日本中世史。

翻訳　亀井ダイチ利永子　Rieko Kamei-Dyche

立正大学データサイエンス学部准教授。専門は日本史、日本文化、英語教育。

亀井ダイチ アンドリュー　Andrew T. Kamei-Dyche

青山学院大学地球社会共生学部准教授。専門は日本出版文化史。

表紙デザイン　水戸部　功

本文デザイン　中村竜太郎

英文詳説日本史
JAPANESE HISTORY for High School

2024年 3 月20日　第 1 版 1 刷発行

2024年 4 月30日　第 1 版 2 刷発行

編者　佐藤 信　五味文彦　高埜利彦

翻訳　近藤成一　亀井ダイチ利永子　亀井ダイチ アンドリュー

発行者　野澤武史

発行所　株式会社 山川出版社

〒101-0047　東京都千代田区内神田1-13-13

電話　東京 03(3293)8131

https://www.yamakawa.co.jp/

印刷　株式会社 加藤文明社

製本　株式会社 ブロケード

ISBN978-4-634-59116-5